DATE DUE

SE 29 05			

DEMCO 38-296

Sun Yat-sen

Sun Yat-sen

by MARIE-CLAIRE BERGÈRE

Translated from the French by JANET LLOYD

STANFORD UNIVERSITY PRESS

STANFORD, CALIFORNIA

Sun Yat-sen was originally published as La Chine au XXe siecle: D'une révolution à l'autre 1895–1949.
© Librairie Arthème Fayard, Paris, 1994.

Cover and interior photographs courtesy Hoover Institution, Stanford, California

Stanford University Press
Stanford, California

English translation © 1998 by the Board of Trustees of the Leland Stanford Junior University

Printed in the United States of America
CIP data appear at the end of the book

Published with the support of the French Ministry of Culture

Contents

Note to Reader

ROMANIZATION

In this work, the system generally used to romanize Chinese names is *pinyin.* However, I have kept to traditional usage where it is firmly established; thus Sun Yat-sen (rather than Sun Yixian), Chiang Kai-shek (rather than Jiang Jieshi), Peking (when referring to the pre-1949 period), Nanking (rather than Nanjing), and Canton (rather than Guangzhou).

I have also decided to retain the Cantonese rendering or westernized form of the names of a few important figures: Ho Kai (rather than He Qi), Sun Fo (rather than Sun Ke), Charlie Soong (rather than Song Jiashu).

The other Chinese mentioned in the Notes and the Bibliography are given in *pinyin*, except where authors themselves used a different romanization, in which case their preferred form is retained.

THE VARIOUS NAMES OF SUN YAT-SEN

Like all Chinese, Sun Yat-sen had a number of forenames: the *ming* (personal name) given him at birth, Sun Wen; the *zi* (social name) given him when he entered adult life, Sun Dixiang; several *hao* (literary names) that he adopted later—Sun Rixin, Sun Yixian, Sun Zongshan. Furthermore, the fugitive and outlaw often used protective pseudonyms: in Japan he was known as Naka-yama or Hayashi.

Out of all these names two or three have stuck, not the same ones in China as in the West. The West knows him as Sun Yat-sen (the Cantonese pronun-ciation of the *hao* Sun Yixian). In China, usage is more diversified. Apart from

Sun Yixian, the most current appellations are Sun Wen and Sun Zhongshan. Unlike his other forenames, Zhongshan is often used on its own, without his family name. Literally, Zhongshan means "central mountain," and it symbolizes Sun's eminent position "overlooking the Chinese Republic from on high."

MONETARY UNITS

The taël was the traditional Chinese monetary unit. It corresponded to a weight in silver, which varied by place and sector of activity, roughly 37–38 grams.

The dollar was either an imported silver coin (the Mexican dollar) or a coin minted in China (the Yuan Shikai dollar), which varied in appearance, weight, and name. When other currencies are mentioned, the terms "American dollar," "Hong Kong dollar," "Singapore dollar" are used.

Maps

Sun Yat-sen

Introduction

In October 1979, in Tiananmen Square, Sun Yat-sen's portrait took the place of Mao Zedong's, alongside the great forebears, Marx, Engels, and Lenin. That substitution signaled the beginning of a new era of reforms and opening-up. What better patronage could Deng Xiaoping have found for his policy of the Four Modernizations? Sun Yat-sen (1866–1925) had, after all, been an ardent champion of modernization conceived on the Western model and to be realized with the help of the West. Chinese historians were accordingly encouraged to study the life, thought, and work of the founder of the Chinese Republic and to summon up a new legitimacy from the past that would sanction the power and projects of Deng Xiaoping.

Communist regimes have long since accustomed us to this rewriting of the past to suit the constraints and objectives of the present. In China, this politicized view of history is especially potent because it belongs to a long tradition in which the memory and interpretation of the past are closely linked to the dominant ideology and current government practice. In the days of the empire, historians were government officials employed to preserve and classify documents and establish the correct version of events. Theirs was essentially a moral and didactic task. It was a matter not of bringing to life a particular period or personality but rather of highlighting certain events and actions that could illustrate and uphold Confucian orthodoxy. Anything that did not fit the stereotype was eliminated. The history of individuals was subjected to the same functional approach: personal characteristics, feelings, and aspects were left aside. Only examples of social behavior accommodated by the various networks defined by Confucian morality were considered worthy of attention: essentially, those networks were represented by the family and the bureaucracy. The individual—that is to say the tragic or epic—dimension of history was deliberately ignored.

In this respect, the nationalist regime proved itself as worthy an heir to the empire as communism. Both regimes used Sun Yat-sen as a symbol, representing him as the incarnation of a revolutionary movement conceived in monolithic fashion the better to fit in with an exclusive leadership and a nationalist and socialist line of thought—namely, the doctrine of the Three Principles of the People, as fixed in its latest formulation of 1924, from which all hesitations, limitations, and contradictions were expunged. Both nationalists and communists used historical scholarship as the basis of their political legitimacy and claimed the patronage of Sun Yat-sen in order to sanction regimes born of the revolution: in Taiwan, the "Father of the Nation" (*Guofu*) is the object of a veritable cult; in Beijing, where Marxism-Leninism still constitutes the fundamental ideological reference, the homage paid to the "pioneer of the revolution" makes it possible to claim continuity with the national past.

Thus when, in 1979, the Beijing government called for renewed studies of Sun Yat-sen, it was not trying to encourage any kind of return to historical objectivity. Rather, it wanted to readjust its dogma in such a way as to promote the new policies of reform. Although this process meant emphasizing various aspects of the thought and work of Sun Yat-sen that had so far remained obscure, in principle it was still, notwithstanding, as selective and political an operation as any undertaken earlier. For this reason, this bringing-up-to-date of Sun Yat-sen studies, in spite of its positive side effects, in particular the publication of many of his writings, has received almost no attention from Western historians and has not reconciled them to the figure of Sun.

In the name of a different concept of history founded upon a search for the truth—however elusive—most European and American historians have continued to question Sun's personality and role, stressing the man's weaknesses, the thinker's incoherences, and the revolutionary leader's many failures. The better to destroy the myth, they have launched against it a destructive attack of impeccably researched monographs, underlining the contrast between their own pragmatic and scientific methods and the overall view of their Chinese colleagues.

The historiography of Sun Yat-sen has thus become a prime field of confrontation between two different modes of producing history and, at the same time, an inexhaustible source of mutual incomprehension between Chinese and Western specialists. The study of Sun Yat-sen has been distorted both by the creation of the myth and by the attempts at demythification. Faced with the eminently political constructions of the Chinese historians, Westerners have settled for a positivism justified (and limited) by the demolition of a heroic cult. There being no apparent resolution to this dialogue, Western historiography turned away from Sun Yat-sen. The relaunching of Sun studies in China that began in 1979 produced no echo in the West, where among young historians the rejection of the cult of Sun has tended to become a rejection of the analyses that cult produced: analyses, for example, of the role played by the West in the Chinese quest for modernization, or the role played by coastal China in the nationalist awakening. Sun Yat-sen's omnipresence in Chinese historiography contrasts starkly with his almost total erasure from the historiography of the Western world.

Surely it is time to put an end to this paradox. Between the stereotyped official Chinese histories and the fragmented vision of Western monographs, might there not be room for a measured analysis leading to an overall evaluation of the life and work of Sun Yat-sen? The present work represents an attempt of this kind. Having already devoted a number of studies to the economic and social aspects of the first Chinese modernization (in the early twentieth century), I felt it was natural to turn to the man generally considered to be its promoter, theorist, and embodiment.

Sun Yat-sen, a Cantonese raised in Hawaii and Hong Kong, was a pure product of maritime China, the China of the coastal provinces and overseas communities, open to foreign influences. The travels, encounters, and education that the young peasant received in missionary schools initiated him into the modern world and aroused in him a desire to give China a rank and role worthy of it in that world.

At first he was associated with the secret societies and devoted himself to organizing peasant rebellions; but eventually he got himself accepted by the emerging intelligentsia and became the leader of a nationalist and republican revolutionary party, the Revolutionary Alliance, designed to prepare the downfall of the empire. After the 1911 revolution Sun Yat-sen was fleetingly president of a republic that quickly degenerated into a dictatorship and then into anarchy. Inspired by an unshakable faith in the Chinese national destiny and in his own mission, Sun Yat-sen then struggled to organize a base in Canton where he could rally the forces of progress and seize power from the generals in Peking. In 1924, the hostility of the Western powers forced him to accept an alliance with Soviet Russia, and it was from this model that he drew his inspiration for the reorganization of his party, the Guomindang, and the reformulation of his doctrine of the Three Principles of the People.

On the basis of these data, his eulogists have constructed an exceptional destiny for him: that of a charismatic leader, theorist, and man of action inspired by an ardent patriotism and fully aware of what was at stake in modernization, yet prevented from implementing his program by (according to the nationalist version) the shortcomings of his entourage or (according to the Marxist-Leninist version) by the backward nature of the socioeconomic context.

A simple account of the events of Sun's life produces a very different picture, and it is just such an account that I have primarily tried to provide. Drawing upon two fundamental works published quite recently in the West (by Harold Z. Schiffrin and Martin Wilbur), and following the chronology, I have tried to reconstruct the career that turned an adventurer of the Southern Seas (Part I) into the founding father of a republican regime (Part II), and eventually the leader of a great nationalist movement (Part III).

All biographers face the problem of the context in which their subject developed. In the case of a political leader or a military commander, the difficulty lies in establishing the correct balance between the man himself and the history in which he was involved. Suetonius taught the Western world the art of distinguishing between imperial biography and imperial history, between private life and public life, between the individual and the hero. But in China, where biography is still often close to hagiography (or demonology), the first problem for the historian is to identify the true historical role of his or her subject.

The Sun Yat-sen who emerges from a factual account is a muddled politician, an opportunist with generous but confused ideas, interested first and foremost in conquest and power games. This Sun Yat-sen made little impression on the course of history. In opposition, he was usually impotent, and in the very brief periods when he held the responsibilities of leadership (as President of the Republic at the beginning of 1912, or as head of various provisional governments in Canton, between 1917 and 1924), the power of decision eluded him. Nor was he a great theorist. His doctrine of the Three Principles of the People had neither the originality nor the intellectual rigor of either Marxism or the great political texts of Chinese Reform—by men like

Kang Youwei and Liang Qichao. Sun Yat-sen, it would seem, was not one of those protagonists of history, one of those major actors, whose intervention changes the course of both events and thought. His destiny cannot match that of his contemporary Lenin, whom he dreamed of emulating.

If the cult figure is swept away, what remains of Sun Yat-sen? Nothing, or very little, would be the reply of many of his critics, satisfied or exhausted by having toppled the idol.

But they would be wrong. The real Sun Yat-sen, not the frozen image presented by his eulogists but the man revealed by his adventures and words, his successes and his failures, is a figure of the contemporary world: a communicator, a kind of media genius, born for jetliners, the Fax, and television, despite having had to content himself with steamers, the telegraph, and the press. He did not stamp his mark upon the history of his time. The China of the early twentieth century is not "the China of Sun Yat-sen" in the sense that the France of the later seventeenth century is still known as "the France of Louis XIV." But Sun himself was fashioned by the historical context in which he lived and which he has come to embody: that of China moving toward modernity.

The problems of change, of imitating the Western model, of rejecting or adapting tradition, usually arrived at discursively through intellectual debate and the thinking of men of letters, are in this case conveyed through the destiny of a man who instinctively grasped the aspirations of his time, understood their force, and crystallized them into practical programs. At the end of the empire he thus made antidynastic hostility the hobbyhorse of the opposition; then, during the 1920's, somewhat belatedly focused on anti-imperialist nationalism, contributing in both instances to the mobilization of support for the revolution, if not to the success of the revolutionary project itself.

His intuitive gifts enabled him from the outset to seize upon fundamental developments as they were only just beginning. He foresaw the danger that technocracy might represent to democracy, stressed the role of infrastructures (transport, energy) in economic modernization, and looked forward to a new style of diplomatic and international economic relations based upon cooperation that bypassed or absorbed old hostilities. These "utopias" of his, at which his contemporaries heartily jeered, now seem to be so many prophecies.

Sun Yat-sen's acute perceptiveness was favored by the ex-centric position that he occupied, on the periphery of his own society. He was born at the southernmost part of Guangdong, the coastal province farthest from Peking. He grew up in Hawaii, studied in Hong Kong, and up until 1912—when he was forty-six—he lived outside China, interspersing his visits to Japan and Southeast Asia with trips to the United States and Europe.

But wherever he went he found communities of émigré Chinese merchants, groups of students in quest of training, and exiled intellectuals. His country was what we would today refer to vaguely as "greater China." This community of interlinked expatriate Chinese settlements still connected to the motherland through multiple solidarities—clanic, religious, dialectal, economic—that extended beyond any territorial or national base perpetuated Sun's loyalty to certain aspects of the Confucian culture and at the same time encouraged his conversion to modernity. His travels from one end of the hemisphere to the other, from one link to the next in this vast overseas Chinese network, enabled him to discover the world without breaking with Chinese civilization. He thus looked upon the politics and society of his native country with the critical perspective of a cosmopolitan observer, but without the detachment; he judged China as an outsider but loved it as a son.

Sun Yat-sen was a globe-trotter with a cause. The mission that he assumed or that Heaven had assigned to him—for this egoistic Christian, it came to the same thing—was to save his country. To the service of that ambition he devoted his life, his strength, and the talents with which nature and his education had endowed him: not so much the talents of theorist, organizer, and general (though he certainly did assume all those roles), but those of a communicator.

His extreme geographic mobility nurtured his equally great versatility of mind and temperament. He could cross cultural boundaries as easily as geographical ones, adapt to all societies, all types of men. Some critics have seen this flexibility and plasticity as a mark of inconsistency or even duplicity. But Sun Yat-sen, whose sole strength frequently lay in his powers of persuasion, knew that in order to convince you need to speak the language of the person you are dealing with. He was as capable of operating in missionary circles as in the lodges of secret societies, in merchant guilds as in students' cultural societies, and was as active in Tokyo, London, and San Francisco as he was in Hong Kong, Hanoi, and Singapore.

He took his ideas from wherever he found them and spread them wherever he happened to be, tirelessly pleading his cause with the most varied of publics. Always on the lookout for partners and allies, he tried his luck with Chinese warlords and American bankers, the French military and the Japanese bureaucracy. Certainly these approaches to so many diverse people and the erratic and chance contacts give an impression of, at the least, confusion. Sun Yat-sen had derived his most original ideas from thinkers considered second rate in the West (Henry George, Maurice William) and he recruited his friends among adventurers, fixers, outsiders, idealists, and extremists rejected by their own societies.

But is that not the common lot of those who operate on the frontiers of two or more cultures and manage to establish communication between them? It is not among the elites of scholarship or power that cultural intermediaries or "boundary crossers," of whom Sun Yat-sen presents the perfect model, are recruited, but on the contrary among the half-rejected, the self-taught borne along by faith and great-heartedness, familiar with several cultures but masters of none. Sun Yat-sen was less well versed in the Classics than any lowly mandarin, but he did know how to win the sympathy of English public opinion for the cause of Chinese Reform and how to "sell China" (as one might say, borrowing the vocabulary of advertising) when he was living in London in 1896–97. His views on nationalism, democracy, and socialism were less trenchant than those of any number of contemporary Chinese intellectuals, yet it was through Sun that the inhabitants of Canton, Shanghai, and Peking learned of the ideologies and institutions of the West.

To trace the path followed by Sun Yat-sen is to reconstruct the history of these boundary crossings. It means approaching the process of modernization by swerving away from the royal highways of political and intellectual history and, instead, coming upon it through the back door, having followed along the path of the not particularly prestigious encounters that are the stuff of intercultural communication.

How could the century now drawing to a close under the sign of globalization both cultural and economic, television channel-surfing, and cultural confusion, fail to recognize Sun Yat-sen as its child? How could modern China fail to acknowledge him as one of its founders? Long considered in China itself as an unlucky pioneer or a frustrated utopian, Sun Yat-sen has been dismissed as a man of transition who occupied the stage for no more than an interlude, only until such time as the real hero could make his entrance. Mao Zedong, the man with an iron fist and an assured dogma, got the credit for restoring China's national sovereignty and institutional stability and for launching economic modernization. But notwithstanding the ardor with which the centenary of Mao Zedong (1893–1976) was celebrated, it may well be that in years to come, perspectives will change and, with the anticipated triumph of "Greater China" in the twenty-first century, communism in its turn will appear as no more than a transitory phase in the revolution and modernization prophesied by Sun Yat-sen.

PART ONE

The Adventurer of the Southern Seas,

1866–1905

Until the age of forty, Sun Yat-sen was a man of no importance, a marginal person, one of those adventurers of the treaty ports who live on the fringes of both East and West, trying to make a fortune and establish a career or a destiny on the basis of their ability to move between different languages, different customs, and different beliefs.

As the son of peasants, Sun was from the start excluded from Chinese society, the society of the educated and landowning elites. As a Cantonese, it was quite natural for him to take the path of emigration. Thanks to the protection of an elder brother already settled in Hawaii, exile was not as hard for Sun as for many others, and he had the advantage of being able to attend school. In the Protestant establishments in which he studied for more than ten years, he acquired a half-culture, the ideals of social activism, and a remarkable network of contacts.

His religious education engendered in him a deep and unshakable sense that it would be his vocation to save, not souls, but his country. As an overseas Chinese, familiar with the contemporary world, Sun was well placed to appreciate the gravity of the crisis through which China was passing, preyed upon by greedy foreign powers. But the acculturation that initiated him into modern times did not count in a society given over to the power of the literati. For Sun Yat-sen, a child of the coasts and the open sea and of an extended China exposed to cosmopolitan influences and change, there was no place in the Confucian, bureaucratic empire entrenched on the continental mainland (Chapter 1).

Sun took as his target the system from which he was shut out. He denounced the backward economy, the prejudices of its mandarins, the cruelty of its institutions. And he laid the responsibility for all these evils at the door of the foreign dynasty, the Manchu barbarians who ruled over China. The antidynastic ploy was traditional, but in Sun Yat-sen's case it was wrapped up in pro-Western discourse preaching nationalism and democracy.

Sun's opposition was anchored in the periphery of the official China: in the overseas communities, the circles of merchants and compradors, the lodges of secret societies, the associations of Christian converts. It erupted on the southern fringe of the empire, in the province of Guangdong, where the young revolutionaries plotted against the magistrates and tried to get the peasants to revolt. These incidents led nowhere and had no importance—except for Sun: from being an outsider, he became a criminal, a rebel. He had been an émigré. Now he was an outlaw.

The episode of Sun's kidnapping in London, where the Chinese Legation held him prisoner, made him the hero of a sensational newspaper story, which Sun made the most of to foster his reputation in the West as a patriot and a persecuted liberal progressivist (Chapter 2). His new status won him admittance to Japanese pan-Asiatic circles, which then helped him to launch new, equally unsuccessful insurrections in Guangdong. In his own country Sun Yat-sen was, in 1900, still no more than an unknown or despised outlaw (Chapter 3).

In the last years of the nineteenth century, Sun's fortunes, and those of China, took a new turn. The international expedition against the Boxers brought foreign pressure to a climax and threatened China's survival as a nation. All its structures—ideological, institutional, social—had been undermined. The China of the treaty ports and overseas communities, until then despised for its acculturation, now became a model whose values of nationalism, Westernism, and modernism appealed to a new generation of intellectuals.

Sun Yat-sen rallied to his support the sons of the very literati-officials who had rejected him earlier. In 1905, in Tokyo, with the founding of the Revolutionary Alliance, Sun at the age of thirty-nine finally became the revolutionary leader that up until then he had merely claimed to be (Chapter 4).

This success sanctioned not so much the perseverance of a single man but the rise to power of maritime and coastal China, in the face of the old rural and bureaucratic empire.

ONE

The Formative Years, 1866–1894

Sun Yat-sen was born into a very modest peasant family, raised in Hawaii by an elder brother with a flourishing shop, and educated in colleges in Hawaii and Hong Kong. He was not an intellectual. He was no more attached to the tradition of the Chinese literati nurtured by years of study of the Classics, than he was to the Western culture of Hawaii and Hong Kong, neither of which, at the end of the nineteenth century, represented that culture's finest flower. But neither was he an ignoramus. Caught between two intellectual worlds, he tried to make his own way. He spoke English and wrote Chinese, and he had read widely and had studied the rudiments of Western medicine. He derived his real education not from intellectual speculation but from the observation of the realities of his time.

China was at this time in a perilous state as a result of having been forcibly opened up to foreigners and also owing to the decline of the ruling dynasty. But in China's treaty ports a new society and a new culture were in the process of emerging: foreign trade was booming and there was a lively foreign presence that stimulated a universal desire to get rich quickly; it was a triumph of pragmatism. This coastal civilization, which included not only the mainland communities but also those of the periphery (Hong Kong, Macao) and overseas, stood in contrast to the rural, bureaucratic, Confucian tradition of the provinces of inland China. Canton, Hawaii, Hong Kong, and Macao, where Sun lived during his formative years, were among the major centers of this new civilization. Sun himself appears to have been a pure product of it.

The story of Sun's youth is thus not so much that of the schools he attended, the books he read, and the ideas that he mastered; rather, it is about the encounters he had, the friendships he made, and the links that he established. Sun became part of a whole series of social circles that were to remain loyal to him throughout his career, starting, of course, with his family circle and the village and provincial communities of Guangdong, continuing with the émigré community of Hawaii and the network of Chinese converts to Christianity and, through them, groups of missionaries, foreign protectors, and advisers, and leading as time passed to the Chinese elites of the treaty ports, and even to the secret society lodges.

With consummate skill, Sun Yat-sen moved easily within this complex network of contacts that sometimes overlapped, sometimes clashed. But always, however, his humble birth and unorthodox education prevented him from moving into the world of the literati, the mandarins, and the gentry—still, for a man aspiring to a public role, the only world that counted in China.[1] Perhaps the most humiliating snub occurred in 1894, when Sun was refused admittance by one of the most powerful imperial mandarins, Li Hongzhang (1823–1901), then governor-general of Zhili.[2] Its effect upon this young Cantonese was either to commit him to the path of opposition from the periphery or to confirm him in that potentially novel and radical commitment.

CHINA IN CRISIS: THE ENFORCED OPENING-UP, DYNASTIC DECLINE, AND SOCIAL MALAISE

The Enforced Opening-up

Beginning in the mid-nineteenth century, the burgeoning capitalism of the West increasingly forced China to open up its markets to world commerce and integrate its empire in the international order planned and organized by the European powers. To better prevent conflicts and to preserve both peace and the supremacy of the empire, these powers set about destroying the traditional Chinese system that limited interaction among different peoples. With their immense technological progress in the fields of transport, armaments, and industrial production the Western powers could readily force China, however unwillingly, into the process of opening-up.

The process was initiated with the First Opium War in 1839 and it continued during the next six decades, culminating in the international expedition to put down the Boxer rebellion in 1900–1901. There were many reasons why it took so long. The Western side was hampered not only by the limited scale of the technology initially employed, the aim being not to conquer

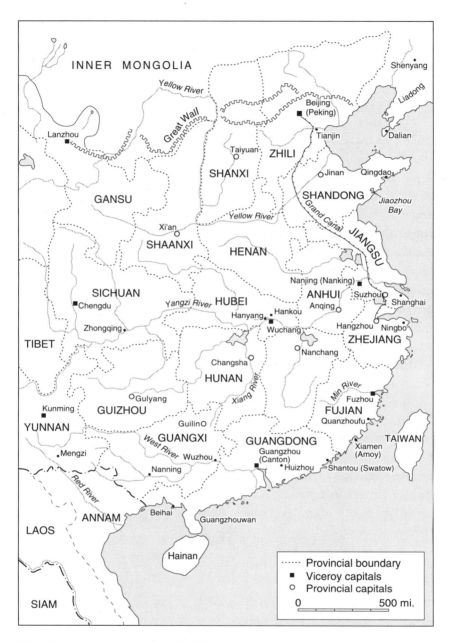

The Chinese provinces at the end of the empire

China but to force it to trade with the European powers and recognize their existence, but also by the rivalry among the various powers. On the Chinese side, the opening-up process was slowed down both by the extreme coherence of the traditional system and by its surprising flexibility, which for several decades enabled it to survive the fatal blow dealt it by the Opium Wars.

The treaties and conventions that brought the Opium Wars to an end (in Nanking in 1842, Tianjin in 1858, and Peking in 1860–61) gave the foreigners a collection of rights and privileges that for nearly a century provided them with a legal framework for their penetration of China. A number of cities were opened to them, where they acquired the right to reside, buy property, and engage in trade. Foreigners in these treaty ports benefited from the rights of extraterritoriality and were liable only to the jurisdiction of their respective consuls. The treaties also established free trade by canceling all forms of official and monopolistic organization on the Chinese side and establishing uniform and moderate customs dues (5 percent *ad valorem*) on imports. Foreign goods were also granted dispensation from internal taxation (*lijin*) in return for the payment of a modest transit tax upon entering Chinese territory. Finally, the treaties allowed missionaries to pursue their religious and social activities, initially only in the treaty ports but subsequently throughout the country.

In practice, the privileges granted by the treaties were given ever broader interpretation. Thus, the concessions—originally simply zones of residence for foreigners in the treaty ports—soon assumed the right of self-government and became veritable foreign enclaves. From the point of view of international law, these privileges represented a grave infraction on the sovereignty of the Chinese empire in that it was deprived of its jurisdiction over part of its resident population and prevented from governing certain portions of its territory and establishing its own customs tariffs.

The Dynastic Decline

The progressive foreign penetration revealed the weakness of the imperial power. It was embodied in a dynasty of Manchu origin, which the Chinese still regarded as foreign despite its having been altogether swamped by the Chinese culture. In the nineteenth century, this dynasty did not produce any great emperors of the caliber of those who had been the glory of China in the preceding century. Following the splendid économic growth of the sixteenth to eighteenth centuries, stagnation had set in and from the 1820's on crises multiplied. Besides the deflation and the commercial contraction that affected the most developed regions of eastern and southern China, there was an increasingly dangerous imbalance between population and agricultural production. In 1850 the population of China rose to 450 million, as a result of the exceptional demographic surge of the preceding centuries, while agricultural production, following the settlement and colonization of the southern and western regions and in the absence of any technological revolution, seemed incapable of further development. Popular feeling reflected these difficulties, and with foreign intervention abetting, discontent eventually erupted in vast rebellions, the most serious of which, the Taiping movement, spread quickly through southern and eastern China between 1851 and 1864. The dynasty seemed on the point of collapsing. But it recovered, thanks mainly to the energy and loyalty of a few Chinese high officials and military generals determined to save the Confucian culture and political order; thanks also to help from the Westerners, who preferred a stable, if weakened, power to uncontrollable rebels.

The stay of execution that history afforded the Manchus coincided with the Tongzhi era (1862–75). In the cyclical concept of traditional Chinese history, this reign appears as a period of restoration (*zhongxing*) that temporarily interrupted the dynastic decline. The rulers of the Tongzhi era restored order and proceeded to rehabilitate the regions devastated and depopulated by the rebellions and their repression. They did not, however, launch any program of reform and modernization comparable to that of the Meiji period of Japan.

The delay in confronting the Western challenge was to a large extent occasioned by the delay in perceiving it. Although the Opium Wars had forced China to open up to trade and diplomatic relations with the West, they had not shaken the mandarins' confidence in the superiority of the Confucian ideology and the sociopolitical system that stemmed from it. The Westerners were only one more species of barbarian, who, if they could not be repulsed, would simply have to be tolerated on the edges of the empire. They could be allowed both to manage their own affairs and to participate, with second-rank status, in the economic and administrative activities of the state and might thereby even accede to civilization (by definition, Chinese). In short, the mandarins in their ignorance of world affairs looked upon the system of treaties, which the foreigners regarded as a "charter of privileges," as nothing more than "a series of restrictive measures."[3]

Nonetheless, some mandarins were anxious to know more about the West—not that they conceded it the slightest intellectual or cultural superiority, but they could not help recognizing its military superiority. The progress of what might be called Chinese westernization was extremely slow. A program for sending Chinese students to the United States, introduced in 1870, was halted in 1875. The reports and memoranda written in the 1880's and the early 1890's by the first Chinese diplomats in Europe testify to the ignorance and bewilderment of these privileged observers. Public opinion— that is to say the opinion of the literati and the imperial officials—remained hostile to the opening-up and was critical of Sino-Western contacts. Efforts to adapt institutionally to the establishment of regular relations with the West remained extremely limited. The Office for the General Administration of Affairs concerning Various Countries (Zongli yamen), considered by the Westerners as a Ministry for Foreign Affairs, was in truth no more than a subsidiary and marginal cog in the Chinese administrative system.

A few important regional leaders, either viceroys[4] or provincial governors, did draw more pertinent conclusions from these early contacts with the West, and from 1860 on adopted modernization policies, known as the Western Affairs Movement (Yangwu yundong). They were just as good Confucians as the court mandarins and were equally convinced of the superiority of Chinese culture, but they recognized the weakness of the imperial armies and appreciated the efficiency of modern weaponry. Borrowing the technology of the West would be a way of protecting the established order more successfully.

This first, essentially conservative Chinese attempt at modernization was characterized by a lack of coherence and continuity, which in part also explained its failure. There was no organized plan for the setting up of arsenals and construction sites, and a viceroy's transfer to another province or his appointment to other duties was likely to jeopardize the development of whatever industries he had just established. The results of a whole decade of efforts were disappointing. Under the influence of Li Hongzhang, the modernization movement did spread during the 1870's to the mining, steel, textile, and modern transport industries, following the sensible idea that China could not strengthen its military might (*qiang*) without at the same time developing its wealth (*fu*), that is to say without setting up the infrastructure indispensable for a modern economic surge. In 1885, China's defeat in the Sino-French war, born from French colonial expansion in Tonking, revealed the meagerness of the results achieved by the renovated modernization program but did not lead to any change in orientation or methods. Quite apart from the shortcomings of the strategy adopted, the causes of failure no doubt lay also in the instrumental concept that guided this modernization effort, which could be summed by the famous Chinese saying: Western knowledge for the practical application, Chinese learning for the essential principles (*xixue wei yong, zhongxue wei ti*). The leaders of the Western Affairs Movement sought to adopt foreign techniques without in any way changing the values of the Chinese tradition.

This semicommitment to modernity was not of a kind to inspire any politics of real change, so in the end the Western Affairs Movement had little real impact on the Chinese economy and society. If anything, the movement probably only strengthened the power of the major provincial governors, who controlled the embryo of modern production, and increased their autonomy in relation to the central government. So it was that even several decades after being opened up, China had changed hardly at all. The trappings of power had been restored. After the death of the emperor Tongzhi,[5] the government in Peking was dominated by the conservative Manchu princes in his entourage and, increasingly, by his mother, the dowager empress Cixi who, having acted as regent in the name of her son, now, in the Guangxu period (1875–1908), ruled in the name of her nephew. The foreign presence remained confined to the south and east of the country, extending along the coast from Canton to Shanghai, and it was essentially commercial in character. For the imperial bureaucracy, an illusion of grandeur still survived. More surprisingly, the power of China continued to inspire a certain respect on the part of the witnesses and partial cause of its decline, the Westerners.

Social Malaise

In truth, society had by no means recovered its stability. Between 1860 and 1890, the general anxiety and malaise found expression in particular in a series of attacks upon missionaries. Though these were carried out by the xenophobic and superstitious masses and involved killing missionaries and looting

reforms likely to ward off the dangers and ensure national development. Compradors, journalists, and former students of foreign institutions were all capable of doing so. But in contrast to what was then happening in colonized countries such as Algeria and India, where the local elites reinforced their own prestige and power by collaborating with the French or the English, the very contacts that these early Chinese theorists of modernization established with the foreigners caused them to be despised by the dominant class, the mandarins. The ideas of these pioneers could find no legitimation or, consequently, application, unless they were promoted by some prestigious official integrated into the traditional hierarchy. For instance, Li Hongzhang recruited a number of experts as private advisers, to promote the Western Affairs Movement. But unless they benefited from patronage such as this, the modernizers of coastal China were held at a distance and could exert no influence on the conduct of affairs of state.

Limited though it was to a very narrow band of the Chinese territory—the coastal strip extending from Tianjin to Shanghai, Canton, and Hong Kong—isolated from the dominant cultural and political tradition, the coastal civilization nevertheless flourished with remarkable vigor in the second half of the nineteenth century. It perpetuated the tradition of a seafaring China of pirates, traders, and adventurers who, as early as the sixteenth and seventeenth centuries, were already serving as intermediaries between the Confucian empire and the foreigners—Portuguese, Japanese, and Dutch—who were clustering round its shores. But this civilization, always regarded with distrust by the imperial power, which found it hard to control, had in the past known only fleeting periods of expansion that coincided with periods when the authority of Peking was temporarily in decline. It had never managed to throw off the bureaucratic yoke for long enough to develop solid political structures of its own or to set itself up as an autonomous force capable of influencing the ideology and practice of the imperial authorities. Now, in the second half of the nineteenth century, the establishment of foreign colonies and concessions in Chinese territory created pockets of relative security where compradors, pioneers, and adventurers could elude the control and repression of the imperial bureaucracy. It was in this "refuge of the concessions" that contact with foreigners made it possible for this cosmopolitan and entrepreneurial China at last to take off.

This coastal civilization of the treaty ports and their immediate periphery was the link to the overseas Chinese communities. Chinese emigration to Southeast Asia, Australia, and the Pacific (known in China as the Countries of the Southern Seas, Nanyang) was an ancient phenomenon. But the constitution of European colonial empires in the nineteenth century created in these regions new perspectives of employment and enrichment; and the Chinese—about 7.6 million of them by the end of the century—made the most of their opportunities. Not all made their fortunes, but many managed to carve out important roles for themselves in the economic life of their adoptive countries, acting as intermediaries between the colonizers and the local populations. The imperial government held them at a distance, suspecting them of favoring a return of the old Ming dynasty, but the émigrés nevertheless maintained family and religious links with their native provinces, essentially those of the south and the southeast. As the treaty ports developed, these links became closer.

The coming and going, the importance attached to material profit, and the vigor of a nationalism stimulated by permanent confrontation with a non-Chinese world all combined with clanic and family solidarities to create a symbiosis between coastal China and the scattered elements of the Chinese diaspora that was so far-flung both geographically and politically. It was in this China of the coast, the sea, and overseas, this "blue," open China, which the reformists and democrats of 1989 were to oppose to the "yellow" China of the continental loess and the Confucian tradition,[6] that Sun Yat-sen grew up and developed.

THE CHILDHOOD AND YOUTH OF SUN YAT-SEN, 1866–1894

Cuiheng, the village in which Sun Yat-sen was born in November 1866, is situated in the Pearl River Delta. The port of Macao is only forty miles to the south, beyond reddish hills that have no doubt not always been as bare as they are today, since they gave the district its name of Xianshan (Perfumed Mountains).[7]

In this tropical countryside, the low-lying alluvial fields were used to grow rice, but only crops of vegetables and potatoes could be produced on the pebbly edges and the sloping earth of the hills that barred the horizon. Life unfolded at the rhythm of age-old agricultural tasks. Herded by a child in a wide-brimmed hat, grey buffalo with gentle movements would pull the plow, wallowing in the ditch water or pasture along the narrow, raised paths that marked the flooded fields. Winding through the hills flowed rivers with amazingly clear water and along their banks fishermen would be stationed, some of them in skiffs made from branches. But in this southern China—the China of all our stereotypes—life was hard for the peasants. Most lived in abject poverty, and Sun Yat-sen's family was no exception. "I am a coolie and the son of a coolie. I was born with the poor," Sun once declared.[8] "Coolie" should be understood in its wide sense of all those who earn their living by the sweat of their brows, through "bitter work" (*kuli*).

Sun's father, Sun Dacheng, owned too little land to support his family and was obliged to supplement his meager resources by a variety of means: as a tailor in Macao, a journeyman, a porter. His mother was a hard-working peasant, despite her bound feet: in 1879 she was to travel to Honolulu to visit her elder son, Sun Mei. He was fifteen years older than Sun Yat-sen and had left the village in 1871 to seek his fortune in Hawaii. His father was aware of the perils in store for the young emigrant—he had already lost two of his own brothers who had gone off to work in the gold mines of California— but poverty dictates the rules, and besides, the young man was proving un-controllable. Sun Yat-sen also had a sister; many years later he still fancied he could hear the little girl's cries of pain as they began to bind her feet to break the bones.

Sun Yat-sen spent his first thirteen years in Cuiheng. Little is known about them. Presumably he shared the life of the village children, working with his father in the fields. It is known that, from time to time, he attended the elementary school organized and funded by a number of local families. There, under the schoolteacher's rule, the children would learn to read by memorizing—aloud and all together but not necessarily in unison—the textbook, *Classics in Three Characters.*[9]

Sun's peasant childhood came to an end with his brother's triumphant return to the village, having made his fortune, to visit his parents and marry the girl they had chosen for him. It was at this point that Sun Yat-sen's departure was decided. The following year his mother accompanied him to Honolulu. On their way, the travelers paused in Hong Kong, where, as Sun recorded, "I admired the ships and the huge expanse of the sea, and my desire to learn of the West and explore the vast world increased."[10]

The islands of Hawaii had already been open to Western commercial and religious influences for more than half a century. Apart from sandalwood, their principal resources were rice and sugar cane, the production of which had increased greatly since the signing, in 1876, of a treaty of reciprocity with the United States. The modern blocks of Honolulu housed banks and trading companies. Its port bustled with the comings and goings of foreign ships. The local monarchy presided over these changes, but the influence of the United States was growing ever stronger. Sun discovered a new world in the process of modernization and stamped by Western influences. He could easily have lived on the margins of this world as many other emigrants did, participating in the wealth and dynamism and contributing to it, without ever stepping outside the environment of the Chinese community.

But his elder brother, Sun Mei, decided that the adolescent should first complete his education. There being no Chinese establishment on the island of Oahu, Sun Yat-sen was enrolled as a board pupil in the Iolani school, a missionary school under the patronage of the Anglican Bishop Alfred Willis. The students were mostly Hawaiians and half-castes; all the teaching was in English. Sun Yat-sen attended the Iolani school for three years. He learned English and was even awarded a second prize for grammar at the prize-giving of July 1882. Attendance at daily prayers and Sunday service was compulsory and Sun Yat-sen became initiated into the Christian rituals and hymns and the reading of the Bible. He learned to identify Christianity with progress and began to distance himself from the worship of the domestic gods practiced in his brother's house and to think of being baptized as a Christian.

In the autumn of 1882, along with other children from the missionary school, Sun moved to Oahu College, run by American Congregationalists, to continue his initiation into Western knowledge, in particular the rudiments of medicine and law. But Sun Mei, irritated by his younger brother's plan to convert—which to him meant betraying their ancestors and rejecting their Chinese identity—withdrew his support and in 1883 sent Sun Yat-sen back to Cuiheng.

What had the village, with its closed horizon, its popular cults, and superstitious practices, to offer this sixteen-year-old boy who had been exposed to new learning and beliefs? Everything in the village provoked Sun's indignation and mockery. He created scandal by attacking the local temple, with the help of his friend Lu Haodong, a native of Xianshang who had been educated in Shanghai. The two young iconoclasts vandalized the wooden statues of the protective deities, much in the manner of the Taiping rebels whose memory was still very much alive among the Cantonese. The indignant villagers were certain that the foreigners had poisoned Sun Yat-sen's mind. His family, although extremely irritated by him, made it possible for him to escape the village and return to his studies, this time in Hong Kong.

In the spring of 1884, Sun entered the Government Central School (now Queen's College), a secondary school for middle-class children of all nationalities, in which the English curriculum was complemented by the teaching of Chinese. The two and a half years that he spent at the Government Central School were marked by important developments in his personal and family life: his baptism into the Christian religion, his first marriage, a dramatic confrontation with Sun Mei, and, at the level of public life, the deeply felt humiliation of the Chinese by the French in 1885.[11]

Sun Yat-sen was baptized by an American Congregationalist, Dr. Charles Hager, a recent arrival in Hong Kong, at the same time as the companion of his escapades, Lu Haodong. A real friendship seems to have linked the young minister to his convert Sun, whose religious zeal he praised and who was soon accompanying him on his missionary tours. They even went to Cuiheng, where Sun's family offered them several days' hospitality. Owing to the success of its elder son, the family home had become one of the most comfortable in the village. After the incidents of the previous year, Sun must have needed considerable courage to proclaim his faith publicly in this way. A photograph taken at this time shows a young man aged about eighteen, clad in a high-necked Chinese robe and a traditional cap. His serious face and astonishingly direct gaze give him the air of a man of conviction, not an agitator. Following custom, Sun agreed to the marriage that his parents had arranged with the daughter of a merchant's family, Lu Muzhen (1867–1952). Left in the village, in the house of her parents-in-law, this young woman was to bear and raise Sun's children but share hardly at all in the life of her husband, who soon left again to study and travel. Marriage in traditional China was founded not upon romantic love but upon a sense of filial piety and one's duty to carry on the ancestral line.

Sun Mei, meanwhile, was still hostile. Learning of his brother's conversion, he summoned him to Hawaii, meaning to set him back on the right path by cutting off his means of support. But Sun Yat-sen could now find help from new friends among the Christians, in particular the Reverend Frank

Damon, also a Congregationalist. These friends made it possible for him to return to Hong Kong in 1886. Sun Mei, too, relented, and the supplies of cash were resumed. But the several months' long visit to Hawaii had brought Sun's secondary studies to a close and he left the Government Central School without a diploma.

Sun now faced an uncertain future, with a very limited choice of training and career. His peasant origins barred his admission to any modern institutions in China, in particular the naval academies of Jiangnan (Shanghai) and Fuzhou. So his fleeting dream of becoming a naval officer evaporated. Both Dr. Hager and Reverend Damon seem to have expected Sun to make a brilliant career as a preacher. Sun had probably encouraged them in this idea, for the funds that he requested from the Hawaii Christians were supposedly to allow him to return to Hong Kong to study theology. But there was no seminary in Hong Kong, so Sun Yat-sen gravitated toward medical studies, apparently with no particular vocation but with an ardent desire to improve his understanding of the Western sciences. With the help of a letter of introduction from Dr. Hager, Sun was accepted into the Medical School of the Canton Hospital, which was headed by Dr. John Kerr, its founder, of the (American) Presbyterian Church's Foreign Missions. Sun was joined there by his old village friend Lu Haodong, and he also became friendly with another fellow student and baptized Christian, Zheng Shiliang. Zheng, the son of a rich Shanghai merchant, who had been educated at a German missionary school in Canton, had many contacts in the secret societies of eastern Guangdong, the region from which his family hailed, and the three friends appear to have discussed China's destiny frequently, though without yet reaching any definite conclusions.

After one year in Canton, Sun moved to Hong Kong, where in October 1887 he enrolled in the College of Medicine for the Chinese. This was a new college that had just been established as an offshoot of the London Missionary Society, under the patronage of one of the most eminent representatives of the anglicized elite of Hong Kong, Ho Kai (He Qi, 1859–1914). The director of the college was a remarkable Scottish-born doctor, Dr. James Cantlie. Sun Yat-sen was indeed the first student to enroll, and he would be among the first to graduate, in 1892. In his five years at the college, Sun acquired the bases of medical science and practice; and at least as important, he expanded his understanding of both Western and Chinese culture and extended his network of contacts, at the same time continuing to reflect upon and discuss the necessary modernization of his country. His closest friends during this period were Chen Shoabai (1869–1934) a Christian from Canton, well versed in the Chinese Classics and the blood-brother of Sun Yat-sen, whom he had joined at the College of Medicine; Yang Heling (1867–1931), the son of a rich Cuiheng family who was engaged in business in Hong Kong; and, introduced by Yang, You Lie, a clerk of Cantonese origin, who had been initiated into the activities of the secret societies while visiting Shanghai. The young men often met in Yang's shop, to continue the passionate discussions that nobody around them took very seriously. "Our discussions went on forever. We would talk of revolution, yearn for revolution, study revolution. . . . We were known as 'the Four Great Bandits.' "[12]

A VAST NETWORK OF FRIENDS AND CONTACTS

It is difficult to assess the level of the medical qualifications that Sun acquired at the College of Medicine. Neither the British Hong Kong authorities nor the Portuguese authorities of Macao recognized the diploma. During the brief period when Sun actually worked as a doctor, first in Macao, then in Canton, the medicine that he practiced was half-European, half-traditional. His mentor, Dr. Cantlie, had a high opinion of the capabilities of his favorite student and subsequently earnestly encouraged him to complete his training in England. But Sun did not intend to become one of the Chinese pioneers of Western science and technology. Though the work of these men played an important role in the modernization of coastal China at the end of the nineteenth century and the beginning of the twentieth, such careers were relatively obscure. Moreover, the specific, limited, and gradual impact of such a profession was not the sort of impact the ambitious Sun had in mind for himself and his country.

The most obvious benefit that Sun derived from his college training was the formation of a complex and solid network of social relations that he would soon use to serve his own interests and those of his cause. The men he met rather than the books he read were what most influenced his thinking. The network of connections he would rely on in his activities was also that of those who had shaped his thought.

Sun was open and adaptable, always skillful at suiting his discourse to the situation so that he could cope with the divergences and contradictions of those around him. On an intellectual level, however, one cannot easily work out how he synthesized the various influences he came under. Certainly his patriotism and his opposition to imperial policies were clear by the time he emerged from his years of training, but his political thought was still hesitant and ill-defined.

The first circle in which Sun set about gaining control was that of his family. Family solidarity is, to be sure, part of the Chinese tradition, but its effect is generally to subordinate the individual and his ambitions to the interests of the group as defined by its older members: the father and the elder brother. In Sun Yat-sen's case this situation was reversed, and, after a few difficulties, it was the family that put itself at the service of the young man. After the crisis of 1883, when Sun returned to the village and mutilated the temple statues, his father had agreed to send him back to Hong Kong to pursue his studies. Sun's elder brother, in spite of his conservatism and hostility to Christianity, in the end accepted Sun's conversion, and from then on never failed to provide regular and generous funding for the activities of his younger brother—not only for his studies but also for his first political organization, for which Sun Mei acted as an effective propagandist in the Chinese community of Hawaii. Sun Mei also took on his brother's family responsibilities. In 1895, after Sun Yat-sen's failed Canton rebellion, Sun Mei arranged to have his mother, now a widow, and also Sun Yat-sen's wife and three children, come to live close to him on the island of Maui, and thereafter he supported them all. Long before Sun Yat-sen became any kind of celebrity, his family made it possible for him to live free from material worries and devote himself entirely to his political plans. In this respect, his story is particularly atypical and quite at variance with the cultural and social stereotype so characteristic of modern China, that of the young man who sacrifices his own aspirations and talent through filial piety and family discipline.

The other traditional network that Sun Yat-sen was able to use to his profit was that of the regional solidarities that linked together people from the same village, district, or province.

His friendship with Lu Haodong, which went back to his village childhood, was cut short in 1895, when Lu, a fine figure of disinterested patriotism, was executed after the failure of Sun's first attempt at a revolutionary insurrection, in Canton. Yang Heling, whose shop in Hong Kong had served as a meeting place for the "Four Great Bandits," seems not to have had a significant part in Sun's subsequent activities, but he was always loyal. Was this an effect of the traditional Chinese system of personal relationships (*guanxi*)? Or was it due to the charisma of the future revolutionary leader? Sun always seemed to have the knack of reactivating contacts, even many years later, whenever he felt the need to do so. So it was that a cousin of Yang's, settled in Taiwan, was to help Sun's partisans stir up unrest on the island following its annexation by the Japanese in 1895.

The circle of regional solidarities widened considerably at the district level. By the first half of the twentieth century, the Xiangshan district had already produced numerous compradors, many of whom later pursued fine careers as entrepreneurs and modernizers in Hong Kong, Canton, or Shanghai. Xiangshan also produced large contingents of emigrants: to list the names of outstanding figures who originated in Xiangshan is to recite a Who's Who of pioneering China, from Shanghai to Canton, Hong Kong, and as far afield as the overseas communities. In a society run by traditional rules, particularly in the shifting and geographically far-flung society of peripheral and external China, it was crucial to be able to place one's associates, to know about their families and contacts and also where to find them, if necessary. Sun would thus often refer back to Xiangshan, whether to gain access to important men such as the great comprador Zheng Guanying, adviser to the viceroy Li Hongzhang, or to rally partisans to his cause. It is, for example, remarkable that roughly half the members of his first revolutionary movement, created in 1894–95, were natives of this district.

At the provincial level, regional solidarities were of course looser—it should not be forgotten that by the end of the nineteenth century Guangdong had about 30 million inhabitants—but they were nevertheless very real, and they provided Sun Yat-sen with a spontaneous, natural framework for his activities. In the first decades of his career, the overwhelming majority of the Chinese whom he met and recruited or with whom he collaborated were Cantonese. When the right moment came, in 1904–5, Sun was ready to move beyond this regionalism, which was by then in danger of changing from a basis of support into an impediment to his political career and plans. But even after he had entered upon his national destiny, in his political thought and strategy he was to continue to ascribe a special role to Guangdong and the Cantonese.

Sun Yat-sen also owed much of his popularity and support in many overseas communities to the Cantonese background that he had in common with many émigrés or *huaqiao*. And his popularity was also founded on his personal and family links with Hawaii, which provided him with introductions to cousins and acquaintances who, amid the mobility that characterized the diaspora, had been led to other regions in the Nanyang or America.

The network of Protestant missions run by English and American preachers, around which Chinese converts gravitated, played an essential role not only in Sun's education but also in his early career. Through more than thirteen years of schooling, starting with his arrival at the Iolani School in 1879, moving on from one establishment to another, from Hawaii to Canton to Hong Kong, Sun was a student, a protégé, of the Protestant missionaries.

This group had in 1880 or so begun to reorient their activities, switching from religious proselytizing to wider forms of social action, including education. They were among the first to introduce Western history, geography, science, and technology into China. They also endeavored to make the Chinese public—not only the pupils of religious schools and the experts of coastal China but also the mandarins and liberati with open minds—realize that Western civilization had more than just technology to offer: It had values to communicate, too, and its success lay not just in its scientific superiority but in its ability to mobilize the energies of its peoples in collective action and to organize their political participation in a context of respect for democratic institutions and individual liberties.

Through their teaching and their published works and through the remarkable personalities of missionaries such as Timothy Richard and Young Allen,[13] the Protestants were closely associated with the awakening of modern China and its first reformist and nationalist aspirations. Of all the missionaries who figured in Sun Yat-sen's youth—from Dr. Hager who baptized him in 1884 to the American Reverend Damon who helped him face the anger of his brother, and old Dr. Kerr who admitted him to the Medical School of the Canton Hospital in 1866—the most influential seems to have been Dr. Cantlie, whose favorite student Sun became at the Hong Kong College of Medicine between 1887 and 1892.

James Cantlie was born in 1851 into a family of very modest agricultural laborers that worked hard to raise its eleven children. He studied first literature and philosophy at Aberdeen University, then medicine in London. He was a man deeply cultivated in a vast field of subjects and also possessed of a generous, even impetuous temperament, not afraid to challenge convention. The broad views that he held of his profession as a doctor made him an indefatigable social activist. In Hong Kong, he took a personal interest in Sun Yat-sen, taught him cricket as well as medicine, took him to visit leper villages (in the course of a medical inquiry that was awarded a prize), and helped him to perform a number of delicate surgical operations during Sun's brief period of practice in Macao. James Cantlie was on several occasions to play an extremely important role in the life and career of Sun Yat-sen.

Sun was adept at making the most of these networks of missionary friends. Dr. Hager's letter of introduction to Dr. Kerr had helped him gain admission to the School of Medicine of the Canton Hospital, at a reduced tuition. It was likewise on the recommendations of missionaries that Sun Yat-sen obtained an entrée to the circles of journalists and diplomats in the treaty ports and, later, to American and European political circles.

The Chinese converts to Christianity who were part of missionary society formed a closely knit group within which Sun Yat-sen found many sources of support. Most of his childhood friends, student companions, and the participants in his first political discussions were Chinese converts—Lu Haodong, Zheng Shiliang, and Chen Shaobai, who was up to be Sun's lieutenant for ten or more years. Chen, Cantonese-born, had attended the Canton Christian College, the principal missionary establishment in southern China, set up in 1888 by the American Presbyterian Mission, and he was also schooled in the Classics. From him, and also from Chinese pastors—in particular Qu Fengzhi in Hong Kong—Sun acquired some knowledge of the Chinese Classics. This network of Cantonese Christians was subsequently to prove very useful to Sun in his private business ventures: part of the funds for the Pharmacy of East and West that Sun set up in 1893 in Canton were provided by Qu Fengzhi. It also helped him in his political activities: the first revolutionary uprisings that Sun organized in Guangdong in 1895 and 1900 received active backing from local pastors and other Christians.

Finally, Sun Yat-sen gained admittance to Hong Kong's circle of anglicized Chinese elites, among them Ho Kai, the founder of the College of Medicine, who was not above taking a hand in some of its teaching. This remarkable man influenced the thinking of the young Sun and enabled him to make numerous contacts with the Chinese and English "establishment" of the colony.

Ho Kai was a second-generation pioneer. His father, who had emigrated to Malaysia, had converted to Christianity, and subsequently, with the aid of the London Missionary Society, had embarked upon the career of a preacher, then launched himself successfully into business. He was a cultivated man who made sure that his son Ho Kai received an excellent Sino-British education in the Government Central School (where Sun Yat-sen studied from 1884 to 1886), then in the Faculties of Medicine and Law in Aberdeen, Scotland. Upon returning to Hong Kong in 1882, Ho Kai, as a member of the Legislative Council and all the official commissions, had become one of the Chinese community's principal representatives with the colony's British authorities. He also set up a number of foundations, in particular that of the Alice Memorial Hospital (so named in memory of his English wife), the management of which he entrusted to the London Missionary Society and to which, in 1887, he added the College of Medicine. Ho Kai's dream was to modernize China along Western lines, and he figures prominently in Sun's early political activities, as an inspiration, strategist, and influential connection to British journalistic and diplomatic circles in Hong Kong.

Sun Yat-sen does not appear to have had many contacts in his youth with the secret societies whose henchmen he was later to mobilize for his revolutionary uprisings. He was certainly aware of the tradition of loyalty to the Ming dynasty and of opposition to the Manchu invaders that had survived for two centuries in the Triads of southern China.[14] Deplored by the imperial authorities and their bureaucracy and deserted by the mandarins and literati, most of these loyalist groups became fraternities and mutual assistance societies that attracted the poor and the outcast. Force and violence were their means of action, secrecy their protection. In the 1850's and 1860's, the Taiping revolt had been sustained by their hostility toward the established society; and the Taiping tradition was still very much alive in the Cantonese countryside. Sun Yat-sen must have learned something about it in his village, certainly at one point from his friend Lu Haodong, who had told him of the Taiping leaders who, after a superficial conversion to Christianity, had made the "destruction of idols" and the struggle against superstition the bases of their dogma. Sun and Lu may have regarded their attack on the Cuiheng temple as a sort of continuation of the popular rebellion of three decades earlier. In Hong Kong, Sun's friends nicknamed him Hong Xiuquan, after the Taiping leader. Zheng Shiliang, whom Sun met at the Canton Medical School, was in fact a high-ranking Triad dignitary, and he drew Sun's attention to the subversive potential of the secret societies. Up until 1894, however, Sun Yat-sen does not seem to have established relations with them.

All these groups and social networks, here presented one by one, overlapped or opposed one another in a complex fashion. Many family, Cantonese, and émigré circles overlapped or identified with one another: for instance, the circle of modernized elites of the treaty ports, that of the missionaries and converts, and that of the diplomats, journalists, and foreign businessmen. But many divergences and oppositions also existed: between the family circle and the circle of Chinese Christians (as is testified by Sun Mei's hostility to the baptism of his younger brother); between secret societies perpetuating the most arcane superstitions and modernized Chinese elites of the treaty ports and Hong Kong, who dreamed of introducing their country to scientific progress and the social and political institutions of the West; and between the xenophobic secret societies and the foreign missionaries against whom they were forever launching armed attacks.

One cannot but admire the ease with which Sun Yat-sen moved in all these circles, using them for his own purposes without ever being drawn into their purposes. This skill of his seems to have been quite exceptional, even in a society founded upon the systematic exploitation of interpersonal relations; and it grew ever more remarkable as his career proceeded.

However, there was one point that was common to all the social circles familiar to Sun Yat-sen, namely, their marginality with respect to the dominant currents in the Chinese society of his day. The peasantry from which Sun's family came was so looked down upon by the literati and the mandarins that it was hardly possible for the scion of a villager's family to aspire to any public role. And the imperial authorities mistrusted the overseas communities, suspected of loyalist sentiments toward the Ming dynasty, geographically distant and presumed to be contaminated by the foreign societies into which they had had to fit. The populace and gentry alike reviled and feared the Christian missionaries, and despised converts. The traditional dominant classes neither recognized nor appreciated the modernized elites of the ports, dismissing their foreign diplomas as worthless and criticizing them for their new ideas, their acculturation, and their ignorance of the Classics. In the eyes of the literati-officials, their contacts with the Westerners alone set them apart from the great current of Chinese civilization. They were relegated to the dubious category of compradors, traders, adventurers, and outlaws. As for the secret societies, the literati-officials regarded them as refuges for marginal people, and their practices, which were developed outside the established ideology and order, attracted the same kind of reprobation as those of the Mafia do in our own societies.

So, even if Sun Yat-sen had found a firm footing in the society that surrounded him, winning recognition for his talents and establishing many friendly and protective relations, in the eyes of the dominant classes of Chinese society he was still an outsider. The social integration that Sun Yat-sen had so strikingly achieved was thus limited; a jealously guarded tradition reserved the kind of success that Sun had imagined for those who won honors in the mandarin examinations, the perpetuators and agents of the Confucian ideology. Sun's popularity with the elites of the treaty ports meant nothing at all to those of the imperial bureaucracy, who, of course, in the last decades of the nineteenth century, still held the power. Certainly they assumed a monopoly over not only exercising their power but also reforming it—that is, if any reforming was to be attempted.

Sun Yat-sen left from the years of his studies no writings of a kind to shed light on the evolution of his political thought during this period. The testimony of his contemporaries is conflicting. As a result, a whole polemic has developed around the question of whether Sun Yat-sen was a reformist in those days or had already become a revolutionary.[15]

As has already been noted, Sun Yat-sen was not a man to attach much importance to ideas for their own sake. He was not particularly concerned about intellectual coherence and theoretical problems. He was exposed to extremely contradictory influences, and he seems to have welcomed them all without bothering about conceptual problems and speculations. But there is no doubt that his whole geographical, social, and political environment led him to see and sense the decline into which China was sinking. He was later to declare, in a speech delivered at the University of Hong Kong in 1923, that in his student days the good administration of the colony had opened his eyes to the corruption and backwardness of Guangdong, where he regularly returned for his vacations.[16] Even bearing in mind Sun Yat-sen's unfailing tendency to flatter his audience (in that case, the representatives of the colonial establishment), it seems quite likely that such a comparison must indeed have struck the young patriot. We also know—for he later often alluded to the fact—that he was acutely upset by the humiliating defeat inflicted upon China in the war of 1884–85. According to his *Autobiography* (written in 1918), it was even at that point that he came to the decision to overthrow the dynasty that was incapable of protecting China.[17] Although that declaration, formulated forty years on, should perhaps be taken with a pinch of salt, it still seems likely that the defeat impressed upon Sun the urgency of the need for change.[18]

On the nature and orientation of that change Sun Yat-sen does not seem to have had any clear plan. Should they, as the Triads preached, fight against the Manchu dynasty in the name of loyalty to the old Ming emperors? Some of Sun's friends, Zheng Shiliang among them, pointed out to him the huge destabilizing force that could be represented by these secret lodges with their already organized and committed members trained in violent and clandestine action. Or should they help the Manchu dynasty to reform and modernize China by adopting Western techniques and institutions? In an article published in February 1887 in the *China Mail*, which Sun must certainly have read, the distinguished Hong Kong philanthropist, Ho Kai, pleaded for reforms far more fundamental than those attempted under the aegis of the Western Affairs Movement.[19] It was not enough to import arms and fasten "bolts" on China's doors; first it was necessary to change the institutions, recruit competent officials initiated into the modern world, and reform education. The reason for China's decline was really not so much its military weakness as its failure to adapt, and to overcome the decadence of its ways of life, its society, and its internal organization.

In the missionary school in Hawaii, Sun Yat-sen had been taught the history of Europe and the United States. He dreamed of Washington and Napoleon and perhaps already of a Chinese republic. But as it happened, it was not an intellectual debate that got him to make or to confirm his choice among all these options, but a demoralizing social experience. His lack of success with the great imperial mandarin Li Hongzhang, to whom he went to explain his ideas and offer his services in 1894, turned the peasant outcast into a rebel ready to engage upon an antidynastic and anti-imperial struggle.

THE ATTEMPT AT SOCIAL AND POLITICAL INTEGRATION: THE PETITION TO LI HONGZHANG, 1894

Although the coastal Chinese with special skills who, through their studies, travels, and personal contacts had become initiated into the Western world, had no chance of a career in the mandarin bureaucracy, some nevertheless gravitated to its margins. The mandarins were in the habit of engaging a number of advisers, working without official titles, to help them in their administrative and political tasks. In particular, in the second half of the nineteenth century, some viceroys who were receptive to the idea of a partial modernization of China set about recruiting, on a personal basis, experts whose function was to enlighten and assist them. In the entourages of the great mandarins, what amounted to brain trusts (or think tanks) were thus set up, composed of compradors, translators, and journalists. Their direct access to the high-ranking officials whom they served increased their own social prestige, and their influence carried weight not only within the framework of the treaty ports but also, indirectly, even within the traditional sociopolitical institutions.

In this way, some of the greatest thinkers and entrepreneurs of modern China were to be found in the entourage of the viceroy Li Hongzhang. Some occupied subordinate positions: Yan Fu (1853–1921), for example, who after 1895 emerged as one of the principal political philosophers of his time. After his education in the modern school attached to the arsenal of Fuzhou, he had traveled in Europe, spending two years in England. Upon his return to China, where he was not accepted for a career in the administration, he took employment in the service of Li Hongzhang. The great comprador Zheng Guanying (1842–1923) was also a protégé of the viceroy, who entrusted him with the establishment of a modern cotton mill of mixed status in Shanghai, to be supervised by officials but managed by merchants (*guandu shangban*). Li Hongzhang also employed another comprador, Tang Tingshu (1832–92), who worked for the British company Jardine and Matheson, to manage the China Merchants' Steam Navigation Company. A journalist, Wang Tao (1828–98), formerly assistant to the English sinologist James Legge, whom he helped to translate the Classics and accompanied on his travels in Europe, also belonged to this little group: the articles that he published first in Hong Kong, then in Shanghai, were attentively studied. Some of these experts belonged to the great merchant or literati families: one was Ma Jianzhong (1844–1900), the scion of a dynasty of Shanghai shipowners of Catholic upbringing, who was the first Chinese to obtain the baccalauréat diploma in France and whom Li Hongzhang made his personal secretary; another was Xue Fucheng (1839–94), who, with an uncompleted degree, entered the service of Li Hongzhang and was later, in the early 1890's, sent as a diplomatic representative to London and Paris.

These men were the real thinkers behind the Western Affairs Movement, to which Li Hongzhang gave his backing. Their thought extended far beyond the framework of the movement itself, which was subjected to many political and administrative constraints. As early as 1875, the comprador Zheng Guanying was calling for the free development of trade and industry and deploring the harmful effects of bureaucratic interference in the economy. In 1879, Xue Fucheng pleaded for the development of national capitalism, the only effective protection against Western imperialism.

After the Chinese defeat at the hands of the French in 1884–85 and the appearance, in February 1887, of Ho Kai's article in *China Mail*, these experts came around to the idea that the modernization of production must be accompanied by political reform. The arguments put forward by Ho Kai were taken up and developed by Zheng Guanying, whose *Warning to an Apparently Prosperous Age* (*Shengshi wei yan*), published in 1893, made a profound impact. The reformists were all in agreement in condemning absolutism and calling for some kind of representative government. They sought their model in Great Britain, Germany, and Japan (which in 1889 had adopted a new constitution). As partners of progress, they insisted upon the need to develop education, but they were certainly not radicals: the notions of liberty, equality, and democracy were far from their minds. The political participation that they recommended was limited to a tiny, wealthy, and educated elite. They remained loyal to the Confucian doctrine, even if they rejected the politico-social order connected with it. And however much they wished to repulse imperialistic aggression, they were still prepared to accept foreign aid to develop the Chinese economy and set up new institutions.

At the turn of the 1880's, reformist ideas of this kind were circulating in the major treaty ports and also in Peking, where these more enlightened officials, reestablishing links with the secular tradition of "disinterested proposals" (*Qingyi*)—that is, political debate within the bureaucracy itself—began frankly criticizing governmental policies. The autocratic imperial regime had never encouraged public opinion, but "disinterested proposals" did from time to time appear, usually in periods of crisis serious enough to alarm the literati and officials and to point up the weakness and uncertainty of the imperial government and the upper administration. Such was, precisely, the situation of China in the second half of the nineteenth century, following the wars over the opening-up of China and the Taiping revolt.

In the course of the decade of the 1880's, the movement of discussion and criticism spread beyond the capital to the provinces, drawing in increasing numbers of not only officials but also important local figures: rich merchants, landowners, literati without official posts. These local elites, accustomed to operating within the framework of community interests (*gong shi*), organizing philanthropic and public works, social assistance, and local militia, were now extending their attention to problems of national interest. It was apparent that the struggle against imperialism, nepotism, and the corruption and favoritism practiced by the imperial court must involve the participation of the "people," or at least of an enlightened fraction of them. This politicization of the local elites, most noticeable in the coastal provinces of Jiangsu, Zhejiang, and Guangdong, was stimulated by the press of the treaty ports, in particular the Shanghai daily, *Shenbao*. The frustrations of scholars and officials thus fused with the growing ambitions of local elites and new influences from the coast, in a demonstration of public opinion seeking moderate reformism.

It was this reformist current that Sun Yat-sen tried to become part of in the early 1890's. He approached a number of official figures in an attempt to win recognition for his skills as a specialist familiar with foreign knowledge and to gain admittance to the circuit of mandarin experts who ran the Western Affairs Movement. But it was not easy for a peasant's son educated in missionary schools and equipped only with a diploma regarded as worthless in Chinese eyes to attract the attention of imperial officials or local "notables." Sun's first approach, in 1890, was a letter to a degree holder (*juren*)[20] named Zheng Zaoru (d. 1894), who had formerly served as minister to Japan and the United States and had managed the customs service for Tianjin under Li Hongzhang. Presumably on the strength of their common geographical origins, Sun was able to establish relations with this high-ranking figure, but got nowhere. He next made contact with Zheng Guanying, one of the chief inspirers and rank-and-file leaders of the Western Affairs Movement (also a protégé of Li Hongzhang), and a native of Xiangshan. Some authors believe they can detect a touch of Sun's influence in Zheng's famous pamphlet, *Warning to an Apparently Prosperous Age*.

In 1894, deserting medical practice for good, Sun Yat-sen launched himself into the career of a professional politician and prepared a long petition, which he decided to present in person to the viceroy Li Hongzhang in Tianjin. Accompanied by his childhood friend Lu Haodong, Sun set off for Tianjin by way of Shanghai, where he made contact with the reforming journalist Wang Tao and secured letters of introduction to the viceroy. But Li Hongzhang denied him the hoped-for interview. The publication of the petition in the September–October 1894 issue of *Globe Magazine* (*Wanguo gongbao*), a Shanghai missionary publication very popular in reformist circles, was small consolation.[21] Shortly thereafter, Sun Yat-sen left China for Hawaii, where his revolutionary career was to begin.

Historians have produced many glosses on Sun Yat-sen's journey to Tianjin and his petition to Li Hongzhang, though Sun in his *Autobiography* does not mention either his petition or Li Hongzhang and attributes that trip to the north to a desire to assess the strength of the Manchu regime with his own eyes. The petition was not particularly original: it presented the general themes of the reformist literature and newspapers already developed by Ho Kai and Zheng Guanying: the strength of foreign nations lay not only in "the solidity of their ships and the force of their cannons" but also in free trade, the use of human skills, and the exploitation of natural resources. Sun particularly emphasized the importance of education, which made it possible to recruit men of talent, and agricultural progress. He was clearly well briefed on reformist plans. Did he at this point sincerely support them? He himself traced his commitment to revolution to the Franco-Chinese War of 1884–85, almost a decade earlier. Indeed, a number of historians have suggested that Sun's trip to Tianjin may have had secret revolutionary purposes. Others interpret the text as showing the common ground between Sun and the reformists.

The key to the riddle no doubt lies not so much in the history of ideas as in considerations of a social and much more immediate nature. It does seem that Sun Yat-sen's motivation in this episode was his desire to brazen his way into that world of mandarins and literati-officials to which, by reason of his birth and education, he presumably had no entrée. He knew that he was not capable of composing the essays in eight parts (*bagu*) in which every scholar presenting himself as a candidate in the imperial examinations was supposed to be skilled. However, in his petition to Li Hongzhang he set out his own qualifications in the domain of Western affairs: "I have passed English medical examinations in Hong Kong. . . . In my youth, I experienced overseas studies. The languages of the West, its literature, its political science, its customs, its mathematics, its geography, its physics and chemistry—all these I have had the chance to study."[22]

It was an altogether proper *curriculum vitae* for a request for employment in the category of experts and advisers. Unfortunately for Sun, Li Hongzhang placed his confidence only in experts of good family whose studies abroad usually constituted merely a complement to a classical education. The mediocrity of the post given to Yan Fu up until 1895 itself shows that Li Hongzhang was not prepared to grant his trust and patronage to products of a foreign education who could claim no social standing.

It seemed to Sun, having completed his education, that the doors to fine Chinese society and the paths to influence and power were to remain closed to him. Thence forward, he took no interest in the reformist themes that ought to have served as his passport to the bureaucratic and social elites. He flung himself into violent opposition, which, over the years, he converted into revolutionary doctrine and revolutionary action.

The Symbolic Creation of a
Revolutionary Leader, 1894–1897

China's defeat in the war against Japan in 1894–95 ushered in one of the darkest periods in its history. It revealed the weaknesses of the empire to the whole world and encouraged the European powers to rush madly into the zones of influence and the concessions. At this point, China owed the preservation of its integrity solely to the determination of the foreign powers to maintain among them a balance of forces and ambitions.

The threat of partition for the country provoked two outbreaks of resistance of very different kinds: on the one hand an attempt at Westernizing reform led by the literati, with the encouragement of the emperor Guangxu; on the other, a movement of popular xenophobic rebellion, supported initially by a number of local authorities and elites, then by the court, and opposed by the intervention of the combined foreign powers. All these events affecting the national destiny took place in northern China. In the Sino-Japanese conflict, only the Beiyang fleet (Northern Fleet) was engaged in the naval battles. The regionalization of the war effort, a reflection of the attempts at modernization, was in fact one of the principal causes of the defeat.

After this, the Reform Movement was centered in Peking, where it gravitated around Emperor Guangxu, who patronized the initiative of the Hundred Day Reform in 1898. The Boxer uprising developed in Shandong and Zhili. In 1900, when the court chose to ally itself openly with the Boxers and declare war on the foreign powers, the governors of the provinces of the Yangzi and the South dissociated themselves from this move, refusing to commit the regions in their charge to the disturbances of the rebellion and the foreseeable reprisals from the foreigners. The North went for fundamentalism, the South for pragmatism: it was an opposition, both geographical and cultural, that was to continue to characterize the series of crises that swept through China in the twentieth century.

Sun Yat-sen, a man of the South, excluded by his birth and upbringing from the interprovincial network of literati and mandarins, took no part in those events. He followed them from afar: from Hong Kong and Guangdong in 1895, from Hawaii, the United States, and London, where he was traveling, in 1896 and 1897, and from Japan, where he lived virtually without interruption from 1897 to 1900.

Distanced as he was from the stage upon which China's destiny was being played out, Sun tried to regain a grip on the course of history. In 1894, when he created a small group of partisans, he announced a program and objectives that would have done admirably for a political organization. The armed attack on Canton, which he organized in 1895 with the help of the secret societies, resembled all the others that periodically alarmed the local gentry and the magistrates in their walled cities, but it was converted through the magic of words into a revolutionary insurrection. One year later, the kidnapping of Sun by the Chinese legation in London became a sensation. Displaying a real flair for public relations and an innate confidence in his own destiny, Sun used it to create a "heroic image" of himself, that of a patriot laboring for the salvation and reorganization of his country, the image of a national leader—which he was still far from being.

THE NATIONAL CRISIS

When the Sino-Japanese War broke out on August 1, 1894, the Chinese empire still possessed some credibility. Its weakness had been only partially revealed by the facts. There were many signs of the economic and political crisis, but the imperial regime had put down the great rebellions of 1860–70, and it had managed to maintain the autonomy of its administration and the appearances of power in the face of Western intrusion. The urgent need for change, particularly for institutional change, was evident to only a small fraction of the bureaucracy and the literati society.

The foreigners shared the Chinese illusion of an imperial authority still alive and upheld by its vast continental territories and the country's huge population. Or perhaps they simply chose to foster the illusion, the better to ensure the balance of their own forces in East Asia. At any rate, in 1894 their observers, like the mandarins, were expecting a Chinese victory over Japan.

The rapid and total defeat of the Chinese forces was sanctioned by the treaty of Shimonoseki (April 17, 1895), which imposed a large indemnity on the imperial government, the secession of various territories (including the island of Taiwan), and granted the Japanese—and by virtue of their most-favored-nation status, all the foreign powers—the right to establish industrial firms in the treaty ports. The Sino-Japanese conflict, a direct consequence of European expansion, totally upset the old equilibrium in East Asia and toppled the hierarchy of relations up until then founded on the recognition of Chinese cultural superiority. The victory admitted Japan to the ranks of the great powers. Treated on a footing of equality by its European and American partners, Japan was thenceforth to practice an analogous policy of exploitation and aggression, except that this was rendered even more daunting by Japan's geographical and cultural proximity.

The treaty of Shimonoseki signaled an unprecedented acceleration in foreign penetration into China. All the European powers grabbed portions in the "carving of the China melon" (*guafen*), that is to say, the dismemberment of the country, and Japan was now in there with them. In the course of the "battle for concessions," the powers tried to satisfy their own respective ambitions, at the same time arranging for them to be mutually compatible. The new privileges now claimed and obtained related to the construction of railways, which the imperial government had in the past refused to authorize. By building these railways, the foreign powers hoped to be in a better position to exploit a market until then denied them. They also hoped to push farther into inland China and there to carve out economic and political zones of influence. Leased territories were ceded to them along with the railways. Unlike the earlier concessions in the treaty ports, over which the Chinese had always retained at least the theoretical right of sovereignty, these leased territories were foreign enclaves in which the concessionary state possessed all regalian rights (of justice, policing, defense). In the years 1897–98 a number of zones of influence took shape: German in Shandong, Russian in Liaodong to the south of Manchuria, French in the southern provinces of Guangdong, Guangxi, and Yunnan. Great Britain, a latecomer to these maneuvers, gained recognition for its special economic interests in the provinces of the lower Yangzi.

This new wave of imperialist penetration stimulated the patriotism and the reformist zeal of a number of literati. They were headed by Kang Youwei (1858–1927), a highly cultivated Cantonese who, in an iconoclastic study published in 1891, *Confucius the Reformer* (*Kongzi gaizhi kao*), tried to rework the tradition in order to adapt it to the needs of modern times, identifying (or inventing) an idea of progress in the classical heritage. While remaining faithful to the fundamental values of Confucianism, Kang Youwei called for institutional changes inspired by the Western and Japanese experiences and for the establishment in China of a constitutional regime of a kind to ensure the people's participation in power. These ideas were diffused by the press, then developing rapidly, and by the study groups that were springing up throughout the provinces. They won many supporters among the provincial elites and literati. The most brilliant of Kang Youwei's disciples was another Cantonese, an extremely talented essayist, Liang Qichao (1873–1929).

In 1895, Kang appealed directly to Emperor Guangxu, to whom he addressed a number of memoranda. Eventually, in the summer of 1898, he managed to attract his attention and obtain his protection. Kang Youwei's suggestions now turned into edicts. In the course of the Hundred Day Reform, from June 11 to September 21, more than one hundred edicts appeared, reorganizing the education system, reforming the administration, the army, the navy, the police, the penal code, the postal service, and encouraging the development of the railways, mines, trade, and industry. But this whirlwind of reforms was merely a matter of paperwork. The high-ranking mandarins, threatened by so many upheavals, rallied to the empress dowager Cixi who, in a military coup d'état, thrust aside the emperor, declared herself regent, and annulled all the recent edicts. Several of the reformers were executed. Kang Youwei and Liang Qichao fled to Japan.

The reformist fiasco and the restoration of conservative power coincided with the xenophobic Boxer uprising, which spread turmoil through the northern provinces. In the countryside, where contacts with Westerners were limited, the hostility toward foreigners was turned against the Christian missionaries and their converts. It was they who were blamed by the peasants for all that was wrong in their poverty-stricken lives. Popular discontent fostered the activity of the secret societies, particularly that of the Boxers (Yihequan). Originally antidynastic, the Boxers now became antiforeigner. Some even went so far as to replace their old slogan, "Destroy the Manchus; restore the Ming," with a new one: "Support the Manchus; exterminate the foreigners." You would have to have an extremely solid faith in historical determinism to detect any marks of modern protonationalism in these fanatics who went in for incantations and magical practices to make themselves invulnerable to bullets.

The rapid spread of Boxer activities in Shandong, then in Zhili, can be explained by the protection and complicity the Boxers got from some of the local elites and high-ranking provincial officials, who saw them as a good way to enforce their own ideas of cultural preservation and social conservatism. In June 1900, the entourage of the empress adopted this strategy, openly supporting the Boxers, who were then besieging the legation quarter in Peking, and declaring war on the foreign powers. However, the governors of the central and southern provinces, conscious of the suicidal nature of this policy, officially dissociated themselves from it, declaring that this was not an anti-foreigner war but an internal rebellion. This fiction allowed the powers to spare the dynasty after the victory of their joint military expedition, but it did not save China from the humiliating protocol of 1901, or from having to pay a huge indemnity of 450 million taëls.

At this point, the empire owed its survival to the advantage the foreign powers saw in the existence of a regime that, without obstructing their ambitions, allowed them to harmonize them. The Manchu dynasty's refusal to cooperate with the reformist movement along with its direct responsibility for the Boxers' catastrophe and the consequent degradation of China's international status led to growing disaffection on the part of the general Chinese population and also the literati. Grafted on to the fundamental antinomy between imperialism and nationalism, anti-Manchu hostility, which had remained sporadic since the seventeenth century, revived with new vigor at the turn of the 1890's–1900.

The Boxer rebellion, well known because of its political manipulation by Dowager Empress Cixi and her entourage, constituted just one of many expressions of the profound malaise gripping the countryside and of the insecurity that reigned there. Recurrent natural calamities, whose effects were steadily worsening as a result of the failure to keep hydraulic equipment in good running order and the degradation of the ecological environment, were compounded by the misfortunes of war. Hundreds of thousands of soldiers had been sent to fight against the Japanese in Manchuria. Demobilized without pay after the treaty of Shimonoseki, these formed roving bands, looting and holding for ransom whole towns and villages. Rumors of imminent foreign invasion were rife, causing panics in which whole populations took to flight. Along with the attacks against missions and missionaries, there were hunger riots and revolts against taxation and forced labor. In this climate of violence, when troops of outlaws several thousand strong were attacking towns whose walls and militia did not always suffice to protect them, the secret societies quickly regained the importance that they appeared to have lost following the repression of the White Lotus insurrection in the North (1804) and the Taiping in the center and the South (in 1864).

The secret societies were a refuge for all the rejects of Chinese society—from ruined peasants to failed literati and including vagabonds and out-and-out bandits—and their immediate aim was the survival of their members. They were closed societies ruled by an internal code of honor, and since their chief reason for being was mutual aid, they were more a safety valve for the government than a threat to the Confucian order of which they were definitely a part. Although credited with certain romantic aspirations toward justice and equality, most appear to have been simply criminal organizations. Whatever values they did adhere to seem to have been strangely archaic. How could loyalty to the Ming dynasty or fanatical xenophobia and the rejection of all Western input possibly alleviate China's misfortunes or answer its needs at this point, at the very end of the nineteenth century? Although deeply rooted in the peasantry, the secret societies possessed a considerable power of de-stabilization. Their ability to foster disturbances and their anti-Manchu orientation threatened to endanger the dynasty in the event of its losing the support of the local elites who had so far remained loyal to it out of fidelity to the Confucian culture and order that it embodied.

But now the attitude of these elites was changing. From 1895 on, their social activism developed rapidly, taking an increasingly political turn. In the provinces, members of the gentry, retired officials, rich merchants, and literati without official posts, who had by long custom devoted themselves to the management of community affairs (gongshi), were beginning to abandon their philanthropic works to create commercial and industrial organizations, modern schools, associations against the binding of feet, and discussion and study groups. In doing so, they felt they were contributing to China's progress. More and more, local initiatives were geared to national perspectives.

Through their upbringing and their integration into interprovincial networks of literati and great merchants, these elites were now led to involve themselves in the political affairs of the country. The misfortunes of the time stimulated their mobilization. Through the intermediary of their discussion societies, the elites were associated with the changes attempted during the Hundred Day Reform. Their ranks were swelled by former high-ranking officials who were discouraged by the failure of the reforms and by the humiliating defeats suffered at the foreigners' hands, and now, despairing of ever being able to bring about change through the central bureaucratic apparatus, chose to abandon their official careers and devote themselves to reflection and political debate and to engineering individual local reforms whenever the chance arose. These elites were demanding that the people (that is, to say, themselves) be associated with political power—not to control it, of course, but to guide it toward the necessary changes. They resented the imperial court for disregarding their suggestions and continuing to limit itself to policies and a style of government that were quite inadequate to the internal and external crises. Furthermore, after 1898, Manchus had been appointed as the principal advisers to Dowager Empress Cixi, and in the wave of reaction following the failure of the Hundred Day Reform a number of provincial Chinese officials had been replaced by Manchus, who were deemed more reliable. The political opposition consequently took on a racial connotation.

The old hostility was rearoused. The reformism that from 1895 to 1898 had prompted the elites to offer the government their cooperation now began to give way to more or less avowed opposition. This opposition did not challenge the legitimacy of the imperial power, but it was sharply critical of the government policy developed between 1898 and 1901 and the authorities set in place after Empress Cixi's coup d'état. As the social activism of the elites turned into political commitment, growing frustrations nurtured alienation from the authorities. Demands became more radical, coinciding on a number of points with those of the leading figures of the treaty ports, with whom the provincial elites maintained many contacts. The military defeat, the failure of the reforms, and the Boxer catastrophe extended to the privileged classes as a whole attitudes that, one or two decades earlier, had been entertained only by the small minority of Chinese in contact with foreigners.

The radical groups that made their appearance in Hunan, Shanghai, and Guangdong after 1898 were the harbingers of a rising tide of antigovernmental and antidynastic opposition. The theorists of this new era were Yan Fu, Tan Sitong (1865–98), and Liang Qichao. These talented writers who had emerged from the current of reformism and had distanced themselves from Confucianism spoke of new ideas such as a desire for progress, for a rational organization of the state, for rights for individuals, and for equality between nations. The time for a switch to revolutionary action seemed to be approaching.

Sun Yat-sen had played no part in all these events and changes. Excluded from the class of degree holders, who would not admit him even as an adviser, outside the currents mobilizing the local elites, and incapable of taking part in the philosophical and philological contests in which the political thinkers of the day were debating their ideas (as subtle connoisseurs of the classical texts, they used their own critical interpretations of these to introduce and legitimate their new ideas), Sun Yat-sen turned to forms of direct action. His money came from the overseas Chinese, his men from the secret societies.

Sun was not bothered by the contradictions forced upon him by a strategy that in order to serve a radical modernist project inspired by the West mobilized secret societies that were not only antidynastic but also antiforeigner and superstitious. All the same, he had not given up hope of obtaining from the literati the recognition that he must have if he were to convert his activity as a marginal opponent into a destiny for himself at the national level. Because he could not crash the formidable social and intellectual barriers that blocked his way, Sun Yat-sen took to circumventing them and, with the help of his many networks of relations and at the cost of many ideological oscillations, set about obtaining from Europe and Japan the recognition that he could not get from the Chinese reformist and radical elite. Purely symbolic though that recognition was, it was soon to prove one of his main advantages as he strove to establish his authority at the heart of the opposition.

THE EARLY STAGES OF A PROFESSIONAL CONSPIRATOR

After his journey to Tianjin and his unsuccessful attempt to win the attention of the viceroy Li Hongzhang, Sun Yat-sen gave up his medical activities to become a professional agitator. In November 1894, in Hawaii, he founded his first organization, the Revive China Society (Xingzhonghui), which moved to Hong Kong in 1895. The Revive China Society was a group of conspirators linked by their social or geographical origins and by their shared dissatisfaction with the established order. It was less concerned with politics and long-term perspectives than with immediate action. Its aim was to raise the money and the men needed for an uprising in Canton. It was now, for the first time, that Sun Yat-sen revealed his remarkable skill at mobilizing all the networks of relations he had constructed and orchestrating them to serve his conspiracy strategy. However, the organization of the uprising itself certainly left much to be desired: internal quarrels, lack of coordination among the conspirators, and betrayals all contributed to its failure. The uprising was repressed in October 1895 before it had even had time to break out.

The Creation of the Revive China Society

What a contrast between Sun's journey to Shanghai and Tianjin in early 1894, to deliver his memorandum to Li Hongzhang, and his return to southern China a few months later! Sun and Lu Haodong had left Tianjin in a somber mood, and the disorders that broke out in the provinces after the Sino-Japanese conflict erupted in August deepened their pessimism. Making only a short stop in Hong Kong, Sun Yat-sen set sail for Hawaii toward the end of the summer. It was there, on November 24, that he founded the Revive China Society.

The charter of this organization, written by Sun Yat-sen and no more than thirty lines long, was essentially a patriotic declaration. It began by stressing the danger China faced, threatened as it was by foreign ambitions and the weakness and incompetence of the Manchu government, and went on to invite courageous men to "give new life" to the country. It did not mention any overthrow of the dynasty for the establishment of a republican regime. These points were perhaps made explicit in the secret oath that members of the new association had to swear, but we do not know the wording of the oath, only that it was taken with one hand placed on the Bible—a strange adaptation of the ritual of the secret societies to the Christianized environment of the overseas Chinese.

This first organizational cell that Sun set up in Hawaii with the aid of his brother consisted of some twenty people, all of whom were émigrés linked to Sun or his family by special ties; some were Cantonese natives of the Xiangshan district, or business contacts of Sun Mei, or former fellow students of Sun Yat-sen: merchants, clerks, interpreters, craftsmen—people who were usually considered politically passive. Their motives were no doubt patriotic, their reasons those of friendship for the Sun family, Christian ideals in the case of some, the hope of good business in the case of others (the charter envisaged the possibility of investments in the form of repayable shares once the movement was successful). Still others may have been influenced by developments in Hawaii itself, where a republican constitution had been adopted in 1894.

The political mobilization of this little group of émigrés—however summary its charter—has a particular significance in Sun's career, not only because it was its starting point and his first success but also because it illuminates the importance of the networks of relations so characteristic of his methods. It also marks the entrance of ordinary émigrés into the field of Chinese politics from which they had until then been excluded and in which they were to play an increasingly important role in the opening years of the twentieth century.

It was with the founding of its Hong Kong branch that the Revive China Society took on its importance and its historical significance.[1] This branch was set up on February 18, 1895, and gathered together many of Sun's old companions and fellow students, including Lu Haodong, Chen Shaobai, and Zheng Shiliang. It also absorbed another group, the Literary Society for the Development of Benevolence (Furen Wenshe), whose eminently Confucian name masked its true antidynastic and revolutionary orientations. The fusion of this society with Sun's Revive China Society provides the first example of the takeover tactics that Sun was often to practice, always ready to welcome the collaboration of competing organizations, provided his own personal supremacy was recognized.

The Literary Society for the Development of Benevolence was at that time three years old. Most of its original sixteen members were Chinese employees of English shipping companies; most had attended local missionary schools; some were Christians. The leader was Yang Quyun (1861–1901), born in Hong Kong into a family from Fujian that had spent some time in Malaysia. Yang had served an apprenticeship in the Hong Kong naval dockyard, and then, after learning English and teaching for a time in a local college, he had entered the China Merchants Steam Navigation Company and had moved from there to a post of responsibility in a British company. His chief aide in the society was Xie Zhantai (Tse Tsan Tai), who was then twenty-five years old. Xie was Cantonese by descent, born in Australia, to which his family had emigrated and where he had been baptized into the Christian religion. Having returned to Hong Kong at the age of fifteen, he had completed his education at the Government Central School, once attended by Sun, and had then entered the public works department of the colonial administration.

The family origins and social and professional experiences of the members of the Literary Society for the Development of Benevolence were thus very close to those of Sun and his friends. They were all strangers to the world of the literati-officials. None had received a traditional Chinese education: they had picked up their training in the course of their travels, in the foreign schools they had attended and through professional experiences that had also brought them into contact with foreigners. Like Sun, many of them had links with émigré communities. Their political commitment was born of their own perception of the backwardness of China compared with the material prosperity and administrative efficiency of the British colony. There were thus several reasons for Sun Yat-sen and Yang Quyun to pool their efforts.

It is not known what arguments Sun used to persuade Yang to join the Revive China Society. But he was to face many difficulties in imposing his leadership in competition with Yang, whose ambition and self-confidence matched his own. The choice of a president for the new organization was deferred until October 10. On that day the confrontation between the two men and their respective partisans had a positively murderous air. The compromise, which gave the presidency to Yang Quyun but the on-the-spot direction of the Canton uprising to Sun Yat-sen, did not totally allay the two leaders' mutual suspicions and distrust, for each felt the ambition of the other to usurp his own authority and legitimacy.

In establishing the Revive China Society in Hong Kong, the group had made certain changes in the original charter. Although the patriotic, reforming, and modernizing lines remained as before, criticism of the dynasty and the bureaucracy was made more specific. The idea of the need for a national effort of the people in association with the ruling classes and the invitation to foreigners to join the organization and suggest models introduced a few radical touches into the otherwise conventional text.

Was that text complemented by a secret oath "to overthrow the Manchu dynasty, restore China, and establish a republican regime," as was later claimed by certain witnesses and, following them, historians such as Feng Ziyou and Chen Xiqi? Here again, as with the founding organization in Hawaii, no documentary proof exists, either to show that there was an oath or, if so, what it consisted of. With hindsight, witnesses and historians have been tempted to date some form of commitment, attested later on, to the very earliest days, but this is speculative. Moreover, even if the antidynastic and republican convictions of Sun Yat-sen and Yang Quyun and their immediate entourage do seem established, it is not known whether they were shared by the 153 persons (including the 112 recruited in Hawaii) who then made up the membership of the Revive China Society.

We do know, however, that some of the sympathizers of the society, and not the least important of them, declared themselves in favor of a very different program. Apart from the circles of employees who formed the main body of the Hong Kong recruits, the Revive China Society was also supported by a few of the colony's major personalities who donated funds and acted as spokesmen for it in the English-language press, seeking to rally the sympathy of the British authorities both on the spot and in London.

Of this group of members, Ho Kai, the important reformist figure with whom Sun had been linked ever since his studies at the College of Medicine, was the most in the public eye. But the Revive China Society could also count on the support of Huang Yongshang, the scion of a great anglicized Hong Kong family originally from the district of Xiangshan. In 1846, Huang Yong-shang's father had been one of the first Chinese to go to the United States for study. Upon his return, he had sat on the colony's Legislative Council and had become one of those "King's Chinese" whose acculturation did not necessarily stifle their patriotism. Huang Yongshang was one of the first to join the Revive China Society, and, to help prepare for the Canton uprising, he sold one of his apartment blocks for the sum of 8,000 (Hong Kong) dollars. His family was related to Ho Kai's, and it may have been through Ho Kai's mediation that Huang Yongshang got to know Sun Yat-sen. But most historians believe that Huang Yongshang was closer to Yang Quyun. Throughout this whole period Yang, already well known in business circles, took upon himself the task of raising funding from the Chinese elites of the colony.

Ho Kai's role became that of an eminence grise to Sun, Yang, and their friends.[2] He attended meetings of the society—though he was not a member—and he allowed it to benefit from his good relations with the local, English-language press, particularly the *China Mail,* in which, in 1887, he had published his influential article on reform. As early as March 10, 1895, Thomas A. Reid, Ho Kai's friend who was editor-in-chief of the *China Mail,* printed a series of articles that presented the Revive China Society under the name of the Reform Party and set out details of its program.

According to these articles, this program reflected the ideas of Ho Kai very directly: The article of May 23, 1895, also attributed to Ho Kai a plan for constitutional reform. When the Manchu dynasty was toppled, a constitutional monarchy, not a republican regime, would be established. The bureaucracy would be reorganized and admittance to it would be gained through examinations of a technical rather than a literary nature. To combat corruption, officials' salaries would be increased. Judicial reforms would be introduced; modern education, religious tolerance, and economic development would be encouraged. Local councils would be elected directly by the people, a national assembly by indirect suffrage. New ports would be opened to foreign trade and the levying of taxes would be entrusted to a Sino-foreign administration, modeled on the Maritime Customs Service.

All these ideas seem a long way from the revolutionary, nationalistic, and republican stance attributed to the Revive China Society. Chinese historians have tried to explain these contradictions by pointing out the need to conceal the radical character of the Revive China Society from the Hong Kong authorities, who might have been alarmed by it. It is probably simpler—and, to my mind, more accurate—to infer that intellectual speculations and long-term policies were less pressing considerations than the need to organize immediate action. The objective of Sun Yat-sen and his companions was to take possession of the town of Canton. To that end, they planned a complex strategy designed to combine forces as diverse as the Anglo-Chinese "establishment" of Hong Kong, the secret societies of Guangdong, and the gentry and elites of Canton. Through the intermediary of various organizers, the Revive China Society told each party concerned whatever was most likely to win it over. Small wonder the various messages did not coincide.

The reformist program publicized in the *China Mail* in truth represented but one aspect of the collaboration now effected between the Chinese elites of Hong Kong and the colony's entrepreneurs and administrators. The latter were keen to see the Chinese market open up more and would not have hesitated to use force if the need arose. But on this point they clashed with the government in London, which had no intention of becoming involved in internal Chinese affairs and feared the complications and responsibilities that armed intervention would create.

The opposition between the expansionist ambitions of the local residents and the prudence of the metropolis is a constantly recurring feature in Great Britain's politics in the Far East, as it is in the politics of France at the turn of the nineteenth and twentieth centuries. The aid solicited by *China Mail* for the Revive China Society was, in the eyes of Reid and the other British in Hong Kong, simply a substitute for the application of force of which they dreamed but which London's opposition ruled out. For them, lending support to a rebellion willing to cooperate closely with foreigners was another way of achieving their constant goal: greater access to China for their business ventures. For the nationalists that the Chinese reformists also were, this was no more than a preliminary stage. They reckoned that the restoration of Chinese sovereignty involved a prior internal measure of reform. Once modernization had been achieved, thanks to the example and the aid of the Westerners, China would be restored to its legitimate place in the concert of nations.

In spite of the *China Mail*'s pleas to Britain not to repeat the mistake of not having helped the Taiping, British diplomacy stuck to its general line of support for the dynasty. The British vice-consul of Canton told London: "There is no sign suggesting this to be a revolution in the Western sense of the term, that is to say a change of government initiated by the upper or middle classes. The bold prophecies of a certain Hong Kong newspaper concerning this uprising are nothing but dreams."[3]

Notwithstanding the tone of respectability bestowed by Ho Kai and the far from disinterested local British press, in the eyes of international diplomacy Sun Yat-sen and his companions remained mere adventurers.

The Unsuccessful Canton Uprising

The relations mediated by Zheng Shiliang between the Revive China Society and the secret societies of the Triads and the role it had assigned to them in the Canton uprising bring us back to China's traditional and endemic forms of subversion.

In that summer of 1895, Guangdong, like other Chinese provinces, had been very disturbed. In June and July, a rebellion of two to three thousand men, mostly secret society members and inhabitants of the "green forests" (*lülin*), that is to say brigands, broke out in the eastern prefectures. In September and early October, there were more disorders. The insurrection in Canton planned by the Revive China Society for October 26 was thus but one more in a series of rebellions from which, in the eyes of the authorities, it in no way differed.

Using the money raised by Yang Quyun in Hong Kong, the Revive China Society was supposed to recruit 3,000 mercenaries in the coastal regions of Guangdong. The forces were to muster in Hong Kong and Kowloon, from where the mercenaries would travel by boat to Canton, taking arms and munitions with them. Upon landing, the commando would separate into four columns to attack various civil and military offices. Its action would be supported by other columns converging upon Canton along the tributaries of the Pearl River, led by Liang Big-Gun, a notorious bandit chieftain. In the town itself, the detonation of several bombs would add to the confusion and facilitate the action of the rebels.

As in many cases where an armed attack on a town is planned, the rebels had tried to make sure of the complicity of a number of leading local figures inside the town. This task had fallen to Sun Yat-sen, who had maintained contacts in Canton that went back to the period of his medical studies. To cover his activities, Sun Yat-sen made use of an official permit believed to have been granted him by Li Hongzhang's offices on the occasion of his journey to Tianjin the preceding year, and at the beginning of October he set up an Agricultural Study Association. In the manner of the many reformist educational enterprises then being organized by the gentry in every province, this society declared its aim to be to promote popular education and agricultural progress. In its charter, which he wrote, Sun Yat-sen presented himself as an enlightened modernizer: "In my youth, I traveled abroad and studied methods of government and civilization in the West. I read widely and studied modern science in depth, paying particular attention to agriculture and botany."[4]

The society was favorably received by officials and gentry, several dozen of whom decided to patronize it. But not all were dupes of Sun Yat-sen's professed goals. Like so many other traditional rebellions, this one could claim its own particular aberrant scholar, full of ambition and dreaming of exploiting the disturbances to found a new imperial dynasty, to his own advantage. For this was indeed the dream of Liu Xuexun, a holder of the highest degree in the government examination system, that of a doctor of the imperial palace (*jinshi*) and also the organizer of a lottery that took bets on the results of, not horse races, but the official examinations. Liu Xuexun was an extremely wealthy man. How did this monarchist come to be a contact of Sun's? Perhaps he had once been a patient of his, or perhaps their common origins from the Xiangshan district had been enough to bring them together. We do not know. Nor do we know what persuaded Sun to take such a man into his confidence. It is not unreasonable to suppose that the funds managed by Liu must have given considerable food for thought to the political agitator always in quest of backing for his activities.

The Agricultural Study Association, which was founded when the preparations for the insurrection were already well advanced, does seem to have been designed purely to camouflage the true nature of Sun Yat-sen's project. Nevertheless, the charter of the society was in direct line with Sun's previous reformist texts, and the relations that he established with Liu Xuexun were to be lasting ones and to resurface at a number of turning points in his career. Quite apart from the immediate utility of the Agricultural Study Association to the conspirators, its formation may reflect Sun's enduring aspirations to win recognition from the gentry and the literati.

But most of Sun's support came from a more solid and better organized network of relations, that of the Chinese converts to Christianity. He chose as his general headquarters a bookshop specializing in religious literature, with a Presbyterian chapel in its back room. Sun turned this into the seat of his Agricultural Study Association and also an arms cache. Both the proprietor of the shop, Zuo Doushan, and its manager, Pastor Wang Zhifu, were members of the Revive China Society.

Clearly, this Christian involvement in the insurrection is explained by the relations and friendships that Sun maintained in circles he knew well and in which he was careful always to present his aspirations as an expression of his religious ideals. He may also have hoped to improve his own and his companions' security by placing himself under the protection of the missions, well known to do all they could to ensure immunity for their flock, if necessary even setting in train diplomatic interventions to this end. More generally, the Christian involvement illuminates the role missionaries played in the diffusion of Western models among the least favored strata of the Chinese population. For humble folk, who never traveled abroad and had no access at all to the writings of the literati, local missions offered a chance to learn about the West, and Christianity represented the religious aspect of their faith in the ideologies, institutions, and methods of government of that Western world.

The geographic dispersion and the wide variety of social and political alliances that were such features of the preparation of the conspiracy imposed a need for perfect organization, impeccable coordination between its various leaders, and closely guarded secrecy. The truth of the matter was quite different. On the morning of October 26, when Sun's men had already gathered on the wharf of Canton to greet the boat from Hong Kong, take delivery of their weapons, and join forces with the mercenaries from the colony, Yang

Quyun telegraphed to say that the "cargo" was delayed by twenty-four hours. At this, Sun Yat-sen decided, out of prudence, to put off the whole operation and disbanded his own mercenaries. But the telegram sent to Hong Kong with this information reached Yang too late. About 400 men, along with the weapons, had already embarked on the *S.S. Powan* on the evening of October 27. The British authorities learned of this too late to prevent the operation but warned the Canton government. The hunt for conspirators was already on in the town, and meanwhile, at dawn on October 28, the *S.S. Powan* was met by the garrison troops under the command of the magistrate of the prefecture.

This botched affair and the startling contrast between the solemn declarations and complicated preparations on the one hand and the total absence of any action on the other may seem risible, all too reminiscent of an operetta revolution: most of the mercenaries were considered not to be responsible for their actions and were simply sent back to their villages; only half a dozen or so conspirators fell into the hands of the authorities. But among them was Lu Haodong, Sun's childhood friend, the scourge of village idols. Even under torture he refused to give the names of his accomplices and he died proclaiming his beliefs: "If the Manchu are not destroyed, the Chinese cannot be revived . . . and even if I, one isolated individual, am killed, it will not be possible to kill all those who will rise up and follow me."[5]

Sun Yat-sen managed to escape in a sedan chair to Macao and from there to Hong Kong. But the authorities of Hong Kong had set a price on his head. After six months of intense activity, the Revive China Society found itself without funds, without arms, and deserted by its Guangdong supporters. All that was left of the organization was its staff office. And even this was more divided than ever—with Sun Yat-sen blaming Yang Quyun for the whole fiasco—and was soon disbanded. Its members left Hong Kong to avoid extradition, for which the Canton authorities were clamoring. For the next five years, the Revive China Society no longer existed as an organization.

The Canton conspiracy was just the first in a list that, by 1911, included ten others, all failures. My reason for lingering to describe the 1895 conspiracy in detail is that it included all the elements of the strategy Sun Yat-sen repeatedly employed thereafter: the use of an external base beyond the reach of the imperial authorities, the appeal to mercenary troops financed by the donations of a few rich patriots, the systematic search for foreign aid, to obtain which Sun Yat-sen was always prepared to make not insignificant concessions. The repeated failures of Sun's schemes underline the limitations, already detectable in 1895, of a voluntarist strategy that was too careless about organization and concentrated on immediate results, neglecting propaganda for the purchase of mercenaries and entrusting to bandits summoned from their green forests the application of a modernist and Western program conceived in the treaty ports.

THE BIRTH OF A REVOLUTIONARY LEADER

When he set sail for Japan on October 30, 1895, in order to escape an imminent extradition order, Sun Yat-sen was entering upon sixteen years of exile—sixteen years during which he was banished from Hong Kong and was unable to return to China (except once, briefly, on the occasion of an insurrection in Guangxi in 1907). So it was in the lands abroad where he traveled—visiting Japan, Hawaii, the United States, and England between 1895 and 1897—that Sun Yat-sen pursued, or rather constructed, his destiny as a revolutionary leader, fashioning the criminal wanted by the imperial police into a hero fighting for the salvation of his country. The very persistence of that police effort helped to turn Sun, *a posteriori*, into the principal leader of the Canton conspiracy and the Revive China Society, while Yang Quyun fled to Southeast Asia and South Africa, more or less forgotten for the next three years.

But the essential role in Sun Yat-sen's metamorphosis fell to his British friends and protectors. In the mirror that they held up to him, the Cantonese adventurer appeared as a revolutionary thinker, a strategist of vast designs. Only too pleased to slip into this new personality, Sun Yat-sen worked hard to develop the necessary characteristics and, to a certain extent, to conform to its behavior pattern. The reading and discussions in which he engaged in London broadened his intellectual horizon and sharpened his political awareness. Now all he had to do—and it would be the most difficult challenge—was get his compatriots to accept his new image.

The first stage in this metamorphosis took place not in London, however, but in Japan. On November 12, when he landed at Kobe, accompanied by Zheng Shiliang and Chen Shaobai, Sun learned through the Japanese press that the Canton uprising had been a "revolution" (*geming*). Until that moment, in his mind it had been no more than a rebellion (*zaofan*), a movement of popular protest. In the Chinese tradition, rebellions, directed against corrupt mandarins or cruel landlords, were local affairs, sometimes led by great-hearted heroes—outlawed scholars or fighters against injustice in the Robin Hood mold—but always regarded with scorn and repugnance by the representatives of Confucian morality and order. In the Chinese political vocabulary, the term "revolution," which up until then Sun had studiously avoided, meant the end of a dynastic cycle: the point at which the emperor, having forfeited heaven's mandate, was toppled by a popular insurrection and replaced by a new leader whose skills and virtue marked him as the "Heaven-designated" emperor (*Tian ming*), the founder of a new dynasty. Because these revolutions were, according to Confucius, part of the accomplishment of history, scholars considered the popular insurrections that accompanied dynastic changes to be legitimate.

Sun Yat-sen, hesitating as he was between whether to reform or to destroy the imperial regime, had never imagined that the Chinese crisis could be resolved by a change of dynasty. "Revolution" had never seemed to him the right word for what he had set afoot. What he now discovered from the Japanese press was that "revolution" could be used in the modern sense of violent action leading to an institutional and social upheaval. Seizing the opportunity to reconcile the prestige and legitimacy of the old concept with the radicalism of its modernized ideological meaning, Sun Yat-sen now opted for this term: his party would henceforth be the revolutionary party (*gemingdang*).

He made the most of his stay in Japan to alter his personal appearance. He cut off his queue, stopped shaving his forehead, allowed his mustache to grow, and discarded his long Chinese robe for a European suit. A respectable Chinese was thus transformed into a Japanese gentleman of the Meiji period. Was this simply a precautionary measure, as his chroniclers suggest? With imperial agents still hunting for him even abroad, Sun no doubt did hope to elude them more easily in his new character. But the change in appearance was also highly symbolic. Wearing a queue was, after all, not a custom of Chinese origin: it had been introduced by the Manchu conquerors in the seventeenth century and could be considered as a sign of servitude. Cutting off his queue therefore represented a gesture of emancipation, a total break, with no going back, a declaration of war on the Manchus. As for the adoption of European clothes, was this not an outward sign of Sun's modernizing and Westernist beliefs? It would be hard to overestimate the importance of appearance and clothing at this time of transition and confusion. In this domain, preferences stemmed more from the choice of a civilization than from personal fancy.

Sun Yat-sen did not stay long in Japan. He made a few efforts to reactivate contacts made with the Cantonese community of Yokohama during a stop-over on his journey from Hong Kong to Hawaii less than a year earlier; and he created a local branch of the Revive China Society, thirteen members strong. But the criminal on the run rather alarmed the worthy merchants who had received the young rebel with sympathy. Leaving Chen Shaobai in Tokyo and sending Zheng Shiliang (whose name the imperial police had apparently not discovered) back to Hong Kong, Sun Yat-sen set off for Hawaii.

From January to June 1896, he made the most of the asylum provided by his brother, in whose home he met up again with his mother, now widowed, his son, Sun Fo (Sun Ke), born in 1891, and two younger daughters. The members of the family still living in Cuiheng had been obliged to flee following the failed Canton conspiracy, for, as is well known, in China the principle of collective responsibility directs the long arm of the law. Unable to arrest Sun Yat-sen, the imperial police might well have seized his kin. Once again, one cannot help admiring Sun Mei's Confucian sense of family obligations, thanks to which his younger brother found himself relieved of all moral as well as financial responsibilities toward his close relatives.

The Kidnapping in London

The Canton disaster had somewhat cooled the ardor of the Revive China Society members in Hawaii. Sun was hoping for greater success among the Chinese communities of the United States. But the three months he spent traveling from San Francisco to New York, constantly watched and followed by imperial agents, did not produce great results. Sun Yat-sen then accepted an invitation from his old professor, Dr. Cantlie, and on September 30, 1896, he arrived in London.

Sun spent his first two days in London visiting tourist sights and renewing his friendship with the Cantlies. His every movement was carefully noted by the private detective hired by the Chinese legation to shadow him. Gong Zhaoyuan, who headed the legation, intended to seize Sun, with the help of the legation's British secretary, Sir Halliday Macartney (1833–1906). Sir Halliday, who was related to the head of the first British mission to Peking in 1793, was an old China hand; he had fought against the Taiping, and under the protection of Li Hongzhang had worked in the (modern) arsenal of Nanking before being appointed secretary and interpreter to the Chinese legation that was set up in London in 1877. Loyal to the mandarins who employed him, Macartney always endeavored to reconcile his professional obligations and his principles of an English gentleman. But the Sun Yat-sen operation entrusted to him by Minister Gong was to try him sorely. The plan was to seize the fugitive and return him secretly to China to face punishment.

Shortly after Sun arrived, the Foreign Office, in response to a query from the Chinese legation, let it be known that it would resist any extradition request. The legation had by now been in existence for nineteen years and, their understanding of diplomatic conventions having progressed somewhat in that time, its Chinese officials no longer considered taking justice into their own hands: in 1877 Macartney had had great difficulty in persuading the then minister, angered by a servant's crime, that to do so would not be covered by diplomatic immunity. On the other hand, in the opinion of the legation mandarins, kidnapping and enforced deportation were legitimate means of allowing imperial justice to prevail.

On October 11, Sun Yat-sen disappeared: he was imprisoned in the Legation, with no means of communicating with the outside world. How did he get there? Nobody knows. The incident gave rise to the most contradictory explanations and indeed continues to do so. According to Sun Yat-sen's testimony, given immediately after he was freed, he was abducted, or rather lured by a ruse to the entrance of the Legation, which he had not identified, and was bundled inside in the course of a scuffle, then overcome inside the building. According to the Chinese diplomats, Sun Yat-sen went of his own free will to the Legation, in quest of information. Alerted by his questions, the legation staff apprehended him on his second visit. A third, later, version also exists, based upon oral statements made by Sun Yat-sen's companions, according to whom Sun Yat-sen had told them that he had indeed gone willingly and with his eyes wide open to the Legation, out of defiance and revolutionary ardor, and had only invented the story of the kidnapping to make the legation's attitude more reprehensible.

Each of these versions has its supporters,[6] and each incorporates a number of considerable improbabilities: how could Sun Yat-sen not have recognized the Chinese Legation, which was close to the Cantlies' home and past which he had walked on several occasions before the Cantlies strongly recommended that he should give it a wide berth? It is inconceivable that Sun Yat-sen, on the run from imperial spies for several months past and with a price on his head, would have risked entering the lions' den. Such a concept of patriotic fervor would have been of a naïveté bordering on plain stupidity. More might have been known had the private detectives hired to shadow him done their job properly. But, whether as a result of the inclement weather or quite simply human error, Sun's guardian angels had lost his trail on that fateful Sunday.

While his jailors were busy organizing his secret transfer to China, Sun Yat-sen, fearing poison, refused all the dishes prepared for him by the legation cook, lived on bread and milk, and endeavored to alert his friends, Dr. James Cantlie and Dr. Patrick Manson. But the door of his room was guarded, the windows were nailed shut, and all the messages he entrusted to the Legation's steward, George Cole, who was watching over him, were passed on to Macartney. After a week's efforts, however, Sun Yat-sen managed to persuade Cole to help him—by appealing to class solidarity and declaring himself to be the leader of a Chinese socialist party, the steward later claimed. Sun Yat-sen, on the other hand, subsequently claimed that it was to the Christians of Armenia then being persecuted by the Turks that he had likened himself, to arouse Cole's compassion: in Victorian England, Christian pity probably was more highly prized than proletarian sympathy, and Sun was concerned to win the compassion and sympathy of the public. Perhaps the decisive argument lay in the twenty pounds sterling that Sun Yat-sen handed over to Cole, with the promise of a further thousand to follow.

After a long week, news of the kidnapping finally reached Dr. Cantlie, to whom the steward himself brought a note in Sun's hand: "I was kidnapped into the Chinese Legation on Sunday and shall be smuggled out from England to China for death. Pray rescue me quick. . . . O! woe to me!"[7]

A Heroic Image

In five days, Dr. Cantlie, aided by his colleague and friend Dr. Manson, organized a masterly operation to mobilize the administration and the media. English Sundays are not a good time for diplomatic decisions, and Cantlie's first representations to Scotland Yard and the Foreign Office were frustrated by the absence of officers in positions of responsibility and by indifference on the part of their subordinates holding the fort. In despair, Cantlie turned to *The Times* with an article that the paper's editors decided to keep in their pending drawer until they could assess official reactions. On the Monday, these were made clear: the Chinese Legation was placed under surveillance, ships leaving for China were searched, and the Foreign Office contacted Macartney, urging him to persuade Minister Gong to release his prisoner. If Gong did not comply, London would demand his recall for violating diplomatic privileges.

Governmental reaction was the more vigorous since it was by now buoyed up by public indignation. On October 22, *The Globe*, preempting *The Times*, published a special edition carrying a long interview with Cantlie. On October 23, every morning newspaper picked up the story of Sun's kidnapping. The Legation was now besieged by not only the police but also a mob of journalists, photographers, and curious onlookers. Inside, the representatives of Scotland Yard and the Foreign Office, along with Dr. Cantlie, joined efforts to obtain Sun's immediate release. In the late afternoon he at last left the Legation and took refuge with his friends the Cantlies to escape the pack of reporters.

His retreat did not last long. Having become a *cause célèbre* in the space of five days, Sun sought to make the most of this unhoped-for chance to project himself onto the public stage, establish his reputation, and fix his image. He wrote to the newspapers and gave press conferences, granted numerous interviews, and won universal support. This was not the oriental conspirator of the legation's description, but a respectable patriot. His features were "of a delicate cast" and he "spoke very good English," the London journalists reported. "He is a remarkable man with enlightened views . . . and with a keenness of expression and frankness of feature seldom seen in a Chinese," the *China Mail* of Hong Kong added, for good measure. At the request of H. A. Giles, a sinologist and professor at Cambridge University, who was preparing a Chinese biographical dictionary, and with the aid of an English-speaking friend (probably Dr. Cantlie), Sun produced an account of his adventures in a brief autographical work entitled *Kidnapped in London*. This was published in England at the beginning of 1897 and by May of that year was on sale in Shanghai. It was to play an important part in the Far Eastern diffusion of the "heroic image" created in London.

After his release, Sun Yat-sen stayed on in London for eight months, until the beginning of July 1897, making the most of his time in exile to study and to develop his contacts. He had no difficulty fitting in with a particular kind of society life, and was a regular guest at the table of Dr. Cantlie, who also gave him the run of his library. He accompanied the doctor and his wife to Sunday service at Saint-Martin's-in-the-Fields and mingled gracefully in circles of educated Victorian bourgeois whose religious convictions and far-flung travels inclined them to take an interest in how the world was evolving.

There can be no doubt that Sun Yat-sen learned a great deal from listening to conversations such as one that took place in the home of the Bruces, a family friendly with the Cantlies, at a dinner given on October 25 in honor of a Mr. Weay, recently returned from South Africa. This gentleman told his listeners of the wars waged by Sir Cecil Rhodes and the British South Africa Company to annex the rich territories of local sovereigns, of the fall of Bulawayo in 1893, and of Dr. Leander Starr Jameson's raid on the Transvaal in 1895. A dozen or so years later, Sun Yat-sen, then tackling the problems of nationalism, was to dwell at length on the case of South Africa. Outside the Cantlies' immediate circle, Sun made a number of other friends. One was Rowland J. Mulkern, an Irish nationalist who was a professional soldier and a member of the Restoration Party. He had already expressed his sympathy and admiration for Sun following his abduction, and he sometimes acted as a bodyguard as Sun moved around London; in 1900 he was to take part in the second insurrection that Sun organized, in Huizhou.

According to the testimony of the private detective who, at the request of the Chinese legation, continued to shadow Sun, and likewise of Dr. Cantlie, Sun Yat-sen spent most of his time in the British Museum, "reading books on all subjects relating to politics, diplomacy, law, and military and naval affairs."[8] He made a number of new acquaintances there—among them half a dozen or so Russian political exiles, one of whom, Felix Volkovsky (1846–1914), became his friend. Volkovsky, the editor of a monthly entitled *Free Russia*, had recently got his freedom after seven years' imprisonment in the fortress of Saint Petersburg and eleven years in exile in Siberia. He presented a model of endurance to Sun Yat-sen, who was full of historical impatience and optimism. When asked how long he thought it would be before the revolution triumphed in China, Sun thought it wise to moderate his ardor and replied "thirty years." His Russian friends were thinking in terms of a hundred years for their country. Meanwhile, they translated Sun Yat-sen's *Kidnapped in London*, and a Russian version appeared in 1897.

Also at the British Museum, Sun Yat-sen would sometimes go to talk with Robert K. Douglas, a former member of the consular service in China, now a curator in the department of Oriental printed books and manuscripts and a professor at King's College, London. It was in Douglas's office that, in March 1897, Sun met a Japanese botanist, Minakata Kumagusu, then employed in vacation research work. When Sun asked him about his ambitions in life, he is said to have replied, "My wish is that we Asians will drive out [of Asia] all Westerners once and for all."[9] This early first encounter with Japanese pan-Asianism was to be a source of inspiration to Sun Yat-sen and a valuable aid in his activities.

Did this period of intellectual expansion really coincide, as Sun Yat-sen later claimed in his *Autobiography*, with a first version of his doctrine of *The People's Three Principles*?

> After escaping from danger in London, I stayed in Europe to carry out studies of its political practices and make the acquaintance of its leading politicians. What I saw and heard made a tremendous impression upon me. For the first time I understood that, though the European powers achieved national wealth and power (*fuqiang*) . . . they were not able to give their peoples full happiness. . . . I now wanted to create a single-effort, eternal plan which would simultaneously solve the problems of socialism, nationalism, and democracy. The Three Principles of the People which I advocated were perfected from this [idea].[10]

Undoubtedly Sun Yat-sen's social and intellectual experiences in London had a lasting influence and were in a sense the first threads of his future doctrine, but in 1896–97 that doctrine was a long way from taking shape. To judge from the texts he published at that time, Sun Yat-sen was still thinking in reformist terms of the sort that had guided some of his earlier actions such as the petition to Li Hongzhang and his recourse to the patronage of Ho Kai. The first of those texts,[11] entitled "China's Present and Future: The Reform Party's Plea for British Benevolent Neutrality," appeared in the *Fortnightly Review* on March 1, 1897.

In order not to alarm public opinion, whose hero he had become, Sun Yat-sen, employing a few factual distortions, struck a reassuring note: "Before I adopted the study of medicine, my early years were spent in intimate association with members of the Chinese official class. . . . Thus I have had every opportunity and incentive to study the subject on which I am now writing."[12] Sun went on to attack the corruption and incompetence of the Manchu dynasty and the ineffectiveness of the technological modernization preached by Li Hongzhang. He called for the establishment of a good government, set up by the Chinese themselves, with the advice and help of the Europeans during an initial phase. This sounds like an echo of the programs elaborated by Ho Kai in 1887 and 1895. Though Sun purports to represent a Reform Party, he explains nothing about it apart from implying that it has rallied extensive support, even from the literati. All the powers, in particular Great Britain, needed to do was observe a "benevolent neutrality" and the Manchu government would collapse.

The second text, also discovered only recently, is entitled "Judicial Reform in China."[13] It was published in London in July 1897. In it, Sun paints a somber picture of Chinese judicial practices, describing the cruel tortures and the corruption. Sun had of course come to recognize in his interviews with journalists that the British public reacted with horror to such practices. People had listened incredulously to his account of his narrow escape from assassination in the Legation, and how his mummified body was to have been sent back to Peking to be "executed." No civilized country could support such barbarities: "The laws of China, as enforced with the sanction and support of England, are a blot upon Creation and a disgrace to all humanity."[14] So let London withdraw its support for the imperial government; then the Reform Party could introduce a European style of judicial system in China.

Sun's articles were clearly meant to win over the British establishment. Subtly, they blackened the imperial regime and presented Sun Yat-sen as a moderate reformer, enlightened, eager to derive inspiration from the European model, and supported by much of the Chinese population, including the literati. Even if Sun Yat-sen did not really expect aid to be forthcoming— or at least not immediately—he did want to be able to count on some tacit recognition and a "benevolent neutrality."

Sun was trying to capitalize upon the media attention secured by his kidnapping and turn it into a diplomatic and political advantage, but he underestimated the British government's inflexibility. Though the government had reacted sharply to the violation of human rights and international law committed on its own territory by the Chinese legation, it was not on that account prepared to change its general practical line in East Asia. It did not even lift the banishment order placed on Sun Yat-sen by the Hong Kong authorities in March 1896. Sun's optimism, naïveté, and perhaps vanity had led him to overestimate the significance of all that had been done to help him at the time of the kidnapping, which, he told a friend, "shook the entire country and agitated Europe and every country in the world."[15] Once the wave of public interest subsided, he found himself, as before, an exile on the run, the richer only by some extra reading, a few more contacts, and, above all, a splendid image forged by the English press and public opinion.

That image, which he had not been able to capitalize on in England, Sun Yat-sen now decided to try to turn to good account in the East. This man, who did nothing the way others do, was about to reverse the game of mirrors that relations between China and foreigners so often became. He was to reverse the ploy of creating an image of the Chinese reality with no concrete foundation and exclusively designed for export. Instead, he armed himself with the myth fabricated—with his enthusiastic cooperation—in London, and set out to dominate the Chinese reality and impose himself as leader of an opposition on which, for the time being, he had no grip at all.

THREE

The Symbolic Creation of a Revolutionary Movement, 1897–1900

In August 1897, Sun Yat-sen settled in Japan, a country with which his contacts had so far been limited to a few brief visits to the Cantonese community in Yokohama. Now Sun took on Japanese society itself, and for the next three years he was Japanese. He changed his name to Dr. Nakayama, made numerous approaches to various political circles, and formed some deep personal friendships. He was very impressed by the Meiji modernizers and they became the inspiration for his theoretical thinking and the source of concrete assistance in his subversive activities.

Indeed, Sun Yat-sen's Japanese friends and advisers were as important in his career as the Anglo-Saxon missionaries of his early education—perhaps even more important. His friendship for some of them, such as Miyazaki Torazō (Tōten, 1870–1922), was particularly spontaneous and warm. In these relationships, there was a shared racial and cultural closeness that relieved Sun Yat-sen of the show of Christianity that had been a necessary feature of his relations with the Hong Kong establishment and the London society of the Cantlies. The similarity of the problems faced by China and Japan, both threatened by the West, provided less slippery terrain for an entente than any Sino-British cooperation that affronted Chinese nationalistic sensitivities.

The formation of close ties between Sun Yat-sen and the Japanese went ahead the more rapidly because it was desired on both sides. Sun's hope of finding political and financial support in exile was matched by the wish of his Japanese comrades to organize pan-Asian solidarity against the Westerners. The Japanese saw in Sun Yat-sen, still haloed by the celebrity conferred upon him by his being kidnapped in London, a hero capable of "regenerating China."[1] Their quest for such a hero also led them to the reformists Kang Youwei and Liang Qichao, who had found refuge in Japan after the collapse of the Hundred Day Reform in November 1898.

Japan thus became the location for a meeting with the literati who directed and embodied the opposition of the Chinese elites. Sun Yat-sen had of course long desired such a meeting, and the Japanese, keen to see all members of the Chinese opposition united in their efforts, did all they could to bring them together. Their lack of success was due more to irreconcilable personality clashes than to ideology. Sun Yat-sen's charisma and London celebrity did not weigh very heavily against the prestige of Kang Youwei, who was revered as a lettered sage and an adviser to the prince; and Sun's usual strategy of alliance or fusion in order to take over the strength and influence of his rivals turned out not to work with a man such as Kang Youwei, who possessed an ego as formidable as Sun's own.

The rivalry that, from 1900 on, succeeded the efforts to establish closer ties with the reformists helped Sun to clarify a number of points in his political plans. And as he became certain about his anti-Manchu nationalism and his republican aspirations, these choices established an apparent symmetry between the powerful reformist tendency and the revolutionary current that effectively made Sun Kang's rival and thereby conferred upon him an equivalent symbolic status. It seems, in truth, that for Sun, as for Mao Zedong after him, the prime virtue of a dogma or ideology was simply its utility.

Thus, in spite of the aid of the Japanese, Sun Yat-sen remained isolated. The succession of intrigues to which he devoted himself, in the Philippines in 1898, and in Hong Kong and Singapore, and finally the unsuccessful uprising in Huizhou (Waichow), in eastern Guangdong, in October 1900, seemed in many ways like a return to his starting point. What with the mobilization of secret societies, the attempts at bargaining with the colonial authorities of Hong Kong and the mandarins of Guangdong, and the appeals to his Christian networks, Sun Yat-sen's destiny seemed to be taking him round in a circle. The reality refused to coincide with the fiction; and the revolutionary movement continued to exist solely in the person of the man who claimed to be its leader and in his immediate entourage.

THE JAPANESE ENTER THE SCENE, 1897

Already in the spring of 1897, Sun Yat-sen, in the course of his conversations with his friend Minakata Kumagusu in London, had begun to perceive the strength of the pan-Asian current. During the autumn following his arrival in

Japan, Sun made contact with some of its principal organizers. The meetings were arranged by friends of Sun, by Chen Shaobai in particular and by the pastor Qu Fengzhi in Hong Kong.

The apparent idyll of Sun's relations with his Japanese mentors at the turn of the century has been the subject of a number of widely diverging interpretations. Many observers and historians, with hindsight and in view of Japanese policies of aggression in later decades, have detected in it signs of Machiavellian duplicity on the part of the Japanese, seeking to encourage instability in China the better to promote the grandeur of their own country. Seen from this point of view, Sun's role might seem that either of an auxiliary used by Japanese imperialism or of an adventurer led on by purely personal ambition.[2] The research carried out by the American historian Marius Jansen and by Japanese sinologists makes it possible to adopt a more moderate view, to gain a more precise understanding of the context that encouraged the development of relations between Japanese and Chinese nationalists, and to analyze the common style of thought, life, and action that, for some of them, turned those relations into friendship.

Ever since the point at which, at the end of the nineteenth century, the Tokyo government began to intervene actively in China, its politics were marked by many contradictions. After its victory in 1895 and while the battle for concessions was raging, the Boxer uprising was spreading, and the threat of a dismemberment of China was looming, Japan aspired to play its own role among the other foreign powers and to take its own share of the booty. It accordingly took part in the allied expedition against the Boxers of 1900. At the same time, however, it feared a possible partition of China, and in Japan the slogan "Preserve China" (*Shina hōzen*) became far more popular than the Open Door doctrine formulated by the English and the Americans.[3]

These politics, which were to become even more tortuous later, were not— or not solely—a matter of duplicity.[4] They constituted a response to the extremely diversified intellectual and political atmosphere of the time that existed in spite of the authoritarian nature of the Japanese regime. Just as Japan was emerging as one of the great powers and was taking part in imperialist conquests, a strong countercurrent made itself felt. This laid the emphasis upon the Japanese and, more generally, Asian tradition and reacted to the "Yellow peril" theme so fashionable among the Westerners with an appeal to repel "the Whites." This pan-Asianism, from which those who made the political decisions had ostensibly distanced themselves, developed quite freely on the periphery of official circles yet in direct liaison with them. A few major figures and party leaders supported it. Government policy oscillated according to the respective strengths of these pressure groups.

Because pan-Asianism could be interpreted in many different ways, its partisans could come not only from the Right, the nationalists, the expansionists, and the conservatives, but also from the Left, the liberals, the partisans of constitutional reform and human rights, and the radicals fighting for the oppressed peasantry. At its origins lay an acute awareness of the cultural identity of Japan and the cultural links that bound it to China. Under the patronage of Prince Konoe Atsumaro, the president of the Chamber of Peers, a movement was formed for the study of the Chinese language and civilization. This led, in 1898, to the creation of the Society for the Common Culture of Asia (Tōa Dōbunkai), the objectives of which were to preserve and at the same time reform China and to strengthen Japan's role at a regional level. In effect, thanks to the various institutes that it opened in China and the many inquiries that it launched in these, this society came to play the role of an information agency as much as that of an organization for research. It attracted to it a mixed bag consisting of every specialist in Chinese affairs, every researcher, every spy, and every adventurer in the vicinity.

But apart from the cultural loyalty that everyone professed, choices diverged. The patriotic societies, refuges for former samurai who were frustrated by the Meiji reforms, set themselves up as the guardians of national prestige and the Eastern values that they were anxious to preserve by means of an aggressive foreign policy. They were headed by Tōyama Mitsuru (1855–1944), from Fukuoka on the island of Kyushu, to the south of the Japanese archipelago. Tōyama, born into a family of samurai, had grown rich taking part in the exploitation of the local coal mines. He had never held any official post, but he did use much of his personal fortune to finance the activities of small ultranationalist groups that claimed to support pan-Asianism—in particular the Society of the Black Dragon (Kokuryūkai), founded in 1901 by Uchida Ryōhei (1874–1937), who was later to become one of the principal organizers of the Japanese fascist movement. This society's program called for the extension of the territory of Japan as far as the Amur River in Siberia.

The pan-Asian cause was also taken up by the liberals of the Meiji era, who favored economic and institutional modernization after the Western model but at the same time wished to rid Japan and East Asia of the European and

American presence. At the head of this liberal nationalist Left was Ōkuma Shigenobu, who, backed by a new class of urban entrepreneurs, led the Progressive Party and combined the functions of Prime Minister and Minister for Foreign Affairs from 1896 to 1898. Ōkuma thought that Japan, having been the first to modernize, had a moral obligation to protect China against Western aggression and help it reform its institutions. China should not delay its awakening. If only a "hero" would arise, patriotism would be revived and China would be restored to its place among the great powers. This "Ōkuma doctrine," formulated in 1898, invoked Japan's cultural debt to China and maintained that the time had come for Japan to show its gratitude by holding the West at a distance and helping a "Chinese hero" to save his country. Following in Ōkuma's footsteps, Inukai Ki (1855–1932), a journalist and a liberal statesman, entered into close relations with Sun Yat-sen.

Cooperation between the Cantonese exile and the high-ranking officials and politicians of pan-Asian inclinations was, of course, arranged by intermediaries. Men as much in the public eye as Ōkuma and Inukai could not become directly involved in subversive activities. The intermediaries whom they recruited were adventurers, former samurai who as a consequence of the Meiji revolution had lost their status and, in some cases, their resources. With no official position or personal fortune, these men worked for anyone willing to employ them: the government, political parties, patriotic societies. But they also felt they were working for an ideal. These good-hearted mercenaries or, as they called themselves, men with a noble project (*shishi*), placed at the service of pan-Asianism all the loyalty, generosity, and devotion inherited from their ancient feudal code of honor. Outstanding among them was the fine figure of Miyazaki Torazō, whose sincere idealism had always harmonized with Sun Yat-sen's and who became Sun's closest adviser.

The sympathy between the two men might be explained by their common traits of character and their similar family and social circumstances. Miyazaki, born in 1870, had received his early education in a private, liberal school where the teachers nurtured him on the history of the French and English revolutions. As an adolescent, he went through a religious and moral crisis, converted to Christianity, persuading his two elder brothers to do likewise, learned English, and grew up among first Baptist missionaries, then Congregationalists. His brothers and he desired the regeneration of China, for the greater glory of the yellow race, and pondered the question of how to alleviate the poverty of the peasants, which was made plain to them by the farmers who came to their family home to voice their griefs. A second crisis of conscience led to a total break with Christianity. Miyazaki Torazō then set off on a series of adventurous expeditions to China and Siam, his main objective being to be useful, to help others, and to discover a goal in life. It was Inukai Ki who, in 1896, presented him with this when he entrusted him with funds from the Ministry for Foreign Affairs and with the mission of traveling to China to develop contacts with those opposed to the regime and with rebels, and to seek out a "hero" capable of saving his country. Like Sun Yat-sen, Miyazaki was the product of a society at a stage of transition. He had rubbed up against Christianity, and he had adopted some Western models, even while seeking to reject the Western presence. He was as passionate a patriot as Sun Yat-sen.

Miyazaki was not alone in the quest for a hero. Hirayama Shū (1870–1940) worked at his side. He too enjoyed the trust of Inukai Ki, and was often to be called upon to cooperate with Uchida Ryōhei and the men of Tōyama Mitsuru. The alliance between these liberal idealists and the ultraconservatives of Fukuoka was certainly a strange one. But here, too, ideas seem to have played a less important role than feelings and grudges, interpersonal relations, and social status. It was as if opposition to the Meiji government could only be formulated through nationalist claims—which could easily become chauvinistic and expansionist—and as if what all these frustrated former samurai were seeking in the pan-Asian ideal and adventure was really a remedy for their own nostalgia.

Although not all Miyazaki's companions shared his political purity, what they did all have in common with him, as with Sun, was a particular way of life, on the margins of society. They were professional conspirators for whom adventure was not only a quite natural way of earning a living but also an ethic that seemed self-sufficient. These were no ordinary agents but men whose hearts were in their work; some of them became sincerely attached to the "hero" whom they were supposed to invent.

The meeting between Miyazaki and Sun Yat-sen was arranged by Chen Shaobai; the Japanese agent was taken by friends in common to visit Chen Shaobai in Yokohama before setting sail for southern China, where Hirayama Shū was already waiting for him. Chen told Miyazaki about the Revive China Society and Sun Yat-sen and showed him a copy of *Kidnapped in London*, which he had just received. Favorably impressed by Sun's personality, as it emerged from that work of self-glorification, Miyazaki then set off on his mission, which took him to Hong Kong. The contacts already made by Hirayama, mostly with secret societies, proved disappointing. Memories of the Sino-Japanese War were still painful; and mouths remained obstinately closed. The two Japanese agents then turned to the Revive China Society, using addresses provided by Chen Shaobai. They were given a warm welcome by Pastor Qu Fengzhi, who received them in his church after Sunday service, showed interest in their offers of aid, and told them of Sun's imminent return to Yokohama. Upon hearing of this, Miyazaki and Hirayama returned to Japan.

The first meeting between Miyazaki and Sun Yat-sen took place in the home of Chen Shaobai (while he was away organizing anti-Japanese resistance on the recently annexed island of Taiwan). In the course of this decisive tête-à-tête, Sun made a lasting conquest, and one worthy of admiration, for Sun spoke no Japanese and Miyazaki had but a poor grasp of English and even less Chinese. The two men therefore conversed in writing, through the characters used by both to transcribe their respective mother tongues.

Sun's declarations, as reported in Miyazaki's memoirs, developed the themes of the anti-Manchu struggle, the overthrow of the imperial regime, and the establishment of a republican system based on traditions of local autonomy. Sun Yat-sen, adapting to the personality of his interlocutor in his usual skillful way, spoke of "the hero who would rise up," and modestly proposed his own services. Forgetting his recent enthusiasm for Great Britain and its respect for laws and rights, he now violently denounced Western imperialism: "Because our territory is so huge and our people are so numerous, we are like a piece of meat on the butcher block. The ravenous tiger who devours it . . . will come to dominate the world."[5] He wound up the conversation with a request for aid to organize a successful revolution that would "help the four hundred million of China's masses . . . wipe out the insults that have been heaped on the yellow peoples of Asia . . . [and] protect and restore the way of humanity (*rendao*)."

A pinch of anti-imperialism, another of pan-Asianism, loads of enthusiasm, optimism, and a great strength of conviction had done the trick: Sun Yat-sen had passed the test and Miyazaki had found his hero. He lost no time in introducing him first to Hirayama, then to Inukai: "Instead of a report, I have brought you a live example."[6] Both approved his choice and shared his favorable impression.

Now taken under Inukai's wing, Sun Yat-sen was installed in Tokyo in the company of Miyazaki and Hirayama, whose tutor in Chinese he was supposed to be. During the winter of 1897–98, he was introduced to many political figures, nationalists such as Tōyama Mitsuru, who also became his protectors, parliamentary representatives, even Ōkuma Shigenobu himself. The latter, however, was somewhat reserved: his preference went to the reformists and Kang Youwei, who were then enjoying great success. After Empress Cixi's coup d'état in September 1898, Kang sought refuge in Tokyo and the Japanese acted as intermediaries in an attempt to bring him and Sun Yat-sen together. Their aim was to strengthen the Chinese forces of opposition by uniting them and turning them into a powerful instrument of national regeneration, which they could themselves control. This Japanese policy gave Sun Yat-sen another chance to establish contacts with the literati circles of opposition that had up until this point systematically ignored him.

THE FIRST MEETING BETWEEN SUN AND THE REFORMISTS, 1898–1899

Japanese mediation was not prompted solely by political calculation. It was also a response to a desire to reconcile the sympathies that bound the Japanese, as partners, to more than one group of like-minded Chinese. Although Sun Yat-sen had been immediately welcomed and recognized by the adventurers and the men working in the field, such as Miyazaki, the principal patrons of the pan-Asian current felt more drawn to Kang Youwei. It is true that the Chinese reformists did not conceal their admiration for the Meiji revolution, which they had repeatedly invoked as the example to follow during the Hundred Day Reform of 1898. The slogan "Know the shame of not being Japanese" was frequently adopted in schools open to new ideas.

The Meiji reformers were really more comfortable with the Chinese reformists, who upheld Confucius and the Classics and were loyal to a reformed monarchy, than they were with Sun Yat-sen's vague republicanism. The theme of cultural identity developed by Japanese sinologists and the Society for the Common Culture of East Asia had more to do with the Chinese literati than with the former pupils of Christian missionaries. The favorable reception accorded by the reformists to one of the first pan-Asian pamphlets, of the Daitō Gappō ron (Federation of the Greater East), published in Japan in 1893 and translated a few years later into Chinese, testified both to their support for the great theme of Asian solidarity in the face of the invasion of the whites and to their acceptance of Japanese leadership in the necessary resistance to foreigners and likewise in equally necessary internal reforms. It is clear that the Chinese reformists were aware of the threat of Japanese imperialist expansion that underlay their belief in pan-Asianism; but in 1897–98 they chose to ignore it, faced with what they considered to be the more pressing danger of China's being carved up by the Russians and the Germans.

It was therefore hardly surprising that the Japanese leaders looked with a favorable eye upon the attempt of the Hundred Day Reform or that, when it had failed, they offered help to the reformist leaders. Liang Qichao, who had found refuge in the Japanese consulate at Tianjin, was taken to Tokyo aboard a Japanese gunboat. Miyazaki Torazō was detailed to make contact with Kang Youwei, who had fled to Hong Kong, and to invite him, too, to Japan. Upon his arrival in Tokyo in November 1898, Kang Youwei was treated with the consideration due the head of a government-in-exile. He was received by important people: Ōkuma Shigenobu, Prince Konoe Atsumaro, Inukai Ki. The deep sympathy that linked Sun and Miyazaki was matched by the lasting friendship that developed between Ōkuma and Kang. In both these relationships the interplay of social and intellectual affinities was no doubt just as important as their respective ideological choices.

The Japanese provided both Sun and Kang with funds, and endeavored to bring the two men together and to encourage them to fuse their groups, hoping thereby to produce a powerful opposition party. Although Sun, always in quest of social recognition and advantageous alliances, welcomed this plan, Kang was immediately hostile. He considered the revolutionary leader to be an "uneducated bandit," and he could not forgive him for humiliating China when the English had helped him to regain his liberty after the kidnapping in London in 1896. Once before, in the early 1890's in Canton, Sun, at that time much taken by the reformist ideas, had tried to get himself received by the famous scholar, but without success. In Tokyo, in November 1898, when he tried to welcome Kang, who had just landed, Sun had no better luck and was again rebuffed.

Everything made for distance between Sun and Kang, who considered each other as, respectively, "uneducated" and a "corrupt Confucian."[7] Kang regarded Sun as a rebel without dignity, won over by Western materialistic ideas.

Sun regarded the legitimation of reform by means of a reinterpretation of Confucius and the Classics, to which Kang had devoted so much effort, as a scholastic and pointless exercise. These divergent opinions were exacerbated by a mutual jealousy, each seeking to promote his own authority, and by the apparently insurmountable differences between their social origins and intellectual backgrounds.

Unlike his Japanese mentors, Kang Youwei did not accept that the realization of his political plans might involve the collaboration of men such as Sun Yat-sen and Miyazaki Torazō, whom he considered to be mere adventurers. Although invested with the trust of Ōkuma and Inukai, Miyazaki was as unsuccessful as Sun at winning acceptance from Kang. In Hong Kong, for example, in the autumn of 1898, when Kang was an exile on the run, he had preferred to negotiate his departure for Japan with the Japanese consul rather than with Miyazaki, who had been sent to meet him for precisely that purpose. It was this intransigent elitism along with his unaccommodating haughtiness, as much as Peking's protests against the asylum granted to its proscribed literati, that eventually led the Japanese to withdraw their support of Kang Youwei. In the summer of 1899 he accordingly left Tokyo for Canada, where he founded the Society to Protect the Emperor (Baohuanghui). His departure opened up the possibility of cooperation between his principal lieutenant, Liang Qichao, and Sun Yat-sen.

Liang Qichao was a Cantonese scholar and a disciple of Kang Youwei, who until this point had lived in his master's shadow. He was a journalist, a popularizer, and an educator rather than a politician. Once free of Kang's authority, Liang Qichao proceeded to draw closer to Sun and his group. He adopted some of their ideas, cooperated in a number of specific ventures, and renewed negotiations with a view to uniting the two opposition groups.

The school for further education that Liang created and organized in Tokyo in 1899 accepted not only former pupils whom his master had begun to train in Changsha—a group of emigrant radicals who oscillated between reform and radicalism—but also young Cantonese from the Yokohama community. Liang was in this way continuing the efforts initiated in 1897 by both the reformists and the revolutionaries, all intent upon providing the Chinese Yokohama with modern teaching, dispensed in an establishment financed by Sun and given a very Confucian name by Kang Youwei: the School of Great Harmony (Datong xuexiao).

Meanwhile, the theses defended by Liang in the newspaper he established as soon as he arrived in Japan, *Public Opinion* (*Qingyibao*), were becoming increasingly hostile to the Manchu dynasty. Liang cosigned a number of articles with Sun Yat-sen and was considering becoming the second-in-command, under Sun himself, of a unified movement of opposition to the dynasty. Was Liang really on the point of switching camps? Kang Youwei certainly feared so: at the end of 1899, he ordered him to rally the Chinese of Hawaii and the United States and join up with the Society to Protect the Emperor. Liang chose submission and did as he was told, but not without first obtaining from Sun Yat-sen a letter of introduction to his brother, Sun Mei, asking him to help Liang with his political tasks in Hawaii.

So at this point, in spite of Japanese patronage, Sun Yat-sen had still not managed to establish close relations with the literati opposition. Kang Youwei had yet again rejected him, and Liang Qichao, after a gesture of collaboration, had let him down. Unable to latch on to the reformists' capital of prestige and fame, Sun was forced to revert to his old strategy of local, armed uprisings, appeals to émigré communities for funds, and the mobilization of secret societies. But with the creation of the Society to Protect the Emperor by the reformists in exile, who were also in quest of funds, Sun now found himself faced with daunting competition: in many communities, the prestige of Kang Youwei, the emperor's former adviser, threatened to win out over his own. Nor was Sun any longer alone in seeking support from the secret societies: other opposition groups, including some reformist ones, had become aware of the potential usefulness of these armed bands that already had their own system of organization and were accustomed to taking violent action.

Nevertheless, as he faced his rivals, Sun Yat-sen held one extremely valuable advantage: the money and men with which the Japanese were now willing to supply him, having decided that he was the most capable and the most inclined to serve their pan-Asian designs.

BACK TO THE STARTING LINE

Sun Yat-sen's activities at the turn of the century took place in a wider geographical field, rendered more complex by the intervention of the Japanese agents, the activism of exiled reformists, and the mobilization of the secret societies. His operations, up until then limited to the triangle formed by Hawaii–Japan–Hong Kong/Guangdong, were now extended to the Philippines (in 1898–99), Singapore, and Taiwan, and, more sporadically, the Yangzi valley.

Anxious not to waste any of the possibilities of maneuver created by the Boxer catastrophe, Sun Yat-sen now put a multilateral strategy into operation. He courted the great mandarins of the central and southern provinces who were hostile to the alliance between the imperial court and the Boxers and tempted by a separatist policy, negotiated with foreign powers for whose protection he was prepared to pay with many territorial and political concessions, mobilized secret societies, which he regarded as his instruments for seizing power, and reactivated the Revive China Society and the revolutionary base in Hong Kong. The multiplicity and divergence of these undertakings reflected the confusion of an extremely disturbed period during which the old order was crumbling not only in China but throughout East Asia, which had also become an object of European and American cupidity.[8]

Sun Yat-sen's intense activity during these years was made possible by the aid he was receiving from the Japanese. A few powerful political patrons provided him with money, and a dozen or so adventurer-advisers, including the faithful Miyazaki, assisted him in a practical way in his negotiations with high-ranking separatist mandarins, secret societies, and some reformists, often transporting arms and carrying messages. The Sino-Japanese revolutionary axis initially set up in the name of pan-Asian solidarity thus for a while functioned to Sun's benefit. But in October 1900 it was deliberately destroyed by leaders in Tokyo who had finally become convinced that Japanese expansionism could be better served by other means.

Intrigues in Southern China, and to the South of China

In 1898–99, the pan-Asian Japanese and the Chinese revolutionaries tried out their strategy in the Philippines in the service of an anti-American guerrilla, Emilio Aguinaldo. In its struggle against Spanish domination, the Philippine independence movement had in the spring of 1898 obtained the support of the United States. But when the United States appeared bent on replacing the domination of the former colonizers with their own, Aguinaldo turned to the Japanese pan-Asians. During a meeting with Miyazaki in Hong Kong he asked for assistance, and he also sent an emissary to Sun Yat-sen, then in Japan. Sun's warm support was convincing, and the Japanese offered Aguinaldo their help. Inukai instructed Sun to arrange for the purchase and transport of arms. These were dispatched a few months later, preceded by half a dozen Japanese "military advisers" (one of whom was Miyazaki). The ultimate aim of this venture was apparently to make the Philippines, once liberated and after the departure of the Americans, into a revolutionary anti-Manchu base. But like many noble attempts (including the Canton venture), the plan failed—stopped by a storm and a shipwreck.

Sun Yat-sen had to return to Chinese realities. In default of a Philippine base, he would work to reanimate revolutionary activity in Hong Kong, for this had flagged considerably. The main leaders of the Revive China Society had, of course, left Hong Kong at the end of 1895. Yang Quyun, after traveling in Southeast Asia and South Africa, had joined Sun in Tokyo in the spring of 1898. Not all activity had ceased in Hong Kong: some of Sun's old partisans remained, in particular You Lie, who kept busy recruiting and indoctrinating Triad members, and Sun had kept in touch with former partisans through the intermediary of his Japanese friends, Miyazaki in particular. Now, in 1899, activity was relaunched with a new newspaper, the *Chinese Daily* (*Zhongguo ribao*), and a major campaign to mobilize the secret societies.

After his experience in London, Sun was well aware of the force of public opinion, and wishing to compete with the reformists, using their own weapons, propaganda and the press, he entrusted Chen Shaobai with the creation in Hong Kong of a daily newspaper to serve as the mouthpiece of the Revive China Society. Chen Shaobai, it will be remembered, was one of the few intellectuals in Sun's entourage. The money was provided by Japan, and, to begin with, the venture benefited from the valuable support of the prominent Hong Kong reformist Ho Kai, and later on from that of Li Jitang, a son of one of the colony's rich traders, who in 1900 became a member of the Revive China Society. In spite of a series of financial crises, the newspaper thus managed to continue publication right up until 1913, manifesting a truly exceptional longevity for an opposition organ of the period. However, its influence was much greater in Canton than in Hong Kong.

In 1899–1900 the Boxer crisis made the Hong Kong authorities more tolerant of the dynastic opposition, and the *Chinese Daily* made the most of this to multiply its attacks on not only the Manchus but also Kang Youwei's reformist

Society to Protect the Emperor. Beyond the personality clash, ideological divergences began to take more definite shape. But Sun's pragmatism and his historical impatience always led him to favor direct action above all else.

While busy reactivating his revolutionary base in Hong Kong, he was also renewing and extending his contacts with the secret societies. The secret societies were already highly agitated. Even before the eruption of the Boxer rebellion in the North, the Triads of the southern provinces had encouraged many peasant insurrections, particularly in Guangxi, poverty-stricken and crippled by taxes, where in 1897–98 several thousand rebels had risen up, led by Li Liting. Sun's old companion Zheng Shiliang, who had already served as an intermediary between the Revive China Society and the Triads in 1895, now returned to the campaign. Chen Shaobai invited one of the principal leaders of the Cantonese Triads to Hong Kong, and it was he who presided over the initiation ceremony in the course of which Chen Shaobai received the honorific title White Fan (the equivalent of that of a military adviser). This time, however, the contacts and negotiations were not limited to the Triads of Guangdong and Guangxi. For the first time, Sun's agents ventured farther north and established relations with the Society of Elder Brothers (Gelaohui), which was active and powerful throughout the Yangzi valley, particularly in the provinces of Hunan and Hubei. For this extension of his network, Sun Yat-sen relied partly on his Japanese advisers and companions and partly on a Hunan reformist with radical tendencies, Pi Yongnian, whom he had met in Tokyo.

Hirayama Shū, the friend and adventuring companion of both Miyazaki and Sun himself, had been the first to make contact with the Society of the Elder Brothers, in 1898. In the following year Pi Yongnian took over from him in Hunan and Hubei. Pi Yongnian was accompanied on this mission by a young Cantonese recruit to the Revive China Society, Shi Jianru, a touching figure in the revolutionary movement who, only six months later, was to die in tragic circumstances at the age of twenty-one. The fact that Shi Jianru was not the son of a peasant or a trader was a sign of the times. He belonged to a wealthy family of literati and his grandfather held one of the highest official degrees. He had begun by studying the Classics but at the age of nineteen, in 1898, had entered the Canton Christian College. Following a line of development parallel to that of the founders of the Revive China Society, he had been converted to the revolution at the same time as to Christianity. But it was through the intermediary of the Japanese agents, in particular the representative of the Society for the Common Culture of East Asia, in Canton, and later through Miyazaki himself that Shi Jianru came to work with Chen Shaobai and the Hong Kong members of the Revive China Society.

The activities of Sun's agents led to a gathering of the leaders of the Triads and the Society of Elder Brothers, in Hong Kong, at the end of 1899. It was the first time that these secret societies had come into contact with each other. In the course of negotiations conducted by Chen Shaobai, they agreed to form an alliance with the Revive China Society and to recognize the authority of Sun Yat-sen. Sun hoped that the rallying of the Elder Brothers would assure him of operation bases outside Guangdong and thus give his movement a more national character. He also made the most of the added prestige that the recognition of the secret societies conferred upon him to assert himself as the official head of the Revive China Society, whose president Yang Quyun had remained in title (although less and less in fact) ever since 1895.

This political advantage was short-lived, however. It was not long before Sun had to realize that the amalgamation and unification of the secret societies was hopeless. The alliance concluded between the two groups was loose in the extreme, couched in very ambiguous terms. The Revive China Society's initiative was based on the personal relations of a handful of agents, including Chen Shaobai and Pi Yongnian, and on the promise of subsidies. The rallying of the secret societies to Sun in no way implied their adoption of a revolutionary and republican program. They remained faithful to their anti-Manchu tradition and their own ancestral rituals.

The alliance, baptized the Association for the Rebirth of the Han (Xinghanhui), was sealed with libations of wine and pigeon's blood. As a sign of the rejection of imperial authority, a new seal was engraved and taken to Tokyo by Miyazaki and Chen Shaobai, to be presented to Sun Yat-sen. However, any agreement between, on the one hand, men whose sole dream was to overthrow a usurping dynasty and, on the other, a man who aspired to establish a republic, was bound to be a matter of convenience. Each side hoped to use the other, the one to acquire money and arms, the other to recruit fighting men. The subsidies that Sun Yat-sen had promised were a long time coming, and in the spring of 1900 the Society of Elder Brothers transferred its allegiance to the reformists and the Society to Protect the Emperor. The defection of the Society of Elder Brothers and the withdrawal of Pi Yongnian, who retreated, discouraged, to a Buddhist monastery, deprived Sun of access to the Yangzi and drove him back once more upon his own province of Guangdong.

The disorders created throughout China by the Boxer catastrophe not only encouraged the mobilization of the secret societies but also prompted regionalist and autonomist reactions on the part of the powerful governors-general of central and southern China, who were anxious to preserve their own provinces both from popular unrest and from its inevitable foreign repression. As we know, these governors-general, dissociating themselves from the imperial court's policy of alliance with the Boxers, refused to recognize Peking's declaration of war on the foreign powers, on June 21, 1900. They wanted to come to an agreement with those powers and to sign a pact of mutual defense of the Southeast, thereby ensuring the maintenance of the status quo in their own territories. Some of them may have entertained the idea of going even further and making the most of Peking's disarray to establish a separate power. One case in point appears to have been Li Hongzhang, who, in semi-disgrace, had in November 1899 become the governor-general of Guangdong and Guangxi. The Hong Kong authorities and the British government could not remain indifferent to such a plan. No more could Sun Yat-sen. And in the summer of 1900 an extraordinary series of negotiations took place between Canton, Hong Kong, and London, negotiations in which what was at stake was no less than the secession of southern China.

We know how much Sun Yat-sen relied on his network of relations and how skillful he was at getting this to serve his own interests and those of his cause. The man he now used to mediate with Li Hongzhang was none other than Liu Xuexun, the Cantonese scholar who had once run a lottery. He had played a part in the Canton uprising of 1895, and since then he had become one of Li Hongzhang's principal collaborators. At his call, Sun set sail on June 8, 1900, accompanied by his Japanese advisers, who were to act for him in Hong Kong, since he could not land because of the ban laid upon him. The Japanese opened negotiations with Liu Xuexun, but it soon became apparent that Li Hongzhang, requested by the imperial court to return to Peking to help resolve the Boxer crisis, had abandoned his separatist plan the better to prepare himself for a national destiny. In spite of the insistent pleas of Sir Robert Blake, the governor of Hong Kong, who regarded a Li-Sun alliance as the best means of protecting Guangdong as well as the colony and its British interests against possible popular unrest, Li Hongzhang could not be prevailed upon to change his mind, and on July 17, 1900, he left for Shanghai.

This episode without follow-up, like so many other episodes in Sun's life, spotlights the versatility of his strategy as a leader capable of carrying on simultaneous negotiations with bandits, heads of secret societies, high-ranking imperial mandarins, and representatives of the gentry. It also marks the appearance of an abiding theme whose importance was to grow steadily as Sun's career unfolded: the idea of Canton as an autonomous base, the laboratory for a revolution that would later spread to the rest of China.

The failure of the negotiations with Li Hongzhang did not discourage Sun Yat-sen. He now, on his own this time, relaunched the idea of a republic of southern China, which he planned to establish in the wake of armed intervention by the British. At this point, the Boxer disturbances and the foreign powers' international expedition made any hypothesis seem feasible. Sun hoped to rally the governor of Hong Kong, Sir Robert Blake, to his idea. Ho Kai once again, but for the last time, served as his intermediary and devised a plan. His Plan for a Pacific Government returned to the usual reformist themes: federalism, local autonomy, a role as advisers for the diplomats of the great powers, and China to be opened up totally to foreign economic interests. Blake seemed to approve of the plan. But London had quite different ideas about the defense of British interests in China and soon put an end to all these speculations.

The negotiations between the governor and the exile were but one link in a long chain of contacts maintained between the revolutionary movement of southern China and the colonial authorities. They once again throw into relief the disagreement between the colonial officials on the spot and their hierarchical superiors of the Colonial Office and above all the Foreign Office in London. Not only did imperialism in China speak in several tongues, it also, whether that tongue was English or, as we shall see, French, spoke with several voices. As for the differences already manifest in 1895 between the discourse of Ho Kai and the plans of Sun Yat-sen, that had progressively deepened in the context of a nationalism that had become more general and radical by 1899. Whatever concessions Sun Yat-sen might be ready to make to the foreigners in the name of pragmatism and the immediate interests of his cause—concessions that, as we have seen and will see again, could go a long way, even as far as the secession of sovereign rights or of certain portions of the national territory—the revolutionary leader retained a lofty idea of his country. It was inconceivable that he should ever subscribe to the desperate declaration made by Hong Kong legislative councillors Ho Kai and Wei Yu in 1899:

"We would prefer to see China partitioned at once and good government introduced by the powers. National death is preferable to national dishonor, corruption, and degeneration."[9] It is true that Ho Kai, like the other anglicized elites of Hong Kong, was conditioned by his divided loyalties toward on the one hand China, on the other Great Britain. But Sun Yat-sen loved only China and would limit himself to treating with Great Britain. After 1900, the paths of Ho Kai and Sun Yat-sen separated definitively.

By now, after the failure of all his efforts, Sun Yat-sen could depend only on his own forces, that is to say the local secret societies, the Triads, financed and armed thanks to subsidies raised abroad, and led by members of Revive China Society. In the autumn of 1900, he therefore returned to his old strategy and launched a new insurrection in Huizhou, in eastern Guangdong.

The Huizhou Uprising, October 1900

Like the failed Canton uprising of 1895, the Huizhou uprising, five years later, appealed to the Triads for aid. But in 1900, the role of these societies seemed at once more important and more autonomous. It was no longer simply a matter of the Revive China Society's using whatever finances were available to hire the services of several hundred armed men. Now the plan was to make the most of a peasant insurrection, set off by the secret societies, to attack the prefecture of Huizhou and the provincial authorities of Canton. This was the first occasion to pose an essential problem that was to dominate the history of the Chinese revolutionary movement and its thinking right up until the dynasty was finally toppled in 1911. The problem was that of the relations between the secret societies and the revolutionary party.

Those relations varied according to places and periods. A number of different policies, some of them contradictory, were frequently pursued simultaneously: the strategic integration of the insurrectional potential of the secret societies into plans to subvert the regime; the ideological rallying of a traditional opposition that could sometimes be persuaded to drape the republican colors over its age-old antipathy toward the Manchus; concessions on the part of the revolutionary leaders who, in order to make sure of powerful allies, would be willing to go along with the archaic rituals of the secret societies and back their calls for the restoration of the ancient order. In this respect the Huizhou experience was particularly significant.

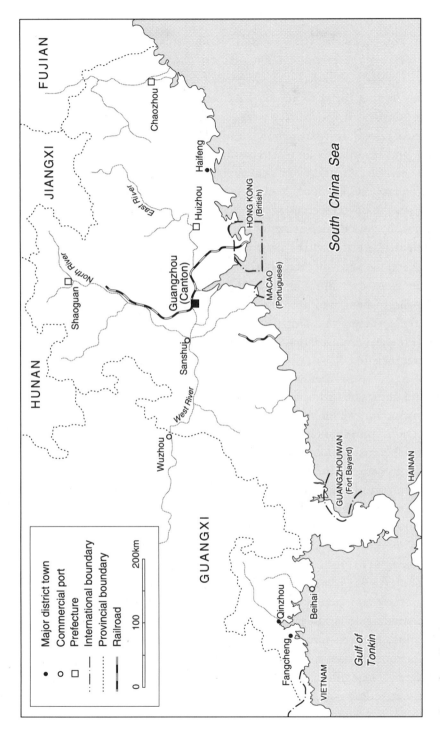

Guangdong Province

The existence of the secret societies usually attracted the attention of observers only at the eruption point of these vast peasant rebellions whose violence regularly exploded in the history of the Chinese dynasties. Yet their activities formed the very web of daily life for a whole section of Chinese society. In principal, the societies were open to anyone, and they recruited not only social rejects such as vagabonds and cashiered soldiers but also artisans, traders, and smugglers whose activities ran along parallel lines and were frequently complementary. Even local gentry were not above joining: officers, minor literati, and landlords might all seek to strengthen their influence and ensure their own protection in this way. Kernels of informal power thus developed beyond the structures of the governmental administration, with a network that overlapped the networks of the small towns and markets. In between, on the one hand, the villages given over to sporadic violence between different clans or militias and, on the other, the regional and provincial metropolises where the imperial officials faced opposition from local literati and elites, small and middling trading centers that escaped the direct control of the imperial administration constituted the principal points of support for the secret societies.

Ever since the eighteenth century, eastern Guangdong, rich from its produce and salt trade, had been a favorite region for the Triads active in smuggling operations, which fostered recurrent episodes of social turbulence. The insurrections were spontaneous, numerous, dispersed, but linked to the network, itself extremely loose, of secret society lodges and organizations. Sometimes, as in 1854, at the time of the insurrection of the Red Turbans, the movement spread. The rebellion that erupted in one town would spark off others in the neighborhood. And when the contagion spread in this way, the rebel forces would converge upon the larger urban centers and might even threaten the provincial capital, Canton, as happened in 1854. Government forces managed to crush the revolt but not to destroy the network. In times of repression, the rebel forces would disperse and the insurgents would return home to their respective towns and villages where they would be reabsorbed into the trading or farming activities of an infrabureaucratic world ruled by the relations between various autonomous forces, which eluded direct interventions from the state authorities.

In eastern Guangdong, the history of the Triads was closely connected with that of salt trading and smuggling. From the second half of the nineteenth century on, mafiosi-type activities intensified as did the imperial government's efforts to apply the monopoly more strictly; in response to this, the resistance of salt traders and smugglers increased. Many of the rebellions began in the town of Tanshui, which was the main center for the salt trade and the seat of the salt tax office. The terrain around Tanshui was particularly favorable to such rebellions in that the local population of Hakkas—Han colonists settled there at a later date than the other inhabitants—were frequently the victims of discrimination.

At the turn of the century, the decline of the imperial system and external setbacks stirred up turbulence among these popular forces. Although the Boxer rebellion has become a part of Chinese history, it was by no means the only movement to spread through the countryside. The provinces of Guizhou and Guangxi provide one example of places where an insurrection of several thousand rebels took place in 1898. Guangdong was also extremely turbulent. The Revive China Society no doubt turned to the Triads of eastern Guangdong and chose Huizhou as the center of the uprising it was planning because Zheng Shiliang, Sun Yat-sen's old companion and his principal intermediary with the secret societies, had many contacts in this region, the home of his ancestors. It became Zheng Shiliang's task to alert the Triads, assemble their leaders and their troops, which were to form the "principal force" in the uprising, and hold them in readiness for action. In accordance with the classic pattern of popular mobilization by the secret societies, the insurrectional movement was to begin in a number of country towns in the Guishan district, then converge first on Huizhou, then on Canton.

At this date, the Revive China Society boasted twenty-three members from the Triads. Most were the heads of lodges, relatively educated people: lower gentry members (such as chemists) or émigrés who had pursued careers abroad, as had Huang Fu in Borneo. Even though close relations between the Triads and Sun Yat-sen's group were usually conditional upon distributions of subsidies to them, financial considerations did not necessarily exclude political interests, at least at the level of some heads of lodges. A common hostility to both Confucianism and the Manchu dynasty also encouraged their cooperation.

Sun Yat-sen did not pronounce officially on Confucianism until 1924, at which date he praised it, paying homage to its role in the formation of the national culture. But his initiation into Christian values and Western civilization, combined with his rejection by dominant Chinese elites, did not dispose him favorably to the relations of subordination (of a son to his father, a subject to his prince) taught by Confucianism. Hostility to the Confucian social order had been perpetuated in China both among certain scholars who exalted the figure of the knight errant, a righter of wrongs, and among humble folk for whom this bringer of justice took on the features of a great-hearted bandit, a sort of Eastern Robin Hood. This anti-Confucianism, more psychological than erudite, may have provided common ground for agreement between the popular insurgents, the lower gentry who organized them, and the republican marginals and their Japanese advisers from the samurai class whose own code of honor was similar on many points to that of these dispensers of justice of the Chinese tradition.

But it was above all hostility to the Manchu dynasty that created a bond between the secret societies and Sun Yat-sen. There were, to be sure, considerable differences between the popular variety of anti-Manchuism and the republican variety. On the one hand, an oral tradition urged that the foreign invaders be crushed and the ancient Ming dynasty restored; on the other, was a systematic analysis showing the damage done to China by the reign of this parasitical dynasty. On the one hand, the secret societies placed their faith in symbols: their insurgents desired to restore to fashion the headgear (without the queue), the robes, and the official titles that had been in use in the sixteenth and seventeenth centuries; on the other, the republicans were appealing for national mobilization in the name of popular sovereignty.

In the ardor of the common struggle, the various anti-Manchu strands do seem to have intermingled. In a statement published by the Hong Kong press during the Huizhou uprising, the insurgents' leaders declared, "We are not Boxers, we are great politicians of the secret societies . . . who wish to oust the Manchu government and establish a government of popular sovereignty," thereby realizing "hopes frustrated for three hundred years."[10] Intermingling their usual slogans with rallying cries borrowed from the Revive China Society, they called for popular sovereignty, the development of international trade in China, and neutrality on the part of the foreign powers.

Sun Yat-sen and his group similarly borrowed much from the secret societies, making use of both their rituals and their conspiratorial techniques such as passwords, rallying signs, and oaths of allegiance. Of course, we may well wonder whether these were no more than purely tactical borrowings, designed to consolidate their links with the secret societies whose fighting forces were needed to support their own cause. The initiation ceremony of Chen Shaobai, in Hong Kong in 1899, in which the honorific title White Fan was conferred upon him, took an extremely simplified, almost casual form: no blood was taken from the neophyte, no libations of wine were mixed with blood.

It is impossible to tell exactly what role was reserved for the secret societies in this strange alliance that threw them alongside the republicans. In the articles that Sun wrote in London in 1897, he was already referring to "hidden forces at work in China" and "the deep discontent" that might cause a mass uprising, and he was certainly more tolerant than many members of his entourage regarding the primitive habits and strong body odor of the fighting companions he had chosen. Yet by 1905 he was criticizing the secret societies' inability to cease quarreling and unify their action. Later, in 1919 and again in 1924, he was to refuse to allow the history of the secret societies to be included in the official historiography on the Republic and the Guomindang, declaring that they had remained "very despotic," with very marked hierarchical differences, and that they manifested "no trace of the republican principle of the idea of popular sovereignty."[11]

Meanwhile, however, Sun needed their aid and was counting on their men, although the story of the Huizhou uprising suggests that he considered them only a supporting force. He did integrate the secret societies into his strategy, but he was above all counting on Japanese military aid and financial support from the overseas Chinese communities. These strategic choices of his contributed, among many other factors, to the failure of the Huizhou venture.

The Failure of the Uprising

According to the initial plan, the insurrection of the secret societies of eastern Guangdong, with the object of besieging Huizhou, was to be coordinated with an attack on the provincial administration offices in Canton itself, where the direction of operations was entrusted to one of the founding members of the Revive China Society, Zheng Shiliang, who was also an important leader of lodges in Hawaii. In 1895 he had joined Sun Yat-sen to take part in the first Canton uprising. He was now assisted by Shi Jianru, the twenty-one-year-old defector from the Cantonese gentry, who brought to the endeavor all the sincerity of his convictions and an ardent spirit of self-sacrifice. As in 1895, the conspirators were supported by the networks of Christian converts associated with the missionary teaching institutions such as the Canton Christian College. Chinese priests and pastors and converted students intermingled with the conspirators, among whom was also to be found the bookseller Zuo Doushan, whose shop had served as an arms store and meeting place in 1895. According to the reckoning of the official historiographer Feng Ziyou, 30 percent of the conspirators involved in the subversive plans for Huizhou and Canton had been recruited among Christian converts, 70 percent among the Triads.

This cooperation between the Christians and the Triads, under the aegis of the Revive China Society, runs counter to the preconception of the existence of a radical hostility between the secret societies and the foreign missions and their converts, a radical hostility that was certainly expressed during this same period in the Boxer uprising, for example, and in many other local insurrections as well. Yet the alliance was in truth not so very surprising. The converts may also have been regarded by their compatriots as members of an unorthodox sect, marginal people among other marginal people. The secret societies' hostility toward the missions was fanned by xenophobic literati, concerned to defend both their privileges and their cultural identity. In Guangdong, wide open to foreign influences and heavily influenced by the millenarist tradition of the Taiping, Triads and Christians seem to have had little difficulty in getting along together in their attack against the established order.

As we have seen, during the summer of 1900 Sun Yat-sen had left Japan to seek the support necessary for the uprising. His travels took him first to Hong Kong (where he did not land), then to French Indochina, Singapore, and Shanghai. But his efforts were frustrated by an unwillingness to receive him in many quarters: on the part of foreign authorities, Chinese mandarins with autonomist tendencies, and reformists alike. In the émigré communities, particularly Singapore, Sun Yat-sen's requests for funds had in many cases been forestalled by Kang Youwei and his Society to Protect the Emperor.

However, when Sun Yat-sen returned to Nagasaki, new possibilities seemed to be opening up on the Japanese side. Seeking to make the most of the troubles in China to extend their influence there, the Japanese were planning to gain a foothold in Amoy (Xiamen), a treaty port in the coastal province of Fujian, facing Taiwan, which had been a Japanese colony since the treaty of Shimonoseki in 1895. Wary of upsetting the other powers, the Japanese preferred to implement their plan through another party. In early October, the governor of Taiwan, Gotō Shimpei, accordingly offered Sun Yat-sen funds and military advisers to seize Amoy. Sun visited Taiwan and revised his plan for an insurrection in eastern Guangdong, substituting Amoy for Huizhou as the rebels' objective.

This strategic decision clearly reveals the priorities of a leader who placed more faith in foreign aid than in the mobilization of popular support. An attack on Huizhou would have represented the normal outcome of a rural insurrection, developing through well-established networks of complicity, founded on local trading links between secondary markets, country centers, and towns. To divert the Triads to Amoy and Fujian meant not only subjecting them to a long march of over three hundred kilometers across rugged terrain, but also cutting them off from their social links and turning a popular insurrection into an expedition of outlaws, leaving the decisive role to foreign intervention. The Huizhou uprising involved both those strategies, first the one, then the other, for the revolt erupted spontaneously on October 6 and developed as foreseen in the initial plan, up until the arrival of Sun's new directives a few days later.[12]

In its early stages, the Triads' uprising presented all the features of a classic rural insurrection. Under the direction of Zheng Shiliang, several hundred men gathered in the small town of Sanzhoutian (in the Guishan district), which was situated a few kilometers from the sea and was used as a base by pirates and smugglers. In the field, these men would only obey their own leaders, and the presence of the Revive China Society essentially boiled down to that of Zheng Shiliang, who transmitted his orders through the intermediary of the lodge leaders. Coordination and discipline were entrusted to the "straw sandals" (cao jie), messengers drawn from the various lodges. In a movement of mounting mobilization, the insurrection spread rapidly from the little town of Sanzhoutian to neighboring centers. Government troops were routed at Shawan and the insurgents reached Zhenlong, only twenty kilometers to the south of Huizhou. In all the villages and hamlets they passed through, or took, they received a warm welcome. Apparently well disciplined and taking care not to attack any Christian missions, they rallied hundreds of inhabitants to their ranks: in ten days their numbers had risen to ten thousand men.[13] Now all they had to do was join up with their "brothers" from local Triads who were waiting for them in the suburbs of Huizhou and farther west, and then converge upon Canton.

It was at this point, on October 17, that, upon receiving Sun's new di-

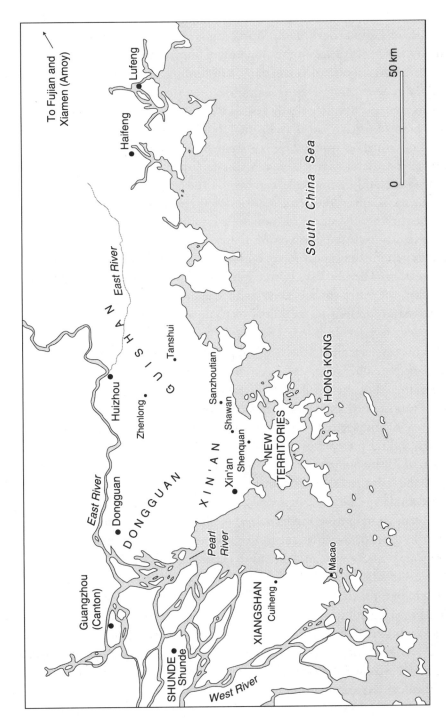

The Pearl River delta

rectives, Zheng Shiliang's men turned toward Amoy. On their long march through unfamiliar terrain they were harrassed by government troops and became exhausted and discouraged. The last remnants of hope evaporated on October 23, with the news that the Japanese, fearing the Russian reaction, had finally given up the idea of establishing a footing in Amoy and had canceled the promised aid. Zheng Shiliang and the principal Triad leaders had little choice but to flee to Hong Kong and leave their men to return to their towns and villages.

This rural insurrection of an altogether traditional type had managed to hold off government troops for seventeen days. It had won the active support of much of the population. Could it have gone on to further success and become a threat to the provincial authorities? Probably not, for with time the government forces could have mustered more troops and weapons. But the fact remains that the impetus of the popular uprising was deliberately broken by Sun Yat-sen, in the name of a strategy based upon foreign intervention: in this instance, Japanese. Why did Sun Yat-sen release his prey to snatch at a shadow? Perhaps because he felt that his vast designs would never be achieved through small local victories, perhaps because he had no confidence in social forces—of a peasant and mostly rural society—over which he had no means of direct control.

A postscript to this setback is provided by the tragic epilogue in Canton. Keen to help the peasant insurrection by creating diversionary disturbances in the provincial capital, the young Shi Jianru organized an attack on the governor of Guangdong. On October 28 there was a bomb explosion, but the governor escaped unscathed. In the course of the police repression that followed, Shi Jianru was arrested. He was beheaded on November 9, having shown the same courage as his self-sacrificing predecessor, Lu Haodong.

In their Hong Kong refuge, the leaders of the Revive China Society eluded the justice of the empire but not the secret agents of its police. Yang Quyun was struck down in his own classroom and Zheng Shiliang died suddenly after a meal, from a heart attack according to the official report, from poisoning all his friends believed.

Sun Yat-sen had returned to Japan. Now, as 1900 drew to a close, he was once again alone and powerless: rejected by the reformists and in competition with them, ignored by the British authorities, betrayed by his Japanese protectors, and left without his best lieutenants. But no setback could discourage

Sun. Whether it sprang from the strength of the man's will or from his visionary dreams, an extraordinary perseverance was one of the fundamental traits of his character. Every setback produced a new plan. In 1900, the Huizhou failure engendered a new strategy. Without renouncing the idea of sporadic attempts at subversion and infiltration from Hong Kong or other frontier bases, Sun Yat-sen recognized the limitations of a policy that was producing more and more actions leading nowhere, forcing him increasingly into the category of adventurer and outlaw and making him almost totally dependent upon foreign aid that was slow to arrive. Sun Yat-sen already knew that in China all legitimacy, including revolutionary legitimacy, depended upon the support of at least some intellectuals. So far he had failed to win it.

In those early years of the century, the rapid radicalization of Chinese political life and the nationalist commitment of the student generation were finally to provide Sun Yat-sen with his long-awaited historical opportunity. The leader of the Revive China Society at last no longer had to profess to be a reformist in order to win acceptance and recognition. It was as a revolutionary that he was about to rally to him youthful forces impatient for action and intellectuals capable of laying down the theoretical bases of a doctrine and a party.

FOUR

The Awakening of Chinese Nationalism and the Founding of the Revolutionary Alliance, 1905

The early years of the twentieth century saw the beginnings of a series of profound social changes that came to constitute the first phase of a revolutionary process that was to continue until 1949. The scale of these changes, which occasioned the emergence of new social groups and upset the relations between society—or at least its elites—and the authorities, has led historians to minimize not only the importance of the 1911 revolution, which they dismiss as no more than a change in the political decor, but also, in consequence, the importance of the influence of the revolutionary movement that preceded it.

It is not only Sun Yat-sen's role that they challenge, but also the very place of his party in the history of a transformation that he accompanied but did not direct. "This was a revolution bigger than all its leaders. . . . The revolutionary movement is important less for what it contributed to the events of 1900–1913 than for the revolutionary tradition that it created."[1] This kind of revisionism expresses a rejection, almost unanimous on the part of Western historians, of all schemata of interpretation drawn from the European and American revolutions, which seek to turn 1911 into the Chinese 1789 and Sun Yat-sen into some latter-day Washington or Bonaparte.

So let us forget 1789 and concentrate on the China of 1900. After the Boxer catastrophe a consensus finally emerged among leaders and elites on the need to preserve, or recover, national sovereignty and to modernize not only China's production apparatus but also its institutional system. Nationalism and modernism were now goals widely accepted, but diversely interpreted. Taking over the ideas of the reformists whom it had executed or removed, the imperial power launched a New Policy (Xinzheng) for the authoritarian transformation of society and the economic and political system. It thus posed as the architect of modernization and the nation's defender.

This initiative on the part of the government, the sincerity and efficacy of which remain controversial, had consequences of major importance. It precipitated developments that it was then expected to resolve, accentuated the politicization of the local elites, and hastened the emergence of new social groups—the Western-style intelligentsia and entrepreneurs. Many circumstances combined to abort this Chinese Meiji a few years later: it had been attempted too late; centrifugal forces were too strong; the central government was too weak financially; and finally, and above all, anti-Manchu feeling was increasing. It had always existed, latently, in the secret societies and certain literati circles in southern China, without ever seriously diminishing the power of the sinicized Qing dynasty that had been ruling China since the seventeenth century. But in the early years of the twentieth century that feeling was revived, and it spread, particularly among the degree holders who up to this point had remained faithful to the dynasty out of Confucian loyalty. Now the anti-Manchu opposition could express itself openly and violently in the press, pamphlets, and political literature.

Through a strange historical quirk, the now revitalized anti-Manchu tradition also encouraged nationalist sentiments born of reaction against Western aggression. Far from being accepted as the guide and initiator of a policy of modernization and anti-imperialist resistance, the hapless sinicized Manchu dynasty took the place of the Western powers as the Chinese nation's number-one enemy.

The identification of nationalism with the anti-Manchu tradition was bound to condemn the New Policy and the would-be reforming empire to failure. However, that identification was neither immediate nor general. Some of the most implacable critics of Western imperialism, such as one of the founders of modern Chinese political thought, Liang Qichao, always rejected it. It eventually became accepted by the majority of Chinese elites from the moment when, in about 1908, reform seemed doomed to fail by the change of sovereign, the lack of money, and the resistance of local bureaucracies. Until then, reactions had been much more varied and many elites had been willing to collaborate in the New Policy launched by the central government.

On the other hand, within the new intelligentsia and the circles drawn toward it, the equivalence between nationalism and anti-Manchu feeling was already accepted by 1903. It was this development that made it possible for Sun Yat-sen, a declared enemy of the dynasty for the past ten years or more, to turn the relative unification of the revolutionary movement to his advantage and to create the Revolutionary Alliance (Tongmenghui) in 1905.

The decision of the Chinese intellectuals to adopt anti-Manchuism as the dominant ideology of the opposition provided Sun with his long-awaited chance to gain recognition as a leader of national stature. Yet it was also that decision that gave rise to many of the ambiguities of Chinese revolutionary thought and action, and likewise to the false successes of 1911–12. Notwithstanding the constant insistence with which Chinese historiography identifies Sun Yat-sen with the revolution, the question that arises is whether the exploitation of anti-Manchu feeling, which served Sun's career so well, did not destroy—or at least deflect—the initial impetus of the revolution itself.

THE NEW POLICY OF THE REFORMIST EMPIRE

The upheavals that affected Chinese society in the first years of the twentieth century owed far more to the initiative of the tardily reformist imperial power than to Sun Yat-sen's propaganda and attempted revolutionary uprisings. But the New Policy implemented by the court did strengthen a social activism of initially uncertain political tendencies and fostered a multiform opposition, part of which rallied to Sun Yat-sen.

The imperial edict of January 29, 1901, denounced the evils of China in terms that appeared to have been borrowed from the reformists of 1898, urged the adoption of foreign models, and announced a general program of reforms. In the years that followed rapid steps were taken to implement it. Most bore the stamp of the Japanese model by which they were inspired. Education was one of the domains most deeply affected. The traditional academies had to make way for modern schools, organized under the authority of a Minister for Education and with a curriculum that included the Western sciences. As early as 1902, students were being encouraged to go off to complete their education abroad, particularly in Japan. In 1905 the discontinuance of the examination system, which for thirteen centuries had closely associated intellectual activity (conceived as the study of the Classics) with officialdom, radically altered the social status of the literati and favored the rise of a modern intelligentsia.

The reform of the army ran parallel to the reform of education: recruitment through the examination system was abolished, provincial military academies were created, and young officers were sent to be trained in Japan. The New Army (Xinjun), the creation of which was decided in 1903, was to be organized and equipped in the Western manner and placed under the centralized control of an Army Ministry. All these measures, accompanied by the rise of nationalism, helped to improve the traditionally weak prestige of the military institution. The recruitment of officers could now be extended to the sons of gentry. The young officers of the New Army shared the same social origin, the same kind of foreign education, and the same political ideal as the members of the emergent intelligentsia. The cultural divide that used to separate the literati and the military was now shrinking.

The creation in 1903 of a Ministry of Commerce, with very wide powers, also testified to the central government's determination to take over the direction of economic modernization, defining its objectives and indicating the means to be employed. In order to put its policies into operation, the imperial government also launched administrative reforms designed to define and strengthen the role of the central ministries, and judicial reforms based on the introduction of new civil, criminal, and commercial codes. It had plans to standardize the currency and weights and measures, and to centralize fiscal administration. Finally, in 1906, the imperial court announced its decision eventually to adopt a constitutional government.

What distinguished this New Policy from earlier attempts at modernization was its centralizing and national nature. As is well known, the Meiji revolution and Bismarck's reforms, the inspiration for this Chinese revolution, were only successful because of the existence of strong government. The imperial court's choice of authoritarian reform, initiated and controlled at the top, was therefore not particularly original. However, it was made very late in the day and at a time when the Peking government was severely weakened financially and when, as soon as it became a matter of changing the status quo, its authority was hard to impose in the provinces. In spite of the support it received from some of the great governors-general, reform came up against the discreet but effective resistance of a local bureaucracy whose prerogatives were under threat. To get around that resistance, the imperial government tried to rely directly on the social forces that were the most involved in the process of modernization and the most likely to profit by its success. It endeavored to create the necessary local points of support for its action by rallying the old elites and at the same time encouraging the rise of new social groups. The state, which customarily had entered into dialogue for the most part solely with its own bureaucracy, clearly now felt the need to communicate more openly with society.

This interventionism hastened developments already set in train decades earlier. We have noted the progressive tendency of local elites to move from the management of traditional philanthropic and educational activities into more modern ventures and projects with a national scope connected with defense, economic development, and fiscal matters. The politicization of the public sphere (*gongshi*) was speeded up by the introduction of the new institutions set in place by these reforms. The modern schools, agricultural societies, and chambers of commerce created by imperial decrees were attached not so much to the official bureaucratic structure as to the sphere of autonomous projects managed by the local elites. The new institutions extended the domain and means of action of these elites, who in this way became directly associated with the national objectives of modernization.

The leaders who used to be found in philanthropic societies were now involved in the chambers of commerce, and those who used to be in the traditional academies were now connected with the modern schools. So the transformation of the institutional framework had not much altered the class of local officials and gentry, even if some intellectuals, having benefited from a foreign education, now joined their ranks. The interconnections between local preoccupations and national ones thus increased greatly, and under the influence of the nationalist fervor shared by all the elites, the sphere of community interests became the hub of the political mobilization of society.[2]

Initially, that is to say from 1901 to 1905, that mobilization was not systematically aimed against the imperial dynasty, whose proclaimed objectives were generally accepted, even if certain measures, such as the discontinuance of the examination system, aroused fleeting resistance. However, it is also clear that local officials, though acting as Peking desired, nevertheless refused to allow the government full control or even to acknowledge that it could force them to cooperate. They were certainly partisans of a modernization policy, but they wished to run it on the basis of agreement with the government, not in obedience to its orders. The reform thus put a strain on the structure of the political system and relations between the state and society, or at least the social elites among whom activists were then being recruited. The revolution of 1911 was to stem from the disaffection and growing hostility of these elites toward the central power, reviled because it was Manchu.

The extreme rapidity of the revolution, which in just over one decade swept the traditional elites from apolitical social activism into launching a challenge against the imperial government, is to a large extent explained by the influence of new social groups. It was owing to the policy of reforms that these arose, but in general they remained hostile to the established regime and exerted a crucial influence upon public opinion.

The entrepreneurial class emerged, in the treaty ports, from the fusion of a number of elements: wholesalers engaged in foreign trade, bankers, industrialists, and compradors, not forgetting overseas traders investing in China either of their own volition or at the request of the imperial power, and anxious to make the most of their wealth and their know-how. From 1904 on, these new entrepreneurs came together in the chambers of commerce just set up by the government. As a class, they differed from the old merchant class in the openness of their attitude to the contemporary world, their aptitude for innovation and for making money through this, and their ability to make tradition serve new objectives. In the treaty ports, however, the initiation of this emerging business class into the modern world often took place in circumstances of dependence and humiliation. Its nationalism was expressed as early as 1905 through its organization of the first major antiforeign boycott, directed against the United States and its discriminatory immigration policy. But the resentment against foreigners was only too ready to change into hostility against a regime judged to be incapable of defending the economic and general interests of the country.

The officers of the modern armies and the students from the new schools were very small minority groups: those attending the new schools (all grades included) are reckoned to have numbered 100,000 in 1905, and in 1906 the number of officers being trained came to no more than 1,500; that of cadets, 3,500. Their importance stemmed from the part that both groups were to play in introducing China to new ideas around which many forms of opposition would crystallize. Many of those officers and students were the sons of local elites, and the nature of their activities and preoccupations now allowed them to escape from their original class, the gentry, while preserving many links of solidarity with it (so, when they fell foul of the imperial police, very many of these young opponents of the regime were saved through the intervention of their families). Many of the army officers were former students who had "discarded their pens to take up swords," the better to serve their country. The reform of the army made it easier for them; and public opinion encouraged them. Entrusted as they were with defending their country, they felt themselves to be invested with special responsibilities. But because they were usually placed under the command of older, corrupt superiors who did not share their preoccupations, they felt frustrated both in the exercise of their profession and in their patriotic aspirations.

It was a frustration that many students shared. The government certainly had taken steps to make room in the administration for those who had studied abroad: special examinations had been organized to grant them the necessary equivalent grades. But as their numbers swelled, the process of integrating these young people into the traditional society became increasingly difficult. Their education had in many cases alienated them from Confucian values and disengaged them from the network of obligations that had been imposed upon the old literati. Many now had a somewhat muddled sense of their responsibilities. Among the best of them it was geared not to the old Chinese status quo but to a national future imagined in the most radiant of colors, and it thus bred revolutionary radicalism.

THE BIRTH OF REVOLUTIONARY RADICALISM

The émigré circles of Tokyo constituted the principal source of the revolutionary radicalism that mobilized an important fraction of the modern intelligentsia and was to serve as a link between the opposition of the local elites and that of the professional rebels.

The Chinese Students in Japan

The flood of Chinese students to Japan at the beginning of the twentieth century (500 in 1902, 13,000 by 1906) was a consequence of the New Policy, which encouraged the training of modern elites abroad. It was also a response to the admiration felt by young Chinese for the patriotism, spirit of national unity, and political and diplomatic success of their neighbors. Most of the earliest candidates for such training held scholarships, the majority provided by the provincial authorities, a few by the central government; there were also some who were sent abroad to study at their families' expense.

Once they arrived in Tokyo, they were taken in charge by associations of their provinces of origin, the most active of these being those of the provinces of central and southern China, Hunan, Jiangsu, Zhejiang, and Guangdong. These associations provided moral and psychological support for their members and also a framework for their first political activities. The ephemeral magazines that they published—the *Circle of Students of Hubei* (*Hubei xueshengjie*), *Zhejiang Wave* (*Zhejiang chao*), *Jiangsu* (*Jiangsu*), *New Hunan* (*Xin Hunan*), etc.—expressed, through provincial solidarity, the beginnings of national awareness. "Love for our country must start with love for our province," declared the *Circle of Students of Hubei* in its first issue.

The intellectual guide of these young people's thinking was Liang Qichao. In the *New People's Miscellany* (*Xinmin congbao*), which he had just created, Liang was no longer content with the radical interpretation of the tradition favored by Kang Youwei. Moving far beyond the reformist themes of 1898, he now harbored new preoccupations, took an interest in Western history and philosophy, and became an admirer of Darwin and Descartes. He appealed to the Chinese to free themselves from their past, and compared China to "a ship just leaving the shore." He deplored the decline of Chinese institutions, the poverty of the people, the corruption of officials, and, above all, the aggressive policy of the foreign powers. The clear, dazzling, passionate style of this inexhaustible journalist and essayist delighted the students. In their own publications, they echoed the principal themes aired in the *New People's Miscellany* and repeated Liang Qichao's attacks on imperialism, economic imperialism included.

In 1903, one diplomatic incident—Russia's refusal to evacuate southern Manchuria, which it had occupied during the Boxer crisis—was all it took to crystallize student radicalism. In the university quarter of Kanda, in Tokyo, the Chinese students' clubhouse became the meeting place for all young patriots. Provincial affiliations merged into national aspirations. The young people joined forces to create a Resist Russia Volunteer Corps. This crisis provided the opportunity for student leaders to play their first public roles. Among them was Huang Xing (1874–1916), who was to become one of the principal leaders of the Revolutionary Alliance and, later, Sun Yat-sen's rival.

The Chinese authorities, who had resolved the diplomatic crisis by their own means, were alarmed by the development of this student unrest. At their request, the Japanese government had the Volunteer Corps dissolved, only to see it promptly replaced by an Association for Military Education, which purported to encourage patriotism and military training for citizens but in fact inclined toward violence and terrorism.

The 1903–5 period was characterized by two developments in student radicalism: on the one hand, it moved into direct action in China itself, where the former Tokyo militants returned to organize many revolutionary groups; on the other, anti-imperialist nationalism turned into anti-Manchu nationalism. The coincidence of these two developments suggests that, faced with the demands of revolutionary action, the young intellectuals could not avoid the decision made by Sun Yat-sen a few years earlier, namely, to form alliances with the secret societies on the basis of a common anti-Manchu program.

The history of the revolutionary groups to some extent bears out that interpretation. It testifies to the efforts made to mobilize the striking power of the secret societies. Like Sun Yat-sen's nationalism, the anti-Manchu nationalism of the students stemmed from a strategy of mobilization applied to a traditional society. Yet that opportunist argument is not entirely satisfactory, for the 1903–5 period saw the publication of many anti-Manchu pamphlets that were remarkable either simply for their violence or—in particular those of Zhang Binglin—for the theoretical aspects they sought to confer upon anti-dynastic sentiments: Anti-Manchu nationalism was no longer simply a historical ploy (or distraction); in its own right it now entered the history of thought of modern China.

Revolutionary Groups in China and the Development of a Tokyo-Shanghai Axis

The flowering of revolutionary groups, linked with the return of Chinese students from Japan, took the form of the creation of a dozen or so associations most of which lasted only for a year or two.[3] These revolutionary groups were concentrated in the Yangzi region, in the larger towns, particularly Shanghai, where the presence of the foreign concessions made it easier to foil the surveillance of the imperial police and where the young radicals trained abroad now linked up with local students and intellectuals.

Although the groups kept in contact with one another, they seldom managed to coordinate their respective activities, so these remained for the most part limited to a provincial framework. They took the form of violent but mostly abortive ventures such as attempted political assassinations or armed uprisings. Police repression was efficient, and, for all their ardor, these young radicals were not seasoned fighters. That is why they sought allies in the secret societies—though without much success. But a few groups did acquire more importance. One was the Society for China's Revival (Huaxinghui), founded in Hunan in December 1903 by Huang Xing; another was the Restoration Society (Guangfuhui), created in Shanghai in 1904.

The Society for China's Revival recruited its first members from among the students lately returned from Tokyo. To extend its influence to the general population, it set up intermediary organizations designed to establish relations with the Society of Elder Brothers and the military—hoping that this might make it possible to avoid the misunderstandings that could arise from a direct meeting between the young intellectuals and the ignorant masses. The Society for China's Revival was relatively successful in its approaches to the cadets of the military academy of Wuchang, the capital of Hubei province. Its only program was the overthrow of the dynasty, its only strategy an armed uprising planned for Changsha (Hunan) in the autumn of 1904. When this miscarried, Huang Xing was forced to seek refuge in Shanghai, then go into exile in Japan.

Meanwhile, Shanghai, with its many modern educational institutions, most dating from before the New Policy, did not need to wait for the return of its Tokyo students to establish itself as a center of radicalism. In 1902 the Chinese Educational Association (Zhongguo jiaoyuhui) was organized by Cai Yuanpei (1867–1940), a great traditional scholar deeply disappointed by the reformist failure of 1898, and Zhang Binglin (1869–1936), soon to establish himself as the master thinker of the first generation of Chinese revolutionaries. Although the association had as its declared aim the translation of Japanese teaching handbooks, it was actually a subversive organization that supported student strikes and patronized a Patriotic School (Aiguo xueshe) designed for the training of revolutionary militants. Its methods of action were sometimes inspired by those adopted by the Tokyo students, with whom the association was in contact: sending telegrams of protest, forming volunteer corps, and so on. On the whole, however, it gave priority to the writing of pamphlets and to propaganda.

This Tokyo-Shanghai axis, engendered by the constant interaction of both men and ideas between the two, was given more concrete political expression by the founding, in Shanghai, in 1904, of the Restoration Society. Its organizers, former Chinese students in Japan, set out to intensify revolutionary mobilization in the lower Yangzi region. The abortive outcome of the uprising planned for Changsha by Huang Xing (in which the Restoration Society had been involved) put an end to the Shanghai activities of this group. But the society survived until 1912 in Zhejiang, where it founded schools, infiltrated the secret societies, organized assassination attempts, and intermittently collaborated with Sun Yat-sen.

None of this agitation led to particularly concrete results. But it did establish the foundations for a revolutionary movement, which spread from Wuhan throughout the Yangzi valley.[4] The small groups set up in 1903–4 paved the way for the many societies, clubs, and associations that were to light the fires of the victorious insurrections of 1911. In both cases, the same diversified strategy was adopted, with a similar geographic and social scattering of separate organizations, each pursuing its own autonomous action and united solely by their common objective.

The small groups formed in 1903–4 also played an important part in the eventual weakening of imperial power, encouraging local officials to move on to political and dynastic opposition. The shift effected by these officials, who moved from ambiguous collaboration with the New Policy into determined opposition to the central government, reflected the evolution of general public opinion as it became increasingly receptive to the revolutionary propaganda that the radical intellectuals continued to use as their chief weapon.

The Golden Age of the Pamphleteers

Unlike the earlier movements of rebellion led by Sun Yat-sen, the flowering of radical groups was accompanied by an abundant flow of political literature. Criticism of the dynasty soon became one of its essential themes. Anti-Manchu opposition, until then a domain reserved for the secret societies and certain backward-looking literati circles, now began to emerge as a political doctrine. The students had started off by associating hostility to imperialism (the main cause of their initial mobilization) with a critique of the dynasty that had failed to protect the country from that imperialism. Very soon, however, the logic behind that approach was submerged by the rising tide of what was, quite simply, racial hatred.

The most famous anti-Manchu pamphlets, many of them written by very young people, were lyrical compositions that appealed above all to passion. However, in Zhang Binglin, a scholar of great talent, anti-Manchuism found its theoretician. A number of "affairs," the most famous of which was that of the *Subao* (Jiangsu Journal) in 1903, were to bestow national, even international fame upon the works of these propagandists, especially those of Zou Rong and Zhang Binglin, whom their contemporaries nicknamed "the Mazzinis of China."

After the Resist Russia movement of 1903, the Tokyo student press, the titles of which have been listed above, took to manifesting national ambitions. The *Circle of the Students of Hubei* thus became the *Voice of China* (*Han sheng*). This press now devoted more and more space to the problems of imperialism, increasingly laying the blame for China's weakness quite openly on the Manchu dynasty. The same themes were echoed in hundreds of other revolutionary publications, many of them very ephemeral, that appeared in Shanghai in 1904 and 1905. Two famous pamphleteers, Chen Tianhua and Zou Rong, were to develop this nationalism further, diverting toward the Manchu dynasty the hostility previously aimed at the Westerners.

Chen Tianhua (1875–1905), a native of Hunan province, took an active part in the Resist Russia movement. At the end of 1903 he returned to China to help Huang Xing create the Society for China's Revival. It was at this point that he produced two texts, both of which met with resounding success: *Wake Up!* (*Meng huitou*) and *Alarm to Arouse the Age* (*Jingshi zhong*). The tone was vehement, the logic clear. Obsessed by the threat that foreigners represented to the "yellow race" (here assimilated to China), Chen Tianhua called for resistance from his compatriots: "A dog cornered against a wall will always turn around and take a few bites. Are we, 400,000,000 of us, not able to match a dog? . . . All press ahead. Kill the foreign devils. . . . If the Manchus help the foreigners to kill us, then first kill all the Manchus. Kill! Kill! Kill."[5] Two years later, in December 1905, Chen Tianhua committed suicide in the course of a conflict between the Chinese students and the Japanese authorities. He did so in order to save the honor of his compatriots, who stood accused by the local press of "being changeable and devoid of will."

Zou Rong's style was even more inflammatory. He was a young Chinese student who in 1903, after a brief stay in Tokyo, published *The Revolutionary Army* (*Gemingjun*), in Shanghai. In this pamphlet he denounced not only the weakness of the Manchus in the face of foreign aggression but also, and above all, their discriminatory policies toward the Chinese and their intrinsic corruption. He attacked all these "barbarians" and "thieves," called the dowager empress Cixi a prostitute, and referred to the emperor by his personal name (which rated as a crime of *lèse-majesté*). He exalted the revolutions in the West "which advanced from barbarism to civilization." It was a cry from the heart of an eighteen-year-old who had lived his whole life in his native province, only recently discovering the modern world in Shanghai and Tokyo. There would be no point in seeking for penetrating analyses here, but we can admire his youthful enthusiasm, his eagerness for change, his passion for new ideas, and his clear, vigorous style, close to spoken Chinese; and we may be moved by his incantations: "Revolution! Revolution! Achieve it, then you may live, fail in it, then you may die"[6]—a sadly prophetic exclamation, for two years later Zou Rong died in a Shanghai prison, where he had been incarcerated for writing this pamphlet.

The youth of these two pamphleteers, the wholeheartedness of their enthusiasm, and their tragic destinies make them both symbolic representatives of the Chinese revolution in its early years. They played an essential role in arousing anti-Manchu feeling. However, it was left to a real scholar to produce a theory for anti-Manchuism and to turn dynastic opposition into an ideology.

The Theorization of Anti-Manchuism

Zhang Binglin (1869–1936) was a great scholar, born into a wealthy and cultivated Zhejiang family which had preserved the tradition of the Ming loyalists.[7] For seven years the young man was educated in a famous Hangzhou academy where he acquired a solid knowledge of the Confucian Classics and also took an interest in the ancient currents of thought (*zhuzi*) that had flourished in China before the foundation of the empire, from the sixth to the third centuries. He was receptive to certain Western influences and became initiated into the most purely metaphysical aspects of Buddhism, as developed by the Mahayana school. The national crisis that erupted in 1895 prompted Zhang Binglin to abandon his career as an erudite researcher in order to embrace the reform party and journalism. After the failure of the Hundred Day Reform, he sought refuge first in Taiwan, then in Japan, where he met Sun Yat-sen, but collaborated with Liang Qichao.

The Boxer catastrophe caused Zhang Binglin to move into the antidynastic opposition. In the 1902 revised edition of his collection of essays, *Urgent Advice* (*Qiushu*), and his *Reply to Kang Youwei on the Subject of the National Revolution* (*Bo Kang Youwei lun gemingshu*) Zhang accused the Manchus of having precipitated the decline of China: not only did they not defend the country against the Western aggressors, but for more than two centuries they had persistently worked to obscure the cultural and historical consciousness of the Chinese.

Zhang Binglin's theory on the national revolution (or restoration) (*minzu guangfu*)[8] was partly based on the views of the philosopher Wang Fuzhi (1619–92), a Ming loyalist much in vogue in the 1890's. Protesting against the establishment of the barbarian dynasty of the Manchus, Wang Fuzhi provided an essentially ethnic definition of China, founded upon the mythical Yellow Emperor. Zhang Binglin returned to that racial notion. But under the influence of the Western social sciences, in particular Herbert Spencer and Auguste Comte, he gave it a wider meaning, not just biological but also, and above all, cultural. He stressed the importance of the historical process in the formation of the nation. In his view, history was the very soul of the nation: by falsifying and obscuring the past, the Manchu regime had deprived the Chinese of their collective memory and thereby of their national consciousness. To reverse that oppression, it was necessary to rediscover the sources of the Chinese culture by revitalizing historiography (this was to be the aim of the Movement for the Preservation of the National Essence, which was to assert itself from 1905 on) and, on a more immediate political level, to eject the Manchu dynasty.

For all his emphasis on cultural factors, Zhang Binglin did also despise the Manchus as a barbarian, inferior race, asserting that "Culture does have its ethnic origins." In China, its source was the Han people. Yet, far from assimilating themselves to the Han and adopting their civilization, the Manchus' policy toward them had been consistently discriminatory: "They have not wedded China; they have violated her."

Zhang Binglin was no closet revolutionary, however. In April 1902, in Tokyo, he helped to organize a meeting to celebrate the memory of the last Ming emperor. "We shall gather in tears to commemorate the fall of China," Zhang said in his inaugural address, comparing the fall of the Ming dynasty to the fall of the nation. The following year, he became directly involved in the *Subao* affair. This erupted in Shanghai, where the newspaper, published in the International Concession, had become the organ of the radicals. Zhang Binglin, the great theorist of anti-Manchu nationalism, was one of its principal collaborators, and he made the most of the chance to multiply his diatribes against the imperial government and to spread the news of Zou Rong's pamphlet, *The Revolutionary Army*. Though far apart in age and education, the two men shared the same anti-Manchu fervor, and Zhang Binglin had been willing to write a preface to the young man's work. Sustained by their common political faith, they were also to face the ordeal of imprisonment together.

The Chinese authorities demanded that the miscreants be handed over. The municipal council of the International Concession refused to allow them to be extradited, thereby interpreting the extraterritorial status of the concession in a most presumptuous manner that was violently contested by the imperial officials. The polemicists were tried by the Mixed Court of the International Settlement (under foreign authority) and got away with sentences of no more than two to three years' imprisonment.

The fame of Zhang Binglin and the youth and martyrdom of Zou Rong (who died in prison in April 1905), the long procedural wrangle between the Shanghai Municipal Council (of the International Settlement) and the imperial officials, and the political and diplomatic implications of what was at stake all combined to publicize the affair in the Chinese provinces as well as in Shanghai and Tokyo and the circles of foreign residents. The radicals could not have hoped for better publicity for their anti-Manchu propaganda. Zou Rong's pamphlet was translated in the foreign press and published in Tokyo and Hong Kong: according to Feng Ziyou, over a million copies of it were in circulation. When Zhang Binglin left prison, in June 1906, the crowd that had gathered at the gates acclaimed him as a hero. Thanks to the vast publicity that it showered upon Zou Rong and Zhang Binglin, the *Subao* affair appears as one of the founding events of the revolutionary movement. After concealing or minimizing the affair for many years, Chinese historiography now seems to be recognizing its true importance. This stems in particular from the role played by the episode in the recognition by the imperial officials as well as public opinion of the existence of a revolutionary tendency quite distinct from the reformist movement.

However, the repression sparked off by the *Subao* affair now hampered the development of the radical activities in Shanghai and the provinces of the Yangzi region. At the beginning of 1905, after the failure of the planned uprising in Changsha and when Huang Xing had been forced to flee and Zhang Binglin was in prison, the chances of the revolutionary project seemed all the more compromised in that the reforming empire was showing a certain vigor and its New Policy was winning a measure of credibility.

Even Liang Qichao, who in many respects may be considered the originator of student radicalism, was rejecting methods of violence and the anti-Manchu struggle that he had recommended with such success in the *New People's*

Miscellany. Alarmed by the turn taken by student unrest in Tokyo, held back by the links that still attached him to his master Kang Youwei, and, above all, convinced that any internal disorder would simply provide the foreign powers with new opportunities for meddling and aggression, Liang Qichao rallied to the plan for a constitutional monarchy and gradual change. A few years later, he even agreed to collaborate with the Qing court's reformers.

This example must have given many radicals pause for thought, among them Chen Tianhua, whose fiery pamphlets had inspired student ardor in 1903–4 and who now, in 1905, was on the point of following Liang and rallying to the reforming Manchus. He had taken refuge in Tokyo in January, but now planned to travel to Peking to present the imperial officials with a petition that he had just drawn up. In it, Chen gave priority to the anti-imperialist struggle over the antidynastic opposition: the Manchus could be forgiven for belonging to a foreign race, provided they now proved themselves "good patriots." Chen Tianhua's apostasy was narrowly averted by the intervention of Huang Xing and other Hunan radicals. But the fact remained that the many setbacks and the frustrations both of impatience, lack of organization, and divisions were discouraging the radical students. Many could see no solution except individual heroism and self-sacrifice. The traditional political ethic, by which martyrdom had the power to discredit the authorities and mobilize men's minds against them, paved the way for nihilist, then anarchist influences. From 1903–4 on, individual terrorism became for some students the weapon "par excellence" in a "revolution conceived as an age of planned assassinations."[9]

For those who rejected such extreme means, the solution that was about to emerge would be closer ties with Sun Yat-sen, who, standing aside from the unrest of Tokyo and Shanghai, had been working at polishing up his image as the man for the job, capable not only of winning over people's minds but also of mobilizing resources and organizing action.

SUN YAT-SEN IN SEARCH OF EXTERNAL AID, 1903–1905

Sun Yat-sen appears to have had little to do with the events that fired the patriotic circles of Tokyo and the Yangzi provinces in these early years of the twentieth century. From 1900 to 1902 he was living in Yokohama among its

Chinese traders, far from the student agitation in the capital. From 1903 on, except for returning for a brief period to Japan from June to September 1903, he was traveling. At the time of the great mobilization against Russian encroachment, Sun was in Hanoi, where he remained from December 1902 to May 1903. While the *Subao* drama was unfolding, he was living in Hawaii (September 1903–March 1904). At the end of 1904 he went to the United States and then, at the beginning of the following year, to Europe. Not until July 1905 did he return to Japan.

Sun's absence can be explained by the prejudices that intellectuals continued to harbor against him, and also by the distrust that they themselves inspired. According to Zhang Binglin, "the Chinese students in Japan thought he [Sun] was an uncultured outlaw, hard to get along with, and they did not associate with him."[10] Chinese students in Europe in 1905, where Sun Yat-sen was trying to arouse support, even reported him to the Chinese legation in Paris. They were perfectly willing to take part in the revolution but were not prepared for the shame of entering into alliance with Triads and the Society of Elder Brothers, for, after all, they said, "are we essentially students or bandits?"[11] For Sun Yat-sen, this betrayal simply confirmed the distrust awakened in him, a few years earlier, by the volte-face of Liang Qichao.

Little is known of Sun Yat-sen's activities in Yokohama between 1900 and 1902. Perhaps he was assailed by the same discouragement that overwhelmed his old friend Miyazaki Torazō after the Huizhou setback. For a while, Miyazaki turned to drink, took to the road, and made his way across Japan singing ballads—and writing his memoirs entitled *The Thirty-three Years' Dream (Sanjū-sannen no yume)*. At the end of 1902, however, Sun Yat-sen was again in action. His strategy had not changed. Disdaining the new forces that were growing stronger with the rise of intellectual radicalism and the mushrooming of revolutionary groups, he continued to place his hopes in the mobilization of overseas Chinese communities, aid from foreign powers, and the support of secret societies. His objective seems to have been to reconstruct the fragile coalition that had enabled him to launch the Huizhou uprising, with a view to setting up other insurrections along the southern frontiers of China.

But Sun Yat-sen was now faced with numerous rivals in the field of political opposition. In the Yangzi provinces, radical groups were establishing many links with secret societies, hampering the liaison that Sun had tried to establish with them early in 1900. In the émigré communities, where the principal contributors of funds were to be found, Sun Yat-sen now ran up against the influence of the reformists and the popularity of Kang Youwei and his Society to Protect the Emperor. On the other hand, the quest for aid from foreign governments, which Sun continued to pursue, seems to have been an original and atypical ploy in this period dominated, among reformists and radicals alike, by intense anti-imperialist mobilization.

The "French Connection"

The six months that Sun Yat-sen spent in Hanoi, from December 1902 to May 1903, established the bases of cooperation with certain elements in French political, diplomatic, and military circles, which were to bear fruit from 1905 on but particularly in 1907.[12] Sun had already sought and to some extent obtained aid from foreign powers such as Great Britain and Japan. Why did he turn to France in 1902?

One reason for this new orientation was that Japanese policies themselves had changed and were no longer according priority to the Chinese revolution. Since 1898 Japan's international status had been transformed. Japan was now a great power, a player in the international diplomatic game. Its alliance with Great Britain in 1902 conferred upon it a prestige and respectability that were further to increase with its victory over Russia in 1905.

In these circumstances, collaboration, even of an indirect nature, with adventurers such as Sun Yat-sen no longer seemed such a good idea. The Meiji leaders preferred to support the reform carried out by the Manchu dynasty, which openly took them as its models. In 1901 they began sending advisers to the Peking government and in return obtained from it numerous concessions. Increasingly, their interests coincided with preservation of the established order in China. The patriot adventurers who a few years earlier had been dreaming of a Chinese revolution to promote pan-Asianism and Japanese expansion were now more concerned to halt Russia's progress in Manchuria and northern China. The Black Dragon Society, so called after the Chinese name for the Amur River, laid the emphasis on the cultural renewal of Asia and pressed for war against Russia. With the agreement of a number of military leaders, the Japanese adventurers were now planning to foster unrest in the Irkutsk and Lake Baikal region, in order to disrupt the operation of the Trans-

Siberian Railway and weaken its logistic capacity. Sun Yat-sen was no longer the hero, no longer the leader whom it was important to help. And even though his closest friends, such as Miyazaki Torazō, were still loyal, they could no longer assure him of the aid of official circles.

In Sun Yat-sen's strategy, France's role was therefore to take over from Japan's declining support. Sun's choice of France was without doubt dictated by that country's clearly expressed ambition to extend its influence in the direction of the provinces in southern China (Guangdong, Guangxi, Yunnan), the better to protect its possessions in Tonking. At a time when Chinese public opinion was mobilizing against the creation of a French sphere of influence in the South, Sun Yat-sen was planning to make the most of that imperialistic greed, with a view to obtaining the aid that he needed.

It was thus upon his own initiative that, in June 1900, he requested an audience with Jules Harmond, the French ambassador in Tokyo. According to Harmond's report, Sun Yat-sen asked him for arms and military advisers, proposing in exchange to grant France concessions in the southern provinces that would be wrested from imperial control. This move was part of an extremely complex series of maneuvers undertaken by Sun during this period, immediately after the Boxer crisis. On the one hand, in league with the governor-general of Hong Kong, Sir Robert Blake, Sun was trying to get Li Hongzhang, the viceroy of the two Guangs (Guangdong and Guangxi), to defect and set up a secessionist government. At the same time, however, he was thinking of profiting from a possible foreign invasion (in this case, French) of those same provinces. Sun juggled both strategies in the course of his trips to Hong Kong and Southeast Asia that summer. When he arrived in Saigon on June 21, 1900, he was carrying a letter from Ambassador Harmond, addressed to the governor-general of Indochina, Paul Doumer.

Franco-French Divergences and Sun Yat-sen's First Setbacks, 1900–1903

Paul Doumer, governor-general of Indochina since 1897, had behind him a career as a politician, deputy, and Minister of Finance. As soon as he took up his post in Indochina, he declared himself to be a man of action, determined to consolidate and extend the French presence in the Far East. He made the most of the increasingly favorable disposition of public opinion and the French Parliament regarding French colonial aspirations, and he himself took care to foster that climate of approval by using his political relations and organizing press campaigns and pressure groups such as the Committee for French Asia, created in 1901 under the chairmanship of the former Minister for Colonies, Eugène Étienne. In his program report of March 22, 1897, Doumer stressed the incompleteness of the pacification of Tonking, the weakness of the general government, and the poor administrative organization of the Indochinese territories. In the course of the years that followed, he took steps to remedy those deficiencies, obtaining the means to do so by creating a general budget for Indochina, fed by the colony's own resources.

One of his main preoccupations was the defense of the territory. He wanted to keep in check the Japanese ambitions "which are a threat to all nations with interests in Asia, particularly France," as he wrote in his report of March 1897. He also wished to be ready "to profit from the redoubtable crises and possible dislocations" that could not fail to arise in China.[13] He accordingly gave his ardent support to the 1898 policy of breaking up China and creating a French sphere of influence in the southern provinces, founded on the concession of the leased territory of Guangzhouwan, in western Guangdong, and the Tonking-Yunnan railway.

The Chinese provinces bordering on Tonking, which were poor and mountainous, edged and conveniently protected the French possessions. They also provided a possible zone of expansion in the event of the collapse of the Chinese empire. The policy of the French government at this time was to limit itself to economic expansion, preserving good relations with the Chinese imperial regime. Doumer would have liked to go further and faster, and he had in mind the military conquest of Yunnan, which, he claimed, was "geographically linked to our Indochina." In May–June 1900, he believed the time for action had come, when the French general consulate in Kunming (Yunnan-fu) was besieged by xenophobic bands urged on by the local mandarins. Doumer regarded this as another legation siege. In Paris, one section of the press set about inflaming public opinion, and Auguste François, the besieged consul of Kunming, hit the headlines in *L'Illustration*. The governor-general of Indochina massed his troops on the border between Tonking and Yunnan. However, neither the Minister for Colonies nor the Minister for Foreign Affairs approved of Doumer's plans. He was forbidden to allow his troops into Chinese territory. And Auguste François, in Kunming, was told to avoid all provocation so as to give him no pretext for intervention.

The timing of Sun Yat-sen's efforts to meet Paul Doumer could thus not have been worse. Alerted by a telegram from Harmond, the Minister for Foreign Affairs and the Minister for Colonies, hostile to any support for subversion in southern China, warned Doumer off, and Sun's request for an interview was denied. Sun was permitted to meet one of the governor-general's high-ranking officials, to whom he explained his plans: in the long term, the overthrow of the Manchus, in the short term the formation of an independent government for the South. But he received no promise of support.

However, the governor-general had not given up his expansionist designs on Yunnan. On the occasion of the opening of the railway linking Hanoi and Langson, in July 1900, he complained of the way in which the Minister for Foreign Affairs was sticking spokes in his wheels and told Auguste François, who was present at the ceremony, "If I do not soon get the satisfaction I am demanding, I shall leave for Paris and I shall be taking my horse-whip with me!"[14]

In the following year, the conflict hardened between the governor-general, claimed by his opponents to be deliberately creating incidents along the frontier, and the authorities in Paris, who were determined to maintain a status quo deemed to be in the national interest and to pursue their penetration into southern China by exclusively economic means. The Kunming consul, now back at his post, was a victim of these political contradictions. Each of the frontier provocations, which he dismissed as "Doumerian follies," made his position more perilous and further excited the people's xenophobia. With the help of the local mandarins, who now regarded the consul as their "best guarantee against the Indochinese threats,"[15] Auguste François did what he could to ease the situation. Being convinced that Doumer's plans were deluded, he denounced the aggression "against a province that will burn our fingers" and poured mockery upon the greed of those sitting in their carpet-slippers in Paris and dreaming of an Eldorado in Yunnan where he, in the course of numerous forays, had come across nothing but rocks and monkeys.

Meanwhile, Doumer was becoming ever more active: "His press cries out for battle and his agents are busy."[16] The governor-general now resumed contact with Sun Yat-sen, inviting him to visit the colonial exhibition that had opened in Hanoi in November 1902, and holding out to him the hope that he would this time be received. Sun Yat-sen accordingly set sail on December 13, 1902, and, probably after a discreet stop in Shanghai to obtain a new visa, arrived in Hanoi a few weeks later—too late to meet Paul Doumer, who had just been recalled to France.

Sun Yat-sen nevertheless installed himself in Tonking for the next six months, during which he established contacts with the entourage of the new governor-general, Paul Beau. But Doumer's successor, a former minister to Peking, was a diplomat through and through, and his views faithfully reflected those of the French government. In Kunming, Auguste François could breathe again. As for Sun Yat-sen, whom the governor arranged to have received by his secretary, he was still not heeded. His requests for aid, his plans for a federal republic in southern China, and his promises of concessions for France were ignored by the colonial authorities, whose only concern was to keep the revolutionary leader under surveillance and to strengthen controls on the transport of arms in the direction of the Chinese frontier.

Trapped amid the oscillations and contradictions of French colonial policy, Sun Yat-sen was thus for the second time fobbed off and denied a proper audience. However, the markers established in 1900 and 1903 were to make it possible for him to resume dialogue with the French authorities—this time more fruitfully—when he passed through Paris in 1905.

Sun Yat-sen's Visit to Paris in the Spring of 1905 and Boucabeille's Mission

When Sun Yat-sen arrived in Paris in February 1905, after organizational meetings in Brussels and Berlin, he reactivated his network of contacts and was interviewed by a number of officials at the Ministry of Foreign Affairs, among them, in all probability, Raphaël Réau, who had worked in the Hong Kong consulate. Réau understood the troubled situation in southern China and had already met Sun Yat-sen in 1903, when he had been interested in his plans. Two memoranda preserved in the archives of the Quai d'Orsay record the exchange of views in the spring of 1905.[17] The texts are not signed, but a handwritten note added in the lower margin states that they were written by Réau. In these interviews, Sun Yat-sen elaborated upon his usual themes. France ought to replace Japan as the principal support of the Chinese revolutionary movement, with the major objective of establishing "a federated republic of the provinces of southern China." In exchange for military and financial aid, Sun declared himself prepared to facilitate France's penetration of southern China by mobilizing his partisans and the secret society leaders.

He explained that "in the provinces of Guangxi and Yunnan, the people are openly hostile to the French. It would be easy for us to change that spirit of hostility rapidly into real sympathy, to the enormous benefit of your policies and your various commercial and industrial enterprises" (memorandum of February 9). In the report's own words, the "famous agitator" held "enormous power" in these provinces and he seemed "to have put together the most detailed plans." He and his movement represented "important factors in the Chinese question."

Raphaël Réau's analyses were favorably received by at least two high-ranking officials, Philippe Berthelot, the secretary of the Quai d'Orsay, and Paul Doumer, both of whom Sun probably met in person. We have already seen where the colonial party's ambitions lay. Furthermore, in 1905, the Russo-Japanese war had caused tension between France and Japan and it was natural enough that any plan to substitute French influence for Japanese in southern China should attract attention in the Ministry of Foreign Affairs and likewise in the Ministry of War.

The result of these interchanges was the creation, in May 1905, of the Intelligence Service on China, one of whose tasks was to collect information on the evolution of the situation in southern China, the activity of the Japanese in that region, and military measures to be taken in Tonking. The Intelligence Service was headed by Captain Boucabeille, with its headquarters in the Peking Legation. However, it was not dependent upon the diplomatic representatives there, since it had to avoid compromising them. In practice, the Intelligence Service was autonomous, and it sent its reports directly to the Ministry of War, then run by Eugène Étienne, the former minister for colonies and one of the principal leaders of the colonial party. This intelligence operation, which continued until October 1906, opened up the means for close cooperation between a small group of French officers, on the one hand, and Sun Yat-sen and his Cantonese entourage, on the other. It gave Sun the opportunity to mount an astonishing propaganda campaign designed to present him as the direct inspiration behind the troubles disrupting the central and southern provinces, and the supreme authority recognized by rebels of all persuasions—in short, as a heavyweight partner and worthy recipient of both logistic and diplomatic support from the French government.

On his way to China, Captain Boucabeille stopped at Hanoi, where he met the interim governor-general, Broni, who had probably been involved in the contacts made with Sun Yat-sen in 1902. At the same time, Boucabeille made sure of the cooperation of the commander of armed forces in Indochina. Although the Intelligence Service was officially established in Peking, its activities were in practice to be managed and controlled by Hanoi. The interview between Boucabeille and Sun Yat-sen took place on October 11 on board the steamer *Caledonia* in the port of Shanghai. What was said by the two men in the course of this conversation, which lasted no less than eight hours? The French and the Chinese sources are in disagreement. According to Boucabeille, he himself expressed the personal opinion that the French government was ready to support Sun's party, provided it could be shown that it represented a powerful and effective organization. He claimed that he accordingly asked Sun to help him and his lieutenants to verify the magnitude of revolutionary mobilization on the spot and to evaluate its chances of success. Chinese sources credit Boucabeille with more categorical declarations and firmer commitment. The French officer is said to have presented himself as the representative of the Minister for War and to have declared the Government of Paris to be ready to supply Sun with immediate aid if the time was ripe.

Whatever the truth of the matter, the agreement reached between Boucabeille and Sun was to make it possible for Sun to organize several intelligence missions between the winter of 1905 and the summer of 1906; they were carried out by Captains Claudel, Vaudescal, and Ozil. To act as guides to these French officers and to organize their interviews with local rebels, Sun Yat-sen placed at their service a number of his own trusted men. Huang Xing also helped the foreign inquirers through his own network of relations with the secret societies and officers of the New Army. Boucabeille and his collaborators, with the exception of Vaudescal, were rapidly won over to the cause of Chinese revolution, which they likened to that of the French Revolution and in which they saw "a good way to save the country."[18]

With a somewhat naïve enthusiasm, these young officers transposed their own ideal of republican progress to China, whose wretchedness they were just discovering. Their reports gave a very favorable account of Sun Yat-sen and his actions: "Sun is an extremely intelligent man; he has the support of both the students and the secret societies; [he] has established his supreme authority over all rebel elements." Boucabeille saw the situation through Sun's eyes and exuded optimism. However, he ran up against the radical hostility of Edmond Bapst, the French minister in Peking, who rejected his reports and refused to have anything to do with a man he considered at best an amateur and at worst an adventurer. It was an opinion that most French diplomats shared.

Thus, when, in the autumn of 1906, the imperial government, assessing correspondence and photographs seized by its police, officially complained about the subversive activities of the officers in southern China, the French authorities disowned Boucabeille. He was recalled to Paris, and on October 16, the Intelligence Service was suppressed. The abruptness of this epilogue can probably be partly explained by recent political changes in Paris itself, where the Sarrien cabinet was about to fall, then did so on October 19. Its fall brought, in its train, the departure of the Minister of War, Eugène Étienne, Boucabeille's principal protector. In the Clémenceau cabinet that was now formed, priority was given to European and Franco-German problems, not to expansion in Asia.

The failure of Boucabeille's mission and the change of government shattered Sun Yat-sen's hopes of getting French support. To calm down the imperial authorities and restore its credibility in their eyes, French diplomacy now became hostile to Sun and proceeded to preach nothing but prudence to the general government of Indochina. Was Boucabeille simply manipulated by certain French politicians interested in exploring a new strategy of expansion in Asia? Or was it on his own personal account that he tried to exploit divisions in the politico-bureaucratic system in which he worked, so as to realize his personal ideal and collaborate with the Chinese revolutionaries? Was the Boucabeille affair part of an official double game or was it simply an example of political adventurism? Given the state of the documentation, it is hard to say. Besides, the one possibility does not necessarily rule out the other.

Hard pressed by his need for funds and diplomatic support, Sun Yat-sen had collaborated with the most determined colonialist forces in the French political world. Recourse to the Chinese émigré communities would surely have been far more natural than an alliance with the expansionist imperialists of old Europe, but on that side, too, Sun's efforts met with numerous obstructions.

The Attempted Conquest or Reconquest of the Chinese Overseas Networks

We have already noted the importance of the Chinese overseas communities in Sun Yat-sen's early career and, more generally, in the formation of national consciousness and the beginnings of revolutionary mobilization. Yet neither the economic situation of these émigrés (which was often difficult) nor their intellectual training (which was, for the most part, cursory) predisposed them to political commitment. Their intervention in the public life of modern and contemporary China has, in fact, remained extremely limited, except for precisely those dozen years preceding the revolution of 1911.

Their early exposure to the modern world, and the regional and family links that bound many of these émigrés to Sun Yat-sen and his Cantonese entourage do not suffice to explain the extent to which the overseas communities were mobilized at this time. It resulted from efforts made by the entire Chinese opposition in exile. At no other time in the twentieth century have so many intellectuals been led, by choice or constraint, to live outside China. The new exiles naturally enough turned to compatriots who had long been installed in these foreign countries that they themselves hardly knew. From these earlier émigrés they obtained the funds necessary for their subversive or propaganda activities, and for introductions to foreign political authorities who might be persuaded to support their action.

The support of these communities was thus very important to the various currents of opposition. Sun Yat-sen, who had been the first to seek that support, now had to face competition from Kang Youwei and the reformist party; and redoubtable competition it was, for in these communities Kang Youwei enjoyed the prestige of a scholar and an adviser to the prince. His accession to power during the Hundred Day Reform of 1898 had won him the respect due a former (and possibly future) prime minister. The reformist cause could also count on the huge talent of Liang Qichao. Besides, the patriotism of the rich traders who dominated the émigré communities tended to favor a peaceful transformation rather than revolutionary upheavals.

The rivalry between Sun Yat-sen and Kang Youwei was to take increasingly violent forms, in an increasingly vast geographical area. Initially, Sun Yat-sen had only been interested in the communities of Hawaii and Japan. From 1900 on, impelled by the challenge from Kang Youwei, he strove progressively to extend his field of action to the United States, Singapore, and French Indochina.

Sun and Kang used exactly the same methods of mobilization, imposed upon them by the social structures of the émigré communities which, in a foreign environment, reproduced the traditional Chinese social organization. To rally public opinion, the propagandists of the opposition would address themselves on the one hand to the merchants and gentry who presided over the professional guilds, the regionalist associations, and the educational institutions and, on the other, to the secret societies that were powerful among the workers, laborers, and clerks who constituted the bulk of the émigré populations.

When Sun Yat-sen arrived in Yokohama in June 1903, after leaving Tonking, he found no more than ten or so partisans still loyal to him. All the rest had passed under the influence of the reformists. Even the president of the local cell of the Revive China Society in Yokohama, the bookseller Feng Jingru, who had supported Sun consistently ever since 1895, was now financing the publications of Liang Qichao. To raise the money indispensable to his great plans, Sun Yat-sen therefore set off, on September 26, 1903, for Hawaii, which he had not visited since 1896 and where his family was still living. Liang Qichao had been in Hawaii in the spring of 1900 and had managed to turn around public opinion completely in favor of the reformists—indeed, Sun Yat-sen's brother, Sun Mei, was now president of the cell of the Society to Protect the Emperor. Besides making very underhand use of the letters of recommendation given him by Sun Yat-sen, Liang Qichao had been skillful in exploiting his Cantonese origin, his prestige, and his eloquence. His speeches had fanned the enthusiasm of Sun's former partisans to "white-hot heat." Nor had Liang hesitated to borrow his rival's strategic ideas: for example, he recommended an armed insurrection in Guangdong—to save Emperor Guangxu and the reform. He had even gone further than Sun in that he had actually joined certain local Triads, the better to gain acceptance in the Chinese community. This was a step that Sun had never taken, even though he used the Triads to promote his cause.

Sun therefore had to try to win back his partisans. He turned to the only network that Liang had apparently not challenged him for—that of the Chinese converts. Chinese pastors organized the many political meetings in which Sun Yat-sen, contradicting Liang, recommended the overthrow of the Manchus and the founding of a republic. Sun had no qualms about taking up his rival's challenge in the very field in which the latter's excellence was well established, that of eloquence and propaganda. It was fair repayment for the man who, a few years earlier, had borrowed Sun's ideas of resorting to armed insurrection and cooperation with the secret societies. Thus it was that, in the autumn of 1903, Hawaii witnessed Sun Yat-sen's debut as a political orator.

According to a Western journalist, he "punctuated his words with forcible gestures" and the audience was quite carried away.[19]

Encouraged by this early success, Sun moved into the attack in what was for him a new field: the press. To rebuff the criticisms of a local reformist paper, he acquired a gazette of traditional style and converted it into a revolutionary organ. On December 29, 1903, it carried a long article by him entitled "Refutation of the Newspapers of the Society to Protect the Emperor" (Bo Baohuan bao), in which he declared anti-Manchuism to be the criterion of all patriotism and repudiated the idea of transforming China politically in gradual stages. He set the reformist current and the revolutionary current squarely in opposition, the better to identify them clearly as a way of invalidating Liang Qichao's strategy. He claimed that, after 1898, Liang had sought to use violence in the service of the constitutional cause and had profited from the resulting confusion to place himself at the head of radical opposition. However, Sun explained in "A letter respectfully warning my fellow countrymen": "It is a mistake to say that 'pao-huang' [the protection of the emperor] is an assumed name for carrying out revolution. In everything there must be conformity between things and names. . . . Liang is a man with two ways of talking, like a rat looking both ways."[20]

The violence of the attack reflected more than simply a clash of ideas. In Sun, it was prompted by a desire to rid himself of a rival who, over the past years, had won recognition as leader of the radicals and at the same time rallied the votes of not only intellectuals but also many émigré communities and secret societies.

As we have seen, in 1903 Liang Qichao had already begun to go into reverse gear and renounce the use of violence. This volte-face, really a quasi-abdication, allowed Sun to lay claim to the exclusive leadership of the revolutionary current, and this proved more effective than his polemic in the Hawaii press. But the polemic also made its mark. Sun Yat-sen recovered the trust of his old partisans (including his brother). And he managed to raise some funds by offering "patriotic bonds" at $10, redeemable for $100 after the revolution.

These successes encouraged Sun Yat-sen to turn his attention to the Chinese communities in North America, among which Kang Youwei had been very active ever since founding the Society to Protect the Emperor, in Canada, in July 1899. To facilitate his task, Sun Yat-sen, abandoning his former stance, joined the Triads, whose Hawaiian lodges maintained many contacts with the

United States. This ploy was no doubt inspired by Liang Qichao's behavior, and it set Sun Yat-sen's relations with the secret societies on a new footing. Up until this point, Sun had used these societies as instruments—or at best as partners—in his military actions, leaving his subordinates to make the necessary contacts with them. From now on, he recognized their autonomous existence, and, practicing what would nowadays be called "infiltration," he tried to get these organizations to serve his own political ends. Armed with letters of recommendation from the local lodges to the Triads in San Francisco, on March 31, 1904, Sun set sail for the United States.

His first success was simply managing to set foot on American soil. The recent exclusion laws made it difficult for Chinese citizens to enter the country. Sun Yat-sen had taken the precaution of acquiring false papers that declared him to have been born in Hawaii and to be therefore eligible for American citizenship. But upon arrival in San Francisco on April 6, 1904, he was recognized and denounced by employees of the Customs Service who happened to be Chinese members of the Society to Protect the Emperor. The intervention of a Chinese pastor and the head of the local Triads helped to extricate Sun Yat-sen from this tricky situation. The cooperation between Chinese converts and secret societies, upon which Sun Yat-sen had relied so heavily at the time of the first attempts at insurrection in Guangdong, now once again played in his favor.

But this success was short-lived. Neither Sun's stay in San Francisco nor the tour that, starting in June 1904, he made to a dozen or so large American cities (among which were Los Angeles, New Orleans, St. Louis, Atlanta, Philadelphia, and New York) brought him much satisfaction. Yet, having learned from his recent experience in Hawaii, he had certainly made good use of propaganda. He had ten thousand copies of Zou Rong's anti-Manchu pamphlet, *The Revolutionary Army*, printed and distributed, and he also took over the organ published by the San Francisco Triads, the *Great Harmony Daily* (*Datong ribao*), summoning one of his own disciples to run it.

Still with the help of the converts' network, Sun organized a "grand meeting" in a Presbyterian church in San Francisco, during which he set out his political plans and tried, unsuccessfully, to sell his "patriotic bonds" and recruit new members. Sun then changed his tactics. Giving up the idea of implanting the Revive China Society in what was obviously an unfavorable environment, he decided to use the Triads as a front organization through which he could collect funds and increase his influence. To strengthen the control of the pro–Sun Yat-sen San Francisco lodge over the whole network of American lodges (most of which were then supporting the reformists) and to get them to give him the funds they had been supplying to Kang Youwei and Liang Qichao, Sun drew up a new Triads charter. In it, he redefined their objectives and associated them with those of the Revive China Society, as described by the famous secret oath (the overthrow of the dynasty, the restoration of China, the establishment of a republic). He then went on to propose an idea that he had already mentioned several times since the summer of 1903 but was only to explain fully later on—namely, the equalization of land rights (*pingjun diquan*). The lodge members were to promise to cooperate with whoever respected these objectives, and to oppose all others—meaning, of course, the reformists, who were described as "traitors to the Han."

Though Sun patiently explained these ideas in the course of his four-month tour, they did not arouse much enthusiasm, nor was his plan to centralize the Triads under the direction of the San Francisco lodge successful. The other local lodges continued to act as autonomous cells, in accordance with their own interests and impulses.

By the end of September 1904, Sun Yat-sen reached New York City, "full of cares and anxiety," according to Dr. Hager, his old mentor in Hong Kong, with whom he now resumed contact. But this did not keep him from launching an offensive, aimed at American public opinion and the government, with the publication of *The True Solution to the Chinese Question,* a pamphlet that he composed himself, in English. As in the articles published in London in 1897, after his kidnapping, Sun Yat-sen here took a reassuring line. He avoided anti-imperialist themes, denounced the Manchus as the ones really responsible for the Chinese crisis, and called upon the United States to support a revolution conceived on the American model. As always with Sun Yat-sen, the tone varied according to the audience: it was violent and antiforeigner when he addressed the Triads, moderate and full of consideration when he addressed the American public. Nonetheless, his pamphlet elicited little sympathy from the readers at whom it was directed.

On the whole, these two years of travels, interviews, lectures, and contacts had achieved little, apart from Sun's recovery of influence and control over the Chinese communities of Hawaii. Nevertheless, during this period Sun had continued to get himself known—if not always recognized—in increasingly numerous and diverse émigré communities. His usual operational techniques, founded on networks of relations and friends, had been supplemented by the resources of propaganda. In this respect the rivalry of Liang Qichao had been helpful, for it had forced Sun to extend his strategic repertoire. The newspapers that he controlled still amounted to no more than a fragile press network, but it was relatively integrated, with strongholds in Hong Kong, where the *Chinese Daily* appeared, Hawaii, which printed the *New Honolulu Journal* (*Tanshan xinbao*), San Francisco, with the *Great Harmony Daily*, and finally Singapore, where Sun's old companion You Lie from 1903 to 1905 produced the *Daily for Closer Relations with the South* (*Thoe Lam Jih Pao*; in Mandarin, *Tunan ribao*). These four papers defended the same anti-Manchu and republican program, attacked the reformists, sent one another articles, and interchanged editors. They made it possible for Sun to make his political presence felt even without resorting to any personal contact.

Sun Yat-sen had thus pursued his self-assigned mission. He had made many contacts with foreign diplomats and officials and with the leaders and lodges of émigré communities. No potential leader of the opposition could boast such varied experience, except possibly Liang Qichao. But in 1903 Liang had abdicated the role of guide to intellectual radicalism that had been de facto his. This left Sun Yat-sen as the most authoritative representative of the anti-Manchu opposition, which he had always promoted as the only legitimate expression of modern nationalism, having understood that only this opposition could bring together all the subversive forces at work within China and outside it. However, he still needed to win acceptance from the radical intellectuals; and this meant overcoming the double barrier of his distrust of them and their scorn for him.

CLOSER RELATIONS BETWEEN SUN YAT-SEN AND INTELLECTUAL CIRCLES AND THE FOUNDING OF THE REVOLUTIONARY ALLIANCE, 1905

The founding of the Revolutionary Alliance in Tokyo, in August 1905, marked a very important turning point in Sun Yat-sen's career and also in the history of the Chinese revolution. Sun Yat-sen now became what he had for years been claiming to be: the leader of a revolutionary movement of national proportions, within which the most varied of social groups were integrated. Sun won recognition in this role as a result of his reconciliation with the émigré intelligentsia. The recognition that he had striven in vain to obtain from the gentry and the literati class eventually came to him, not without delays and difficulties, from the radical students who had emerged from that class.

A Difficult Reconciliation

A whole series of circumstances was to make it possible to rise above the social impediments that had so far stood in the way of a meeting between the Cantonese adventurer and the small revolutionary groups of Tokyo. On the side of the students, the failure of the attempted scattered uprisings in the Yangzi provinces in 1903–4 had forcefully driven home the need for unified action. The presence in Tokyo of the principal activists, who had fled China and its police when their plans failed, made concerted action not only possible but sensible. As soon as they had arrived in Japan in early 1905, the head of the Society for China's Revival, Huang Xing, and his adjutant, Song Jiaoren (1882–1913), had thought of founding a united organization. But why, when it came to finding a leader for it, did the choice of the young radicals fall upon Sun Yat-sen, whom many of them despised? For these representatives of a traditional system no more than marginally reformed, Sun's education amounted to no education at all. Yet, quite simply, no other choice seemed possible.

Liang Qichao's now definite defection to reformism and the dynasty had deprived the students of the source of their inspiration. The fact that Sun Yat-sen was invited to take his place may have been due to his age: most of the activists were no more than twenty years old and their older comrade Huang Xing was only thirty-one, whereas Sun Yat-sen was getting on for forty and he certainly had the longest revolutionary career behind him. In 1902, the publication of Miyazaki Torazō's *The Thirty-three Years' Dream*, translated into Chinese in 1903, helped to cast a flattering light on Sun Yat-sen's past action. Furthermore, Sun could claim experience of a wide variety of social circles and, above all, international contacts entirely beyond these young people, all brought up within a universe that in most cases stretched no farther than their native province, Shanghai, and Tokyo.

In the Chinese cultural and political context of the period, it was extraordinary that intellectuals should now acknowledge the authority of a leader from the peasant class. And, as we shall see later, as an ideologue and theorist of the revolution, Sun Yat-sen clearly did not always inspire confidence in his new partisans. What they seemed to expect from him was leadership of an essentially pragmatic nature, which would protect them from much-feared foreign intervention and satisfy their historical impatience by sparking off a victorious insurrection as soon as possible. But even that is not certain. In China, as elsewhere, it sometimes happened that the official president of a movement was not its principal leader but someone simply required to confer credibility and prestige upon the organization, by virtue of his presence alone, or even just his name. According to Song Jiaoren, one of the principal activists and a cofounder of the Revolutionary Alliance, some of the intellectual radicals were willing to allow Sun Yat-sen only an essentially symbolic role: he was to attract the attention of the authorities and the public, while the real action would be pursued by others. "Revolution means conspiracy," Song said. "We should seek the practice of revolution and not merely the name. . . . We should wait for [Sun Yat-sen's] arrival [in Tokyo], and let him bear the name of the organization, so that we may return to China to await opportunities for a rising."[21]

Also, Sun Yat-sen's attitude and analysis of the situation had changed in a way that made it easier for the radical intellectuals to acknowledge him. Sun's first efforts to establish closer ties with the intellectuals had been aimed at dominant elite figures, literati, and mandarins, and had been made in a reformist atmosphere. Both Li Hongzhang and Kang Youwei had spurned all cooperation with him, driving him to confirm his own choice of revolutionary strategy. As he saw it, such a strategy need not necessarily require the participation of the intellectuals. Convinced as he was that China was on the eve of a great popular insurrection similar to that of the Taiping, Sun Yat-sen had been chiefly concerned to find funds and troops. The students could provide neither and seemed to him ill-suited to organize action on the ground. Liang Qichao's volte-face in 1900 must finally have convinced him that intellectuals were not to be trusted.

From 1902–3 on, however, Sun's ideas seem to have begun to change, possibly because he was then starting to make systematic use of propaganda, the press, the written word. His progress toward this position had been slow, punctuated by sporadic contacts with a variety of persons and activist groups. In the spring of 1902, Sun Yat-sen was invited by Zhang Binglin to take part in the ceremony planned to commemorate the collapse of the Ming dynasty. In the summer of 1903, during the few months that he spent in Japan between his return from Hanoi (in June) and his departure for Hawaii (in September), Sun Yat-sen organized a secret military academy in Aoyama to train Chinese students excluded from the Japanese institutions.

If Sun at this point associated himself with the nationalist and guerilla aspirations of the students in Tokyo, it was no doubt in the hope of enrolling them among his partisans. The Aoyama cadets had to swear the same oath of loyalty as members of the Revive China Society, and to this was added an article demanding the equalization of land rights (*pingjun diquan*), without further definition or explanation. The fact that the fifteen or so cadets who were enrolled were almost all Cantonese is an indication of the limited results of Sun Yat-sen's attempt at rapprochement at this point, for its effects were more or less restricted to provincial forms of solidarity. The military academy of Aoyama did not last more than four months, anyway.

More interesting were Sun's attempts, during this same summer of 1903, to establish himself as an ideologue and theorist in the eyes of the young radicals and to identify his cause with theirs. It was in one of their papers, *Jiangsu*, that he elected to publish an essay entitled "On the Preservation or Dismemberment of China" ("Zhina baoquan fenge helun").[22] In it Sun Yat-sen adopted the nationalist vocabulary that Liang Qichao had made fashionable among students. He expounded the theme of the inability of the Manchu dynasty to protect—let alone reform—China. Above all, he presented himself as an expert in international relations and, while denouncing imperialism, at the same time maintained that certain sectors of foreign public opinion were definitely favorable to China, sectors that, properly handled, could head off foreign military intervention against the Chinese Revolution, when it happened. Even if Sun Yat-sen wrote that article hoping to rally the students to him, he clearly did not expect great results from it, for in November 1903, before it was published, he left Japan for Hawaii. Raising funds among the overseas communities seemed to him a more urgent and more promising task than recruiting followers among intellectual circles.

No doubt his lack of success among the Chinese communities in the United States made Sun Yat-sen look more favorably upon collaboration with the young radicals. Significantly enough, this began, not in Tokyo, but in Europe, where he spent the spring of 1905. Sun was to capture the citadel of the intellectual émigré community working from outside.

There were far fewer Chinese students in Brussels, Berlin, and Paris than there were in Tokyo—one hundred at the most. Those most active came from Hubei. Their meeting with Sun Yat-sen came about as a result of the mediation of one of their compatriots, Liu Chengyu, whose anti-Manchu radicalism had already drawn attention to himself in Tokyo in 1902–3 and who at Sun's request took over the direction of the new revolutionary organ in San Francisco, the *Great Harmony Daily*. Discussions between Sun and the Hubei students were held first in Brussels, then in Berlin. Their respective points of view proved hard to reconcile. Whereas Sun represented the secret societies as the only trustworthy forces for the revolution, the students insisted on the importance of the intellectuals and the army. After three days of discussion, Sun came round to the students' point of view, conceding to these young elites the special role to which they were laying claim.

This unification of attitudes allowed Sun to establish the bases of a new revolutionary organization that, later, after the founding of the Revolutionary Alliance in Tokyo, was to be called the European Bureau of the Revolutionary Alliance. Now, for the first time, opposition currents from very different circles came together in the name of anti-Manchuism, under the leadership of Sun: secret societies, modernized elements from the treaty ports, and intellectual circles. Sun organized the fifty or so members he had managed to recruit according to the usual procedures of the secret societies, with esoteric oaths and rituals. But hardly had his organization been set up than it was betrayed and denounced to the Chinese legation in Paris. Perhaps the extremely moderate reaction of the minister, Sun Baoqi, was an indication of the change in public opinion, including that of the mandarins, since the episode of the London kidnapping in 1896. Perhaps it was explained by the contacts that Sun was then establishing with French political circles. It was a betrayal that really presented no threat to Sun's safety, but all the same it fueled his bitterness and his doubts as to whether the intellectuals were capable of making a revolution work. Hardly had the new organization been formed than it had to be purged, after which only about fifteen members were left.

The European interlude had both a practical and a symbolic importance. It was the Chinese students in Europe who alerted the radical circles of Hunan-Hubei in Tokyo and their organizers Huang Xing and Song Jiaoren, advising them to make contact with Sun Yat-sen as soon as he returned. And it was in Brussels and Berlin that Sun for the first time managed to overcome the social prejudices and provincialism that had previously limited his action and to get his authority acknowledged by radical intellectuals.

The Founding of the Revolutionary Alliance

After all these long preliminaries, once Sun Yat-sen was back in Japan (July 19, 1905), it took him and the Tokyo intellectuals no more than one month to find a common language and unify their organizations. The Revolutionary Alliance was officially founded on August 20, 1905. The rapidity with which this decision was reached was largely due to the very active mediation of the Japanese. The Japanese advisers who in 1900 had striven in vain to bring the reformists and the revolutionaries together managed, in 1905, to fuse all the anti-Manchu currents of opposition. Miyazaki Torazō was the person who organized Sun Yat-sen's first meeting with the leading student activists. It was usual for such meetings to take place in the home of some Japanese sympathizer. Miyazaki and one or two other advisers were present and probably took part in all the preliminary transactions. Of the seventy founding members of the Revolutionary Alliance, the only three foreigners were Japanese and one of them was, of course, Miyazaki.

Immediately upon arriving back in Japan Sun Yat-sen had organized a series of interviews with the principal activists, Huang Xing, Song Jiaoren, and Chen Tianhua. The meeting of July 28 took place in the offices of the magazine *Twentieth-Century China* (*Ershi shiji zhi Zhina*), the organ of the Society for China's Revival, in the presence of the principal members of that society and Miyazaki. Sun Yat-sen spoke of the need for unity, the role of intellectuals in the revolution, and the active strength of the secret societies. The following day, the members of the Society for China's Revival discussed what form the projected fusion should take: should it be amalgamation, or federation, or what? Some were opposed to any kind of union. Eventually each person was left free to choose and almost all decided to join the Revolutionary Alliance. Similar deliberations do not appear to have taken place in Sun's party, the Revive China Society, the organizational structures of which were then rapidly declining.

The decision to found a new party under Sun's leadership was taken on July 30, at a larger meeting attended by seventy people, held at the headquarters of the ultranationalist Japanese Black Dragon Society. The name chosen for the new party, Tongmenghui, evoked the terminology of the secret societies, just as the way it was organized—with an oath, passwords, and so on—was inspired by their conspiratorial practices. The intellectuals' recognition of Sun Yat-sen was consecrated at a large meeting chaired by Song Jiaoren, at the Fuji Restaurant, on August 13. More than seven hundred students crowded into the hall or stood outside, to hear Sun. It was the first time he had ever spoken publicly in Tokyo and his speech was greeted with huge ovations.

As always, Sun was able to tell his audience what it wished to hear. Rejecting any idea of gradual progress, he flattered the impatient nationalism of his youthful listeners, promising them "artificial" progress—that is to say, speeded-up progress, which would enable China to achieve in twenty years, or even fifteen, what Japan had taken thirty years to bring about. China would be able to reach directly for the most perfect form of political organization, a republican regime. Sun used one of his favorite analogies, that of a steam engine: nobody would even consider modernizing Chinese transport by importing out-of-date machines, so why choose, as the reformists did, a regime of constitutional monarchy, which had represented no more than a transitory stage in the political evolution of the Western world? This voluntarist concept of progress was obviously bound to please the elites. And the decisive role reserved for "men of determination" could not fail to draw in these children of the former ruling classes. The message of nationalism and optimism went over well, and the students who used to despise the "uneducated adventurer" gave him a triumphant reception.

On August 20, the Revolutionary Alliance was officially founded at a meeting held in the home of a Japanese member of parliament. Three hundred people listened to Sun as he read out the new party's charter, and swore loyalty to the People's Three Principles: the overthrow of the Manchus, the restoration of China, and the adoption of a republican regime, complemented by the clause concerning the equalization of land rights. A committee of directors of thirty members was then elected and assigned to the management of three departments: executive (the only one that ever really functioned), legislative, and judicial. Sun Yat-sen was elected as the Revolutionary Alliance's president, Huang Xing as its vice-president. Tokyo was chosen as the central headquarters of the new party, which was to establish a network in China under the direction of five regional offices (only two of which, those of Southern and Central China, were ever created), to which would be added the four offices for Europe, Southeast Asia, the United States, and Hawaii, The Hunan-Hubei group brought as a dowry its newspaper, *Twentieth-Century China*, soon reorganized under a new name, the *People's Journal* (*Minbao*). The Revolutionary Alliance was thus "groping toward all the attributes of a modern political party: a hierarchical structure, a program, a propaganda arm, and a plan for action."[23]

But the Revolutionary Alliance was far from being a modern political party, and Sun's victory was soon to be limited by the very nature of the organization over which he presided without really controlling it, an organization that identified itself no more with him than he with it.

The Institutional Fragility and Ideological Weakness of the Revolutionary Alliance

From the outset, the Revolutionary Alliance was saddled with a number of features that soon turned into handicaps. The Japanese mediation that forced the alliance came at a time when the Tokyo authorities and the adventurers in their service no longer considered the Chinese revolution to be any more than a low priority. Although Miyazaki's own sincerity is beyond doubt, it does seem paradoxical to have chosen the premises of the Black Dragon Society for announcing the official foundation of the Revolutionary Alliance. The head-quarters of this ultranationalist, reactionary group, from which so many fascist militants were to emerge in the 1930's, certainly provided a very strange baptismal font for the new revolutionary organization. Sun Yat-sen still trusted his Japanese entourage; but the students, exasperated by the discrimination from which they suffered even in Tokyo, and alarmed at the rise of Japanese chauvinism, were ready to turn their backs on the cooperation that was now, anyway, being offered them even more reluctantly. Already there were signs of the contradiction that was later to become increasingly acute between, on the one hand, Sun Yat-sen's abiding sympathy for the Japanese, and, on the other, a revolutionary nationalism that favored a struggle against the encroachments and imperialism of Japan.

Other handicaps also combined to weaken the cohesion of the Revolutionary Alliance and Sun's control over it. The Revolutionary Alliance took the form of a quite loosely knit federation of three principal currents—the Revive China Society and the Society for China's Revival, soon joined by the Restoration Society. The Revive China Society was by no means the most important of these. Of the seventy founding members of the Revolutionary Alliance (those who attended the meeting of July 30), only ten belonged to Sun's direct entourage (three of them were Japanese). And of the thirty members of the directing committee, only two had belonged to the Revive China Society. The break with the original party appears even deeper when one considers the geographical and social recruitment of the Revolutionary Alliance. Of the 963 members enrolled in 1906, a majority of 863 were intellectuals, students living in Tokyo, from various Chinese provinces. The Cantonese, who had made up almost all the membership of the Revive China Society (271 out of 286 identified members), now constituted only a minority of 112 members.[24] So Sun Yat-sen could no longer depend as he had formerly done upon provincial solidarities to impose his authority. Nor could he impose his own former lieutenants upon this party of intellectuals. The days of the Four Great Bandits of Hong Kong were long gone. Not one of his companions of the early days was at Sun Yat-sen's side in the Revolutionary Alliance.

The Revolutionary Alliance's president would therefore have to adapt to the new party's make up—intellectuals who spontaneously felt closer to figures who had emerged from their own circles, such as Song Jiaoren and Huang Xing. Huang, co-founder and vice-president of the Revolutionary Alliance, had the look of a rival right from the start. Sun would also have to come to terms with the centrifugal and autonomist forces at work within the Revolutionary Alliance, in particular those of the Restoration Society, which, in spite of rallying formally, continued to pursue its own particular activities in the province of Zhejiang.

It has been said that Sun Yat-sen's great strength was his ideological contribution to the Revolutionary Alliance, for it was he who brought it the doctrine of the People's Three Principles that made possible at least the formal unification of the various currents. In truth, although the People's Three Principles—nationalism, democracy, and social progress—were set out in the party's charter, their content was left vague. Adding the equalization of land rights to the initial anti-Manchu and republican program had raised a few objections but very little serious discussion. According to Song Jiaoren, the students who gathered in August 1905 to hear Sun were not interested either in democracy or in social progress.[25] They were mobilizing purely for the overthrow of the Manchus, the key watchword whose ambiguity we have already noted. The institutional fragility of the new Revolutionary Alliance was matched by the party's ideological weakness.

Nevertheless, as it stood, the Revolutionary Alliance represented a very precious instrument to Sun. It conferred legitimacy upon his claims and at last made it possible for him to bring to life an image that had up until then been nothing but words. He was now an undisputed national figure, a credible and respectable politician whom the intellectual elites acknowledged as their leader. Furthermore, within the Revolutionary Alliance he would meet not only with rivals but also with collaborators whose talents as theorists, polemicists, and on occasion strategists, far superior to his own, he would be able to use.

With the foundation of the Revolutionary Alliance Sun Yat-sen was thus provided with a united source of dynamism that had been largely developed without him and had mustered forces that he did not control. His genius lay in having been there at the right moment and having said the right things to fire that dynamism and orient it to suit him. The foundation of the Revolutionary Alliance did not upset Sun Yat-sen's own strategy, which was invariably to remain based upon foreign aid, contributions from overseas, and secret society insurrections; but it did provide Sun with some key cards in the implementation of that strategy.

Sun and Song Qingling in Tokyo, October 1915, shortly after their marriage

Sun Yat-sen and his son, Sun Fo, in Honolulu, 1910

Mikhail Borodin

Kang Yuwei

Homer Lea

Sun Yat-sen with leaders of the Guomindang, warlords, and others

Sun Yat-sen and his wife in Kobe, November 1924

PART TWO

The Founding Father?

1905–1920

The fifteen years from 1905 to 1920 were Sun Yat-sen's years of maturity, the years of his forties and his early fifties, full of activity, new ventures, successes and failures. It is a period of capital importance for the history of China, for it witnessed the overthrow of the age-old empire and the institution of a republican regime of the Western type, which coincided with the climax of Sun's political career: for in January 1912 he was elected president of the new Republic. Was the revolution that Sun had hoped for really the fruit of his own efforts? Was Sun Yat-sen the true "Father of the Nation" and the Republic that embodied that nation, as was proclaimed by the official title *Guofu* that was bestowed upon him after his death?

Sun Yat-sen played a decisive role in the founding of the Revolutionary Alliance in 1905 in Tokyo. He gave the new party an ideology, the People's Three Principles, around which the various anti-Manchu currents crystallized. This institutionalization of the opposition around the person and the thought of Sun took place with the active participation of the young émigré intelligentsia of Tokyo. It represented an immense success for Sun. The fugitive rebel had become a political chief in exile (Chapter 5).

But that success changed neither Sun's temperament nor his revolutionary strategy. Sun Yat-sen was not, nor ever would be an apparatchik. Happy enough to make use of his title as president of the Revolutionary Alliance, Sun nevertheless soon abandoned the party he had just created to a chaotic destiny, in order to launch himself into a series of abortive insurrections along the southern margins of the empire. His life continued to be one long journey, the journey of a conspirator, or of a traveling salesman of the revolution, in quest of aid and money to finance his insurrectional strategy (Chapter 6).

For Sun, as for the Revolutionary Alliance, the revolution that erupted at

Wuchang on October 10, 1911, was simply a missed appointment with history. Neither the party nor its president played any role in sparking off the events that were to lead to the collapse of the empire. Yet both were to manage quite quickly to regain a measure of control over these events and to get co-opted by the rebels. So it was that Sun became the president of a provisional Republic, with shaky authority. He remained in that post for only six weeks. Then he turned away from the political struggle to cultivate a utopian dream and to absorb himself in grandiose plans for industrial expansion.

The 1911 revolution represented a short-lived triumph of fine words over the all too evident reality of a backward China dominated by its traditional elites. Soon it was replaced by the military dictatorship of Yuan Shikai. In the background to the failure of the revolution can be glimpsed the failure of Sun Yat-sen, who not only could not control but could not even keep up with the change that he had so long desired (Chapter 7).

By 1913, Sun Yat-sen was back in exile in Japan, a refugee with all credit and prestige gone. Isolated, but still ambitious, he became the object of many manipulations. When Yuan Shikai's death in 1916 made it possible for him to return to live in China, he plunged into the melee of warlords, hoping to establish his power in Guangdong, then eventually had to take refuge in Shanghai. This long march through the desert seems in many respects an inglorious end to a shattered career.

The young China that arose and took over the problems left unresolved by the earlier generation—national sovereignty, political participation, economic development—had no interest in Sun Yat-sen. New men and new ideas asserted themselves. If Sun Yat-sen had disappeared in 1920, his name would by now probably have been forgotten (Chapter 8).

FIVE

Sun and the Revolutionary Alliance

Although Sun's name is closely associated with that of the Revolutionary Alliance, the history of the party and that of its president do not merge. Accustomed to wield his own power personally, Sun could not tolerate seeing it dependent upon an institution and, in all likelihood, limited by the statutes that institution had given itself. He made no attempt to turn the Alliance into the instrument of his own policies but continued to found his authority upon the networks of friends, partisans, and contacts that he systematically maintained and extended.

Sun's attitude was not just an expression of his own personal concept of the exercise of power; it can also be explained by the difficulties that the opposition encountered as it struggled to organize itself in representative institutions, abiding by a hierarchy and rules willingly recognized. In spite of the statutes it had created for itself, the Alliance continued to be dominated by rivalries between provincial factions and by personality clashes. Within this divided party, soon weakened by many rifts, Sun could only exert a contested authority. His power lay elsewhere: in the skill he brought to the direct mobilization of the resources necessary to revolutionary action.

Sun Yat-sen's history between 1905 and 1911 thus continues along the familiar lines of travels in foreign lands in search of funds to finance the many insurrections that he launched in southern China. The existence of the Alliance no more altered his strategy than it affected his style of leadership.

When they called upon Sun Yat-sen to be president of their party, the students in Tokyo had been hoping to make use of his experience and relationships. They soon realized that the man they were dealing with was too much for them. Far from identifying himself with the party, Sun Yat-sen tried to make the party identify itself with him. "How could there be an Alliance without me?" was his response to his critics. In all his deals, Sun Yat-sen made much of the name of the Revolutionary Alliance. But he did so in order to use it rather than to be of use to it. As he saw it, an institution has no existence without whoever embodies it, and that happened to be himself. So he used the Alliance to increase his own prestige and credibility, to improve what would nowadays be called his image, and to strengthen his position both in China and outside it. The contributions of some party members who were endowed with great intellectual capacities had made it possible for Sun to present himself as the theorist behind the People's Three Principles, and to move on from the armed conspiracy of banditry to that of revolutionary strategy. The Alliance had also provided Sun Yat-sen with a splendid visiting card, that of president (*zongli*), which meant that the traveling salesman of the revolution was now able to introduce himself as the man in whom the power of the future republic rested.

Although Sun Yat-sen's relations with the Revolutionary Alliance have attracted the full attention of historians (with the hagiographers as concerned to construct a cult as the revisionists are to demolish it), the role played by the revolutionary movement that Sun and the Alliance together organized is still unclear. It will remain so until the nature of the 1911 revolution itself has been analyzed. The detailed studies devoted to Sun Yat-sen and the Revolutionary Alliance contrast sharply with the uncertain knowledge we have of the actual evolution of Chinese society and institutions at the beginning of the century. And a historian cannot help thinking of Virgil's hero (or at least Virgil as revised and corrected by the Perrault brothers)[1] who, having descended to the Underworld, encounters the shade of a carter, cleaning the shade of a cart, with the shade of a sponge. The historian is bound to wonder whether he or she, too, has not strayed into a kingdom of illusions as a result of concentrating upon these "few men, often at odds with each other, within a rather small and divided organization which was in turn only one of many revolutionary groups which even added together . . . may not have accomplished very much."[2]

Whatever the answers future studies provide to these questions, the history of Sun Yat-sen and his collaborators and rivals in the Revolutionary Alliance is still the history of intelligent and generous-hearted men tackling the problems of their time—problems that, almost a century later, are still those of our own time: the rise of nationalism, cultural interactions, the constraints of modernization, utopian aspirations. Though in the eyes of a historian it is not unimportant to know whether or not their action was crowned with success, in the eyes of the social critic, the philosopher, or simply the curious observer lurking inside every historian, their failure or success matters less than their attempt, and the thoughts and hopes that it engendered.

SUN YAT-SEN, THE CONTESTED LEADER OF A DIVIDED PARTY

The Revolutionary Alliance was created by amalgamating already existing provincial organizations. It constituted a kind of federation within which members were loyal not to the central leadership but to the local leaders of the various regional groups. The looseness of the structure inevitably encouraged a factionalism that was further compounded by ideological and political struggles.

Regionalism and Factions Within the Revolutionary Alliance

The Alliance did not recruit its members directly, on an individual basis, but indirectly, through the affiliation of the provincial groups that were the organic cells of the party.[3] The unity of the Alliance as well as the authority of its president thus depended first upon the cooperation of these groups and the loyalty of their leaders. The Alliance consisted of three main groups: that of the natives of Hunan and Hubei, led by Huang Xing and Song Jiaoren; that of the natives of Zhejiang-Anhui, represented by the scholar Zhang Binglin and the secret society head Tao Chengzhang; and, finally, the Cantonese who surrounded Sun Yat-sen.[4]

The members from Hunan were the most numerous, supported by their neighbors from Hubei. Together, they made up 263 of the Alliance's 863 Tokyo members in 1905–6. These militants, from inland provinces that until the end of the nineteenth century had remained cut off from all foreign influences, manifested a touchy nationalism, great distrust of Westerners, and an abidingly strong attachment to tradition, and they maintained close ties with the gentry from whom most of them were descended.

Their local leader, Huang Xing, was thirty-one years old. He came from a modest but educated family, had embarked upon classical studies, and had qualified for the lower degree (*xiucai*) in his native Hunan. He had continued his education at Wuchang, the capital of the neighboring province of Hubei, where in the late 1890's he had followed courses at the semi-modern academy. In 1902 he had been selected by the provincial government of Hubei to go to Japan to complete his education. Along with his prestige as a talented scholar who combined a modern education with a solid classical training, Huang Xing enjoyed the reputation of a man of action, acquired through his creation of the Society for China's Revival in 1903 and his planning for the abortive conspiracy of Changsha. Song Jiaoren, at his side, eight years his junior, came from a similar background. He was the son of a small-scale landowner who had also begun by studying the Classics and passing the bachelor's examination and then, at the beginning of 1903, had entered the Wuchang School of Civil Studies (Wuchang wenputong zhongxuetang), created within the framework of the educational reforms. Then, seized by revolutionary fervor, he had helped to set up the Society for China's Revival and to prepare for the Changsha conspiracy, before fleeing to Japan where, in early 1905, he founded the newspaper *Twentieth-Century China*.

The Zhejiang-Anhui group, gathered in the Restoration Society, did not join the Alliance until 1906. Its nationalist and antiforeigner tendencies reflected the influences of its two main leaders, both natives of Zhejiang. The scholar Zhang Binglin, whose role in the diffusion of anti-Manchuism from 1902–3 on we have already considered, was convinced of the superiority of Chinese culture and the relative uselessness of material progress. He stamped his group with a character that was curiously traditional in the context of the Revolutionary Alliance. Tao Chengzhang (1877–1911), much involved with the secret societies of Zhejiang, came from a family of lower gentry. Like most of the Chinese students in Tokyo, he had received a solid classical education before embarking, in a quite superficial fashion, upon modern studies. He was an excellent organizer who seemed relatively little influenced by Western ideas and whose social and cultural conservatism was in accord with that of Zhang Binglin, with whom he collaborated closely within the Alliance.

The Hunan-Hubei and the Zhejiang-Anhui groups both came from the Yangzi valley and were linked by a common strong attachment to tradition and by their collaboration in the abortive plan for an uprising in Changsha in 1904. Both geographically and culturally, they were closer to each other than to the third group in the Alliance, the people from the province of Guangdong.

The group of Cantonese (112 of them in 1905–6) constituted Sun Yat-sen's power base in the Alliance. Its members, too, were for the most part students, born around 1880; many of them had won scholarships from their provincial government. Like their fellow students from Hunan and Hubei they had received a classical education and had passed government examinations and had been admitted to gentry status as bachelor (*xiucai*) or provincial graduate (*juren*). But coming as they did from a province long open to the outside world and international relations, or in some cases having been born into émigré communities, they were distinguished by their cosmopolitanism, their interest in the West, and their desire to cooperate with it. Unlike Sun Yat-sen's first disciples, the early members of the Revive China Society, the second-generation Cantonese revolutionaries did not come from the despised (by the Chinese) circles of the treaty ports, but from the families of scholars and merchants. Some of Sun Yat-sen's adjutants later became politicians or professional revolutionaries: Hu Hanmin (1879–1936), for example, a degree holder, was sent with a provincial government grant to pursue his law studies in Tokyo; his fellow student Wang Jingwei (1883–1944), a provincial graduate, went on to acquire a diploma from the Tokyo Institute of Administration and Public Law (Hōsei daigaku); and Feng Ziyou (1881–1958), whose father, a bookseller in Yokohama, had rallied to Sun back in 1895. Others, having obtained their diplomas, returned to make their careers in Guangdong, where, thanks to the system of equivalence introduced by the reformers, they were able to obtain official posts while at the same time pursuing their secret and part-time revolutionary activities. One such was Zhu Zhixin (1885–1920), another Chen Jiongming (1878–1933).

In this breeding ground of Cantonese intellectuals, Sun Yat-sen recruited a whole series of competent and loyal collaborators who were to be a great help to him, especially in the field of propaganda. From 1905 to 1907, Hu Hanmin, Wang Jingwei, and Zhu Zhixin rated among the most brilliant and most prolific polemicists on the *People's Journal* and played an essential role in the creation of the ideology of the People's Three Principles, while in Hong Kong Feng Ziyou was almost singlehandedly running the *Chinese Daily*. Family connections further reinforced this group of Cantonese, which included some brothers and cousins (such as Hu Hanmin and Hu Yisheng) and sons-in-law and fathers-in-law (such as Feng Ziyou and Liu Yutang, a leading Hong Kong trader whose monetary contributions periodically bailed out the *Chinese Daily*).

Over and above these geographical, social, cultural, and family links, provincial factionalism affected fundamental ideological and strategic beliefs. The various groups held divergent views on the matter of tradition (more respected by the Yangzi revolutionaries than by those of Guangdong) and on foreigners: whereas the Cantonese were ready to ask for their financial, political, or even military help, the other groups in the Alliance were far more reluctant to do so.

The problem was particularly acute where the Japanese were concerned. The Tokyo revolutionaries tended to regard them with mistrust, whereas Sun Yat-sen's personal links with them went back a very long way. Neither the Zhejiang nor the Hunan leaders liked the slogan "same culture, same race" (*dōbun, dōshu*), which Sun Yat-sen and Hu Hanmin had borrowed from the Japanese pan-Asian movement. In the summer of 1907, Zhang Binglin was elected president of the Alliance of the Oppressed Nations of East Asia (Dongya wangguo tongmenghui), which assembled in Tokyo émigrés from India, Burma, Indochina, the Philippines, and Korea but excluded the Japanese, who were regarded as imperialists. Song Jiaoren passionately denounced Japanese imperialism and the pan-Asian arguments it hid behind: "Some powers [Japan], however, utilizing geographical and racial affinity intend to swallow up China and, day after day, seek for an opportunity to deceive us. . . . The arch-enemy of our country—past, present, and future—is Japan," he wrote in his paper, *People's Stand* (*Minlibao*) on February 8, 1911.[5]

Regional factionalism also played a part in the clashes over the strategy for seizing power. Although all the revolutionaries agreed on the need for an armed conspiracy, those from the Yangzi valley, with the extremely remarkable exception of Huang Xing, rejected the priority that the Cantonese claimed for southern theaters of action, and were of the opinion that uprisings breaking out closer to the geographical and political center of the empire would prove more decisive in toppling the Manchu dynasty.

The ideological and political disagreements within the Revolutionary Alliance were thus molded by the traditional structures of primary solidarities. The persistence of the latter within the Revolutionary Alliance gives the proclaimed institutionalization of the revolutionary movement a somewhat illusory air. In the struggles soon to tear the party apart, people took sides according to these solidarities, which, though never mentioned in any of the speeches (for they were taken for granted), underlay all the decisions taken.

The First Clashes and the First Rifts, 1907–1909

The first clash between Sun Yat-sen and the vice-president of the Alliance, Huang Xing, took place in February 1907. The reason: the design of the flag that would be the party's emblem. Sun Yat-sen was satisfied with the old flag of the revolutionary party, designed long ago by his childhood friend Lu Haodong: a white sun against a blue background. Huang Xing wanted the flag to have a Chinese character symbolizing the policy of the equalization of land rights. The violence of the disagreement over such a minor matter took everyone by surprise, and it revealed a strong clash of personalities. According to Song Jiaoren, who was close to Huang Xing, Huang was very bitter about Sun's attitude: "Sun has never been sincere, open, modest, or frank with others, and his way of handling things is almost dictatorial, and intransigent to an unbearable degree."[6]

These problems came to the surface a month later in connection with a far more serious problem having to do with the circumstances surrounding Sun Yat-sen's departure from Tokyo. Giving in to pressure from the Manchu government, the Japanese authorities decided to expel Sun Yat-sen. To sweeten this bitter pill, they accompanied the order with profuse diplomatic apologies and a large sum of money. Many of the party leaders took offense at not having been consulted or informed, and they regarded the Japanese money as a bribe to get Sun Yat-sen to leave without causing trouble. They spoke of Sun's arrogance and cast doubt on his honesty. Zhang Binglin was so indignant that he took down the portrait of Sun that hung on the wall of the office of the *People's Journal* and spoke of hounding him from the presidency of the party.

Tumult broke out again in June, after Sun's departure, over a contract for the purchase of arms that Sun had arranged with a view to organizing a revolutionary uprising in Guangdong. The leaders back in Tokyo were alarmed to see Sun pursuing his strategy of southern uprisings, which they themselves disapproved of, and they accused him of buying weapons that were outmoded. The Cantonese tried to mediate but without success, for in this crisis, as in earlier ones, Sun rejected any reconciliation and in his turn accused Zhang Binglin of having revealed the party's military secrets by sending a noncoded telegram to try to stop the arms purchase.

Relations between Sun and the Tokyo leaders went from bad to worse. In October, Sun Yat-sen personally entrusted his friend Miyazaki Torazō with the task of representing him in Tokyo to make financial arrangements and negotiate the purchase of arms; and he formally excluded the other Alliance leaders from all military secrets.

Later, the conflict came to a head around the *People's Journal.* Since the prohibition of its circulation in China, its funding had become increasingly uncertain. Its appearance was threatened, and eventually, in October 1908, the Japanese banned it. At no point did Sun Yat-sen intervene to help resolve the financial difficulties, nor did he support Zhang Binglin when Zhang had to stand trial as the paper's editor. Worse still: in 1909, Sun Yat-sen engaged in what amounted to a poaching operation when he took over the name *People's Journal* for a new organ whose editorship he entrusted to the faithful Wang Jingwei. This "false" *People's Journal* (*wei Minbao*) ceased publication after only two issues. But in the meantime relations between Sun and the Tokyo group had reached breaking point.

In truth, Sun had ceased to take an interest in the *People's Journal* ever since he lost control of it, that is to say since his departure from Tokyo in March 1907 and the departure soon after of his faithful Cantonese followers Hu Hanmin and Wang Jingwei, both of whom had played a large part in the preparation of the early issues. After this, the *People's Journal* passed under the exclusive direction of Zhang Binglin, and Sun transferred his hopes (and his funds) to the *Renaissance Daily* (*Zhongxing ribao*), which began to appear in Singapore. During the winter of 1907, Tao Chengzhang, sent by Zhang Binglin, traveled to Singapore to ask Sun for $3,000 for the *People's Journal.* Not only did he receive no satisfaction, he also found himself forbidden to make any personal efforts to raise the necessary funds from the overseas communities. Ignoring this, Tao Chengzhang continued his tour through Southeast Asia, taking the opportunity to denigrate Sun to those who were forthcoming with funds, some of whom—the non-Cantonese—gave him a sympathetic hearing.

Sun riposted by calling Tao Chengzhang an agent of Kang Youwei and, some say, by setting assassins on his trail. The war of words reached its climax with the imprecations hurled by Zhang Binglin against the "young gangster" (*shaonian wulai*), attacking his behavior, his luxurious habits, and his abuses of trust. He claimed that Sun was promising those who gave him funds that he would grant them mining and railway concessions and trading monopolies, and was thereby personally disposing of the resources of the future republic.

Exacerbated by political attacks and personal insults, the conflict ended in an open break. In November 1909, while Zhang Binglin was fulminating against the false *People's Journal*, accusing Sun Yat-sen of having sabotaged the true one, and requesting the overseas Chinese to stop giving the Cantonese leader funds, an open letter from Tao Chengzhang was circulating throughout Southeast Asia, denouncing Sun Yat-sen's high-handed dictatorial style and again calling for his expulsion from the party. Zhang Binglin and Tao Chengzhang were determined to destroy Sun's carefully constructed image and ruin his credit and that of his Cantonese entourage among the overseas communities. In this they were partly successful; however, the Revolutionary Alliance, already much weakened, now foundered altogether amid all these quarrels.

Sun Yat-sen Without the Alliance

Sun had never based his power on the Alliance as an institution. To win recognition and obedience, he relied on the personal contacts he was so skilled at establishing and the international networks that he never ceased to keep active. Long before his expulsion from Japan he had already decided to establish his power base in Southeast Asia, close to the potential providers of funds and possible theaters of operation.

In April 1906, in Singapore, the Alliance's Southeast Asia Bureau was founded in his presence. That summer, local sections of the Revolutionary Alliance multiplied in the Malay Peninsula, following visits made by Sun, who always favored face-to-face meetings. To Sun's mind, the general headquarters of the Alliance were not in Tokyo but wherever he himself happened to be residing: in Hanoi from March 1907 to January 1908, in Singapore for the next few years, in Penang from July 1910 on. Sun never stayed long in any one place, but he kept in touch through his entourage of Cantonese whom he trusted and who were directly responsible to him.

Throughout his many travels, Sun Yat-sen was in regular contact with his partisans, as can be seen from the abundant correspondence preserved in his *Complete Works*. In this way he kept himself informed on how the situation was evolving in various parts of the world. He even drew up a twenty-seven-page list of secret codes to be used when telegraphing urgent messages and distributed copies of this to his principal lieutenants. Sun Yat-sen was a man who worked through contacts and communication, producing a remarkably modern interpretation of the traditional Chinese priority given to personal relations. In this respect, as in others, he was in advance of his time. One cannot help thinking how successful he would have been as a media personality had he lived in the age of television.

Up until the major conflicts of 1909, the Alliance, from which Sun had never derived the substance of his power, did nevertheless provide him with a useful reference, an honorable visiting card. After those conflicts, Sun acted as though the Alliance no longer existed, which for all practical purposes was true. In San Francisco, which he visited in early 1910, he asked the new disciples he had recruited to swear loyalty not to the Alliance but to the Revolutionary Party of China (Zhonghua gemingdang). Sun's own presence at the oath-swearing ceremony underlined the personal nature of the promised allegiance.

All these initiatives, which ran counter to the Alliance's statutes, were taken with no consultation whatsoever with the Tokyo leaders. In June 1910, in the course of a brief meeting held secretly in Yokohama (for Sun was still banished from Japan), Sun told those leaders: The Alliance "has long since been dissolved. Those who felt strong enough to do so could organize independent establishments of their own."[7] That was certainly what he himself was busy doing. On his return from Singapore, in July, he noted that, as a result of the Tao Chengzhang's campaign, many former members of the Revolutionary Alliance were turning away from him. At this point he decided to move the Revolutionary Alliance's Southeast Asia Bureau to Penang, which now became his new general headquarters, and to proceed to re-enroll party members. His aim was to create an organization united around his own person.

The other leaders had not waited for the challenge Sun issued in Yokohama to create or revitalize their own organizations. In 1907, the revolutionaries originating from the Yangzi region, who were hostile to Sun's southern strategies, created the Society for Common Progress (Gongjinhui) which, while acknowledging the supreme authority of the Revolutionary Alliance, pursued its own autonomous and, in many cases, competitive action. The same was true of the Restoration Society, one of the constitutive organizations of the Revolutionary Alliance, which from 1908 on resumed its own activities, spurred on by Tao Chengzhang. However, none of these organizations was as prestigious as the Alliance, particularly in the eyes of those overseas who provided funds. That is why, in 1910, the Tokyo leaders decided to relaunch the Revolutionary Alliance, hoping to make it serve their own strategies.

The Revolutionary Alliance Without Sun Yat-sen

The principal forces behind the rebirth of the Alliance were the provincial leaders of the middle and lower Yangzi, now regrouped around Song Jiaoren. The party was reborn in the form of the Revolutionary Alliance Central China Bureau, established in Shanghai in August 1911. It will be remembered that the statutes of the Alliance provided for the creation of regional offices in China, only one of which, for the South, had actually been set up. The purpose of the Central China Bureau was to coordinate the activities of the revolutionary groups mushrooming in the Yangzi valley.

Although, strictly speaking, the formation of this office was in conformity with the Alliance's statutes, in truth it represented another declaration of war on Sun Yat-sen and his Cantonese entourage, who lost no time in expressing their disapproval through Hu Hanmin. The response that this attracted left nobody in any doubt about the sentiments of the Tokyo group:

> The headquarters [of the Alliance] are in Tokyo, but the *zongli* has been constantly wandering about in the South [Southeast Asia] and the East [Europe and America], continuously without a fixed address, and has never given it any attention. What sort of *zongli* is he? The maintenance of the Tokyo Office entirely depended on the contribution of the residing colleagues, who had never resorted to bragging and deceit in order to raise funds. But you, in the name of the Alliance, had obtained from the overseas Chinese huge funds.[8]

Clearly, references to the Alliance continued to persuade the émigrés to loosen their purse strings. And it was in order to channel this wealth in their direction that the Tokyo leaders sought to revitalize the party, at the same time withdrawing it from Sun's authority.

The announcement accompanying the official inauguration of the Bureau, in July 1911, criticized the past weaknesses of the Alliance, its lack of cohesion, and its faulty leadership, all of which Song Jiaoren and his comrades proposed to remedy. In truth, they were hoping to turn the Central China Bureau into the Alliance's leading arm and to replace the authority of the president, Sun

Yat-sen, with that of a central executive committee of five members, subject to annual reelection. The announcement made it clear that this collective leadership was designed to "rectify the inclination towards partiality and to prevent the rise of tyranny."[9]

This announcement focused attention upon ideological differences between the Alliance and the Central China Bureau. Although the latter certainly included in its program the toppling of the Manchus and the establishment of a republican regime, it made no mention of the third principle, that of the welfare of the people, or the "people's livelihood," defined at the time by Sun Yat-sen as the equalization of land rights. Keen to create an opposition front that was as wide as possible, the leaders of the Central China Bureau were no doubt unwilling to alienate the local elites, who were almost invariably landowners. In the extremely influential newspaper, *People's Stand*, which he ran in Shanghai from October 1910 on, Song Jiaoren tried, on the contrary, to rally the constitutionalist opposition. Abandoning the systematic denigration of the Manchu race and the attacks against Liang Qichao, Song Jiaoren now stressed the threat of foreign intervention and pleaded for moderate republicanism. He still claimed that revolution was necessary, but argued that it should avoid useless lacerations.

The "zonal strategy" that he now recommended was designed to cater to this need. Of the three zones in which a revolutionary uprising might take place (the zone close to the capital, the central Yangzi zone, and the southern zone of Guangdong and its neighboring provinces), Song Jiaoren favored the central zone. An uprising in the capital zone would be decisive and would make a rapid seizure of power possible, but it would be difficult to organize and its chances of success would be slim because this region was situated at the very heart of the apparatus of imperial power. The southern zone, much less well controlled by that apparatus, presented a better chance of success for revolutionary uprisings, but the seizure of power in such a distant region could not, on its own, bring about the collapse of the Manchu regime. (It is worth noting that Sun Yat-sen, for his part, would have settled for secession, at least as a first stage.) For these reasons, Song Jiaoren considered the best choice for a theater of operations to be the central zone, that is, the Yangzi valley; the revolutionaries enjoyed relative freedom of movement there, and because it was closer to the capital and had good connections to it, a victorious insurrection could spread northward rapidly.

The Revolutionary Alliance, all too frequently presented as the party of Sun Yat-sen, thus turns out to have been an extremely loose federation of revolutionary groups, some of which over the years became openly hostile to the Cantonese leader. Sun Yat-sen was nevertheless able to profit from the existence of the Alliance, in particular from the cooperation of its intellectuals amid the unifying fervor of its early days. The revolutionary ideology of the People's Three Principles, which these intellectuals created at that time, was elaborated under the influence of Sun Yat-sen and has remained linked with his name.

THE CREATION OF A REVOLUTIONARY IDEOLOGY: THE PEOPLE'S THREE PRINCIPLES

The revolutionary ideology of the People's Three Principles was first formulated in the Manifesto of the Revolutionary Alliance, which dated from the creation of the party and, as revised in the autumn of 1906 by Sun Yat-sen with the help of Huang Xing and Zhang Binglin, became known as the Revolutionary Program of the Revolutionary Alliance (Zhongguo Tongmenghui geming fanglüe). The major lines of the manifesto were developed in the *People's Journal.* Its articles, the work of a number of different writers, reveal personal, sometimes contradictory views. Nevertheless, they do constitute a body of doctrine, the People's Three Principles, generally considered to express the political thought of Sun Yat-sen.

Sun Yat-sen, however, took very little part in the preparation of those texts. He inspired a few ideas, and left the composition to the constellation of intellectuals by whom he was surrounded from 1905 to 1907. The doctrine was elaborated very rapidly. Each new issue of the *People's Journal* carried its crop of articles. This remarkable effort of theorization was not an isolated phenomenon: it was part of the flowering of the first golden age of modern Chinese political thought and coincided with the rise of the constitutionalist, anarchist, and socialist currents of thinking.

All the problems then preoccupying the Chinese intelligentsia were tackled by the editors of the *People's Journal*: the confrontation between tradition and modernity, culture and nationalism, the relations between power and society. The texts testify to the brilliant intellects of their authors, their solid, classical culture, and their increasingly precise understanding of Western thought. One has to admire the legal sense of Wang Jingwei, Song Jiaoren, and Hu Hanmin, and the erudition of Zhang Binglin.

Yet their speculations were inspired by a particular political project, and this was Sun Yat-sen's creation. It was a matter of drawing a line, erecting an impassable ideological barrier between the revolutionaries rallied to Sun Yat-sen and their formidable reformist rivals, led by Liang Qichao. The articles in the *People's Journal* were so many blows dealt at an enemy to be attacked by all possible means, including physical disputes in the course of meetings. The polemic was the more violent for the very reason that positions between the two groups were so close, particularly on problems such as the defense of national interests and the need for public participation in power. The preoccupation with polemics dominated the *People's Journal* in its early days, that is, in the period when Sun's influence was at its peak, from the autumn of 1905 to the autumn of 1907. It encouraged a number of new developments in Chinese revolutionary thought—which was, it seems, often more intent on inventing differences in order to establish its own originality than on thinking along lines based on the observation of contemporary realities.

Liang Qichao was the most incisive Chinese political thinker of the early twentieth century. His analyses covered a vast field ranging from anti-imperialism to popular mobilization, very close to that in which the thinking of the revolutionaries of the Revolutionary Alliance evolved. In order not to follow in the footsteps of their adversary or set up camp on terrain he had already occupied, Sun's disciples were forced into a number of intellectual contortions: they replaced anti-imperialism with anti-Manchu racism as the basis for modern nationalism, identified democracy exclusively with a republican system, and so on. Most of the problems they tackled were analyzed from the point of view of the Revolutionary Alliance's hostility to Liang Qichao. When, toward the end of the decade, Sun Yat-sen's influence over the Alliance was totally gone, what was left of the Alliance's program could be seen to be much closer to Liang Qichao's propositions, as is clear from Song Jiaoren's articles in the *People's Stand* in 1910–11.

On Sun Yat-sen's initiative, a rift was deliberately created, for overt political purposes, between the reformists and the revolutionaries. But at this level of ideas, the gap was sometimes almost imperceptible between, on the one hand, those whom the revolutionaries tried to portray as false progressivists and, on the other, themselves, who claimed to be the only true patriots and democrats. In fact, on many points, particularly on relations with foreigners, the thinking of the Revolutionary Alliance inspired by Sun seemed more timid than that of Liang Qichao.

However unsatisfactory a historian of ideas may find the Revolutionary Alliance's attempts at theorization, they were of great political importance. In particular they were to provide Sun Yat-sen with the ideological framework that he had lacked up until this point. Conversely, thanks to Sun Yat-sen, with his indefatigable activity, his charisma, and his many networks of contacts, the People's Three Principles right from the start eluded the limits of purely intellectual circles, and as the years passed and the doctrine itself evolved, it became a beacon whose importance was considered by its advocates to be every bit as great as that of Marxism or Liberalism.

The People's Journal: The Laboratory and Platform of the People's Three Principles

The first issue of the *People's Journal* appeared on November 26, 1905. The Japanese authorities suspended its publication after issue 24, dated October 10, 1908. In the course of those three years it was run by two successive editorial teams. The first, responsible for the first five issues, was composed of a group of Cantonese intellectuals including Feng Ziyou, Hu Hanmin, and Wang Jingwei, and men from the Yangzi provinces, notably Chen Tianhua (who, before his suicide in December 1905, adopted a number of different names to sign seventeen articles in the first issue) and Song Jiaoren. In the autumn of 1905, when the Revolutionary Alliance's Manifesto and a number of articles on its program were appearing, the journalists were in daily contact with Sun Yat-sen. He himself dictated certain texts and was the inspiration behind most of the rest. His influence was particularly apparent in the systematically violent character of the attacks launched against Liang Qichao and the Society to Protect the Emperor.

When, in June 1906, Zhang Binglin was released from the Shanghai prison in which he was detained following the *Subao* affair, four emissaries from Sun Yat-sen met him and took him back to Tokyo, where the students gave him a hero's welcome. In November, he took over the direction of the *People's Journal*. Zhang Binglin placed his literary talent at the service of the war of words and, in the polemic in which the Revolutionary Alliance and Liang Qichao and his *New People's Miscellany* were set in opposition, he firmly embraced the Alliance's cause. His comrades nicknamed him "the erudite revolutionary," and certainly his ambition was to raise the tone of the debate. In the numerous commentaries that he published in the *People's Journal* (two out of three of whose articles were signed by him between November 1906 and October 1908), he strove to strengthen the theoretical bases of the People's Three Principles.

At first, Zhang Binglin's collaboration increased the success of the newspaper; 7,000 copies were now being printed and sold both in China and in overseas communities. From the spring of 1907 on, however, many material difficulties developed. The ban placed on the paper in China undercut its profits; and Zhang Binglin could no longer count on subsidies from Sun Yat-sen, who had lost interest in the paper once he had left Tokyo.

The fact that the line adopted by the paper now took a new turn was not just coincidence. Zhang Binglin gave more and more space to his moral and philosophical preoccupations. To raise China out of its decadence, he wanted to cultivate a kind of revolutionary virtue founded upon certain Buddhist principles and to promote the idea of "national essence" (*guocui*), as expressed by traditional scholarship. Increasingly, his antipathy for the West broke through, as did his skepticism regarding material progress. These new orientations, Sun Yat-sen's absence, and the organizational decline of the Revolutionary Alliance all combined to make the *People's Journal* in its later period appear increasingly as the organ—"the throne," Sun mockingly called it—of Zhang Binglin himself. To analyze the People's Three Principles, we therefore need to turn to the early issues of the paper.

Nationalism (minzuzhuyi) and Anti-Manchuism

The Alliance's Manifesto represented one of the earliest expressions of modern Chinese nationalism in which the individual was identified with a political unit that transcended the particularities of clans and provinces. But the birth of national consciousness did not eliminate provincial loyalties, which expressed themselves through the organization of separate political groups all pursuing their own special activities. On the contrary, as we have seen, those loyalties remained extremely vigorous within the Alliance itself. But they all flowed into the movement for national unity.

The dialectic between centrifugal forces and the affirmation of Chinese unity was certainly no new phenomenon. For centuries, the literati had combined their membership of a provincial society, to which they were attached by dialect, family, and economic links of solidarity, with their participation in Confucian culture, conceived within a universal framework (*tianxia*, literally "whatever exists beneath the sky"). However, that Confucian pair, provincialism-cosmopolitanism, had become distorted from the second half of the nineteenth century on, as a result of the progressive discovery of the specificity, hence limitations, of Confucianism, which now came to be regarded as a historical and regional phenomenon, and, in opposition, the equally gradual emergence of the concept of the nation (*guomin*).

This concept did not win recognition all that easily. On the one hand, the emergent nationalism was in some danger of being subverted by a provincialism which, in the context of the decline of Confucian values, often appeared to elites as a refuge and their preferred field of action, reform, and progress; on the other, the concept of a nation imposed a remarkably restrictive framework upon the ideas of literati accustomed to think in universal terms. To opt for the nation was both to set oneself above provincial links of solidarity and at the same time to give up the intellectual satisfactions of a Confucian universalism that had been outstripped by the evolution of the modern world. It was a tricky venture to embark upon, particularly under the pressure exerted by confrontation with the West and foreign aggression. The nationalist current that developed from the second half of the nineteenth century on was sustained by a variety of sources: a traditional sense of cultural superiority, the xenophobia of the secret societies, and a number of ideas borrowed from Western thinkers. The violent anti-imperialist reaction provoked by the Boxer rebellion speeded up its evolution. But in 1903 that reaction took a new turn and there was a surge of anti-Manchuism which, under the influence of Sun Yat-sen and the Revolutionary Alliance, then became the pivot of the new Chinese nationalism.

The Alliance's Manifesto declared at the outset the need for a national revolution (*guomin geming*), to be undertaken by all members of the nation (*yiguo zhi ren*) and to unfold in two stages; stage one would be the expulsion of the Manchus, stage two the restoration of Chinese sovereignty. The Manchus, barbarians from the East, from beyond the Great Wall, had conquered China and imposed servitude upon the Chinese, who "remained for two hundred and sixty years a nationless people" (*wangguo zhi min*). Once the

Manchus were ousted, it would be possible "to restore Chinese sovereignty" (*guangfu Zhonghua*). "China is the China of the Chinese. Its government must return to the Chinese." The Manifesto accordingly called for the re-establishment of a national state (*minzu guojia*).

Nothing in any of these passages of the text referred to the Western presence: the conquerors and oppressors were the Manchus. This shift from nationalism to anti-Manchuism and the exclusive assimilation of the one to the other might have had the air of an archaic resurgence, a return to the rebel ideology of the secret societies, had it not been accompanied by profound thinking on concepts such as race, the state, and the nation. I note in particular an article by Wang Jingwei entitled "A Nation of Citizens" (*minzude guomin*), which appeared in issues 1 and 2 of the *People's Journal*, and others too, signed by Hu Hanmin, Chen Tianhua, Zhu Zhixin, and Zhang Binglin. These authors turned away from the simple argument developed by Zou Rong in 1903, which blamed the Manchus for their nonresistance to foreign aggression and thereby turned anti-Manchuism into another expression of anti-imperialism. The principal counts on which the Manchus were now condemned were the oppression to which they had subjected the Chinese, their inferiority as a race, and their inability to implement change and ensure progress.

The theme of oppression was probably the one most fully developed by the revolutionary literature. The Manchus were blamed for having deprived the Chinese of their own identity by forcing them to adopt customs such as the wearing of the queue, for having isolated them from the outside world the better to dominate them, for having ousted them from the upper administration, and for having practiced discriminatory policies that undermined their civic rights and private property: in short, they had conquered China by violence and had reigned over it as tyrants. This argument varied slightly depending upon whom it was addressed to. In *The True Solution to the Chinese Question*, written in English at the end of 1904 by Sun Yat-sen, who was then living in New York, the Manchus were accused of having deprived the Chinese of material progress and of law and equality and of not having behaved in the manner of Western democrats. Wang Jingwei, for his part, illustrated his list of charges with a great abundance of historical examples. But in general the argument of oppression thinly masked the racial hatred with which it tended to be confused.

For many revolutionaries, including some of the most eminent, the essence of anti-Manchuism was quite simply the scorn and hatred that the Chinese reserved for "others," for "barbarians." Chen Tianhua was content to invoke the authority of the Classics, in this case the *Zuo Zhuan*, to justify the basis of that hatred: "If he does not belong to our race, his spirit is bound to be different."[10] The Manchu government could not be anything but bad, Hu Hanmin added, because "it is not a Chinese government, but the government of a foreign tribe. . . . Its defects are rooted in the nature of this race and cannot be eliminated or corrected."[11]

Zhang Binglin was one of the first to attempt to rationalize this racism by referring to the ethnology, sociology, and history of Europe and Asia. In his essay "Urgent Words," written in 1903, and later in his *Anti-Manchu Declaration* (*Tao Manzhou ji*), Zhang rejected the idea that a foreign dynasty could ever acquire any legitimacy through Chinese acculturation. According to him, "Every culture has its ethnic origin." Race is defined not by biological features but in terms of consciousness. The gap between the Chinese and the barbarians is as wide as that between men and beasts (*shou*). What distinguishes the Chinese is that they possess a culture. The restoration (*guangfu*) of China thus depends upon its returning to its own national identity, which is founded upon its unique, specific, historical culture, indissolubly linked with the presence of the Han race. This culturalism and "ethnocentric nationalism"[12] of Zhang Binglin's was subsequently to propel him into more and more conservative positions.

Wang Jingwei, in his article, "A Nation of Citizens," already cited, tackled the problem of race from a politico-juridical angle, which led him to elaborate the concept of a nation-state. He defined a nation (*minzu*) as "a stable human group possessing common characteristics." He distinguished this from nation (*guomin*), conceived as a community of citizens dependent upon a state (*guojia*), and posed the problem of whether a nation in the ethnological sense of the term (*minzu*) ever coincides with a state. If it does, it installs a spontaneous reign of liberty and equality between members of the same race, animated by fraternal sentiments. But in China, the retarded minority of the Manchu conquerors was as far distant from the Chinese as "the sky from the earth," leaving the defeated with no alternative but to undergo enforced assimilation.

The racist argument helped to confirm the absolute necessity for revolution, ruling out any possibility of reform by a government that, being Manchu, was naturally bad and could only remain so. Although the imperial court sent a mission of parliamentary inquiry to Europe in 1905 and in September 1906 announced its decision to adopt a constitution, the Revolutionary Alliance gathered all its strength to fight against such competition, and it did not bother with overcomplicated arguments. Zhu Zhixin declared, "The line dividing the races is the basis for the Manchus' inability to establish a constitution."[13] Wang Jingwei resorted to a slightly more complex argument. He showed that the constitutional attempt simply masked a ploy to retain power and that the policy of centralization by which it was accompanied was in truth designed to limit the influence of Chinese high-ranking provincial officials and to strengthen the control exercised by the Manchu court: "The constitution is bait, centralization is the hook." Wang Jingwei argued that even if the Manchu government took over the objectives of the revolutionaries, it would never be able to fulfill them because it was not possible "that the horse will sprout horns or the ram give milk."[14]

Anti-Manchuism, generated by the resentment provoked by foreign aggression, was thus over the years turned into a weapon to use against Liang Qichao, the reformists, and the reforming policies of the imperial government. This avatar of nationalism has perplexed plenty of historians, including those of the People's Republic of China. Although no one denies the central place occupied by anti-Manchuism in Chinese revolutionary thought before 1911, most historians prefer to consider it more a strategic choice than a true ideological position. To rally the popular Chinese masses so profoundly hostile to the dynasty (as is shown by the virulence of the secret societies), the revolutionaries are said to have chosen anti-Manchuism as a theme capable of federating all the opposition. In other words, it is claimed, anti-Manchuism was not so much an ideology as propaganda.

That argument of opportunism cannot be dismissed: the first successes of the 1911 revolution were won in the name of the struggle against the Manchus. But on both the ideological level and the level of longer-term political evolution, the emphasis laid on anti-Manchuism was to lead to confusion and weakness. In many respects, the choice of the Manchus as the principal target of the revolutionary movement does seem to be a diversionary tactic. It made it possible to set in the place of an unassailable foreign imperialism a prey already much weakened: the imperial dynasty. As Liang Qichao relentlessly pointed out and as history was later to show, the fall of the dynasty would resolve none of the problems then facing China. However, the anti-Manchu project appealed to popular feelings, facilitated mobilization, made it easier to confound rivals, and held out hopes for rapid successes.

Anti-Manchu fervor also enabled revolutionaries to avoid tackling such painful questions as the significance of tradition and the importance of cultural heritage in the construction of a modern nation. It allowed them to avoid the dilemma between culturalism and nationalism, which is common to a great many Third World countries. The examination of questions such as these was to be left to the next generation, that of the intellectuals of May 4, 1919. At the beginning of the twentieth century, the revolutionaries were content to blame the Manchus for all their country's troubles.

Yet some analyses (those of men such as Wang Jingwei, for example) show that some progress was being made in understanding the modern world and elaborating the concepts of state, nation, and collective identity. Anti-Manchuism, made the Alliance's top priority under Sun's influence, contributed not at all to the formation of a theory of nationalism. Quite the reverse. But it did coincide with popular feeling and facilitated patriotic mobilization. Sun Yat-sen's pragmatism and political sense—some would say his demagogy—made it possible to convey a message that might otherwise have remained simply an object of debate in intellectual circles.

It was an effective strategy to the extent that the revolution of 1911 would result from the concerted action of all sources of anti-Manchu opposition. But it was suicidal to the extent that the message thus diffused was then emptied of content and that the thinking thus deflected had not prepared for the future, since it had failed to tackle the most fundamental problems: relations with a Western world that was both a model and a threat, and what attitude to take toward a cultural heritage whose very richness represented both an advantage and a handicap. The blending of nationalism and anti-Manchuism contained the seeds of not only the revolution's first successes but also the setbacks that immediately succeeded them.

The Principle of Democracy (minquanzhuyi)

In the view of the Revolutionary Alliance, the sole possible application of the principle of democracy was a republican regime. In the early 1900's, when no more than a handful of republics actually existed (France, the United States, Switzerland), that may be found surprising. As we have already seen, for Sun Yat-sen the choice of a republic corresponded with his desire to adopt the form of political organization that he judged to be the most modern and therefore the most likely to deliver the right results. The analogy that he frequently used between the republican regime and the most up-to-date models of steam engines illuminates the essentially nationalist approach to constitutional change (in the widest sense of the term) that was adopted by most of the members of the Revolutionary Alliance. The reorganization of relations between the state and society, the participation of the masses in political life, the recognition of the importance of law, the redistribution of powers within the government, and the status of property had as their essential, ultimate ends social cohesion and a reinforcement of state power capable of ensuring the might and greatness of China. Seen in the Darwinian social perspective adopted, explicitly or not, by most of the editors of the *People's Journal,* nationalism was conceived as the principal force of popular modernization, while republican democracy was regarded as the most effective instrument of Chinese reconstruction.

In this respect, notwithstanding the violence of the polemics, Sun Yat-sen seems to have been very close to his rival Liang Qichao. Although the one opted for a revolutionary break, the other for the path of gradual reform, what they both expected and hoped for from political and institutional change was modernization supported by the action of a state that would be transformed in its structures and would maintain relations of a new kind with society.

That goal of modernization is clearly expressed in the utopian vision of the Chinese Republic produced in an unfinished novel by Chen Tianhua, *The Roaring Lion (Shizihou),* published in installments in the *People's Journal.* Chen envisaged "a large city, with wide streets of white stone, spotlessly clean, lined with seven-storey houses. Electric streetcars were weaving back and forth along the street. Overhead was an iron bridge, well traveled by pedestrians. Beneath the ground ran trains." He imagined that "even London and Paris were not like this." The fiftieth anniversary of the "restoration" [of Chinese rule] was in progress. An *Almanac of the Republic* revealed that "this paradise had 300,000 schools, 60,000,000 male and female students, a standing army of two million . . . 700 warships, several tens of vessels that plied under the water or through the air, and 300,000 *li* of railways."[15]

The Republic is described here in purely material terms, as a symbol of the triumph of technological progress and China's transformation into a great modern power. However, spurred on by the criticisms and objections of Kang Youwei and Liang Qichao, these revolutionaries pressed on beyond that vision: they looked for theoretical justifications for the choice of a revolution and a republic.

To support their arguments, they appealed to not only the Chinese Classics but also Western thinkers, chiefly seeking from them elements of a kind to reinforce their own state-based conception of the change. For Chen Tianhua, as for Wang Jingwei, the principle of democracy resided in the people, whose loyalty should go, not to a sovereign or a dynasty, but to the state. The idea that the nation belonged to the people was diffused under the influence of Jean-Jacques Rousseau, whose works had been translated into Japanese and on whom Liang Qichao had produced an essay in 1902. Zhang Binglin acknowledged his debt to Rousseau, whom he called "the father of human rights and liberty."[16] Chen Tianhua dismissed the French *philosophe*'s contribution to modern political thought, but he emphasized that the *Shujing* and Mencius had already made popular consent the basis of all legitimate power. He even attributed to a Chinese author of the seventeenth century, Huang Zongxi, a theory of popular power that had prefigured *The Social Contract*.[17]

It is striking to note that from their first reading of Rousseau Chinese revolutionaries such as Chen Tianhua and Wang Jingwei had retained not only the principles of equality and liberty but also the idea that the general will takes priority over the liberty of the individual and that, if need be, the latter must be made to submit to the will of the social body. That constraint implies no infringement of individual liberty, since the general will is engendered by the free expression of individual opinions, and by obeying that will the individual is in fact obeying only himself. Nurtured on a political culture wary of the individual, always considered to be a carrier of egoistic tendencies, the Chinese revolutionaries praised Rousseau for having substituted collectivism (*tuantizhuyi*) for individualism (*gerenzhuyi*) (Wang Jingwei) and proclaimed that what they sought was "the freedom of the group . . . not the freedom of the individual" (Chen Tianhua).[18]

The theoretical debates then taking place among the Chinese intelligentsia were also greatly influenced by German political thought. Wang Jingwei relied on the German jurist Georg Jelléneck (1851–1911) to counter Liang

Qichao's idea, inspired by other German thinkers, that the state is identified with a monarch and only that monarch can arbitrate between the various interests of its citizens.[19] For Wang Jingwei, the state possessed a distinct legal personality produced by the general will. And the people were not an object of government, but possessed both rights and duties.

In opposition to Liang Qichao, who denounced the omnipotence of the legislative body and the parliamentary absolutism that he considered to be inherent in the separation of powers, Wang Jingwei invoked Montesquieu: far from wishing to damage the unity of the state, Montesquieu sought to preserve it by preventing absolutism and by attributing to the legislative, the executive, and the judiciary powers autonomous domains within which they functioned in liaison with one another. Finally, Wang Jingwei maintained, still in opposition to Liang Qichao, that the representative system was in practice the only truly democratic one, although he did recognize, along with Liang (and Rousseau) that, theoretically, democracy presupposed the direct exercise of sovereignty by the entire people. However, the representative system does not deprive the people of its prerogatives and pass them to those to whom it entrusts its mandate. Parliament simply "represents the people in the exercise of its rights." Wang Jingwei further stressed the importance of the law and human rights. The laws represent the general will of the people. The state must be governed by its laws. This state based on law is radically different from the government through virtue recommended by the Confucian tradition, and it alone, Wang claimed, has the means to control those in whose hands power lies.

Through his debate with Liang Qichao, Wang Jingwei thus introduced his readers to a set of problems long familiar in the West: the expression and representation of the general will, the responsibility of those given a mandate to those who gave it to them, and the imperative and impersonal nature of laws. Sun Yat-sen made almost no contribution to this exercise in theoretical elaboration. On the other hand, he alone—or almost alone—seems to have been concerned to translate those general principles into institutions. In 1906, Sun Yat-sen proposed a constitution based upon a distinction between five powers. To the three powers defined by Montesquieu, Sun added a power of control, intended to prevent the legislative assembly from dominating the executive body, and a power of examination, used to organize the recruitment of officials, so as to eliminate influences—political patronage and various forms of clientism—that might place incompetent men in positions of responsibility.[20]

The *People's Journal* provided no other details relating to the future republican constitution. On the other hand, as early as 1905, in the manifesto of the Revolutionary Alliance, we find the idea that, after the victory of the revolution, the establishment of democracy and the Republic will need to be deferred in order to avoid chaos and foreign intervention. The republican regime would be introduced gradually, over a nine-year period of transition, divided into three stages: first a military government that would eliminate the evils of the *ancien régime* (the opium, the corruption, and so on); next, a provisional constitution that would institute the election of local officials and regulate relations between the military government and the citizens; then, finally, the Republican constitution. That transitional military government sounded very like the enlightened despotism (*kaiming zhuangzhi*) recommended by Liang Qichao, but it incorporated its own risks of slipping toward dictatorship; and Liang Qichao made no bones about criticizing it on that account.

This whole debate on democracy was dominated by the initiatives of Liang Qichao and, to a lesser degree, by those of the reforming empire. It was Liang who threw down the challenge, arguing that China was not ready to adopt a republican regime; that the population, insufficiently familiar with democratic procedures, would be bound to turn to a strongman; and finally that the establishment of a republic implied a revolution and this would inevitably bring with it violence, chaos, and ultimately foreign moves of intervention that would be fatal for China. It was not the republican regime in itself that Liang criticized, but the idea of China's adopting that kind of regime.

It was accordingly on this front that the revolutionaries concentrated their response, trying to show on the one hand that plenty of aspects of the Chinese tradition predisposed China to embrace republicanism and, on the other, that only by revolution could the regime be changed.

From Sun Yat-sen to Wang Jingwei, and from Chen Tianhua to Hu Hanmin, nearly all the leaders of the Revolutionary Alliance made efforts to discover democratic antecedents in the Chinese tradition, upon the basis of which it would be possible to establish the republic for which they all longed. In an article that he published in Hawaii in the winter of 1904 to refute the reformist arguments, Sun Yat-sen pointed out that from time immemorial the Chinese clans and villages had enjoyed total autonomy in the management of their own affairs, in the field of education, public works, and so on. The adoption of republican parliamentarianism would simply extend to political and administrative officials a system already widely practiced among the population. Hu Hanmin argued that the establishment of a republic ought to be easier in China than elsewhere since the people would not have to struggle against both a monarchy and a nobility, for the nobility had long since disappeared. In Wang Jingwei's opinion, too, the spirit of the republican system suited the Chinese people. In the most ancient period of its history and up until the Warring States period (403–221 B.C.), it had cultivated the principles of equality, fraternity, and liberty and had considered the sovereign and the citizens to be linked by reciprocal rights and duties. The latent presence of these democratic elements in the Chinese culture was bound to facilitate the graft of ideas and institutions borrowed from the West.

It would be pointless to reopen this intricate historical debate. But what is worth noting about this return to sources is the desire of these intellectuals to integrate a cultural tradition of which they were proud into a future imagined in colors borrowed from the West. In this respect, the generation of the 1905 Manifesto certainly was a transition generation. Although more open than the reformists of 1898 to foreign concepts and systems, it shared with its immediate predecessors a respect for traditional formulations and references. It was only from the time of the May Fourth Movement in 1919 that some Chinese intellectuals began to welcome innovations from the West for what they were, no longer bothering about national precedents.

The declaration that revolution was absolutely indispensable to break the dynastic cycle and establish a democratic regime stemmed to a large extent from nationalist anti-Manchu propaganda. For the rest, the arguments of the revolutionaries rested upon an optimistic vision of the future, typically that of Sun Yat-sen. He described it in the speech that he delivered in Tokyo in 1906 to celebrate the first anniversary of the founding of the *People's Journal*: the Manchus would fall without much resistance, the revolutionaries would remain united and would oppose the rise of chaos. Foreigners would realize that it was in their interests, as well as China's, to refrain from any intervention. In short, the revolution was necessary, but it would soon be over and would occasion no more than a minimum of disorder.

This was a far cry from the exaltation of revolutionary violence for its own sake, as it was to be celebrated by the young Mao Zedong in 1927. In preaching the need to destroy in order to innovate, the revolutionaries of 1905 were satisfying the demands for an anti-Manchu struggles that underpinned their strategy, and also the need to distinguish themselves from their principal rival, Liang Qichao. But in truth they shared the latter's concern for order and his desire for a strong state, as can be seen from their plan to introduce the republican regime gradually, from the limits they hoped to impose upon the revolutionary process itself, and from their authoritarian concept of social change, the third panel of their program.

The Principle of the People's Livelihood (minshengzhuyi)

The expression "the people's livelihood" (*minsheng*) first appeared in the declaration signed by Sun Yat-sen (but written by Hu Hanmin) that introduced the first issue of the *People's Journal* in the autumn of 1905. Sun used it again in the major speech that he delivered on October 17, 1906, at the celebrations to mark the first anniversary of the paper, and it also appeared in many articles, the most important of which were written by Feng Ziyou and Zhu Zhixin.

Sun Yat-sen had, of course, not waited for the creation of the Revolutionary Alliance to declare the need for social change, but until this point he had relied on the Sino-Japanese term generally accepted for socialism, *shehuizhui*. Why was it that, from 1905 on, he preferred the expression "the livelihood of the people"? The significance of this change is not altogether clear. In the *People's Journal*, the principle of the people's livelihood was used as a synonym for socialism. The application of this principle was supposed to preserve China from the evils that had accompanied material progress in the West, and to enable China to "harvest in one go the fruits of a revolution at once political and social."

More precisely, the third article in the program of the Revolutionary Alliance referred to a plan to nationalize the land, or for the equalization of land rights, which Sun Yat-sen had already mentioned in 1902–3 and which he was to elaborate and explain in 1905–6 with the help of Feng Ziyou and Zhu Zhixin. The principal aim of this project was not, as might have been expected, an agrarian reform involving the redistribution of land in order to remedy the poverty of the peasants in the vast expanses of rural China. Rather, the emphasis was laid upon taxing unearned increments from the sale of urban or suburban land, with a view to slowing down building speculation. This paradoxical decision can be explained by the influence then exerted both in the West and in Japan by the theories of the American reformer Henry George (1839–97) and Sun Yat-sen's enthusiasm when he learned of them. Certainly it was Sun who suggested, or insisted, that other members of the Revolutionary Alliance should rally to George's ideas, even members like Zhu Zhixin, who had already begun to discover Marxism.

These days Henry George is a more or less forgotten figure, but in the last decades of the nineteenth century he was a widely read author whom Engels himself took the trouble to refute. The theory that he put forward in his work *Progress and Poverty* (1879) was inspired by the situation in California where the building of new towns had resulted in a steep rise in the prices of land for building and had provoked much speculation. To fight against these phenomena, which he judged to be unhealthy, Henry George suggested introducing a single tax that would be levied on the "unearned increment," that is, the increase in land values resulting from social progress and public investments. The state's appropriation of income from land would make it possible to do away with all other taxes and would thus contribute to the enrichment of the country and the workers, at the same time promoting equality at the heart of society. For Henry George, unequal access to landownership was the greatest source of injustice in the distribution of wealth.

Henry George's theories were very popular among the English liberals and socialists, particularly the Fabians. By the time Sun was living in London, Georgism was already rather old hat, but it was still talked about, and the British press gave detailed coverage to Henry George's 1897 campaign for the office of mayor of New York City.[21]

Engels criticized Henry George for his exclusive emphasis on land problems and for the narrowness of a program capable at the very most of encouraging local reformism. But George's ideas also spread to Germany, and in 1898 an association was formed there in favor of the single tax. One of the members of this association, Dr. Wilhelm Schameier, became the commissar for town planning in Jiaozhou (Shandong), where, from 1906 on, he applied George's system in the territory leased to the Germans. The system was also used in the United States, Canada, Australia, and even Japan. In 1906, Miyazaki Torazō's elder brother, who was in contact with Japanese socialist circles, published a study in which he developed George's principal ideas.

During his stay in London in 1896–97, in the course of his travels in Canada and the United States, and in discussions with his Japanese friends and advisers, Sun Yat-sen had thus had ample opportunity to learn about Henry George's theories. But why was Sun so beguiled by them that he made them the basis of his entire program for social change? Property speculation certainly did exist in Shanghai and Hong Kong. But compared with the wretchedness of the Chinese peasantry, ground down by land rent and usury, it represented no more than a minor evil.

Should we assume that, in his long exile, Sun Yat-sen had eventually lost contact with the social realities of China? That is by no means certain. In truth, it was not so much the cosmopolitan émigré, but rather the visionary in Sun Yat-sen who was so fascinated by Henry George's theories. Sun paid less attention to reforms that could bring immediate relief to the peasantry than to those designed to prevent the evils of future urbanization linked with industrialization, for he was singularly skilled at projecting himself into the future. He could imagine himself in a Chinese republic like that described by Chen Tianhua, and in such a republic the system of a single tax on unearned increments from real estate could have a number of advantages. It would make it possible to ensure greater equality between citizens, and at the same time, economic development under the aegis of the state would prevent social revolution even as it increased national wealth. The system would thus give China a chance not only to catch up with the West but even to outstrip it, since the latter had never managed to resolve its social problems.

From 1906 to 1912, Sun frequently returned in his speeches to the system of a single tax and explained exactly how he thought it would work. Landowners would themselves estimate the value of their land, and the state would receive a one percent tax on the declared value. If the need arose to build railways or roads, for example, the state would reserve the right to buy back the land at its declared value. Clearly, Sun Yat-sen did not envisage general nationalization. In fact, his plan appears far more moderate than that of Henry George, who had fixed the single tax at a much higher rate in such a way as to absorb all the unearned increment on the land. In effect, Sun's plan combined an individual's eminent right to own land with a practice of expropriation when this was in the public interest.

The principle of the people's livelihood and the theories of Henry George were adopted and defended by revolutionaries such as Wang Jingwei and Zhu Zhixin, who were well acquainted with the history of socialist thought in Europe, from Bismarckian social reformism right across the board to Karl

Marx's *Communist Manifesto*. That fact alone speaks volumes about the pres-tige and influence of Sun Yat-sen among the Tokyo intellectual circles in 1905–6.

As early as the winter of 1905, Feng Ziyou published in the revolutionary press of both Hong Kong and San Francisco an article entitled "The principle of the people's livelihood and the future of the Chinese political revolution," which was then reprinted in the *People's Journal*.[22] In this article Feng set out Sun Yat-sen's ideas and developed them. Socialism was born in the West from the industrial revolution, which had created a deep rift between the rich and the poor. The exploitation of the majority of the people by a handful of capitalists, whose fortune rested upon the monopolization of wealth—starting with the land—was a form of barbarity. To avoid such decadence, it was necessary for the social revolution to begin as soon as possible and develop alongside the political revolution. In its initial form, which would coincide with the establishment of a military government, right after the revolution socialism would take the form of a state socialism (*guojia minshengzhuyi*), inspired by the experiments of Bismarck and the Japanese reformers of the Meiji era. Its basis would be the nationalization of land, that is, the equaliza-tion of land rights, according to the method of a single tax, as recommended by Henry George. Only later, with the establishment of true democracy, would the country move on to forms of the pure or extreme socialism preached by nihilists and anarchists, which for the time being would be undesirable. Feng Ziyou naturally made an effort to discover Chinese antece-dents for the policy of the equalization of land rights: these ranged from the ancient and half-mythical system of collective property (*jingtian*) to the es-tablishment of public granaries by the Taiping rebels in the second half of the nineteenth century.

An analysis of Feng Ziyou's article confirms the general characteristics of Sun Yat-sen's version of socialism: they are those of moderate reformism, managed in an authoritarian fashion by the state, and designed for the greater benefit of society and greater power for the nation.

The principle of the people's livelihood, like the principles of nationalism and democracy, sparked off an argument with Liang Qichao. In light of the latter's criticisms, the positions of Sun Yat-sen and his entourage were con-firmed and occasionally refined. Liang Qichao condemned Sun Yat-sen's so-cialist program in a series of articles published in the *New People's Miscellany* in

1906. One of those articles, entitled "Is the Social Revolution Necessary in the China of Today?" constituted a direct reply to the program Sun set out in his major speech on October 17.[23]

Liang Qichao developed his argument along two contradictory lines. On the one hand, he declared that the social revolution, indispensable in the Western world that was prey to all the evils of industrialization, was not needed in China, where for the time being the fundamental problem was production, not distribution. He then proceeded to recommend developing a Chinese capitalism capable of resisting imperialism, for without this China would sink into chaos, succumb to aggression, and would then possess only "two classes: foreigners and Chinese."

Liang criticized Sun Yat-sen's program not only for the danger it presented to national independence but also for the brake that it would impose on economic development. The accumulation of resources in the hands of the officials responsible for managing the public sector could only lead to corruption and stagnation. Carried away by political considerations and a desire to alienate from Sun Yat-sen the rich overseas traders for whose patronage the reformists and the revolutionaries were competing, Liang Qichao ascribed to his rival a plan more radical than it really was. He was out to scare off a particular political clientele and to discredit Sun Yat-sen in its eyes. Liang Qichao further turned against Sun Yat-sen the arguments he had already used against Henry George. He accused him of paying attention exclusively to the agrarian problem and failing to understand the role of capital, the essential motivating force of development.

To judge by the reply produced by Zhu Zhixin,[24] the revolutionaries were very sensitive to the first of those categories of criticisms, which threatened to alienate the support of the wealthy overseas Chinese. However, Zhu Zhixin pointed out, those criticisms concerned pure socialism, the kind that favored general expropriation and the rise to power of the lower classes. What the Revolutionary Alliance was defending was something very different: "State socialism," which would be applied in a very progressive fashion and would attack only monopolies. The second of Liang's criticisms, which questioned the socialist nature of the principle of the people's livelihood, elicited almost nothing in the way of refutation. Yet it is worth noting that on this point Liang was joined by many contemporary socialists, in particular the Japanese, in spite of their favorable dispositions toward Sun Yat-sen, and also the Chinese intellectuals most preoccupied by the problems of social change, who were gradually to draw closer to the anarchist groups then flourishing in Tokyo and Paris. Nevertheless, Sun Yat-sen himself never ceased to consider himself a socialist and was throughout this period in contact with the Second International.

The Conspirator

The creation of a revolutionary party explicitly posed the problem of the seizure of power and the strategy that would achieve it. After 1905, as before, Sun Yat-sen was counting on an armed conspiracy and on uprisings that would be led by local men on the ground. The students and the organizers of the Revolutionary Alliance would not be involved in this insurrectional phase. Their time would come later, when it became a matter of constructing the Republic.

Their exclusion was no doubt dictated by Sun's distrust of intellectuals and also by the limited control that the Cantonese leader exercised over the Revolutionary Alliance and by his bad relations with its other leaders from 1907–8 on. Yet it does appear that on this point all the revolutionaries shared Sun's view, and that they, like him, were hoping to seize power without entertaining any ideas of creating a counterpower by developing their own organizations and establishing their own institutions, as the communists were to do in the 1920's. Everyone in the Alliance—Sun Yat-sen, his comrades, and his rivals— was hoping above all to use the premobilized secret societies and bands of outlaws to do their heavy work. They made little attempt to indoctrinate these groups and were content to control them by appealing to bonds of personal loyalty or, quite simply, by paying them money. For this revolution that was supposed to be so modern, they employed a strategy of armed conspiracy that was of an extremely traditional nature.

There were, however, some leaders of the Revolutionary Alliance who were more inclined than Sun to favor propaganda work among units of the New Army and in schools and other local institutions. Toward the end of this period, in 1910–11, their influence may have affected Sun Yat-sen's attitude, for at this point he did begin to ascribe a more important role to the Alliance organizers, making them responsible for rallying a number of urban groups to the insurrection. These strategic disagreements, which we would today consider so important, do not seem to have led to conflict between Sun and the other Alliance leaders.

On the other hand, dissension did break out over where insurrectional action should occur. There were many who wished to give priority to a theater of operations in the Yangzi region, and Sun Yat-sen himself did not immediately rule out this plan. In 1906, he was even considering organizing a whole series of insurrections in the region, and associating his French advisers in the operation: the idea was that, working within the framework of the Boucabeille mission, they would make many contacts on the ground. The French authorities disowned the Boucabeille mission in the autumn of 1906. A few months later, serious uprisings, organized by the secret societies in the mining districts of Jiangxi and Hunan, proved abortive; and in July 1907 a conspiracy organized in Anhui by one of the leaders of the Restoration Society turned into a disastrous failure. All these setbacks, compounded by the police repression that followed them, combined to convince Sun that the southern provinces offered a more favorable terrain. His expulsion from Japan in March 1907 further removed him from central China, both geographically and politically.

Sun Yat-sen thought that the advantages of the southern provinces lay in their geographical distance from the capital, which made it more difficult for Peking to establish its control there, in the strength of their traditional anti-Manchu feeling, in the vitality of their secret societies, and in their long-established contacts with the outside world and their easy access to the émigré communities and foreign countries likely to lend their support to antigovernment rebellions. These southern provinces were already disturbed by many troubles: in Yunnan and Guangxi, which suffered from severe drought in 1902, the secret societies had raised what amounted to peasant armies, which in 1904 mustered as many as 20,000 men. In Guangdong, agitation had become endemic. "Never has Sun held so many trump cards. . . . Will he know how to use them?" the French consul in Shanghai wondered in February 1907.

Between 1907 and 1911, the official history lists eight rebellions in south or southwest China, all organized by Sun or associated with his name. They all shared the same objective: the creation of a revolutionary base centered in Canton, where, with foreign aid, it would be possible to establish a separatist government, a federated republic of southern China that would pave the way for the foundation of the future Chinese Republic.

In 1907–8, these insurrections were still local in character. Some were hardly distinguishable from the customary kind of peasant revolts or bandit raids. They erupted far from Canton, on the margins of western Guangdong and Guangxi, on the borders between the Chinese Empire and French Indochina. Most were organized by Sun Yat-sen and his staff headquarters in Hanoi, with the more or less open aid of various French political circles or interest groups. The presence of this "Indochinese sanctuary" and the intervention of the French, though discreet, alarmed the Peking government, and in 1908 it succeeded in persuading the colonial authorities to banish Sun Yat-sen and his companions. Sun's expulsion and the withdrawal of French aid slowed down insurrectional activity in southern China, but by February 1910 it flared again with the mutiny of the New Army in Canton. An even larger uprising broke out in Canton little more than a year later, in April 1911.

Those two insurrections in the provincial capital implied the participation of not just secret societies and bandits but new social groups that had emerged with the reforms—modern officers and officials. They also provided a more important role for the Revolutionary Alliance cadres. Do they indicate a shift in Sun's strategy? Do they represent the beginning of a swing away from the traditional armed rebellions that sporadically expressed discontent, within the framework of the status quo, toward revolutionary insurrection underpinned by more widespread social mobilization, with a view to imposing political change?

THE INDOCHINESE SANCTUARY AND THE FRONTIER REBELLIONS, 1907–1908

The rebellions that broke out in May and June 1907 in eastern Guangdong were minor incidents repressed in a matter of days, very similar to the Huizhou uprising of 1900 in geographical location, organization (managed by secret societies working in extremely loose liaison with Sun Yat-sen), and the social groups involved (salt traders and smugglers, joined by peasants). The next insurrections, labeled in the official history as the "fifth, sixth, seventh, and eighth revolutionary attempts by Sun Yat-sen," all took place close to the

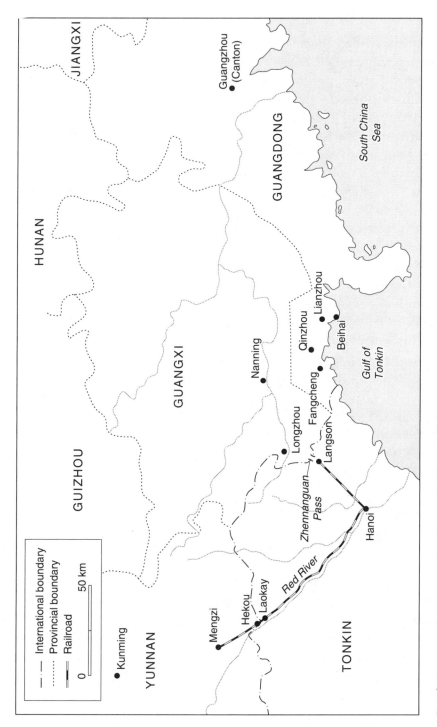

Revolutionary insurrections on the China-Indochina borders (1907–1908)

Sino-Indochinese border, in western Guangdong, Guangxi, and Yunnan. All these were directly organized or supported by Sun Yat-sen and his staff headquarters in Hanoi.

On the edges of the Chinese southern provinces and Tonking, mountainous country extends for hundreds and hundreds of kilometers, intersected by narrow gorges and inhabited, in 1907–8, by a thinly scattered population that included many non-Han tribes. This was frontier country in every sense. Life there was hard, subjected to the constraints of harsh nature, and dominated by brutal forces. The political authorities were far away. The region was friendly territory for outlaws, who in China had always sought to protect themselves by settling on the margins of provinces in order to exploit the weaknesses of uncoordinated and ill-planned repressive measures. These southern borders of the empire offered the further advantage of being close to a foreign frontier. In spite of the Franco-Chinese treaty of 1885, which sanctioned French sovereignty over Tonking, and in spite of operations of pacification carried out by the colonial authorities in the course of the decades that followed, the Sino-Indochinese frontier remained extremely porous, constantly crossed by bands of outlaws, brigands seeking loot or refuge, and deserters from the imperial armies. Insecurity was general. Every village in this Far West was a fortified camp. The opium trafficking sharpened greed and bred violence. Opium, the main crop of these enclaved provinces of southern China, found a particularly profitable outlet in the French colony. Since 1899, in fact, the opium trade had been monopolized by a general government careful to keep official prices very high, creating a situation from which the traffickers in parallel markets obviously profited.

It was among the leaders of these wild bands that Sun Yat-sen recruited his allies, leaving them to direct operations in the field. One of the boldest was Wang Heshun. He was born into a poor family in Jiangxi province, and after 1885 had taken part in the last-ditch struggles continued by the remnants of the Black Pavillions[1] against the French presence on the borders of Tonking, Guangxi, and Guangdong. Transferring from the imperial army to the Triads, Wang Heshun encountered Sun Yat-sen, joined the Revolutionary Alliance in 1906, and installed himself in Hanoi, where he got along extremely badly with the president's entourage. But that did not really matter, since, except for Huang Xing, the organizers of the Alliance held no operational responsibilities in the insurrections of 1907–8.

The setting was classic: an isolated, wild region, inadequately controlled by the authorities, dominated by opium trafficking and the violence of the secret societies. What was less classic was the close presence[2] of a revolutionary leader intent upon making the most of the connivance of foreign authorities to foment and organize rebellion. The Indochinese sanctuary from which Sun Yat-sen and his staff headquarters operated had been set up as a result of contacts and agreements already several years old.

It will be remembered that, in the winter of 1902–3, Sun Yat-sen had visited Hanoi, where he had met a number of figures in the colonial government. In the course of conversations with Hardouin, the head of the governor-general's office, Sun seems to have obtained permission to live in Hanoi and even to pursue his revolutionary activities there, provided he did so relatively discreetly. The French refused to authorize the transport of arms to the frontier, but they did not deny the revolutionaries access to it. That reticent tolerance reflected the disparity of the opinions held in the various French political circles.

Notwithstanding official French policy, which favored cooperation with the imperial government, the partisans of expansion were always ready to use Chinese revolutionaries to bring about the downfall of the Manchu government for their own purposes of economic exploitation. Certainly in Saigon and in Hanoi, among the colony's officers, entrepreneurs, and adventurers, the expansionist party was the stronger, and it did all it could to help Sun Yat-sen by providing money, military advisers, and probably arms as well. The money reached Sun by various means, partly through the intermediary of the comprador of the Banque de France in Saigon. His military advisers seem to have been French officers on leave, "borrowed" from the French army. Traffickers negotiated the purchase of arms for Sun, although deliveries were occasionally stopped by the colonial authorities. The expansionist party could count on a measure of sympathy from the diplomatic corps, in particular that of the French consul in Mengzi (Yunnan), Raphaël Réau, and also in government circles in Paris, wherever Paul Doumer was still active. But it could not flout the official policy of moderation and prudence too openly. It was therefore hoping for a victorious insurrection that would present the government in Paris with a fait accompli, satisfy a number of individual interests, and result in the success of its own concept of national grandeur.

French policy with regard to Sun was affected by all these contradictions: it was a policy of compromise, unstable, and not very clear. The general government of Indochina refused to hand Sun Yat-sen over to the imperial police, who were demanding his extradition, and gave in only to the extent of placing him under surveillance and curtailing his freedom of maneuver. Within those limits, the Indochinese sanctuary offered Sun Yat-sen and his companions the not inconsiderable advantages of personal security, financial assistance, technical advisers, and in the event of a successful insurrection, the prospect of immediate diplomatic and military aid. It was up to Sun Yat-sen to prove himself.

The first of the border insurrections broke out on September 1, 1907, in Fangcheng, a market town in western Guangdong, quite close to both Guangxi and Tonking.[3] The revolutionaries were keen to make the most of the disturbances agitating the region, where for several months past sugar cane planters had been protesting against the imposition of an extra tax. The revolutionaries were also relying on the complicity of two local military leaders, General Guo Renzhang, garrisoned in the district city, Qinzhou, and Colonel Zhao Sheng, stationed not far away. General Guo was a personal friend of Huang Xing, and Colonel Zhao was a member of the Revolutionary Alliance who, having been expelled from the New Army of Jiangsu for spreading revolutionary propaganda, had in 1906 enrolled in the New Army of Guangdong.

Sun Yat-sen sent emissaries to make contact with both these officers. French instructors (probably recruited by Raphaël Réau in Mengzi) were set to teach the rebels how to handle guns. The insurgents were headed by the secret society leader Wang Heshun. They seized the town of Fangcheng and murdered the local magistrate. But in the absence of the reinforcements expected from the two officers, Guo and Zhao, the rebels then dispersed, and Wang Heshun returned to Hanoi. The involvement of Sun Yat-sen and his emissaries had done nothing to alter the traditional character of the Fangcheng rebellion, which was dominated by the actions of the secret societies. Contrary to the hopes that Sun Yat-sen and Huang Xing had placed in the "revolutionary officers," neither rallied to the rebels; they even played an active part in the operations for reestablishing order, alongside troops sent especially for the purpose from Canton.

The rebellion that broke out three months later, in December 1907, at Zhennanguan, was an integral part of a more general plan of insurrection the objectives of which were three strongholds defending the route from Tonking to Yunnan and Guangxi. The relative complexity of the initial plan, the role it assigned to transport vehicles, and the choice of the strongholds, close to the Tonking-Guangxi and the Tonking-Yunnan railway lines, suggests the part played by French advisers working with Sun. However, the operation launched in December 1907 involved only one—but the most important—of the strongholds targeted by the earlier plan.

The Zhennanguan pass, situated in southwestern Guangxi, had a strategic importance underlined by the presence of a garrison of several hundred men and several cannons. The pass was to be traversed by the Tonking-Guangxi railway, of which only the Hanoi-Langson portion had so far been built. At the news that the local rebels had seized Zhennanguan, Sun Yat-sen took the train as far as Langson, accompanied by Huang Xing, Hu Hanmin, a French army captain (on leave), and a few others. After a long march and a night climb, on December 4 they reached the fort. But contrary to their expectations, they found no stock of arms, only one Krupp cannon with which the French captain, after many efforts, succeeded in bombarding the imperial troops' positions. So Sun Yat-sen returned to Hanoi to negotiate a loan to buy arms. A French bank promised him money, on condition the rebels demonstrated the viability of their operation by capturing Longzhou, the administrative center closest to Zhennanguan and the first important station on the line that was to extend the railway from Hanoi to Langson into Chinese territory. But by December 8 the recapture of the Zhennanguan fort by regular Chinese forces put an end to these negotiations.

This "sixth revolutionary attempt" was the only one in which Sun Yat-sen—briefly—himself took part and was on the spot. The presence of a French officer alongside him and the active part that the latter played in the battle are an indication of the interest taken in the operation by certain elements—idealists or adventurers—of the colonial army. The location of the insurrection close to the Hanoi-Langson railway line, the bank's conditional offer of funds, the fact that most of the fleeing rebels (arrested, then released by the French authorities once they reached the Tonking frontier) had been recruited from among the coolies working for the Compagnie du Chemin de Fer de Yunnan all point to the active involvement in the rebellion plan of certain business groups.

This escalation of French intervention did not pass unnoticed by those, on both the French and the Chinese sides, who feared its consequences. In

Longzhou, Colonel Pelofi, resolutely hostile to the expansionists and their protégé, helped the local magistrate to foil the rebels' plans. In Peking, the imperial government made numerous diplomatic protests, and, under pressure from the French Minister for Foreign Affairs, Sun Yat-sen was expelled from Tonking in March 1908. However, he left behind him Huang Xing and Hu Hanmin, to organize the last two insurrection attempts on this border.

The first of these, in March–April 1908, once again took place in western Guangdong, still troubled by antifiscal revolts and still policed by General Guo Renzhang, whom the rebels still hoped to rally to their cause. What was new about this attempt at insurrection was the part played by the expeditionary force of two hundred or so men that Huang Xing brought with him from Tonking. Led by overseas Chinese and swelled by several hundred local peasant recruits, this force kept on fighting for two weeks, until a skirmish (probably accidental) with the regular soldiers put an end to any hopes of Guo Renzhang's rallying to them. This officer seems, in truth, to have acted purely as a mercenary, his decisions oscillating according to the size of the recompense he would receive: whatever was an offer from Sun's representatives was clearly judged to be insufficient.

The last border insurrection was perhaps the most remarkable and the most likely to have succeeded. It erupted in April 1908 at the Hekou fort, which guarded one of the main routes between Tonking and Yunnan. A garrison of 2,500 men was stationed there. On the French side of the border was the town of Laokay, an important station on the Yunnan railway line, which now extended into Chinese territory as far as Mengzi, where Raphaël Réau was consul.

In many respects, the Hekou insurrection was a repeat of that of Zhennanguan, with which it had originally been planned to be coordinated. In both cases the role of the consul Raphaël Réau and that of the Compagnie du Chemin de Fer du Yunnan seem to have been very important. The company, then threatened with bankruptcy, was trying to extend the construction of the railway line into the richer regions of central Yunnan, a service that would be more profitable. A successful insurrection, spreading from Hekou to Mengzi and Kunming, would have provided it with the means to complete its construction plans. The part played by Paul Doumer and his party in launching the company, and their designs on Yunnan, were prompted by a combination of economic and political ambitions.

The unique feature of this last border uprising was, right from the start, the fact that many regular soldiers rallied to it, bringing the number of rebels to several thousand. Huang Xing had come to lead them. He wanted to move on Mengzi, where supplies of arms awaited them and where he was counting on aid from Raphaël Réau. By establishing the credibility of the revolutionaries, the capture of Mengzi would also open up the coffers of the Bank of Annam to them. And the Compagnie du Chemin de Fer du Yunnan had promised that, if successful, the rebels could use the railway to transport their weapons. Never had the situation looked more promising. But the mercenary rebels refused to budge until they were paid. The arrest of Huang Xing, who had returned to Hanoi in search of funds, and his expulsion from Indochina condemned the insurrection to failure. It also brought an end to French funding for Sun Yat-sen and his efforts at insurrection.

The strategy of border insurrections adopted by Sun Yat-sen in 1907–8 probably had no chance at all of success. In the view of Lyon Sharman, one of the first and principal foreign biographers of Sun, it represented the "height of futility." After all, how great a threat to the imperial government, with its headquarters over two thousand kilometers away, were a few hundred outlaws rampaging through the countryside or attacking some isolated fort? Even within the Revolutionary Alliance, this strategy, with its long string of failures, provoked angry criticism. Zhang Binglin reproached Sun Yat-sen for never having "really deliver[ed] a significant blow to the Manchus" and for having "created a terrorist image for the revolutionists." In his view, the "sporadic attacks from the border region, while wasting our precious resources, have no chance of making [our revolution] successful."[4]

Over and above the personality clash between Zhang Binglin and Sun Yat-sen, the opposition between their respective strategies reflected all that separated a man of letters from a provincial rebel. Zhang Binglin's education predisposed him to reason within a national framework. He could conceive of no political action except at the level of the central government, and of no insurrection except one directed against that government. Sun Yat-sen, who had grown up far from Peking, alien to both the Confucian ideology and its bureaucracy, preferred to engage in local actions, limited to be sure, but easier to organize for the very reason that they were local. He placed his trust in a unifying, dynamic force capable of extending early successes and, with people increasingly rallying to the cause, eventually propelling the whole of China into revolution. Even today, the question of whether China should be changed by starting at the top or by starting at the bottom, by the government in Beijing or by the coastal zones, continues to divide both leaders and observers. In 1908, Zhang Binglin and his Tokyo comrades, realizing that Sun would persist in refusing to abandon his southern strategy, decided to set about implementing their own plans in the Yangzi region.

Sun Yat-sen's border strategy also raises the problem of his collaboration with the French. The material extent of that collaboration is still hard to determine, even though it is presumed to have been considerable. Officially, the French authorities denied it, rejecting the accusations of the imperial government, which, it claimed, was being misled by anti-French reports from the viceroy of the provinces of Yunnan and Guizhou.

Those official denials reflect not only the incorrigible hypocrisy of all State diplomacy but also the relatively widespread disapproval that the alliance with the Chinese rebels generated among top French administrative and political spheres. Some of those who lent a hand with subversion and supported Sun Yat-sen were motivated by generous political sentiments. They were guided by their hatred of absolutism and obscurantism and by their enthusiasm for the Republic, the symbol of all progress. They wished to bring China what they considered to be the benefits of the French Revolution. Idealists of this kind were undoubtedly to be found among officers such as Boucabeille and Ozil. But the expansionist ambitions of the party clustered around Paul Doumer, the greed of the mining and railway companies of Indochina, and the political ambitions of those who supported them in Paris constituted the principal bases of these border intrigues. In 1908, the abrupt withdrawal of the French aid that had sanctioned Sun Yat-sen's string of failures was also provoked by a fear that the subversion encouraged in southern China might soon spread to Tonking, where a number of anti-French incidents had given rise to alarm. What was the point of promoting the French presence and French interests in Yunnan and Guangxi if these sapped French security in Indochina?

How did Sun Yat-sen reconcile the nationalist ideal, which he had made the first and principal article of his program, with the imperialistic designs of his French friends? I have already drawn attention to the paradoxical strategy of the man later to be dubbed "the Father of the Nation" (*Guofu*) who, in the heat of action, was perfectly prepared to compromise the resources and sovereignty of the future Chinese Republic in order to secure by no means disinterested foreign aid. Even if we bear in mind tactical preoccupations, even if we take into account Sun Yat-sen's pragmatism, voluntarism, and optimism and concentrate on his point of view of immediate efficacy, this alliance with the French expansionist and colonialist circles remains hard to explain. The fact is that this alliance prevented Sun Yat-sen from drawing support from the nationalist Vietnamese current, whose rise, from 1907–8 on, provoked many anti-French incidents in Tonking; it also helped to turn most of the leaders of the Revolutionary Alliance against Sun Yat-sen, because they were hostile to all foreign aid. Furthermore, more generally, it isolated the Cantonese leader from Chinese public opinion, which was becoming increasingly aware of the dangers of imperialism in all its forms, including economic and financial ones.

Sun Yat-sen's recourse to French aid confers upon his strategy an opportunist, adventurist character easily associated with the traditional nature of frontier rebellions involving foreign money and local mercenary bandits. Not only did the strategy not lead to success for the revolution, it also seems to contradict the very spirit of the People's Three Principles. The withdrawal of French aid compelled Sun Yat-sen to rethink his strategy and recenter insurrectional action upon Canton, with closer involvement for the other organizers of the Revolutionary Alliance and representatives of new social groups. Was traditional rebellion now about to give way to revolutionary insurrection?

THE CANTONESE UPRISINGS, 1910–1911: A CHANGE IN STRATEGY?

In February 1910, after two years of relative calm, insurrectional activity revived in southern China with the mutiny of the Cantonese New Army. This New Army was made up of two regiments, which complemented the forces of the traditional reserve units. Between 1907 and 1908 the first of the two regiments had been under the command of Colonel Zhao Sheng. After the failure of the frontier insurrection of Fangcheng, in western Guangdong, in which his regiment was for a time involved, Zhao Sheng had been transferred to Canton and eventually dismissed from his regiment on account of his revolutionary sympathies. But Zhao's successor, too, had been won over to the anti-Manchu opposition and was a member of the Revolutionary Alliance. It is hard to tell to what extent he had managed to rally the junior officers and men of his regiment to his cause. Judging by the local gentry's indignant reactions to the repression that followed the mutiny, it seems likely that the men of this First Regiment had been recruited from among students and sons of local elites who were, no doubt, like most of their fellows, fired by nationalist, anti-Manchu, anti-imperialist fervor and keen to be in the vanguard of change.

At any rate, propaganda work with the New Army seems to have made sufficient impact for the Revolutionary Alliance Cantonese to decide to play the card of military revolt. To prepare for the revolt and to supervise it, the Revolutionary Alliance opened a South China Bureau in Hong Kong, run by Hu Hanmin. The Bureau raised funds: 8,000 Hong Kong dollars were sent by Sun Yat-sen, then touring the United States, and 20,000 were contributed by the traders of Hong Kong. Soon Hu Hanmin was joined by Huang Xing and Zhao Sheng. These leaders were considering bidding for the support of the bandits and secret societies when clashes between the police and the soldiers broke out during New Year festivities. The revolt then erupted spontaneously, and prematurely. As a result, the First Regiment of the New Army was dissolved.

The abortive outcome of this military rebellion, recorded by the official historiography as "Sun Yat-sen's ninth insurrectional attempt," was a great disappointment to the militants of the Alliance, and many of them left. In Hong Kong, membership fell from 2,000 in 1909 to less than 200 in 1910. Feng Ziyou, who for the past four years had been the chief organizer of the Alliance in Hong Kong, went off to pursue his career as a journalist in Vancouver, British Columbia. Wang Jingwei opted for individual terrorism and devoted himself to preparing for an attack on the Prince Regent. This took place, unsuccessfully, in April 1910.

But still Sun Yat-sen did not lose hope. The success of his American tour encouraged him to prepare for a new insurrection of unprecedented size. He wanted to make a big splash, to confound his critics. To ensure its success, he was prepared to mobilize all his financial resources and all his networks of influence.

The new uprising called for more systematic preparation than any of the earlier attempts. Huang Xing took charge of this on the spot, acting in accord with Sun Yat-sen, who was traveling in the United States. We have already noted the part played by Huang Xing in earlier insurrections. He was a soldier, an operator in the field, and he had frequently led the rebel troops, negotiated with secret societies, and organized retreats. But this leader of men also possessed the qualities of a strategist and a political leader. Even as he rallied to the plan for a local uprising, he would be thinking of insurrection within the framework of a more widespread revolutionary strategy and trying to fit a seizure of power in Canton into a plan of general revolt. For this native of Hunan, Canton was simply a starting point where it would be a mistake to linger. Although he was still loyal to Sun Yat-sen, his own particular version of the latter's southern strategy was innocent of all regionalism.

Huang Xing's original style is conveyed in a letter that he wrote on May 13, 1910, in response to a missive from Sun Yat-sen, the text of which has not been preserved. On three essential problems—foreign aid, the role of the army, and the coordination of the Cantonese insurrection with revolutionary action in progress in the Yangzi valley—Huang Xing formulated proposals rather different from those upon which Sun Yat-sen's insurrectional strategy had been founded in 1907–8.

Sun had always looked upon foreign aid as an essential condition for revolutionary success. Having lost his French support, he had turned to various American financial circles, which had promised to provide him with arms and instructors. Huang Xing agreed to receive and to stock the arms, but he protested against the arrival of foreign mercenaries. For him, the success of the revolution depended above all upon the mobilization of national forces and, in particular, on the rallying of units of the New Army. In spite of the setback in Canton in February 1910, Huang Xing remained convinced that it was possible to rely on the anti-Manchu feeling of most of these units and also upon the esprit de corps that would spread the movement from one province to another. Sun Yat-sen's strategy was limited both geographically and socially by the configuration of the networks of influence under his control. The most extensive of these networks, the secret societies, in the end turned out less of an operational asset than had been expected, on account of its weak internal coherence and the unreliability of its leaders.

The New Army, which was implanted throughout the country but represented one of the most fragile links in the chain of imperial institutions, seemed to Huang Xing to be a far more promising network. As with the secret societies, the New Army constituted an already existing organization—with the difference that it had been established and armed by the imperial power itself. What was needed was to reverse its loyalties. Surely the young officers trained in Japan would be more receptive to the patriotic and revolutionary slogans than Triad leaders, who only thought in terms of immediate self-interest. In Huang Xing's plan, propaganda recovered a role, as did, along with it, the leaders of the Revolutionary Alliance: not only the Cantonese leaders, that is, Sun's immediate entourage, which had organized the frontier insurrections of 1907 and 1908, but also the leaders from the Yangzi provinces. True, those leaders had rejected Sun Yat-sen's authority and were pursuing their own activities, preparing for the establishment of their own headquarters with the opening of the Alliance's regional Central China Bureau, planned for Shanghai. Nevertheless, Huang Xing urgently argued to Sun, "If we are modest and willing to listen to the opinions of others without prejudice, there is no one who would not be happy to work with us."[5]

With cooperation, Huang Xing was hoping to secure, if not centralization, at least a harmonizing of their revolutionary efforts. He accordingly suggested sending emissaries to the Yangzi leaders, in particular to Song Jiaoren. For even if he preferred the choice of the provincial capital as the site of the next insurrection to some isolated fort on the frontier, Huang Xing was thinking that immediately after the capture of the town, the revolutionary armies should be sent northward, one to Hunan, the other to the provinces of the lower Yangzi.

Huang Xing's proposals were not in contradiction to Sun Yat-sen's general ideas, but they were aimed at correcting practices that had become bogged down in regionalism, idiosyncrasy, and a certain isolationism. They reaffirmed the political purpose of armed insurrection; they restored a role to propaganda and ideology and established a direct, concrete, immediate connection between local initiatives and the national revolution. What the textbooks call "Sun Yat-sen's tenth attempt at revolutionary insurrection" was probably the only one that truly deserved that name.

Preparations thus went ahead under the direction of Huang Xing and with the aid of Sun Yat-sen, who, on June 15, 1910, met his adjutant in Yokohama, where he handed over "a full suitcase" of banknotes. These preparations clearly involved general party mechanisms that had not been brought into play by the border insurrections organized by Sun Yat-sen with no more than a harmful of his immediate entourage members, in a most uninstitutional fashion and with no financial transparency at all. Admittedly, the conference held by Sun Yat-sen in Penang in November 1910 was attended only by his closest partisans: his Cantonese entourage and a few Malaysian sections of the Revolutionary Alliance. The Tokyo militants were not even informed of it. But the conference did give its approval to Sun Yat-sen's southern strategy, estimated a budget for it, and allotted tasks. In the course of their tours round the overseas communities during the following three months, the Alliance leaders proceeded to raise HK $187,000.

At the beginning of January 1911, Huang Xing set up his general headquarters in Hong Kong. The plan of operations, as fixed at the Penang conference, was reminiscent of that of the 1895 uprising. The attack made by a commando force brought in from Hong Kong was to coincide with simultaneous uprisings of outlaws, secret societies, and, this time, military units.

Huang Xing set about assembling the 800 members of the commando force. These "dare-to-die" were not, as in 1895, bandits and secret society members but overseas Chinese (traders, coolies, intellectuals), joined by some Cantonese and other provincials. Huang Xing and the officer Zhao Sheng were to share the command. Arms bought in Japan, Saigon, and Siam were delivered to Hong Kong and sent clandestinely to Canton. To facilitate the transfer, forty secret cells, each working in isolation, were set up in the provincial capital. Two rice shops, opened especially for the occasion, provided revolutionaries in search of quarters with a safe meeting place. So as not to arouse suspicion, the business of renting accommodation was carried out by false couples seemingly organizing their weddings, and the transport of arms was carried out discreetly in the carefully curtained sedan chairs of the brides-to-be.

Members of the Alliance surfaced to spread propaganda. Chen Jiongming, a deputy in the provincial assembly as well as a member of Huang Xing's staff headquarters, launched a revolutionary newspaper, *Aye*, which printed a number of articles by Zhu Zhixin, up until this point known in Canton only as a professor. The New Army was one of the principal targets of this propaganda, which did not hesitate to pay one dollar to every soldier who rallied to the revolutionary cause. Emissaries were dispatched to central China to warn the Yangzi revolutionaries to hold themselves in readiness.

On April 23, Huang Xing went to Canton to take command of the uprising, then imminent. He found the situation not at all favorable, owing to the revolutionaries themselves; the very extent of the preparations and the rumors that had accompanied them had alerted the imperial authorities, and new troops had been brought in as reinforcements. The initiative of one isolated revolutionary, from Malaysia, who on April 8 assassinated a Manchu general, added to the confusion. Huang Xing, no longer certain whether he should or should not bring in his "dare-to-die" from Hong Kong, issued a series of orders and counterorders. Finally he decided to engage in action on April 27, even though not all the reinforcements had arrived. After a short-lived success, during which the offices of the general government were captured, Huang Xing was wounded and his small force was overcome by loyalist soldiers. By the time the "dare-to-die," led by Zhao Sheng and Hu Hanmin, landed in Canton in the late afternoon, the rebellion had already been crushed.

To Sun Yat-sen this new failure represented a very heavy defeat. Particularly large sums of money had been committed, and members of the Canton revolutionary network—Chen Jiongming, Zhu Zhixin, and many others— had blown their cover. The authorities had taken the threat very seriously, which no doubt accounted for the severity of the repression: 86 executions. The official historiography recorded only 72 victims. In 1918, a memorial was raised to them in the northern suburbs of Canton, at Huanghuagang, which thereby became one of the key spots of the revolution and, as Wu Zhihui put it, "the Holy Land of the Republic of China."[6]

The number of victims, and the presence among them of students recently returned from Japan, suffice to explain the cult surrounding the martyrs of Huanghuagang. That cult and the glorification of the April uprising (known as the March uprising in Chinese sources using the lunar calendar) also were the consequences of a deliberate political decision: namely, to turn the defeat into a success, making the Canton uprising appear as a prelude to the victorious insurrection of Wuhan, a few months later. Once history had justified Sun Yat-sen's rivals and set the crown of success upon their strategy founded upon the mobilization and insurrection of the Yangzi provinces, it was important to attach this sorry Cantonese episode to the triumphant march of the revolution and to reaffirm the role played by Sun Yat-sen and his entourage in the final victory. "Although the Revolution of March 29 failed, its effect was one hundred times greater than the capture of the city," Hu Hanmin declared in his *Autobiography*.[7] But, in truth, the failure of April 1911, coming as it did after so many others, once again brought into question the validity of the southern strategy and dealt a new blow to Sun's authority and prestige.

SUN YAT-SEN AND THE MONEY FOR THE REVOLUTION

Although the attempted insurrections of 1907–11 were initiated by Sun Yat-sen or associated with his name, Sun himself was never present on the battle-field except on one occasion, and he only sporadically took a direct hand in their preparation. It was his companions who were responsible for the propaganda, for contacting the secret societies and rebel officers, and for the armed operations. Sun Yat-sen, the revolution's traveling salesman, was meanwhile combing the world in search of funds. From 1905 to 1911 his life was one of protracted wandering. Frequently pursued by the police, the revolutionary leader went from one country to another, going right around the world several times over. He had no fixed residence, not even a general headquarters. But up until 1910, he regularly returned to Singapore, the seat of the Revolutionary Alliance's regional Southeast Asia Bureau.

The revolution's accounts are by no means transparent. Records are fragmentary but fuller for some campaigns, such as that undertaken to finance the Canton insurrection of April 1911, and they are frequently more precise on incoming sums of money than on outlay. It was, after all, important to register sums that would one day have to be repaid, with their donors recompensed. But as for the money used to buy the services of the brigands and secret societies, for corrupting the military and officials, and for paying secret agents—those sums disappeared leaving virtually no trace. Contrary to the accusations of Zhang Binglin and the Tokyo leaders, Sun Yat-sen does not seem to have diverted for his personal use any of the large sums that passed through his hands. He considered it natural that he should live off the revolution money, but his life was simple and entirely devoted to his political activity.

It is estimated that between 1907 and 1911, Sun Yat-sen raised HK $600,000. The money came from various sources, in the first place from the subscriptions paid by members of the Revolutionary Alliance. But at one American dollar per person, for a membership of probably fewer than 10,000, the Alliance's own resources were clearly limited. The main funds thus came from donations and loans. Most of the providers of funds were members of Chinese overseas communities. Many were people of quite modest means: clerks, employees, shopkeepers of Cantonese origin. Then there were students, the scions of well-to-do families pursuing their studies in Japan or in the West, and Chinese Christians, and second-generation émigrés who had made their careers in the United States. Sun Yat-sen appealed to all these groups in the name of anti-Manchu racism. He aroused their enthusiasm with promises to renovate China and turn it into a glorious, powerful nation, capable of protecting its émigrés.

More unexpectedly, Sun Yat-sen would also appeal to their commercial sense and their taste for speculation and would sell them revolutionary bonds. These bonds were IOU's for very high interest loans. The future republican government undertook to repay several times the sum invested. As early as 1895, the statutes of the Revive China Society were proposing to sell $10 bonds repayable by the Republic at $100. In 1905, Sun Yat-sen had bonds printed in Japan for a nominal value of 1,000 Chinese dollars, which he tried to sell at $250 apiece. It is known that during his stay in Indochina from October 1905 to February 1906, Sun Yat-sen tried to sell patriotic bonds to the wealthy Chinese traders in the local community. One of his French friends, Z. Léoni, from Saigon according to some sources, from Paris according to others, printed bonds in both French and English, destined for possible foreign donors. They bore the signature of the President of the Chinese Revolutionary Government, Sun Wen, and were to be redeemable from the Canton Treasury after the revolution.

The most successful fund-raising operation was that launched in San Francisco in early 1911, to prepare for the April uprising in Canton. Bonds of a nominal value of $10, $100, and $1,000 were sold at less than half price and found many buyers. In Canada alone, their sale raised about U.S. $35,000.

Finally, Sun Yat-sen could also count on the generosity of a few rich protectors: businessmen, financiers working either for themselves or as intermediaries handing over subsidies paid by certain foreign governments. The most loyal of these wealthy patrons was Zhang Renjie (Zhang Jingjiang, 1877–1950), whom Sun first met in 1906 on a French steamer during one of his many sea trips. Zhang Renjie was born into a wealthy family of silk wholesalers, in Zhejiang. Well educated and with an open mind, the young man had obtained a post as an attaché to the Chinese legation in Paris. He made the most of his stay in the French capital and the relations afforded him by his official functions to launch himself privately into the antiques and exotica trade. Being of progressivist inclinations, he sought out the company of the Chinese intellectuals in Paris, among whom he found a number of anarchists.

Won over by the personality and political program of Sun Yat-sen, he joined the Revolutionary Alliance. Zhang Renjie had many connections in Parisian society and in political and financial circles, and the exceptional size of some of the funds he donated to the Alliance between 1907 and 1911 suggests that he may sometimes have been laundering and passing on secret funds advanced by the colonial party, which was planning to use Sun for its own ends.

The motivations of the providers of Sun Yat-sen's funds thus varied widely. In his pursuit of the quest for money upon which he had embarked before 1905, Sun always did his best to play upon the aspirations and appetites of those whom he met. But as the years passed, that quest acquired a rather different orientation. The Chinese merchants of Singapore, Malaysia, Canada, and the United States took on more importance than those of Hawaii and Japan. And American adventurers took over from the earlier French idealists and colonialists.

The Base in Singapore and Malaysia, 1906–1910

The Chinese communities of Singapore, dominated by rich merchants, were initially reformist. The revolutionaries who took refuge there in 1900, after the disastrous uprising in Huizhou, such as You Lie, found it hard to get a hearing. But after 1901, a radical tendency emerged in direct response to events in China, in particular the *Subao* affair. You Lie cooperated with this current, seeking to strengthen it and eventually win it over, by creating the *Daily for Drawing Closer to the South*. You Lie sent Sun Yat-sen, then in San Francisco, the first copies of the newspaper and told him of the turn taken by Singapore opponents to the Manchu regime. All Sun Yat-sen had to do to win their allegiance was meet them on his return journey to Japan, in June 1905. By April 1906, Sun was in a position to set up the Revolutionary Alliance's regional Southeast Asia Bureau, in Singapore. For the next four years, Singapore and Malaysia were to constitute one of the turntables in Sun's life of revolutionary activities.[8]

At first, Sun enjoyed the support of some of the major traders or their sons. Teo Eng-hok, the president of the Alliance's regional office, belonged to an overseas family from Guangdong; his father was a rich wholesaler of cotton materials. Tan Chor-nam, the vice-president, was the son of a large-scale timber trader with commercial relations in Shanghai and the treaty ports of southern China. Goh Say-eng, who in 1910–11 was to organize the Malaysian revolutionary movement, was the son of a match manufacturer. It was not by chance that men such as these were recruited: Sun Yat-sen attributed particular roles to particular social groups. Just as he counted on the secret societies to get the armed uprising to triumph, and on the intellectuals to set up the republican regime, he considered that it was up to the overseas merchants to provide the money necessary for all these undertakings—and it was of course pointless not to target the richest of them.

But in this field, Sun Yat-sen still ran up against stiff competition from the reformists. In 1906, the Party to Protect the Emperor could claim several hundred thousand members and an organizational network far denser and better structured than that of the Revolutionary Alliance: eleven regional offices, and 103 local sections in North and South America as well as in Australia, the Dutch East Indies, Malaysia, and Singapore. Like Sun Yat-sen, the reformists appealed to the patriotic sentiments of the overseas communities, and often they obtained a better hearing than he did from the local elites.

In Singapore, much of the energy of Sun and his Cantonese entourage was thus absorbed by the struggle against the reformists who were favored on the spot by their longer-standing implantation. The polemic fought out in 1905–6 in Tokyo between the *People's Journal* and the organs controlled by Liang Qichao was continued between 1907 and 1910 in Singapore by the *Renaissance Daily* (revolutionary) and the *Union Times* (reformist). The tone of the debate had changed: theoretical preoccupations now gave way to practical and personal considerations, and defamatory abuse tended to take the place of reasoned arguments. In China, a leader's personality often played a more important part than an ideological line and a political program in determining one's affiliation to a party. The newspaper war was also waged by means of sabotaging the opponents' meetings, and on occasion even by physical clashes such as those that marred the proceedings of November 19, 1908, when the reformists, who had decided to observe official mourning in honor of the dowager empress Cixi and Emperor Guangxu, came to blows with the revolutionaries.

Sun Yat-sen and his Cantonese friends Wang Jingwei and Hu Hanmin would try anything to win over the merchants of Singapore and Malaysia to their cause. Sun Yat-sen embarked on even more canvassing tours. In 1906 he visited the mining centers of Malaysia, proceeding through personal contacts rather than mass meetings and relying on native-place sentiment (many immigrants were from Guangdong), dialectal affiliations, and family loyalty. Wang Jingwei appeared at public gatherings organized in Singapore by the *Renaissance Daily*. In 1908–9, he delivered eight speeches, six of them devoted to nationalism and celebrating the anti-Manchu resistance of the southern provinces in the seventeenth century and the heroism of the Taiping in the nineteenth century. There was no mention of democracy or of the "livelihood of the people," for it was pointless to alarm a clientele consisting mainly of merchants.

Results did not match expectations. The wealthy merchants were not forthcoming. Under pressure from reformist attacks and having lost face over his Indochinese setbacks, in 1909 Sun Yat-sen was beset by serious financial problems. It was with difficulty that he raised the funds needed for the publication of the *Renaissance Daily* and even the money necessary for the journey, when he decided to seek aid in Europe and America.

In his absence, from May 1909 to June 1910, the situation of the Revolutionary Alliance in Singapore continued to deteriorate, the *Renaissance Daily* ceased to appear at the beginning of 1910; and following the failure of the New Army's uprising in Canton, in February, the local leaders were tempted to abandon all political activity. Upon his return a few months later, Sun Yat-sen tried to reestablish the Alliance's regional office, using tactics already tried out in California: the adoption of a new name, the Chinese Revolutionary Party (*Zhonghua gemingdang*), and the swearing of a personal oath of allegiance.

But his attempts were opposed by the local revolutionaries. So on July 20, Sun Yat-sen decided to transfer the Alliance's regional office to Penang, in Malaysia, and for the next few months this was his general headquarters. It was from Penang that Sun organized the strategy and the funding of the Canton uprising of April 1911. He paid for it personally, for his statements were so violent that they alarmed the British authorities, who in November expelled him from the territory. However, he left behind him Huang Xing, who in the space of a few days managed to raise 50,000 (Singapore) dollars. That success created a precedent that had the effect of stimulating the zeal of the Chinese communities in Canada and the United States, from whom Sun Yat-sen thereupon received 707,000 (Singapore) dollars.

Finally rid of the competition of the reformist party (which had been in decline since 1909), Sun Yat-sen thus did manage to mobilize sizable financial resources among the overseas communities. It represented a huge success, but it had been slow in coming. In the meantime he had not failed to explore other forms of aid.

The Appeal to American Financiers and Mercenaries, 1910–1911

The American interlude of 1910–11 reads like something out of a second-rate thriller serial. The scenario went as follows: somewhere in between California and New York adventurers were dreaming of bringing down a third-world government, then dividing the spoils between them. They were conspiring to find the money, arms, and men necessary for their plan. At the center of this intrigue was a cripple, a hunchbacked dwarf named Homer Lea (1876–1912). As an amateur strategist, Lea dreamed of changing the world map and presenting his fellow citizens with a new field of economic expansion: China. At first, Lea set his sights on Sun's great rival, Kang Youwei. Aided by his knowledge of Chinese, which he had acquired at Stanford University, Lea made contact with the Society to Protect the Emperor in San Francisco and was admitted into Kang's entourage. He styled himself "General" and set about training units of cadets recruited from among the young Chinese of America. In 1905, he got Kang Youwei to accompany him on a trip to inspect the cadets of New York and Philadelphia. But from 1909 on, the decline of the Society to Protect the Emperor obliged Lea to look around for another partner. It was now that he co-opted Sun Yat-sen. For once, it was not Sun who took the initiative: he simply entered the scene as a second string to Lea's bow. Very soon, however, the character he played eclipsed Lea's. Sun presented himself as the leader of a Revolutionary Alliance that boasted a membership of 30,000 intellectuals and students in China and overseas and that could, moreover, count on the support of 30 million Triad members. Alongside General Homer Lea and President Sun Yat-sen, the trio of players was completed by Charles Boothe. He was a former banker, now retired in California but still with links to military circles in New York and happy to take an interest in the benefits that could accrue from the toppling of the Peking government.

The conspirators' plan was simple. Mercenary officers would be sent to southern China to train the revolutionary forces. Arms bought in the United States would be stockpiled in western Guangdong until such time as the insurrection occurred. Homer Lea would be the commander-in-chief. Charles Boothe would supply the money.

The budget for this operation was calculated at U.S. $3.5 million, then—at Sun's demand—raised to $10 million. Sun would control all expenses. Boothe, dubbed "exclusive financial agent for overseas," would have the task of extracting loans from the bankers of New York. Under the future republican regime, the investors would be rewarded by being appointed as customs commissioners or postal administrators and by the concession of commercial monopolies and mining rights in Manchuria; and a special role would be reserved for them in the economic reconstruction of China.

This plan never even started to get off the ground. Charles Boothe did not raise any funds. Sun Yat-sen, who was in need of money for his personal requirements, was reduced to asking Homer Lea, whom he knew to be hostile to Japan, to mediate with the War Department to negotiate the purchase of secret diplomatic documents in his possession that concerned a possible Japanese attack on the United States.

Several points are worth retaining from this tale: Sun Yat-sen's apparent eagerness to follow any available trail, even of the most risky nature, and his acceptance of any and every condition set by his partners in return for possible aid, even if those conditions directly restricted the sovereignty and independence of the Chinese Republic. In this respect, this American interlude simply underlined the misgivings created by Sun's earlier cooperation with the French colonialists. How could a nationalist leader be prepared to alienate the rights of a country that he claimed to be restoring to its original dignity and power?

Sun's eulogists invoke tactical imperatives and the paramount importance of the short term. To portray Sun Yat-sen as a precursor to Lenin is grossly to exaggerate the dialectical skill of a man of action and contacts, accustomed to react to the immediate circumstances without bothering too much about the contradictions produced by his successive decisions. Sun Yat-sen was prepared to sell his country to foreigners—in order to lay hands on the money that would help him to save it from those very foreigners. Was this treason? No, for if there was one consistent trait in Sun Yat-sen's quicksilver political personality it was the love he bore his country. If an explanation is really essential, one could possibly invoke naïveté or duplicity.

But it is probably wiser not to try to substitute our own logic for Sun's. We should accept the idea that his stratagems were those of a politician constantly on the alert and, above all else, determined to resolve difficulties as and when they presented themselves. His aim was to create a revolution. It would be up to the future Republic to take care of its republican difficulties. Rather than stemming from dialectical argument or from Machiavellian calculation, Sun Yat-sen's connivance with foreigners seems to have been prompted by the shortsighted philosophy of "take each day as it comes" and to be stamped with a pragmatism that has continued to characterize Chinese politics throughout the twentieth century.

SEVEN

The (Adoptive) Father of the Chinese Republic

The man whom historians consider the founding father of the Chinese nation and whose name more than any other they associate with the revolution of 1911 and the establishment of the Republic in fact played no direct part in the chain of events that, leading on from the Wuchang insurrection of October 10, 1911, to the imperial edict of abdication of February 12, 1912, brought about the collapse of the Manchu empire. After heading or inspiring a whole series of antidynastic uprisings, Sun Yat-sen missed his rendezvous with history and it was only from afar, *in absentia*, that he took part in the downfall of the imperial regime.

Yet history seemed to be offering him another chance when, upon his return from the United States and Europe at the end of December 1911, he was co-opted by the principal leaders of the revolution and elected president of a Republic that he had always longed for in his heart, even if he had not brought it about in his works.

Just a few weeks later, Sun Yat-sen abandoned his power to Yuan Shikai, a high-ranking official and general of the Manchu empire. That abdication is at odds with the proclaimed power of the revolutionary movement; and that contradiction, among many others, forces one to question the analyses of an official historiography more concerned to exalt the 1911 revolution as a founding event and source of legitimacy than to illuminate the relations between the social and the politico-military forces in play.

Even if the balance of forces can explain Sun Yat-sen's abdication from power, it sheds no light upon his attitude or upon his almost total eclipse from the political scene in the following year, from the spring of 1912 to the spring of 1913. While the young Republic strove to assert itself and adopted Western parliamentary and democratic institutions, Sun stood aside. He took little part in the great public debates on the issue of federalism or centralism and that of a presidential system or ministerial responsibility. He left others to organize the strategy of the revolutionary party and to defend the republican ideal against the dictatorial ambitions of Yuan Shikai. When these ambitions were eventually asserted openly, in the spring of 1913, Sun Yat-sen reentered the political melee with a belated start that proved powerless to prevent the failure of the second revolution, in the summer of 1913.

Just as he reached the peak of his political career (for never again would he obtain the functions of leadership at the head of the Chinese state), when his former rivals in the revolutionary party gave way before him and his fame was drawing thousands to take part in the public meetings and official ceremonies over which he presided, Sun Yat-sen seemed to want to pull back. Yet he was not a man to be intimidated by success or to disclaim the credit for a victory that fulfilled all his aspirations even if it was not exactly his own efforts that it crowned.

What did happen? According to the explanation most frequently proferred, Sun Yat-sen's patriotism, his sense of national unity, and his fear of foreign intervention led him to sacrifice his personal ambitions and efface himself before Yuan Shikai, whom he judged to be more capable of ensuring the future of the young Republic. But that argument is not altogether satisfactory, either in its implications of exceptional qualities of modesty and abnegation in a person with such a highly developed ego, or in its assumption of such gullibility in an old campaigner and seasoned political professional with a wide understanding of men and their ambitions. The eclipse of Sun Yat-sen during this crucial period is bound to raise many questions.

Did the professional conspirator feel inadequate once he was called upon to exercise power? Was the former adventurer of the treaty ports carried away by the official pomp and ceremony? Did the master manipulator, so skilled at creating images and bringing visions to life, allow himself to be taken in by the promise of republican appearances? Or did Sun Yat-sen consider that with the toppling of the Manchus he had accomplished his mission and could thereafter desert the political battle to devote himself to another battle, more important in his eyes, namely, that of economic modernization?

Sun Yat-sen's paradoxical attitude, his errors of judgment, and the apparent flagging of his energies should not be traced solely to the complex nature of his character and his frequently distorted view of reality. They also reflect the ambiguities of a revolution that, under the cloak of progressivist and Wester-nist discourse, was essentially the work of conservative social forces: the gentry and the local elites, merchants, officers, and officials. The close-on two years that separate the Wuchang insurrection (October 1911) and the crushing of the Second Revolution (August 1913) represent a moment of truth when the utopian vision, nurtured and diffused by the intellectual revolutionaries, of a republican, democratic, wealthy, modern China was confronted by the monumental problems of an underdeveloped country, still dominated by its traditional elites. How could the fall of the Manchus on its own possibly have reconciled the vision with the reality? The revolutionary party now paid the price for the ideological misguidedness that had allowed it to give absolute priority to the anti-Manchu struggle, which had resulted in the belief that the overthrow of a dynasty was both the necessary and the sufficient condition for national renewal.

As the figurehead of republican opposition and the leader most responsible for its anti-Manchu choice, Sun Yat-sen was also the principal victim of the contradictions and ambiguities of a revolution that was not really a revolu-tion. The grafting of the dream upon the reality, which led to the collapse of the empire and the founding of the Republic, confirmed Sun Yat-sen's sym-bolic role but did not provide him with the means of deepening and develop-ing the transformation thus begun. The revolution of 1911, that ephemeral triumph of words over facts, may have encouraged Sun Yat-sen to cultivate a utopia, to turn away from day-to-day politics in order to absorb himself in his extraordinary plans for industrial and railway expansion.

Yuan Shikai's shows of force at the beginning of 1913 shook Sun Yat-sen out of his dreaming or torpor. At this point he took a stand as the defender of republican legitimacy; but in the eyes of public opinion he was by now already no more than a conspirator, a troublemaker. It was, in truth, not so much Sun's shortcomings or the maneuvers of Yuan Shikai, the aspiring dictator, that got the better of the revolutionary illusion, but the obstinacy of hard facts.

The events of 1911–13 are frequently analyzed in terms of revolution and counterrevolution, republicanism and Bonapartism, but they are ill-served by these classic schemata. Did the confused situations in China, in which the most heterogeneous aspirations and experiences jostled together (often de-scribed in abusive terms borrowed from a Western vocabulary and point of view), really offer a decent chance to democracy, let alone to socialism? Did it really leave room for the initiatives of any sincere republican, even one much more farseeing and energetic than Sun Yat-sen?

A MISSED RENDEZVOUS: SUN YAT-SEN AND THE INSURRECTION OF OCTOBER 1911

The insurrection that broke out on October 10, 1911, in Wuchang or, according to Chinese terminology, the insurrection of the Double Ten (the tenth day of the tenth month), was not, as Sun Yat-sen suggested, "a sheer accident."[1] It was the work of groups of local revolutionaries who had recruited men from the New Army and also enjoyed support from both the secret societies and the urban elites. The links between these local organizations and the movement led by Sun Yat-sen and the Tokyo group were extremely tenuous. So far as they did exist, they were relayed on the one hand by Huang Xing in person, on the other by the Central China Bureau of the Revolutionary Alliance, founded in July 1911 by Song Jiaoren. But neither Huang Xing nor Song Jiaoren believed the insurrection would succeed. And later, when they did go to Wuchang, neither managed to establish his authority over the military government of Hubei that had emerged from the insurrection. While the revolutionary movement was spreading through the country in October and November, taking the form of provincial secessions, a second center of direction was created in Shanghai and Nanking, under the control of members of the Revolutionary Alliance, most of whom were natives of the Yangzi region.

But Sun Yat-sen continued his travels in the United States and Europe. Was he sulking because he had lost the initiative? Did he share the doubts of his Cantonese entourage, particularly Hu Hanmin, about the chances of a revolution set off by the gentry and the military? Or was he searching abroad for the diplomatic and financial support that might enable him to take control of the situation?

A Headless Dragon: The Insurrection of the Double Ten

The failure of the uprising of April 1911 in Canton marked the end of the string of insurrectional attempts made by the Revolutionary Alliance under

The 1911 revolution (provinces independent in December 1911)

Sun Yat-sen's leadership. After this, the initiative slipped away from the Cantonese, and the center of revolutionary action shifted to the Yangzi valley. During the summer, Sichuan was disturbed by vast demonstrations against the government policy of rail nationalization, for patriots feared that this would open the way for new foreign encroachments.

For ten years or more, the small revolutionary groups of Hubei had kept constantly active.[2] Pursued by the police, time and again they had been dissolved only to be reborn instantly under different names. On the eve of the insurrection they were gathered together in two principal societies, the Literary Institute (Wenxueshe) and the Progressive Association (Gongjinhui). The former recruited its members from among the officers and men of the New Army units stationed in Wuchang. The latter represented a provincial extension of a dissident organization of the Revolutionary Alliance that had first emerged in Tokyo in April 1907 and had gone on to collaborate closely with the secret societies and also to attract members of the gentry and intellectuals. The gap separating the two organizations was more social than ideological. But in September 1911, in response to their leaders' appeals, the revolutionaries of Hubei rose above their differences and agreed to unite in their efforts to prepare for the uprising.

The links that these small groups maintained with the Revolutionary Alliance were of a personal rather than an institutional nature. Their collaboration had always been episodic, prompted by the contacts that some local leaders always kept up with the non-Cantonese circles of the Alliance, in particular with Huang Xing and Song Jiaoren. Two such leaders were Sun Wu and Ju Zheng, both members of the Progressive Association who had completed their studies in Japan. A few of the local revolutionaries belonged both to the Progressive Association and to the Revolutionary Alliance. The proliferation of these organizations, their elasticity, which defied police repression, their deep roots in a variety of social circles, which, however, did not rule out changing patterns in their supporters or occasional unity when particular objectives were in view—all these features suggest the vitality of a movement with a direct hold over Chinese society as it was at that time. Whereas the Revolutionary Alliance was particularly characterized by its ideological ambitions, the Hubei-Hunan revolutionary movement was above all kept going by its activists.

It was that activism and dynamism that Song Jiaoren was keen to channel when he created the Central China Bureau of the Revolutionary Alliance in August 1911. He wanted to impose the authority of this office upon all the many revolutionary groups of the Yangzi region, which in the past had paid no more than lip service to the Alliance. Through his editorials in the *People's Stand*, Song Jiaoren also tried to broaden the political horizon of these local groups and to link the immediate objective—the overthrow of the Manchus—to a project for the establishment of a democratic and constitutional government. Out of political realism, in order to rally constitutional local elites to the anti-Manchu cause and thereby ensure the rapid success of the revolution, Song Jiaoren kept quiet about the principle of the people's livelihood. Eager to limit both the duration and the geographic spread of revolutionary disturbances, he planned, with the support of the army, to create an insurrectional center in Hubei and to establish liaison with the northern provinces as soon as possible. This plan, as well as the creation of the Central China Bureau of the Revolutionary Alliance, had received the approval of Huang Xing, who, however, counseled prudence.

Prudent Song Jiaoren certainly was. His own view, as a good organizer, was that two or three more years would be needed to complete all preparations. But the revolutionaries of Wuchang were impatient for action. On October 10, the Wuchang garrison rebelled. Neither Huang Xing nor Song Jiaoren had time to rally Wuchang itself; its revolutionary leaders were absent, either on the run or wounded. The troops entered the fray on their own and in a single night overcame the resistance of the authorities. But the leaderless rebels were like a "headless dragon." They got hold of one of the garrison's officers, Li Yuanhong, and forced him to assume the functions of military governor of Hubei—the head of the first revolutionary government was simply a political prisoner!

The Military Government of Hubei

More than two weeks elapsed before Song Jiaoren and Huang Xing arrived in Wuchang. In the meantime, the military government had been consolidated and its authority had extended to the Wuchang, Hanyang, and Hankou triple cities. By October 11, the New Army insurgents had solicited and obtained the support of the local gentry and their representatives in the provincial assembly of Hubei.[3] These local elites, who over the years had been playing an increasing role in the management of local affairs, had progressively also become more interested in problems of national importance, in particular within the framework of the reforming empire's New Policy. In October 1911, when the insurrection took both militant republicans and imperial officials by surprise, the provincial deputies, strong in the knowledge of their institutional legitimacy and with a definite sense of their position as social representatives, were, in contrast, quite ready to seize the initiative. With the circumstances abetting, these staunch constitutionalists, who were calling for the defense of national interests and wider political participation, had no trouble at all turning themselves into moderate republicans.

The president of the provincial assembly of Hubei thus became civil governor alongside Li Yuanhong. Close collaboration was also set up with the merchants, who advanced loans and helped with the maintenance of order. The military government had, furthermore, obtained from the foreigners a promise not to intervene: on October 18 the consular corps had proclaimed its neutrality.

By the time the Alliance leaders arrived in Wuchang, all they could do was integrate themselves into the already existing governmental structures, thereby setting their seal of approval upon this heterogeneous coalition of revolutionary activists and local elites gathered in support of the garrison, which remained loyal to its leader Li Yuanhong. Huang Xing became the commander-in-chief of the revolutionary army, under the authority of Li Yuanhong, and thus had to accept responsibility for the military defeat at the hands of the imperial troops, who recaptured Hankou on November 1, and Hanyang on the twenty-seventh. Song Jiaoren returned to the lower Yangzi to create a second revolutionary center. As so often happened in China, the struggle for power was expressed geographically, being reflected in the creation of new centers of political gravity that shifted from one place to another.

The Emergence of a Second Revolutionary Center:
The Shanghai-Nanking Axis

In the weeks following the Wuchang insurrection, the revolution spread through central and southern China, where it took the form of a series of provincial secessions. In Shanghai, at the beginning of November, an attack led by Chen Qimei (one of the leaders of the Central China Bureau of the

Revolutionary Alliance) against the Jiangnan arsenal gave the revolutionaries control of the city. They were supported by the elites: members of education societies, the chambers of commerce, the municipal commissions of the Chinese city, and the provincial assembly. The influence of these same elites prompted the governors of the lower Yangzi provinces—Jiangsu and Zhejiang—also to proclaim their independence.

Although the revolution of the lower Yangzi was dominated by local elites just as that of Wuchang had been, these were not the same kind of elites. In Shanghai, and to a lesser extent in the delta provinces, merchants, compradors, and modern or semimodern entrepreneurs outnumbered the gentry and literati. In a metropolis that constituted both the bridgehead of foreign economic penetration and the bastion of Chinese capitalism, the traditional elites were gradually giving way to a business class committed to the same program of national independence, republican democracy, and economic development as the Revolutionary Alliance. The power of Li Yuanhong in Wuchang rested upon an alliance between the army, the gentry, and the secret societies: in Shanghai the situation was different and depended upon cooperation between the Revolutionary Alliance and this new business class. With its Double Ten insurrection, the Wuchang faction had acquired a head's lead. But soon its authority was challenged by the leaders in Shanghai.

At the beginning of November, when fourteen provinces had already seceded, the establishment of a central government became a matter of urgency, to prevent the development of regional rivalries and to preserve an appearance of national unity to the foreign presence. It was over the organization of this central provisional government that Shanghai and Wuchang clashed.

In the end, Nanking, which had just been conquered by revolutionary forces, was chosen as the seat of the provisional government. The assembly of provincial delegates met there on December 14, 1911. It consisted of forty-four members, representing seventeen provinces.

While awaiting the conclusion of the negotiations taking place between the revolutionary and the imperial sides, the Nanking assembly had to choose a provisional head of government. The Wuchang faction supported Li Yuanhong; the Shanghai group favored Huang Xing, and the assembly was as unable to come to a decision as it was to determine the powers of this future leader. Some, headed by Song Jiaoren, demanded that those powers be limited by the existence of a responsible cabinet; others pleaded for a regime of the presidential type. In mid-December, the situation seemed blocked by the rivalry between the Shanghai and the Wuchang groups and, within the Shanghai group, by a conflict between Song Jiaoren and more moderate elements of the Alliance, such as Zhang Binglin.

In this confused situation, witnessing the end of one world with no sign of a new order emerging to succeed it, nowhere—neither in Wuchang nor in Shanghai—was there any mention of Sun Yat-sen.

Whatever Had Become of Sun Yat-sen?

In early October, Sun Yat-sen was traveling in the United States, still in quest of funds. When he reached Denver, Colorado, at the foot of the Rockies, Sun deciphered a telegram from Huang Xing. It was already one week old, but he had not yet been able to read it because he had not had his secret code key with him. He now learned from the telegram that an uprising was being prepared in Wuchang and that funds were needed for it. Tired after his journey, Sun put off answering it for the moment. So he was completely taken by surprise the next morning when, just as he was going to breakfast, he read the main newspaper headline, "Wuchang Occupied by the Revolutionaries."

In 1917, when Lenin, then living as an exile in Switzerland, heard of the February Revolution, which had broken out in Petrograd, he could not rest until he found himself back in Russia, even if he had to travel in a German train to do so. In 1911, Sun Yat-sen, in Denver, rushed to buy a ticket for New York and London. A surprising reaction. Sun Yat-sen has himself offered an explanation in his *Autobiography*: "In twenty days I could land in Shanghai and take part in the revolutionary struggle, but at that point the diplomatic front was more important to us than the firing line. I therefore resolved to address myself to matters of a diplomatic order."[4] Sun Yat-sen sensed, with reason, that the attitude of the foreign powers would be crucial. Their neutrality could ensure the success of the revolution. Their active help and financial support would be trump cards in the struggle for power. No doubt Sun Yat-sen was thinking of repeating the operation that had served him so well after his kidnapping in London in 1897 and was counting on success and prestige acquired in foreign capitals to impose his own authority upon his compatriots.

In London, where he arrived on October 20, Sun Yat-sen was reunited with his old friends Dr. Cantlie and his wife. He also met up with Homer Lea. In spite of the collapse of his great plan for subverting the imperial regime, the American adventurer had decided to place his skills as a general at the service of Sun, who was thus presented with his "Lafayette."[5] At any rate, Lea appears to have taken an active part in Sun's attempts to raise financial and diplomatic help for the nascent Chinese Republic.

Homer Lea acted as intermediary in contacting the representatives of the International Banking Consortium,[6] suggesting that they should divert the funds destined for the Manchu dynasty to the future Republic. Lea also, through the mediation of Sir Trevor Dawson (of the Vickers, Sons and Maxim Company, which hoped to receive orders for arms once Sun had become "President of the United States of China"), arranged for a memorandum to be submitted to the Foreign Office proposing an alliance between Sun Yat-sen on the one hand and Great Britain and the United States on the other.

Cosigned by Sun and Homer Lea, the memorandum declared that Sun, once he had become president ("about which there can be no doubt"), would grant numerous privileges to Great Britain and the United States in exchange for their friendship and support: the new president would place the Chinese navy under the command of British officers and take a representative of the London government as his political adviser. This "bluff" (Harold Schiffrin), very much in Sun's style, did not impress the Foreign Office. Two days after learning of the memorandum's contents, Sir Edward Grey telegraphed Peking to say that it was Yuan Shikai who seemed to be the man of the moment. The subsequent decision of the Foreign Office to remain neutral and make no loans either to the Manchus or to the revolutionaries resulted from an evaluation of the risks (including that of a conflict between the powers present in China), and not from Sun's intervention. All that Sun obtained was permission to break his return journey for a few days in the British colonies, Singapore and Hong Kong, from which he had until then still been banned.

Sun's brief stay in Paris, at the end of November, was hardly more fruitful. Sun did meet some important political figures, including Georges Clemenceau, and on November 24 one of his emissaries met Philippe Berthelot, then assistant director of the Asia department at the Quai d'Orsay. But all Sun obtained was a confirmation of the neutrality of the French diplomatic service, prompted, like that vouchsafed by the British, by reasons of general political expediency. In the case of the Quai d'Orsay, however, it may be that the reports of the French consul Raphaël Réau, Sun's long-standing friend and protector, had from the start tipped the scales toward nonintervention. His reports certainly presented the Wuchang insurrection as a true revolutionary movement, not to be confused with any scattered recurrences of Boxerism.

While in Paris, Sun Yat-sen also tried to obtain loans. On November 23 he met Stanislas Simon, the director of the Banque de l'Indochine. But Simon simply repeated that there would be no loan to the Chinese authorities until the political situation had stabilized. The principle of this nonintervention had been approved at a meeting of the International Banking Consortium in Paris on November 10. Sun Yat-sen had to be satisfied with the assurance that at least the enemies of the revolution would receive no support.

Sun Yat-sen thus set out on his return journey empty-handed. But it did not matter—the rumor of his contacts with Western leaders and other figures of importance bestowed an aura of prestige upon him. His compatriots made his return a triumphant one.

SUN YAT-SEN AND THE FOUNDING
OF THE CHINESE REPUBLIC

Sun Yat-sen's return to China marked the zenith of his career. He was elected president, and on January 1, 1912, he proclaimed the founding of the Republic. He headed the provisional government of Nanking until the following March. For the only time in his life, Sun Yat-sen was called to exercise supreme power at the head of a government that declared itself to be (and soon became) united and national. It was a difficult and perilous task, for which Sun Yat-sen's wanderings in foreign lands had hardly prepared him. His competence and experience could not rival those of Yuan Shikai, the imperial general and high official to whom Sun seemed determined to defer. But first, what he wanted from his rival was an assurance that republican institutions would be maintained. The trial of strength that then took place between the two men ended with Sun bowing out. His extraordinarily serene and willing self-effacement sheds a new light on the revolutionary leader's personality and at the same time affords a glimpse of a power struggle less favorable to the revolution than might be suggested by the extent and rapidity of the political upheavals that had taken place in the short space of a few months.

Sun Yat-sen's Return

Making the most of the London authorities' lifting of the banishment order, Sun Yat-sen returned to China, making a halt in Hong Kong, where he arrived on December 21, 1911. Many figures of note were there to greet him, including a number of Sun's Japanese companions. One of them was, of course, Miyazaki Torazō. The Japanese adventurer-advisers who had been so active over the past decade, had taken little part in the first few weeks of the revolution. Their initiatives had been paralyzed not only by the confused and contradictory policies of the Tokyo government but also by the absence of Sun Yat-sen. For years, Sun had absorbed all their attention and energies, and they had developed few contacts with the leaders of other nationalist and revolutionary currents. Sun Yat-sen's return now gave them hope of regaining a foothold in the revolution. But the presence at Sun's side of his American military adviser, Homer Lea, was not at all favorable to them. Homer Lea harbored a deep hostility toward Japan, whose expansionist ambitions he had castigated in a best-seller, *The Valor of Ignorance*, published ten years earlier. Nevertheless, he could not prevent the Japanese from accompanying Sun on the last leg of his journey to Shanghai or stop them joining his entourage.

In Hong Kong, Sun Yat-sen also met representatives of the merchant guilds of Canton. According to Albert Maybon, he even boasted to them of being able to secure foreign loans without mortgages and at very low rates. He declared himself convinced that "the powers will refuse [our Republic] nothing."[7] Because Sun Yat-sen was returning from afar and had been in contact with many important foreign figures, the Cantonese merchants trusted him and took him at his word. Finally, Sun Yat-sen was also reunited with his Revolutionary Alliance Cantonese supporters, in particular Hu Hanmin, appointed military governor of Guangdong after the secession of the province in November.

Hu Hanmin's presence in Hong Kong was more than just a gesture of courtesy and loyalty. It was prompted by a precise political aim: to prevent Sun Yat-sen from going to the Yangzi provinces and getting himself elected president by the Nanking assembly. The argument that now developed between the two leaders echoes some of the polemics that had already set the Cantonese in opposition to Song Jiaoren within the Revolutionary Alliance. It also raised fundamental problems that were to remain at the heart of all the thinking on revolutionary strategy for the next fifteen years. According to Hu Hanmin, the personal ambition of Yuan Shikai and the strength of the armed forces under his control could not fail to reduce Sun Yat-sen's possible presidency to no more than that of a figurehead. It would therefore be better to set up a provisional government in Canton and there muster enough troops to get the better of those in the North, thereby ensuring real victory for the revolution. Hu Hanmin discounted as negligible any support that the Revolutionary Alliance could give Sun Yat-sen in the parliamentary and institutional battle. In his view, the seizure of power could only be achieved through armed victory. And the highest priority was to make sure of the means of that victory.

While recognizing the sense of this analysis (which subsequent events were soon to confirm), Sun Yat-sen argued that the priority was the anti-Manchu struggle and emphasized the urgent need to preserve the neutrality of the foreign powers. He did not trust Yuan Shikai either, but he thought that, even if his sincerity was suspect, the rallying of this high-ranking official would make the immediate toppling of the Manchu dynasty possible—which action he believed to be the essential objective of the revolutionary struggle. The rallying of the general would also make it possible to put an end to civil disturbances that were likely to encourage redoubtable intervention on the part of the foreign powers. These arguments have all the hallmarks of the historical opportunism, impatience, and optimism that are so characteristic of Sun Yat-sen. It is also interesting to note how far he had come, this adventurer who in the past had dreamed of a breakaway southern Republic but who now could see his destiny only as that of a national leader. After a long argument, Hu Hanmin rallied to Sun Yat-sen's plan. So the two men arrived together in Shanghai on December 25, 1911.

The revolutionaries saw Sun's return as a means to ease the pressure and resolve the crisis produced by the rivalry between Huang Xing and Li Yuanhong. Up until this point nobody had even considered making Sun Yat-sen head of state. Everyone regarded him more as a plenipotentiary minister, a fund-raiser, and a specialist in foreign affairs. But a provisional presidency for Sun would make it possible to wait for Yuan Shikai to rally to them and at the same time would solemnly confirm the political standing of the South and China's entry into the republican era.

It was grey and cold in Shanghai that Christmas Day. Nobody was waiting for Sun at the Huangpu wharf swept by a strong wind. The first rendezvous arranged was with Wu Tingfang (1842–1922). He was a well-known jurist, a preeminent reformist figure who had formerly been Li Hongzhang's secretary. The previous year he had returned from the United States where he had served as minister, and had rallied to the revolution. It was he who was negotiating with the northerners. And it was his telephone that rang, announcing the news of Sun's return. Wu Tingfang was at the time accompanied by a young Australian journalist, a correspondent on the *New York Herald.* His name was William H. Donald (1875–1946) and he was subsequently to become one of Sun Yat-sen's closest advisers and friends.

Accompanied by another Chinese diplomat and revolutionary, the two men went to meet Sun, whom they found sitting by a small fire with a humpbacked dwarf, Homer Lea. The deformity of the "American general" was seen as a bad omen and deeply shocked the Chinese visitors. The interview was as glacial as the weather. Despite all his efforts, the young Australian journalist could neither dissipate the gloom nor get a conversation going. When he asked Sun Yat-sen how he envisaged the political future of China after the overthrow of the Manchus, he received the brief reply, "We shall have a Republic," with no further comment or details. As they left, with the Chinese revolutionaries giving free rein to their indignation and wondering how they could conceal the unfortunate presence of the American dwarf, Donald was wondering about the magnetic personality that was attributed to Sun Yat-sen by his followers but of which the journalist had detected no hint.

Two days later, on December 27, it was the former general staff of the Revolutionary Alliance, who, all differences ignored, came to cluster round Sun. The Cantonese (Hu Hanmin, Wang Jingwei) rubbed shoulders with the Hubei-Hunan leaders (Huang Xing, Song Jiaoren, Ju Zheng) and those from Jiangsu-Zhejiang (Chen Qimei, Zhang Renjie). This consensus had not been reached without difficulty. Song Jiaoren was afraid that Sun, the dreamer, would lead the revolution into an impasse; had it been up to him, he would have forbidden Sun even to set foot in Nanking (at least that is what he confided to a Japanese adviser and memorialist, Kita Ikki). But in the end he rallied to Sun's candidacy. The same could not be said of Zhang Binglin, whose hostility was not disarmed and who would have been inclined to allot the presidency to Huang Xing (for his merit), Song Jiaoren (for his talent), or Wang Jingwei (for his virtue), rather than to Sun.

Once approved, with varying degrees of enthusiasm, by the leaders of the

Revolutionary Alliance, Sun's candidacy was supposed to rally the votes of the provincial delegates gathered in the provisional parliament in Nanking. But there was one hitch: what form was the new republican regime to take? The guidelines of the Organization of the Provisional Government of the Republic, the constitution hurriedly set out in Wuchang at the beginning of November, were not at all precise. Song Jiaoren, who invoked democratic principles and probably mistrusted Sun Yat-sen and perhaps also the future president, Yuan Shikai, pleaded for a parliamentary regime with ministerial responsibility. He proposed that the post of prime minister should go to Huang Xing. But there were many in the party who suspected Yuan of nurturing personal ambitions. Sun Yat-sen himself favored a presidential regime: "In the parliamentary system the chief of state does not have real power. . . . At this time of emergency, we cannot adopt a political system which restricts the power of the man we trust."[8]

Though the debate on ministerial responsibilities versus presidential power concerned a crucial political choice, it was also of a kind to involve violent personal rivalries; and it continued throughout the first two years of the Chinese Republic, crystallizing ideas and orienting strategies. In December 1911, the debate was only just beginning, amid considerable confusion: after adopting a number of contradictory positions, the leaders of the Revolutionary Alliance and the provincial delegates eventually decided on a presidential system.

It was thus as a head of state theoretically endowed with extensive powers that, on December 29, 1911, Parliament installed Sun Yat-sen as president, voting him in by 16 votes to 1. On January 1, 1912, Sun arrived in Nanking to inaugurate both his mandate and Year 1 of the Republic.

Sun Yat-sen, President of the Republic, January 1–February 15, 1912

Sun Yat-sen's presidency lasted only forty-five days—just enough time to complete the negotiations between the North and the South and to obtain the abdication of the young Manchu emperor Xuantong.[9] Though he bore the title President, Sun Yat-sen was by no means in control of the situation. His nominal authority did not extend to the northern provinces; his real authority was barely imposed upon those of the South. It was not he who led the spokesmen for peace and union between North and South, for they had already begun their task before his return to the Chinese political scene. In conformity with the implicit contract concluded by the negotiators and backed by the revolutionaries, as soon as the news of the imperial abdication of February 12 reached Nanking, Sun Yat-sen announced that he was resigning to allow Yuan Shikai to be elected president of the provisional republic of the united North and South. But in his forty-five days as president, Sun Yat-sen, at least nominally, oversaw the introduction of the republican regime, the adoption of the solar calendar, and the replacement of the imperial dragons by a flag with five horizontal colored stripes: red, yellow, blue, black, and white.

The presidency could not, in a month and a half, and lacking the means as well as the time, achieve very much. It would have taken a firmer and more enlightened leadership than Sun Yat-sen's to make the most of the opportunity. He was for the first time faced with the trials of power, and if those trials confirmed a number of the man's qualities, it cannot be said that they revealed those of a head of state.

Success did not seem to change Sun: he remained personally modest and invariably full of patriotic and civic fervor. His installment as president took place without great pomp. Apart from the oath of investiture, the only official ceremony took place at the Ming tombs, in the countryside close to Nanking. The monuments stood in ruins: "Broken bricks and crumbling walls, cracked vaults. . . . Grandeur lies only in the memory and in the place, at the foot of a high mound planted with trees and surrounded by hills."[10] Here, Sun Yat-sen paid homage to the founder of the Ming dynasty who, in the fourteenth century, had wrenched China from the Mongols, and he pledged himself likewise to eject the new foreign dynasty, the Manchus. Sun Yat-sen had worked without respite to root revolutionary and republican fervor in Ming loyalism, so it was hardly surprising to find the first president of the Chinese Republic placing himself under the patronage of the long gone Emperor Hongwu (1368–98).

Sun Yat-sen installed himself in the *yamen*[11] of the former governor-general. Although he treated himself to an automobile, probably the first ever seen in Nanking, he was otherwise not extravagant. He remained "welcoming, open . . . saying yes to everyone, listening to all the advice."[12] The portraits of this period show him amid the radiance of his maturity and success, combining dignity with simplicity. The journalists who approached him mention "his serious, thoughtful air"[13] and his "quiet, reserved manners."

He seemed to carry within him the calm that follows a duty accomplished, a mission fulfilled. His *Autobiography*, which he wrote in 1918, in fact ends with an evocation of that January 1, 1912: "I had achieved my essential aim, the aim of my whole life: the creation of the Chinese Republic."[14]

It was a republic only in name, of course: everything still remained to be done. Sun Yat-sen chose a cabinet that brought together a group of matchless figures. Alongside the faithful Huang Xing, who was entrusted with the portfolio for War but in effect assumed the responsibilities of a Prime Minister, were other revolutionaries: at Foreign Affairs Wang Zhonghui, "a very brilliant man . . . a scholar of quite exceptional attainments . . . a Doctor of Civil Law, a Barrister-at-Law of the Middle Temple, and the author (in English) of a translation and annotation of the German Civil Code,"[15] who had mastered not only Japanese but also English, French, and German; at Education, the talented man of letters Cai Yuanpei. Former reformists and constitutionalists also rallied to this first republican government: Zhang Jian, one of the pioneers of the development of the textile industry in Shanghai, was responsible for managing Industry; Wu Tingfang, to whom the reforming empire had entrusted the revision of the Chinese Penal Code, became Minister for Justice. A number of other competent administrators, appointed to Internal Affairs, Finance, and so on, completed the collection of ministers. From the point of view of the quality of its members, this first cabinet eclipsed most of those upon which the Chinese Republic was to rely in the years, indeed the decades, that followed.

But a collection of talents does not necessarily add up to a team. The ministers did not work together. Some never really took up their responsibilities. Sun did not govern with them, or with the provisional Parliament. The provincial delegates censured him in particular for issuing military bonds representing a value of $300,000, repayable in three months' time, on his own initiative and with no prior consultation or preparation and without making any provision for their reimbursement. Did Sun do that because he questioned the legitimacy of these provincial delegates chosen by local authorities of uncertain status? Or was it because it seemed to him that the consolidation of the Republic cried out for an authoritarian government? Whatever the reasons, Sun made in all only three appearances in the elegant hall adorned with plaster arches and illuminated by electric chandeliers in which Parliament met.

The distrust was mutual. Nobody knew what Sun was up to. The lack of information and communication fueled rumors and encouraged suspicions. The very presence of the Cantonese was irksome—they were too lively, too young, too much at ease, too cliquey. The stream of applicants, many of them overseas Chinese, was alarming; Sun had promised them jobs or rewards in his fund-raising days and they now came to claim their due. The influence of foreign advisers was even more alarming—Americans, including Homer Lea, and, worse, Japanese. The Japanese were not popular in the revolutionary camp, and they were positively feared by the Shanghai businessmen who supported the government in Nanking. Their presence also greatly bothered William H. Donald, who had become an adviser to the president: "Every day the trains disgorged new hordes, among them scores of Japanese who settled down in the yamen as if by right. They brought their bedding, their cooking and eating paraphernalia and milled and wandered about like herds of sheep."[16] The army was obliged to intervene before all these squatters, Japanese and others, were ejected. But the affair of the Japanese loans, which erupted in January–February 1912, was far more grave, for it isolated Sun Yat-sen from Parliament, from the gentry and merchants of Shanghai, and from most of the revolutionary leaders.

Ever since Sun Yat-sen had come to power, the circle of his Japanese advisers had been growing. Idealistic adventurers such as Miyazaki Torazō, who had accompanied the revolutionary leader in his career for many long years, had been joined by businessmen, in particular representatives of the Mitsui Company, which was pursuing an active policy of economic expansion in China. Mori Kaku (1883–1932), one of the principal designers of this policy, was paying Sun Yat-sen particularly devoted attention.

Having returned empty-handed from his tour in the United States and Europe, Sun Yat-sen needed to find funds to pay the revolutionary troops concentrated in the lower Yangzi valley. The resources of Jiangsu (of which Nanking was the capital) and the contributions of the Shanghai business class did not suffice for the upkeep of these contingents from many different provinces. Already in January 1912, the Japanese had obtained two loans for Sun, one of 150,000 yen, the other of 300,000 yen from Mitsui. It was the negotiation of a third, much larger loan, for Hanyeping, that brought on the crisis.

The Hanyeping company, created in 1908 by the merging of three businesses—the arsenal of Hanyang, the iron mines of Taye (Hubei), and the coal mines of Pingxiang (Hubei)—had inherited a difficult situation, linked with the former bureaucratic management of its various components. On the eve of the 1911 revolution, under the direction of the great entrepreneur and minister, Sheng Xuanhuai, the affairs of the Hanyeping company were somewhat improved. Japanese credits (among others) had contributed to this: the imperial steelworks of Yawata, in Kyushu (Japan), were extremely interested in the seams of iron at Taye. The Mitsui company acted as intermediary. In exchange for guaranteed deliveries of iron and the right to oversee the management of the company, the Japanese offered a new loan of 12 million yen to Hanyeping. The revolution and the flight of Sheng Xuanhuai interrupted the operation, but negotiations resumed with Sun Yat-sen. He was inclined to hand over the joint management of Hanyeping entirely to the Japanese, who in return would immediately make available to the Nanking government a credit of 3 million yen, taken out of the 12 million destined for the company.

The resistance of the managing board of Hanyeping, the discreet opposition of French diplomacy, anxious to preserve unity of action within the framework of the international consortium, and Sun Yat-sen's resignation foiled the plan. But in spite of the secrecy that had surrounded the negotiations carried out by Sun Yat-sen and Huang Xing in person, the project had seriously alarmed political circles in Nanking and financial and industrial circles in Shanghai. Parliament, indignant at not having been consulted, denounced this betrayal of national interests. The Minister for Industry, Zhang Jian, handed over his resignation, in a letter addressed in early February to Sun Yat-sen and Huang Xing, and then seized the chance to issue a grave warning against Japanese expansionism:

> Of all the commercial enterprises, iron mills in particular should not be made joint ventures with foreigners. Even if this is done, it should not be done with the Japanese. They have patiently and earnestly plotted our ruin for many years. . . . The republican government . . . must look after the people with the best policy at its command. How could it forfeit the boundless riches of the future?[17]

The authorities in the provinces where the businesses planned to be offered as collateral were situated protested in chorus. Faced with this revolt, Sun Yat-sen could count on the support only of his loyal Cantonese. And even Hu Hanmin's justifications rang rather hollow. He invoked the imperious pressure of circumstances and referred to a personal code of integrity that had more to do with revolutionary morality than with the conduct of public affairs:

> [Huang Xing] has been trying to support the armies with a pair of bare hands. . . . He is not unaware of the undesirability of making this deal [on Hanyeping] . . . but he is desperate. . . . The Provisional Government is merely a revolutionary organization on a larger scale. . . . The criterion of judgment is whether the action is motivated by personal gain or for the sake of the cause.[18]

The argument lacks force, but the diagnosis seems fair enough. Notwithstanding the advances that Sun Yat-sen had made toward the constitutionalists—the rallied New Army officers and the Shanghai business circles—the transformation of the revolutionary camp into a national government had not really taken place. The provisional government remained a hotbed of personal, factious, and regionalist oppositions. Its divisions, weakness, and incompetence played straight into the hands of a rival better prepared for the exercise of power by long years of practice in positions of public responsibility.

Sun Yat-sen's Resignation and the Transfer of Power to Yuan Shikai

Yuan Shikai (1859–1916) was one of the principal political figures in the declining imperial government. He had been associated with the New Policy of the Qing court and had set up the New Army of the North (the Beiyang army) and worked to reform the administration. The death of the dowager empress Cixi and the accession to power of Manchu princes hostile to the reforms had resulted in his being eased out. When called upon for help by the imperial court, after the Wuchang uprising, Yuan Shikai had no intention of saving the regime. His objective had been to find a compromise that would allow him to reestablish peace and unity and then to seize power. To display his strength, he had mounted an attack and, in November 1911, had recaptured Hankou and Hanyang from the revolutionary forces. After this victory, he had halted the advance of the imperial troops, in order to open negotiations. These had officially begun in Shanghai on December 18.

The revolutionaries were agreed upon giving the functions of president to Yuan Shikai in the event of his deciding to turn against the dynasty. The offer was made to him by Li Yuanhong and was confirmed by a telegram from Sun

Yat-sen on November 13. The establishment of the provisional government made no difference to the position of the revolutionary leaders. On January 1, 1912, the day of his own investiture as president, Sun Yat-sen cabled as follows to Yuan Shikai: "Although I have accepted this position [of president], for the time being, it is actually waiting for you. . . . I hope that you will soon decide to accept this offer."[19] That strategy reflects the absolute priority that the revolutionaries gave to the anti-Manchu struggle. It also constituted the only policy acceptable to all the extremely disparate parties involved in the rebellion.

The rise of Yuan Shikai thus initially resulted from a consensus, a deliberate choice reached even by the southerners. Yuan seemed to everyone to be the man capable of resolving the crisis produced by the Wuchang uprising, and of obtaining the abdication of the dynasty, avoiding civil war, and preserving national unity by preventing the intervention of foreign powers.

The negotiations begun in mid-December did not make easy progress. Yuan Shikai, who had at his disposal powerful armed forces, resorted to threats and intimidation. He also enjoyed the increasingly openly declared support of a number of the great foreign powers (particularly Great Britain), all keen to have their own interests protected by a "strongman." He was helped by the absence of a candidate in the revolutionary camp, for the authority of the provisional government had failed to establish itself over all the factions and over the mass of southern rebels. Did Yuan Shikai resort to corruption? At the time, there were persistent rumors of sweeteners offered to the delegates of the provisional Parliament of Nanking. Sun Yat-sen himself, as well as other revolutionary leaders, was said to have received huge sums of money. Presumably at least some of this was used to defray the expenses of the provisional government and to pay the southern troops. It has been claimed that, "certainly money changed hands in this period but it was probably no more than a lubricant, not a determining factor."[20]

On February 12, an imperial edict announced the abdication of the young emperor. The actual text of the edict was prepared in Nanking and passed on to Yuan Shikai. But an extra paragraph was added in Peking, entrusting Yuan with the responsibility for bringing about unification with the South and for setting up a Republic. This text, which seemed to make Yuan Shikai the heir to the empire, was in danger of investing him with a legitimacy quite in conflict with the legitimacy the revolutionaries were planning to confer upon him in an election by the provisional Parliament. Yuan Shikai made no attempt to do without that parliamentary election, and so, while vowing to keep tight control over the future president, the revolutionaries proceeded to abandon themselves to the joys of victory.

In Nanking, on February 15, Sun Yat-sen announced his resignation. The whole town celebrated the end of the empire, the coming of a recognized republican regime, and China's refound unity: "Of the forty-five days of the presidency of Souen-Wen [Sun Yat-sen] in Nanking, none was more representative, more joyful, more conscious of the past and of hope for the future."[21] Once again, a general descent was made upon the Ming tombs where governmental staff, the consular corps, and delegates to the provisional Parliament mingled with some thousands of soldiers, to celebrate the motherland. After fireworks, music, and gifts, the solemn declaration of unity was read out "like a prayer, from the high terrace." In the afternoon, President Sun Yat-sen gave a grand reception in his palace "and to everyone, with the wine flowing, he sang the praises of Yuan . . . the friend of the Republic, the devoted and valued servant of the cause."[22]

In accordance with Sun's wish, the provisional Parliament elected Yuan Shikai president. The publicized amity nevertheless concealed plenty of mutual suspicion. The revolutionaries had wanted to make use of Yuan Shikai to hasten and facilitate the overthrow of the dynasty. This had now been accomplished. But had not Yuan Shikai equally made use of the revolutionaries to get the secessionist southern provinces to rally when, in December, they might have resorted to armed resistance to oppose any attempt to regain control by a central government? Who was the principal beneficiary of this united, republican operation?

The truth soon emerged. Although he was resigning, Sun Yat-sen was resolved not to hand over his powers before all possible precautions had been taken to guarantee the maintenance of republican institutions. He appended to his resignation a number of conditions: Nanking was to remain the capital, and after his election the president was to come there to take up his functions. Only then would Sun's resignation take effect. In the meantime, Parliament was to promulgate the Constitution of the provisional government to which the new president would have to swear loyalty. In the six weeks between the announcement of Sun Yat-sen's resignation on February 15 and his abandonment of his functions on April 1, the Southerners tried to enforce their conditions and Yuan Shikai maneuvered to elude them. The outcome of these struggles set the seal upon both Sun Yat-sen's failure and, in the slightly longer term, the failure of the provisional Republic itself.

Sun Yat-sen's first precaution as a way of preventing possible treachery on the part of Yuan Shikai, installing the new republican capital in Nanking, had a good many advantages besides its symbolic value expressed in the ceremonies organized around the Ming tombs. Primarily this choice would remove Yuan Shikai well away from the military and bureaucratic networks in the North and install the young Republic in a social and economic environment propitious to its consolidation. Aware of the trap, Yuan Shikai pleaded the difficulty of moving the central administration, the reluctance of the foreign powers to finance new legations in Nanking, and, finally, the need to keep an eye on the Mongol and Manchu regions where foreign plots could be hatched and bring counterrevolution in their wake.

The transfer of the capital to Nanking was Sun Yat-sen's own idea, and at first he had some difficulty in getting it accepted by some of the revolutionary leaders and also by Parliament. Song Jiaoren, among others, who was well aware of the difficult situation in Manchuria, was afraid that such a move would signal the abandonment of the regions that lay beyond the Great Wall. Quite apart from the immediate political implications, the location of the capital certainly did carry great symbolic significance: to choose Peking was to seek to carry on with the imperial policy of conquest and hegemony in eastern Asia; to choose Nanking was to revert to a more self-centered tradition and to give formal recognition to the revolutionary origins of the regime. On February 15, at the same time as electing Yuan Shikai, the members of Parliament voted against the transfer. It reconsidered and changed the vote in favor only after Huang Xing threatened to send in troops to convince recalcitrants to change their minds.

The agreement of Yuan Shikai was of course needed. The arrival of a delegation sent to him in Peking coincided with a popular riot, the first to erupt there since the beginning of the revolution. On the evening of February 28, gunfire resounded in the Tartar city[23] and the sky glowed red. The editor-in-chief of the *Peking Daily* declared, "This was the only tragic moment of the revolution."[24] Among the foreign community, which had not forgotten the Boxer attack, alarm escalated. International troops were sent in to help the isolated residents of the Catholic Beitang Mission. Shelter was sought in the legations quarter; and the town was abandoned to mutinous soldiers and looters. Then, as suddenly as the riot had erupted, order returned. Yuan had a few wretched coolies executed and calmed down his troops with soothing words.

But the danger had made Chinese and foreigners alike shudder and had clearly demonstrated the need to keep the president in Peking. Many suspected Yuan Shikai himself of having started the riot, although no proof was ever found to bear out these accusations. All the same, Sun Yat-sen and the Nanking leaders were obliged to give up the idea of transferring the capital. It was therefore in Peking that, on March 10, Yuan Shikai was invested as president.

All that remained to block Yuan Shikai's ambitions was the barrier represented by the republican institutions. The southern revolutionaries accordingly did their best to strengthen them. The provisional Parliament, which, so as not to limit Sun's power, had until then rejected the principle of ministerial responsibility, had no hesitation in reversing that decision now that it was a matter of establishing firmer control over the power of Yuan Shikai. On March 12, Parliament promulgated the provisional Constitution, distinguishing and defining the legislative, judiciary, and executive powers. Executive power was exercised by the president together with the cabinet, all of whose members had to be approved by Parliament. The assent that Yuan Shikai for a while gave to this constitution made it possible for Parliament to vote for its own transfer to Peking and for Sun Yat-sen officially to relinquish his responsibilities on April 1.

The fragile consensus based on these reciprocal concessions did not halt the conflict that set the "strongman" of the North against the republicans of the South. But from now on that conflict took the form of an institutional struggle—presidential prerogatives versus ministerial responsibilities—complicated by interparty maneuvering. On the republican side, it was Song Jiaoren who led the offensive, with both courage and flair. Sun Yat-sen meanwhile disappeared almost completely from the political scene.

THE NEW ECLIPSE OF SUN YAT-SEN,
SPRING 1912—SPRING 1913

Sun Yat-sen's new eclipse coincided with one of the most disturbed but (in terms of experience) also one of the richest and most fertile periods of the

Chinese Republic. It coincided with the testing out of the new ideas and institutions borrowed from the West. China was now trying to become familiar with interparty exchanges, parliamentary practice, and the organization of elections. For all the inevitable distortions and confusions, this first year of the republican regime witnessed one of the strongest advances of democracy ever known in twentieth-century China.

During this period, Sun Yat-sen was absent from the political scene. He had lost power to Yuan Shikai and it was not long before he lost control of the opposition to Song Jiaoren. Those were now the two figures who dominated the course of events. Yuan, the longtime official, favored authoritarian modernization, and to this end he employed all the political tricks he had learned in the imperial palace as well as his solid talents as an administrator and a military commander. Song, one of the very few Chinese revolutionaries to have understood the meaning and practice of parliamentary institutions, was ready to prove that it was possible to rely on those institutions to guide China along the path to political and socioeconomic change.

Sun Effaces Himself from Political Life and Its Debates

After presidential powers passed to Yuan Shikai, the political opposition organized itself around the defense of the republican institutions, with a view to securing rigorous application of the constitution. The first ministerial cabinet was a coalition that included no more than four ministers from the Revolutionary Alliance. It was set up at the end of March 1912 by Tang Shaoyi (1860–1938), lasted a few weeks, then, in June, collapsed, a victim of its own internal dissensions and also of its conflicts with both the president and Parliament. That first failure convinced Song Jiaoren of the need for a realignment of the political forces and led to the formation of the Guomindang (Nationalist Party) in August 1912. His aim was to mobilize public opinion in readiness for the national elections called for by the March 1912 provisional constitution in order to create a parliamentary majority capable of controlling the executive. The Guomindang's successful showing in a poll conducted in the winter of 1912 represented a personal success for Song Jiaoren and gave the Chamber a majority of 269 nationalist deputies (out of a total of 423). Sun Yat-sen, however, was no more than distantly associated with this campaign faultlessly led by Song Jiaoren, whose forceful progress seemed unstoppable and who was emerging as the unchallenged leader of the opposition—until, that is, he was laid low, riddled by the bullets of Yuan Shikai's hired assassins, on March 20, 1913.

Following Sun Yat-sen's resignation, the revolutionaries soon lost all control over the executive. The man in whom Yuan Shikai placed his confidence and whom he had chosen to form a cabinet was Tang Shaoyi, a Cantonese who had contributed to the success of the exploratory talks between North and South and was prepared to cooperate loyally with the revolutionaries. In the course of his mission to Nanking at the end of March 1912, Tang Shaoyi negotiated the formation of a coalition cabinet that included four members of the Revolutionary Alliance (one of whom was Song Jiaoren). However, the nature of the ministries they were assigned (Justice, Education, Agriculture, Industry) made their participation more or less symbolic. The portfolio for War, crucially important in the disturbed context of the time, did not go to Huang Xing. The many conflicts that soon arose between the President and his Prime Minister led to the departure of the latter in mid-June and, soon after, to the collapse of the government. After this, the revolutionaries refused to take part in any coalition cabinet, and meanwhile Yuan Shikai opposed the formation of a politically homogeneous collection of ministers, favoring competence as the sole criterion for their selection. Thus prevented from exerting any pressure on the executive, the influence of the revolutionaries, if it was to remain legal, could only be developed through Parliament.

In the spring of 1912, the Chinese political scene, as reflected by Parliament, was both fragmented and unstable. In accordance with the regulations of the March Constitution, the number of members of Parliament had been increased to over one hundred, and this had weakened the Revolutionary Alliance. The assembly was dominated by constitutionalists and bureaucrats from the old consultative National Assembly (established in 1910 by the reforming empire), and a number of dissidents from the Revolutionary Alliance had joined them. The members of this Parliament, at first split into many tiny groups of uncertain definition, had eventually, in the course of 1912, grouped themselves into two main parties, the Republican Party (Gonghedang) and the Democratic Party (Minzhudang). Both were radically hostile to the revolutionaries, on account of old personal rivalries more than ideological differences, and their professed attachment to republican institutions was becoming tempered by a leaning toward enlightened despotism, which Yuan Shikai would soon turn to his advantage. In such a situation, it was to be Song

Jiaoren's task to reorganize, then transform the Revolutionary Alliance into a majority party capable of imposing its policies through the parliamentary vote.

As we have seen, in 1909–10 the Revolutionary Alliance, having splintered into various currents, had almost totally disintegrated. The presence of the Alliance in the 1911 revolution hardly made itself felt at all except through the role played by the Central China Bureau and thanks to the intervention of the activists of Hubei-Hunan and the lower Yangzi. The success of the insurrection, the return of Sun Yat-sen, and his election to the provisional presidency encouraged the reestablishment of a measure of consensus between the factions and the reemergence of the Alliance as a unified organization. The two thousand delegates assembled at what amounted to a refoundation congress in Nanking on January 22, 1912, renewed their commitment to the doctrine of the People's Three Principles, entrusted power to a collective leadership dominated by the personality of Song Jiaoren, and considered the problem of changing the Alliance from a clandestine revolutionary organization into an open political party. Hu Hanmin, who in December 1911 had vainly advised Sun Yat-sen to install himself in Canton, was convinced that the revolution was not yet over and that the Alliance should remain an instrument of armed struggle and subversion. Song Jiaoren believed, on the contrary, that now that the military phase of the seizure of power was over, the Revolutionary Alliance should win recognition as an official formation and should take part in national political life in accordance with the modalities provided for in the Constitution.

Song Jiaoren thus continued to work for openness, as he had consistently done ever since 1910, in Shanghai, at the head of his newspaper the *People's Stand* and through many operations of mediation between the provincial assemblies (dominated by their gentry and local elites) and the revolutionaries, during the uprisings of 1911. But he met stiff resistance. Sun's Cantonese entourage accused him of being "nothing but Yuan's yes-man." The refounded Revolutionary Alliance remained attached to its original objectives, reaffirmed and even radicalized at a further congress held in March 1912. It wanted to ensure national unity, develop local government, apply a socialist program, make education compulsory, install equality between the sexes, fight for the international status of China—and so on.

However, from April 1912 on, the position of the Revolutionary Alliance was weakened by the transfer of the government to Peking and by Sun's resignation. In Parliament, the majority had swung to the Republican Party led by Li Yuanhong. But that party could not be depended upon to control Yuan Shikai's actions or to force him to "knuckle under or resign." Song Jiaoren therefore returned to his plan to open up the Revolutionary Alliance, proposing an amalgamation between it and various small moderate republican parties. This time the project received the agreement of Sun Yat-sen, Huang Xing, and other revolutionary leaders who were alarmed by the increasingly overt ambitions of Yuan Shikai.

The Guomindang held its foundation congress on August 25, 1912. Sun Yat-sen presided over the executive committee, with Huang Xing at his side. But the real leader of the party was its Number Three, Song Jiaoren. The rallying of the gentry and wealthy merchants was achieved thanks to the moderation of its programs, from which Song had deleted the "people's livelihood" and equality between the sexes. On the other hand, Song had managed to extend the social bases of the party by winning the support of some of the local elites who had ensured the success of the rebellions and secessions of the autumn of 1911. While some members of the old Revolutionary Alliance continued to cry treason, Song was preparing to mobilize the party and win the first national elections.[25]

The provisional constitution of March 1912 had stipulated that elections should be organized before January 1, 1913, to designate members of the National Assembly (formed of a Senate and a Chamber of Deputies) and to renew the members of the provincial assemblies. Despite the restrictions that limited the vote, these elections truly did constitute a national consultation. More than three hundred political parties and organizations took part in it. There were 40 million registered electors, twenty times as many as for the elections to the provincial assemblies in 1909. The political debate was open and free and was recorded by the press. In many respects, this poll seems to have been more democratic and more meaningful than any that followed.

The shattering victory of the Guomindang was all the more remarkable on that account. The organizer of this victory was Song Jiaoren. During the months when the operations for getting out the vote were taking place (December 1912–February 1913), Song made use of the Guomindang to mobilize the local elites. He himself took part in the electoral campaign, organizing many meetings in Hunan (his native province), Hubei, and the lower Yangzi valley. In his speeches, he attacked the politics of Yuan Shikai, showing that he was incapable both of resolving the financial problem and of preventing the detachment and independence of (outer) Mongolia. He argued for a system of ministerial responsibility, for the election of provincial governors, and for regional autonomy. His message was well received by the elites, whose political awareness was rooted in their commitment to community interests.

The electoral success of the Guomindang designated Song Jiaoren as Prime Minister. It was with that position and with the support of Parliament that Song was intending to obtain Yuan's submission and take the direction of the country in hand.

The assassins sent by Yuan to the Shanghai railway station on March 19, 1913, put an end to the irresistible rise of Song Jiaoren. They also put an end to the most vigorous attempt at parliamentary democracy that China has ever known. That attempt was carried through by the energy and political intelligence of a man barely thirty years old, a leader who had a remarkably modern air to the extent that he preferred collective leadership to personal power and placed his trust in institutions and parliamentary practice rather than in networks of personal relations. His attempt was also animated by the lessons learned in the course of the past decade: by the political thinking of radical intellectuals and by the great movement of social and political organization led by local elites. Finally, it coincided with an exceptional liberation of Chinese society. Echoed in the ever expanding press, the debates on the problems facing society and the principles of political organization ranged far beyond the framework of the parties and they ignited public opinion. Song Jiaoren's own contributions to those debates were essential, whether they addressed the matter of the role of Parliament, ministerial responsibility, or the balance to be maintained between the indispensable authority of the central power and the provinces' legitimate aspirations for autonomous government.

Subsequently, the nationalists were to criticize Song Jiaoren for his moderation, his alliances with the elites, and his abandonment of the most radical objectives of the Revolutionary Alliance. Even at that time, Hu Hanmin consistently opposed Song and his politician's politics in the name of a utopian radicalism that the constraints born of revolutionary success had done nothing to modify. But why was the voice of Sun Yat-sen not heard?

Loyalty to Yuan Shikai and the Deferment of Socialism

Sun Yat-sen's withdrawal in the spring of 1912 was prompted by a desire to preserve national unity and to prevent foreign invasion. It may also have reflected the real balance of forces—in particular armed forces—between the North and the South.[26] But what is the explanation for Sun Yat-sen's eclipse in the following year? And for his reiterated support of Yuan Shikai on a visit to Peking in the autumn of 1912? Why did he give up all opposition? Although he never rejected or criticized the action of Song Jiaoren, he never associated himself with it. Was that out of a repugnance for the order of power-sharing and collective leadership, or was it out of loyalty to a socialist ideal that his own entourage continued to recommend most vociferously? Did the exhausted fighter allow himself to be seduced by all the official pomp or was it that he preferred to escape from a situation that he could not control, taking refuge in his own utopian ideas and the elaboration of huge development plans?

After the fall of Tang Shaoyi's cabinet, in June 1912, relations between Yuan Shikai and Parliament became strained. To dissipate the unease, Yuan Shikai invited the southern leaders to meet him in Peking. When Sun Yat-sen arrived in the capital, on August 24, a magnificent official reception was held for him: "All the troops [form] a guard of honour when he passes. He [is] received like a king. He has [been given] as a residence a palace built in the European style, designed for the reception of visiting sovereigns and princes." During these two weeks, Sun Yat-sen was treated solely to "the joys of triumph." He took part in many public meetings, "speaking directly to the people, to inform it of its rights, to rekindle its patriotism." Thousands of admirers flocked to hear him. "His fame [surrounds] him like a halo which [seems] to radiate a magic influence on to the crowd."[27] Sun Yat-sen and Huang Xing, who had joined him in Peking, held huge banquets, with exquisite fare prepared by the presidential kitchens. The princes of the imperial family were invited and took the opportunity to declare their support for the Republic.

In between the official functions and festivities, Sun Yat-sen was continuing to meet with Yuan Shikai. In the course of his stay in Peking (from August 24 to September 20), the revolutionary leader had thirteen meetings with President Yuan Shikai, some of which lasted for several hours. The most diverse questions were tackled: industrial development, defense, foreign affairs, even agrarian reform. Sun Yat-sen was somewhat surprised to discover that Yuan Shikai seemed to understand his own political views very well and that their "ideas were more or less the same." After Sun returned to Shanghai, he summed up his impressions in a speech addressed to the local office of the

Guomindang: "I believe [President Yuan] is really a man of ability. . . . I definitely believe in his sincerity. . . . His mind is also very clear. He understands world problems quite well. His ideas are also quite new, though the way he governs is rather old-fashioned. . . . President Yuan is just the right man."[28]

The seal was set upon this consensus by a joint announcement published on September 25, 1912, proposing an eight-point program: a centralized government, demilitarization, an open door to foreign capital, reconciliation between the parties, and political stability. Some observers thought the Republic was entering upon a phase of consolidation. Was that Sun Yat-sen's view? Did the triumphal reception he received in Peking heal the wounds received in 1894 from the failure of his journey to Tianjin and the hoped-for interview with Li Hongzhang? Whatever the case may be, now that he was recognized and lauded by the establishment, he seems to have turned away from politics. The lengthy task implied by the consolidation of the regime did not interest him; he preferred to pass the responsibility to others. He would turn his efforts to a field that he considered far more important, that of social and economic modernization: "Having finished the task of bringing about a political revolution, I am now devoting my thought and my energies to the reconstruction of the country in its social, industrial and commercial conditions."[29] However, this social revolution yet to be achieved was no longer envisaged by Sun Yat-sen in quite the same terms as before 1911.

In 1913, Yuan Shikai was to blame the resumed civil war on Sun Yat-sen, accusing him of having fomented trouble in the name of socialism and equality. At about the same time, Charles Albert, the French socialist, would be asking, "While they held power, why did the Chinese revolutionaries not make the most of it to carry through a few major social reforms?"[30]

Yet Sun Yat-sen's message had not changed: it was that of a moderate socialist seeking, not to redistribute wealth or to get the "have-nots" to rise up against the "haves," but rather to protect China against imperialist monopolies and capitalistic speculations, to ensure a balanced development, beneficial to all social classes, and thereby to prevent the emergence of an industrial proletariat ready to wreak violent revenge. On his tour of Guangdong in the spring of 1912, Sun repeatedly declared: "Ours is a socialist republic and we intend to follow socialistic principles. All the leaders are genuine socialists."[31] The revolutionary leader then proceeded to continue to recommend agrarian reform à la Henry George to his Cantonese audiences.

Nevertheless, it is clear that in practice Sun did sacrifice the immediate implementation of social reforms to unity and peace both internal and external. At any rate, in the summer of 1912, he did not publicly condemn the Guomindang's abandonment of the principle of the people's livelihood. And through his silence he seemed to lend his approval to the reduction of socialism to a project of industrial development piloted by the state and based upon the generalization of education and reform of the fiscal system—the form of socialism, in short, that had allowed the new Guomindang party to win the support of the elites in favor of modernization. Subsequently, hagiographers of Sun Yat-sen were to plead the constraints of the circumstances and cast doubt upon the wholeheartedness of his rallying to the Guomindang's state-controlled modernizing program. In truth, Sun Yat-sen's behavior, whether confused or ambiguous, provides ample grounds for both theses.

Having sought in vain for alternative solutions, Sun Yat-sen and Huang Xing agreed to the Guomindang program and were even willing to act as patrons of the new party. But the Guangdong militants, following Hu Hanmin, refused to rally to it. These remained faithful to the Revolutionary Alliance and its program, which they tried to put into practice, making the most of the large measure of autonomy, or quasi-independence, then enjoyed by the southern provinces. Hu Hanmin did not trust Yuan Shikai at all, disapproved of the formation of the Guomindang, and remained determined to consolidate the revolution and socialism at least in his own province, where the Revolutionary Alliance had come to power, at least until such time as circumstances would allow the experiment to be extended to the entire country. For Hu, the fall of the imperial regime did not signal the success of the revolution. Though the North had rallied to the Republic, the military governor of Guangdong remained faithful to the strategy of a southern base as defined a few years earlier by Sun Yat-sen, even if Sun himself now seemed to prefer a policy in the national interest.

Surrounded by former Tokyo students, such as Zhu Zhixin and Liao Zhongkai (1878–1925), and local activists such as Chen Jionming, Hu Hanmin formed a provincial government with a program directly inspired by the objectives of the Revolutionary Alliance: socialism, agrarian reform in the Henry George manner, international equality, and the struggle against imperialism, to which were added a number of more concrete aims: universal education, equality for women, compulsory military service, the democratization of the army, and so on. This Young China depended on the support of modest townsfolk—shopkeepers, employees, teachers, students, journalists, discontented former officials—all of whom the Revolutionary Alliance worked hard to mobilize. The Cantonese section of the Revolutionary Alliance refused to dissolve itself and merge with the Guomindang, and kept up a very active party life, publishing its own newspaper and holding many meetings.

Matching their actions to their words, the new leaders of Guangdong embarked upon a policy of radical change. They wanted to sweep away tradition, free individuals from all impediments, and launch them "upon the conquest of wealth." They had temple statues destroyed, discontinued the teaching of the Confucian Classics in schools, favored mixed education, ordered houses to be disinfected after deaths, fixed the liquidation of accounts for the end of every three months (instead of, as traditionally, at the time of the great festivals of the lunar calendar), and considered making monogamy compulsory. "There is too much of the past within these walls," lamented these lovers of the future, impatient to set up a new Chicago in the place of Canton.[32] They prepared a program of major public works; the creation of roads, tramway lines, drainage systems, covered markets. They even tried to apply the agrarian reform written into the program of the Revolutionary Alliance.

In July 1912, the provincial government launched a major operation involving the exchange of title deeds to property for deeds fixing the market value of the land. In accordance with the procedure recommended by Henry George, the determination of that value was left to the landowners themselves. The final purpose of this was to fix a proportional land tax or, if necessary, a takeover of the land by the authorities for public use. But the absenteeism of landlords, many of whom were overseas Chinese living abroad, hampered the operation. Pressed by financial needs, the utopians turned sectarian. Having initially abolished taxes, they then reintroduced a fiscal system of an inquisitorial and crushing nature, and confiscated the property of guilds and associations. Panic-stricken gentry and wealthy merchants departed to seek refuge in Hong Kong or Macao.

Did the Revolutionary Alliance of Guangdong try to get Sun Yat-sen to sanction their policy? They may well have, for Sun visited Canton at the end of April 1912. He received an extremely warm welcome from many different social circles which, at banquet after banquet, acclaimed his speeches. Even the Catholic missionaries feted the revolutionary leader "to peals of bells and the sound of the fanfare of the Sacred Heart," and the Bishop of Canton, "bemitred and carrying the cross," stepped up to the altar to lead a *Te Deum* in his honor.[33]

Sun delivered speech after speech. At a banquet held in his honor by the editors of nineteen Canton newspapers, he returned to the theme of agrarian reform, which ever since 1905 had constituted a key piece in his system:

> In the first place, it will be necessary to open offices to record all the title deeds to land and receive the land taxes. . . . Secondly, the government will reserve the right to pronounce upon expropriation, for public use, of all necessary land . . . so the first thing to do is to increase land taxes in proportion to the value declared by the landowners. It will no doubt be objected that I am increasing the charges that weigh upon the people, but my reply to that is that I am, at a stroke, abolishing all indirect levies, taxes, and charges. . . .
>
> Most of the money received will be used for the development of public instruction, all children will be obliged to attend school from the age of eight onward. Generous scholarships will be given. Next, a retirement fund will be set up for old people who, after the age of fifty, will have to rest. Think together for yourselves of ideas for humanitarian and national works to which the republican state should commit itself.[34]

Hu Hanmin, who wanted Sun's support, was one of his most loyal collaborators. Many family links and ties of friendship bound Sun to his native province, as did the memory of his political struggles there, which went back to 1895. But since the revolution, Sun Yat-sen had been thinking of his own future purely in terms of a national destiny and of the future of China solely in terms of national unity. He now took no interest in the peripheral power base that Guangdong represented, and he had no desire to tie in his lot with that of a marginal group of militants. The only concrete help that he gave Hu Hanmin's government was to rid him of the opposition of Sun Mei.

Sun Yat-sen's brother had become a dissident. After his many years of loyal service to the revolutionary cause, he had been hoping to acquire an important post in the Cantonese provisional government. There was, after all, such a thing as family solidarity. But for Sun Yat-sen, as we have seen, that solidarity operated strictly one-way, exclusively in his own interest. So he vetoed the appointment so much desired by his brother. Since then, Sun Mei had been living in Macao, where he ran a dissident branch of the Revolutionary Alliance and where, with the financial support of the Cantonese merchants who had taken refuge in the port, he was trying to enlist bandit leaders whom the success of the revolution had put out of work. The Canton authorities were fearful of collusion between Sun Mei and the Peking government. A visit to Macao by Sun Yat-sen on June 22 was enough to restore order to the situation.

Apart from that gesture, which was a family as much as a political matter, Sun Yat-sen's contribution to Cantonese radicalism remained purely verbal. Was that why Cantonese radicalism failed? In truth, the resolute hostility of the big merchants and the gentry probably played a far more determining role in bringing about the collapse of the Cantonese Revolutionary Alliance and its rallying to the Guomindang at the beginning of 1913.

Nevertheless, Sun's apparent indifference to this provincial experiment should not lead us to conclude that he was no longer interested in active socialism. The part that he took in the debates of the Chinese Socialist Party (Zhongguo shehuidang), in October 1912, on the contrary testifies to his abiding desire to turn his aspirations for equality and justice into political reality.

The Chinese Socialist Party emerged in November 1911, out of a small study group created in Shanghai a few months earlier. Its founder and leader, Jiang Kanghu (1885–1945), was a young scholar who knew Japan well, had traveled in the West, and defended a humanist, generous-hearted socialism that appealed for morality and education rather than a class struggle. Jiang had been strongly influenced by anarchism and this remained vibrant within the party, finding expression in, for example, attacks against the family and insistence upon equality between the sexes. The intellectual and social fervor of the immediate aftermath of the revolution stimulated the growth of the new party, which was soon 400,000 members strong.

Sun Yat-sen played no part in the creation of the Socialist Party, but he seems to have given it a sympathetic welcome and some financial aid in the spring of 1912. After his resignation, in April, and while the former Revolutionary Alliance was preparing to give way to the Guomindang, Sun may even have considered assuming the leadership of the Socialist Party. At any rate, he was present in Shanghai when the second annual congress of the party was held there in mid-October, and he addressed the congress at length in three speeches (October 14, 15, 16) each lasting about four hours. The texts of those speeches were published in the press and later collected in a pamphlet entitled *Lectures on Socialism*; its thirty-three pages constitute Sun Yat-sen's most explicit profession of faith at this period.

Held at arm's length by the Guomindang, whose electoral preoccupations he did not share, and cut off from the Cantonese radicals by his collaboration with Yuan Shikai, was Sun Yat-sen hoping to make the Socialist Party a new instrument of influence and power? To judge from the first of the three speeches, it might well be thought so. In it, he exhorted the Chinese socialists to organize themselves into a proper political party, as their European and American comrades had done. The Socialist Party, which "has been formed under a democratic regime . . . should have no activities outside the political sphere and should from this day forth organize itself as a powerful political party and, from its position of political strength, apply its socialist program."[35]

What was the position envisaged for this party on the Chinese scene? Was it to merge into the single great party that Sun sometimes seemed to yearn for? Or was it to become integrated into bipartism—also a possibility sometimes recommended by the versatile leader? Sun did not explain himself. In his second speech, he returned to the more familiar theme of a pacific transition to socialism under state direction, and he rounded off his thoughts with a series of philosophical musings, seemingly inspired by Rousseau, on the theme of the earth, which "supported the human race" and was "the property of society," and on machines and inventions, fruits of the human genius that nobody had any right to appropriate as private property.[36]

The socialist ideal was thus still very much alive for Sun Yat-sen in that autumn of 1912. His expression of it even acquired a lyrical quality seldom evident in his earlier writings. But if he was indeed intent upon a political maneuver, it certainly misfired. Sun Yat-sen's exhortations to the party to politicize itself were met with resistance by a membership composed of young people sensitive to anarchist influences and hostile to any hierarchy, who set more store by the practice of virtue (vegetarianism, chastity, self-sacrifice) than by political mobilization. The second congress ended with these anarchist elements splitting away, after which the party declined rapidly until, in the summer of 1913, it was banned by Yuan Shikai.

After his resignation, Sun Yat-sen thus seems to have been isolated, stripped of initiative. He distanced himself from the moderate and electorist currents of the former Revolutionary Alliance and also from the radical Cantonese Left and the young progressive intelligentsia. He refused to take part in the experiment of real socialism upon which Hu Hanmin had embarked in Canton, and he failed to mobilize around himself the scattered members of the Socialist Party, committed to idealism and self-sacrifice. He seemed paralyzed by the loyalty he had deliberately promised to Yuan Shikai, a loyalty that he considered to be essential for the construction of the Republic. Yet, to judge by his speeches, he had not renounced socialism. Perhaps the choice of utopianism that he now made was essentially an implicit recognition of his inability to resolve his own contradictions.

Big-gun-Sun (Sun dabao)

Big-gun-Sun: this was the nickname given to the Sun Yat-sen with dreams of constructing some 100,000 miles of railways, costing billions of dollars. A lot of fuss about nothing, in the view of his compatriots. Delusions of grandeur, scoffed the foreigners.

To avoid the social conflicts the ravages of which he had seen in the West, Sun Yat-sen wanted to stimulate industrial development of a kind that would bring labor and capital together instead of setting them in opposition. But industrialization presupposed the establishment of a modern transport system. It was to this concrete task that Sun Yat-sen now decided to devote himself. It was in Yuan Shikai's interest to encourage the project: on September 9, 1912, Yuan appointed Sun Yat-sen Director of Railways, with funds of 30,000 yuan a month and full powers to "set up plans for a national railway network" and to negotiate with foreigners for the financial backing.

One week later, Sun Yat-sen left Peking in a special train, to visit the northern provinces and begin to set up plans for the future railway lines. It was certainly a strange progress—in a carriage that had belonged to the dowager empress Cixi, with yellow curtains and trimmings of blue velvet embroidered with gold dragons and peonies. Sun was accompanied by a throng of fund-raisers and officials of the new government, among them his old friend from Shanghai, the former pastor Charlie Soong, whom he had appointed as treasurer for the railways. Charlie Soong's eldest daughter, Ai-ling, was also on the train, organizing Sun's English secretariat and not to be confused with other pretty girls whose sole function was to provide company for the travelers. This extremely disparate team also included the Australian journalist William H. Donald, who since the Revolution had attached himself to the southerners.

The convoy made many stops. At each station, Sun Yat-sen was greeted by a band, took tea with the local dignitaries, and made speeches. While the train was in motion, he conversed with his friends and advisers or busied himself planning the future railway network. In a letter to G. E. Morrison, another Australian journalist, who had become an adviser to Yuan Shikai, Donald provides an unforgettable picture of Sun absorbed in his railway visions:

> A large map of China was on the wall opposite him. A tea table held a bowl of water, a packet of cotton wool, a Chinese writing brush and an ink slab. . . . "Oh," said Dr. Sun . . . "I propose to build two hundred thousand *li* of railways in ten years. . . . I am marking them on this map. You see the thick lines running from one provincial capital to another? Well, they will be trunk lines. The others are laterals and less important connections."
>
> "Tsk, tsk!" Sun would say, and he would take a piece of cotton, dip it in the water, wipe out a crooked line and mark a straight one in its place. This went on every morning for days, the little railway builder sitting before his map, making a new line here, straightening this one, straightening that one. . . . At last, all the capitals were linked by trunk lines, all the prefectural cities connected by smaller lines and there were branches in all directions.
>
> "Doctor, that line circling Tibet can never be built. You can build it with brush and ink—and that's all. Some of the passes over which your railway would run are fifteen thousand feet high."
>
> Sun arched his eyebrows. "There are roads, aren't there," he said, more as a statement of fact than a question.
>
> "Not roads, Doctor. Just narrow, rough trails. They go spiraling up into the sky. They're steep, so steep a strong yak can hardly climb them." "Where there's a road, a railway can be built," Sun answered softly.[37]

Sun Yat-sen was counting on foreign capital to finance his network. He would need no less than sixteen billion francs, if we are to believe the figure mentioned in an interview that he gave to the French journalist Fernand Farjenel. It was to seek the loans necessary for the realization of his project that Sun Yat-sen left for Japan, on February 11, 1913. He was still there when the news of Song Jiaoren's assassination reached him.

A BELATED REAROUSAL: SUN YAT-SEN AND THE FAILURE OF THE SECOND REVOLUTION, 1913

The news of the assassination of his old comrade Song Jiaoren jolted Sun Yat-sen out of the political passivity into which he had withdrawn the previous spring. The vigor of his rearousal matched the enormity of the provocation and the indignation provoked by the crime. It was also, possibly in particular, explained by the influences Sun Yat-sen had encountered during his stay in Japan. He had been received there as the honorable representative of the Chinese Republic. But the Japanese with whom he held many discussions had applied themselves to undermining his hopes of cooperating with Yuan Shikai. They sought to get him to share their growing hostility toward the Chinese president and urged him to make a new show of revolutionary intransigence.

The intransigence which, following Song Jiaoren's death, prompted Sun Yat-sen to call for the armed intervention of the southern forces against Peking contrasted sharply with the moderation of the other revolutionary leaders. Most of them, even the most radical, such as the Cantonese Hu Hanmin, rallied to Huang Xing's point of view and at first favored an institutional and legal solution to the crisis. They were fearful of the imbalance of military forces, did not wish to be seen as spoiling for civil war, and, above all, rejected any idea of collusion with Japan. The extremely lively debates that followed in the revolutionary camp highlighted all that would be politically at stake in a North-South conflict and also all the contradictions between, on the one hand, a revolutionary nationalism at last liberated from the anti-Manchu commitment and, on the other, the pan-Asianism that was favored by Sun Yat-sen but was regarded more generally as the Trojan horse of Japanese imperialism.

The divisions among the revolutionaries gave Yuan Shikai time to prepare for the clash. The "reorganization" loan that he had obtained in April 1913 from the International Consortium, without even informing Parliament of it, enabled him to strengthen his military forces. When the Second Revolution broke out in July 1913, Yuan Shikai had no difficulty in crushing the movement, which was poorly organized, poorly armed, and lacked popular support. Sun's belated jolt of reactivation succeeded merely in hastening the establishment of a dictatorship and forcing the revolutionaries once again into exile and impotent opposition.

Sun's Journey to Japan, the Prelude to the Second Revolution

When he arrived in Japan on February 13, 1913, Sun Yat-sen received a particularly warm welcome. He was treated not just as a high official of the Chinese Republic but as almost a head of state. He traveled in a special railway coach, was accommodated in the very best hotels, and met with the principal bankers, court dignitaries, ministers, and former ministers. "He has been treated with probably greater honour than has ever before been shown to the representative of any other country not of princely rank."[38]

The relations established in the days of exile and the aid received for earlier revolutionary activities do not suffice to account for this dazzling reception. In fact, Sun's old fighting comrades were not at all in the forefront of the Japanese who clustered round him in the spring of 1913. Miyazaki Torazō was hardly mentioned. The friends from the bad old days effaced themselves before the bureaucrats, the financiers, and the great industrialists.

The Tokyo government had fallen into line on the policy of support for Yuan Shikai adopted by the great Western powers, mainly on the initiative of Great Britain. However, there were many Japanese political and economic leaders who were worried by the declining role played by their country in China and also by the new Chinese president's open hostility. Furthermore, they deplored Japan's membership of the Consortium (dating from June 1912). The liberty of action previously enjoyed by Japanese firms had suffered from it. National economic interests would be better served by direct military or diplomatic intervention. The objective would be to topple Yuan Shikai, either by force or by subversion, and to replace his centralizing and modernizing regime with regional powers from which a Japan unencumbered by a British alliance could obtain considerable concessions.

Sun Yat-sen's visit came at just the right moment to give substance to these plans. How could the magnificence of his reception and the solicitude of his hosts fail to dispose in their favor a man who, already in January 1912, when he presided over the provisional Republic in Nanking, had been prepared to agree to the extension of Japanese interests in southern and central China? In these circumstances, it was not hard for Sun Yat-sen and his hosts to find a common language. The thanks that Sun now expressed for past aid provided an opportunity to sketch in the possibilities of future collaboration, founded upon pan-Asian solidarity: "Japan is my second home . . . Japan, which I knew would prevent the European powers and America from dividing the melon among themselves. . . . The patriots of your country have led and taught me and I deem Japan my second fatherland and your statesmen my mentors. China awaits your help."[39]

As Sun saw it, pan-Asianism legitimized the special privileges that Japan might be granted in China. The revolutionary leader denounced the "imperialism which may be called the barbarous civilization of Europe and America" and expressed his wish that "Asia be governed by Asiatics."[40]

In more concrete fashion, Sun Yat-sen negotiated with Shibusawa Eichi (1840–1931), a leading Japanese businessman, the founder of many firms in China, who two decades earlier had financed the invasion of Korea and paved the way for its annexation by Japan. These negotiations began on February 24 at the headquarters of the Mitsui company. Their object was to create the Industrial Company of China (Zhongguo xingye gongsi); its purpose would be to exploit Chinese mines and other raw materials with the help of Japanese companies such as Mitsui and Mitsubishi. The chairmanship of the company would fall to Sun while the vice-chairmanship and real management would be the responsibility of a Japanese diplomat and entrepreneur, Kuruchi Tetsukichi (1870–1944). This was a chance for the Japanese to relaunch their attempt to take control of Chinese mining resources that the shareholders of the Hanyeping Company had foiled the previous year.

Would the assassination of Song Jiaoren provide Sun with opportunity to recover the political initiative and the Japanese businessmen with the chance to implement their plans of expansion on the Chinese mainland? That would depend on the attitude of the other revolutionary leaders and the military commanders who controlled the provinces of southern and central China.

Disagreement Between Sun Yat-sen and Huang Xing

The assassination of Song Jiaoren was the first of a series of violent actions by means of which Yuan Shikai would manage, within a few months, to impose his dictatorship. One of the main reasons for Yuan's success was the support given him by the foreign powers. So far that support had been discreet, but on April 26, 1913, it was openly manifested with the granting of a loan of 25 million pounds sterling by the International Consortium. The loan was in principle intended for the reorganization of the Chinese administration. Violating Article 19 of the provisional Constitution of 1912, which obliged the government to submit all financial measures to Parliament for its approval, Yuan Shikai signed this contract on his own authority. Moreover, he certainly intended to use the funds to consolidate his own power, by force if necessary. Although the new Parliament (set up by the elections of the previous year) manifested its opposition in a massive vote, it deterred neither Yuan nor the Consortium. The danger of a dictatorship loomed clearly. Sun Yat-sen issued a solemn warning to the foreign powers: "This tyrannical and unconstitutional action had added to the intense indignation aroused by the murder of Sung Chi'iao-jen [Song Jiaoren]. . . . A terrible revolution seems inevitable."[41]

Since his return to Shanghai on March 25, Sun Yat-sen had been urging an open break with Peking and an armed confrontation with Yuan Shikai. He had no confidence at all in the efficacy of a parliamentary opposition exposed to the police pressure that the government could apply. He argued for the political and military mobilization of the provinces of the Center and the South, which he wanted to persuade to declare their independence and perhaps even create a separatist government.

But Sun Yat-sen's only power lay in his influence. Though he was nominally president, he did not control the Guomindang, whose organizational network was, besides, very loose. The leadership of the party was effected through the cooperation of a group of men among whom Sun Yat-sen appeared simply as *primus inter pares.* Some of these "barons," such as Sun himself and Huang Xing, owed their authority solely to their prestige and their revolutionary pasts. Others derived their power from their control of a territorial base or of regional armed forces, as did Hu Hanmin, the military governor of Guangdong, and Li Liejun (1882–1946), the military governor of Jiangxi. To launch an offensive against Yuan, Sun Yat-sen needed the consent and active collaboration of all these leaders. But with the exception of Li Liejun, they were all extremely reluctant. To be sure, they were aware of the threat that Yuan Shikai represented to the institutions of the Republic, but they were unwilling, at least for the time being, to resort to arms to stop him. They pointed to the unequal balance of forces: the southern troops were ill-prepared, fewer in number, and inferior in quality to those of the North. They also invoked reasons of principle: to declare the independence of the southern provinces and to take up arms again against the troops of Peking would be to strike against national unity and against the very existence of the Republic. It had been born amid the violence of a revolution; but in 1911 that violence had been justified, for it was founded upon the nation's unanimous aspiration to recover its identity. In the spring of 1913, violence might appear to be partisan, made to serve a struggle for power and therefore dishonoring for whoever resorted to it.

This whole debate brought back to the surface the old problem of the relations, at once contradictory and complementary, between the China of the South, looking out to sea and dominated by the forces of change, and the China of the North, open to the steppes, the symbol and refuge of the imperial ideology of hegemony and centralization. However attached they were to the republican idea, the democrats of the South were, in 1913, reluctant to attack "the strongman of the North," the embodiment of the continuity and unity of the nation. Faced with the Peking regime, the only other solution was independence for the provinces or possibly a separatist Southern Republic—either way, division for the country. How could patriots countenance this? And what would be the reaction of public opinion, the opinion of the elites who had made the 1911 revolution possible? The overthrow of the Manchu dynasty had left intact the powerful ideological bases of the imperial order. The precepts of Confucian morality continued to rule people's consciences, even those of revolutionaries. The virtuous men who had risen up against the Manchu invaders would be nothing but troublemakers if they rebelled against the Chinese Republic. This argument, which Yuan Shikai had promoted for propaganda purposes, had struck a chord among his adversaries. It was clear, furthermore, that in the event of a new civil war the foreign powers would abandon the neutrality they had observed in 1911. What they wanted was order and they had already decided which camp to back.

Sun Yat-sen thus found himself isolated when he argued for his policy of intransigence. Later, in a letter to Huang Xing, he reminded him of the meeting of March 26 in which the principal leaders of the Guomindang had welcomed their president back from Japan and discussed how they should react to the "Song affair" (*Song 'an*):

> You said that we were now a Republic and that laws were now effective. You recommended that we should adopt a calm attitude and abide by a legal solution. . . . You thought that the forces of the South were not strong enough and that war, once declared, would inevitably bring about great calamities. I was not in agreement with you then, but you would not listen to me.[42]

Did Sun Yat-sen's resolution stem from his greater political foresight, as the official historiography suggests? Perhaps he finally did lose his illusions (*huan xiang*) and came to understand, before the rest of them, that only force could halt Yuan Shikai in his advance on dictatorship. Also, possibly his attitude as

an overseas Chinese, alien and hostile to the Confucian world that had rejected him, made it easier for him to spurn a coherent ideology of an essentially imperial nature, based on centralization. His determination may also be
explained by the aid that he was counting on receiving from the Japanese. But
that very trust placed in Japan affronted the nationalism of other revolutionary leaders, who were inclined to regard it as positive betrayal. It was not a new
disagreement, but in the dramatic context of 1913, it took on a more acute
aspect.

Although the position of the Tokyo Ministry of Foreign Affairs was still
aligned with that of Great Britain and the International Consortium and a
high-ranking Japanese diplomat visiting China had already warned Sun Yat-
sen and Huang Xing of this, there were plenty of other important Japanese
figures or adventurers who were ready to support any opposition to the Peking
regime and who were urging Sun Yat-sen to make a break. In Tokyo, Ōkuma
Shigenobu and Inukai Ki were attacking Yuan Shikai for his policy of centralization, which they considered to be contrary to the tradition of autonomous
management by local elites, and were pleading for a loose federalism that
would favor the manifestation of democracy (and also, of course, the development of Japanese interests).

On the spot, in China, negotiations continued between Sun and his Japanese advisers, foremost among them Mori Kaku, one of the principal execu-
tives of the Mitsui company and the New Industrial Company of China. In
order to secure Japan's diplomatic or military aid, Sun Yat-sen was prepared,
successively, to make the yen valid tender on Chinese territory, to entrust to a
Sino-Japanese bank the management of the mines and railways in the provinces of central and southern China, and even to abandon Manchuria in
exchange for 20 million yen and equipment enough for two divisions in
weapons and other military supplies. Addressing his compatriots, whom he
wished to convince of the need for cooperation with Japan, Sun tirelessly
returned to the theme of Greater Asia, declaring, "I have realized that the
protestations of friendly sentiments of Japan are not superficial, but come
from the bottom of their hearts."[43] Sun's plan now contained two, mutually
supportive, projects: alliance with Japan, and war against Yuan: "If Japan
helps us, we shall be victorious," he maintained.[44]

The provocative behavior of Yuan Shikai, determined to make the most
of his position of strength and of the largesse provided by the Consortium, eventually made the southern revolutionaries adopt the policy of war

favored by Sun Yat-sen. But most of them did so reluctantly, and the disagreements between them aggravated the unfavorable balance of forces, leading to rapid defeat.

The Failure of the Second Revolution and the Flight of Sun Yat-sen

In two weeks, July 12–29, it was all over. Up until June the Guomindang had endeavored to temporize. It even declared itself ready to vote in favor of the Reorganization loan if only Yuan Shikai would submit it to Parliament for approval. But Yuan, very sure of himself, no longer wished to negotiate and instead initiated a trial of strength by sacking the military governors of Jiangxi, Anhui, and Guangdong. Although they had been officially appointed by Peking, these governors had really been installed by the revolution: either they had been elected by local gentry (from the provincial assemblies, the chambers of commerce, and so on) or they had been confirmed by them in posts that they had won by fighting for them. The illegal arrangement of the Reorganization loan had undermined the institution of Parliament, which, in spite of Song Jiaoren's efforts, had not yet managed to root itself in political practice and in which few Chinese, even among the revolutionaries, placed much trust. The battle to have the loan ratified by Parliament had thus taken on a mainly symbolic character. On the other hand, the Center's control over the provinces was an issue of major importance. By revoking the Guomindang governors, Yuan Shikai was threatening the territorial bases upon which the party's power was founded. To be sure, the Guomindang's control over those provinces could only operate with the frequently renegotiable collaboration of the governors themselves; but in the absence of more established organizational structures, that control, though indirect, remained the only material basis for the power of the Guomindang.

Peking's reassertion of its authority did more than simply exacerbate the strained relations between Yuan and the revolutionaries; it also called into question the autonomy won by the local elites, which Song Jiaoren and the Guomindang had sanctioned. But the defense of provincialism as the vector of democracy and nationalism, which had ensured the electoral success of the Guomindang in 1912, was in the following year no longer enough to mobilize the elites, disappointed by the performance of local representative institutions and now beginning to feel twinges of nostalgia for a unifying central power that provided funds and guaranteed public order. In 1913, the Guomindang was no longer able to count on the support of all those, such as dissatisfied officials, merchants, and the military, who had risen up against the Manchu court in 1911. It was reduced to its own forces, that is, the troops controlled by its militants and sympathizers.

In early July, the governors revoked by Yuan Shikai declared the independence of their respective provinces: Jiangxi, Anhui, and Guangdong. With varying degrees of reluctance, other provinces followed suit: Hunan, Fujian, and Sichuan. Hostilities broke out in Jiangxi on July 12, then spread to Shanghai and northern Jiangsu, where the crack troops of Nanking, under the command of Huang Xing, were defeated by Yuan's soldiers. On July 29, Huang Xing decided to evacuate Nanking, the keystone of the southerners' military strategy. Sporadic fighting continued. Once abandoned, Nanking held out against the northerners' attacks for another month. During that time, Sun Yat-sen left for Japan, where he landed on August 8 and was soon joined by Huang Xing and the other revolutionary leaders. By early September Yuan Shikai had crushed all the rebellions. He crowned his victory by getting Parliament to elect him president for five years and inaugurated his mandate with a dazzling ceremony on October 10, 1913, the second anniversary of the 1911 revolution. Sun Yat-sen, the founder of the Republic, was now nothing but an exile.

Whose fault was it? the defeated wondered. Sun Yat-sen blamed Huang Xing's hesitations, which had divided the party and delayed the launching of an offensive against Yuan. And it is quite true that Huang Xing had always been doubtful of the outcome of a fight that he reckoned to be not just unequal but suicidal for the nation. His premature abandonment of Nanking reflected that pessimism. They *could* go on with the struggle, he had said, "Yet I think that it is a useless and ruinous struggle, and should we carry it to the bitter end, it will . . . despoil and devastate our fair land."[45]

An analysis of the situation fully justifies Huang Xing's reservations. Public opinion, that of the local elites, which had supported the insurgents of 1911, condemned those of 1913. Not that it harbored much sympathy for Yuan Shikai, but it did condemn violence and anarchy: "Since Shanghai is a trading port, not a battlefield . . . whatever party is the first to begin hostilities will be considered an enemy of the people."[46] Those are the terms in which the Shanghai Chamber of Commerce sent packing northerners and southerners alike and outlawed any rebellion.

It was Sun Yat-sen and the other revolutionary leaders who were generally considered to be the troublemakers in the conflict in which they opposed Yuan Shikai; and it was his consciousness of that responsibility that so paralyzed Huang Xing. But Sun Yat-sen was not bothered by that. He refused to recognize that in 1913 the weakness of the revolutionary ideology and organization was such that the alternative lay between Yuan or chaos. With no faith in the parliamentary system, Sun Yat-sen was content simply to call for an armed struggle against Yuan Shikai. "Tao Yuan!" (Down with Yuan!) was the simple slogan on the banners of the southern rebels.

The absence of any political perspective or ideological aspirations and the very personalization of the conflict and the predominant role played in it by individual affiliations, geographical solidarities, and personal allegiances or animosities reduced this Second Revolution to an armed clash between rival factions, a prelude to the era of the warlords. Taking into consideration the complexity created by the vastness of the Chinese territory, the movement of 1913 has more the air of a putsch than of a revolution. It was the military governors and the generals at the head of the troops who took the decisions. The rest was just a matter of money and soldiers.

Faced with the threat of dictatorship that Yuan Shikai's successive acts of violence introduced, Sun Yat-sen thus did in the end react. Scorning the mechanisms of institutional opposition, in which he had never believed, lacking the support of a real revolutionary party since he had made no attempt to organize one, and deprived by the fall of the Manchus of his main theme for popular mobilization, Sun Yat-sen was content to return to the insurrectional strategy and adventurist practices upon which he had depended so often before 1911. And as had been true then, the inadequacy of his military and financial resources led him to failure and exile.

Although his name is closely associated with the 1911 revolution, Sun Yat-sen affected the chain of events that led China from the imperial monarchy to the Republic hardly at all. What is more, his experience as a head of state and his acceptance by his country and its people, who acclaimed him, do not seem to have changed the nature of his political commitment. He still appears as an adventurer, a dreamer—and one not particularly skillful at using the power to which he laid claim. Behind the failure of this abortive revolution looms the failure of a leader who proved incapable of controlling, or even keeping up with the change for which he had yearned. He had not really bothered to define the modalities that would make it work or the orientation that it should adopt.

EIGHT

Crossing the Desert, 1913–1920

The failure of the 1911 revolution left Sun Yat-sen isolated and uncertain. Of all the crises he had weathered, that of the years 1913–20 was the most profound; and of all the setbacks he had known, that of the Second Revolution, of 1913, was the most dismaying. At the age of fifty, he found himself once again exiled in Japan, but no longer as the symbolic leader of an opposition full of hope. Now he was a refugee who had forfeited all credibility and authority, manipulated by Japanese agents and ignored by the rising forces of Young China—the radical intelligentsia and the nationalist masses. Vainly he sought in his conspirator's past for the recipe for new revolutionary successes.

The difficulties of his apparently shattered political career were now compounded by a personal and family crisis: Sun decided to leave his wife and remarry. His new wife was Song Qingling, a woman young enough to be his daughter; she was in fact the daughter of one of his best friends. To cope with this kind of crisis, Chinese society offered concubinage, while Western society offered divorce. But Sun and his new wife, as westernized Chinese and Christians, were positioned midway between these two societies: neither the ancient customs of the one nor the legal practices of the other could help them. As a result, Sun's remarriage scandalized both the foreign missionary establishment and the Chinese elites of the treaty ports.

Sun, seemingly unperturbed, continued to declare his confidence in the success of a new revolution that would rid China of the dictator Yuan Shikai. But when that revolution took place, in 1916, and the southern provinces rose up from the Protection of the Country (Huguo), it was not Sun who led the movement; indeed, he took almost no part in it at all. Never had the separation been so great between his words, still dynamic and optimistic, and his actions, increasingly marginal and cut off from what was taking place.

Following Yuan Shikai's death in June 1916, when China was beginning to sink into the chaos of internal wars, Sun threw himself into the fray, as one warlord among many others, but one who lacked both troops and a territorial base. The magic of his rhetoric, his references to the constitutional and republican ideology (over which he by no means held a monopoly), and foreign funds (which many of his rivals also enjoyed) were not enough to impose the military government that he headed as Grand Marshal, in Canton, in 1917. The Constitution Protection Movement (Hufa) to which he then tried to attach himself mobilized nothing but personal ambitions that competed with Sun's own and were better armed.

From 1918 to 1920, Sun stayed in the French Concession of Shanghai. He lived there as a studious recluse, uninvolved in the debates over the New Culture that were firing intellectual circles and untouched by the great nationalistic demonstrations that aroused the urban population at the time of the May Fourth Movement of 1919. Sun continued to meditate upon the reasons why the 1911 revolution had not borne fruit and to dream up postrevolutionary developments oriented totally toward economic modernization. In his *Plan for National Reconstruction* (*Jianguo fanglüe*), written at this time, he returned to a number of themes dear to his heart, describing, for example, the construction of an immense network of railways. But the utopia that, in 1912–13, had led the Director of the Railways astray now took on a new intellectual dimension. Liberated from the management of actions, Sun raised himself to a prophetic vision of the future. Had this adventurer and conspirator now found his true vocation in utopian socialism and theoretical philosophy?

THE NEW EXILE AND THE CRISIS OF
THE FIFTY-YEAR-OLD

Sun's low-key welcome when he arrived in Japan in early August 1913 was a far cry from his triumphal progress there a few months earlier as the Director of Railways representing the young Republic of China. His contacts and supporters melted away in official circles and business circles alike, for everyone was now backing the chances of Yuan Shikai.

The Balance Sheet of a Defeat

Sun was deeply depressed by what he considered to be the humiliating failure of 1913. Sun's comment, "There wasn't one party man killed in the battles of the Second Revolution,"[1] was not quite accurate, but it reflected his view of the betrayed revolution: it was the revolutionaries themselves who were mainly responsible for the defeat; they were guilty of indiscipline and "had acted independently." In other words, they had not followed the directives of Sun, the only one to see things clearly. The defeated leader set out his re-criminations in a letter to the revolutionaries of Southeast Asia, dated April 18, 1914: "During the period of the Nanking provisional government, although I had the honor to be president, I was no more than a puppet. I could decide nothing." That was a true assessment, but later the drift of the letter becomes more specious: if the revolutionaries had listened to Sun, they would have refused to keep the capital in Peking, and, above all, upon Song Jiaoren's death, they would have begun hostilities against Yuan immediately, in March 1913, thereby avoiding a delay that Sun, incorrectly, thought was the principal cause of the failure of the Second Revolution.[2]

Sun Yat-sen was living quite comfortably in Tokyo, but he did not have enough money to help his comrades in exile to feed and clothe themselves, keep themselves warm, or resume their political struggle. The several thousand Chinese revolutionaries who found themselves back in Tokyo in 1913 were a disunited bunch. Many were discouraged and believed that Yuan Shikai was now firmly established in power. "We are passing through a period of crisis." Huang Xing observed. Some decided to travel. Li Liejun, the former Guomindang governor of Jiangxi, went off to Paris. Not long after, Huang Xing left Tokyo for the United States.

Even before the Guomindang's dissolution by Yuan Shikai in November 1913, it had ceased to exist as a party. No leader had come forward to replace Song Jiaoren at its head and disagreements between its northern and southern organizers had multiplied, as they had even within those two factions. Although he was its titular president, Sun Yat-sen was never regarded by anyone, least of all by his enemies, as the head of the party. Before actually banning the party, Yuan Shikai had at first demanded that it expel from its ranks all the militants compromised by the Second Revolution; Huang Xing, Li Liejun, Chen Jiongming, and a number of others were all named, but no mention was made of Sun Yat-sen. Similarly, when Yuan decided to strike at the leadership of the opposition, he put a price of $10,000 on Huang Xing's head, but did not refer to Sun.

Ignored by his adversaries, Sun was also now deserted by his partisans. The disagreements between him and Huang Xing over the urgency of an armed uprising against Yuan were followed by a new clash over the principles upon which the revolutionary party should be reorganized. Sun's intransigence ruled out any compromise solutions. Huang Xing then left for the United States. Even the faithful Hu Hanmin was subjected to many fits of temper by his mentor, and the loyal Miyazaki now only paid rare visits to his old fighting comrade. Should we believe the diagnosis made by the banker and future Minister of Finance, Kong Xiangxi (H. H. Kung, 1881–1967)? He was at this period particularly well placed to observe Sun in Tokyo, since both were visiting one particular family there, namely, the Song, the one preparing to marry the elder daughter, the other the younger. Kong Xiangxi remarked: "Some think that his dangers and anxieties have affected his nervous system."[3] It is true that his testimony should perhaps be taken with a pinch of salt. It appears in a secret memorandum sent to G. E. Morrison, Yuan Shikai's adviser, which was designed to whitewash Kong, who had recently returned to China, from any suspicion of associating with the revolutionaries. However, the existence of a personal crisis is confirmed by the turn now taken by Sun Yat-sen's private life.

Sun Yat-sen and the Mid-life Demon

A man aged fifty, or almost, meets a beautiful young woman of twenty-three and decides to abandon his wife and children and rebuild his life with her. It is a common story. What is less common in this case is the personality of the heroine, Song Qingling, and also the fame of her family and the fact that it had been closely linked with Sun for the past twenty years. An elopement led up to a secret marriage, which the absence of a prior divorce condemned in Western eyes, while the absence of parental consent condemned it equally in Chinese eyes. The glare of scandal suddenly focused upon the private life of a politician whose history had until then involved solely his public career.

Chinese biographers are never inclined to evoke the private lives of public men. Virtually nothing is known of Sun's private life before this romantic episode. From his first marriage, arranged by his parents in his village, Sun Yat-sen had three children, one of whom was a son, Sun Fo (Sun Ke). But it was Sun's elder brother who looked after Lu Muzhen, his peasant wife, who moved to Hawaii as early as 1895, and his children. Sun, meanwhile, traveled, lived in Japan, where he entered into a number of liaisons, one of which produced a daughter whom he never acknowledged. In traditional China, marriage was a social contract. Sun had done his duty by ensuring the subsistence of his wife, through the generosity of his brother, just as she had done hers by giving birth to a son who would continue the line.

After the 1911 revolution, Sun Yat-sen moved his family to Shanghai, and he and his wife were reunited. Although excluded from Sun's public life, as was customary in traditional China, Lu Muzhen did mingle with some of the president's friends. Among these were the Song, who valued and respected her, in spite of her lack of education. After the 1913 failure, Lu Muzhen followed Sun Yat-sen to Tokyo, where the Song family also took refuge.

The revolutionaries of the early twentieth century had already experienced the sentimental frustrations that the younger generation of the May Fourth Movement of 1919 denounced with vehemence, condemning the system of arranged marriages and pleading for unions freely consented and founded upon mutual love. Among the first revolutionary generation, some tried to resolve this modern aspiration for a romantic union by resorting to the traditional concubinage. Thus Huang Xing took as his second wife the young militant who sheltered him and nursed him after the failure of the 1911 Canton uprising. It was she who, from then on, accompanied and assisted him in all his political activities, relegating to the shadows his first wife, who nevertheless retained her status and role and even gave birth to another child. But for Sun Yat-sen, the identity of his chosen loved one, who came from a modern, westernized bourgeois family of Shanghai, completely ruled out that solution.

The Song family is part of legend as well as of history. According to the latest of its chroniclers, its destiny bears comparison only with that of the Borgias.[4] It included a number of the men who shaped the face of China in the first half of the twentieth century: Sun Yat-sen, who married the second daughter, Song Qingling; Chiang Kai-shek, who married the youngest, Song Meiling: ministers and financiers such as the scion of the house, Song Ziwen (T. V. Soong), and Kong Xiangxi, who married the eldest daughter, Song Ailing, herself famous for her talents as a speculator and money manager and the one whom some consider to have been the mainspring of the family's success.

The father, Charlie Soong (Song Jiashu, 1866–1918) was a Cantonese self-made man. His apprenticeship as the son of a trader took him from Hawaii to Java, then to Boston, where he arrived as a stowaway on an American ship. He was lucky enough to be adopted and protected by its captain, who recommended him to the Methodist community of the South. With the financial assistance and patronage of Julian Carr, a rich capitalist from Durham, North Carolina, Charlie Soong then embarked upon his education and the study of theology. From 1882 to 1885 he attended Vanderbilt University in Tennessee. But upon returning to Shanghai, in 1886, his missionary vocation deserted him. He turned to business, but retained his Christian faith and his patronage from missionary circles. He acquired a small printing press and began producing cheap Chinese Bibles for the American Bible Society. Later his business diversified and he married a Christian girl from one of the best Shanghai families. By 1893–94 he was a wealthy entrepreneur, respected in both Western and Chinese circles in the city.

His house, in a residential sector of Hongkou, resembled the residences of the South that Charlie Soong had had a chance to admire while in the United States. It had wide verandahs and all the commodities of modern civilization, from running water and bathrooms to pianos. It became home to four children, three girls and a boy, born between 1890 and 1897. Two more sons would follow later. Their mother kept a close eye on their religious education.

Song Qingling, whose western Christian name was Rosamund, was the second daughter, born in 1892. Like her elder sister, Ailing, she was sent at an early age to the smartest foreign school in the International Concession, the McTyeire School for Girls, run by Methodist missionaries. In 1907, Song Qingling and her younger sister, Meiling, went to the United States to study, first at a school in Summit, New Jersey, and then at Wesleyan College in Macon, Georgia, from which Song Ailing had graduated. The photographs of Song Qingling at this time show a very beautiful face with a high brow, delicate and regular features, and a pensive expression. Song Qingling may not have had the vitality of her elder sister, but beneath her quiet grace and her elegance, a compound of gentleness and reserve, lay a strong taste for patriotic ideas and intense feeling. When, still at Wesleyan College, she learned of the revolution, she wrote an article for her college magazine entitled "The greatest event of the twentieth century," in which she praised China, "a vast empire and an ancient culture," which had found "liberty and equality" and would now be able to "play its part" in the progress of the human race.[5] When she returned to Shanghai in the spring of 1913, it was with considerable emotion that she prepared herself to meet the man who, in her eyes, embodied the revolution and the future of China.

It would not be hard to meet him, for the former president of the Republic was an old family friend whom Song Qingling and her brothers and sisters had always regarded as an "uncle." Charlie Soong's friendship with Sun went back to 1894, when the young Cantonese rebel had stayed in Shanghai on his way to Tianjin, where he had hoped to meet Li Hongzhang. Everything predisposed the two men to get along well: their common Cantonese origin, their Christian faith, their foreign education, their familiarity with the English language, and, finally, a common political ideal. A few years later, Charlie Soong's villa in Hongkou and the offices of his printing works, in the International Concession, became meeting places for the revolutionary leaders. In July 1905, Charlie Soong was in Tokyo. Then he went off to raise funds for the Revolutionary Alliance from his old protector, the millionaire Julian Carr. His mission was highly successful, and in 1906 Charlie Soong handed over funds of considerable magnitude to Sun Yat-sen.

Until 1911 the political and friendly links between Sun and Soong were kept secret, but after the revolution they were openly revealed. Once Sun had become Director of Railways, he summoned Charlie Soong to be his treasurer; Ailing, Soong's eldest daughter, became his secretary, dealing with his English correspondence.

Even then the politician, perhaps feeling disappointed or weary, was looking for a young woman to comfort him. Sun fell in love with Song Ailing and wanted to marry her. His adviser, the Australian journalist William Donald, in whom he confided, sought to dissuade him. But to all his objections, Sun replied, "I know it, I know it. But I want to marry her just the same." Sun went to ask Charlie Soong formally for his daughter's hand; and Soong showed him the door, reminding him of their common Christian faith and the nature of the sacred bonds of marriage: he had not raised his children with care only to see them fall into a life of licentiousness.[6] A year or so later, in Tokyo, where the Song family, compromised by its collaboration with Sun, had been obliged to take refuge after the Second Revolution, Song Ailing married the young banker Kong Xiangxi, with whom she shared a love of money and skill at accumulating it.

Sun Yat-sen turned his passion for Song Ailing upon Song Qingling. The girl worked as a secretary for him, taking over from her elder sister after the latter's marriage in the spring of 1914. The liaison remained a secret until Charlie Soong announced his intention to return to Shanghai and Song Qingling refused to leave. She was forced to. In Shanghai she was locked in her room. But she escaped through the window and went off to join Sun Yat-sen in Kobe. The Song family hastened to pursue her but arrived too late: the marriage had already taken place on October 25, 1915.

The scandal broke. No divorce had been declared. Sun had simply announced that he considered himself divorced from his first wife. For devout Christians like the Songs, the marriage was not valid. It was an affront both to their religious principles and to Chinese tradition. Sun Yat-sen was nothing but an adulterer and a bigamist, and Song Qingling had acted in defiance of filial piety and parental authority. The clash was violent, the break shattering. Disapproval was also manifested in the missionary community and among Christian converts. No longer was Sun Yat-sen sought out as an orator in the churches, no longer was he cited as a model. His old network of relations extending to England and America was weakened. He was even obliged to plead his cause with his old friends the Cantlies:

> I can see from your last letter that you have not been informed of my remarriage which took place in Tokyo three years ago. My wife was educated in an American college and is the daughter of one of my oldest collaborators and friends. I am living a new life and making the most of all that I have previously lacked: a real home and the presence of a companion and collaborator.
>
> My ex-wife did not like travelling and so never accompanied me abroad when I was a fugitive. She wanted to spend her life close to her old mother and always encouraged me to take a concubine, following the old custom. But the girl with whom I have fallen in love is a modern girl who would not have accepted such a situation, and I myself was unable to give her up. There was therefore no other solution possible except to agree to a divorce with my ex-wife.[7]

Little by little the storm died down. Song Qingling made her first public appearance at her husband's side in late 1917, in Canton. Thereafter she was constantly to be seen with him, acting as his translator and collaborator, sharing both his trials and his successes. She became a political personality, the "First Lady" of a modern China to the birth of which the revolutionaries devoted themselves. She was militant, but not suffragette. She often appeared in Western dress of sober elegance: suits of a single shade, with a cloche hat. A photograph taken in December 1924 shows her on the deck of a ship bound for Tianjin, accompanied by Sun Yat-sen, already ravaged by the cancer that was to carry him off three months later. Wrapped in a splendid fur coat, wearing dainty, high-heeled shoes and a hat perched coquettishly over her face, the young woman shines with a grace shadowed only by the sadness in her eyes. That was the vision of her remembered by Deng Yinchao (Zhou Enlai's wife), who on that day was lost in the crowd of those welcoming and acclaiming the presidential couple. Half a century later, she was to recall that vision, alongside Song Qingling's coffin: "I saw you—erect, slim, graceful, young, beautiful, dignified, tranquil."[8]

To honor Sun's memory, the communist regime was to give his widow the title of vice-president of the People's Republic of China, a title that she retained until her death in 1980. In 1981, it was possible to visit Song Qingling's private residence in Beijing, to the northwest of the Forbidden City. High walls sheltered a vast house, furnished in the modern style, where a number of works of English literature were still to be found. One is moved at the thought of the solitude of this elegant woman of cosmopolitan culture and tastes, living out her life in a China laid waste by the crimes and convulsions of the Cultural Revolution.

The approval conferred with hindsight by Chinese public opinion and historians alike upon this new union of Sun's, which was even described as an "ideal marriage,"[9] should not make us forget the dramatic circumstances in which it started or the difficulties that beset it. For it was not solely the force of tradition that caused those difficulties. Sun and his wife had to cope with the ambiguities of a process of modernization fashioned by the prejudices of missionary puritanism. It was not too long before Sun managed to get his remarriage accepted by his entourage and public opinion. However, the effect of his various political initiatives at this time was simply to accentuate his isolation and marginality.

THE STRUGGLE AGAINST YUAN SHIKAI, 1913–1916:
SUN, THE SOLITARY KNIGHT ERRANT

After the Second Revolution of 1913, Yuan Shikai, strengthened by the support of the Western powers and the Beiyang (Northern) militarists, installed an authoritarian regime with dictatorial tendencies, which practiced a centralizing policy designed to complete the institutional and economic modernization of the country. In November 1913, what was left of the Guomindang opposition party was dissolved. At the beginning of the following year, Parliament was dismissed, as were all provincial and local assemblies. In May 1914, the 1912 provisional constitution was annulled and a new constitution was introduced, doing away with all mechanisms that imposed any control over the executive power and extending the duration of the presidential mandate indefinitely. The revolutionary interlude of 1911 had enabled the local elites to acquire power and had made possible the triumph of self-management that they applied to institutional and economic modernization. Now Yuan Shikai reverted to the New Policy (Xinzheng) of the Qing court (1901–11) and tried to impose change from above. But his ambitions went beyond fulfilling the old imperial policies: he soon began to think of ascending the throne himself. At the beginning of 1915, he encouraged the creation of a Peace Protection Society (Chou'anhui), which launched a campaign in favor of an imperial restoration. On December 12, Yuan officially announced his desire to become emperor and fixed the following January 1 as the beginning of his reign.

In the face of what in the first years seemed to be the irresistible rise of the "strongman," his potential opponents—important local figures, southern generals linked with the Guomindang, professional revolutionaries—reacted in disorder and confusion. Some were tempted to rally to an opposition, others favored a wait-and-see policy. Sun Yat-sen was virtually alone in calling immediately for a new revolution, though this did more credit to his zeal as a conspirator than to his political acumen. He founded the Chinese Revolutionary Party (Zhonggua gemingdang) and made a series of attempts to get insurrections going, each more ineffectual than the last. The financial aid that he sought from Japan further increased his isolation. In early 1915, when the whole of China reacted passionately against Japan and its Twenty-one Demands, which revealed its declared colonialist ambitions, there were many, even among his friends, who regarded him as a traitor.

A few months later, after Yuan's semicapitulation to Japan and the proclamation of his imperial ambitions caused Chinese public opinion to turn against his dictatorial regime, Sun Yat-sen was too isolated to place himself at the head of the antimonarchical movement, baptized the Movement for the Protection of the Country (Huguo), which mobilized the provincial and military elites of southern China and some of the generals in the Beiyang clique. Throughout these years, an ever widening discrepancy developed between Sun Yat-sen's domineering and voluntarist words and a political situation with which he was increasingly out of touch.

From Revolutionary Plots to Leninist Strategy: The Founding of the Chinese Revolutionary Party in 1914

The organization of the Chinese Revolutionary Party began to take shape at the end of 1913 and was completed with the publication of a manifesto on September 1, 1914. After the failure of the Republic, Sun seems to have lost confidence in the efficacy of Western parliamentary institutions and to have decided that China was not yet ready to adopt them. His criticisms were mainly directed against the Guomindang. Song Jiaoren had wanted to turn the Guomindang into an open, democratic party, but his efforts had been subverted by the absorption of a crowd of opportunists and conservative bureaucrats and paralyzed by the development of factionalism. Once it had abandoned the program devised by Sun (the People's Three Principles, evolution in Three Stages of Revolution, and the organization of the Five Powers), the Guomindang, bogged down as it was in all kinds of compromises, inevitably failed to manage the postrevolutionary period. So it was not the Revolutionary Alliance's plan for government that Sun was criticizing for weakness or lack of realism, but rather Song Jiaoren's policy of cooperation with local elites. Yet when that policy had come to grips with the major social forces, it had produced some fine results—as long, that is, as it had been managed by a politician of great talent.

In Sun's view, salvation lay in a return to more traditional forms of organization. He wanted to re-create a centralized and disciplined revolutionary party, reestablishing loyalty and absolute obedience to the leader in the way that such loyalty existed in the secret societies. He planned to insist upon an oath of personal allegiance from all members of the new party.[10] Each would promise to "sacrifice his life and liberty to the salvation of China and its people." All would sign the text of the oath and authenticate their signatures by appending their fingerprints. Sun Yat-sen hoped by these means to safeguard his own authority against the rival ambitions that had led to the disintegration of the Revolutionary Alliance. He was convinced that retaining personal power was justified because he had, he thought, always been right, even if he had not always managed to get his voice heeded: "I dare say that, but for me, there are no guides to the revolution. . . . There are many things you do not understand. . . . You should blindly follow me."[11] "Unless comrades unite and obey me, personally, the revolutionary cause is bound to fail," he told the revolutionaries of Southeast Asia.[12]

But if the practice of oath-swearing likened the Chinese Revolutionary Party to the secret societies, the monopoly of political power attributed to the party coincided with certain Leninist principles of organization. Having learned from the experience of 1912, Sun Yat-sen was now careful to specify the conditions in which power was to be exercised *after* the victory of the revolution. He retained the schema of the Three Stages of Revolution, devised as early as 1905, but now modified its content. Although he kept the first stage—that of military power, indispensable for the postrevolutionary restoration of order—he now envisaged the second stage as a tutelage exercised by the party. In effect, in this new plan, the first and second stages merged into a period described as "revolutionary." Whereas in the 1905 plan the management of state affairs after the revolution had been entrusted first to a military government, then to authorities designated by a provisional constitution, the 1914 plan assigned the party a monopoly over power until such time as a constitutional regime was established. Furthermore, whereas the 1905 plan had limited the duration of each of the first two stages to three years, the 1914 plan set no time limit upon the "revolutionary" period of the party dictatorship.

To avoid any disaster like the one that, in Sun's eyes, had caused the destruction of the Revolutionary Alliance in 1911, the status of each party member was to be determined by the date when he joined. Those who joined the ranks of the party before the beginning of the revolution were to be "original members" and would later become "privileged citizens." Those who rallied after the beginning of the revolution but before the establishment of the new power would be "adjutant members" and would become "deserving citizens." Those who waited for victory of the revolution before joining the party would be "ordinary members," with the status of "progressive citizens."

This classification, which would apply throughout the (indeterminate) duration of the revolutionary period, implied a gradation of political rights. Whereas "privileged citizens" would be endowed with "special powers," "deserving citizens" would be allowed to elect or be elected to public posts, and "progressive citizens" would be allowed to take part in elections but not to present themselves as candidates; citizens who were not party members would have no rights and would be excluded from public life.

The program of the Chinese Revolutionary Party returned to the Revolutionary Alliance's People's Three Principles, minus the first of those, nationalism, for Sun reckoned this had already been achieved with the overthrow of the Manchus. What remained to be established were democracy (in the long term) and the people's "livelihood."

In the immediate instance, Sun Yat-sen planned to seize power through the direct action of a small group of pure and determined revolutionaries, financed by funds from overseas. He was thus returning to his old strategy of the early Cantonese days, but with the important difference that the secret societies now were excluded. Before 1911, Sun had made use of their anti-Manchuism, and their collaboration had assured him of at least a measure of military force and popular involvement in the earliest revolutionary insurrections. Now, however, the conspiracy was to be self-sufficient: in this respect Sun seems to have been more in line with the tradition of revolutionary plots than with Leninist strategy.

Sun's proposals encountered strong resistance from many revolutionaries, in particular Huang Xing. Huang certainly recognized the need to reorganize the party but conceived of that reorganization as paving the way for a united front against Yuan Shikai: "Only if we include various factions in order to aid our development can our party seemingly not need to be overwhelmingly crushed."[13] He did not reject the principles of unity, discipline, and obedience to the leader, but he could not stomach the personal nature of the allegiance that Sun Yat-sen demanded. Many comrades joined him in these criticisms. They also opposed the distinctions introduced between different categories of militants and regarded the promise of a privileged status to the longest standing of them as an insult to their democratic and patriotic zeal. They also very much disapproved of the dictatorial power that Sun's plan conferred upon the party during the revolutionary period. In their view, it was not the party's business to act as the people's guardian; that would be contrary to democracy and would lead to the reestablishment of the tyranny of absolute power.

Sun Yat-sen defended himself by invoking the Classics and the justification that any emperor too young to govern should be guided by his minister; the emperor represented the people, the minister the party. At this point, another justification rises unbidden to mind: one that Mao Zedong was prone to use, that of the buffalo (the people) led by the child (the party). Sun Yat-sen also drew upon Western philosophers, in particular Robert Michels and his book *The Political Parties* (first published in German in 1911), which stressed a militant's duties of obedience in democratic formations.

The main obstacle to the rallying of the revolutionaries was the idea of swearing that oath to Sun, and it was upon this point that they entered upon negotiations. The revolutionaries would have been prepared to swear loyalty to "the president elected by the party." But Sun's intransigence—or that of his immediate entourage—made such a compromise impossible. The result was that Huang Xing did not join the new party, and his refusal was followed by the refusal of most of the other principal revolutionary leaders—ideologues ready to sacrifice themselves personally in heroic endeavors, like Wang Jing-wei, fighters in the field such as Chen Jiongming, and former southern military governors such as Li Liejun and Bo Wenwei. All these men chose to continue the battle outside the framework of the Chinese Revolutionary Party. The new party managed to attract only a few hundred of the several thousand activists exiled in Japan. At the foundation meeting, on July 8, 1914, only eight of the Chinese provinces were represented and no figure sufficiently prestigious could be found to fill the post of vice-president, originally destined for Huang Xing, alongside the president, Sun Yat-sen.

Thus deserted by his old fighting companions, Sun Yat-sen turned to a new team. It was dominated by a group of adventurers and henchmen very different from the intellectuals who had formed the staff office of the Revolutionary Alliance. Their leader was Chen Qimei (1876–1916), whose authority stemmed from his strong personality, his intelligence, and his courage. Chen was about ten years younger than Sun, a rather frail man, with owl-like spectacles, still with something of an adolescent air about him. He was a born organizer, a man of action, a conspirator ready for anything, even assassination. As a native of Zhejiang, he felt at home in Shanghai, where many of his compatriots had come to make their fortunes. His friends included rich bankers and compradors, the former president of the Shanghai Chamber of Commerce, Li Houyu, and the millionaire antiques dealer Zhang Jingjiang, once involved in an anarchist group in Paris, whom Sun had originally rallied to his cause during a chance encounter on a steamer. Zhang was nicknamed Quasimodo by the French in Shanghai, but it was neither his club foot nor his dark glasses that made him "a sinister character."[14] What made him fearsome was the power that he derived from his relations with the Shanghai underworld and with Du Yuesheng, the leader of the Green Gang (Qingbang), the city's toughest criminal organization.

Chen Qimei had studied at the Tokyo Police Academy in 1905–6 and had joined Sun and the Revolutionary Alliance. When he returned to China, he continued his revolutionary activities in Zhejiang and Jiangsu. In November 1911, he led the attack on the Jiangnan arsenal and overcame the Manchu garrison in Shanghai. When he became the city's military governor, he recruited his ministers from among the leading merchants and gentry. But in July 1913 he was unsuccessful in his attacks against the troops loyal to Yuan Shikai, holed up in the arsenal. He returned to Tokyo, where he shared Sun's bitterness and his analysis of the defeat, which he too blamed on Huang Xing's hesitations.[15] Like Sun, he was impatient to resume the struggle: "The opportunity invariably arises from being created and never from being awaited," he declared.[16]

Under the influence of Chen Qimei, who favored an insurrection in the province of Jiangsu and those farther north, in Shandong and Manchuria, Sun Yat-sen at last forsook his old strategy centered on Guangdong and the southern provinces. Shanghai now became the hub of the activities of Sun's partisans. They found refuge there in the foreign concessions, rediscovered old contacts that went back to the period of the revolutionary government of 1912 or even further, and enjoyed the protection afforded by the Japanese consulate and also, presumably, by the powerful mafiosi societies such as the Red Gang (Hongbang) and the Green Gang. On the ground, the leader was Chen Qimei, who knew the men and the terrain. He acted in Sun's name, but he appears to have enjoyed total freedom of decision.

In his train Chen Qimei brought a young lieutenant, ten years his junior, named Chiang Kai-shek. Like Chen Qimei, Chiang was a native of Zhejiang, and he had been under Chen's protection and guidance since 1906. The two men were linked by deep friendship and had become sworn brothers in 1913. Chiang Kai-shek, now an artillery officer, had trained at the famous Japanese military academy of Shimbu Gakko from 1908 to 1911. Chen Qimei probably brought him to the Revolutionary Alliance. He came under fire for the first time under Chen Qimei's command in Hangzhou, which he won over to the revolution in November 1911, and subsequently in Shanghai, to which he brought a regiment of the revolutionary army of Jiangsu. In July 1913, he led the ill-fated attack on the arsenal.

But this was also an officer who had no hesitation in engaging in operations that were closer to banditry than to the orthodox military art. The police archives of the International Concession contain several warrants for Chiang's arrest for crimes that include armed robbery.[17] Though these affairs have never been properly sorted out, there appears to be no doubt that it was Chiang Kai-shek who, on February 15, 1912, with his own hand executed the revolutionary leader Tao Chengzhang, firing at him from point-blank range as he lay on his sickbed in the Sainte-Marie Hospital.[18] This act rid Chen Qimei of one of his chief rivals, the head of the Restoration Society, who had at first rallied to the Revolutionary Alliance but then split away from it. Was Chiang acting on Chen's orders, as is suggested in a report by the French consul, Dejean de la Bâtie? Or did he liquidate Tao Chengzhang on his own initiative, in a fit of fury? The young Chiang was notorious for his bursts of uncontrollable anger and for the life of debauchery that he led in the Shanghai brothels, in the company of Zhang Jingjiang and other well-known figures of the underworld and under their protection.

Virtually the only intellectuals still faithful to Sun were Dai Jitao and Zhu Zhixin. The former was his personal secretary and his Japanese interpreter, a partisan of anti-white pan-Asianism and of a Sino-Japanese alliance directed against the West. The latter had been one of the protagonists in the polemic against Liang Qichao in the *People's Journal* and was also a hero of the Canton uprising of April 1911. He was an ideologue given to action, a "model revolutionary"[19] who in 1920 was to fall victim to his own spirit of self-sacrifice, but whose influence seemed on the wane faced with the impetuosity of Sun's new trusted followers, impatient for action.

The Chinese Revolutionary Party, a small affair, thus did not replace either the structures of the former Guomindang or its personnel, inherited from the Revolutionary Alliance. The overseas cells that were so crucial to revolutionary finances still considered themselves to belong to the Guomindang, as indeed did some of its former leaders. In 1914, however, the opposition between these currents and the new party remained moderate. All that changed at the beginning of 1915, when the Tokyo government presented its Twenty-one Demands. Whereas the Guomindang currents reacted violently to this aggression against national sovereignty, Sun continued with his policy of cooperation with Japan, thereby exposing himself to many accusations of treachery from his former friends as well as from his enemies. Such a suicidal attitude perhaps calls for a closer look at the nature of the relations between Sun and the Japanese since the failure of the Second Revolution.

At Cross-Purposes with Nationalist Mobilization

With Yuan Shikai supported by the advisers and money of the International Consortium, no opposition could hope to succeed without foreign aid. In the common front presented by the foreign powers, Japan pursued a vacillating policy, divided between official support for Yuan and discreet support of his adversaries. Sun therefore turned to the Japanese once again. But he still had to convince them that he truly was the man for the situation, the one most likely to topple Yuan.

The outbreak of war between Germany and the Allied Powers seemed to Sun to present a favorable opportunity. "Europe will not have time to bother about the East and the traitor [Yuan] will no longer benefit from foreign loans and military equipment," Sun wrote on September 1, 1914. "This is our chance to rise up and make our stand."[20] Japan, too, saw an opportunity—a chance to regain the initiative in the Far East and to relaunch its own autonomous policy of expansionism in China.

On November 29, 1914, Uchida Ryōhei, the Black Dragon leader, addressed a memorandum to the Japanese government concerning a solution for the Chinese question, in which he sketched out a plan for an alliance with a China delivered from Yuan Shikai and placed under Japanese protection. He recommended supporting two rebel groups likely to help to topple Yuan: the monarchists of the North, grouped around Prince Su, who could be helped to establish a separatist kingdom in Manchuria and Mongolia; and Sun Yat-sen and the southern revolutionaries.

Sun Yat-sen, no longer the exclusive negotiator with the Japanese authorities, was ready to make any concessions in order to regain Tokyo's favor and support. His conciliatory eagerness is evident in the letter he sent in June 1914 to the Japanese Prime Minister Ōkuma Shigenobu.[21] After evoking the familiar themes of geographic, racial, and cultural proximity and Japan's aid to the Chinese Revolution, Sun declared that it was natural that that aid should now again be requested. In return for such aid, he offered to make sure that Japan enjoyed a quasi-monopoly of the Chinese market. This vast market and the natural riches of China would support Japan's prosperity, just as in the nineteenth century India's resources had supported the expansion of Great Britain. And Japan would even be spared "the trouble and expense of stationing troops!" Clearly, none of this was possible as long as Yuan held power. But now the revolutionaries were seeking support, and if Japan was willing to provide it, it would derive great benefits.[22]

In this letter, Sun thus wrote as an apologist for Japanese imperialist expansion and to a certain extent made himself its instrument. The enormity of the concessions promised is a measure of the urgent need for the hoped-for aid. Okuma's government did not respond to this letter, but the promises Sun made did apparently encourage the Japanese to formulate their Twenty-one Demands and at the same time gave them a means of applying pressure upon Yuan in order to extract from him the concessions already offered by his rival.

The Japanese demands were presented to the Peking government on January 18, 1915. They were divided into five groups; the first four related to territorial concessions in Shandong, southern Manchuria, and eastern Inner Mongolia; the fifth referred to the appointment of Japanese military and political advisers to the Chinese government, which would thereby be reduced to a puppet regime.

The exorbitant nature of these demands provoked a violent patriotic reaction in China, and the dangerous emergency had the effect of uniting a number of political forces behind Yuan Shikai. The revolutionaries were themselves tempted to join this national united front. Even for those who proclaimed themselves republicans, the dictatorship had ceased to be the major problem. At this point, many exiles returned, out of hatred for the aggressor. They were encouraged to do so by Yuan's propaganda, which made many offers of amnesty and reparation. Only Sun Yat-sen, Chen Qimei, and their immediate circle remained committed to cooperation with Japan. Their opponents made the most of this chance to cry treason; and Kong Xiangxi himself suggested that his quasi-brother-in-law was being manipulated by the Japanese:

> China may refuse to sign the twenty-one demands, but Japan's great continental scheme, which includes even India, will be only delayed, not thwarted, if she can nourish local insurrections or import ready-made ones. For the broad success of this scheme it is necessary that she have under her protection and influence prominent Chinese revolutionists or suspects. . . . The name and prestige of Dr. Sun Yat-sen are worth more to Japan than several divisions of an army.[23]

Carried away by their concern for national safety, the Chinese of Southeast Asia sent off their donations to the former Guomindang governors, Li Liejun and Chen Jiongming, who were reckoned to be more patriotic than Sun; some even sent them directly to Yuan Shikai. Sun, totally isolated, refused to budge from his position. On March 14, 1915, he sent the Japanese Minister for Foreign Affairs a letter in which he offered the Tokyo government even greater concessions than those claimed in the Twenty-one Demands.[24] The negotiations taking place between Yuan and the Japanese worried him. Fearing a compromise, he hastened to raise the stakes by presenting new proposals. China would submit for Japan's approval any diplomatic agreement concerning Asia, made with any third power; it would use Japanese armaments in such a way as to facilitate military cooperation; it would give priority to the appointment of Japanese advisers to both the central government and local governments; and finally, it would set up a Sino-Japanese bank with many branches, to finance economic cooperation, and Japanese capital would receive priority in the sectors of mines, railways, and coastal trade. Japan, in return, would help China to get rid of its bad government and to reestablish the nation upon solid bases.

Although it is hard to imagine what more the Japanese could have desired, they were quite aware of the extent of Sun's weakness and isolation and refused to negotiate. What is significant is the obvious gap that separated Sun Yat-sen from Chinese public opinion, by then burning with patriotic indignation.

In May 1915, after several months of negotiation, Yuan Shikai gave way to the Japanese pressure and signed his acceptance of the Twenty-one Demands, minus group 5, concerning the appointment of Japanese military and diplomatic advisers. Even so, the Chinese nationalists now withdrew their support of Yuan and shifted their hopes, not to Sun Yat-sen, but to his rivals in the Guomindang movement.

It was more than a year before Japan decided to change its policy and abandon Yuan Shikai, by then judged to be irremediably compromised by his attempt to restore the empire. In the spring of 1916, Sun Yat-sen finally received at least a measure of the aid he had been working for. It was not exclusive: other leaders of the opposition also benefited—for example, the monarchists of Manchuria and some of the southern generals. Nor was it to be unconditional: the agreement of February 26, 1916, in exchange for funds (1.7 million yen, equivalent to U.S. $700,000), insisted upon rapid success on the ground and specified that if this was not achieved payments would be discontinued. Sun Yat-sen quite evidently had lost his position among the Japanese as the sole important representative of the opposition, and his persistence in seeking Japanese aid had damaged the reputation of the Chinese Revolutionary Party both in China and in the overseas Chinese communities. Nor did the other members of the anti-Yuan coalition who shared in the Japanese largesse along with Sun suffer the same condemnation as he did. In Sun's case, scandal probably attached not so much to the aid actually received but rather to the timing of his negotiations and his offer of the most excessive concessions, coinciding as they did with the grave national crisis which, in early 1915, mustered the whole of Chinese public opinion against Japanese aggression.

Quite apart from these coincidences, the old rift between Sun and the most anti-imperialist of the revolutionary currents had again opened up. In 1907, anti-Manchu propaganda had served him as a patriotic umbrella. After 1911, when Sun considered the national problem settled, his idea of Sino-Japanese cooperation, even if inspired by the most opportunistic and Machiavellian of strategies, seemed at best a grave political mistake and a serious miscalculation of the deepest currents of Chinese public opinion, at worst a betrayal. It certainly helped to increase Sun's isolation and to prevent him from reaffirming his authority over the vast coalition that, in 1916, united all forces hostile to Yuan Shikai in the Movement for the Protection of the Country (Huguo).

The Movement for the Protection of the Country (Huguo) and the Marginalization of Sun Yat-sen

After the failure of the Second Revolution in 1913, the emerging dictatorship of Yuan Shikai met no more obstacles within China itself. And among Yuan's exiled opponents, Sun Yat-sen alone believed in the possibility of an immediate counterattack. In the next two years, up until the end of 1915, he tried again and again in an erratic series of plots to set up revolts, but they all aborted no sooner than formed. They testified more to the old fighter's disarray than to his combative spirit.

In January 1914, Sun Yat-sen gave his blessing to Chen Qimei's expedition to Manchuria. Not much is known of this expedition, but the plan probably involved having the revolutionaries make contact with Prince Su's monarchists and help establish the separatist kingdom of Manchuria that some

Japanese leaders already had in mind. It is known that, unlike Song Jiaoren and a number of the other revolutionary leaders, Sun had never evinced any passionate nationalism with regard to these regions of the northeast. Perhaps that was because they had formally been the territory of barbarian tribes, only annexed to China at the beginning of the twentieth century. Sun considered that these territories were "not all of China," if they were lost, "the true China," the China of the Han, would still remain.[25]

When, after a few weeks, Chen Qimei's expedition came to nothing, Sun Yat-sen rallied somewhat reluctantly to a plan for an uprising in the region of Huizhou, in eastern Guangdong, arranged by Zhu Zhixin, who had formed an alliance with wandering bands of demobilized soldiers and landless peasants. It is interesting to see Zhu Zhixin here taking over from Sun, who had tried to launch an insurrection in the very same region in 1900, with the backing of the Triads. But by November 1914, Sun no longer believed in the role of the secret societies and "primitive rebels," nor did he any longer give priority to the southern front. Under Chen Qimei's influence he had moved on to embrace a different conspiratorial strategy, focused, this time on the lower Yangzi valley.

In November 1915, the assassination of an admiral with a counterrevolutionary past, followed in December by an unsuccessful attempt to sabotage the Chinese fleet anchored in Huangpu, marked a resumption of Chen Qimei's revolutionary activities in Shanghai. After the mutiny on the battleship *Potemkin* had led into the Russian Revolution and even before the cannon of the cruiser *Aurora* had affected its development, Sun Yat-sen had realized how important a role the navy—by then the modern arm *par excellence*—might play in a seizure of power. His plan now was to rally the fleet, then, from the ships, bombard the arsenal and other targets of strategic importance, with a view to seizing Shanghai. But the operation launched on that December 5 was so badly prepared that, in spite of the participation of Japanese officers, it proved a total fiasco. The press of the International Concession poured ridicule on the operetta-style battle: instead of aiming at the targets indicated, the sailors fired their cannons into the sky, and all the isolated rebels could do was take to flight. This futile act of terrorism utterly discredited Sun Yat-sen in the eyes of Chinese public opinion at the very moment when the official announcement of the plan to restore the empire, on December 12, united against Yuan Shikai nearly all the political and military leaders who had up until then either accepted his dictatorship or resigned themselves to it.

The moving spirit of this operation, ready to turn into armed resistance, was General Cai E (1882–1916). Cai E was a native of Hunan who had studied at the famous military academy in Tokyo, Shikan Gakko. There, he became friendly with about forty cadets from Yunnan, inspired like himself by intense patriotic zeal. Although this group was close to the Revolutionary Alliance, which a dozen or so members joined, it differed from it in its belief in the priority of nationalism over revolution and of the anti-imperialist struggle over the antidynastic one. Once back in China, Cai E pursued a brilliant military career. By the age of twenty-nine he was a general and was in command of units of the New Army stationed in Yunnan. After the 1911 Revolution broke out, he declared the independence of the province and established an authoritarian government there, with himself at its head.

Although often represented as a disciple of Sun Yat-sen, Cai E developed his own line of political thought, influenced by Liang Qichao and inspired by the history of modern Germany.[26] Cai E wanted to make the army the instrument of reform and turn the Chinese into a "martial people." He chose a provincial framework to put his ideas into practice: for a while he even dreamed of establishing a new Prussia in the southwest. But after the 1911 revolution, his rallying to Yuan Shikai was not a matter of making the best of a bad job, as it was for the other revolutionary leaders. His decision was a response to his conviction that China needed a strong government and a centralized political system. And later, in 1912–13, what Cai E deplored were not Yuan Shikai's infringements of democracy but the instability of his political cabinets, the weakness of the Executive, and the divisions of Parliament, which was constantly disrupted by partisan maneuvers.

To Cai E, the army, set above the political melee, represented a guarantee of unity, strength, and progress. Cai E and his officers did not take part in the Second Revolution of 1913. The official historiography explains his nonparticipation by the fact that he was far away at the time, but it was altogether in line with Cai E's political logic. Nevertheless, at the end of 1913, Yuan Shikai, fearing Cai E's independent character and his freedom of maneuver, recalled him from Yunnan by moving him to an honorific post in Peking. Tang Jiyao (1881–1927), the new military governor of the province, who replaced him, shared Cai E's ideas, however, and the influence of the Yunnan army, as an institution, therefore persisted.

This was the army that launched the antimonarchic movement organized by Tang Jiyao and soon joined by both Cai E, who had escaped from Peking, and the former Guomindang governor Li Liejun. At first, the movement had an essentially military character, fueled by the patriotic and republican zeal of the officers. On December 25, 1915, the rebels made a solemn appeal to the other provinces, inviting them to join the struggle against Yuan. Their ultimate objective was the reestablishment of a strong and reunited Republic. In the immediate instance, they were above all concerned to form a national front, and preferred to call themselves the Army for the Protection of the Country (Huguo), rather than the Republican Army. They accordingly strove to integrate all the various opposition forces.

Sun Yat-sen did not take part in that coalition. Learning from the setbacks of 1912, he refused to ally himself with generals and bureaucrats whose republicanism was doubtful and who, above all, were not prepared to recognize his authority. He was constantly warning his own partisans against the appearance of a "second or a third Yuan Shikai, unless they assumed control themselves."[27] On the ground however, the initiative certainly did belong to the southern generals, who now moved on to the offensive in Sichuan.

In the spring of 1916, Sun, using the Tokyo loan, tried to organize insurrections in Shanghai and Shandong, for both these regions were of intense interest to the Japanese and he was sure that their capture would bring him millions more yen. But on May 18, 1916, the assassination of Chen Qimei, by Yuan's killers, cut short an operation in Shanghai that could already be seen to be hopeless. And in Shandong, Sun's emissary pulled off no more than a fleeting success. His mission was to make his way along the railway line from Qingdao to Jinan and from there to rally Peking. In Qingdao itself he was helped by logistic support from the Japanese, now occupying what used to be territory leased to Germany. When the expedition got going, rebel general quarters were systematically set up in the railway stations of the Qingdao-Jinan line, also controlled by the Japanese. Liaison between Sun and his troops was assured through various Japanese consulates, and supplies of funds were made available by the Yokohama Specie Bank. In March 1916, Sun even had no qualms about appealing to Japanese officers to eject from Shandong opponents of Yuan who did not recognize Sun's authority, such as the former Guomindang governor Bo Wenwei.

Sun Yat-sen was aware that his systematic recourse to Japanese aid would prove extremely unpopular with Chinese public opinion, in which nationalism had continued to be strong ever since the crisis of the Twenty-one Demands. He accordingly urged discretion upon the expedition leader: "Outwardly, we must shun any connection with the Japanese."[28] Yet even with Japanese aid, success on the ground was slow in coming. In May 1916, Sun Yat-sen, who had just arrived in Shanghai, therefore decided to end his splendid isolation and he officially joined the anti-Yuan coalition forces.

Was it the realization of his weakness that led Sun Yat-sen to recognize his strategic failure in this fashion? Or was it that the disappearing of the conspirator Chen Qimei made it possible for Sun Yat-sen to resume a more personal political style, one founded upon negotiation and infiltration and more of a kind to turn defeats into victories? We lack a sufficiently long historical perspective to be able to judge, for on June 6, 1916, the sudden (but natural) death of Yuan Shikai upset the entire Chinese political scene.

SUN, GRAND MARSHAL OF CANTON, OR THE UPS AND DOWNS OF A WARLORD WITHOUT AN ARMY, 1917–1918

The death of Yuan Shikai made an ephemeral restoration of republican institutions possible. The vice-president Li Yuanhong assumed the functions of president. He reconvened the Parliament dissolved in 1913, and reintroduced the Constitution of 1912. But the man he chose for prime minister, General Duan Qirui, who represented the northern clique of militarists (Beiyang), wanted to follow Yuan Shikai's example and use the army to seize power. The confrontation between the president and the prime minister stiffened in 1917, when the two men took opposite positions on the question of China's participation in the world conflict. This crisis broke out in the summer of 1917. Duan Qirui was able to get rid of Li Yuanhong and send Parliament packing, but he had difficulty imposing his authority within his own clique, and, on top of this, the general confusion was aggravated by an attempt at a Manchu restoration, which rapidly miscarried.

While a succession of violent coups went on in Peking, the generals of the South reasserted their independence and tried, without much success, to organize themselves into a common political system. It was at this point that northern China and southern China definitely began to go their separate ways, mostly in conflict with each other. Meanwhile, within both camps, those who held increasingly fragmented power took to thinking first and foremost of their own interests. The era of the warlords had well and truly begun.

In a political context of this kind, there was little place for a leader whose strength lay essentially in ideas and in his ability to mobilize partisans and financial resources in the name of those ideas. While still true to his convictions—he was to act in the name of the Protection of the Constitution (Hufa)—Sun Yat-sen adapted to the constraints of the times. He placed his faith in armed might, negotiated with the militarists, and ended up virtually indistinguishable from them. Being a general without troops, however, he was soon sidelined in the war games that came to dominate politics more and more.

Sun and the Protection of the Constitution (Hufa)

In 1916, Sun thought that now that Li Yuanhong was president and Parliament had been recalled, China would be able to embark directly upon the constitutional era. Jettisoning the idea of the transition periods provided for in the program of the Chinese Revolutionary Party (which, since it scarcely existed, it could not have introduced), Sun accordingly recommended "reestablishing the provisional Constitution of 1912 and relying on the representative assembly of the people," that is to say, the 1913 Parliament. This was still dominated by the old Guomindang majority, which Sun now, after having rejected it in 1913, looked to for support.

Sun made his comeback to the political scene in the spring of 1917, on the occasion of the debate over whether or not China should finally throw in its lot in the World War. This debate set in opposition the prime minister Duan Qirui and the president, Li Yuanhong, who was supported by the parliamentary majority and much of the press and public opinion. The issues of internal politics that were involved were in truth probably of more importance than the diplomatic issues at stake. By arguing for China's entry into the war, Duan Qirui hoped to obtain from Japan financial and military aid that would help him, not to send reinforcements to the Allies, but to establish his own power in China. In Tokyo, the new cabinet of Terauchi Masatake supported this policy, believing it to be more favorable to Japanese interests than the brutal aggression practiced in 1915–16.

The debate began in February 1917, after the United States broke off relations with Germany and suggested that neutral powers, of which China was one, should do likewise. In early March, Duan Qirui tried to use intimidation to get Li Yuanhong and Parliament to approve the breaking off of diplomatic relations. It was at this point that Sun Yat-sen intervened with his recommendation that China should maintain its neutrality: "Whether a country can promote her status depends on her own strength. For China, to join [the Allies] will result in domestic disorder rather than improvements."[29] The purely diplomatic and international aspects of the problem were set out in a pamphlet that a relatively late historiographical tradition attributes to Sun Yat-sen but that in truth seems to have been the work of Zhu Zhixin. This pamphlet, entitled *The Question of China's Survival (Zhongguo cunwang wenti)*, was written in April or May 1917, probably in consultation with Sun. It is extremely hostile to Great Britain, denounces Russia as potentially the most dangerous enemy of all, and returns to the theme of the Sino-Japanese common culture and common interests. It considers Germany to be less aggressive toward China than Russia and declares that China would have less to lose from victory for the Triple Alliance than from victory for the Entente.

The only way for Duan Qirui to impose China's entry into the war was to resort to force. In April, at Tianjin, he gathered together the generals and military governors of the Beiyang clique. On May 11, he sent "petitioners" to lay siege to Parliament. Threatened by 5,000 soldiers, Li Yuanhong was on June 12 forced once again to dissolve Parliament. He then himself abandoned his presidential functions. Throughout this crisis, Sun Yat-sen did everything in his power to save the republican institutions, calling for the punishment of the rioting "petitioners" and begging the generals of the south and the southwest to launch a punitive expedition against the factious members of the Beiyang clique:

> The military governors of the provinces . . . cannot take refuge in neutrality. For neutrality means separating oneself from the central government . . . and from what country, what master, what regime are the partisans of neutrality trying to separate themselves? If they want to separate from the Republic, they will be censored by 400 million people.[30]

Sun made contact with the Minister for the Navy, Cheng Biguang, who was thinking of getting the fleet to intervene against the North, and proposed transferring the central government to Shanghai. In the end, he left for Canton, escorted by two warships. Upon his arrival in the southern port on July 17, Sun was greeted by members of Parliament from Peking, local deputies, and the military governor of Guangdong. The important speech that he delivered to them returned to the need to resort to force to save the institutions of the Republic and to protect national unity. Canton would serve as a refuge for the legitimist government ejected by the militarists of the North, and as a military base for the reconquest of power and of the country:

> To reestablish a true Republic, we need to have at our disposal two forces: the army and the navy. . . . It is impossible to reestablish a true Republic . . . without recourse to the armed forces. . . . What I am expecting from you today, dear sirs, is that you will invite all units of the fleet to assemble here, and you will ask Parliament to come and sit in Canton and President Li Yuanhong to come here and resume his functions.[31]

Faced with routed parliamentary representatives and generals preoccupied with defending or increasing their own power, Sun Yat-sen played the card of republican legitimacy and national unity. Not without success. On July 21, the Minister for the Navy ordered the fleet—about fifteen ships—to leave Shanghai for Canton, where 130 parliamentary representatives, about one-third of the total number, had gathered.

Whatever the political talent and persuasive force with which Sun was credited, there were other explanations for these successes. Sun had at his disposal funds that made the departure of the fleet possible and also allowed the invitation to the parliamentary representatives to be financed. Where did this money come from? A secret report produced by the German consulate general in Shanghai and discovered in the Potsdam archives after World War II mentions contacts between that consulate and Sun Yat-sen between March and August 1917. The interests of the Germans lay in overthrowing or destabilizing the government of Duan Qirui, which was poised to enter the war on the Allied side. They knew of Sun's hostility to that policy and had no doubt noticed that the opinion expressed in *The Question of China's Survival* was relatively favorable to Germany. Cao Yabao, a friend and partisan of Sun's, acted as intermediary. Sun asked for two million Chinese dollars, to buy the army and the navy. There is no positive proof that he received the money, but all the evidence suggests that he did, including a number of confidences that the military governor of Guangdong let slip to the United States consul general.

The declaration of war on Germany that the government of Canton (controlled by Sun Yat-sen) made on September 13, 1917, must have dashed the hopes of those German diplomats. They had believed that they were using Sun—and Sun had used them. If this episode of the German funds is authentic—and I believe it is—it illuminates the eminently opportunistic nature of the advances that Sun would make to foreigners to get their support. The revolutionary leader does not appear to have felt the slightest bit committed to the exorbitant promises that he made in order to obtain money. In fact, he seems to have regarded lying for a good cause as a mark of political skill and patriotic ardor. Foreign observers, inclined as they were to take such texts and declarations literally, found it hard to understand this variable geometry of the truth and complained of treachery. This difference in comprehension may well constitute one of the principal sources of misunderstanding between the East and the West where Sun is concerned. At any rate, the declaration of war made by the Canton government confirms *a posteriori* that it was essentially the internal politics of China that were at stake in the spring of 1917 in the debate over whether or not the country should intervene in the world conflict. Once the problem of Duan Qirui was out of the way, purely diplomatic considerations do not seem to have presented any obstacle to Sun Yat-sen and the parliamentary representatives gathered in Canton.

There were too few of those representatives to form the quorum required by the Constitution. Their group constituted no more than a rump parliament, with uncertain authority. It was nevertheless from them that Sun Yat-sen sought to derive his legitimacy when, in the absence of Li Yuanhong, he had himself elected head of a military government whose objective was to organize a punitive expedition against the northern warlords and to restore the 1912 Constitution. As part of the plan that aimed to transfer the legal government of the Republic to the South, Sun Yat-sen had finally established a separatist government in Canton, to rival that in Peking. But how could the aura of legitimacy conferred by his election by the rump government and his declared loyalty to the Constitution possibly suffice for Sun to impose his authority on a China split asunder, in which political life was increasingly being reduced to the relations of military strength between local potentates?

The Grand Marshal of Canton

With his plumed kepi, his fringed epaulettes, the festoons of braid across his chest, his insignia, and his white gloves, Sun Yat-sen looked very grand! But the title of grand marshal that he assumed, to emphasize the military nature of his mission and his government, only illuminated the weakness of his real authority. In early September, the grand marshal appointed his ministers and the commanders of his armed forces, most of whom never bothered to take up their functions. The president's orders never made it beyond the precinct of the cement factory in which he had set up his offices and where idle officials whiled away the time playing chess. The trouble was that Sun's military government had been grafted on to other power structures that he could neither integrate nor supplant.

When Sun arrived in Canton in 1917, the provinces of the south and the southwest were organized around two poles: the Greater Yunnan region, incorporating Guizhou and part of Sichuan, under the authority of Tang Jiyao, and a Guangxi-Guangdong axis, controlled by the militarists of Guangxi, led by Lu Rongting. These generals had taken part in the Movement for the Protection of the Country in 1916, and it was owing to that movement that they had been able to extend their dominion over the provinces neighboring their own. In June 1917, they had also taken up position against Duan Qirui's show of force in Peking and had threatened to launch a punitive expedition against the Beiyang clique. In the meantime, Lu Rongting had proclaimed the military and administrative independence of Guangxi-Guangdong and had immediately made the most of this to lift the bans placed on the opium trade and gaming houses, the better to tax them.

While Lu Rongting was planning his exploitation of the two provinces under his control, Tang Jiyao was drawn to "greater Yunnanism" and expansion toward Sichuan and the Yangzi valley. The political sympathies of these generals inclined them toward, not Sun, but former Guomindang governors such as Li Liejun or the ex-imperial general Cen Chunxuan, with whom they had collaborated closely at the time of the Movement for the Protection of the Country in the preceding year. In fact, contacts established between these various characters before Sun arrived in Canton had already led to a plan for a United Council of the Provinces of the Southwest. Sun's arrival upon the scene, with his military government, upset the interplay between these regional politico-military forces.

Those who had already held power were not prepared to submit to the grand marshal, even in the name of the common ideal of Protection of the Constitution. On September 2, just after Sun's election, Lu Rongting sent a telegram to the parliamentary representatives and the gentry and merchants of Canton. It ran as follows: "With the president still in,[32] there is no need to set up another government. The rather confusing title of Grand Marshal is particularly subject to question. We, simple and plain, merely work conscientiously, without any ambition for power and we shall not take wrong steps. Therefore we are not willing to comply with the present move."[33]

The southern generals thus continued to recognize the Peking government, which Sun refused to regard as constitutional once Parliament had been dissolved. Lu Rongting and Tang Jiyao were content simply to denounce the factious prime minister Duan Qirui. As they saw it, the punitive expedition should help the Peking government to extricate itself from the influence of the Beiyang clique and to resume its functions normally. In their view, the establishment of a separatist military government in Canton served not so much the Protection of the Constitution, as it did the personal ambitions of Sun Yat-sen.

The abstention of the principal military commanders reduced the grand marshal's government to an impotence clearly perceived by Sun himself, who complained of "the somewhat unstable position," and also by the members of his entourage. One was Zhang Binglin (now reconciled with Sun after a decade of disagreement), who suggested going to Kunming (Yunnan) to make one last attempt to win over Tang Jiyao, since, he said, "this is like a game of *weiqi* (Chinese chess); one should rescue an encircled situation outside the encirclement."[34] But Zhang Binglin's attempt failed.

Sun Yat-sen now looked for other sources of support. He turned to the rump parliament. But the most powerful of its cliques, the Society for Political Studies, which consisted of the former Guomindang deputies, was not susceptible to Sun's influence. Besides, many of the deputies had begun to disperse and those who remained "were dreaming of personal success." They lived in the hotels of Canton: "Gathering together all day long, they merely exchanged reliable and unreliable information on how to form useful connections."[35]

Among the armed forces, Sun Yat-sen could count on the Canton garrison, under the command of Chen Jiongming. But twenty or so battalions did not amount to much against Lu Rongting's 100,000 soldiers stationed in Guangdong, with whom bloody clashes were increasing. Sun Yat-sen decided to protect the garrison troops from these encounters by sending them off to fight in Fujian. The only military forces to have welcomed Sun Yat-sen with enthusiasm upon his arrival in Canton were the Yunnanese contingents, about

20,000 men stranded in Guangdong by the decline of the Movement for the Protection of the Country in 1916. The territorial base occupied by these troops was not large enough to keep them in supplies and they had been obliged to depend on handouts from Lu Rongting. So, in spite of their sympathy for Sun Yat-sen, they did not support him when, exasperated by the lack of cooperation from the Guangxi militarists, he had their offices bombarded by a gunboat steaming up the Pearl River.

One gunboat does not make a fleet. The other ships had gone off to anchor twenty or so kilometers downstream from Canton, at Huangpu, upon the orders of the Minister for the Navy, Cheng Biguang, who was anxious to distance himself from Sun. The isolation of the military government steadily increased. Sun's pressing appeals for funds to the overseas Chinese went unanswered. According to the analysis of one high-ranking Cantonese official, Sun's government was "an empty one, with neither soldiers nor funds. . . . When it can no longer manage, it will dissolve entirely."[36]

In May 1918, Sun's failure was confirmed by the reorganization of the military government, on the initiative of the generals of the southwest, with the support of the navy and a majority in the rump Parliament. A military directory of seven members was substituted for the grand marshal, to head a Confederation of the Provinces of the South and the Southwest. Sun was appointed as one of the directors but he refused to take up his functions and departed to Shanghai, leaving the field in the hands of the Guangxi clique.

Sun's attempted graft upon the militarist structures of the south and the southwest had not taken. Neither the (declining) power of his political personality nor his adoption of a constitutional ideology (over which he by no means held a monopoly) was sufficient to impose Sun's authority in a China where power now passed through the barrel of a gun. Reduced to temporary inaction, the old leader withdrew to Shanghai, where he took time off to think and write.

SUN'S RETIREMENT IN SHANGHAI AND
THE RISE OF HIS UTOPIAN THINKING

The two years spent in Shanghai, from the spring of 1918 to the autumn of 1920, gave Sun a chance to catch his breath, make the most of his harmonious married life, read, and set out his ideas in writing.

A Studious Retreat

Sun settled at 26 rue Molière, in a quiet quarter of the French Concession. A photograph of this period shows him at the age of fifty-two, his face thinner, his hair receding, with a white mustache and a serene air. He had abandoned the uniform of the grand marshal for the robe of a scholar. He is looking through some newspapers.

Song Qingling worked at his side. Together, they revised the retranscribed notes of Sun's speeches, with a view to publishing them. It was a delicate task, for when he spoke in public, Sun would allow himself to be carried away by the inspiration of the moment. "It all depended on the political situation and the audience. I would be as nervous as a cat, sitting next to him on the platform and wondering what was coming next," Song Qingling recalled later.[37] Formalizing the definitive text implied not only restructuring it but clarifying political choices often left open by the orator, who was always anxious not to put off any of his listeners. Sun would warn Qingling, "We have to be very careful how we go at things. . . . Do it the Chinese way— roundabout—never directly at the goal."[38] He toned down his criticisms of those from whom he hoped to obtain aid and worked the text of his manuscripts in such a way as not to introduce dissent among his partisans.

To relax, Sun Yat-sen and Song Qingling would play croquet on the lawn of their little villa and would entertain their friends and sympathizers. They seem to have patched things up with the Song family. At any rate, they helped Charlie Soong to entertain his former protector from North Carolina, Julian Carr, whose funds had helped to finance the Revolutionary Alliance. Two banquets were organized in Carr's honor at the villa in the rue Molière.

Sun's Passivity with Regard to the New Culture and the Nationalism of the Masses

This life of studious leisure might have seemed to suggest Sun's retirement from politics. Out of touch with the development of the New Culture, then all the rage with the radical youth of China, Sun seemed to be turning increasingly to the past, whether recent or distant. Not content with having donned the robe of a scholar, he opposed the young intellectuals, such as Hu Shi and Chen Duxiu, who wanted to establish a foundation for democracy by opening up the paths of culture to the people. While the magazine *New Youth* (*Xin Qinnian*) was urging the substitution of the spoken language (*baihua*) for the literary language (*wenyan*) in written texts, Sun Yat-sen rejected such a development (comparable to the replacement of Latin by French or English, after the Renaissance). In his eyes, the classical literary language was an integral part of Chinese culture; it guaranteed the continuity of that culture and likewise of the nation and the state.

Sun Yat-sen's indignant reactions to the iconoclasts of the new generation may have been sincere. A number of indications suggest that, like so many aging members of the establishment, he was becoming reconciled with tradition. On the other hand, it may be that his orthodox protestations were above all designed to ensure him of the support of certain conservative politicians. Whatever the truth of the matter, the effect of his attitude was to marginalize him utterly in the social developments and the cultural revolution that were then causing such an upheaval in Chinese political life.[39] But, as we know, Sun had never had much time for small circles of intellectual radicals. Already in Tokyo, he had avoided them until such time as the formation of the Revolutionary Alliance had thrown him and them together. In all likelihood, moreover, the young intellectuals felt little active sympathy for or even curiosity about this leader of an unsuccessful revolution, trapped in his narrow political strategies, who persisted in thinking in terms of military alliances and an offensive against the North.

In spite of the presence at his side of Song Qingling and his son, Sun Fo, Sun had almost no contact with the new youth of China. He was no more than a spectator in the great movement of mobilization that filled the streets of Shanghai in June 1919 with thousands of students, shopkeepers, and workers, united in their support for the demonstrators in Peking who were likewise protesting against the humiliation inflicted on China by the Paris Peace Conference.[40] When Sun did address this youthful audience the following October, it was to remind it that China's difficulties called above all for a political solution. It was not enough to develop education, the economy, and regional autonomy; without an armed revolution, they would never get rid of the old bureaucrats, the leftovers from the imperial court, and its shady politicians.

Five years later, in October 1924, when his alliance with Soviet Russia was confirmed, Sun was to criticize the excessive liberty in schools and within the party and again stress "the need for individual sacrifice." It may be that his recent alliance with the communists had inspired this retrospective severity. But it was, in truth, very much part of the ideological and strategic development of Sun's thought following the Second Revolution. What was preoccupying him in the autumn of 1919 was not so much a New Culture founded on science and democracy, but how to reorganize the revolutionary party.

Since Sun's return to Shanghai in May 1916 and his rallying to the united antimonarchical front, the Chinese Revolutionary Party had been moribund. On the other hand, in both China and overseas, many parliamentary representatives and militants continued to consider themselves members of a Guomindang that now lacked any kind of legal structure. On October 10, 1919, Sun Yat-sen therefore announced the creation of the Chinese Nationalist Party (Zhongguo Guomindang). It was not exactly a resurrection—the old party of 1912 had been simply the Nationalist Party (Guomindang)—but this party was similar. It appeared to be a matter of closing an unfortunate parenthesis and abandoning a sectarian form of organization, oriented toward conspiracy, in order to return to a more open practice of political militantism.

The liberalization Sun now favored involved suppressing the personal oath of loyalty and the distinction between the various categories of militants who, earlier, were to have been more privileged or less so according to the length of their membership of the party. Those were issues that had been particularly upsetting to some of Sun's old companions. The statutes promulgated on November 9, 1920, assigned to the party the task of implementing the People's Three Principles and establishing a constitution founded upon the Five Powers. It was in effect a return to the Revolutionary Alliance. There were limits to this liberalization, however, and Sun Yat-sen still harbored a narrowly personal concept of power. As president of the party (*zongli*), he reserved for himself full authority. He wanted to be followed blindly both as theoretician and as strategist: "My San Min Chu I [Three People's Principles] and the five-power Constitution can also be known as Sun Wen's revolutionary [principles]. Therefore, to obey me is to submit to the revolution which I advocate. And if one follows my revolution, naturally one should [also] obey me."[41]

The reorganization of the party was thus more formal than real. It did not question the role of Sun, who was as keen as ever upon his own, personal authority. Although this loss of contact with reality may have led Sun to a strategy somewhat out of touch with the changing times, it did, on the other hand, open up to him paths of utopian reflection in which he could give free rein to his imagination and his visionary gifts.

Sun's Utopian Thought Takes Off: "The International Development of China"

The works written by Sun Yat-sen between 1918 and 1920 appeared in the form of articles, most of them published in the party's new magazine, *Reconstruction* (*Jianshe*), founded in August 1919. Whereas at the time of *People's Journal* Sun Yat-sen had tended to leave the writing to the intellectuals in his entourage, he now took to copious self-expression. His articles were subsequently collected into a work entitled *Plan for National Reconstruction* (*Jianguo fanglüe*).

The problem that obsessed Sun Yat-sen was that of the republican failure following the overthrow of the Manchu dynasty. He had imagined that it would be hard to get the empire to fall but easy to implement the revolutionary program. The first part of his *Plan for National Reconstruction*, entitled "Psychological Reconstruction," attributes the impotence of the revolutionaries to their fear of moving on from thought to action.[42] They had been influenced by the ancestral axiom according to which "knowledge is easy, action difficult"; and this had atrophied their energy and will. Sun's plan had been perfectly calculated to lead China on to the path of progress; but the revolutionaries themselves, "slaves of the theory that action is difficult," took it into their heads to regard that plan as a utopia of empty words, instead of taking on the responsibility that fell to them in the reconstruction of China.[43] As Sun now saw it, the failure thus lay not in the politico-social context, let alone in the excessive ambition or inadaptability of his program, but in the mental paralysis of the revolutionaries: "The truth is that the force of the mind is immense." It was this force that Sun now wanted to transform and convert from being a brake into the very motor of action. For this, all that was needed was to reverse the terms of the traditional theory and establish that it is easy to act, but difficult to know. Once the Chinese accepted this truth, "they would no longer consider [his] program as utopian or empty words. In millions, with a single heart, they would arise to make up for their delay . . . and construct a nation with an enlightened government that would give the people peace and happiness."[44] For, difficult though it is to know, that was a difficulty already surmounted by Sun Yat-sen himself; so the militants could simply place their trust in him.

Sun Yat-sen thus cleared himself of any blame for mismanagement or political incompetence and, what is more, justified himself in doing so on the score both of his aspirations to absolute authority and of his penchant for elaborate, vast program. His most perceptive biographer, Lyon Sharman, denies Sun any creative or visionary qualities. In his eyes, Sun is simply a "programatist" whose imagination was not applied either to the men who surrounded him or to the forces that he set in movement, but became immured within a purely rational exercise oriented toward ideal goals. But is that not exactly the way that the utopian socialists proceeded? Sun Yat-sen, by virtue of his visions and the accuracy of some of his intuitions and premonitions, deserves a place alongside men such as Saint-Simon and Fourier.

As early as 1912, Sun's railway construction plan had provided a first glimpse of his modernizing ambitions. At the time, the plan had seemed all the more ridiculous because it was put forward by the Director of the Railways, who was himself responsible for the administration of the network. In 1919, relieved of the burden of management, Sun Yat-sen threw himself unstintingly into his creative fervor. In the second part of his *Plan for National Reconstruction*, called "Material Reconstruction," which by 1920 had already been separately published in English under the title *The International Development of China*, Sun Yat-sen set out his grandiose plan for Chinese modernization.[45]

With the passion of a demiurge, Sun modeled the future China, recommending "gigantic methods," wiping from the map whole towns (such as Xiaguan, a large suburb of Nanking), cutting across 100-kilometer-wide loops to rationalize the course of the Yangzi, and making provision for "the establishment of a direct rail link between Zhili [the province of Peking] and Capetown [South Africa]." These plans were supposed to be realized thanks to the reconversion of the industry of the United States and the European powers, which, with peace restored, would devote 25 percent of their erstwhile annual war budget to financing Chinese modernization.

Not surprisingly, this economic romanticism provoked criticism from contemporary observers such as the American minister to Peking, Charles R. Crane, who ridiculed "these impractical and grandiose schemes."[46] But Sun Yat-sen's visions deserve better than that kind of dismissal. They are anchored in a recognition of reality: the reality of the poverty of China "where many people die of hunger." Sun Yat-sen attributed that poverty to "nondevelopment . . . crude methods of production, and the wastefulness of labor." "The radical cure for all this is industrial development" on the model of "Europe and America, which are a hundred years ahead of us."

The significance of the Western model is reaffirmed on every page of *The International Development of China*. The great northern port that Sun Yat-sen dreams of seeing rise in the Gulf of Bohai is to be "as important as New York." The rationalization of the Yangzi would stimulate trade as much as or more than the construction of the Suez or the Panama canals. This euphoric vision, unconcerned with the intermediary stages and technology, stemmed from Sun's continuing desire to move fast and adopt the most modern methods.

Many of the first-generation Chinese revolutionaries share Sun's voluntarism and historical optimism, and these ideas were to continue to resurface in the political thought of the twentieth century. More unusual was the confidence that Sun placed in the West: it was with it, not against it, that he hoped to take up the challenge of modernization. He appealed for foreign capital and equipment, soliciting what was not yet known as scientific and technological expertise: "During the construction and operation of each of these national undertakings, [they] will be managed. . . by foreign experts. . . . As one of their obligations these foreign experts will have to undertake the training of Chinese assistants to take their places in the future."

In an age characterized by an explosion of nationalist movements and a proliferation of anti-imperialist struggles, this appeal for international cooperation was extremely bold. The idea of foreign aid contributing to Chinese development ran counter to the diplomatic practices of the nineteenth century that had aimed to turn China into a "prey for militarist and imperialist powers" and "a 'dumping ground' for the overproduction" of the "commercial nations." Similarly, it stood in contrast to the nationalist policies adopted by the reformers of the Western Affairs Movement, who had been obsessed by a desire to strengthen China, the better to contain and eventually dominate Europe and America. According to Sun, the cooperation between China and foreigners should be founded upon mutual interest. It was not really aid that he was soliciting: "The profits of this industrial development should go first to pay the interest and principal of foreign capital invested in it." With its abundant natural resources and raw materials and its cheap labor, and with the contribution of foreign funds, China would become "an unlimited market for the whole world," a "New World, in the economic sense," playing an essential part in international trade. Accordingly, "the nations which will take part in this development will reap immense advantages."

At the time when Sun Yat-sen formulated these proposals—which were as distant from traditional sinocentricism as from anti-imperialist nationalism—public opinion was not yet ready to accept them. Not until the second half of the twentieth century would the problem of international economic cooperation between industrialized nations and developing countries find a place at the heart of political debate.

Sun Yat-sen's condemnation of imperialism thus did not imply a simultaneous rejection of capitalism. Capitalism was still considered to be the creator of wealth and progress. That was why Sun wanted to "make capitalism create socialism in China." That formula, with which Sun's essay ends, may be understood to mean cooperation between the capitalist West and a socialist China. But in a broader sense it also suggests coexistence between socialist and capitalist sectors within China itself. Right from the start, Sun recognized that "all matters that can be and are better carried out by private enterprise should be left in private hands." The essay only tackled national enterprises, so we may conclude that any activities not mentioned—agriculture, commerce, services—were to continue to be the concern of the private sector.

The public sector was to include the development of the railway network, the colonization of virgin land, the construction of canals, the management of rivers, and the establishment of ports. These were the projects to which Sun Yat-sen was particularly committed. In some sectors, such as the cotton industry and small mining industries, private enterprise was already active; the state would continue to develop these branches, not seeking to eliminate private enterprise but, on the contrary, encouraging it by means of specially designed legislation and fiscal measures.

Endeavoring to take into account the forces of spontaneous capitalist development—what he calls "unconscious progress"—Sun thus ended up describing, or rather intuitively apprehending, something that could operate as a mixed economy system. But he clearly preferred a public sector that would be planned in such a way as to achieve the best results at the least cost. The main purpose of *The International Development of China* was to set out just such a plan.

Sun's plan was organized around six programs, giving priority to the development of transport and energy. The first and the third programs, devoted, respectively, to northern China and southern China, laid particular emphasis upon the construction of railways. Not that this prevented Sun from returning to that subject in his fourth program, which is entirely devoted to the development of the rail network. In similar fashion, the expansion of the coal and iron mining industries, treated at length in the first program, is again tackled, in more systematic fashion, in the sixth program.

The priority given to heavy industries, which Sun calls "the key and basic industries," is, however, by no means absolute. In his fifth program, Sun recommends the development of "those industries which provide every individual and family with the necessaries and comforts of life." These consumer industries constitute "the principal group of industries," and they must begin to be developed forthwith, without waiting for the construction of their infrastructures to be completed.

Sun Yat-sen gives no precise details about how this public sector should be managed. He refers to "a central authority" and "national control." He adds that the state will have to be sure to subsidize the price of coal, or "the price of coal should be reduced as low as possible, so as to give impetus to the development of various industries." The state will have the right to preempt land for the building of towns, at a fixed price, in accordance with the schema devised by Henry George, whose influence persists here.

Sun Yat-sen's great modernization project is conceived within a regional framework, and his first three programs are, respectively, devoted to the provinces of the North, the Yangzi valley, and the South. Each of these regional systems is to be focused on a "great seaport" that will link it to the outside world and the international market. Within the framework of each regional system, a network of transport routes combining railways, canals, roads, and rivers will link the hinterland to the main port. For example, the "Great Northern Port" (to be built close to Tianjin) is to serve as the outlet for half a dozen provinces and also for Mongolia and Sinkiang.

Sun Yat-sen, taking the West as his model, thus saw the coastal zones and their great ports as the principal poles of future development. However, he did not neglect the future of inland regions; these would fuel the activity of the "great ports" and would also themselves benefit from the coastal development. For instance, the rail network of the southwest, necessary for the growth of

Canton, "would play an essential role in the prosperity of the whole region." Transport routes would represent the most important instrument in a regional integration that would satisfy the criteria of economic rationality, such as the implantation of industries in the zones producing raw materials, as well as the desire to raise living standards in regions inhabited by hundreds of thousands of people. The planned distribution of investment would make it possible to harmonize the imperatives of national growth with those of regional development.

Finally, to facilitate cooperation between China and foreign countries, which was the key to Chinese modernization, Sun Yat-sen recommended the creation of an international organization that would serve as sole representative with the Chinese authorities. Contracts of a kind to ensure the realization of Sun's Six Programs would be drawn up in consultation with this organization. In this way, the economic rivalry between the foreign powers present in China could be eliminated and the country's progress in peace and independence would be assured. Having ruled out "commercial warfare" between the powers, Sun Yat-sen tackled the "class struggle," which he defined as "a struggle between labor and capital." Because of its industrial backwardness, China had not yet reached this stage and this was to its advantage. It should make the most of it by ensuring that all producers—workers and entrepreneurs alike—cooperated as associates in the task of national construction.

Indeed, Sun emphasized in his conclusion, cooperation was "the primary force of human evolution." But this did not mean the Wilsonian sort of cooperation of a League of Nations, which Sun seemed to evoke in his earlier pages. Instead, at the end, returning to traditional Chinese concepts, he was looking forward to the coming of *Datong*, or the age of Great Harmony.

Anyone familiar with the development of contemporary China will have identified in the plans described above many of the policies put into operation by Deng Xiaoping within the framework of the Four Modernizations: opening up China to the West, using foreign technological and financial expertise, assigning a special role to the coastal outposts, getting a public sector to coexist with private enterprise, valuing consensus and social stability. In this respect, Sun Yat-sen appears as a harbinger. Although his thought is at times somewhat extreme, he developed it with force and originality. His vision is anchored in the Chinese experience and transcends it in the name of a logic and norms borrowed from Western achievements rather than from any Wilsonian or Confucian humanism, although both these thinkers are cited.

Sun Yat-sen regarded himself as a man of action, but whatever action he achieved was usually marginalized as utopianism or as being bogged down in intrigue. In this essay devoted to the theory of modernization, Sun does seem to have hit upon the miraculous balance of pragmatism and idealism that is essential for progress.

PART THREE

Sun's Last Years: National Revolution and Revolutionary Nationalism

1920–1925

In the last years of his career, Sun Yat-sen adopted a policy of cooperation with Soviet Russia and the Chinese communists. That cooperation, which Sun made official one year before his death through the First National Congress (or Reorganization Congress) of the Guomindang, continues to give rise to contrary interpretations. For communist historians, this was a fundamental decision that makes Sun the precursor of the 1949 revolution and, *a posteriori*, justifies all the ups and downs of his career, conferring upon it the grand status of a destiny. The nationalists, in contrast, consider that, for Sun, cooperation with the Soviets and the Chinese communists simply represented a tactic dictated by the circumstances. It was just an episode that the leader's premature death has frozen into a fixed image, and to which one should beware of attaching too much significance.

Sun Yat-sen's activities in his last years provide support for both theses. He was intensely active, involved in many initiatives that developed within a variety of frameworks. He was directing the Guomindang, fixing its ideological orientations and establishing the principles of its organization. He was managing his provincial base in Guangdong. He was elaborating and attempting to implement a strategy—essentially military—for seizing power nationally. He was engaged in diplomacy of the most eclectic nature, always in quest of the indispensable foreign support. So many simultaneous endeavors involved a number of contradictions and it is from these that the communists and the nationalists derive their respective arguments.

These chaotic years lived under the sign of a twofold urgency—the ever pressing urgency for national reunification and emancipation, and that imposed by his incurable disease—were also years in which Sun Yat-sen produced another (the last) interpretation of the People's Three Principles, which his death was to render definitive. As always, Sun's theoretical elaborations were entangled with his political maneuvers. His thought seems to have oscillated in conjunction with factional setbacks, alliances of convenience, and financial and diplomatic constraints. One contradiction follows another, giving the impression of a certain incoherence or even a hint of duplicity. Herein lies the essential difference between modern Western practice, in which the politician considered responsible identifies himself (or is assumed to) with what he says and what he does, and Chinese practice, dominated by the forceful personality of a leader whose role is above all symbolic. However devious his political actions, whatever the glaring inconsistencies of his declarations, in his own view as well as that of the Chinese public, Sun Yat-sen never ceased to embody the ideal of national unification and liberation. Although linked with a long revolutionary career and indubitable talents as a propagandist and communicator, Sun's personal aura by now seemed to operate in a quasi-autonomous fashion. To speak of charisma is just a way of recognizing the limits of analysis.

The succession of events recounted in the following three chapters shows us not a politician at the peak of his career, but a leader isolated, sometimes at bay, scheming against adverse fate, manipulated by those he tried to use—and always ready to tell those whose aid he seeks whatever it is that they expect to hear from him. In the past, Sun had been Christian with the missionaries, Confucian with the literati, a comprador with businessmen. Now he became anti-imperialist and antimilitarist with the agents of the Communist International (Comintern). Was he any more sincere than in the past? The question is beside the point. Political efficacy justified any path taken to achieve it. As for moral integrity, that was measured by personal honesty and loyalty to the essential objectives—democracy, modernization, justice, and social harmony—with which Sun never ceased to identify and be identified by his fellow citizens. Of course, the many articles and treatises Sun published during this period were for the most part written for particular circumstances (many were hasty transcriptions of speeches made to party members, the military, workers) and framed to suit a particular political, factional, or diplomatic context. So for the most part it would be pure exercise to select from them what may appear to be proofs of any one particular ideological orientation. The speeches vary according to an oscillating strategy that was now pro-Soviet, now pro-Western, and "proof" for either orientation is bound to be detectable somewhere.

Yet beyond such circumstantial variations, there does emerge what has to be described as a political philosophy, founded upon long-term objectives. Although very directly influenced by the many ups and downs in his action-packed career, Sun's thought is consistently organized around a handful of major axes and it is upon these that his doctrine rests. The better to seize upon those major axes and distinguish between what is episodic and what is fundamental, I have decided to leave the study of the doctrine itself to Chapter 10, at which point we shall pause for a longer view. In Chapter 9, which is devoted to Sun Yat-sen's last attempts to seize power and apply his program, I shall simply indicate the circumstances that led him to reformulate his People's Three Principles, meanwhile trying not to lose sight of the fact that, although he placed his thought at the service of politics, to suit circumstances, in other ways it truly did govern Sun and his actions: it was, in short, a servant that ruled him.

It could almost be said of Sun Yat-sen's last political action—his journey to Peking in the winter of 1924–25—that, had death not intervened to cut it short, it would have opened up a new chapter in his career. However, even death did not terminate Sun's role. Quite the reverse. It opened up the way for a mythical construction whose influence on Chinese political life far surpassed any exerted by Sun Yat-sen in his lifetime. So it is that Chapter 11, devoted to Sun's death and transformation, is in a sense more important than any other in this whole biography.

NINE

Sun Yat-sen, Soviet Advisers, and the Canton Revolutionary Base, 1920–1924

From 1920 to 1925, Sun Yat-sen was driven by one overriding ambition: to reconquer political power in Peking and, as president, to unify and pacify China. In his strategy for reconquest, he tried to use Guangdong as his territorial base, and for the greater part of those five years (except during the second half of 1922) he did manage to retain control of it. Sun seems to have regarded this base as a springboard that would facilitate an immediate seizure of power in the North: a territory that would provide him with soldiers and money, and where he could implant a government with national pretensions as a rival to the government in Peking and of a kind to receive recognition, hence also financial aid, from foreign powers. This plan set Sun Yat-sen in opposition not only to the Western powers, which were hostile to what they considered to be a rebellion, but also to the Cantonese, who refused to take on the military and financial responsibilities for a reconquest of the North and, in June 1922, ejected Sun from Canton.

In January 1923, following a victory scored by his mercenaries, Sun was able to reinstall himself in the provincial capital. But his power remained precarious: local negotiations and wars absorbed his time and his strength. It was to consolidate his base and increase his chances of success in Peking that the revolutionary at this point accepted the aid that Soviet Russia was offering him.

This was of course not the first time that Sun had resorted to foreign aid, but this time he was not dealing with agents—either cynical or idealistic—of Western or Japanese imperialism, isolated individuals, disowned at the first hint of danger by the governments that had secretly encouraged them. Sun's new partner was a revolutionary state acting through the intermediary of the Comintern, a structured organization with a powerful striking force, served by men of exceptional talent. So the Soviet aid that made it possible to consolidate the base in Canton also profoundly changed its character. From being a territorial base it became a revolutionary base. Its objective now was not simply to supply the needs of a diplomatic and military reconquest of the North, but to light a fire whose flames would eventually engulf the whole country. At this point, Sun's historical impatience ran up against the long-term strategy of the Sovietniki, the Soviet advisers who were agents of the Communist International.

SUN AND THE PROVINCIAL BASE OF CANTON, NOVEMBER 1920—OCTOBER 1923

From 1920 to 1923, Sun Yat-sen tried to use the Canton base as the instrument of the nation's destiny. Putting off the implementation of his democratic and social program, he gave priority to negotiations with the militarists of the North. He became involved in the interplay of alliances between the warlords, and launched a short-lived military expedition to the provinces of the Yangzi valley.[1]

The national nature of his ambitions precipitated a clash between Sun and the members of his entourage who wanted to apply socialism "here and now," and another between himself and the Cantonese gentry and merchants, who were not at all keen to finance the diplomatic and military reconquest of the North. A combination of Cantonese regionalism and pragmatic socialism was personally championed by Chen Jiongming. He favored changing Guangdong into a "model province," later to be integrated into various federalist structures. It was Chen who ejected Sun Yat-sen from Canton in June 1922.

Yet again a refugee in Shanghai, Sun continued to negotiate with the North and to seek diplomatic support from the West, while at the same time considering the possibilities of an arrangement with the Soviets and launching a partial reconquest of Guangdong, using a mercenary force. Sun was not yet prepared to make an irrevocable choice. But what he required of all the paths that he explored was that they should lead to Peking.

Once back in Canton, in February 1923, Sun set up a general headquarters for his future expedition to the North. But he remained paralyzed by the hostility of local circles and the silence and lack of trust of the Western countries. It was at this point that he put the finishing touches on his plan for cooperation with the Soviets, who, he hoped, would give him the means to resolve the situation.

Sun Yat-sen's Nationalism Versus Chen Jiongming's Provincialism

The militarists of Yunnan and Guangxi, who in May and June 1918 had ousted Sun and assumed power in Guangdong, were soon fighting among themselves. When their regime crumbled, the Cantonese troops that had taken refuge in southern Fujian reconquered the province, led by Chen Jiongming.

Chen Jiongming had a long revolutionary career behind him, but his relations with Sun Yat-sen, though of long duration, had never been particularly good. He was born in eastern Guangdong in 1878 into one of the enlightened provincial elite circles that later played a crucial role in the revolution of 1911. He came from a family of large landowners, passed the lower official degree, and then, in 1906, began to attend the extremely elitist academy of law and political sciences in Canton. Most of the teachers at the academy had been trained in Japan. One of them introduced Chen Jiongming into local revolutionary circles. He was elected to the provincial assembly of 1909, took an active part in the reform policy, and won great popularity when he succeeded in getting gambling and opium banned. It was at this point that he became interested in anarchist ideas that were to have a lasting influence on him.

In 1911, Chen Jiongming won the only major battle of the revolution fought in Guangdong. When he was made vice-governor of the province, he ensured the military security of Canton. In 1913, after the failure of the Second Revolution, Chen Jiongming went into exile but refused to join the Chinese Revolutionary Party and swear personal allegiance to Sun Yat-sen. Later, he took part in the Constitution Protection Movement and supported Sun's military government in Canton.

Between 1918 and 1920, while Sun was living in seclusion in Shanghai, Chen, who had taken refuge in Changzhou, made this "the Moscow of southern Fujian."[2] In the twenty-six districts (*xian*) that he controlled, he organized the building of roads and schools. He invited the anarchists to collaborate in a program of education, encouraged freedom of the press, and was prepared, himself, to write articles for the *Fujian Star* (*Minxing bao*), in order to spread the nonviolent anarchist ideas of Pyotr Alekseyevich Kropotkin. In October 1920, when Chen Jiongming reconquered Canton from the Guangxi troops, he planned to establish a government of his own there, to put into practice a policy of economic development, democratization, and social justice, on a provincial scale. Chen's regionalism was fueled by a deep attachment to eastern Guangdong, the cradle of his family and the scene of his first social and political experiments. But he aspired to be the protector of the whole of the province, and his slogan, "Guangdong for the Cantonese," won him all votes. His provincialist ideal was incompatible with the constitutionalist ideology that had inspired Sun's action and military government in Canton in 1917–18, and accordingly, after his reconquest of Canton, Chen Jiongming advised Sun to stay in Shanghai.

Sun had the support of the navy and a few local troops, however, and also that of the Cantonese revolutionaries Wang Jingwei and Liao Zhongkai, and on November 28, 1920, he managed to return to Canton. But the compromise he reached with Chen Jiongming only led to a difficult coexistence for these two men set in opposition by their different political beliefs and rival ambitions.

Sun Yat-sen's first idea, upon his return, was to resuscitate the military government over which he had presided in 1917–1918, within the framework of the Constitution Protection Movement. But realizing how little support there was for this project, he abandoned constitutionalism, though without giving up the hope of establishing a national government. He managed to persuade 225 members of the former parliament (produced by the 1912 elections) to meet in Canton on April 7, 1921, and to proceed to the election of a president. The absence of a quorum obliged Sun to take the title of Extraordinary President. These moves aroused the opposition of Cantonese public opinion; and local trade unions and members of the provincial assembly joined their protests to those of Chen Jiongming. Sun was consequently forced to negotiate, to accept the principle of autonomy for the provincial government, and to recognize the power that Chen Jiongming already exercised over the management of local affairs in his capacity as governor of the province and commander-in-chief of the Cantonese army. As a symbolic gesture, Chen accepted two ministerial portfolios in the new national government. Sun Yat-sen succeeded in arranging for his son, Sun Fo, to recover his functions as head of the Canton municipal government.

For about a year, this compromise enabled the two leaders to pursue their own objectives, separately. Chen Jiongming consolidated the security of the Cantonese base by chasing the Guangxi troops back to their native province, the eastern portion of which he conquered. Meanwhile he was busy modernizing and democratizing the political institutions of Canton. He promulgated a Provincial Constitution, which limited military expenses to 30 percent of the budget and reserved 20 percent for education. He established many schools and colleges, financed programs for further training, and encouraged students to go abroad (particularly to the Franco-Chinese Institute at Lyons, run by former members of the Paris anarchist group). And finally, Chen Jiongming encouraged the rise of Cantonese trade unionism, which was largely dominated by his anarchist friends.

Sun remained uninvolved in these undertakings. He devoted himself solely to his project for national unification, simultaneously engaging in negotiations with the Northern militarists and the warlords of the Yangzi valley, preparing for a military expedition and making many attempts to set up diplomatic contacts. Sun's negotiations with the militarists were conditioned on the one side by the increase in interclique conflicts, on the other by the rise of the autonomist and federalist movement that was such a feature of national political life in the early 1920's.

The Anfu clique, which since 1918 had enforced a brutal but relatively efficient government in Peking, was toppled by a coalition of two other cliques in July 1920. From this time on, the central power over which former coalition parties took to fighting became strictly nominal and the provinces fell more than ever prey to whatever mercenaries managed to impose their authority there. Sun Yat-sen was maneuvering to impose his own authority not only among the major warlords struggling for control of Peking but also among the chief military leaders who, in the provinces of central and southern China, were trying to organize themselves in such a way as to protect their independence. In the North, Sun Yat-sen negotiated with the Zhili and Fengtian cliques,[3] led, respectively, by General Wu Peifu and General Zhang Zuolin. He was ready to ally himself with whichever of these two would agree to reserve him the presidency of a new national government. This is made quite clear by Canton's Minister for Foreign Affairs, in an interview given to *North China Herald* on April 29, 1922: "Whosoever comes to an understanding with us will have to agree that he [Dr. Sun] be provisional president pending the convocation of a parliament and regular elections. We should make no further stipulations."[4] Since Wu Peifu was also ambitious to be the national president, in April 1922 a deal was struck with Zhang Zuolin. It was an unfortunate choice, for the Fengtian clique was almost immediately defeated by the Zhili clique.

Once victorious, Wu Peifu called for the simultaneous resignation of both presidents: Xu Sichang in Peking and Sun Yat-sen in Canton. Wu Peifu claimed to be thereby paving the way for pacific reunification. But on June 2, 1922, while the president in Peking yielded under pressure, Sun Yat-sen, in Canton, roundly refused to quit: "Why should I resign when I am the constitutional President of China?" he said to the United States consul.[5] When Wu Peifu, seeking to re-create the unity and constitutional legitimacy that had briefly prevailed after the death of Yuan Shikai, recalled the president Li Yuanhong and the 1917 Parliament to Peking, Sun refused to recognize this "puppet regime" whose ardent defender he had himself been only five years earlier.

Although Sun's negotiations with the North were explicitly dictated by tactical considerations, those that he was pursuing with the militarists of the Center and the South proceeded under the cover of the autonomist and federalist movement. This movement had by this time mobilized a large segment of public opinion. The ideology of provincial self-government, to which many of the revolutionary or radical elites and enlightened gentry of 1911 had remained faithful, had received new impetus from the rallying of many of the radical intellectuals who had been disappointed by the failure of the May Fourth Movement of 1919. Across the board from moderates to anarchists and including liberals, a consensus seems to have emerged in favor of a federal solution that would make it possible to restore national unity and at the same time allow the provinces to choose the form and pace of their own development. Federalism was even preached by numerous warlords, particularly by those who controlled the central and southern provinces. For these, federalism appeared both as a program capable of consolidating the social basis of their power (by assuring them of the support of the local elites) and as a political strategy that would enable them to fend off the powerful Northern militarists, who were tempted to expand toward the Yangzi.

Sun Yat-sen had refused to associate himself with the policy of provincial autonomy adopted by Chen Jiongming in Guangdong. But on the other hand, he did seek support from the autonomous movements in other provinces, in order to weaken the authority of Peking. In the autumn of 1920, he was trying to negotiate an alliance with the autonomous Hunan of Zhao Hengti and, through Hunan, also with Sichuan and Yunnan. However, the failure of these intrigues pushed him into adopting a strategy of military conquest.

In October 1921, the Extraordinary President got his project for a Northern expedition approved by the rump parliament of Canton. He placed himself at the head of operations and, with a weak force of men, moved toward the frontiers of Guangxi, from where he planned to attack the autonomists of Hunan. This move created high tension between Sun Yat-sen and Chen Jiongming, who as a nonviolent anarchist condemned any recourse to military force and was still counting on federalism to achieve unity. The Northern expedition, which Chen Jiongming refused to finance with provincial funds, soon found itself bogged down. At Guilin (Guangxi), where he established his headquarters for the winter of 1921–22, Sun Yat-sen waited impatiently to be able to swing into action.

As always, he was counting on foreign aid to attain his internal political objectives. Immediately after assuming his functions as Extraordinary President, Sun Yat-sen had published a *Manifesto to the Powers*, in which he presented his opposition to Peking as "a struggle between militarism and democracy, between treachery and patriotism," and urged recognition of his government.[6] Sun saw himself, and wanted foreigners to see him, as the sole president of the true Republic of China. What was at stake in this move of his was clearly, in the first place, the legitimacy of a national government about which the vast majority of Chinese knew nothing and which foreign aid might help to get them to recognize; and second, the financial manna represented by the customs surpluses controlled by the foreigners, which hitherto had found their way to the Peking government.[7]

However, at this point, the international context was not favorable to Sun Yat-sen. In the aftermath of the Washington Conference (November 1921–February 1922), the foreign powers, with the exception of Soviet Russia and Germany, had fixed upon a common policy toward China, whose sovereignty, independence, and territorial and administrative integrity they reaffirmed. They had reached agreement upon a timetable designed to lead to the revision of the customs tariff and, subsequently, to the suppression of privileges of extraterritoriality. In order to facilitate these developments, they wished to stabilize and strengthen the central government—which to them meant the government in Peking. The foreign powers were not of a mind to consider dealing with any other political agent. They regarded Sun Yat-sen as a rebel, and the establishment of his separatist government in Canton, in the spring of 1921, as a move likely to deepen the country's divisions and further weaken the central power. So Sun Yat-sen's many diplomatic efforts were all met with more or less hostile rejection.

Sun Yat-sen's opposition to China's entry into the war on the side of the Allies in 1917 had cost him the support he used to enjoy in American public opinion. The judgment passed by the press was severe. The *New York Times* regarded him simply as "a discredited politician," "a shifty and unscrupulous spokesman of the southern party."[8] Diplomats said much the same, though less directly. The American minister to Peking, Charles R. Crane, described Sun as a man with "impractical and grandiose schemes," who showed "great personal vanity." Many regarded him as "an unscrupulous adventurer, more than willing to [sacrifice] the interests of the nation to his own ends."[9] At the State Department, the Far East Office shared those official judgments. So it was not surprising that the letters that Sun Yat-sen sent to President Warren G. Harding remained unanswered and his efforts to obtain financial aid from American businessmen were blocked by the Washington administration. In January 1921, the State Department refused approval for an agreement struck between Sun and a Chicago *financier* named George H. Shrank that proposed to place bonds issued by "the Republic of China" on the American market: no government that was not officially recognized could issue bonds. Similar objections interfered with a deal arranged later that same year (September 21) between the Canton municipality and the Rabbit Engineering Corporation of New York: on the Chinese side it had been made nominally by "the government of the Republic of China," and Washington refused to guarantee transactions between American citizens and "the Canton government as a political entity acting independently of the central government."[10]

Sun Yat-sen encountered similar intransigence on the part of the British, for whom the existence of a separatist government in Canton threatened not only Chinese unification but also the social and economic stability of Hong Kong. There were still the Japanese; but since the death of Yuan Shikai, Sun Yat-sen had ceased to represent a political advantage for Tokyo, which preferred to treat directly with the Northern warlords. As for France, whose influence in China had declined following the World War, it seemed unable to come up with the crucial aid.

Sun Yat-sen then had the idea of turning to Germany and Russia, neither of which had attended the Washington Conference and both of which found themselves excluded from the new world order dominated by the Anglo-Americans. In 1921, Sun concentrated on negotiations with Germany, picking up and renewing the attempts at cooperation first made in 1917. The reopening of German diplomatic missions in China made contacts easier. These were developed in Canton itself with Vice-Consul Wagner, and in Germany through one of Sun's emissaries. Sun's objectives were the same as ever: to obtain recognition for the Canton government, and also funds. At the beginning of 1922, when secret negotiations were proceeding and there was talk of a visit to Canton by Admiral P. von Huitze, the former German minister to China, Sun Yat-sen decided to incorporate Soviet Russia in the future agreements and to work for a triple Sino-German-Russian alliance.

By this time, late 1922–23, Sun Yat-sen had already made a number of contacts with Soviet emissaries. In December 1921, in Guilin, he had even received a visit from Hendricus Sneevliet, the official representative of the Comintern, better known as Maring. (We shall be returning later to these first contacts that opened up the way for cooperation between Sun Yat-sen and Soviet Russia.) The project of a triple alliance nursed by Sun was not really a part of this revolutionary cooperation, but was dictated by essentially geo-strategic preoccupations. Pinned down as he was in his southern base, Sun Yat-sen needed allies in the North if he was to succeed in the military conquest of Peking. His Northwest plan, upon which he was meditating from 1920 on, envisaged an offensive coordinating an attack of revolutionary forces from the south with a Soviet intervention in Sinkiang, in outer Mongolia, or Manchuria. A triple alliance offered the possibility of military supplies from Germany and, thanks to Russia, control of key regions close to Peking. But when, in September 1922, these secret negotiations were discovered and the *Hong Kong Telegraph* carried the headline, "Plan for Triple Bolshevik Alliance," the German government promptly denied the entire operation. Sun himself acknowledged the existence of the alliance plan, but he denied that it could ever have been founded upon a "Bolshevik ideal."

By the early 1920's Sun Yat-sen had thus still not managed to create for himself the kind of international role that would compensate for his political isolation in Guangdong and for his marginalization on the Chinese political scene. When the inevitable crisis with Chen Jiongming came to a head in the spring of 1922, Sun found himself bereft of both internal and external support.

In April, Sun Yat-sen, irritated at not receiving backing from the provincial authorities of Guangdong for his Northern expedition, decided to strip Chen Jiongming of his functions as governor and commander of the Cantonese forces. This had little effect on Chen's authority. He had returned to Canton wreathed in glory from his victories in Guangxi and was now at the height of his career—having the support of local gentry and merchants and the trade unions, and being courted by the Northern warlords, in particular Wu Peifu, and also by the Comintern emissaries Grigori Voitinski and Maring. The two latter regarded him as "not only a revolutionary general . . . but a brilliant organizer, receiving the sympathies of the masses, popular."[11] Finally, his troops, or rather those of his lieutenant Ye Ju, held the town of Canton.

The rift provoked by Chen Jiongming's symbolic sacking rapidly became increasingly serious. Its effects spread beyond the local balance of power and combined with another crisis that took on national proportions. Wu Peifu had called for the resignations of both President Xu Sichang in Peking and Sun Yat-sen in Canton. With the support of a number of prestigious intellectuals, and in the name of national unity, Chen Jiongming now joined his voice to those demanding Sun's departure. Sun's continued refusal to comply now made him seem in the eyes of both Chinese and international public opinion nothing more than a politician greedy for power, and, to borrow the words of the American minister to Peking, "the one outstanding obstacle to reunification."[12]

Sun Yat-sen himself did not seem to realize the full extent of his isolation. He responded to his critics with provocation and intimidation. He ordered Ye Ju's troops to withdraw from Canton within ten days and threatened that if they did not obey, "I have eight-inch guns with poisonous shells which are capable of entirely finishing their sixty batallions in three hours."[13] The bluff failed. On June 16, Ye Ju had Sun's residence shelled. Song Qingling has left an account of this dramatic episode:

> About two o'clock on the morning . . . Dr. Sun roused me . . . telling me to hurry and dress, that we were in danger and must escape. . . . I thought it would be inconvenient for him to have a woman along with him, and urged him to

leave me behind for the time being. . . . He . . . left all fifty of our bodyguard to protect the house. Then he departed alone. Half an hour after he had gone, rifle shots rang out. . . . The enemy fired downhill at us from two sides, shouting "Kill Sun Wen! Kill Sun Wen!"

As day broke, our men began to reply to their fire with their rifles and machine guns, while the enemy employed field guns. . . . Our captain advised me to leave. Four of us . . . crawled along the bridge passage to make our escape. The enemy soon concentrated fire on this passage and flying bullets whistled about our heads.

After several hours, the fugitives managed to reach the gardens leading to the back of the residence buildings. But they found no more than precarious shelter there:

> From eight in the morning till four that afternoon, we were literally buried in a hell of constant gunfire. . . . Our iron gates were soon smashed and we were confronted by the bloodthirsty bayonets and revolvers of the soldiers who rushed, however, not for our persons, but for the bundles in our hands. . . . Quickly, we seized our chance and ran toward two currents of wild crowds of troops. . . . I succeeded in making an escape. . . . I was absolutely exhausted and begged the guards to shoot me. Instead, they dragged me forward, one on each side supporting me.

Song Qingling in this way managed to reach a farm, then the next day, disguised as an old peasant woman, made her way to a friendly house where she spent another night. "Shelling never ceased the entire night and our relief was enormous when we heard cannon shots at last from the gunboats. Dr. Sun, then, was safe."[14]

Having taken refuge on the gunboat where his wife and a few loyal followers (including Chiang Kai-shek) joined him, for several weeks Sun Yat-sen tried to negotiate, but he quickly found that the Cantonese were on Chen Jiongming's side, that nationally his credibility had been severely damaged by his refusal to resign, and that all his democratic rhetoric paled in comparison with his rival's achievements in Guangdong. He asked for foreign intervention. American diplomacy refused to mediate on the grounds that this in itself would "dignify and magnify Sun Yat-sen and assure him of prestige in the future."[15] Great Britain would do no more than place a gunboat at Sun's disposal. This enabled him to leave the Pearl River on August 9, in order to reach Hong Kong and, from there, Shanghai.

Sun regarded his expulsion from Canton as "a misfortune for the Republic," which he attributed not to his own political mistakes but to "a decline in moral integrity" that made possible the rebellion of "a follower of over ten years."[16] Sun's ego was clearly as strong as ever, but with age it was becoming tinged with Confucian moralism. His failure and his return to Shanghai thus did not lead to any reorientation of his policy.

Sun's New Retreat to Shanghai and the First Steps Toward Cooperation with the Soviets

Unlike Sun's first period of retreat in Shanghai, from 1918 to 1920, essentially devoted to reflection and writing, his second was marked by intense political activity consisting of an endless succession of negotiations, lectures, contacts, and interviews: "His home [had] become a Mecca for political leaders of all shades of opinion and the scene of numerous dinners in which politics [was] the main dish."[17] Sun was simultaneously continuing to negotiate his peaceful return to Peking, exploring the option of the Soviet alliance, requesting aid from the Western powers, and buying generals and mercenaries who could reconquer Canton for him.

Immediately upon his return to Shanghai, Sun Yat-sen published two manifestos in which he defended himself against the charges being brought against him by the Northern generals, part of Chinese public opinion, and certain Western diplomats. The separatist government he had established in the South had not added to divisions in China. It was a constitutional regime that should have opened up the way to unification. Sun made Chen Jiong-ming responsible for that failure and suggested to the Northern warlords a new plan for civil peace and reconstruction. He recommended restoring the authority of Parliament by convening in Peking all deputies, including those of the rump parliament of Canton. He also called for general demilitarization by dismissing the troops or converting them into teams of workers. Finally, he proposed a reorganization of the political system that would make room for a large measure of local autonomy.

At this point, Sun seems to have had the backing of the Zhili clique and its leader General Wu Peifu, a dominant political figure whose control extended to most of the northern provinces and as far south as the Yangzi valley. Wu Peifu enjoyed British support, and his professed liberalism had also won him that of a large section of Chinese public opinion. For several months Sun Yat-sen carried on negotiations with Wu for his return to Peking, although this did not prevent him from simultaneously parleying with Wu's rival, Zhang Zuolin, the head of the Fengtian clique, from whom he appears to have received some funds.

As failure in these negotiations loomed, Sun Yat-sen's plan for pacific reunification was modified, to assign a greater role to Western intervention. In a circular telegram addressed to the leading militarists on January 26, 1923, Sun Yat-sen returned to his plan for a voluntary demilitarization of troops, but accompanied it by a mission of good offices, to be entrusted to a foreign power. This mission would be responsible for overseeing the demobilization operations and also for raising and using international funds for the economic and political reconstruction of the country. Over the months that followed, this theme of voluntary demobilization and foreign participation in the restoration of order in China was to resurface repeatedly in Sun's plans. It constituted one of the leitmotifs of his political philosophy in the last period of his life, even when his strategy of cooperation between the Guomindang and Soviet Russia was becoming a success.

Yet again, Sun Yat-sen appears contradictory and utopian and in advance of his time. This confidence placed in the international community to help to restore order from which, eventually, it would itself benefit testifies strongly to his remarkably modern concept of diplomatic relations. In the same way as, throughout *The International Development of China*, Sun already perceives the importance of economic cooperation, and in his plan for reunification he appeals to a policy of active international mediation of a kind that, half a century later, the United Nations Organization would regularly be adopting.

The "friendly power" whose intervention Sun Yat-sen was soliciting was the United States; but American hostility was not disarmed. Sun consequently turned to a closer examination of the Soviet offers that were then beginning to crystallize.

The history of the establishment of close relations between Sun Yat-sen and Soviet Russia is essentially one of Soviet initiatives to which Sun was increasingly receptive. In his contacts with Western diplomacy Sun was the one who made the advances, thinking up political plans and submitting them to the partners with whom he wished to associate. With Soviet Russia, he was more passive. Usually, he was content to react to the proposals put to him. To understand Sun's attitude, then, we must briefly examine the objectives of Soviet policies in China in the early 1920's.

Those objectives were twofold. As a state, Soviet Russia had inherited the national interests of the czarist regime. Notwithstanding the first Karakhan Manifesto of July 25, 1919, which announced the renunciation, without compensation, of all privileges granted by nineteenth-century treaties, Russia certainly meant to consolidate the geostrategic positions held by the Russian empire along the northern frontiers of China. It wanted to ensure the security of its seaboard and Siberia through its continued control over the Chinese Eastern Railway by extending its influence in northern Manchuria and Outer Mongolia.[18] The realization of these immediate objectives depended on establishing relations with the Peking government, which alone had international diplomatic recognition. Whether pinned down in his southern base or living as a refugee in Shanghai, Sun Yat-sen was, in this respect, of no use to Moscow.

On the other hand, he might be helpful for longer-term plans that Soviet Russia was hatching. Disappointed by the poor showing of socialism in Europe, the Moscow leaders had decided to promote the revolution in colonial countries. At the Second Congress of the Comintern in July 1920, Lenin, in his *Theses on the National and Colonial Question*, had underlined the need for the revolutionaries of Asia to collaborate with movements of national liberation, including those of the bourgeoisie, without, however, altogether subordinating their action to that collaboration.

In accordance with these objectives, both immediate and long-term, Soviet strategy in China was thus three-pronged: it involved negotiations with the Peking government, aid for the organization of the Chinese Communist Party, and a search for "bourgeois" revolutionary partners for the constitution of a united front. While diplomatic representatives came and went in Peking (first Adolf Joffe, then Lev M. Karakhan), agents of the Russian Communist Party and the Comintern were covering the length and breadth of China. In the spring of 1920, Grigori Voitinski encouraged the formation of the first Communist cells. In July 1921, Maring, also an agent of the Comintern, helped to organize the founding congress of the Chinese Communist Party. This attracted a bare sixty members—not a very strong revolutionary striking force—and the Soviet emissaries accordingly established more contacts in their quest for allies. They approached anyone who held military power and political influence, from Wu Peifu to Chen Jiongming, including Zhang Zuolin and a few others, and, of course, Sun Yat-sen, though they do not seem to have regarded him with any particular favor.

Some years earlier, Lenin had formed some opinions of Sun Yat-sen. In a

1912 article entitled "Democracy and Narodism in China," Lenin had praised Sun's "sincere spirit of democracy" and his "warm sympathy for the masses," but criticized his petit-bourgeois, naïve ambition "[to prevent] capitalism in China."[19] In another article, written in April 1913, "The Party Struggle in China," Lenin's opinions were harsher: he attributed the weakness of the Guomindang party to the fact that it had "not yet been able to attract sufficiently the broad masses of the Chinese people into the revolution" and he noted the "weaknesses" of its leader, who was "a dreamer and indecisive."[20] By 1921 Lenin seems to have completely lost sight of Sun Yat-sen. "I know nothing of the insurgents and revolutionaries of South China," he declared.[21]

Between 1920 and 1922, however, a succession of more or less authorized representatives of the new Bolshevik power met Sun, questioned him about his plans, told him of the recent evolution of socialism in Russia, and dangled before him the hope of financial and military Soviet aid. Among those agents, Voitinski and Maring played a determining role.[22]

Voitinski, then twenty-seven years old, represented the Eastern Office of the Comintern. Though he was new to China, he had lived for many years in the United States and spoke fluent English, which enabled him to communicate directly with Sun. He was intelligent, charming, unassuming, and all in all inspired his Chinese interlocutors generally with sympathy. In the autumn of 1920, Sun often received him in his villa in Shanghai. Song Qingling would join the two men for tea and enter into the conversation. The Dutch-born Maring, who succeeded Voitinski a year later, was quite a different sort of person to deal with. A number of the Chinese communists complained of his rough manners and scornful attitude. His revolutionary career had until then been mainly in Indonesia. At the second congress of the Communist International in July 1920, Maring had vigorously supported Lenin's theses. He believed in the policy of a united front and was keen to see it applied in China. After preparing for the foundation of the Chinese Communist Party in Shanghai, he had undertaken a long journey through inland China in order to meet Sun Yat-sen in Guilin, the general headquarters of the Northern expedition. The two men were thus able to have several talks in December 1921.

The first conversations between Sun and these Comintern agents seem to have been dominated by very general themes. There was as yet no question of any alliance or aid. The Soviets wanted to know about Sun and his action, and, for Sun, "these scattered contacts, furthermore, were strands in the broader fabric of [his] relations with the foreign world."[23] Sun declared his sympathy for the Russian revolution and for Lenin personally. He was curious to know more of the accomplishments of the new regime and, in particular, of its New Economic Policy. He dreamed of military aid that would help him to conquer Peking and of a strategy that would make it possible to seize the capital in a pincer movement of nationalist armies from the south and Soviet units converging from the north and the northwest.

A combined action of revolutionary forces would be difficult to manage when the partners were so far apart geographically and Sun also thought it prudent to put off an alliance that might provoke reprisal measures by the British. Hostile as it was to the Soviet regime and anxious to protect Hong Kong, Great Britain might well take the Northern expedition in bad part and threaten the Canton base. However significant Sun's interest in Soviet Russia, it does not seem that the Chinese leader was at this point particularly keen on an alliance with his revolutionary brothers.

The opinion of Sun Yat-sen formed by the Soviet emissaries evolved as one followed another and depending upon how well their meetings with Sun went. At the end of 1919, one of Sun's earliest contacts, a Colonel Popoff, described the Chinese leader as "an old-fashioned militarist who saw no way of saving his country except through arms."[24] But two years later, Maring picked Sun out as the indispensable partner in any collaboration with the Chinese national revolutionary forces. Maring's opinion was not accepted by the Comintern without resistance. M. N. Roy in particular, who was hostile even to the idea of a united front, called Sun "a schemer . . . impractical . . . positively reactionary."[25] And at the Congress of the Toilers of the Far East, meeting in Moscow in January 1922 to counterbalance the Washington Conference, Grigori Zinoviev, the head of the Comintern, produced a shower of attacks on the bourgeois style of the Guomindang and Sun's obstinacy in seeking American aid.

During the second half of 1922 and early 1923 the collaboration between Sun and the Soviets took on firmer form. Maring renewed contact with Sun Yat-sen in August 1922 and used the Chinese Communist Party to promote the policy of a united front. Though with some misgivings, Maring and the Comintern invited members of the Chinese Communist Party to join the Guomindang, individually. Their leaders, Li Dazhao and Chen Duxiu set an example by doing so. Relations between Sun and the Soviets also took a more official turn once the Moscow government's new envoy, Adolf Joffe, was sent to Peking. A correspondence of several months preceded Joffe's journey to meet Sun in Shanghai in January 1923.

The increasing number of Soviet moves in Sun's direction, which some historians, such as Dov Bing, attribute to the role played by Maring personally, in fact coincided with the theoretical elaboration of the concept and strategy of a united front.[26] The *General Theses on the Oriental Question*, approved by the Fourth Congress of the Comintern in November-December 1922, emphasized the intrinsic weakness of the Chinese Communist Party, arguing for a temporary compromise with the Nationalists and certain local leaders and recommending the formation of a united front. The front would have as its main task the pursuit of the anti-imperialist struggle, but the Communists could also use it to promote the social revolution. Finally, a resolution of the executive committee of the Comintern, dated January 12, 1923, designated the Guomindang as the exclusive partner of the Chinese Communist Party and directed it to work within the Nationalist Party, meanwhile preserving its own autonomous organization and action. Sun received the Soviet initiatives favorably if somewhat cautiously. He allowed the Communists into the Guomindang but only on an individual basis, for he rejected the idea of an alliance on an equal footing with a small group that he judged to be incomparably less important than his own party. On the advice of the Bolshevik representatives, who were critical of the Guomindang's inability to mobilize the masses, Sun attempted to revitalize the organization of the party. In September 1922, he appointed a commission of members (including the Communist Chen Duxiu) to revise the party statutes and prepare a new program. The new texts were adopted in January 1923, but they made no practical difference.

Finally, Sun Yat-sen entered into correspondence with Adolf Joffe, who, in Peking, was negotiating in the name of the Soviet government for the normalization of diplomatic relations between China and Russia and for a settlement on the contentious issue of the Chinese Eastern Railway. In the course of the autumn of 1922, they exchanged half a dozen or so letters. Sun explained his military plans to Joffe, asked for advisers to be sent to Shanghai, and broached the idea of Chiang Kai-shek's being sent to Moscow to negotiate aid for the Chinese revolution. However, he expressed irritation over Joffe's conversations with the Peking government. Why couldn't the Soviets wait until Sun had ousted the militarists and established his own presidency? Sun was also worried about rumors of a Russian invasion in northern Manchuria and about a plan for an alliance between Moscow and Wu Peifu.

To resolve these misunderstandings, Joffe himself made the journey to Shanghai to meet Sun. The series of their talks, between January 17 and 26, 1923, resulted in a Joint Statement, which, significantly enough, took the form of a diplomatic agreement concluded between a foreign ambassador and a high-ranking Chinese leader. Sun behaved as a head of state and, with the signature that he placed at the foot of the document, Joffe granted him that status. In this declaration, Sun accepted alliance with Moscow, with two reservations. First, there would be no conversion of China to communism; Russia would be content to support China, that is to say Sun, in its struggle for national unification and independence. Second, Joffe repeated Russia's renunciation of all the privileges secured by the czarist treaties (including those relating to the Chinese Eastern Railway). In return, Sun provisionally accepted the modus vivendi that left the management of this railway to the Russians and authorized the occupation of Outer Mongolia by Soviet troops. It is not known whether this declaration was accompanied by a promise of aid. Perhaps this was negotiated a little later, by Liao Zhongkai, a close collaborator of Sun's, whom Sun sent to meet with Joffe, then in Japan. At any rate, it was after that trip that, in March 1923, Moscow decided to send advisers to Sun and to allocate two million Chinese dollars to him.

The Sun-Joffe Joint Statement of Shanghai was to provide the basis of the cooperation between the Soviets and the Guomindang. Yet, in Sun's view, it did not commit the future. For on January 26, 1923, the very same day as the publication of that declaration, Sun sent off his circular telegram setting out his plan for peaceful reunification thanks to the good offices of a "friendly power," meaning the United States.

Sun was aware that the Soviet aid would be conditional upon the services that he himself could perform for Moscow, that is, through his commitment of the political force that he would represent. But, not unreasonably, he considered that, in the China of 1920, that political force was measured primarily in terms of territories and troops. That is why he reckoned that the development of the Soviet alliance should take second place to the reconquest of Guangdong:

I shall be able to develop closer relations with them [the Russians] from now on. But fundamentally we must have a base to rely on before we can do much. Without anything to rely on, even though the young Chinese Communists share their doctrine, what good can these youngsters do? . . . All this tells us that we must secure a base first. To get that we must recapture Kwantung [Guangdong].[27]

But the strategy of a territorial base brought with it various needs. To set up Guangdong as the base for a grand policy of both national and international dimensions, Sun had to secure the neutrality and, if possible, the cooperation of the colony of Hong Kong, which lay so close. Thus, at the very moment when he was negotiating with the Soviets, Sun Yat-sen, who had just managed to eject Chen Jiongming from Canton, was also making a series of overtures to Great Britain.

The Return to Canton and the Overtures to Great Britain

The defeat of Chen Jiongming, ejected from central Guangdong in mid-January 1923, opened up the way for Sun's return to Canton. Sun had purchased this return by financing mercenaries to the tune of 400,000 Chinese dollars.[28] He had used mostly men from Yunnan. It will be remembered that an army from Yunnan had established itself in Guangdong as early as 1916, in connection with the movement for the Protection of the Country, aimed against Yuan Shikai. Initially this army had been well organized and well led, but it had gradually disintegrated. It severed its links with its native province, which thereupon ceased to finance it. It then had to ensure its own survival by exploiting the territories that it occupied and by negotiating with the surrounding powers. Its command had become fragmented to the point where the practical authority of its leader Yang Ximin was converted into an influence of an essentially moral nature. Nevertheless, by virtue of its size, its equipment, and the relative degree of its discipline, in 1922 the Yunnan army was still the major military—hence also political—power in Guangdong. It constituted the core of the coalition that was formed there and that overcame the power of Chen Jiongming; and it provided Sun with his major striking force. This alliance between Sun and the Yunnanese was one of the determining factors, frequently unrecognized (or passed over in silence) in Guomindang's rising power between 1922 and 1924. But it was an alliance that had to be paid for. Sun Yat-sen hoped to be able to count on Hong Kong for this. By mid-January 1923, he was accordingly making a series of overtures toward the British.

He was encouraged in these tactics by a number of members of his close entourage, who had assembled around his son, Sun Fo. This "prince's clique" (*taizipai*) consisted of young men who had a good Western education and were much attached to the objectives of economic and administrative modernization and were partisans of a certain pragmatism. Their concern for efficiency won them the respect of the Cantonese merchants, who from 1920 to 1922 had maintained good relations with the Canton municipal government headed by Sun Fo. The Chinese elites of Hong Kong were similarly well disposed to Sun Fo's group, an attitude that was strengthened by numerous family links. Two of the foremost members of the prince's clique, Wu Chaoshu (C. C. Wu, 1887–1934) and Fu Bingchang, had married daughters of Ho Kai, a prominent figure in the colony at the turn of the century, whose reformist ideas had inspired Sun Yat-sen at the start of his career.

The prince's clique, by reason of its composition and orientation, was hostile to cooperation with the Soviets. Preferring the idea of a Western alliance, it worked hard to establish a liaison between Sun and the Hong Kong authorities. In February 1923, even while in Shanghai, Sun Yat-sen made contact with the British consul general and Minister Sir Ronald Macleay, who was passing through the city. Although Macleay told Sun not to expect any official support from Great Britain, he then advised the Foreign Office to deal tactfully with the revolutionary leader, bearing in mind his influence in southern China and among the Chinese communities of Southeast Asia. The fall of Chen Jiongming and Sun's imminent return to Canton made it politic for British diplomacy to adopt a certain flexibility in this area.

But nothing could have prepared for the degree of enthusiasm with which Sun Yat-sen was received during the few days that he spent in Hong Kong, from February 17 to 21, before going on to Canton. Invited to lunch by the governor of the colony, to tea with the director of the Hong Kong & Shanghai Bank, the main financial establishment, feted by the Chinese merchants and acclaimed by the students, Sun Yat-sen had many opportunities to explain his plans for demobilization and for the economic modernization of Guangdong, and he had every reason to hope for financial cooperation.

Did he allow himself to be carried away by the euphoria that such a triumph must have inspired in him? Did he want to please his audience? Was he moved by the memory of his revolutionary beginnings in the colony? Whatever the reason, on February 19 he delivered a most unexpected speech to the University of Hong Kong. The man who, just four weeks earlier, had been signing an agreement with Soviet Russia, launched into an apologia for the colonial administration of Hong Kong. He evoked the old days when, as a student, he had discovered the benefits of that administration and at the same time, by comparison, all the corruption of the Chinese bureaucracy. He wound up with a eulogy of the English parliamentary system: "We must take England as a model and carry the example of good government to all parts of China."[29]

For a time after Sun arrived in Canton, the euphoria persisted. The prince's clique was in full sail: Sun Fo once again became the city's mayor, Fu Bing-chang supervised the customs department, Wu Chaoshu the department of foreign affairs. Sun referred publicly to "loans under negotiation" in Hong Kong and the prosperity that this capital could not fail to bring to the province.[30] But the rapid deterioration of the military and political situation of the Cantonese base alarmed the hoped-for providers of funds and the mirage of cooperation with Hong Kong faded as suddenly as it had arisen.

What should we conclude from that renewed spurt of enthusiasm for the West, as ardent as it was unexpected, at a point when preliminary talks had already begun on cooperation between the Guomindang and Soviet Russia? In the Joint Statement that he signed on January 26, 1923, Sun Yat-sen had clearly opened up an option, but he had not committed himself to anything. So while the decision to help him was slowly ripening in Moscow, Sun assumed a total freedom of diplomatic maneuver that led him to make moves altogether at odds with the spirit of the declaration. This behavior was not unusual for him, but it was then, and still is, confusing for Western observers and historians, who not without reason find it incoherent if not dishonest. The simultaneous exploration of contradictory paths was partly Sun's response to the divergent constraints of a strategy of intervention in the North that was founded upon control of a territorial base in the South. It also reflected, without ever really rising above them but possibly seeking to exploit them, the clashes in Sun's own entourage, which set the partisans of cooperation with Moscow in opposition to the prince's clique. In short, such behavior has the air of a distinctive style for the management of contradictions, probably as much a feature of Chinese political culture in general as of Sun Yat-sen's own temperament.

SUN AND BORODIN: THE ALLIANCE WITH SOVIET RUSSIA AND COOPERATION WITH THE CHINESE COMMUNISTS

In the autumn of 1923, Sun swung over to the Soviet camp. Not without misgivings: some of his actions suggest that he still had not altogether put aside the idea of some arrangement with the Western powers. But his rallying to the Soviet alliance and the strategy of a united front were from now on to be expressed with enough determination to affect Guomindang policy and, through this, the destiny of the revolution and China as a whole.

Sun's decision seems to have been dictated mainly by the circumstances. To be sure, he admired Lenin and wanted to learn from the Soviets the methods that had resulted in the triumph of the Russian revolution. But given Sun's eclecticism and the wide range of his interests, it is doubtful whether his curiosity and sympathy for Russia would have sufficed to lead him into a somewhat uneasy alliance had it not been for the insecurity of his position and the absence of any alternative solution. At the time, he was still possessed by the same ambitions: namely, to achieve the military and political reconquest of the North, to get his own power recognized in Peking, and thus to unify China under his leadership. The territorial base in Canton was still simply an instrument serving this national policy. But Sun's control over this base had never been more precarious. And this very precariousness itself dispelled all the hopes that, in February 1923, he had placed in aid from Hong Kong. It was also that precariousness that induced Sun to try to increase his financial resources by seizing the revenues from the maritime customs, though by doing so he put himself in open conflict with the foreign powers who, by virtue of treaties and diplomatic practices that went back to the nineteenth century, managed those revenues. In short, in the autumn of 1923, Sun Yat-sen found himself forced to activate the Soviet option and commit himself to cooperation with Moscow.

That cooperation, deeply ambiguous, would probably never have taken off in the way that it did had it not been encouraged, on the Soviet side, by a man of exceptional talent, Mikhail Borodin (1884–1953), the political adviser sent by Moscow, whom Sun was prone to call his "Lafayette." The meeting of these two personalities was to change the course of contemporary Chinese history. Their relations are still extremely mysterious, very inadequately documented on the side of Chinese historiography and illuminated in a purely partisan light by the Soviet archives only recently made accessible. The relations between the two men relate to a fundamental controversy over the very nature of the alliance struck between Sun and the Soviets. Was it a matter of Sun's rallying enthusiastically to the cause of anti-imperialist and antifeudal revolution, or was it a tactical maneuver on both sides, a mere marriage of convenience that each party hoped to turn to its own interest?

If, as I believe, the second hypothesis is the more likely, the relations between Sun and Borodin may serve as a barometer to indicate the degree of mutual manipulation practiced by each of them. Borodin was a subtle psychologist, endowed with great persuasive force, and an indefatigable organizer who strictly applied the Comintern's directives and, of course, held the decisive trump card represented by Soviet military and financial aid. His influence on Sun Yat-sen was profound. Whereas Sun had hitherto always managed to make the skills, capital, appetites, and idealism of foreigners serve his own objectives, it seems that his talents as a manipulator paled before those of Borodin. Who was going to be using whom?

The Meeting of Sun and Borodin, Autumn 1923

The relations between the two protagonists were affected as much by the circumstances as by their respective personalities. At the point when Borodin arrived in Canton, in early October 1923, Sun's authority over his base was extremely fragile and his credibility abroad was completely eroded.

Stunned by the violent and confused atmosphere of clashes between military adventurers, landowners at the head of their local militias, bandits plotting with politicians, and compradors seeking support from Hong Kong, Borodin, on his arrival in Canton, exclaimed, "Canton is a veritable Babel in which one feels completely lost."[31] Sun himself was having great difficulty in forcing even a semblance of respect for his authority. Since his return to Canton at the end of February, he had been trying to consolidate a military base in the delta region. The coalition on which he had depended for his reconquest of the city had very rapidly split apart. The Guangxi units, theoretically Sun's allies, turned against him and, in mid-April, tried to seize Canton. That scare was soon followed by another offensive, this time launched by Chen Jiongming, who still occupied the eastern part of Guangdong. In the north of the province, the borders with Hunan and Guangxi were held by armies hostile to Sun and secretly assisted by the Northern warlord, Wu Peifu. The Guomindang forces (about 100,000 men) controlled only central Guangdong. The Yunnanese mercenaries, who constituted the kernel of these forces, without openly disobeying Sun Yat-sen, simply refused to apply his orders when it came to setting out on any campaign. Sun was obliged to negotiate each and every offensive with their officers, and pay cash for it on the spot.

These mercenaries, constantly in dispute among themselves, were above all concerned to exploit the regions they occupied. Installed in the trading quarters of Canton or in the outskirts of the town, they grabbed all the local resources, increased the taxes on opium and gambling, claimed many rights of seizure, confiscated the railway revenues. Sun could neither discipline these troops nor eject them from Canton, let alone disband them. Besides, the soldiers constituted his regime's only protection, for although they were disinclined to take the offensive, they were quite ready to fight to preserve their control over the zone that provided for all their needs.

To maintain at least some authority over these armies, Sun Yat-sen sought to divide them, playing off the Yunnanese mercenaries against the Hunanese contingents or the Cantonese units. Sun's method of arbitration was to allot the various contingents their respective zones in which to live (and to exploit), reserving the richest regions for the contingents that he wished to favor. This manipulation created an unstable balance which Sun thought had the advantage of avoiding a repetition of what had happened in the summer of 1922, when rebellion on the part of Chen Jiongming alone had been enough to topple the Canton government.

Guangdong was thus given over to the arbitrary violence of soldiers, brigands, and pirates. The Western press painted a catastrophic picture of the situation; and in Borodin's view was equally somber: "Any place in the Guangdong Province picked at random contained the HQ of a warlord. These troops were controlled by dozens of generals, either completely independent or gravitating towards the strongest of them. Bandits had their organizations linked with the warlords."[32] The endemic fighting that ravaged the province was positively medieval: officers were carried in palanquins along cobbled roads, all the equipment was transported on men's backs, towns were surrounded by ramparts and could only be attacked when they were scaled by means of ladders.[33]

Although primitive, this warfare was expensive. And even if the mercenaries grew rich, thanks to the regions that they were given to control, Sun Yatsen no longer knew where to turn for the money needed to get his disparate contingents on the march—money amounting to about one million Chinese dollars per month.[34] His Military Government multiplied taxes, exacted war contributions from the merchants, had them accused of "treason" and arrested, then released on payment of large ransoms (tactfully known as "guarantee deposits"). Property of clans and philanthropic organizations was confiscated and sold. Exactions such as these raised the municipal revenues of Canton from three million dollars in 1921 to nine million in 1923.[35] But they discredited the government. However, Sun had no choice. He had to find the money necessary to keep control of the contingents theoretically under his authority, and he expended most of his energy tirelessly weaving a network of personal links with the various military leaders on whom, in effect, all his power depended. It was the urgency of his financial needs that prompted Sun's attempt to seize Canton's share of the maritime customs surplus, though the move inevitably brought him into conflict with the foreign diplomatic corps.

The administration of the maritime customs, under international management, used most of its revenues for the repayment of foreign loans. But after World War I, a steep rise in those revenues made it possible to set aside a surplus, which the foreign banks returned to the Peking government. In 1919, however, the southern generals had laid claim to and obtained payment of a portion (13.7 percent) of this surplus to their separatist government, that portion being proportional to the contribution from the ports of Guangdong. In March 1920, when the Guangdong government became dislocated, it stopped insisting on its rights. In the memoranda that Sun Yat-sen addressed to the diplomatic corps on September 5 and October 3, 1923, he asked that those payments be resumed, with arrears that he calculated brought the sum owed to 12.6 million Chinese dollars. Sun's arguments were of both a legal and a moral nature: how could it be acceptable that Cantonese revenues paid to the Peking government should be used to finance its war against the South?

Receiving no reply from the foreign powers, Sun Yat-sen threatened to seize the Canton Customs by force. In December, sixteen warships of American, English, French, and other nations were cruising in Canton waters, while on the nationalist side a proliferation of demonstrations erupted, accompanied by press campaigns and appeals to the Chinese in the United States. Then, quite suddenly, the crisis died down, without Sun's obtaining any satisfaction. In the eyes of nationalist opinion, the glory went to Sun, as to a David facing a Goliath. But the episode also highlighted the extent to which relations had deteriorated between Sun and the foreign powers. The silences of the West had become open hostility. Without money and without allies, Sun Yat-sen was all the more inclined to listen to the Soviet proposals, now that these were put to him by the most convincing and beguiling of messengers.

The new Soviet emissary arrived in Canton on October 6, 1923: he was Borodin. "Borodin had the noble look of an old underground Bolshevik. . . . His drooping mustache . . . was the kind Russian workers wore in pre-revolutionary times. His face had a winning frankness. . . . He was tall and wore a tunic and trousers over high boots, [and] spoke in a resonant, deep bass."[36] Mikhail Borodin (his real name was Grusenberg) was born in 1884 into a family of rabbis in Vitebsk (Belorussia). He was arrested after the revolution of 1905, then went into exile in the United States. The October Revolution brought him back to Russia. In 1919 he helped to found the Third International, then became one of its most active agents in Mexico, the United States, and Europe. All who encountered him at this time praised his extraordinary intellectual powers, his encyclopedic knowledge, his brilliant talents as a conversationalist, and his gifts of persuasion: his ability to win "the confidence and regard of the people to whom he was sent."[37]

When, in September 1923, the central committee of the Russian Communist Party selected him to be Sun Yat-sen's political adviser and to implement the strategy of a united front with the Guomindang, Borodin was totally unacquainted with Asia. But he had behind him a very solid experience of revolutionary organization, and his mastery of the English language would enable him to communicate directly with Sun. His credentials amounted to no more than a single note from Karakhan, informing Sun that he was sending him "his personal representative." Karakhan and Borodin arrived almost simultaneously in China, in the autumn of 1923, and they embodied the double face of Soviet politics. Karakhan, in the North, set about reestablishing diplomatic relations with the Peking government: Borodin, meanwhile, in the South, undertook the job of preparing the overthrow of that same government. The two men worked in close cooperation, with Borodin each week sending Karakhan a detailed report of his activities. As an agent of the Comintern, appointed by the Central Committee and established in his post by a representative of the Moscow government, Borodin enjoyed far greater authority than any of the earlier Soviet emissaries.

As soon as he arrived in Canton, Borodin was welcomed personally by Sun. But though the welcome was warm, the two men were not thinking in the same terms. Sun returned to his northwestern plan. He spoke of launching a punitive expedition against Wu Peifu, establishing a revolutionary base in Mongolia, backed up by Soviet Russia; and in the meantime he asked for the military aid essential for the consolidation of his own power in Guangdong. Borodin wanted Sun to fight against imperialism, in alliance with Soviet Russia and the Chinese Communists. In the days that followed, at receptions organized in his honor by members of the government and leaders of the Guomindang, Borodin enlarged upon the same themes. He did so diplomatically, explaining that he had come to place himself at the disposal of the Chinese revolution,[38] and that, where nationalism and democracy were concerned, Soviet objectives coincided with the People's Three Principles. His words nevertheless provoked strong resistance even within Sun's entourage and among local leaders of the Chinese Communist Party, who had not yet rallied formally to the policy of a united front.

Faced with this resistance, and in his very tenuous position, Borodin set about consolidating his influence and power upon the links of personal friendship that he hastened to establish with Sun Yat-sen. He could see that it was only through Sun Yat-sen's authority that he could impose his own. He agreed with the analysis of the Cantonese communists, according to which "Sun Yat-sen . . . was the soul of the Kuomintang, the center around which different elements—even those who often clash with each other—unite."[39] And in a report that he sent to Moscow, he explained: "I cannot envisage the reorganization of the [Guomindang] party without Sun. It is necessary to make use of his leftism, his authority, his desire to create a party."[40]

To win the confidence of the Chinese leader, Borodin professed unqualified admiration for his political thought and action: "In all my speeches, I have emphasized the extreme importance of Sun Yat-sen's leading role in the national revolutionary movement in China, thereby demonstrating to him our desire to consolidate his position as leader."[41] Borodin insisted that Sun was a precursor and that the attention he had paid to socialism as early as the time of the Revolutionary Alliance was a sign of destiny, paving the way for alliance with a Russia that since then had become socialist.

In his confidential reports to Moscow, Borodin was much more candid: "Sun is very backward. He judges very badly in political matters. He . . . often reasons in a simple way like a man on the street. . . . The Chinese politicians too are judged by him from the standpoint of his personal sympathy or antipathy. . . . He considers himself the hero and the others the mob, while in China he is simply an enlightened little satrap."[42]

Borodin's attitude toward Sun reflects a clear intention to manipulate him psychologically. Did Sun Yat-sen, himself such a subtle negotiator and so clever at bending others to his will, really fall into the trap? Or did he simply play along in a game from which he hoped to derive concrete advantages: namely, military aid and financial subsidies? Sun certainly seems to have been fascinated by Borodin's personality, and by the logic and sincerity of his eloquence and the fervor of his convictions. He hoped that Borodin would be able to help him, Sun, to become another Lenin and to make the revolution triumphant in China, as Lenin had made it triumphant in Russia. Very soon he was to have a chance to appreciate Borodin's organizing skills; and it was not long before he was placing his trust in this Soviet adviser. He sang his praises constantly and insisted upon his presence at all party and government meetings, making him the all-powerful adviser to the political office of the Central Executive Committee of the Guomindang.

Yet Borodin's influence over Sun Yat-sen does not seem ever to have become total. Sun was both stubborn and volatile. Before Borodin's influence, that of other members of the presidential entourage paled, but was never altogether eliminated. Promises made to Borodin one day were often reconsidered the next, for Sun would frequently rally to the last piece of advice proffered and give way before the latest pressures to be exerted. Borodin would then be obliged to return to the attack, mount a permanent guard on Sun, tirelessly repeat his arguments, and obtain renewed confirmation of decisions already taken. Meanwhile, the persistence with which Sun, throughout the period of cooperation with the Soviets, would return to certain projects alien or contrary to that cooperation, such as the Northern expedition, cooperation with the West, or alliance with Japan and pan-Asian solidarity, suggests that the president of the Guomindang may have regarded cooperation with the Soviets as a way of attaining more distant objectives about which he reserved the right to remain vague. The personal friendship that rapidly developed between Sun and Borodin was shot through by the complex interactions between two men of great character and experience. The consequence of their relationship was to be a profound upheaval in the basic elements of Chinese political life.

Sun Rallies to the Policy of a United Front

Even the importance that Borodin attached to Sun's personality was itself tactical. But for this good Leninist, the real instrument of the political struggle and the national revolution could only be the party. He had harbored few illusions on the score of the Guomindang and would repeatedly tell the Soviets in his entourage that "it was impossible even to call the Kuomintang a party. From all points of view—political, organizational, and theoretical—it was something very diffuse and undefined."[43] From the moment of his arrival in Canton, therefore, Borodin's priority was the reorganization of the party. He wanted to consolidate its structures and change its methods in such a way as to make it an efficient tool. At the same time, he wanted to get it to acknowledge its anti-imperialistic objectives explicitly and so break definitively with the West. Sun was quite receptive to his desire for reorganization: when meditating upon the causes of the Republican failure, he had often laid the blame upon the compromises made by the revolutionary party and the presence within it of so many opportunists. Already in the winter of 1922–23, while still in Shanghai, he had himself attempted the beginnings of reorganization, but without success: as we have seen, Sun was no party man.

On October 13, Sun gave his approval to the plan submitted by Borodin: namely, to establish new statutes, set up hard-core cells in Canton and Shanghai, then create local structures in the rest of the country, and finally assemble a congress to approve these changes and elect a central executive committee. In the days that followed, the campaign for the reorganization of the party was led with much razzmatazz by Borodin and Sun Yat-sen *in tandem*. On October 15, at a Guomindang rally in the Canton public park, Sun made a long speech in which, returning to a by now familiar theme, he criticized those who, once they managed to become officials, considered their revolutionary task to be over. He then went on to echo Borodin's ideas, recommending government of the country by the party, unification by dint of popular mobilization, and the use of propaganda in preference to weapons.

Borodin, who was present at these meetings, combined praise of Sun closely with the new objectives proposed by the party: "The Kuomintang has a national leader, Doctor Sun Yat-sen. He is capable of uniting China and, if supported by the people, of liberating the country from oppression by foreign imperialists and Chinese militarists."[44] The orators were acclaimed by the crowd. Borodin also mobilized the press and stated in an interview given to the *Trade Journal* (*Shangbao*): "I deeply believe that before long it [the Guomindang] . . . will be definitely capable of making its organization complete. For, when I think that this party has such a great leader as Sun Chung-shan, I know it [will be so]."[45] Even as he pursued his lightning offensive on the Guomindang, Borodin was busy reassuring the Chinese communists, who were still very suspicious of the Guomindang and the united front policy. Between October 9 and 17, Borodin held five private meetings with them, in the course of which he presented the policy of reorganization as a policy of infiltration: "In the press, I spoke of the Kuomintang but to us it means that I was speaking of the increase, in the end, of the influence of the Communist Party. . . . It must never be forgotten that in reality the work [devoted to the stabilization of the Guomindang] is done for the stabilization of the Communist Party, which aim should always be kept in mind."[46]

On October 25, 1923, Sun appointed a Provisional Central Executive Committee of nine members, one of whom was a communist. The task of this committee would be to prepare the party's statutes and program, to oversee the reorganization of the local offices, and to convene a national congress. Throughout the months of November and December 1923 and into mid-January 1924, the Provisional Executive Committee was intensely active, meeting frequently, elaborating texts and always working in close liaison with Borodin, whom Sun Yat-sen had assigned to it as adviser. Sun approved of this activity. He thanked Moscow for having sent him Borodin, whose "warm" and "sincere" aid he much appreciated.[47] In private, however, he harked back to the days of the Revolutionary Alliance, a time when revolutionary fervor burned brightly and comrades were linked by close personal ties. Since those days, the ranks of the party had swelled. The reforms now in progress should help to preserve the original impetus at the same time as procuring all the advantages of Soviet-style organization. The Guomindang would be able to borrow from that type of organization whatever was useful to it, while rejecting its negative aspects: "We may merely yoke up Soviet Russia and mount it," he remarked.[48] That was typical of Sun's attitude (and of the attitude of many of his contemporaries and successors, always keen to imitate foreign models, not for their intrinsic value but for their possible benefit to Chinese practice).

Borodin was clearly not too pleased. Although the Guomindang boasted of having 30,000 members in the province of Guangdong alone, barely 3,000 had actually renewed their membership at the time of the campaign. In Canton itself, twelve local sections had been created around cells of activists, most of them communists. But Borodin was dismayed to discover that there was no real communication between the leadership of the party and the militants on the ground, and that the objectives of Sun Yat-sen's struggle (particularly against Chen Jiongming) had never been clearly explained to the people. The serious political and military crisis that threatened the very existence of Sun's government in mid-November 1923 confirmed Borodin's fears and severely tested the new cooperation between the Guomindang and its Soviet adviser.

Since August, the Yunnan and Guangxi military contingents controlled by Sun had been besieging Chen Jiongming in his base at Huizhou, to the east of Canton. But at the end of October, these contingents lost ground and fell back toward Canton, pursued by their enemy to the very outskirts of the town. The collapse of both the capital and Sun's government seemed imminent.

At this point, Borodin threw his usual caution to the winds. At the meeting of the Provisional Executive Committee on November 13, he criticized the Guomindang leaders for not having mobilized the masses. "The essentially peasant population of Guangdong still has a passive attitude to what is happening at the front!" he declared. To resist Chen Jiongming's attack, Borodin proposed issuing two decrees: the one would declare the confiscation of the property of landowners and its redistribution among those who cultivated it, and the other would limit the working day to eight hours and increase workers' wages. "As many militants as possible would fan out across the countryside using bicycles, motor-bikes, sampans, or cars" to spread the political news to the population and to mobilize it. In the meantime, Borodin organized detachments of volunteers to reinforce the town defenses: about five hundred, most of them trained by communists, set off for the front.

Terrified by the dangerous emergency and swayed by Borodin's eloquence, the members of the Provisional Executive Committee approved all these measures. But they still had to be countersigned by Sun Yat-sen. He, however, could not be found. He simply let Borodin know that his partisans, particularly those living overseas, would never accept the confiscation of land. When at last Sun did consent to receive Borodin, it was to inquire about the possibilities of political asylum in Russia and to discuss his best means of flight.

On the evening of November 18, the military situation was reversed and Chen Jiongming's troops beat a retreat. It is hard to say to what extent this success was due to Borodin's efforts at organizing and mobilizing resistance. Sun Yat-sen was convinced that he had been saved by Borodin and their relations became even closer. Borodin now demanded that Sun Yat-sen become personally involved in putting the Reorganization plan into operation. He was no longer content with the go-ahead given by Sun, who meanwhile remained essentially absorbed by military affairs and rarely put in an appearance at Guomindang meetings. Made the wiser by the failure of his decrees on the confiscation of land and the limitation of working hours, Borodin now feared that some of the Guomindang leaders who were hostile to Soviet influence would block the Reorganization unless Sun himself prevented this. Modest as usual, he himself claimed to do no more than implement Sun's decisions, declaring that without Sun's effective leadership mistakes would be inevitable.[49] It was therefore decided that in future the meetings of the Provisional Executive Committee would take place under Sun's personal chairmanship. Following the military crisis of November 12–18, Sun's support for his Soviet adviser became ever more active and enthusiastic.

Having learned a few lessons from that crisis, Sun Yat-sen now recognized the need for a policy based upon the mobilization of the masses, and he defended the Soviet model against any of his partisans who found it too radical:

> What our party and they advocate are the Three Principles of the People: the ideologies are similar. But our party still lacks effective methods and should study theirs. Since we wish to learn their methods, I have asked Mr. Borodin to be our party's director of training: he is to train our comrades . . . and I hope all comrades will give up prejudices and earnestly study his methods.[50]

Borodin's management of the military crisis had confirmed the excellence of Soviet methods in Sun's eyes. Did the leader of the Guomindang really believe in the promises of his adviser, who was confident of consolidating the Canton base in six months and extending the revolution to the whole of China within one or two years? At any rate, from the end of November on, Sun used all his authority to ensure the success of the policy of a united front and to impose it upon his party. Borodin stood in need of every bit of his help if he was to overcome the increasingly explicit opposition of many members of the Guomindang.

The Reorganization Congress of January 1924

The Reorganization Congress took place from January 20 to 30, 1924, in Canton. Its aim was to legitimate Borodin's moves in southern China and, through this, the policy of the Comintern. Although the congress was under Sun Yat-sen's control, Sun himself acted in large measure as Borodin's spokesman. His influence over the 196 delegates representing the provinces, major towns, and overseas communities was all the stronger because he had himself personally appointed half of them, the remainder having been elected by local party members.

The respect that surrounded the historic founder and leader of the revolutionary party was expressed in the ritual. At the opening ceremony, the delegates first saluted the Guomindang flag three times, then bowed to Sun Yat-sen. Despite his dislike of the discussions, bargaining, and compromises inherent in all such assembly procedures, Sun took an active part in the congress. He made no fewer than eight major speeches. Right from the start, his message was clear. They should follow the Russian model: "Now only Russia has [a method] which can be considered a good example for our Party."[51] On January 25, in the memorial speech he made in honor of Lenin, who had just died, Sun returned to this theme in lyrical mode: "You, Lenin, are exceptional. You not only speak and teach, you convert your words into reality. You have founded a new country; you have shown us the path for the common struggle."[52] The homage is particularly interesting because of the hint of self-criticism by a man whose words had so often remained divorced from facts.

But Sun Yat-sen was not content simply to indicate general guidelines. He vigorously backed up his policies, intervening, reintervening, arbitrating, overruling, taking over the discussion, forcing votes. Did all this activism, rather unusual for Sun, simply reflect the strength of his convictions? Should it not, at least in part, be ascribed to the requests and pressure coming from Borodin, who remained at Sun's side throughout the congress? The president of the Guomindang was, in effect, the Soviet adviser's principal supporter facing an opposition that was crystallizing around three essential problems: the peasant policy, relations with the West, and the admittance of communists into the Guomindang.

The congress was preceded by a series of clashes between Borodin and the party moderates, who were supported by the overseas communities. At the end of November, ten or so Cantonese members of the Guomindang, led by Deng Zeru, presented Sun with a petition in which they denounced "a plot to borrow the body of the Kuomintang (Guomindang) but to infuse it with the soul of the Communist Party."[53] They criticized the new organizational principles inspired by the Soviet model. According to them, those principles were in truth elaborated by Chen Duxiu, the secretary general of the Chinese Communist Party. Possibly because they could not attack Borodin himself, so much was he in Sun's favor, they then proceeded to lay into Chen Duxiu, stressing anything that could render him suspect and hateful to the president of the Guomindang: "Ch'en Tu-hsiu [Chen Duxiu] was formerly Ch'en Chiung-ming's [Chen Jiongming's] favorite. . . . He declared . . . that the Three Principles of the People and the Five Power Constitution had no theoretical basis . . . and accused you yourself [Sun Yat-sen] of being a man of the past."[54] Through the Reorganization, they claimed, the communists were seeking to subvert the Guomindang and impose upon it their own leadership and dogma. By including anti-imperialism in its program, the Guomindang would forfeit any hope of foreign (Western) aid, and by recommending a struggle against militarism, it would isolate the generals who held real power in the country.

This document was important because of the identity of one of its signatories, Deng Zeru (1868–1934). He was a veteran of the revolutionary party, within which he had played a leading role as early as 1907, raising funds in Malaysia and Southeast Asia and demonstrating his unshakable loyalty to Sun Yat-sen during the black years following 1913, as well as in the clash with Chen Jiongming in 1922. His protest against Sun's new political orientation was the first criticism ever voiced by this loyal friend and collaborator of Sun's.

Sun Yat-sen swept the criticism aside. He dismissed it with a few notes scribbled in the margin of the text itself: Chen Duxiu had taken no part in the elaboration of the party's new statutes. "The project . . . was prepared by Borodin at my request and examined by me," Sun Yat-sen declared. It was pointless to fear the substitution of the communist ideal for the principles of the Guomindang, he added, since "there is really no difference between the principle of people's livelihood and communism." Finally, if the young communists had mocked the Guomindang, that was because they wanted to disparage it in order to monopolize Russian aid for themselves. But Soviet Russia had preferred to ally itself with the Guomindang, which represented a social and political force far superior to that of a small group of young radicals: "If we suspect Russia because of our suspicions of Ch'en Tu-hsiu (Chen Duxiu), we shall fall into Ch'en's trap and help him to realize his plan." As for the "capitalist nations," it was pointless to hope for the slightest aid from them: "They will never have any sympathy for the Guomindang." The Guomindang could count only on Russia.[55]

Sun Yat-sen thus sought to reestablish discipline within the ranks on the basis of both doctrinal and strategic arguments. He did not succeed in convincing all his partisans, and one questions whether he himself was in truth totally convinced. On the eve of the Reorganization Congress, the debate was still going strong, but Sun Yat-sen's position had become less intransigent. The final wording of the plans to be put before the congress had been entrusted to a small group of Guomindang leaders, with Borodin at their side. While the Soviet adviser found an unconditional ally in Liao Zhongkai, he came up against criticism from Hu Hanmin and also from Wang Jingwei (despite the latter's leftist reputation). The controversy centered on two main points: the peasant policy and the attitude toward the West.

Borodin wanted the Guomindang program to include the confiscation of land and its redistribution to the peasants. Wang Jingwei was against confiscation on the grounds that it would promote the class struggle in the countryside. The text eventually presented to the congress, though it referred to redistribution, omitted any mention of the provenance of the land to be redistributed.

Borodin also wanted to obtain from the Guomindang an explicit declaration of alliance with Soviet Russia in their common anti-imperialist struggle, a declaration that would make any return to the past impossible and would definitely rule out all hope of Western aid. To those who protested that China, surrounded by hostile imperialist nations, had to remain prudent, he replied with passionate eloquence: "Nations and States are divided into the oppressed and the oppressors. Which of these do you intend to stand with?"[56] In the end, Sun arbitrated in favor of moderation. An anti-imperialist declaration would be "inopportune." When the right time came, Sun would be the first to declare himself against the West. So in these preliminary discussions, Borodin's success was limited, but he had to make the best of it, for fear of alienating Sun's support. And that support was still absolutely indispensable, as can be seen by the turn taken by the debates during the congress.

From the start of the congress, on January 20, up until its suspension, declared on January 25, to observe mourning for Lenin and to honor his memory, the debates mainly concerned the adoption of the Manifesto. The document contained three parts: the first recalled the history of the revolutionary movement and its setbacks after 1911 and concluded with an appeal for national revolution; the second set out the People's Three Principles; the third announced the party's new program.[57] The account of its new aims could only alarm the moderates of the Guomindang, of whom there were many among those attending the congress. Sun Yat-sen set the ball rolling. In his opening speech, on the morning of January 20, he stressed the need to reorganize the party and make it the instrument of the revolution and national reconstruction. In the afternoon of that same day Sun delivered a second major speech, criticizing the laxity shown by the revolutionary party after 1911, when it had accepted conservatives and reactionaries in its ranks. The Manifesto was then read out to the congress delegates. After this, Sun Yat-sen again underlined the importance of this document and, before a vote on it was taken, submitted it to the examination of an ad hoc committee.

Within this committee argument broke out again, as violent as on the eve of the congress. Hu Hanmin spoke for the moderates. The Manifesto reflected the aims of the Comintern, as defined in the resolution passed by its Executive Committee on November 23, 1923. Like the Comintern resolution, the Manifesto attributed the misfortunes of China to imperialism and militarism, redefined nationalism in terms of the anti-imperialist struggle, and pressed for the mobilization of the peasant and working masses. Although the Manifesto did adopt the People's Three Principles and the organization of the Five Powers, its interpretation of these positions (in particular concerning the livelihood of the people, which was given a Marxist-Leninist slant) seemed to the moderates a betrayal of their original principles. Opening the debates of the committee, on January 21, Sun Yat-sen recognized this opposition and tried to calm things down, saying, "I have recently received telegrams from members of the Guomindang living in Southeast Asia. They are wondering whether our program has become communist . . . and, if it has, they are threatening to leave the party." Sun lamented that error of judgment (which he blamed on imperialist propaganda). He then reaffirmed the Guomindang's fidelity to its original principles, which in any case were not incompatible with communism: the livelihood of the people, for instance, "embraced communism, socialism, and collectivism, all at once."[58] In conclusion, he appealed for entente between the moderates and the radicals of the party, between comrades both old and new.

These calming words did not disarm the opposition, however, and the strength of their defiance eventually rattled Sun Yat-sen, who now took to deserting the congress and avoiding Borodin. The two men came face to face in a dramatic encounter on January 23, the day on which the Manifesto was to be submitted to the plenary session. Sun Yat-sen spoke of the anger of the party's veterans and possible reprisals on the part of the Western powers. In his reply, Borodin castigated this "ancestor cult" and the personal interests linked with fund-raising among the overseas Chinese communities. Sun proposed abandoning the Manifesto for a program of national government that would undertake to satisfy the four essential needs of the people: food, clothing, lodging—and transport. This was a crucial moment for Borodin. The withdrawal of the Manifesto would spell ruination for all his efforts and a return to the Guomindang's "empty phraseology." But he did agree that the program of national government should be published at the same time as the Manifesto, though not as a substitute for it, reckoning that although the program was useless in itself, it could not possibly be harmful.[59] In the end, Sun gave way to Borodin's insistence, returned to face the congress, presided over the session, steered the discussion, and managed to get the Manifesto voted through.

This was a great victory for Borodin. But the moderate opposition persisted, and when the congress reconvened on January 28 it relaunched its offensive, this time over the statutes of the Guomindang and the place given in the party to the communists. Anxious to avoid the formation of a party within a party, the opposition wanted to ban double membership and oblige all communists to abandon their original party upon joining the Guomindang. The communist delegates to the congress had chosen Li Dazhao to plead for their cause and the retention of double membership. Complying with recommendations made by Borodin, Li Dazhao made his speech at a plenary session and in the presence of Sun, to whose authority he made many references. It was Sun who had authorized the communists to join the Guomindang and they would remain in it, meanwhile retaining their links with the Comintern, as Sun had allowed. Li Dazhao spoke with modesty and courtesy. He recognized the Guomindang's leading role in the anti-imperialist fight. He proclaimed his loyalty and that of his comrades: "Since we have joined the Party [the Guomindang] and so long as we remain its members, we shall carry out its political program and abide by its constitution and by-laws."[60] In the debates that followed, Sun Yat-sen committed his authority in support of this line. "The communists are joining our party in order to work for the National Revolution. We are therefore bound to admit them. . . . If the communists betray the Kuomintang, I will be the first to propose their expulsion."[61] The delegates did not dare to oppose Sun and the principle of the communists' entry into the Guomindang (*ronggong*) and their double affiliation was voted through by a strong majority.

The congress also approved the party's new statutes, closely inspired by the Soviet model: they instituted a similar hierarchy and similar discipline, founded upon democratic centralism. On one point, however, the statutes of the Guomindang did differ from their model. They established a presidency, endowed with very extensive powers, superior to those of the National Congress and the Central Executive Committee, and they entrusted this presidency to Sun Yat-sen for the whole of his life. This preeminence retained for Sun Yat-sen may have been necessary in order to obtain his active support for the Reorganization or to reassure veterans still loyal to their leader. From Borodin's point of view, it no doubt had the added advantage of strengthening his own power through that of the Chinese leader.

The last task of the congress was to choose the leadership team that would be responsible for implementing the new orientations of the party. The twenty-four members of the Central Executive Committee (CEC) were chosen by Sun and approved by a show of hands from the congress. They included three communists; and among their deputies were seven others. By giving the communists so many posts in the Guomindang's central organization, Sun Yat-sen demonstrated a fine confidence in his allies, or perhaps in himself. Communists also headed some of the main offices of the CEC (organization, peasants, labor) where they acted as directors or, more often, assistant directors. These could be counted upon to steer Guomindang action toward the masses. And they themselves could count upon the support of the left wing of the party, which under Liao Zhongkai's leadership, had made a remarkable breakthrough at the congress. However, the right wing was certainly not eliminated. It still provided two-thirds of the top party officials.

The Reorganization Congress had transformed the Guomindang from "a collection of followers of a national hero to a highly organized party of disciplined individuals united by the acceptance of a common revolutionary program."[62] This evolution had been willed and directed by Sun Yat-sen and, through him, by Borodin. Borodin's triumph must certainly be identified with Sun's. But can the reverse be said to be true? Did Sun's hesitations at moments of crucial decision merely reflect the opposition coming from his entourage or did they betray personal misgivings? Did Sun share the convictions of his Soviet adviser or had he given way to the latter's insistence just to make sure of financial and military aid from Russia? In Sun's eyes, the congress's most important decision may have been the creation of the military academy that he had been dreaming of for years and that he had often urged upon his Soviet advisers. It could well be that, to ensure Russian aid, Sun Yat-sen had acted with an ideological opportunism more than a little reminiscent of the concessions that he had in the past proposed to both the West and Japan.

Such an interpretation should, of course, be studied in the light of the fundamental texts that Sun Yat-sen published in 1924. We shall attempt to do so in Chapter 10. But another way of assessing the depth and sincerity of Sun's new commitments is to compare his declarations of intent with what he actually did following the Reorganization Congress. Sun was to die in March 1925. By January in that year, the cancer that was killing him ruled out public activity of any kind. So there is only the brief space of one year in which to try to discern whether, within the context of a hectic sequence of events, there are signs of a real conversion or, on the contrary, simply indications of an essentially tactical alignment, the ephemeral nature of which was then blotted out by his death.

SUN YAT-SEN AND THE TRANSFORMATION OF CANTON
INTO A REVOLUTIONARY BASE

The congress's votes ratifying cooperation with Russia and the Chinese communists manifested the Guomindang members' confidence in Sun and their respect for him more than their own political convictions. Opposition to this cooperation remained strong among the nationalist leaders, and Sun Yat-sen was to encounter considerable difficulties in the management of a united front disrupted by many crises and undermined by a latent unease. Notwithstanding those difficulties, the very existence of the united front sanctioned an extreme radicalization of Cantonese policies. Sun Yat-sen associated himself with these but in general took no initiatives. Although the moves of the communist and nationalist activists usually received Sun's approval, sometimes they did arouse his misgivings; and Borodin then worked hard to overcome these by means of either persuasion or pressure.

Sun thus appeared to be committed to the implementation of the new political line decided upon by the congress, which aimed to turn Guangdong into a genuine revolutionary base from which a vast movement on a national scale would then be launched to mobilize the masses. Sun proclaimed this to be necessary, but he may well have considered all this recourse to propaganda and organization as a detour, for, in truth, he was still attached to his old dream of reconquering the North. To him, a few military victories and a few skillful negotiations still seemed the shortest route to power. So, to the consternation of his communist allies and his Soviet advisers, in September 1924 he tried to relaunch the Northern expedition, creating a real stumbling block for the united front and a hugely discordant note in the concerted operation of revolutionary mobilization.

Sun Yat-sen and the Problematic Piloting of the United Front: The Crisis of June 1924

After the Reorganization Congress, Borodin was absent from Canton for several months, leaving Sun Yat-sen on his own to direct the smooth running of the united front. In Borodin's absence, the Soviet influence continued to make itself felt through the action of the *sovietniki* and the initiatives of the communists who were now in positions of leadership within the Guomindang. But the opposition persisted in denouncing both the communists' infiltration of the party apparatus and Soviet Russia's grand designs for power. Left to his own devices, Sun proved to be more or less unwilling, or incapable, of coping with these contradictions. In June 1924, when the crisis broke, Sun pressed for Borodin's return, for he depended on it to get the status quo restored. But the unease in the party persisted and the relations between Sun and his "Lafayette" were disrupted by clashes that were subsequently reflected, at a theoretical level, in the contradictory interpretations given to the principle of the livelihood of the people. The stormy history of these few months illuminates both the extent of Sun's commitment and the restrictions imposed upon it by the weight of old friendships, his desire not to upset particular interests, and his loyalty to a number of doctrinal choices brought to maturation by the experience and reflection of an entire lifetime.

In Canton itself, the group led by Deng Zeru continued its campaign against the infiltration of the Guomindang by the communists. Deng found considerable support in the municipal government: the mayor, Sun Fo, and his colleagues, for instance, and also in Sun's immediate entourage. Chiang Kai-shek, who had recently returned from Russia to organize the new military academy of Huangpu (Whampoa), also joined the chorus of those who denounced Soviet afterthoughts: "According to my observation, the Russian [communist] Party does not have any sincerity.... The Russian Party has only one objective in China, that is to build up the Chinese Communist Party as its legitimate heir."[63] A circular letter issued by Sun Yat-sen and dated March 18, 1924, reminded party members of discipline: they had no "individual liberty" and should "strictly observe the party line."[64] But this authoritarian argument did not suffice to calm spirits that were then further agitated by the Soviets' campaign to get a Sino-Russian treaty signed. The treaty, a fruit of Karakhan's negotiations with the Peking government, was designed to establish diplomatic relations between China and Soviet Russia. But the Minister of Foreign Affairs, Wellington Koo (Gu Weijun), wanted to renegotiate its conditions so as to obtain definite recognition of Peking's sovereignty over Outer Mongolia. In the meantime, despite the anger of the Russians, the Chinese government had decided to withhold its signature. It was supported in this by public opinion and even by certain members of the Guomindang. As we have seen, Sun Yat-sen was hostile to the very principle of this treaty. Nevertheless, he was obliged to join the propaganda campaign in favor of its ratification, which Borodin was organizing with the help of the Chinese communists.

But the scandal that precipitated the eruption of the crisis was the discovery in Shanghai, by two nationalist leaders, Zhang Ji and Xie Chi, of internal communist documents that had appeared in the *Journal of the Socialist Youth Corps* and that were explicit about the details of cooperation with the Guomindang: "Hereafter in all propaganda, publishing, people's organizations . . . our party should use the Kuomintang name. . . . But in matters which we recognize as essential and in which the Kuomintang is unwilling to use its name, we will still do them as our party's individual activity."[65] The two nationalist leaders believed that they had here discovered proof of a plot. As veterans of the party and members of its Central Supervisory Committee, they decided to go to Canton at the beginning of June to present Sun Yat-sen and the CEC with a formal Impeachment of the Chinese Communist Party.

Their criticisms, which echoed those of the Cantonese moderates, stressed the discrepancy between the communists' professions of allegiance and their real activities within the Guomindang. They even went so far as to question Sun Yat-sen's authority and role. To be sure, they did not dare to attack the historic party leader directly, but they accused the communists of having deceived him. As is well known, in China the mistakes of the emperor can always be blamed on his evil advisers.

Caught between two fires, subjected to pressure from those clamoring for the expulsion of the communists and also threatened by those same communists with a break with Russia in the event of a rejection of the united front, Sun Yat-sen refused to settle the matter until Borodin returned. After being summoned by several urgent telegrams, the Soviet adviser arrived in Canton on June 20. The exact drift of the conversation between the two men during a private dinner is not known, but rumor had it that Borodin had issued a warning: if the Guomindang was going to interfere with the development of the Chinese Communist Party, Soviet Russia would be obliged to seek other partners in China. A few days earlier, on June 25, in the course of a meeting with the leaders of the moderate opposition, Borodin had recognized that the communists indeed constituted "a party within the [Guomindang] party" but had intimated that this was the price to be paid for Russian aid:

> The Kuomintang as such is dead and buried. . . . New elements, like the communists, acting as a group, have called into being a new Kuomintang, by instilling a spirit of emulation into the old comrades. . . . The central organization of the Kuomintang is still lax and its orders are not obeyed by all party members. The communists cannot be expected to give up their organization under such circumstances.[66]

Was it because of Sun Yat-sen's imperative need for Russian aid or because of the confidence that he truly placed in Borodin and the Soviet model that the status quo was maintained? In any event, it was. According to a circular from the CEC, dated July 3, all those who adhered to the ideal of revolution and the objectives of the People's Three Principles should be considered members of the party, whatever faction they may have belonged to in the past.

Within the Guomindang, however, anxiety remained acute. Letters flooded in from Shanghai and Peking protesting against the intrusions and manipulations of the communists and, in particular, their propaganda urging the ratification of the Sino-Russian treaty. In Canton, Zhang Ji and Wang Jingwei made openly anti-communist speeches, and petitions circulated demanding the expulsion of the dangerous allies. Sun Yat-sen himself seemed won over by this movement. On August 3, in the course of a lecture on the People's Livelihood that he was delivering at Canton University, the president criticized Marxism, refuting the Marxist plus-value theory and rejecting the central role of the class struggle. According to witnesses, when the lecture was over, Borodin had a forceful conversation with Sun, after which the two men parted, looking angry. One week later, in a second lecture on the People's Livelihood, Sun Yat-sen went back on his criticisms and once more asserted that the principle of the People's Livelihood and socialism were equivalent. It was now possible for the crisis to be rapidly defused. In a resolution passed on August 23, the plenary session of the CEC recognized the special responsibilities of the communists within the Guomindang and absolved them from the accusations of factional activities that had been brought against them by Zhang Ji and Xie Chi. Once again Sun Yat-sen had vouched for the communists and the Soviets, in spite of the misgivings of his own partisans.

In the face of Sun Yat-sen's hesitations and U-turns, one might be tempted to exclaim, like Cardinal de Retz, infuriated by the infinite complexity of the intrigues of the Fronde, "What a multitude of movements all in opposite directions! What contrariety! What confusion!"[67] One might even go so far as to declare, along with him, that "quite honestly, in some matters there are some points that remain inexplicable!" But, despite the cardinal's castigation of "the insolence of vulgar historians who would think they were doing themselves less than justice if they left one single event without elucidating its causes," it is hard to resist trying to work out some of Sun's motives. There is no evidence to shed any light on the line of reasoning that he followed; so, really, the most one can do is attempt to see the situation that he faced through his own eyes. That is clearly a risky undertaking, but still, here goes . . .

One of the principal constraints, if not *the* principal one, that Sun Yat-sen had to take into consideration was the imperious and urgent need for the financial and military aid that was beginning to be made available and was bearing its first fruits. And, as we have seen, the Cantonese communists, like Borodin himself, were not slow to point out that such aid was conditional upon the united front's functioning successfully.

Martin Wilbur, the most recent and the most scholarly of Sun Yat-sen's Western biographers, furthermore suggests that Sun derived considerable satisfaction from directing the national movement as a whole and getting his party to profit from the new impetus provided by the communist militants. This extremely plausible hypothesis is, of course, partly based on Sun Yat-sen's own high opinion of himself and his role, but it also rests upon the strategy that the revolutionary leader had already adopted in Tokyo, at the time of the founding of the Revolutionary Alliance in 1905.

In 1924, the young intellectuals who formed the Chinese Communist Party harbored just as many misgivings with regard to Sun Yat-sen, his thought, and his style of action as the young exiles in Japan had at the beginning of the century. By 1924, the gap between Sun and the new intelligentsia was not just one generation, but two generations wide. The literati's disdain of anyone who had not studied the Classics had been succeeded by the scorn that militants felt for a romantic revolutionary and rough-and-ready politician such as Sun Yat-sen. We know that Sun himself had felt little warmth for the students he encountered in Tokyo. And the sympathy that he had expressed for the young activists of the May Fourth Movement (from among whom the first communists had been recruited) had likewise been measured. In a speech made in the presence of the cadets of Huangpu, on November 3, 1924, Sun Yat-sen criticized the lack of discipline of student protesters: "They do not really know what a revolution is," he said.[68] Nevertheless, in both cases, Sun Yat-sen's political sense and his intuitive apprehension of the way a society developed enabled him to recognize the potential importance of these intellectual circles and the fact that it would be in his interest to control them.

So, predictably enough, when he allowed communists into the ranks of the Guomindang, Sun Yat-sen was not content simply to obey the conditions imposed by the Comintern but set about attempting to consolidate his own power. The group formed by the Chinese Communist Party, tiny though it was, represented a harder nut to crack than the earlier circles of young reformists who had been influenced by Liang Qichao. Furthermore, in 1924 Sun Yat-sen no longer held the major trump card upon which his strength had rested in 1905: namely, control over the funds sent to him by the overseas communities. Far from appearing as a provider, he was in danger of being regarded as a usurper by the communists (particularly those of Shanghai), who, notwithstanding the funding provided by the Comintern for the Guomindang, continued to regard themselves as the natural and most important allies of Soviet Russia. In 1924, the unequal balance of forces and the superiority of the hundreds of thousands of nationalist disciples over the several hundred communist militants may have caused Sun to think that he could effect a takeover of the radical intelligentsia, just as he had in 1905. But if he did think so, he was leaving out of account the evolution of the international context, the change in ideological references, and the presence on the scene of Borodin, a strategist with nerves of steel who was working with Sun Yat-sen but not necessarily for him.

Whatever the effects of his impotence or his miscalculated ambitions may have been, Sun's reluctant goodwill made it possible to maintain the united front and, by so doing, to implement a radical policy aimed at turning Guangdong into a revolutionary base.

"Red Sun over Canton"?

Should the "red sun" rising over Canton really have been identified with Sun, as it was in the leading American journal of Shanghai, *China Weekly Review*, on November 1, 1924?

Even if he recognized the need for radical social measures of a kind to mobilize the masses in the service of the revolution, and if he approved of those measures and endeavored to facilitate their application, in general Sun Yat-sen was not taking the initiative here. He did no more than react to things as they happened, more or less giving his approval to the actions of the communists and the left wing of the Guomindang. And where the mobilization of peasants and workers was concerned, Sun Yat-sen even manifested a measure of prudence. He rejected slogans calling for a class struggle, particularly in the countryside. He contented himself with promoting anti-imperialist slogans. On the other hand, in some domains Sun Yat-sen was perfectly prepared to follow, if not to precede, his mentors in the art of revolution—in bringing the university into the party, for example, and in the political indoctrination of the armed forces. In the autumn of 1924, Sun associated himself fully with bringing the Cantonese business circles into line by means of a harsh suppression of the Merchants' Corps and the burning and looting of the commercial quarter of the provincial capital. Whatever reservations he may have expressed with regard to the communist doctrine, on such occasions Sun was looking more and more "red" in the eyes of both Chinese and international public opinion.

In 1930, Borodin was to boast of having been the first, along with the Cantonese communists, to defend the idea that the Chinese revolution should rely on the peasantry, and also of having launched the policy of rural mobilization. In this, he was acting in accord with the directive voted by the Comintern at its Third Congress in May 1923, saying that, in the zones occupied by the forces of Sun Yat-sen, it was absolutely necessary to insist that land confiscation take place. Only this could ensure the victory of Sun's revolutionary army.[69] But, as we have seen, Sun Yat-sen did not favor the policy of land expropriation. On that point, he never gave in to Borodin, neither during the crisis of November 1923 nor at the time of the clashes before and during the Reorganization Congress in January 1924. The program adopted by that congress had therefore made provision for a reform of land rent and the implementation of a policy of credit and major works of improvement. Though it had gone on to declare that the state would give land to cultivators without enough, it was vague about where the land for redistribution was to come from. To move from the economic and social modernization of the countryside desired by the Guomindang to the peasant revolution preached by the communists was a big step. In the course of successive drifts in that direction on the part of local authorities and, it would seem, in the face of Sun's opposition, it was eventually taken.

From the spring of 1924 on, two institutions were made responsible for formulating and applying the policy of the Guomindang in the countryside: the CEC's Farmers' Bureau and the Farmers' Movement Training Institute, which opened in Canton on July 3. Although the Farmers' Bureau was headed by a succession of directors who were members of the Guomindang, it was really controlled by its secretary, Peng Pai (1896–1929),[70] and, through him, by the Farmers' Committee of the Chinese Communist Party and by Borodin. This was the department that, in June, got Sun and the CEC to approve a

"Plan for the first steps of the peasant movement," to prepare for the organization of peasant associations (*nongming xiehui*). The declared purpose of these was "to liberate the working classes on the basis of the People's Three Principals, and to organize poor and exploited peasants." In fact, they were designed to become the instruments of the class struggle in the countryside. Accordingly, they excluded from their ranks large landowners, priests, and moneylenders. Since they were autonomous, they eluded the control of the Guomindang. Eventually, these peasant associations became armed organizations capable of confronting the village militias (*mintuan*) run by the local gentry. They were to be led by activists produced by the Farmers' Movement Training Institute. The first cadre, recruited in early July, numbered thirty-eight students, most of them young intellectuals wanting "to go to the people," who were given political instruction. The second cadre, enrolled two months later and numbering 225, also attended courses in military training.

Although Sun Yat-sen had in June agreed to the creation of the peasant associations and the Institute, by August he was alarmed by the dangers of a radical drift and was issuing warnings to the future cadres whom he went to address in their Institute. Certainly the peasants must be rallied to the national revolution. But the particular features of China's political situation and its social organization made it impossible for China to follow Russian strategy and enter upon a class struggle. On the contrary, it was necessary to use pacific methods and appeal for cooperation: "You must be very cautious in your propaganda. . . . You should especially persuade all farmers to cooperate with the government, and deliberate carefully on the method to solve the relation of farmers to landlords so that the farmer will benefit and the landlord not suffer loss."[71]

In spite of these warnings, clashes between the peasant associations and the village militias that autumn turned into pitched battles. Did Sun Yat-sen take sufficient note of the eruption of this revolutionary violence in the Cantonese countryside, where so many other kinds of violence were already rife? Did he distinguish these social battles from the usual exactions being perpetrated by the troops or by bandits? There is no evidence that he did. Absorbed in other preoccupations, Sun now seldom intervened in rural politics. And by February 1925, when Borodin decided to send in Canton government troops to reinforce the peasant associations in their struggle against the village militias, Sun was in Peking, on his deathbed.

Although Sun was associated only distantly with the agrarian policy carried out by the communists in the name of the Guomindang, he did actively support the mobilization of the workers. Without throwing doctrinal caution to the winds, as he faced up to the hostile West and in order to reinforce his own image as a great patriot, he deliberately drew personal credit from this mobilization.

The Guomindang had taken an interest in the workers' movement long before the Soviets arrived in Canton. Like Cantonese industry itself, with the predominantly handicraft production of its many small businesses, the workers' movement was fragmented and heterogeneous. Guilds, some of which were gathered into federations, operated alongside a few trade unions of a more modern kind, such as that of the seamen. On the whole, trade unionism of a moderate nature prevailed, marked by corporatist traditions and, to a lesser degree, by the anarchist influences of the period when Chen Jiongming had controlled Canton, from 1920 to 1922. For many years, Sun Yat-sen had maintained links with the trade unions, whose principal leader, Ma Chaojun (1885–1977), was one of his most faithful disciples. This former apprentice, who had joined the Revolutionary Alliance in 1905, had taken part alongside Sun in all the great revolutionary battles, from the Canton insurrection of April 1911 to the struggle against Chen Jiongming in 1922. The Guangdong Mechanics Union, which he had founded in 1917 and which he still led, was one of the most powerful of the workers' organizations of Canton. The precocity and remarkable vitality of this movement, which operated throughout the delta region and beyond it too, toward Hong Kong, had already been manifest in the organization of successful strikes in 1919, 1920, and 1922 and in the First All China Congress of Workers, held in Canton in May 1922.

The Chinese Communist Party (founded in 1921) and the Secretariat of Labor that it created had played virtually no part in the rise of this movement. From 1924 on, however, owing to their alliance with the Guomindang and their participation in the leadership of the party, the communists were able to relaunch large-scale worker mobilization in southern China and also work to take control of the principal trade union organizations.

The Labor Bureau of the CEC, created immediately after the Reorganization Congress, was headed by Liao Zhongkai, who combined loyalty to Sun with his pro-Soviet sympathies. It was upon his initiative that the great celebration of May 1, 1924, was organized in Canton. This demonstration, designed as a show of unity, attracted thousands of participants. In his speech to them, Sun Yat-sen once again appealed for a fight for national emancipation, and consigned the theme of the class struggle to the back burner. In a colonial country such as China, he declared, the workers were oppressed and exploited not by local capitalists but by foreign imperialists who controlled the Maritime Customs, took possession of the market, and impeded the rise of national industries. The first step in the emancipation of the workers therefore had to be victory over imperialism. The main item on the agenda was not the struggle between Chinese workers and capitalists but "the political problem, which can only be solved through the People's Three Principles."[72]

A few weeks later, the Shamen strike (July 15–August 20, 1924) provided an opportunity to draw the trade unions into a major patriotic movement and for the communists to intensify their work of organization. The strike broke out in protest against the security measures imposed by the British and French authorities following an assassination attempt in the Shamen concession against M. Merlin, the governor-general of Indochina, who was visiting Canton. The Chinese would now have to show a passport in order to go at night to the Shamen enclave on the bank of the Pearl River, in the heart of Canton, where the French and British concessions were located. Under the terms of nineteenth-century treaties, the concessions made available to the foreigners to set up their houses and their firms remained legally under Chinese sovereignty, although the practices of the nineteenth and early twentieth centuries had in many cases led to de facto independence for these foreign enclaves. But the nationalist fervor aroused in the wake of the May Fourth Movement of 1919 had rendered such abuses intolerable. On July 15, all the Chinese workers of Shamen, from consulate employees to nursemaids and policemen, went on strike. They were supported by twenty-six trade unions coordinated by a strike committee. Sun took the role of mediator. For more than a month he negotiated with the foreign authorities, the Guomindang moderates, the communists keen to prolong the strike and radicalize it, and the workers, who were impatient to return to work but were prevented from doing so by the strike committee's pickets. Finally, the French and British authorities agreed to lift the security measures.

Sun Yat-sen had won an important victory. For the first time he was seen as the spokesman and inspiration for mass nationalism. Not only had he become part of the anti-imperialist movement that permeated and galvanized Chinese (urban) society, but he had placed himself at its head. Never had his prestige seemed greater, even in the Chinese communities overseas.

In this reconquest of public opinion, entered upon in the name of patriotism, Sun was greatly helped by the communist activists' work of mobilization. Since they too profited from the strike by beginning to gain control of the organization of Canton workers, in conformity with the proletarian vocation they had embraced, the movement of the summer of 1924 appears in a sense as a rehearsal. For only a year later, starting in the summer 1925, a great revolutionary strike would for sixteen weeks mobilize the workers of Canton and Hong Kong against the British, allowing the communists to strengthen their position considerably in Canton and within the Guomindang and provoking, in response, violent reactions on the part of the moderate nationalists. At the time of the Shamen strike, while Sun Yat-sen was still in the saddle, the respective objectives of the nationalists and the communists seemed to balance out. The way the situation evolved affirmed the diagnosis made a few weeks earlier by Borodin, when he had rejected the accusations of communist infiltration and cell-creation within the Guomindang and had declared, "As matters now stand, the two parties [nationalist and communist] make use of each other for mutual advantage."[73]

The main characteristics of the system set in place in Russia after the 1917 revolution were the absolute monopoly exercised by the Communist Party, the interpenetration of the party and the state, and the subjection or suppression of all forms of autonomous organization. Sun Yat-sen was inevitably impressed by the efficiency of the system that Borodin extolled to him. He had himself always complained of the laxity of the Revolutionary Alliance and the Guomindang, the egoism and inconstancy of their militants, the individualism of the students, and the independence of the troops theoretically rallied to the revolution. How, then, could he fail to identify with the idea of a party disciplined in the service of its ideology and its political program? Already in 1914, the creation of the Chinese Revolutionary Party had been an attempt to realize Sun's desire to shape a reliable and solid instrument of power. But at that time, the only means he could devise to anchor the obedience that he wanted to insist upon from the militants had been an oath of personal obedience, which most of his disciples had rejected as being humiliating. Now, at the head of a Guomindang renovated and regulated (in theory) by democratic centralism, Sun Yat-sen strove to extend the influence of this party over two institutions: education and the army, for he reckoned control over these to be essential to the success of his revolutionary project.

The doctrinal divergences that prevented Sun from adhering totally to the policy of mobilizing the masses urged by his communist and Soviet allies were of no account when it came to problems of organization and the exercise of power. Sun believed Leninist discipline to be one of the strong points of the Soviet model. It was indeed, he believed, the main reason for the success of the Russian revolution, in contrast to his own failures. One can sense an instrumental concept of the united front taking shape in Sun's mind—a prolongation, as it were, of the idea of the old reformists of the nineteenth century who wanted to borrow "Western methods" in order to put them to work to achieve their own ends, and a premonition of the deliberate pragmatism of Mao Zedong, who was to dismiss dogma as being "less useful than excrement," and to choose to retain from Marxism-Leninism only its efficacy.[74]

As we know, Sun Yat-sen had never felt much sympathy for the student circles that he had taken care to avoid twenty years earlier in Tokyo, with their volatile, unwarlike intellectuals to whom he had been loath to entrust responsibility when he was preparing for insurrectional uprisings in southern China at the beginning of the century. Later, he had stood aside from the happenings of May 1919; and though he encouraged the students, he continued to mistrust the spontaneity of their actions, attributing it to an excess of liberty and suspecting it of leading to chaos. To channel the vibrant strength of youth, which was as likely to result in disorder as in revolution, it was necessary to train the students in the party spirit and to inculcate them with the ideal of the People's Three Principles, along with a sense of discipline. It was with all this in mind that he created the Canton University by merging three local establishments of further education.[75] The president appointed for this university was a high-ranking party cadre, Zou Lu (1884–1954), who combined his functions there with being a member of the CEC and the director of the Youth Department.

Symbolically enough, it was at this university that Sun Yat-sen chose to deliver an important series of lectures on the People's Three Principles, in the spring of 1924. Many other orators—nationalist leaders, Soviet advisers, and so on—also spoke at this university whose students, subjected to this stream of propaganda, soon underwent rapid politicization. This was the first step in the process of linking the university to the party (*danghua*, meaning literally "partification"), a process that, from the 1930's on, was to dominate the educational system of the Guomindang and, later, that of the communist regime.

The establishment of the military academy of Huangpu represented the heart of the apparatus set up by the united front or, at any rate, what Sun Yat-sen considered to be the essential part in that apparatus. As we know, Sun had always conceived of the revolution as an armed seizure of power. In order to recruit for the revolution, he had in the course of his career turned successively to secret societies, bands of outlaws, factious officers, and warlords greedy for guns. But mercenary soldiers thought only of their own interests, and what Sun was dreaming of was a revolutionary army over which he himself could exercise direct control. In fact, this had been one of the first requests he made to the Soviet agents. He had mentioned the matter as early as December 1921, to Maring, and tried again first with Joffe, then with Borodin. There certainly were many armies fighting alongside the revolutionary party in Guangdong, he said, but you could not call them revolutionary armies. They were not inspired by any ideal and their leaders were guided by personal interest. At this point, Sun would proceed to evoke what he considered to be the treachery of Chen Jiongming.

Sun Yat-sen was counting upon Soviet money and advertisers for the establishment of the academy where the ideal revolutionary army (*lixiangshangde gemingjun*) would be trained. And the academy was indeed financed by 186,000 Chinese dollars from the Canton government and 3 million rubles (the equivalent of 2.7 million Chinese dollars) by the Soviets. It received thirty guns from the Canton arsenal, and 8,000 from the Soviets. In terms of both money and men, the creation of this academy represented the principal Soviet investment in China in Sun's lifetime. The first group of four military experts arrived in Canton in January 1924, led by Pavel A. Pavlov, a former czarist officer who had become a hero of the Red Army. Half a dozen more officers joined these in October, led by Vassili K. Blücher, better known by his adopted name, Galin. General Galin had been the commander-in-chief on the Far Eastern front in 1921–22 and was a man of experience, energy, and intelligence (his portrait was drawn unforgettably by André Malraux in his *Les Conquérants*). After Pavel's accidental death, it was Galin who became the chief military adviser to the Canton government, coordinating his work closely with Borodin.

The site chosen for the academy was the small island of Huangpu, situated in the delta, twenty-five kilometers downstream from Canton. A fort had been built there in 1870, and a few pieces of artillery still remained, looked after by the garrison installed at that date. These artillerymen were now so old that they were assisted in their military tasks by their sons, grandsons, and great-grandsons.

In January 1924, the Reorganization Congress had appointed Chiang Kai-shek chairman of the preparatory committee for the academy. In spite of Chiang's misgivings, hostile as he was to the growing influence of the Soviets in Canton, the necessary preparations went ahead. At the beginning of May, Huangpu Academy opened its doors to the first class of five hundred cadets. The new academy, modeled on Soviet institutions, reserved a place of fundamental importance for the ideological training of the future officers. Under the supreme authority of Sun Yat-sen, Chiang Kai-shek took on the military direction of the academy, and Liao Zhongkai became responsible for the political instruction. In addition to departments of General Education, Military Instruction, and so on, there was a political department run by Dai Jitao (a moderate Guomindang member), assisted by the communist Zhou Enlai.

The military instruction was given by Chinese officers, advised by Soviet experts. The many difficulties that arose in the relations between the Chinese and the Soviets did not stem solely from the inevitable linguistic obstacles. Professional and national susceptibilities were also involved, as were problems of "face" and fear of "the red fever" (*chihuo*). The Soviets therefore limited themselves to training the cadets in shooting and teaching them tactics. As A. I. Cherepanov explains, they left political indoctrination to Borodin, who intervened when necessary, using Sun Yat-sen and Liao Zhongkai as intermediaries.

Most of the cadets were young men fresh from college, who had never suffered the debilitating experience of service in the warlords' armies. The Academy endeavored to inculcate a sense of mission and a spirit of self-sacrifice. In the political course, the emphasis was laid on the People's Three Principles, expounded by the old leader Hu Hanmin, and the history of the revolutionary party, taught by Wang Jingwei.

Sun Yat-sen took a close interest in Huangpu Academy. Accompanied by Borodin and the principal party leaders, he presided over the official inauguration of the establishment on June 16, 1924. The speech he delivered on that

day to a young and enthusiastic audience retraced the history of the Chinese
revolution and its setbacks, fixed the objectives of the academy, which was
charged with creating the armed limb of the revolution, and invested its
cadets with a particular responsibility for implementing the People's Three
Principles and winning the final victory. Sun expressed his hope that "it would
be as brilliant as that won by Russia." In his introduction he compared the
fates of the two revolutions, but that was the sole allusion made to Russia. His
discretion in that respect confirms the impression that, in spite of the presence
of the *sovietniki* and cadres such as Zhou Enlai, in its early days the academy
was relatively closed to communist influences and that in Huangpu Sun was
given a clear field.

In Marxist historiography, Sun Yat-sen is portrayed as the representative of
a Chinese bourgeoisie fighting for the national revolution. But while it is true
that the treaty-port merchants and the overseas communities did give him
precious aid at the time of the 1911 revolution, ten years later they felt nothing
but mistrust where he was concerned. The crisis of the Merchants' Corps,
which erupted in the heart of the Cantonese capital in the summer of 1924,
led to a brutal armed clash. This civil war had in many respects all the features
of a class struggle, with workers' pickets and peasant detachments coming to
reinforce the government units that were fighting against the Merchant militias. The radicalization of Guomindang policy under the influence of the
united front certainly helped to precipitate the conflict. But its origins went
further back: for several years, the general insecurity and the many new taxes
and exactions had driven the merchants to arm themselves in order to protect
their property and their lives.

The mercenaries from Yunnan, Guangxi, and elsewhere, on whom Sun
depended for support in order to control Canton, subjected the town and
surrounding region to gross financial exploitation. Even when his own government was tottering under its financial difficulties, Sun was obliged to
sanction or at least tolerate those exactions. The traders, left to look after
themselves, not at all surprisingly resorted to creating self-defense forces. The
first Merchants' Corps had been created in Shanghai in 1905, in imitation of
units organized in the International Settlement. At the time of the 1911 revolution, the Merchant Volunteer Corps had been closely associated with the
dawning of nationalist feeling in the urban classes and the defenses of the local
autonomy from which, according to public opinion, the defense of individual

liberties stemmed. They were banned by Yuan Shikai but were revived during the troubled period of the early 1920's. Neither their immediate objectives of self-defense nor their ideology had changed, but the extremely rapid radicalization of government policy now made the defense of local interests seem to the Guomindang to be a reactionary reflex, designed to preserve the elites.

The scale of mobilization was a response to the ubiquity and urgency of the perils. The number of Merchant Corps volunteers rose from 13,000 in the autumn of 1923 to over 50,000 by the summer of 1924. Most were shopowners and employees in trade. Their firms undertook to pay the cost of their equipment. Some firms financed forces as large as thirty militiamen each, and militias of this kind were organized in as many as a hundred or so towns in Guangdong. In June 1924, these volunteers federated themselves into a provincial body. According to the president of the federation, a comprador of the Hong Kong and Shanghai Bank, the movement was strictly limited to the defense of local interests: "We are tired . . . of . . . the drop of our trade, the inability of raw materials to reach their proper market, the loss to our investments."[76] This economic discontent masked a violent political antipathy to Sun Yat-sen, whom the merchants blamed for having appealed to mercenaries to reconquer Guangdong and then allowed them to grow fat on local resources. They condemned Sun Yat-sen's ceaseless, and expensive, wars against Chen Jiongming and his other rivals. Finally, they were worried about his alliance with the communists and the encouragement given to the workers' trade unions in their opposition to corporatist guilds.

As for Sun, he suspected the merchant militias of seeking aid from his great enemy, Chen Jiongming, who was still holed up in eastern Guangdong and whose autonomist inclinations were in accord with those of the local gentry and merchants, and above all from the British, who were alarmed by the specter of Cantonese Bolshevism.

On August 9, a Norwegian cargo vessel, the *Hav*, arrived in Canton loaded with weapons bought in Europe through British intermediaries and destined to reinforce the Merchants' Corps. Although the importation of these weapons was covered by a perfectly valid license, Sun Yat-sen ordered the cargo to be seized, and it was stocked under guard in Huangpu Academy. The merchants appealed to the (Cantonese) overseas communities, to the Inspector General of the Maritime Customs, to the diplomatic corps in Peking, and to the foreign consulates in Canton. The Canton government issued a warrant for the arrest of the president of their federation. The merchants responded with a general strike that brought business to a standstill. Sun Yat-sen considered bombarding the business quarter of Canton. The consular corps protested and the British threatened naval intervention. On September 1, Sun published one of his most violent anti-imperialistic manifestos. But he took no further action and for a while the crisis died down. Desperately in need of money, Sun even entered into negotiations with the Volunteers, offering to return their weapons to them, at a price.

On October 10, as the unloading of the weapons in the port of Canton got under way, a crowd of demonstrators celebrating the anniversary of the 1911 revolution interrupted their delivery. A bloody skirmish ensued. The merchants again declared a general strike, called for the overthrow of Sun Yat-sen and his government, and announced the speedy return of Chen Jiongming.

The response of the nationalists was to create a crisis cell in the form of a Revolutionary Committee endowed with full powers, with detachments of workers and peasants placed at its disposal along with rural police brigades, the arsenal garrison, the cadets of Huangpu, and other units under direct government authority. The composition of this committee was the subject of another argument between the moderates and Borodin, who wanted to exclude Hu Hanmin and Wang Jingwei. Sun Yat-sen arbitrated in favor of that exclusion, for, he said, the revolution must follow the Soviet model, which Hu Hanmin did not believe in and which Wang Jingwei was temperamentally unsuited to apply. Both were clever at maintaining the status quo but incapable of taking the forceful decisions necessary in a time of crisis. In October 1924, as in November 1923, Sun Yat-sen's faith in Borodin seemed to grow as the emergency became increasingly alarming.

On October 14, the order was given to attack the business quarter of Xiguan. The next morning, at dawn, government units seeking to infiltrate the quarter clashed with marksmen stationed on the stone towers that were used as pawnshop stores. These windowless towers looming above the surrounding wooden buildings constituted so many small fortresses. To dislodge the marksmen, the whole quarter was set ablaze and then looted. A thousand apartment blocks were reduced to ashes. The Merchants' Corps was disarmed, and its leaders fled. Victory was Sun's. But in Shanghai, in the large coastal towns, and in Southeast Asia and the United States, the powerful Cantonese communities that at the turn of the century had been the first to welcome and support their young compatriot were now outraged by his tyranny. The communists, through their official organ, *The Guide* (*Xiangdao*), blamed the drama on the past compromises made with imperialism. They pressed Sun to declare war on Great Britain and to purge the Guomindang of its ultra-rightist and counterrevolutionary members.

Enmeshed in these crises and carried along by their momentum, would Sun give up trying to keep the difficult balance that he had so far—up to a point—managed to maintain between the moderates in his party and the radicals allied with the communists? It certainly looked as though the repression of the Volunteers marked a shift to the Left on Sun's part. Did this mean that he had totally given in to Borodin? In fact, what was occupying Sun's mind in the autumn of 1924, as disease was taking over his body, was neither the revolutionary base nor relations between the Left and the Right. It was his irrepressible fascination with the North.

Sun Yat-sen's Strategic U-turn and the Plan for a New Northern Expedition

The ancient imperial capital, facing the steppes and firmly landlocked, remained the symbolic seat of political power and national unity. Ever since 1911, when his destiny had almost taken a national turn, Sun Yat-sen's eyes had been fixed on Peking. The creation of separatist governments in Guangdong had—at least in his mind—been aimed solely at reunification. The consolidation of a revolutionary base in Canton could fit in very naturally with such a plan, and Borodin was careful to dangle before Sun the perspective of an extension of the revolution to the whole of China in the near future. But, at the end of the summer of 1924, Sun dissociated himself from that strategy.

In the first week of September, he decided to launch a new Northern expedition. He left Canton and moved to the little town of Shaoguan, on the northern frontier of the province, where he set up his headquarters. What possessed Sun to turn his back deliberately on all that had been achieved by the political and military efforts in Canton over the past ten months? He himself provided an explanation, in a letter to Chiang Kai-shek: "I have come to Shaoguan with the intention of abandoning Canton, cutting my bridges, so to speak." The consolidation of the base seemed to him impossible, or perhaps just too slow, for three reasons that he proceeded to enumerate: "In the first place, British pressure. . . . Second, the counter-pressure of our enemies [Chen Jiongming] in the East River region. . . . Third, the greed and arrogance of the expatriate armies. . . . We must give it [Canton] up quickly and look for a living space elsewhere."[77]

But Sun's move was not simply a reflex of flight. It was connected with a strategy of alliance with a number of militarists, against the Zhili clique and General Wu Peifu, who controlled Peking. Sun Yat-sen was hoping in this way to provoke a general realignment of the political forces in the North that might eventually enable him to accede to the presidency.

This decision took Sun's entourage by surprise. Criticism and protest were rife even within the Guomindang. Sun Fo resigned from his functions as mayor, Liao Zhongkai abandoned his post as provincial civil governor, and Chiang Kai-shek refused to allow the cadets of Huangpu to take part in the expedition: only one company was sent to Shaoguan, as a personal guard for Sun Yat-sen. The communist allies criticized this expedition that had "nothing to do with the true revolution of national liberation" and in which "neither the trade unions nor the peasant associations should become involved."[78]

Sun's behavior certainly was inconsequential in relation to the policy announced and applied since the Reorganization Congress. This Northern expedition, the second of its kind, was nevertheless in direct line with the intentions and ambitions Sun had nursed in 1922–23, which his support for the united front had clearly not dispelled. Perhaps all the work of revolutionary transformation undertaken in Canton under the guidance of the Soviets and with Sun's support had had a single objective—in Sun's mind, at least: namely, at last to render possible this military reconquest that he had been planning for so long. In view of the great anti-imperialist demonstrations mobilizing Canton, the floods of revolutionary eloquence pouring over the city, and the violent social claims being made in its suburbs and the surrounding countryside, it is admittedly hard to believe that Sun truly did want to reverse the priorities and was capable of releasing the prey to grasp at a mere shadow. Yet nothing could distract him from his planned expedition—not even the lack of cooperation from his Soviet military advisers, which simply had the effect of forcing him to turn to the mercenaries of Yunnan and Guangxi, or the crisis of the Merchants' Corps, which he was content to manage from a distance.

Does the absolute priority thus given to the reconquest of the North over the revolutionary mobilization of the South call into question the significance of the policy of the united front as practiced by Sun Yat-sen alongside the *sovietniks* and the Chinese communists since the autumn of 1923? Some people think so. But before tackling the controversies surrounding Sun Yat-sen's last months and his posthumous destiny, we must consider his new formulation of the Three Principles, as he elaborated them during the spring of 1924.

The composition of this political credo amid so much activity is part of the history of the revolutionary base of Canton, and it illuminates Sun Yat-sen's attitude at this time. The importance of these texts is, however, greater than that of the circumstances in which they were written. Once they became definitive, as a result of the premature death of their author, they took on a major reference value and made it possible to turn Sun Yat-sen's extremely volatile political thought into a doctrine.

Sun Yat-sen's Three Principles of the People

Strictly speaking, *The Three Principles of the People (Sanminzhuyi)* is the title that Sun Yat-sen gave to his last work, published in 1924. More generally, the Three Principles of the People are understood to be the political doctrine that Sun was constantly elaborating throughout the last two decades of his political life. He used the term for the first time in 1905, seeking to encompass in a single revolutionary project his views on nationalism (*minzuzhuyi*), democracy (*minquanzhuyi*), and the livelihood of the people (*minshengzhuyi*). In the years leading up to the 1911 revolution, the doctrine of the Three Principles of the People was diffused by the *People's Journal* and became the charter of the Revolutionary Alliance. But only the first of its three principles, nationalism—at that time understood as opposition to the Manchu dynasty—was unanimously accepted by the revolutionaries. In 1919, after a long interruption, Sun Yat-sen returned to reflecting upon the concept. From that time on, he was constantly revising and enriching its content.

From 1905 to 1925, then, the Three Principles of the People appear to have been a constantly evolving doctrine, an ideology that continued to change and adapt to new circumstances. At the risk of fixing Sun Yat-sen's very volatile thought in a static mode, I have opted for "freezing the image" for just long enough for a critical exploration of the work published in 1924. Important though it is not to forget the constraining influences of those chaotic times and of a still tentative revolutionary strategy, it is, I think, necessary to identify the major orientations that underlie what some people have no hesitation in calling Sunism.

Why I have selected *The Three Principles of the People* of 1924 as our guideline is not only because of the emblematic character that its title confers upon it, but also because this was the last major work published by Sun Yat-sen and because he himself, in his *Political Testament*, pronounced it fundamental for the exposition of his program, alongside, it is true, three other texts: *The Fundamentals of National Reconstruction (Jianguo fanglüe)*, *The Bases of National Reconstruction (Jianguo dagang)*, and the *Congress Manifesto* [of the Guomindang], of 1924. On many points, these three texts overlap. But whereas *The Fundamentals of National Reconstruction* is a collection of disparate essays, mostly dating from the end of the second decade of the twentieth century, and *The Bases of National Reconstruction* and the *Manifesto* are both brief texts of a programmatic nature, *The Three Principles of the People* is more explicit. It is presented as a work of reflection and synthesis, composed all in one go between January and August 1924. In it, Sun seeks to justify his ideological choices by referring to the philosophical traditions and the historical experiences of, on the one hand, China, and on the other, the West. So, without deliberately avoiding references to Sun's other writings, I shall base this analysis essentially upon *The Three Principles of the People*.

It is a text that is at times strange, very different from the philosophical treatise and theoretical considerations that might have been expected from an inspirer of revolutions. On the score of intellectual speculation and literary qualities, Sun Yat-sen can rival neither the masters of the preceding generation (Kang Youwei, Liang Qichao) nor the protagonists of the May Fourth Movement of 1919, let alone Lenin. But, to be fair to his *Three Principles of the People*, we should bear in mind the conditions in which it was produced. Sun Yat-sen himself invokes them in his Introduction. While he was preparing his treatise on the principles of the people, he lost all his books of reference and all his notes in Chen Jiongming's bombardment of his residence, in June 1922. Thereafter constantly absorbed in political battles, Sun Yat-sen never found time to return to the elaboration of his treatise.

The Three Principles of the People, bequeathed as his testament to the Guomindang, is simply the transcription of sixteen lectures delivered at the Canton University. Although Sun Yat-sen did himself partially revise this transcription, *The Three Principles of the People* smacks of its declamatory origins: the forceful, simplified formulations and the dramatic emphasis of the repetitions convey the fiery oral rhetoric and improvisation of a speaker bent on carrying his audience with him. It is a work of propaganda, a long political tract designed to win followers rather than to instill conviction, an appeal to action rather than to thought. Its purpose is to diffuse a number of ideas rather than to analyze them. As Sun Yat-sen himself declares, for him a principle is not simply an idea; it is "a faith (*xinying*), a power (*liliang*)."[1]

The eloquence that produced *The Three Principles of the People* gave it warmth and impetus. But it also impaired it by introducing imprecisions, incoherences, and contradictions, not to mention intrusive, trivial anecdotes, and ribald stories of ineptitude designed to illustrate the difficulties encountered by the Chinese in determining their own behavior and their relations with foreigners.

Depending on one's mood, one might either pronounce the work to be eclectic—or a hybrid hodgepodge. Chinese cultural pride is mixed with Leninist anti-imperialism, Montesquieu's Laws rub shoulders with Lincoln's precepts, and socialism in the manner of Henry George goes hand in hand with Marxism and traditional Chinese utopian thinking. "In every case, Doctor Sun refers incidentally to some European or American theory, which he absorbs into his own theoretical schema, leaving the latter unaffected" (Jerome Chen). For Sun, as for many Chinese gripped in the vise of modernization, including Mao Zedong, foreign borrowings had to serve Chinese objectives and the importation of new methods and new concepts did not necessarily imply adoption of the systems from which they were extracted: "We cannot decide whether an idea is good or not without seeing it in practice. If the idea is of practical value to us and to the world, it is good, if the idea is impractical, it is no good."[2] This out-and-out pragmatism opened up the way for a syncretism that sometimes degenerates into incoherence. Only Sun Yat-sen's powerful, unshakable optimism saves the text, lifting it above and beyond its contradictions.

What *The Three Principles of the People* conveys of Sun Yat-sen's personality is essentially the force of his temperament. It remains a fundamental work, for it crystallizes the questions, ambitions, and ideas that fueled the debates of the first quarter of this century. It was through this text, later to become canonical, that several generations of Chinese were to come to grips with the modern political thought of their country.

THE PRINCIPLE OF NATIONALISM (*MINZUZHUYI*)

The principle of nationalism is the subject of Sun Yat-sen's first six lectures, given between January and March 1924, and it holds a central place in the thought of this great patriot who was never more moved or more moving than when speaking of the Chinese nation. His discourse on nationalism remains deeply marked by the debates that had surrounded the very birth of the concept of a nation a quarter of a century earlier. The modernists of 1919 considered the concept already established, taken for granted; some of them were even beginning to criticize it. But Sun Yat-sen always felt a need to legitimize it, just as had the scholars and reformists of the late nineteenth and early twentieth centuries.

The Chinese tradition was universalist and so defined the individual not as belonging to an ethnic or social group, or by the practice of a particular religion, but by reference to the progress made in the moral and spiritual quest that is the aim of life and that governs the harmony that should exist between man, society, and the cosmos. China itself is not a country: it is the expression of a culture, or rather of culture itself; the Chinese state is regarded simply as "the unitary structure for the integration of the civilized world, progressively extended to the whole of humanity" (Léon Vandermeersch). The Western image of a "concert of nations," to convey the relations between sovereign, independent, and theoretically equal states stands in opposition to the Chinese tradition's concentric and hierarchical organization of the world, with the heart of civilization, China, at its center, spreading outward to a barbarian periphery: other peoples were destined either to be assimilated or to disappear. Universalism and ethnocentric culturalism conditioned the vision of the world of the ancient Chinese.

The intrusion of Westerners deeply undermined this conceptual architecture. The officials and scholars who at this point leaped in to save China were at the same time anxious to restore intelligibility to the world order, to make it comprehensible by introducing a linear concept of historical evolution and by replacing cosmic influences by the laws of Darwinian competition for survival. The nationalism that flowered at the turn of the century stemmed from this twofold patriotic and philosophic effort. At this date, the presence of a foreign dynasty on the imperial throne facilitated, but perhaps also distracted the quest for national identity. The question of whether to give priority to the antidynastic struggle or to anti-Western resistance became the principal criterion that divided revolutionaries and reformists. Apart from its eminently political aspects, the quarrel that set these two currents in opposition stimulated an essential debate on the biological, social, and historical bases of the nation, on the relations between the nation and the state, and between the

nation and the worldwide community. This thinking, led by men of exceptional culture and talent, from Kang Youwei to Liang Qichao and including
Zhang Binglin, which borrowed from the West but did not entirely repudiate
the East, represents one of the highest points of modern Chinese political
thought during its first golden age (1895–1911).

In those debates Sun Yat-sen played no more than a lateral, not to say
marginal role. His intervention was indirect, mediated by articles published in
the *People's Journal*, from the pens of brilliant intellectuals such as Zhu Zhixin
who, although writing under their own names, rested their authority on the
basis of their frequent contacts with the leader of the Revolutionary Alliance
and presented themselves (or were presented) as his spokesmen.

Twenty years later, when the Manchu issue was a thing of the past, an echo
of those old debates still lingered in Sun Yat-sen's writings. Liberated from
their polemical context and conveyed in forceful, straightforward prose, the
concepts of race, nation, and state had become popular terms in a new, mass
nationalism. In the meantime, however, Sun Yat-sen had taken up the Leninist theory of imperialism, from which he borrowed the idea of the economic
exploitation of underdeveloped countries and also that of the inevitable clash
between colonial powers and oppressed nations.

Linked as they are to successive phases in a checkered career, these various
theories constitute as it were geological strata that remain distinguishable in
the layered whole represented by Sun Yat-sen's political thought. Perhaps what
is most surprising is that this layered whole itself never conceals the tradition
upon which it rests: for that tradition is constantly evoked and invoked. And,
paradoxically enough, it may be this very basis that confers a certain cohesion
upon Sun Yat-sen's nationalism, which in other respects is so very modern.

Race and the "Natural" Bases of the Nation

For Sun Yat-sen, only an appeal to nationalism could save China (*jiuguo*),
that is to say the Chinese race. Racial consciousness had never been entirely
absent from this cultural tradition that prided itself on its universalist vocation. What Frank Dikötter calls "discourse on race"—not to say "racism"—
had autochthonous roots nourished by the perception of not only socio-
cultural but also physical differences. But it was Western aggression that, at
the end of the nineteenth century, placed the problem of race at the center of

the political and philosophical debate. Going back to the distinction, clearly established by Zhu Zhixin as early as 1908, between the nation-race (*minzu*), born of natural forces and historical evolution—that is, constituted spontaneously according to the Royal Way (*wangdao*)[3]—and the nation-state (*guojia*), a product of artificial forces and military intervention—that is, constituted according to the Way of Might (*badao*)—Sun Yat-sen defined nationalism above all as a racial nationalism (*minzuzhuyi*). And he proceeded to list the principal "natural forces" upon which such nationalism was founded.

First: "blood," the blood of ancestors that is "transmitted eternally." Here, the idea of race coincides with "the patrilinear ideology" (Joël Thoraval) according to which all the Chinese are descended from a mythical Yellow Emperor. Next, style of life, language, religion, and customs. Unlike Stalin and Lenin, Sun Yat-sen did not include territorial rooting among the conditions leading to the formation of a nation.[4] Territory seemed to him at the most an attribute of the state and of state nationalism. (In this way, simply by virtue of a definition, Sun Yat-sen integrated or reintegrated into the national community the millions of émigrés established overseas.)

Proceeding from this definition, Sun Yat-sen developed a line of argument very close to that of the reformers of the 1895–1905 period which, incorporating the social Darwinism imported from the West into traditional ethnocentrism, called for the defense and preservation of the Chinese race. The struggle for survival was reduced to the idea of a racial war that conditioned historical evolution. Like the reformers, Sun Yat-sen feared the white peril and warned against it. He wanted to fill his readers with a sense of imminent danger. Taking over the vocabulary of his predecessors, he evoked the specter of racial extinction (*miezhong*) and forcefully drew attention to what he considered to be the demographic decline of China in the face of the rise of the American and European powers: "A hundred years hence, if their population increases and ours does not, the more will subjugate the less and China will inevitably be swallowed up. Then China will not only lose her sovereignty, but she will perish, the Chinese people will be assimilated and the race will disappear."[5]

According to Sun Yat-sen, the concept of race goes beyond biological data and is also founded upon a number of sociological and historical conditions of a kind to create a sense of belonging, what Zhu Zhixin, in his article of 1908, had called the nationalism of the heart (*xinlide guoajiazhuyi*): "Our Chinese nation is one also of great antiquity, with more than four thousand years of authentic history. . . . Through four milleniums . . . we see our civilization only advancing and our nation free from decay."[6] For Sun Yat-sen, what made China unique was the coincidence, ever since the earliest antiquity, between the race and the nation-state. Whereas, abroad, a single race had given birth to several nations, or conversely a single nation might include several races, "China has been developing a single state out of a single race (*yige minzu zaocheng yige guojia*)."[7]

Of course, Sun was not unaware of the presence of ethnic minorities in China: Mongols, Manchus, Tibetans, and so on. For even as, in response to Western aggression, the Chinese were rethinking their relations with the outside world, they were also becoming aware of the presence of the various other ethnic groups that coexisted within the imperial framework. However, the interaction between ethnicity and national identity had not been made clear. On the basis of the numerical weakness of the minorities (which he reckoned at ten million), Sun proclaimed the purity of a race of four hundred million Chinese: "The Chinese race totals four hundred million people; for the most part, the Chinese people are of the Han or Chinese race with common blood, common language, common religion, and common customs—a single, pure race."[8] As early as 1912, Sun Yat-sen had proclaimed the equality of the Five Races under Chinese sovereignty, and in the Manifesto of the Reorganization Congress he had gone as far as to recognize those races' right to self-determination, yet he seems to have counted on a process of cultural assimilation to unify the nation around the Hans.

China's misfortune was attributable to its having lost the treasure (*baobei*) represented by a sense of nationality. The race survived, but the Chinese did not nurture any feeling of loyalty toward the nation-state; they neither identified with it nor felt obligations toward it. They were feeble citizens whom Sun Yat-sen likened to "loose sand" (*sansha*). He blamed this loss of national spirit on a culturalist and cosmopolitan (*shijiezhuyi*) tradition, which China had cultivated the better to extend its universal empire (*tianxiazhuyi*). Sun denounced the treachery of the bureaucrats who had rallied to the Manchu invaders who claimed to be the defenders of the Confucian culture and values. And, echoing arguments used twenty years earlier in the struggle against the reformists, he accused "the scholars and men of letters" (meaning Kang Youwei and Liang Qichao) who argued in favor of cooperation with the foreign dynasty in order to modernize and save the state (*guojia*), without taking into account the subjection of the race beneath the foreign yoke.

The revival of the nation, he declared, must restore honor to the values respected over hundreds and thousands of years, which had created the Chinese identity. Sun Yat-sen defended the old Confucian virtues of filial piety, loyalty, and humanity: "Because of the high moral standards of our race, we have been able not only to survive in spite of the downfall of the state, but we have had power to assimilate . . . outside races. . . . If we want to restore our race's standing . . . we must first recover our ancient morality; then, and only then, can we plan how to attain the national position we once held."[9]

Racial nationalism should furthermore rest upon traditional family and clan loyalties and extend these to take in the entire country. In China, people had for thousands of years been accustomed to seeing a long stream of generations within the same clan. That was something firm and indestructible. By gathering those clans together, it would be possible to "become a great national union—the Republic of China."[10] And it would be possible for the nation-state to be constructed naturally, working from the bottom upward, from the individual citizens up to its central organizations. This was a movement that would grow as it proceeded. Race (*minzu*) would find its spontaneous expression in the state (*guojia*). Unlike in the West, in China the basic social cell was not the individual but the family. This was a great advantage, for the very cohesion of the family cell could serve as a model to encourage the revival of national spirit.

Sun Yat-sen thus introduced his principle of nationalism with a disquisition on race that expanded upon his earlier views and integrated elements borrowed from the West by the great intellectuals of the transition period: the linear concept of historical evolution ruled by the principle of natural selection and the idea of the survival of the races with the most aptitudes. There was nothing particularly original or new in these later additions, which in strong and simple terms repeated the conclusions reached in the debates that had fired the previous generation. Only the theme of the salvation of the country (*jiuguo*), to which Sun Yat-sen still, in the early 1920's, returned as to a leitmotiv, retained all the force and pertinence that it had already possessed in 1898 when the threat of partition had hung over China. This patriotic slogan, which always served as a rallying cry to those alarmed by the presence of foreigners, enabled the Soviet agents and the Chinese Communists to introduce and popularize a new Leninist, anti-imperialist analysis of the relations of strength between China and the foreign powers. Sun Yat-sen's many borrowings from this analysis helped to modernize his nationalist discourse and bring it into line with the contemporary mood.

Nationalism and Anti-imperialism

At the beginning of his revolutionary career, Sun Yat-sen had attributed the misfortunes of China to the Manchu conquest, not to Western aggression. He had denounced the stupidity and barbarity of the Manchus as the cause of China's backwardness. Up until the 1911 revolution, all his attacks were directed against the usurping dynasty, against which he sought the alliance of the enlightened nations of the West. The overthrow of that dynasty consequently appeared to him as the absolute accomplishment of the nationalist principle. China was restored to the Chinese. In the constitution of the new Chinese Revolutionary Party that he set up in 1914, Sun Yat-sen referred to only two principles that still remained to be implemented: democracy and the livelihood of the people. As he saw it, nationalism was no longer on the agenda.

By the early 1920's, Sun Yat-sen's position was altogether different. *The Three Principles of the People* most violently deplored the danger that Western imperialism represented for China. His second lecture on nationalism, given on February 3, 1924, was entirely devoted to a description of the foreign powers' political and economic oppression in China. On February 24, he returned to and developed these same themes in his fourth lecture.

By political oppression Sun meant the amputations perpetrated upon the national territory; and he enumerated all these despoilations. He reminded his audience of the concessions wrested at the time of the breakup of China in the late 1890's, proceeded to list the losses that had followed both the Sino-Japanese War (1894–95) and the Sino-French War (1884–85), then went back to the seventeenth century and recalled the secession to Russia of the territories situated north of the Amur River, not forgetting to mention in passing the Westerners' emancipation or colonization of countries that had formerly paid tribute to China: from Siam to Java, and from Ceylon to Borneo and Nepal.

Since the beginning of the twentieth century, the foreign powers had halted these encroachments, for they had realized how difficult it would be to conquer a territory as vast as the Chinese continent and wished to avoid the rivalries that might have developed between them over the division of such a conquest. They had therefore abandoned political oppression and replaced it with economic oppression, which Sun believed to be even more pernicious because it was more difficult to identify. To help his compatriots to understand to what extent they were the victims of exploitation, Sun Yat-sen presented a detailed picture of foreign economic penetration in China: the seizure of the Maritime Customs Service, the deficit produced by the balance of trade, the printing of bank notes, the control of exchange rates, the domination of maritime and river transport, the abusive taxes imposed in the concessions, the privileged status of Western and Japanese firms. It was a classic, if controversial picture. Sun Yat-sen reckoned China's annual loss occasioned by this exploitation to run to 1.2 thousand million Chinese dollars, although it is well known that Sun had a somewhat emotional concept of statistics. More surprising is his refusal to take into account the Boxer indemnity (450 million taëls, plus interest) imposed upon China in 1900, denunciation of which has been a recurrent theme in nationalist and communist historiography right down to the present day. Sun considered this to have been a "one-shot" exaction involving a "not very considerable sum"!

However inaccurate and open to challenge, this view of the Chinese situation led Sun to the unassailable conclusion that China was a country under foreign domination. Admittedly, unlike many other countries in Asia and Africa, it had not been colonized. But the Chinese were wrong to "disparage the Koreans or the Annamese, calling them slaves without a country (*wangguo nu*)" and priding themselves on the fact that their own country, which was not subjected to any one power in particular, was only a semicolony (*banzhimindi*). That was a misleading consolidation. In truth, China's status was not superior, but inferior to that of a colony (toward which the metropolis at least assumed certain responsibilities). China was "a colony of the Powers" and this made the Chinese "not the slaves of one country but of all." Sun invented the term "hypocolony" (*cizhimindi*) for this ultimate degradation.[11]

From 1923–24 on, anti-imperialism became one of the essential mainsprings of Sun Yat-sen's nationalism and of all his revolutionary thought. "Formerly, the battle-cry of the revolution was the overthrow of the Manchu dynasty. Henceforth, it will be the overthrow of the intervention of foreign imperialism in China."[12] Although Sun Yat-sen made many contradictory statements in the last months of his life where imperialism was concerned, he maintained an opposition to it that was both forceful and unremitting. The theme of imperialism recurred constantly, from the *Manifesto on the Northern Expedition* (September 18, 1924) through to the *Farewell Letter* to Soviet Russia, written on his deathbed in March 1925, in which Sun again evoked "the historic task of the final emancipation of China and other oppressed countries."

Sun Yat-sen's anti-imperialist swerve is generally attributed to the influence of the Soviets, with whom he sealed his alliance in precisely 1923–24. We know that national liberation was the great federating principle of the united front. We also know how hard Borodin had worked to detach Sun Yat-sen from his hopes of cooperation with the West. Echoes of the injunctions tirelessly repeated by his mentor often seem detectable in Sun's rhetoric. They appear, in particular, in the long passages devoted to banking, commercial, and industrial problems and even more in his denunciation of the Washington Conference (1921), whose generous resolutions gave rise among Chinese liberals and modernists to hopes—soon dashed—of true cooperation with a West with mended ways. The violence with which Sun attacked those diplomatic agreements, which "in the space of a morning and with a single stroke of a pen" could annihilate the existence of a nation, smacks more of the irreducible opposition of Borodin, the spokesman of Soviet Russia, at that time excluded from the international community and from the Washington Conference, than of the prudence and ambivalences of a Sun who, in 1924, had still not renounced all his previous year's hopes of American mediation in the Chinese civil war.

But as we have seen, Sun's identification with Soviet views was always partial, always selective. His enthusiastic commitment to anti-imperialism could well have stemmed simply from the coincidence of Soviet discourse and his own personal experience and reflection. Sun's experience ever since the World War was of failures in all his negotiations with the foreign powers and in all his attempts to obtain from the West and Japan both recognition of his own legitimacy and the material aid that was indispensable to him. We should not forget how much his credit had declined in Japan after 1916, the rancor of American public opinion provoked by his opposition to China's entry into the world conflict in 1917, and the distrust aroused in Hong Kong and London by his military operations and his policies (reckoned to be secessionist) in

Guangdong. In the autumn of 1923, the conflict over the control of the Canton Customs had brought out into the open all the hostility directed against Sun Yat-sen by the principal foreign powers.

In a China where politics and military operations were always as one and where nobody could hope to maintain his influence without the help of foreign funds and munitions, Sun Yat-sen now no longer had a choice of alliances. But did he really intend to sever all bridges to the West when he moved toward the Soviets? We cannot be certain. With his versatile temperament, his thick-skinned reactions when rebuffed, and his ability not to regard his failures as a matter of personal honor, Sun was perfectly capable of simultaneously pursuing the most contradictory of projects. His closer ties with Soviet Russia had certainly not put an end to his contacts with representatives of the Western Powers.[13] Like many of his Chinese contemporaries, Sun harbored ambivalent feelings toward the West: for all his sense of being rejected, admiration and a desire to imitate and cooperate lived on. But Borodin was there to remind him that to incline toward the Soviet side was, as Mao Zedong put it a quarter of a century later, to lean to one side only: it was to choose one's camp.

Sun Yat-sen paid heed to that warning, the more so since, being singularly adept at recognizing and formulating the aspirations of the Chinese society of his day, he was aware of the scope of the wave of nationalism among the masses that had been engendered by the May Fourth Movement of 1919. The workers' and students' strikes and the merchants' boycotts were manifestations of a nationalism to which Sun Yat-sen himself had contributed very little. Nevertheless, he had understood that anti-imperialism was now the major force that would determine the country's evolution. He was a historical surfer who knew how to choose his waves. He wanted to be carried forward on the wave of patriotism, become its symbol or, better still, appear as its creator. The violence of his discourse seemed to come not so much from hatred as from a desire to make up for lost time and take control of the surging impetus of the masses.

Still, the fact that Sun Yat-sen rallied to Soviet views did not mean that he accepted the analysis of imperialism and capitalism that Lenin had posited in 1917. He did not go along with the idea that exports of capital to underdeveloped countries created an international monopolistic capitalism that divided the world into zones of influence and created an opposition between the center and the peripheries. As he saw it, the criterion by which to distinguish between friendly and unfriendly nations was not their position on the scale of capitalist development but simply their attitude toward China, or rather toward Sun himself, who, like de Gaulle, tended to identify his country with his own person.

In November 1924, in a major speech delivered in Kobe, Sun Yat-sen thus solicited Japan's aid in the struggle against European and American imperialism, in the name of pan-Asian solidarity. Yet in 1920 pan-Asianism had been formally condemned by the Second Congress of the Comintern. Although directed against the capitalist West, pan-Asianism, if successful, would strengthen Japanese imperialism: it could therefore not be confused with any national revolutionary movement or brought into alliance with one. Sun Yat-sen paid no attention to such strictures. The only reason that his plan for an alliance with Tokyo never came to anything was that it ran up against skepticism and hostility on the part of the Japanese leaders themselves.

For Sun Yat-sen, imperialism was essentially of a political nature. It was not to be confused with the economic oppression (*jingjilide yapo*) that was one of its principal manifestations. Imperialism was engendered by inequality between nations. In China, it grew out of the unequal treaties system, the abolition of which should, in Sun's eyes, be the primary objective. Japan, which had rejected such treaties as early as the end of the nineteenth century, ought now to help its Asian brothers to do likewise. Sun defined imperialism in terms of politics, race, and culture as much as—or perhaps more than—in terms of economics. That no doubt explains how it was that his concept of the anti-imperialist struggle was more inclusive than that of his Soviet allies.

Lenin, in his *Theses on the National and Colonial Question*, had laid down the conditions of support for the struggle for liberation in what was not yet known as the third world: "The bourgeoisie of oppressed countries, even if it supports the national movement, is nevertheless working with the bourgeoisie of the capitalist countries. . . . As communists, we should support bourgeois movements for the emancipation of the colonies only in cases where those movements are truly revolutionary, that is to say . . . where they do not prevent us from preparing the great exploited masses for revolution."[14] For the Soviets and the communists, it was therefore essential that the class struggle should coexist with the anti-imperialist struggle within the framework of the united front. Sun Yat-sen, however, refused to recognize the class contradictions at the heart of the national revolution. He called for unity between all Chinese in order to achieve emancipation: "To raise the position of workers, it is necessary first to raise the position of the nation." As an organized social group, the workers had "responsibilities toward the nation that were even more important than their responsibilities toward their own group."

In short, the primary task was not a struggle against the Chinese bourgeoisie but a struggle to recover Customs autonomy and to abolish the unequal treaties.[15] Here, the priority of the national objective strengthened the need for unity, born of a tradition that aimed for social consensus and social harmony. That tradition, which underlay all Sun's conceptual and lexical borrowings from Leninism, continued to fuel and direct his thinking.

Nationalism and Cosmopolitanism: Their Relation to Tradition

Unlike the iconoclastic radicals of the May Fourth Movement of 1919, who had declared along with Chen Duxiu, "Rather the extinction of our national quintessence than the definitive extinction of our race," Sun Yat-sen adopted an extremely qualified position vis-à-vis the cultural tradition and its relation to modern nationalism. His severe criticisms of the universalist ideas of the scholars of the past led him not to reject but simply to defer aspiration for a unified, pacific, and harmonious world. In the immediate instance, he was counting upon a revival of Chinese culture and on the Confucian moral values (loyalty, filial piety, etc.) to help in the construction of a nationalism that he never defined as an ideology of expansion, but simply regarded as a defensive reflex for survival. He thus liked to regard himself as a re-founder rather than as a grave digger of the old order (Paul Linebarger) and, accordingly, as closer to the great scholars of the transition period than to the iconoclasts of the new generation.

Does this appeal to the past, to Chinese culture, to the national essence (*guocui*) then so dear to the most conservative intellectual circles, make Sun Yat-sen the traditionalist celebrated by his right-wing Guomindang interpreters, such as Dai Jitao and, in his wake, Chiang Kai-shek? The question is beside the point: to the extent that such a celebration was an integral part of the fight for the Chinese heritage, it has more to do with the political history of the 1930's than with the intellectual history of the 1920's.

Might Sun's tardy attraction to the traditional Chinese values have been simply the result of the kind of tender look back at the past that is a feature of most lives drawing to a close? Or did it represent a generational phenomenon, in which Sun's behavior repeats that of the reformists and reformers of 1898, such as Liang Qichao, who, twenty years on, were anxious to return to the sources of their own culture? If nostalgia was indeed involved, in Sun's case it was certainly combined with an intellectual effort that sought to move beyond the contradictions that the reformists of the past had encountered and the rifts to which the intellectuals of 1919 resigned themselves. It was a matter not of saving the tradition by means of modern nationalism, or of installing that nationalism in tradition's place, but rather of constructing a national identity that would make use of the tradition and at the same time transcend it. For Sun Yat-sen, the currents that were projected by the two antinomic poles represented by, on the one hand, the nation, and, on the other, traditional culture, were not mutually alien or invariably hostile. Their interpenetration engendered a dynamic force upon which the formation of the national consciousness both could and should draw.

At first, however, Sun Yat-sen violently attacked the traditional belief that China was the center of the world, the empire of the Middle, the epitomy of human civilization. The cosmopolitanism that had exalted the cultural norm and failed to recognize racial and ethnic particularities had led China to lose its national consciousness: "Nationalism is that precious possession which enables a State to aspire to progress and a nation to perpetuate its existence."[16] Sun traced the destruction of Chinese nationalism to the Manchu empire (seventeenth to twentieth centuries). Once they had made the values of Chinese culture their own, the Manchu conquerors had established their legitimacy in the eyes of the scholars, who promptly rallied to this foreign dynasty. Traditional culturalism had paralyzed any possibility of national resistance to the invasion. It was because the whole of Chinese society favored the theory of cosmopolitanism that, when the Manchus crossed the Great Wall, there was nobody willing to resist them and save the country from ruin. The Chinese of those days were ready to receive anybody as emperor of China because they made no distinction between barbarians and themselves.[17]

However, the source of that cosmopolitanism was the hegemony that ancient China had exercised over all the countries close to it. The Chinese empire had wished to be universal in order to preserve its special position of the nation in the Middle (*Zhongguo*) and to establish the "Great Unity" (*Da*

Yitong) throughout the lands that paid it tribute. Once China had passed under the Manchu yoke, that same cosmopolitanism ruled out the survival of the racial and national consciousness that is so strong among other conquered peoples such as the Jews and the Poles. In this way, "China has had all her national pride crushed out."[18]

If China wished to survive, it had to rediscover the lost treasure and reawaken its nationalism. Neither traditional culturalism nor the internationalism favored by Chinese youth was on the agenda. Cosmopolitanism could not be the doctrine of weak peoples: it was the doctrine of imperialist powers eager to safeguard their privileged position as world arbiters. Now that China had become a dominated country, its only chance of salvation was a nationalist reawakening.

To the extent that the nationalism preached by Sun was presented as an ideology of development that appealed to sentiments of racial and ethnic belonging, it bore a number of similarities to other doctrines that emerged in the same period in more or less analogous circumstances. The Indian socialist M. N. Roy, for instance, detects "the menacing shadow of fascism"[19] hovering over Sun's discourse. But, notwithstanding the distortions that the right wing of the Guomindang was later to imprint upon the Three Principles of the People (such as the creation of the fanatical Blue Shirt militias and the movement of moral rearmament known as New Life), in Sun's own discourse there is no trace of any celebration of the moral virtues of violence or of the cult of the charismatic leader that are so characteristic of fascism. On the other hand, it certainly does use themes purveyed by the Italian nationalism of the second decade of the twentieth century, themes that Mussolini was to refer to as the doctrinal source of fascism: a hostility to cosmopolitanism, the importance of racial and ethnic factors, a desire to make up for having slipped behind other industrialized countries and for spiritual regeneration through a return to the traditional virtues upon which the greatness of the former empire had been founded.

The cultural pride upon which Sun wished to found modern nationalism clung to not only the moral values of the ancient Chinese but also their political philosophy. According to Sun, the latter had already explored all the systems from which the West now derived its inspiration. Anarchism and communism were well-known old systems dating from several millions (*sic*) of years ago. Cosmopolitanism had only just been born in Europe whereas in

China it was talked about more than two thousand years ago.[20] The spiritual civilization of the West could not possibly equal that of ancient China: by affirming the identity of the natural and the human orders, and by founding social harmony, administrative regularity, and the good functioning of the cosmos upon the moral fulfillment of the individual, Confucianism (in the neo-Confucian version produced in the eleventh and twelfth centuries, to which Sun Yat-sen was referring) provided a global explanation of the universe. Sun Yat-sen thereupon proceeded to cite and comment at length upon one of the most famous passages of *The Great Learning*: "Search into the nature of things, extend the boundaries of knowledge, make the purpose sincere, regulate the mind, cultivate personal virtue, rule the family, govern the State, pacify the world."[21] At the heart of this paradigm lies the humanist and nationalist postulate that considers the order of the world to be a moral order founded upon the perfecting of the individual. "Such a deep, all-embracing theory," Sun Yat-sen declared, "is a nugget of wisdom peculiar to China's philosophy of State and worthy to be preserved."[22]

Such a return to ancient morality and learning was nevertheless not enough to restore China to its preeminent rank. It was also necessary "to learn what the foreigners have that is good," that is to say, science: "For European superiority to China is not in political philosophy but altogether in the field of material civilization."[23] Here Sun Yat-sen appears to be closer to the scholars and officials who at the end of the nineteenth century were recommending "Western learning for the practical application, Chinese learning for essential principles," than to the intellectuals of 1919 who were so full of enthusiasm for Science and Democracy, which they regarded as an inseparable pair. In modern China, the temptations of radical westernization, almost invariably followed by a culturalist backlash, have created a permanent undertow in which each generation has in its turn been caught and in which many individual destinies have foundered. But Sun did not pause to consider this contradiction, which others have experienced with such tragic consequences. Sun, the child of Blue China, now took over the discourse of Yellow China,[24] not without imparting to it an impetuosity and optimism that, even in his maturity, never deserted him. The thing to do was to learn from the foreigners not by "following behind them" but by "marching forward with them"—that is, not by proceeding stage by stage but by immediately becoming initiated into the most advanced knowledge. Converting its backwardness into an advantage, China would profit from the experience acquired by others and thereby do better than they. "The latest arrivals would take the front seats."[25] Mao Zedong, inspired by the same sense of historical urgency and the same determined wishful thinking, was also to evoke the privileges of backwardness and to praise the advantages of "the blank page."

If China followed the course prescribed by Sun Yat-sen, it would take it only a few years to recover its ancient position, "the foremost position."[26] But once recovered, that primacy must not be made to serve a brutal imperialism imitating that of the Western powers. On the contrary, it would make it possible to help the weakest nations and to get peace to reign in the world, in other words to apply the old adage, "Administrate the country well, pacify the universe."

Although Sun Yat-sen made nationalism the first priority and the instrument of China's salvation, he does not seem to have ascribed an intrinsic value to it. Nationalism was not a goal in itself, merely a stage. Once that stage was over and China was saved, the utopian paradigm must recover its full force. It would then be up to the Chinese to use their refound power to establish the universal peace, the Great Harmony (*Datong*) that Confucian teaching urges the human race to achieve: "We shall operate on the basis of the moral values and the desire for peace that are peculiar to us, so as to unite the world and found the government of the Great Harmony."[27]

Passing from culturalism to nationalism, and then from nationalism to universalism, did Sun Yat-sen's thought really come full circle? This aspiration to unity—no longer just of East Asia but of the whole wide world—a unity constructed around the Confucian values that were deemed to be superior, and this moral tutelage entrusted to China, did they not in truth constitute an insidious triumph for the very nationalism for whose rejection they claimed to stand? In the early 1990's, China, in its pronouncements on human rights, showed that it was incapable of recognizing any universal values except those for whose definition it was itself responsible. In this respect, the onward march of the century does not seem to have made much difference to the ways that people think. For the universalism to which the nationalism preached by Sun Yat-sen was supposed to lead seemed, even then, to be a universalism that was simply Chinese. The world of justice that Sun evoked was to have China as its center and was to be founded on Confucian morality. The synthesis that, in the wake of so many others, he tried to establish between modern nationalism and traditional humanism would thus lead only to a renewal of the cultural ethnocentrism upon which the Chinese Empire had been founded. But Sun's objective was never to reconcile two concepts of the world, two different philosophical visions of the universe. It was purely to save China and to do so without betraying the past that gave meaning to its quest for its identity. By taking things one step at a time, adopting first a nationalist approach, later a universalist one, and by indefinitely deferring the latter, he thought it should be possible to achieve that goal.

THE RIGHTS OF THE PEOPLE (*MINQUAN*): AN INSTRUMENTAL DEMOCRACY

Sun Yat-sen expressed his trust in democracy early in his career, at a time when most of the major thinkers imparting new life to Chinese political philosophy through the importation of Western ideas were recommending at least a provisional recourse to authoritarianism and enlightened despotism. Well before 1905, when the Revolutionary Alliance included in its program the establishment of a republic, Sun Yat-sen was arguing for the adoption of constitutional democracy, the latest of the Western political institutions to make its appearance and consequently, in his eyes, the best. It is worth re-membering the metaphor that Sun developed in the Hawaii press in 1904: why should the Chinese import outdated locomotives when they could ac-quire more modern engines with a better performance? Similarly, why should they import constitutional monarchy in preference to a republic? In the years that followed, the controversy over the best form of regime remained at the heart of the polemic between Sun and the reformists.

Sun Yat-sen may well have been not insensible to some of the arguments of his opponents, those that drew attention to the low cultural level of the Chinese people in order to justify a gradual process of change, conditioned by the development of education and the formation of political consciousness. But the revolutionary leader's generosity of spirit and impatience were not of a kind to tolerate the delays of history. "Waiting for the muddy waters to clear by themselves would cost too dearly in human lives. . . . I am a man of action," he told Yan Fu, whom he met in London in 1905.[28]

By 1924, the failure of the Chinese Republic, the difficulties of the Western democracies, and the establishment of the Soviet regime in Russia had radically transformed the historical context. Both Sun Yat-sen's thought and his political program underwent considerable changes. But the president continued to place his full trust in democracy—a trust that seemed to stem from faith rather than from judgment and that never made him forget the strategic constraints to which he was always subjected as a "man of action."

He praised popular sovereignty in naïve but forceful terms: "When we have a real republic, who will be king? The people, our four hundred millions, will be king."[29] Although it implied liberty and equality, he did not think that popular sovereignty was founded upon the natural rights about which Rousseau theorized in the *Social Contract*. "We see that democracy has not been Heaven-born, but has been wrought out of the conditions of the times and the movement of events."[30] It is the product of an evolution that sweeps the world toward progress. It is one of the faces of modernity and, as such, seems at once desirable and irresistible. "This world-tendency has flowed from theocracy on to autocracy and from autocracy now on to democracy, and there is no way to stem the current."[31] Such determinism could not disarm his militantism, however; for Sun, democracy was, first and foremost, one expression of the nationalism that was to save China.

"Loose Sand" or Democracy as an Expression of Nationalism

Sun Yat-sen approached his thinking on democracy by way of a meditation on liberty. He noted that in the West it was the struggle for individual liberty that carried along the whole revolutionary movement. This could be explained by the particular historical conditions. Over the centuries, European monarchs had become so powerful that they had managed to control their subjects' entire lives: their opinions, religious beliefs, family and social practices, and economic activities. "The European tyranny in one way and another pressed directly down upon the shoulders of the common people."[32] That is why the people fought for their emancipation. In China, the state's interference in society was always much more limited. Apart from having to pay taxes, the Chinese were subjected to hardly any constraint: they pursued their intra-family relations, their businesses, their religious practices as they saw fit. As individuals, the Chinese had so much liberty that they noticed it no more than the air they breathed. That extremely large measure of social autonomy had even led to the anomaly of their doing as they pleased without bothering about the community. So the problem was not a lack, but an excess of liberty: "We have had too much liberty without any unity and resisting power, because we have become a sheet of loose sand."[33] This aggregate of individuals with no sense of community made China easy prey for foreign imperialism. It made it "the slave of all." And, with the nation subjugated, how could individual freedom exist? Faced with imperialists, it was national liberty that must be defended, at the cost, if necessary, of sacrificing individual liberty. To repulse foreign imperialism, "we must break down individual liberty and become pressed together into an unyielding body like the firm rock which is formed by the addition of cement to sand."[34] China needed above all unity and discipline in order to achieve its national liberation.

Yet the Chinese students were always going on about liberty, believing that the present revolution should imitate that of the Europeans.[35] But the Chinese people paid no attention to what they said. "Because no one welcomes their theory in the society outside, they [the students] can only bring it back into their own schools, and constant disorders and strikes result."[36] The students who launched the May Fourth Movement and the liberal and Westernist tendencies produced by that movement were here condemned out of hand by Sun.

Europe followed its own path. China must likewise follow its own. "The aim of the Chinese revolution and that of foreign revolutions is not the same, so nor are the methods."[37] The Chinese needed to struggle for the liberty of their nation and from this would stem true liberty for the people.

Sun Yat-sen thus opted for the state against the individual. He called for patriotism the better to convince an audience composed for the most part of students who belonged to a generation avid for emancipation. Their more conformist elders—cadres, activists, Guomindang sympathizers—were more prepared to accept a curtailment of individual rights and interests, for Confucian morality had always disapproved of these. Further to the Left, the appeal for order and discipline was bound to accord with the preoccupations of the communists and radical allies, won over to the principles of Leninist organization.

If the anathema expressed against individual liberties clashed with the aspirations of the youthful intelligentsia, the condemnation of local autonomy and federalism ran the risk of affronting the convictions of older revolutionaries. In China, resistance to the abuses and tyranny of the power-holders was usually expressed by insubordination on the part of the local officials and elites. The dialectic between the central government and the regions occupied the political space that is devoted, in the West, to the relations between the state and individuals. Those who advocated liberty thought in terms of autonomy, geographical secession. Conversely, for the supporters of order, the destruction of China's unity could lead only to the negation of all norms and to chaos. The 1911 revolution, which was accompanied by a spate of declarations of provincial independence, bore out this thinking. To counter the rise of the anarchy that, since 1917, had been such a feature of the warlords' reign, much of urban liberal public opinion was in favor of federalism. As we have seen, Sun Yat-sen was hostile to such a solution; and this hostility was not solely a consequence of the power struggle against Chen Jiongming and the Cantonese merchants and gentry in which he was engaged. There were also more fundamental reasons for it, and these he set out in his fourth lecture on democracy.

Reiterating the official discourse of the Confucian elites, Sun Yat-sen invoked the tradition of unity. He deplored the anarchy that had characterized the periods of regional emancipation and waning imperial power: "In times of union, there was order, in times of separation, disorder." In his view, the anarchy introduced by the reign of the warlords was no more than "a temporary disorder," a passing crisis that could not justify any move into permanent division in the form of federalism. Sun Yat-sen refuted the arguments of those who invoked the United States as an example. "The United States' wealth and power have not come only from the independence and self-government of the original states, but rather from the progress in unified government which followed the federation of the states."[38]

Regional autonomy is not discussed in terms of the rights of communities or groups any more than individual freedom is envisaged in terms of human rights. The debate focuses on the strengthening of the nation. The arguments put forward by those who supported federalism have to do with "the wealth and power" of the nation. Sun Yat-sen, who agreed with those primary objectives, was simply arguing that they could never be achieved by resorting to federalism. To liberate itself and achieve fulfillment as a nation, China needed a strong government; and in his eyes, as in those of the former high imperial officials, that meant a unified and centralized government.

In the program of The People's Three Principles, liberty was really not a consideration, either in the form of the individual liberty so ardently advocated by the young, westernized intelligentsia, or in the form of regional autonomy, the bone of contention for the local elites. All that counted was the liberty—that is, the power—of the nation.

Democracy and Elitism: Popular Sovereignty and Governmental Power

Although he recognized the principle of equality, Sun Yat-sen accepted, indeed approved of the existence of a social hierarchy founded, not upon access to property, but upon grades of intellectual aptitude. "Equal position in human society is something to start with; each man builds up his career upon this start according to his natural endowments of intelligence and ability."[39] In the name of, not any kind of right to personal fulfillment but the interest of society in general, Sun Yat-sen rejected egalitarianism, the effect of which would inevitably be to level downward: "If we pay no attention to each man's intellectual endowments and capacities and push down those who rise to a high position in order to make all equal, the world will not progress and mankind will retrocede."[40] The pragmatism that directed Sun Yat-sen's ideological choices thus implied recognizing social inequalities and making use of them.

On the basis of individual capacities, Sun Yat-sen distinguished between three categories of citizens: "those who know and perceive beforehand (*xianzhi xianjuezhe*)," who are the first to discern underlying causes and the way things will evolve; "those who know and perceive afterward (*houzhi houjuezhe*)," who take a little longer to see how things are; and "those who do not know and perceive (*buzhi bujuezhe*)," who never understand anything.[41] The degree of a person's capacities determines his social roles. Those in the first category are "discoverers"; those in the second are "promoters"; and those in the third are "practical men."[42] This distribution of functions must not lead to relations of domination, however. Each individual must, in solidarity with his fellows, strive for the common good and feel responsible for the group: "Although men may now vary in natural intelligence and ability, yet as moral ideas and the spirit of service prevail, they will certainly become more and more equal. This is the essence of equality."[43]

Because of their exceptional talents, those with foresight were given particular responsibilities. It was up to them to take charge of the ignorant masses. "The majority of the people are without vision. We who have prevision must lead them and guide them into the right way."[44] More particularly, it was up to this enlightened minority "to make democracy" and to "give it to the people."[45] Behind those with foresight or "prevision," who were responsible for the material and political progress of society, can be glimpsed the officials, who governed through the impact of their virtues. The better to respond to the needs of modern times, the inventor, or discoverer, had now taken the place of the scholar trained to read the Classics. But there was a direct affiliation between the two, and the main role ascribed to those with foresight certainly seems a modernized version of the magisterial functions exercised by the Confucian elites.

Sun Yat-sen thus wanted to "entrust the great affairs of State to men of value."[46] He wanted a strong government capable of getting the country to progress, following the example provided by Bismarck in Germany. At the same time, he did not recognize the latent contradiction between the role of the elites and governmental power on the one hand and the exercise of popular sovereignty, on the other. Sharply intuitive, he sensed the danger of a technocracy. "At the present time we depend upon experts without being able to control them."[47] He had noticed that Western democracies are wary of the power of their governments and therefore limit it. "In many nations where democracy is developing, the governments are becoming powerless."[48]

To reconcile the privileged role of those with foresight with democratic equality, and governmental efficacy with popular sovereignty, Sun Yat-sen proposed making a distinction between the power (*neng*) of the people and the power (*quan*) of the government. The masses are sovereign: they reign but do not exercise the power. Those with foresight govern, but in the last resort they depend upon the people, who choose them and may dismiss them. To clarify the division of prerogatives for his audience and also the difference in nature between popular power and governmental power, Sun Yat-sen gave two examples. The first was that of a business run by a manager qualified to do so, under the control of the shareholders: "The people of a Republic represent the shareholders, the president of the Republic is the manager." The second example was that of a car driven by a chauffeur to whom the vehicle's owner must allow full freedom of maneuver. "The people are masters of the nation and should act towards the government as I did towards the chauffeur on that ride to Hongkow."[49]

The action of the government is carried out in accordance with the Constitution founded upon the Five Powers (*wuquan xianfa*) to which Sun Yat-sen refers in his sixth lecture on democracy, but of which he provides a more detailed description in the speech he gave to the Guomindang's Bureau of Special Affairs in July 1921. Returning to the classic division between the executive, the legislative, and the judiciary, Sun Yat-sen complemented this by distinguishing between a power of examination and a power of censure, both inspired by the old system for recruiting imperial mandarins and keeping them under observation.[50] Although Sun referred explicitly to the *Esprit des Lois*, his own preoccupations were very different from Montesquieu's. He was less concerned to balance and thereby limit the various powers than to introduce a fundamental distribution of tasks in the interests of greater efficiency. "The Constitution founded on the Five Powers . . . represents the basis for governmental organization. Within the hive, work can be divided up."[51] A government organized in this way is a "complete government." "Once one has this governmental machine . . . it will be possible to do excellent and very thorough work."[52]

However powerful, the government must nevertheless function under the control of the people. The exercise of popular sovereignty rests upon four rights: those of suffrage, revocation, initiative, and referendum. The introduction of the right to revoke government officials and the right of referendum reflects the growing dissatisfaction felt by Sun Yat-sen and his entourage with regard to classic representative systems and their desire to improve those systems by adding to them a number of procedures characteristic of direct democracy. This critique of Western parliamentarianism must have been encouraged by the closer ties with Soviet Russia. But in fact it predated those ties and was reinforced by recognition of the failure of the republican institutions set in place after the 1911 revolution. By 1919–20, Sun Yat-sen and several of his immediate collaborators were already trying to learn more about the mechanisms of direct democracy and were using the periodical *Reconstruction (Jianshe)* to publish many translations of articles and works on the subject.[53]

In the metaphorical vein so characteristic of Sun's style of argument, the four fundamental rights were compared to "four taps, or four electric switches," the use of which would enable the people to oversee the policies of the state.[54] Thanks to the distinction drawn between the Five Powers and the Four Rights, "the foundation of the government of a nation must be built upon the rights of the people, but the administration of government must be entrusted to experts" and the problem of the incompatibility between democracy and efficiency would be wiped out.[55] Sun Yat-sen frequently congratulated himself on the originality of this discovery of his: "I have found a solution . . . and for the first time in the world, this solution is formulated in scientific terms."[56]

One may feel inclined to share the irony of Pascal M. d'Élia, who comments upon this discovery with a sly "Eureka!"[57] At any rate, it is hard to join in the triumphalism of Sun Yat-sen as he glories in his "perfect democratic-political machine."[58] Apart from enumerating the various rights and powers, he gives no details on the functioning of this machine. His metaphorical flights of fancy hardly suffice to explain how the government would itself cope with the imbalances between its Five Powers, imbalances that would inevitably create all kinds of blockages. To judge by the difficulties that most democratic systems encounter in the management of three independent powers, the addition of two more would be likely to complicate the task and lead to paralysis rather than efficiency. (Such a diagnosis is to some extent confirmed by the unwieldy nature of the governmental apparatus of Taiwan, set up in accordance with Sun Yat-sen's prescriptions.) How would Parliament exercise control in practice? Sun Yat-sen specifies neither how often it should meet nor how it would be kept briefed. What sort of relations would there be between Parliament and the Legislative Commission (*Yuan*), whose function within the government was to pass laws? Would the Legislative Commission be responsible to a Parliament elected by the same voters?

The emphasis laid on the liberty of the nation to the detriment of that of individuals or regional communities, the privilege recognized for elites, and the weakness of the mechanisms of popular control all make for a strange way of establishing democracy. "The civic rights that we advocate are not the same as the civic rights advocated in Europe and America," Sun Yat-sen tells us.[59] Quite true. It is clear that Sun Yat-sen was thinking of setting up a strong power capable of leading China toward national emancipation and modernization, not of establishing a system capable of reflecting the views of the majority. But can this democracy in the Chinese manner really be called democracy? The very circumstances in which it was to be established, only following a period—of indefinite duration—of military authority and political tutelage, were bound to increase doubts and to accentuate the resemblances between such a democracy and a dictatorship.

The Problems of Transition: Tutelage and Dictatorship

The idea of a necessary period of transition in between the seizure of revolutionary power and the installation of a constitutional government appeared as early as 1905 in the Manifesto of the Revolutionary Alliance. At that time Sun imagined the introduction of a republican regime taking place in three stages, each lasting three years: initially, a military government would have the task of eliminating the evils of the *ancien régime*; next, a provisional constitution would regulate the relations between the military government and the citizens; then the transition would be completed with the adoption of a republican constitution. In 1914, when the Chinese Revolutionary Party was created, Sun Yat-sen retained this plan but organized it differently, merging the first two stages into a "revolutionary period" of indeterminate duration, during which the party monopolized power.

In April 1924, in *The Fundamentals of National Reconstruction*, Sun reconsidered the definition of the stages of the transition. Once again, he distinguished between a military period (*junzheng*), during which the government would resort to martial law to suppress all counterrevolutionary forces, and a period in which to prepare for the adoption of a constitutional regime. This would be known as a period of tutelage (*xunzheng*), during which the people, under the direction of the revolutionary government, would raise the level of its civic consciousness. Sun Yat-sen justified the need for these transitional periods by invoking the mistakes that had been made following the 1911 revolution. The immediate adoption of a provisional constitution (in 1912) had not allowed enough time to complete the demolition of the old order and had conferred upon the people responsibilities that it was not capable of assuming:

> The first difficulty that resulted from this was that it was impossible to get the new regime to function while the old corrupt practices had still not been abolished. The second difficulty was that those practices were touched up and perpetuated under the new regime. The third difficulty was that the continuation of those old practices made the new regime wither away. In short, it is fair to say: *primo*, that the democratic regime was not able to be realized; *secondo*, that under the false appearance of a democratic regime a veritable dictatorship became established; *tertio*, that even the appearances of democracy eventually vanished.[60]

In order not to fall into the same mistakes, Sun Yat-sen proposed that all traces of the *ancien régime* be eliminated by force during a period of military government and that power should only then be handed over to a tutelary authority responsible for ensuring the political education of the population.

Sun Yat-sen provided only vague and contradictory indications of the nature of this instruction. In 1923, he spoke of creating a revolutionary government whose powers would be fixed by a provisional constitution.[61] In 1924, he appeared to be thinking, rather, of placing that government under the authority of the (Guomindang) party. Although this point was not made clear either in *The Three Principles of the People* or in *The Bases of National Reconstruction*, it is suggested in the speech that Sun addressed on January 20, 1924, to the Reorganization Congress, in which he praised the Soviet model: "We must use the party to construct the State. It is fair to say that the success [of the Russian Revolution] is due to the priority given to the party over the State. . . . We must reorganize ourselves and place the party above the State."[62]

Notwithstanding that claimed Soviet patronage, the tutelary period envisaged by Sun was very different from the dictatorship of the proletariat as defined by Lenin in *The State and the Revolution*. The suppression of the bourgeoisie and the elimination of counterrevolutionaries, for example, both tasks allotted to the dictatorship of the proletariat, are not included among the tasks assigned to the tutelary government, for the destruction by force of the *ancien régime* would already have been completed by the military government. The essential task of the tutelary authorities was to be education of the people. Sun Yat-sen was in agreement with the intellectuals of his time in denouncing and deploring the lack of political awareness in the Chinese population; but far from this leading him to believe that a monarchy or a dictatorship would be necessary, he concluded that what was needed was education. His reaction reflects his Confucian optimism about the perfectibility of human nature and at the same time his republican belief in the virtues of universal education. "Even the cow can be trained to plough the field and the horse to carry man. Are men not capable of being trained?"[63]

Training in the practices of democracy would have to be pursued through the exercise of local responsibilities within the framework of the district (*xian*), which was the lowest level of politics and administration in China. Under the direction of qualified experts sent by the government to help them, the Chinese would in this way become initiated into their duties as citizens at the same time as they embarked upon the work of economic and social development. When every provincial district had reached the stage of autonomy, the Constitution would be promulgated and the national Parliament would be elected. At this point the revolutionary government would have to step down and the final period of constitutional government (*xianzheng*), would begin. The aspect of local autonomy (at district level) that attracted Sun Yat-sen was that it would enable the people "to exercise its rights directly." In that sense, it represented the real foundation of the democratic edifice and operated as a precautionary measure that prevented any adverse development in the representative system.[64]

This priority given to local autonomy distinguishes the Sunist model from the Leninist one, which advocates democratic centralism. It also appears to contradict Sun Yat-sen's own condemnation of the principle of federalism. However, Sun explains, with the perceptiveness that sometimes illuminates his writing like a flash of lightning, it is important not to confuse democratization with decentralization. What the advocates of federalism want is decentralization, that is, the deconcentration of political and administrative powers to the benefit of the provincial bureaucracy. Now, "if the power belongs to the officials, it continues to belong to them regardless of whether there is a centralized governmental system or a federation of autonomous provinces. . . . And the control that a province exercises over its districts reproduces the control exercised by the center over the provinces. . . . In fact, it is even more oppressive."[65] At a theoretical level, Sun Yat-sen's reasoning clashes with the contentious definition that he gives of federalism. But in the Chinese practice of the 1920's, federalism could with good reason inspire mistrust in that it more often than not served to legitimate the maneuvers and ambitions of warlords or local potentates and bureaucrats. That is why Sun Yat-sen recommended building democracy from the bottom up: "In this way national reconstruction will depend upon the people and no bureaucrat or militarist will be able to confiscate it."[66]

But however well founded it may appear, the autonomy of the districts remains hard to reconcile with the existence of the unitary state, centralized government, and virtuous bureaucracy that Sun Yat-sen also yearned to see. Besides, how could such autonomy be reconciled with a political tutelage when no mechanism existed to limit the authority of that tutelage or, above all, to guarantee its disappearance once its task of instruction was completed and the people had been educated? Sun Yat-sen declared, "The transition from political tutelage to constitutional government will be smooth and free of pitfalls,"[67] but that could only be so, one might add, provided the authoritarian or dictatorial power *in situ* agreed to organize its own disappearance (and that is quite a major proviso!). Indeed, it is hard to see what could prevent the power of tutelage from deferring the switch to constitutional government indefinitely.

Might not the plan for a transition in three stages simply lead to the establishment of a dictatorship? Sun's disciples have tried to legitimate the preparatory tutelage on the grounds of his final objective of constitutional democracy. But on those grounds one could equally well identify Stalinism with the socialism that it claimed to be constructing. Sun Yat-sen's way of proceeding was certainly not Stalin's, but his concept of democracy does seem above all destined to legitimate the establishment of an authoritarian regime designed to ensure national development. "How can we turn China into a rich and powerful (*fuqiang*) country? By adopting the Constitution founded upon the Five Powers."[68] The doctrine of the sovereignty of the people is integrated into the program of modernization in such a way as to make it seem no more than auxiliary. With that observation in mind, let us now examine the third principle upon which this program was essentially based: namely, the principle of the livelihood of the people (*minshengzhuyi*), probably the most important and certainly the most original of Sun Yat-sen's three principles.

THE PRINCIPLE OF THE LIVELIHOOD OF THE PEOPLE (*MINSHENGZHUYI*)

Sun Yat-sen's third principle, which lies at the heart of his doctrine, is not easy to grasp. The very absence of a satisfactory translation can be explained by the multiplicity and complexity of the ideas covered by the term *minshengzhuyi*. Sun Yat-sen used this term to designate at once his philosophy of history, the ideal goal that he assigned to social evolution, and the strategy that he recommended for achieving this objective. *Minshengzhuyi* thus has a triple meaning—philosophical, normative, and programmatic—and Sun Yat-sen played upon all these levels of meaning without explicitly warning his public when he was shifting from one to another.

This intellectual confusion was compounded by contradictions born of political necessities. It so happened that the four lectures on *mingshenzhuyi* (the last in the series on the Three Principles of the People) were scheduled for August 1924, which turned out to be the height of the crisis provoked by the Guomindang faction hostile to collaboration with the Soviets and the communists. Because of this, Sun's lectures became crucially important political statements. In the course of the crisis, they served to convey opinions now critical of Marxism, now favorable to communism. As always with Sun, the formulation of doctrine and emergency practicalities were intertwined. On top of all this, the Left and the Right of the Guomindang produced opposed commentaries on Sun's text and even divergent versions of it.[69] Clearly then, we need to be wary when studying the third principle of the people.

What Does "Minshengzhuyi" Mean?

Literally, *min* means "people," *sheng* means "life," and *zhuyi* means "doctrine." Taken word by word, *minshengzhuyi* thus means "the doctrine of the life of the people." That is indeed how the earliest—English—translators understood it, using the expression "the people's livelihood," a formula nowadays considered by specialists to be "clumsy," "rather vague," or "meaningless."[70] Nor are the French expressions used particularly striking for their lightness of touch ("*le principe du bien-être du peuple*") or for their clarity ("*le démisme vital*").[71] However, this English translation will be referring to "the livelihood of the people," since that is the expression favored by the English translation used as the text of reference.

When Sun Yat-sen embarked upon his lectures on the livelihood of the people in August 1924, he had long been considering the theme. As early as 1905–6, in the program of the Revolutionary Alliance, he had presented *minshengzhuyi* as a synonym for socialism (*shehuizhuyi*) and had reduced its application to the adoption of a policy of landownership and taxation in conformity with the prescriptions of the American reformer Henry George. Later, he complemented the program of the livelihood of the people by adding state socialism and the major plan of economic modernization that he described in 1921 in *The International Development of China*. But it was only in 1924 that Sun ventured a new, systematic, and more profound definition of his third principle.

From the very start, this 1924 version of the people's livelihood indicated its difference. Whereas at the time of the Revolutionary Alliance, Sun Yat-sen had identified his principle with socialism, he now associated it also with communism. He declared: "The livelihood of the people is socialism, also known as communism" (first lecture); and then he repeated, "the livelihood of the people is communism, it is socialism" (second lecture).[72]

Had Sun Yat-sen abandoned his own credo for that of his new Soviet and communist allies? And did his rallying to the policy of a united front lead to his ideological conversion? Some have claimed so. But the idea of such a conversion seems hard to reconcile with the systematic refutation of Marxism that appears in his first lecture on the livelihood of the people. These contradictions, which have sometimes caused Sun to be accused of incoherence, can probably be explained by the political constraints of the moment.

In his first lecture, delivered on August 3, Sun Yat-sen, under strong pressure from the moderate wing of the Guomindang, denounced the errors of Marxism. After that lecture he was taken to task by Borodin and led to modify his position in order to save his alliance with the Soviets. In his second lecture, given on August 10, he therefore devoted himself to relaunching the united front policy and, to that end, sought to reassure the Guomindang moderates who "entertain many false ideas, thinking that, with its Three Principles of the People, the Nationalist Party is in disagreement with communism. . . . [Those] comrades understand nothing about the livelihood of the people. Not only can it not be said that communism is opposed to the livelihood of the people, but [it has to be said] . . . that it is its great friend. And if communism is a great friend of the livelihood of the people, why do members of the Nationalist Party want to oppose communism?"[73] Sun Yat-sen was trying to bring together the extremists of both parties by presenting an ideological justification for their collaboration, postulating that the livelihood of the people and communism were identical. On the theoretical level, he was also trying to produce some kind of legitimation for his opportunism by drawing a distinction between Marxism, rejected as unsatisfactory, and communism, understood in a very vague sense, assimilated to the ideal of the Great Harmony (*Datong*) and deferred until some point in a utopian future. This vague communism could accommodate anything grafted on to it: "Communism is the ideal of the livelihood of the people, while the livelihood of the people is the realization of communism. So there is no difference between the two . . . except perhaps in their methods."[74]

This feat of verbal magic, which no doubt did help to restore a temporary calm within the united front, did not mean that Sun Yat-sen's economic and social ideas had undergone a metamorphosis. His 1924 lectures are full of the ideas he had been turning over for years, unaffected by any communist influence.

The Livelihood of the People as a Philosophy of History

The first lecture on the livelihood of the people was devoted to the "social problem," which involved questions about the progress and evolution of society. For Sun Yat-sen, the motivating force of history lay in man's ever renewed efforts to ensure his subsistence. "The problem of livelihood is the problem of subsistence. . . . Livelihood is the central force in social progress . . . and social progress is the central force in history."[75] This declaration of faith was accompanied by a point-by-point refutation of the principal postulates of Marxism. While recognizing the importance of the industrial revolution and the introduction of machinism, Sun rejected historical materialism. "The materialistic conception of history is wrong . . . the struggle for a living and not material forces determines history."[76] The evolution of civilization cannot be defined as adaptation to successive modes of production, through the class struggle. Contrary to what Marx proclaims, "the class struggle is not the reason for social evolution."[77] To be sure, the class struggle exists: it erupts when man can no longer provide for his needs. "It is a kind of disease that appears in society . . . [and] Marx stopped short at the disease affecting social evolution." He did not perceive its cause. "You could say that Marx was just a pathologist and not a physiologist of society."[78] The class struggle seems to Sun Yat-sen to be simply a lamentable deviation in social evolution. The mainspring of that evolution remains harmony. This is a theme he had already raised in *The International Development of China*: "The principal force in human evolution is cooperation, not conflict."[79] It reappears and is developed further in his first lecture on the livelihood of the people: "If society makes progress, that can only be because of the harmony between the economic interests of society's multitudes."[80]

In support of his thesis Sun cites recent progress achieved by Europe and America. Higher taxes on income, the nationalization of means of communication, the rise in the general level of education, and many other reforms had made it possible to increase production and improve distribution, in short to enrich both employers and workers. "So harmony, rather than opposition, is realized between the interests of the capitalists and those of the workers."

Sun Yat-sen also criticizes the Marxist notion of plus-value. If one attributes an exclusive role in the productive process to labor, ignoring the contribution of other social factors, one is bound to go wrong. For instance, Karl Marx's predictions of longer working hours, reduced workers' wages, and higher prices for manufactured goods had not been borne out. Furthermore, Fordism, the principal elements of which Sun proceeded to outline, contradicted Marx's analyses on every point: "Marx did not see things clearly in the past and consequently the opinions that he later defended . . . are mistaken both generally and in particular. . . . He spent several decades studying the social question; what he learned were the realities of the past; as for the realities of the future, he was absolutely incapable of foreseeing them."[81]

Sun's refutation of Marxist philosophy and his interpretation of evolution in terms of a quest for subsistence and social harmony owe much to Maurice William, an American socialist. World War I triggered in this socialist a crisis of conscience from which, in 1920, emerged a book entitled *The Social Interpretation of History*. William, a disappointed disciple of Marx, produced a critique of his master, from which Sun Yat-sen appropriated not only the major ideas but even its vocabulary. Examples of his textual borrowings abound. Perhaps the most striking is the metaphor quoted above, in which Marx is portrayed as a "pathologist" of society. Its source is Maurice William's following comment: "Marx was a social pathologist. He studied social pathology and mistook the phenomenon he observed for the laws of social biology. The manifestations of the class struggle are symptoms of social pathology."[82]

In spite of the numerous cases of word-for-word transpositions from William's text in the first lecture on the livelihood of the people, Sun Yat-sen cannot be accused of plagiarism, for, in passing, he does acknowledge his debt, or at least mentions William's name. However, a comparison of the two works reveals clearly enough that Sun Yat-sen had drawn most of his information from William (on Fordism, on the divisions between various socialist currents, etc.) as well as most of his arguments (on plus-value, the class struggle, and so on). Should further claims be made? William himself asserted that it was upon reading *The Social Interpretation of History* that Sun Yat-sen, previously a convert to Marxism, changed his mind and rallied to the idea of an evolution governed by the universal quest for subsistence and conditioned by social harmony.[83] But that thesis hardly seems plausible. Nowhere is there any hint of a conversion to Marxism on Sun Yat-sen's part, whereas a number of pronouncements made before 1924 on the quest for subsistence and social harmony do exist.

Let us therefore continue to credit Sun Yat-sen with the generation of the philosophical theses upon which the Three Principles of the People are founded, simply adding that reading William had not only confirmed Sun's opinions (as is recognized in his official biographies) but also helped him to clarify, express, expand upon, and argue views that until then had remained intuitive apprehensions rather than doctrines.

The Principle of the Livelihood of the People as Both an Idealistic Goal and a Strategy for Development

"The principle of the livelihood of the people . . . is that the people of the whole nation . . . have a share in the profits of capital."[84] This utopian communism would realize the dream of making "everybody contented and happy, free from the suffering caused by the unequal distribution of wealth and property."[85] Sun Yat-sen assimilated this communism to the Confucian ideal of universal harmony. In fact, it was upon that note that he concluded his second lecture: "When the people share everything in the State, then we will truly reach the goal of the principle of the people, which is Confucius' hope of a "great commonwealth."[86] As described in the *Book of Rites* (*Liji*; fourth to third century B.C.), this world of great harmony will be one in which all under heaven will work for the common good (*tianxia weigong*) and in which universal love will reign. Those most deprived will be looked after. Each person will fulfill his duty and the spirit of greed will disappear. This will not only be a world that allows each person to live "according to his needs"; it will also consecrate the reign of virtue.

To prepare for the coming of this communist paradise, Sun advocates a method adapted to the Chinese condition. "We must base our methods not upon abstruse theories or upon empty learning but upon facts, and not facts peculiar to foreign countries but facts observable in China."[87] Now, the fundamental feature of China was its poverty: "All the Chinese people must be counted as poor. . . . There is no especially rich class, there is only a general poverty. The "inequalities between rich and poor" which the Chinese speak of are only differences within the poor class, differences in degree of poverty."[88]

China's poverty and economic backwardness made the adoption of Marxist methods unsuitable. "The youthful scholars today advocate Marx's way for the solution of China's social and economic problems. But they fail to realize that China now is suffering from poverty, not from unequal distribution of wealth."[89] Sun Yat-sen then proceeded to prove his point with a parable. Evoking the rich Cantonese who dressed up in their furs as soon as winter approached (a warm, tropical winter) and then complained of the dangers of too soft a climate, Sun drew the conclusion that it is pointless "to first wear furs and then hope for the north winds."[90] So what course should one take? "The Nationalist Party made that clear in its program very early on: a) equalize land rights; b) restrict capital."[91]

The 1924 agrarian program to a large extent returns to that set out in 1905–6, which was inspired by the theories of the American reformer Henry George. The agrarian question is tackled through the growing speculation that had grossly inflated land prices from Canton to Shanghai. Sun was indignant at the private appropriation of a plus-value resulting from "the efforts of everyone." And he listed the measures designed to prevent such misappropriation: a survey of real estate properties, declaration of their value, taxation proportional to the declared value, and so on. And that is all that Sun Yat-sen had to say on the agrarian question in his second lecture, which was designed to set out the broad meaning of the People's Livelihood. He did return to the subject in his third lecture, however, delivered on the following August 17. And this time he tackled the fundamental underlying problem, namely, the problem of the ownership and the exploitation of agricultural land. After all, how important was the urban property speculation in a few treaty ports compared with the burden of the land rent that, throughout China, was oppressing millions of peasants?

Sun Yat-sen dealt with this problem in just a few sentences (whereas he devoted long paragraphs to the program of reform inspired by Henry George's ideas). But his tone was vehement. He deplored the poverty of peasants who "by dint of very hard labor . . . produce foodstuffs over half of which are taken from them by their landlords. What is left is barely sufficient to keep them alive. It is totally unjust." There was only one remedy for such injustice: to give the land to the tillers. "If our principle of the livelihood of the people is really to achieve its goal and if the agricultural problem is really to be resolved, 'let the land go to those who work on it.' "[92]

The importance that Sun thus belatedly ascribed to the peasant problem certainly does seem to reflect the influence of his Soviet advisers and his communist allies, whose agrarian radicalism is a well-known fact. But, as we have seen, even if Sun Yat-sen did express approval of the objectives of the agrarian revolution, he did not advocate their immediate and integral application. Hostile to the idea of expropriation of a violent nature, he recommended a gradual reform, the broad lines of which he was to expound a few days later in his address to the Farmers' Movement Training Institute, on August 21 (or 23). On August 17, however, in his third lecture, although he stressed the need for peasant emancipation, Sun Yat-sen hardly devoted any time to considering how that emancipation was to be achieved. Instead, he spoke at length of a program of technical modernization, going into details on its every aspect: mechanization, artificial fertilizers, electrification, the rotation of crops, and so on. Sun evidently placed more hope in increased production, obtained as a result of a technological revolution, than in any redistribution of wealth. At any rate, at this point he seemed to prefer to ignore the revolutionary implications of the slogan he had put forward: land to the tillers. That slogan, borrowed from his Soviet and communist allies, or imposed by them, defined not so much a policy as an ultimate objective, without going into the methods that would lead to it.

The other aim of Sun's program was the limitation of capital. Sun Yat-sen did not seek to do away with private enterprise. Although he deplored the monopolizing of the means of production, he justified the existence of industrial profit by the contribution that entrepreneurs made to production. "We have already recognized the injustice of industrialists and traders monopolizing the values of material [goods] in order to make money." However, "those industrialists work extremely hard and, even if they do make large profits, it is only after purchasing cheaply and selling advantageously, and after many plans and deals."[93] So their gains could not be compared with those of landlords who speculated on the plus-value of real estate.

The fact nevertheless remained that in Europe and in America the development of private capitalism had led to violent, apparently insoluble social conflicts: "If we wait until our trade and industry are flourishing before we start to think of this, we shall be in an even worse position for finding some means to resolve the problem."[94] The experience of the West and especially that of Soviet Russia showed that "forceful procedures" (revolutionary methods and "dictatorship of the common people and producers" advocated by the Marxists) had not produced a solution to the economic problem. It would therefore be better to rely on the "pacific methods" that had enabled America to attenuate the difficulties, if not to eliminate them. The four measures proposed by Sun Yat-sen—social and industrial reforms, the nationalization of means of transport and communication, increased taxation on income and inheritances, and the collectivization of distribution networks—were directly inspired by Maurice William. Understandably enough, Sun Yat-sen, with his desire to avoid a class struggle, had been very attracted by what William claimed to be so many methods of "pacific expropriation." It was therefore by means of legislation that Sun Yat-sen proposed to limit, but not to overthrow capitalism: there was to be no enforced nationalization, no class struggle. "Industrialists already established will suffer no loss," he claimed, for what he was proposing was altogether different from "what, in Europe and America, is called nationalization, which consists in wresting from individuals all the industries that already exist, so as to make them the government's responsibility."[95]

In truth, in the domain of urban economy, just as in that of agriculture, Sun Yat-sen believed not so much in the redistribution of wealth as in increased production. And in a backward country such as China, that increase would depend upon State intervention. "China is poor. . . . Other countries have a surplus of production while China is not producing enough. So China must not only regulate private capital, but she must also develop State capital and promote industry."[96] Sun Yat-sen's admiration for Bismarck went back a long way. As early as 1905–6, the *People's Journal* had been extolling the thought and work of the Chancellor. And in his fourth lecture on democracy, Sun Yat-sen once again returned to the policies of Bismarck, who "practiced State socialism, used the force of the State to enable himself to realize the program of the socialists, and employed a preventative method rather than a conflictual and destructive one." Sun Yat-sen recognized that this was an "anti-democratic maneuver," but nevertheless seemed full of admiration for "the very cunning method that made it possible, within less than twenty years, to transform a weak Germany into an extremely strong nation."[97]

So it was up to the State to "promote industry and use machinery in production." The public sector would coexist with private enterprise and would check the latter's further expansion. "If we do not use State power to build up these enterprises but leave them in the hands of private Chinese or foreign businessmen, the result will be simply the expansion of private capital and the emergence of a great wealthy class with the consequent inequalities in society."[98] State socialism would concern the fundamental sectors of transport, mining, and manufacture. Sun Yat-sen gave no further details on his program of modernization and industrialization, but referred his listeners to the descriptions earlier provided in *The International Development of China*. However, he once again stressed the imperative need to call upon foreign capital and experts. "We shall not be able to promote . . . these great industries by our own knowledge and experience, with our own capital."[99]

In the context of the period, recourse to foreign capital and experts could only mean recourse to European or American capital and experts. Sun's recommendation therefore seems somewhat at odds with his violent diatribes against Western imperialism. In this domain, however, Soviet Russia had already provided an example with its New Economic Policy. Moreover, Sun Yat-sen took good care to consign these borrowings to within the framework of his own program, making them serve his own objectives. "We shall use already existing foreign capital to create the communist world of the future China."[100] Besides, Sun had already explained in *The International Development of China* that cooperation with foreigners could only be established upon a basis of equality.

In the immediate instance, what was most urgent was to strive to establish such relations. Both in the public and in the private sector, economic development involved first of all winning back independence and sovereignty. "We cannot find a solution for the livelihood problem in the economic field alone; we must first take hold on the political side, abolish all unequal treaties, and take back the customs out of foreign control. Then . . . our home industries will naturally be able to develop."[101]

Like Cato, relentlessly bent on the destruction of Carthage, Sun Yat-sen constantly steered his audience back to the problem uppermost in his mind, the great problem upon which, he believed, the solution of all the rest depended: namely, the problem of national emancipation. Far from adopting the Marxist point of view, according to which there are no frontiers to economic development and social movements, Sun Yat-sen (again in agreement with Maurice William) believed that one's standard of life, in the very widest sense, depended not so much upon social stratification but much more on one's nationality. You were poor not because you were a worker . . . but because you were Chinese. He had come full circle: his thought upon the principle of the livelihood of the people reached the very same conclusion as that already suggested by his study of nationalism and democracy.

THE THREE PRINCIPLES OF THE PEOPLE: FROM INTELLECTUAL HISTORY TO CULTURAL TRANSMISSION

The Guomindang party lost no time in turning *The Three Principles of the People* into a canonical text. In the West, in contrast, it has never been rated as one of the great works of contemporary Chinese thought, and no major study has been devoted to it for over half a century. Even before World War II, when the triumphant Guomindang imposed a Sunist cult in China, Western commentators were already proving very critical. It was said of Sun Yat-sen: "He never attained intellectual maturity and he was completely devoid of the faculty of reason. He functioned, mentally, in sporadic hunches."[102] His doctrine was judged to be a mishmash, a jumble, the result of an unruly eclecticism that juxtaposed the most disparate ideas without bothering to make them agree. "In his haste, he was never at pains to reconcile the earlier doctrines which he had borrowed from Henry George and Karl Marx with those which he had acquired at later dates from Dr. Maurice William and Comrade Borodin."[103] The West did not recognize itself in Sun's confused speculations and resented the way he had upset the ordering of its theories, tendencies, and schools of thought. "Sun Yat-sen is typical of the impact of Western ideas upon China. If we do not admire the result of our influence, we must at least recognize it as our handiwork. . . . Sun Yat-sen was typical also of the half assimilation of Western ideas which has been an inevitable but unlovely phase of the transition."[104]

It is true that a Westerner feels somewhat bewildered by the kaleidoscope of Sunist references. Initially, in the second lecture on democracy, Sun declared that the revolutionary slogan of the French Revolution was "Liberty, Equality, Fraternity," just as the slogan of the Chinese Revolution was *The Three Principles of the People*.[105] Later, in the second lecture on the principle of the livelihood of the People, the Three Principles of the People were reduced to Lincoln's famous formula, "Government of the people, by the people, and for the people."[106] Along the way, Marx and Bismarck, and Henry George and

Maurice William were all involved. The defense produced by (Chinese) exponents of Sun's thought is that it is perfectly natural that Western ideas should change somewhat in the course of their transposition, given that Sun Yat-sen decided to associate them with (or some might say subordinate them to) certain aspects of traditional Chinese thought; and there are certainly enough references to the Classics—Confucius and Mencius—in *The Three Principles of the People* to support that view.

In fact, the nature of *The Three Principles of the People* is such that the most divergent interpretations can be justified. And it was, of course, precisely this that dismayed Western historians of political thought. Their mistake perhaps lay in considering Sun Yat-sen's work as a conventional one, as they would have considered the writings of Proudhon, Darwin, or Lenin. But *The Three Principles of the People* is not a conventional work, the fruit of a particular culture and a particular background. It emerged at the frontier of two traditions, Chinese and Western, and at the intersection of many different cultures: Russian, German, French, English, American. A study of it perhaps requires a special approach that can accept that intellectual history may be enriched by the contributions of other disciplines, such as anthropology. Instead of trying to sort out the many influences upon the thought of Sun Yat-sen, influences that are hard to pin down and impossible to grade on a hierarchy, it might be more productive to start from the ideas that he uses and to trace their genealogy. It would then transpire that most of the major themes around which Sun's thought is organized—or at least gravitates—faithfully reflect the thought of intellectuals such as Kang Youwei and Liang Qichao at the end of the nineteenth century and during the first decade of the twentieth. When Sun evokes the necessary subordination of the individual to the needs of the state, when he advocates national unity and governmental centralization, when he argues for economic growth and against a class struggle, and when he draws a distinction between popular sovereignty and governmental power, he is simply taking up positions already adopted by the great intellectuals of the transition.

This fact, which the texts seem to establish firmly enough, has seldom been explicitly acknowledged. For political reasons, it was necessary to preserve a boundary between the reformists and the revolutionaries. It was also necessary to preserve Sun's originality in the eyes of posterity. But the interest of this genealogy lies in what it tells us about how Sun's ideas were transmitted to him. The concepts, (in particular those of liberty, sovereignty, and constitutional representation) that Sun had borrowed from intellectuals more skilled than himself at handling abstractions, are Western concepts, but as seen and shaped by Chinese minds.[107] The intimate knowledge of the Classics possessed by the great intellectuals of the transition had clearly influenced the way in which they had appropriated the new notions from the West. Consider, for example, how Kang Youwei combined the dynamism of social Darwinism with the Utopia of Great Harmony. It may well be that the many references to the Chinese Classics in *The Three Principles of the People* can be explained by the connotions created around the Western concepts used by Sun as a result of their having reached him filtered through the Chinese erudition of members of the scholarly elite such as Kang and Liang.

An approach of this kind may enable us to introduce some order into the apparent confusion of *The Three Principles of the People*. But if so, the intrinsic qualities of the text still hardly justify the exceptional place that most Chinese historians (and some others too) assign to it in the history of twentieth-century political thought. It may be that the importance of *The Three Principles of the People* lies elsewhere: at the level of the diffusion of ideas rather than at that of their elaboration. It stems not from intellectual history in itself, but from the history of transcultural border crossing, the history of all the multiform, random, imperfect contacts that make up the fabric of communication between one tradition and another or one civilization and another.

The great intellectuals, scholars, and thinkers who, in China and elsewhere, create the history of thought, frequently play no more than a limited role in those contacts. Absorbed as they are in their own culture, they have no desire to move outside it, and where that culture is a dominant one they have no reason to do so. Such was the case of Bergson, who declined to visit China when invited to do so by intellectuals passionately interested in his work. But if those intellectuals belong to a dominated nation, pragmatic concerns stimulate their interest in foreign cultures. They react to a situation of historical emergency rather than to a purely intellectual challenge. It was the Western gunboats that forced the Confucian scholars to reflect upon nationalism, democracy, and human rights.

So it is from among more modest figures that transcultural border crossers are recruited, and Sun Yat-sen seems the very epitome of one of these. Geographically, he was extremely mobile, living astride a number of cultural frontiers. His temperament was open and generous; he was avid for action and fired by a quasi-religious faith in his mission; and not only was he of an extremely inquiring turn of mind but he set out on his own to satisfy it. The Protestant missionaries had inculcated him with a sense of progress, pragmatism, and optimism; Heaven had endowed him with eloquence; and *The Three Principles of the People* was his gospel.

The Westerners who influenced him the most were not Marx, not Rousseau. They were other transcultural border crossers like himself, likewise of modest origins and ardent convictions, and self-taught. One was Henry George, a New Yorker exiled in the California of the pioneers, a minor employee in the gas company, who believed himself called by God and dedicated his book *Progress and Poverty* to "those who, seeing the vice and misery that spring from the unequal distribution of wealth and privilege, feel the possibility of a higher social state and would strive for its attainment." Marx was to say of George: "Theoretically the man is utterly backward. He understands nothing about the nature of surplus value."[108] But his book reached hundreds of readers, who were won over by the simplicity of his prose. Sun Yat-sen was one of them.

Dr. Maurice William, whose real name was Ilyin, was also an emigrant, the son of a Jewish tailor from Kharkov who found refuge in the United States, a dentist transformed into a writer by his indignation at the misfortunes of World War I. His *Social Interpretation of History* was written in a style devoid of elegance, matter-of-fact, drawing its persuasive power from its very clumsiness. It was published at his own expense, running to a few hundred copies. How one came to fall into the hands of Sun Yat-sen, then living in China, we do not know.

Cultural transmissions are a matter of chance, accident, random encounters. They thrive on simplifications, hasty understanding, misreadings, and misunderstandings. For the generous-hearted men who promote them, writing is simply another form of action. Even if *The Three Principles of the People* has not won a place in intellectual history, it does represent an essential milestone in the history of such transmissions. And the very defects (oversimplification, repetition, naïve enthusiasm) that depreciate it in the eyes of scholars have ensured its success in China and the Third World.

ELEVEN

Sun Yat-sen's Death and Transformation

Like all those who aspire to power, Sun Yat-sen had the knack of discarding certain ideas in a timely fashion, revising particular commitments, and throwing off the role of party leader the better to take on that of head of state. If Paris was worth a mass to Henry IV, Peking was certainly worth an ideological deviation or a strategic U-turn to Sun Yat-sen.

From the summer of 1924 on, Sun dissociated himself from the policy of establishing a revolutionary base that he had been actively supporting since the previous autumn, and launched a new military expedition to the North. When this expedition failed, he gave up the idea of an armed reconquest of Peking. But he still dreamed of obtaining through diplomacy what he had not been able to seize by force. In November 1924, he accordingly left Canton to go and negotiate with the Peking generals with the aim of securing his own election to the presidency of the Republic. Nothing expresses better than this last journey of Sun's the importance that Peking held in the eyes of the Chinese, even those who, in the furthest extremity of the country, were busy trying to create a new national destiny. The Cantonese adventurer of the early years, who had dreamed of seceded republics in the South, had in the end given way to a politician obsessed by the idea of reunification, which, of course, he could only imagine achieved through his own efforts and to his own profit.

Sun Yat-sen's departure for the North represented an abandonment half-way through a project with a chance of success, a project of Soviet inspiration for which the president of the Guomindang had himself frequently declared his approval and support. Had Sun Yat-sen come to realize, in spite of all Borodin's precautions, that he would lose his grip on Canton? Had he wearied of the constant need to arbitrate between the moderate and the radical factions? Had he sensed his approaching death and decided to force the hand of fate and save time by dispensing with a consolidation of the revolution in Canton? It was a departure that yet again raises the familiar problem of Sun's political coherence and posits a number of possible solutions that we have already had occasion to consider. Was it a matter of a lack of foresight, excessive self-confidence, or naïve optimism, or, on the contrary, of a tactical skill bordering on the Machiavellian? Or was it perhaps the obstinacy of an aging politician no longer capable of discarding the rigid framework of the analyses upon which his career had been founded?

That unexpected dash northward, that winter visit to Peking, the last of all Sun Yat-sen's many journeys, is still surrounded by mystery. At what he expected to be his rendezvous with history, Sun found only death, a death as ambiguous as his life had been and that promptly provoked a clash between those who were to become the guardians of the cult—or rather cults—devoted to him. For even eternity could not convert Sun Yat-sen's checkered career into a solid destiny. Nationalists and communists were to continue to wrangle over the heritage of the man who had come to symbolize the Chinese revolution. And history served only to purvey the stuff that myths are made from. Sun Yat-sen's posthumous destiny reflects above all the ups and downs of contemporary Chinese politics. Seemingly possessed of a quasi-autonomous function, that destiny simply erects an extra screen to obscure our view of Sun Yat-sen's historical personality and role.

THE WINTER JOURNEY AND DEATH IN PEKING

The new Northern expedition announced by Sun Yat-sen at the beginning of September 1924 miscarried even before it got going. On October 23, General Feng Yuxiang turned against his leader Wu Peifu, the dominant figure in the Zhili clique and the main source of support for the authorities then established in Peking. Feng Yuxiang seized the capital and ejected the government. This coup d'état upset the balance of politico-military forces in the North and at the same time removed the purpose of the campaign that Sun was preparing to launch against the southern allies of the Zhili clique, now clearly in a state of disarray. On October 30, Sun Yat-sen therefore abandoned the general headquarters he had set up at Shaoguan and returned to Canton—but not to reinstall himself there. He had decided to make the most of the political realignments and institutional reorganization occasioned by Feng Yuxiang's coup d'état and go to Peking to win acceptance for his candidacy for the presidency of a reunited China. The time was past for military force or revolution. Now was the time for negotiation.

Toward Resumption of the North-South Dialogue

First, however, Sun Yat-sen had to enter into negotiation in Canton itself in order to get this journey accepted by his entourage, his party, and his Soviet and communist allies. But how could he possibly justify the idea of a compromise with the warlords whom the Guomindang propaganda had for months been representing, along with the imperialists, as the major enemies of the revolution and of China?

The idea of going to Peking to try his luck in the race for the presidency was Sun Yat-sen's own. The formal invitation that he received on November 1 from Feng Yuxiang to come and take part in a conference on national re-unification was simply a response to solicitations earlier formulated by the president of the Guomindang himself. By October 27, Sun had already taken the initiative of telegraphing to the Northern generals, with no prior consultation with his entourage. His initiative was all the more surprising in that the situation in the North seemed by no means favorable to a return by Sun to the national political stage.

Feng Yuxiang's coup d'état had, it is true, created a vacuum in Peking and had once again raised the problem of the central power. In ousting Wu Peifu he had got rid of the only figure of national stature, who since the spring of 1922 had dominated northern China militarily and had striven, without success, to extend his influence to the Yangzi provinces. Through his appeals for national reunification, his condemnation of Japanese interference, the protection he afforded certain liberal politicians and intellectuals, and the tolerance that he sporadically manifested toward workers' trade unions, Wu Peifu had even for a time managed to forge for himself the image of a statesman devoted to the public interest, and in the eyes of both Chinese and international public opinion, to establish himself as a rival to Sun Yat-sen. After his departure, the political scene was occupied by a group of big barons such as Zhang Zuolin in Manchuria and Feng Yuxiang in the northwest, none of whom possessed the stature necessary to lay claim to the presidency.

Sun therefore reckoned himself to be the man of the moment: only he had a political program and enjoyed national fame. However, the decision rested with those who possessed military clout; and their candidate was not Sun Yat-sen but Duan Qirui. This former officer of Yuan Shikai, who, like all the Northern generals, was a product of the Beiyang army, had been prime minister in 1917 and had made use of his position to set the Anfu clique in power. Since the defeat of that clique in 1920, Duan Qirui had no longer possessed any military strength, a fact that in itself qualified him, in the eyes of the generals, his protectors, as the man to assume a symbolic presidency. To be sure, he was a somewhat old-fashioned figure, hardly an emblem of the awakening Young China. But Duan Qirui held one strong trump card: the patronage of the Japanese, whom he had already provided with numerous pledges of his docility.

Sun's journey was thus in many ways risky. The official organ of the communists, the *Weekly Guide* (*Xiangdao zhoukan*) expressed concern at seeing Sun fall into what they regarded as a political trap set for him by the imperialists and the militarists;[1] and moderates such as Hu Hanmin were fearful for the very safety of their president.

Despite opposition from so many quarters, Sun Yat-sen managed to win approval for his departure by representing it as indispensable to the triumph of a central revolution (*zhongyang geming*), which had to take precedence over the revolutionary base. At the farewell reception he held for his officers on November 4, Sun claimed that he was not going to Peking in order to seize power. That, he said was the opinion "of people who do not understand the situation":[2] in truth, his aim in going to Peking was to "develop propaganda, organize groups, and create a movement in favor of the application of the People's Three Principles." It was similarly in the guise of a messenger of the revolution that, the day before, the president had appeared before the cadets of Huangpu, to whom he also made his farewells. He told them that he wanted to launch "a great central revolution" (*Yi ge hongdade zhongyang geming*). For a quarter of a century, "the revolution had been confined to the provinces and that is why it had had only a very weak influence. . . . But if it roots itself in the capital, then its influence will be very great."[3] Tailored to revolutionary rhetoric, what was surfacing here was the idea of the central role of Peking in Chinese political life, in opposition to the strategy of the Canton revolutionary base. According to Sun, Feng Yuxiang's military coup d'état opened up the way to this "great central revolution." Once militant action was carried to the North, power would be removed from the militants and bureaucrats and handed over to the Guomindang. In the same speech, Sun claimed that this plan had the support not only of the Nationalist party but also of anti-imperialist forces throughout the provinces.

The preparation of a "central revolution" certainly required support on a national scale. So Sun was seeking a way to obtain this. He moderated the social and political demands formulated during the Reorganization Congress—in part dropped them—and at the same time deplored foreign oppression more forcefully than ever. Moderate democracy and vehement anti-imperialism were the slogans he counted on to open up his way to power, a path that he represented to his listeners, and no doubt also to himself, as the path of revolution.

In his *Manifesto on Going North* (*Beishang xuanyan*), published on November 10, Sun Yat-sen explained that the program of national revolution, founded on the People's Three Principles, had already been set out clearly in the *Congress Manifesto* of January 1924. But in view of the circumstances, he now proposed to replace it with a basic program pressing for the abrogation of the unequal treaties and a clear distribution of power between the center and the provinces, of a kind to ensure both national unity and provincial autonomy. Not only did the latter proposal accord with the aspirations of local elites (which he had so violently opposed in Canton in 1922, when Chen Jiongming had championed them), but he went further than most partisans of autonomy in that he proposed as the unit of self-government not the province, but the district (*xian*), the smallest unit in Chinese administration.

The *Manifesto on Going North* also took up an idea that had been much in vogue in urban liberal circles a few years earlier: that of a national convention (*guomin huiyi*). The idea had first been suggested by Wu Peifu in 1920, then, in October 1921, had been picked up by the Federation of Chambers of Commerce, which had proposed assembling in Shanghai representatives of professional and educational associations and also of the provincial assemblies, with the aim of reconstructing political institutions and planning reunification, the disbanding of troops, and financial reorganization. The plan had been stillborn, however, for the convention, which took place from March to September 1922, produced no results at all.

Sun Yat-sen now returned to this idea of a convention whose task would be

to unify, pacify, and rebuild the country. It would be preceded by a preparatory assembly whose members would be designated by associations of the
modern entrepreneurs, chambers of commerce, educational societies, universities, student organizations, workers' trade unions, peasant associations, the
militarists (or at least those hostile to Wu Peifu), and the political parties. Sun's
1924 plan widened the scope of popular representation a good deal beyond
what the chambers of commerce had had in mind in 1921. But the principle
behind it was the same: namely, that of representation through interest groups
and professional associations, which was probably more compatible with the
state of semimodernized Chinese society than the parliamentary form of
representation tried out in 1913 and 1917 had been. All this was a far cry from
the People's Three Principles, with its successive stages of military control and
political tutelage. The project was of a kind to win over the local elites and the
treaty port merchants, who for several decades had been forming associations
to defend their interests and promote their ideas. It also seemed to be well
received by the Guomindang. Its moderates were bound to welcome greater
openness and a chance to end the intimate on-going debate with their communist allies; and its radicals were probably hoping to gain control of such an
assembly.

Did Sun's pragmatism really give rise to hopes of a rapid extension of
revolutionary power? Some people probably did see the journey to the North
as a chance to moderate and re-root revolutionary power by getting it legiti-
mated by large sections of Chinese public opinion. Others may have dis-
cerned the possibility of an opportunity to implant their own influence in
regions and social groups up until then relatively hostile. In the eyes of yet
others, Sun's departure perhaps presented the advantage of easing the pressure
on Cantonese political life and slowing down the mobilization of the masses.
At any rate, Sun's departure did take place amid a general consensus.

It was not a retreat but, on the contrary, a triumphant departure. On
November 12, Sun's fifty-eighth birthday, the various workers' and students'
associations organized a grand lantern-lit parade: 20,000 people joined it, to
honor the president. Nor did it represent a break with the policy of the united
front. On November 7, in Canton, the commemoration of the October
revolution was particularly brilliant. In the streets, the sailors from the Russian cargo ship *Voroski*, which had brought in arms for Huangpu Academy,
paraded alongside the Cantonese workers and soldiers. And Sun Yat-sen him-

self joined with the Soviet diplomats and advisers in celebrating the success of the Russian revolution, which was represented as a model.

Sun left behind him a reorganized party that was dominated by its most radical elements and, for the first time in its history, commanded extensive popular support, in spite of the impotent hostility of the merchants. He also left a government in the process of consolidation, controlled by the moderates, under the direction of Hu Hanmin. In Sun's absence, revolutionary change and the political and military integration of the Guomindang were to progress. So the journey to the North did not have the effect of doing away with the strategy of the revolutionary base, for this was to be vindicated in 1926 by the launching of a new military expedition, this time a victorious one, under the leadership of Chiang Kai-shek.

Sun's trip had no place in that strategy, not even as a plausible alternative, but it was nevertheless accepted by the Guomindang, the Communists, and the Soviet advisers. It was thus with a group of eighteen supporters that, on November 13, 1924, Sun Yat-sen, accompanied by Song Qingling, boarded ship, bound for Hong Kong, then Shanghai and the North. Among his entourage were high-ranking leaders of the Guomindang, such as Wang Jing-wei and Eugene Chen, and also Borodin. Did all these people really believe that a renewal of the dialogue between the North and the South, broken off in 1917, could succeed? Were they not, rather, concerned to stick close to Sun, ensuring his safety, monitoring the progress of the negotiations and any concessions that might be made to the Northern warlords, and also, perhaps, checking on one another? The failing health of the president prompted reflection upon the imminent problem of his successor and no faction was inclined to leave the way open to a rival one. Sun Yat-sen continued to be obeyed. But like all great men on the way out, he was soon to be used.

Sun Raises the Standard of Resistance to Western Imperialism

Sun made his way northward in short stages. First he paused in Shanghai, from November 17 to 21, then in Kobe, in Japan, from November 24 to 30. By the time he reached Tianjin, on December 4, he was so weakened by his illness that he was forced to take to his bed, never to rise from it again.

Throughout these weeks, negotiations went on with the Northern generals and the warlords of the Yangzi valley. Duan Qirui, who had placed himself at the head of a provisional government in Peking, announced his intention to convene a conference of provincial representatives for the purpose of Reconstruction. Was such a project compatible with that of a national convention, which Sun had already put forward? As the negotiations proceeded, Sun was exalting anti-imperialist patriotism, which he rightly considered to be the theme most popular with the crowds who acclaimed him. He no doubt also reckoned it to be the best revolutionary justification for his trip in the eyes of the radical members of his suite. He was calling in particular for the immediate abolition of extraterritoriality and repudiation of the unequal treaties.

It was the Westerners themselves who, by their provocative behavior, helped Sun to notch up an even higher degree in the exaltation of the anti-foreigner (that is to say anti-Western) discourse, which since 1923 had been kept alive by a whole series of incidents and clashes and had then been even further fanned by the Soviets. Sun's arrival in Shanghai provoked hostile reactions as soon as it became known. An article in the leading local British newspaper, the *North China Daily News,* ran as follows: "Dr. Sun is an undesirable person politically, whose residence in Shanghai now would destroy its neutrality. . . . It is now time to bar the door against Dr. Sun."[4] Sun replied in stinging fashion, pointing out that the Chinese were the hosts here, the foreigners the guests: "As a Chinese citizen, I have every right to reside in my own territory, and the foreigners who are living in China as guests have no authority at all to oppose the presence of their host in any place on Chinese land. So if the foreigners have the audacity to forbid or disrupt my stay in Shanghai, I am determined, with the help of my compatriots, to take radical measures against them."[5] In a telegram addressed to the United States consul general in Shanghai, Sun clarified his meaning: "Would like to say to the foreigners that Shanghai is China. . . . The Chinese are determined that the concessions must be returned."[6]

These pronouncements, burning with anger and indignation, were followed by anti-Western and in particular anti-British attacks of an extremely harsh nature, which Sun had launched during his stay in Kobe—incidents that seemed not so much an emotional reaction but rather a major strategic move with a particular purpose, namely, to obtain the support of Japan in the negotiations with the Northern generals.

Since Yuan Shikai's death in 1916, followed by a succession of increasingly weak central governments in Peking, the Japanese had broken off all relations with Sun. They judged it to be more convenient and more to their advantage to deal with the Peking government, which they alternately financed and threatened. To try to win back Japanese support, Sun had sent ahead Li Liejun, the former Guomindang general from Jiangxi, to test out Japanese reactions to the old pan-Asian theme. It might have been expected that the theme of racial solidarity would have been wholly supplanted by that of revolutionary and proletarian internationalism. Yet here it was again, resuscitated to meet the needs of the moment. Or possibly it had never ceased to haunt Sun.

The latter hypothesis is certainly suggested by the lyrical passion of the speech that the president gave in Kobe on November 28, on the "doctrine of Greater Asia" (*Da Yazhouzhuyi*), which was to be one of his last speeches. He reminded his listeners of the anteriority and superiority of the Asian civilization and of its decline in modern times; he praised the emancipation of Japan, which had repudiated the unequal treaties, thereby arousing great hopes of regeneration among all the nations and peoples of Asia. Japan's victory over Russia in 1905 had been seen as a victory for the peoples of the East over the peoples of the West. Western civilization, which was a materialistic civilization, had established the rule of force (*badao*). But even now that it had itself indisputably become a great power, Japan continued to depend on a regime of virtue and justice and to pursue the Royal Way (*wangdao*), which was the way of Asian civilization. It was therefore Japan's duty to act as the rampart of the East and help China to free itself from the unequal treaties.[7]

This anathema directed against the West was accompanied by more specific accusations brought against the British in an interview with Sun published in the *Mainichi* newspaper: "To [Sun Yat-sen's] mind . . . the Britishers are the worst. . . . It is the British in China who are always creating trouble there. . . . Dr. Sun said . . . Britishers are a curse to China. . . . They hate him and he hates them more than they him."[8] Alone of all the white nations, the new Russia had rejected the politics of colonial aggression formerly practiced by the czars and had rallied to the Royal Way of the East. That was why Europe today rejected it while Sun welcomed it with open arms.

But although the Japanese press had a field day fulminating against Great Britain, and the Kobe public gave Sun a triumphal reception, the Tokyo authorities remained reserved. They refused to issue to the president the official invitation that he was hoping for, in order to go to the capital, and they restricted his contacts. Japan was not prepared either to sacrifice its expansion in Manchuria on the altar of pan-Asianism, or to destroy the system of unequal treaties upon which it, too, depended to develop its interests in China. It had already made its choice. So, while Sun Yat-sen was held at a distance, Duan Qirui's envoys were in Tokyo, negotiating with the Prime Minister and the Minister for Foreign Affairs. Sun's anti-imperialist and anti-Western imprecations, which elicited an enthusiastic welcome for him from the crowds and acclamation from his audiences, failed to rally the Japanese leaders and revived the suspicions of the Northern generals.

There has been much speculation over the sincerity of this violent speech of Sun's. A few weeks later, in Peking, those in his entourage were suggesting that the Japanese translation had distorted the president's thought. But, whatever ulterior motives Sun may have had, he did not succeed, and he was empty-handed when he landed at Tianjin on December 4, 1924.

A Deathbed Under Surveillance

Sun Yat-sen's arrival in the port of Tianjin gave him one last moment of glory. The crowd of students and workers who had come to welcome him acclaimed him when he appeared on the ship's bridge, with his young wife at his side. But the snapshot that immortalized the moment shows a man with a haggard look and with the hand of death already upon him. On the day after his arrival, Sun was forced to take to his bed. Even so, he did not desist from negotiating and was visited there by the Northern generals or their representatives.

The discussions were stormy. Duan Qirui immediately established his distance from Soviet Russia, refused either to include the abrogation of the unequal treaties in his program or to expand the circle of those taking political decisions by including representatives of popular organizations in the Reconstruction conference that he was preparing to convoke. In an interview dated December 7, reported by the Eastern News press agency, Duan Qirui criticized Sun Yat-sen's "idealism," stated that the abrogation of the unequal treaties could only damage China's international credit, and reminded Sun that there were "differences between Peking and Canton."[9] Matching actions to words, as head of the provisional executive, Duan Qirui then proceeded to confirm the validity of the treaties currently in force, in exchange for recognition for his government by the foreign powers. The journey to the North was thus a total failure for Sun Yat-sen: the president was to die defeated.

With his state of health declining, on December 31 Sun Yat-sen was taken by a special train to Peking, where he was hospitalized in the Peking Union Medical College. This establishment, founded by missionaries and funded by the Rockefeller Foundation, provided the most modern medical care in the capital. Sun's presence, along with that of his revolutionary companions and his Soviet advisers, in this place that was so symbolic of Western imperialism in itself sums up the hybrid nature of Chinese modernization, stimulated as it was by the most contradictory of sources. A surgical operation performed on January 26 confirmed the diagnosis of cancer of the liver in its terminal stage. The patient was then transferred to the house of friends. It was there that the last act of his public life was played out: the signing of a political testament under the watchful eyes of his entourage.

As soon as they learned of Sun's state of health, many of his old companions came to be with him in Peking, and an Extraordinary Political Council was formed around Wang Jingwei. Borodin was one of its members. Not much is known about how the Soviet adviser had spent his time following the departure from Canton, except that he did not accompany Sun Yat-sen to Japan. He probably went ahead to Peking. But now he was constantly at the patient's side. Indeed, apart from Wang Jingwei, he seems to have been the only non-family member to be allowed into the sickroom.[10]

The conditions in which Sun's testament was written and signed remain obscure. In the Chinese tradition, as in many others, anything that evokes death is believed to hasten it, so it is not easy to raise the matter of a will or testament at the bedside of a dying man. Nevertheless, on February 24, Wang Jingwei, surrounded by Song Qingling, Sun Fo, and Sun's two brothers-in-law, Song Ziwen and Kong Xiangxi, asked the president to make his intentions known. But Sun Yat-sen was content to listen to and approve a text composed in advance by Wang Jingwei, in agreement with the other members of the Extraordinary Political Council. (Later, the authorities of the Guomindang were to produce another version of this episode, according to which Wang Jingwei wrote the testament at Sun Yat-sen's dictation.) However, at Song Qingling's suggestion, and as if to put off the fatal moment, the signing of the testament was deferred. Not until March 11, on the eve of his death, did Sun, helped by his wife, add his signature to the text drawn up by Wang Jingwei. Countersigned and authenticated by nine people, either members of the family or long-standing companions of Sun, the *Political Testament* thereafter assumed a quasi-sacred character and served as the Nationalist Party's charter:

For forty years, I have devoted myself to the cause of the national revolution, the objective of which is to restore to China its liberty and a rank equal [to that of the other nations]. The experience of those forty years has convinced me that if we wish to attain that objective, we must rouse the popular masses and unite with the peoples of the world that treat us on an equal footing, so as to pursue the common fight. Today, the revolution has not yet triumphed. May all our comrades, guided by my writings, *The Plan for National Reconstruction*, *The Fundamentals of National Reconstruction*, *The People's Three Principles*, and *The Congress Manifesto*, continue the struggle for this victory. And, above all, it is also necessary as soon as possible to implement the plans that I have recently proposed for setting up a national convention and for abrogating the unequal treaties. Those are my instructions.[11]

This *Political Testament* was accompanied by a private will in which Sun Yat-sen bequeathed all his possessions—books, personal effects, and house—to his wife, Song Qingling. This private will, also drawn up by Wang Jingwei, was presented to Sun and approved by him at the same time as the public testament, on February 24, and was also signed on March 11. It testifies to the honesty of the revolutionary leader who, after raising and managing such vast funds destined for the revolution, died with no personal fortune at all. At a time of generalized corruption, that integrity added to Sun's stature and raised him above his rivals, the warlords, whose methods of action and political style he had, in other respects, often adopted.

But on March 11, a third text was also submitted to Sun Yat-sen for his signature, a text that had not been put before him for his approval on February 24. This was a *Letter of Farewell*, addressed to the Central Committee of the Soviet Union:

I am leaving behind me a party which I hoped would be associated with you in the historic work of completely liberating China and other exploited countries from this imperialist system. . . . I have therefore enjoined the Kuomintang to carry on the work of the national revolutionary movement. . . . To this end I have charged the party to keep in constant touch with you; and I look with confidence to the continuance of the support that your Government has heretofore extended to my country.

In bidding farewell to you, dear comrades, I wish to express my fervent hope that the day may soon dawn when the USSR will greet, as a friend and ally, a strong and independent China and the two allies may together advance to victory in the great struggle for the liberation of the oppressed peoples of the world.[12]

This text, prepared with Borodin's approval by a representative of the most radical faction of the Guomindang, was read to the dying Sun Yat-sen by Song Ziwen. Even if Sun did sign it, it was not cosigned by anyone and the principal leaders of the Nationalist Party were never to respect it as they did the *Political Testament*.

The numerous members of the entourage that had been vying for the dead man's signature were soon at loggerheads over his remains. Sun Yat-sen, who had recognized Lenin as his model and Russian communism as his best ally, died on March 12, as a Christian. Some, including his wife, Song Qingling, and his son, Sun Fo, accordingly wanted a Christian funeral. Others, who identified the revolution and the struggle against imperialism with a rejection of Christianity, rebelled at this idea and were planning to turn the mourning for Sun into a political demonstration. Eventually, two separate ceremonies were held on the same day, March 19, 1925.

A Protestant service was held in the Peking Union Medical College, in the presence of the family and their guests. After hymns and readings from the Bible, Kong Xiangxi, Sun's brother-in-law, addressed the congregation, evoking the deep faith of the deceased: "On the eve of his death, Mr. Soun-Wen [Sun Yat-sen] declared that he was a Christian Protestant and had come into the world to fight against the spirit of evil, by proclaiming revolution, as Jesus did long ago."[13] According to a witness, Sun's actual words were: "Just as Christ was sent by God to the world, so also did God send me."[14] This was hardly the image of "the humble and repentant Christian" that the more radical members of the Guomindang were so indignant at seeing substituted for that of "the formidable leader of a revolutionary movement that is destined to restore to China her strength and her independence."[15] To the very end, Sun Yat-sen retained his extraordinary confidence in himself and his mission, a mission totally self-assigned, which in his own eyes and sometimes in the eyes of others made him a protagonist of history, a prophet of the revolution.

But the factional struggle created its own imperatives. So the second funeral ceremony, which took place in front of the imperial palace, in the presence of a crowd of followers and sympathizers, was designed to honor the revolutionary and get the prophet forgotten. The Soviet ambassador to Peking, Lev M. Karakhan, was among those who led the mourners, and his embassy staff surrounded the coffin, while loudspeakers relayed Sun Yat-sen's voice exalting the principle of nationalism.

After three weeks, during which the coffin lay in state while the public filed past it in homage, it was moved to a Peking suburb. Here Sun was given a provisional burial at the Temple of Azure Clouds, amid the pine trees of the western hills, until such time as it could be buried in Nanking, in accordance with his expressed wish.

The presence of Sun Yat-sen, even dying, even dead, had had the power to impose compromise and a semblance of unity upon the heterogeneous factions of his followers. But his disappearance allowed free rein to the infighting among the communists and the radical and the moderate nationalists, all vying for control of the party and the national revolution.

Barely two years after Sun Yat-sen's death, in April 1927, these struggles culminated in the bloody Shanghai coup in which Chiang Kai-shek violently eliminated the communists, and the united front gave way to a civil war that, with a few periods of remission, was to continue until 1949. Defeated by the communist revolution, Chiang Kai-shek and the Guomindang then found refuge in the island province of Taiwan, where, with the cold war abetting and helped by the success of their economic policies, they managed to consolidate their power. The heirs to the man who had dreamed of unifying his country have thus for the past half-century been perpetuating the existence of two Chinas.

The Guomindang and the Communist Party both made equal use of Sun Yat-sen, turning him into the symbol of revolution, national emancipation, modernism, and socialism. To that effect, they created a whole series of conventional images of him: the patriot, the clairvoyant, the champion of progress, the hero. The facts were adapted to the demands of ideology and propaganda. And when, as Lenin had put it, those facts proved too intractable, they were simply swept out of sight.

SUN YAT-SEN SUPERSTAR: THE MYTH OF SUN AND WHAT WAS AT STAKE POLITICALLY

The subordination of history to politics, long a traditional procedure in China, can be adapted with remarkable ease to the needs of the authoritarian and totalitarian regimes of modern times. The manipulation of the historical past, in order to shore up the official ideology and, through this, the political authorities, was a stratagem used, before 1949, both in Nanking (Chiang Kai-shek's capital) and in Yan'an (Mao Zedong's refuge) and, after 1949, both in Beijing and in Taiwan.

Guomindang Orthodoxy

During the Nanking decade (1927–37), Sun Yat-sen became "the uncrowned king of Young China" (Lyon Sharman). The canonic interpretation of his role and thought was fixed on the basis of autobiographical texts or earlier accounts by fervent admirers and followers: the companions of his youth and his lieutenant Chen Shaobai, and the militants of his first revolutionary organizations, Feng Ziyou and Zou Lu. Even at this early date the texts represented Sun Yat-sen as a born revolutionary, and drew a veil over his reformist efforts and his close relations with the anglicized elites of Hong Kong during the 1890's. Already, they were attributing to Sun the credit for having single-handedly guided and inspired the revolutionary movement, ignited the 1911 revolution, brought down the imperial regime, and founded the Republic. No mention of the personality clashes and the conflicts of ideas and interests! From the very first years of the Republic, Sun Yat-sen and his cohorts had fabricated and imposed a monolithic history of the revolution.

This determined self-glorification and desire to appear as the pioneer and sole leader of the revolutionary movement reflected the high opinion that Sun had always had of himself, and it was also politically motivated. It was important to reaffirm Sun's legitimacy and authority, both of which had been severely undermined after the 1913 victory of Yuan Shikai's military dictatorship. At that time, Sun Yat-sen had himself sought to regild the escutcheons of both his own cause and the revolution by deliberately confusing the two.

After Sun's death in 1925 and the establishment of the nationalist regime in 1927, the construction of the myth was pursued with renewed vigor, now served by the Guomindang's entire propaganda apparatus. The important thing at this point was to wrest the heritage of the Chinese revolution, hence also of Sun, from the communist rivals. The policy of the united front and close relations with the Soviet Union, pursued from 1923 to 1925, could indeed lend a certain credibility to the claims of the communists, who were also seeking to reflect the glory of the prestigious father of the revolution. Efforts were therefore made to establish firmly that the history of the Chinese revolution rested exclusively in that of the Guomindang led by its historic founder and leader, Sun Yat-sen. Similarly, the revolutionary ideology was exclusively summed up by that of *The People's Three Principles*, as formulated in 1924. Although Sun had arrived at his conclusions by way of a series of approximations, had been tempted by a whole collection of solutions, many of them divergent, and had constantly modulated the fundamental themes of his ideas as inspired by changing circumstances, his thought was now presented as fixed, shorn of its hesitations and contradictions and as clear and cold as a dogma. All the positions taken up by Sun before 1924 were reexamined in the light of this dogma, every manifestation of which, however embryonic, was traced (or fabricated).

To facilitate his assumption of power and to legitimate his regime, Chiang Kai-shek, who in Sun Yat-sen's lifetime had been far more interested in action than in theory, now represented himself as a zealous disciple and the faithful guardian of his master's thought. To prevent the communists and the most radical wing of the Guomindang from making the political capital that they could draw from references to *The People's Three Principles*, Chiang Kai-shek produced an extremely conservative account of it, repeatedly declaring, "The thought of our [president] is also in the tradition of the unbroken system of Confucianism."[16] To do this, Chiang Kai-shek had drawn on analyses produced by one of the most brilliant of the Guomindang ideologues, Dai Jitao. As early as June 1925, Dai Jitao, who was hostile to what he considered to be the far too close alliance with the communists, had published *The Philosophical Foundations of the Teaching of Sun Yat-sen* (*Sun Wenzhuyi zhi zhexue jichu*). According to his exegesis, Sun had followed in the path of traditional Confucian thought: *The People's Three Principles* stemmed from *The Doctrine of the Mean* (*Zhongyong*) and were combined with the principle of sincerity (*cheng*). In 1933, this interpretation was taken up and further developed by Chen Lifu, one of the foremost leaders of the Guomindang, who collaborated with Chiang Kai-shek in his work entitled *Vitalism* (*Weisheng lun*). In this, Sun Yat-sen was presented as a spiritual thinker, a modern revolutionary faithful to the Chinese cultural tradition. The great movement of mobilization and social control launched in 1934, known as New Life, was placed under the twofold patronage of Sun Yat-sen and the ancient Chinese sages.

Meanwhile, the nationalist government was building the cult of Sun Yat-sen. On June 1, 1929, the coffin of the late president was transferred to the mausoleum of the Purple Mountains, in the neighborhood of Nanking. In the course of a national funeral led by Chiang Kai-shek and the principal nationalist leaders, accompanied by an army escort, punctuated by the sound of cannons and attended by the diplomatic corps and thousands of ordinary citizens, Sun Yat-sen was installed in his last resting place. The monumental character of his tomb, fronted by a huge flight of steps, the beauty of the surrounding wooded hills, and the proximity of the burial mounds of the ancient Ming emperors, to whose shades Sun Yat-sen had prayed at the founding of the Republic in 1912, all combined to enhance the solemnity of the spot and to encourage reverence. The Purple Mountains looked down from afar upon Nanking, the capital of the new government. "In [his] new role as patron saint of Chinese nationalism," Sun Yat-sen "seemed sure to exert greater force and influence from his lofty resting place than he ever had through his activity in the valley below."[17]

Meanwhile, in offices, schools, and barracks, wherever the nationalist authorities exercised close or distant control, the portrait of Sun Yat-sen kept watch, and before it, every Monday, a ceremony took place according to a decreed ritual. After bowing three times before the portrait, those present listened to a reading of the *Political Testament*, by now a canonical text, and then observed a three-minute silence. The study of *The People's Three Principles* had become compulsory in all educational establishments. "It was the code for new generations . . . it became a class textbook. . . . In competitive examinations . . . a candidate needed above all a good grasp of the doctrine of the People's Three Principles."[18] The anniversaries of Sun Yat-sen's birth and death were celebrated as national holidays on which all public services were given the day off.

In 1940, the party founder, up until then known by his title of "president" (*zongli*) was decreed to be "the Father of the Nation" (*Guofu*). During the Sino-Japanese War (1937–45), patriotic ardor prompted the Guomindang leaders to conceal the close ties that for years had linked Sun Yat-sen and his Japanese friends and advisers. Conversely, the Japanese invaders and the puppet governments that they protected proceeded to invoke those same relations in order to legitimate collaboration, and endeavored to represent Tokyo's imperialist policies of Eastern "co-prosperity" as a manifestation of the pan-Asianism preached by Sun Yat-sen. Wang Jingwei, who had become the president of the collaborating government of Nanking, in 1941 published a collection of pro-Japanese texts by Sun Yat-sen, which he entitled *China and Japan: Natural Friends—Unnatural Enemies.*

After Chiang Kai-shek's government took refuge in Taiwan in 1949, the cult of Sun Yat-sen became one of the essential elements in the restoration of legitimacy following the defeat. The omnipresence of portraits of Sun Yat-sen and his citations, gigantic calligraphies of which adorned all public squares and thoroughfares, was noted by all those visiting Taiwan in the 1950's and 1960's. The doctrine of the People's Three Principles, often reduced to the formulae of a catechism, was still used to indoctrinate the new generations. It was also used to justify a social and economic policy in large measure imposed by Taiwan's all-powerful American ally and protector. The agrarian reforms introduced between 1949 and 1955 were thus presented by Chiang Kai-shek as implementing the principle of the livelihood of the people.[19] Taiwan's opening-up to the international market from 1960 on and the growing role of private enterprise, both of which were instrumental in creating the economic miracle, were represented as stemming from the strategy of modernization advocated by Sun.[20]

One may well consider that American aid, the evolution of the international situation, the spirit of enterprise among the local population, and the skill of economic administrators played a more determining role in the Taiwanese success than did the doctrine of Sun Yat-sen. Nevertheless, reference to that doctrine was systematically cultivated by the leaders of the Republic of China in Taiwan. In 1953, Chiang Kai-shek himself went to the trouble of completing the exposition of the livelihood of the people (left unfinished by Sun Yat-sen in August 1924), in his *Supplementary Description of Two Aspects of the Principle of the Livelihood of the People: Education and Leisure.* Still interpreting Sun's thought in Confucian terms, Chiang Kai-shek underlined the importance of a period of transition after the Lesser Tranquillity (*Xiaokang*), characterized by the development of free enterprise and private capitalism, before tackling the final goal of the Great Harmony (*Datong*), founded solely upon cooperation and the satisfaction of the needs of the people.[21]

The Communist Neo-orthodoxy

In the meantime, however, a new orthodoxy had emerged in the People's Republic of China, where Sun Yat-sen, although assigned a more modest place than Marx, Lenin, and Mao, nevertheless figured in the regime's pantheon as a "pioneer of the revolution" (*xianxingzhe*). Here, the essential role ascribed to the cult of Sun seems to have been to link the 1949 revolution, of Marxist-Leninist—hence foreign—inspiration, to the national tradition and the history of a China that, by the late nineteenth century, had already embarked upon the path of modernization and socialism.

With such a perspective, the communists were led to take over a number of points from the credo of their rivals. Like them, they emphasized Sun Yat-sen's quasi-exclusive role in leading the revolutionary movement and establishing its doctrine—at least, that is, up until the appearance of the Communist Party in 1921. They likewise stressed his contribution, judged to be crucial, to the 1911 revolution, which resulted in the abdication of the Manchus and the downfall of the imperial regime. In the communist version of orthodoxy, perforce in line with Marxism-Leninism, Sun Yat-sen appears not so much as a self-made man, carried to the fore by his own personal merit, but rather as the representative of vigorously rising social forces, those of young capitalism and the bourgeoisie of entrepreneurs, known as the national bourgeoisie. The collapse of the Republic in 1913 reflected not, as the nationalists claimed, the waverings of Sun's followers and disciples, but rather the incomplete nature of an economic revolution that had not made it possible for new social formations to assert their power and had thereby condemned the "old democratic revolution" to failure.

There were other nuances, too, that distinguished or opposed the two orthodoxies. The Guomindang orthodoxy kept quiet about the anti-Western sentiments Sun had expressed on numerous occasions; the communist orthodoxy, on the contrary, laid considerable emphasis on his anti-imperialist pronouncements. The Guomindang orthodoxy stressed Sun's concern to preserve the originality of his party and his own doctrines, even between 1923 and 1925 when he was collaborating with the Chinese communists and Soviet Russia. In Peking, in contrast, emphasis was laid upon the relations of trust between Sun and his allies within that first united front and upon the alignment of not only Sun's strategy but also his thinking with the Socialist model offered him by his Soviet advisers. Finally, communist historians made much of, not the People's Three Principles, but the Three Great Policies—alliance with the U.S.S.R., collaboration with Chinese communism, and support for the peasants' and workers' movement—that Sun had adopted at the end of his life.

Although those certainly were the policies that the president got to prevail at the Reorganization Congress in January 1924, the actual concept of the Three Great Policies, which crystallized and systematized those orientations, came later. It appears to have been introduced by the communists and the left wing of the Guomindang during the winter of 1926–27, at a time when both groups were endeavoring to maintain the united front, already condemned by Chiang Kai-shek. So the debate was not about what political choices Sun Yat-sen had arrived at but about the long-term validity of those choices. The Three Great Policies were designed to confer durability and stability upon orientations that the moderates of the Guomindang had considered to be little more than tactical positions of an ephemeral nature. It was a concept forged for the purposes of political combat that the communists had integrated into their own particular interpretation of Sun Yat-sen's doctrine. It even became their principal grid for any reading of the People's Three Principles, for which, in fact, it was to a large extent substituted.

Deng Xiaoping's Reforms and a Renewal of Sunist Fever

The death of Mao Zedong and the accession of Deng Xiaoping in 1978 led to many breaks with the past within the Chinese communist system, but they did not upset the bases of historical practice. More or less the only explanation for the present vogue for Sun Yat-sen in China must be the utility of the Sunist myth, now revived to come to the aid of the policy of the Four Modernizations.[22]

This policy gives absolute priority to the development of economic production and to making up for the accumulated backwardness of this domain in China. The realization of strictly socialist objectives (social justice, equal conditions) has been deferred until such time as modernization has been achieved. To encourage development, the reformers have adopted a strategy that makes a total break away from the economic policy applied since 1949 and takes up a position in total opposition to the theories and practices previously considered as essential to the very nature of the regime. The priority of a protected public sector has been superseded by encouragement for private and collective enterprise ruled by market forces. The ideal of self-sufficiency promoted by the slogan "Rely on your own strengths" has been abandoned in favor of an open-door policy of financial and technical cooperation with foreigners, which operates with most success in the Special Economic Zones that were created in the southern provinces in 1979. This reversal of economic strategy has been accompanied by a shift in values and a shake-up in historical references. In 1988, the well-known television series *He shang* (The River Elegy) struck a blow against the mud-colored, Yellow China that, sheltered by its Great Wall, perpetuated a rural and bureaucratic tradition, and it exalted the Blue China that was the color of the ocean, open, cosmopolitan, enterprising, and rich with the boundless energy of its immense population.

Such a radical change was bound to provoke violent resistance. At this point there were many who deplored what they regarded as the reestablishment of capitalism and the return of Western and Japanese imperialism. The reformers were accused not only of abandoning socialism but also of betraying China and its sovereignty and fundamental interests. The authorities' exaltation of Sun, the model patriot and cosmopolitan modernizer, was thus designed to provide historical justification for Deng Xiaoping and his collaborators. The standing of this prestigious forerunner was supposed to protect them against all those accusations of ingratiating behavior toward foreigners and to legitimate their open-door policy, their appeals to private capital, and the priority they ascribed to the development of the coastal zones. In the longer term, the exaltation of Sun Yat-sen is supposed to create the basis of an entente with the Taiwan regime and eventually prepare for the island's return to the bosom of the mother country. Would not the reunification of China represent the highest of patriotic achievements, one that would block the complaints of all disgruntled nationalists?

The show of new interest in Sun Yat-sen is thus a response to the needs of the reformist strategy. Contrary to what happened in the 1950's, the emphasis is no longer on Sun's alliance with the Chinese communists from 1923 on; rather, it is on the earlier role that he played in arousing national spirit at a time when China was still living under the yoke of the Manchu dynasty and foreign imperialism. Sun Yat-sen is saluted as the promoter of vast plans for economic development, plans that called for foreign aid. It is in this context, for example, that the development of the new port and financial district of Pudong, in Shanghai, for which the Beijing government solicited capital from the West and the overseas Chinese, is regularly presented as the realization of a plan described by Sun Yat-sen in *The International Development of China.*

The reformists take shelter behind the optimistic patriotism of a Sun Yat-sen who was convinced that his country would save a great deal of time by soliciting aid from foreign powers and that it would be entirely in the latters' interest to assist a process of modernization that would not only benefit China but also promote world peace. More generally, Sun's comeback in the guise of a nationalist of the treaty ports and a cosmopolitan modernizer is an indication of the increasing weight that the coastal and southern provinces carry in the Chinese political scene. After the era of the ideologues and bureaucrats from Beijing, Hunan, and Sichuan, the time has come for the revenge of the entrepreneurs and adventurers from the South, the people from Shanghai and Canton.

This is not the place to attempt to evaluate how useful the reference to Sun Yat-sen has turned out to be to the policy of the Four Modernizations. But it is hard to resist a smile at the ironic twist of history that has turned the ghost of Sun against those who once sought to exorcize it. Following the repression of May–June 1989, the dissidents, just as keen as their adversaries to make history serve their purposes, themselves evoked Sun Yat-sen and his revolutionary propaganda and mobilization activities in the Chinese overseas communities, in justification of their own departure to foreign lands where they were hoping to continue the battle.

THE DEMOLITION OF THE HEROIC IMAGE
AND WHAT IS AT STAKE INTELLECTUALLY

The heroic myth created by Chinese historiography has not stood up to the systematic critical analysis undertaken by Western authors and well served by the abundance of archives (diplomatic, colonial, etc.) and other data recording Sun Yat-sen's many cosmopolitan activities, which are to be found in libraries outside China. Two works have played a major role in the destruction of the myth: the one by Harold Z. Schiffrin, which appeared in 1968, covers the early life and career of Sun up until 1905; the other, by C. Martin Wilbur, was published in 1976 but is based on a whole series of earlier works.[23] The former work sheds light upon the handicap that his peasant origin, his overseas education, and his conversion to Christianity constituted for the young Sun who was so eager to throw himself into political activity. It reveals the weaknesses and contradictions in his political thought, which in the early years oscillated between reformism and revolution, attempting to accommodate a modern revolutionary program within the mold of traditional, anti-Manchu slogans. The manipulative skill of the young Sun and his extraordinary self-confidence are not enough to establish him as a revolutionary leader, except perhaps in the eyes of the group that constituted his faithful companions and a few foreign friends. For everyone else, he was, and up until 1903–4 remained, merely an obscure Cantonese adventurer.

His political destiny began to take firm shape with the founding of the Revolutionary Alliance in 1905. But even within the Revolutionary Alliance he had to contend with the authority of other leaders who were equally (or more) prestigious and with the influence of thinkers more brilliant than himself. Far from being the principal instigator of the 1911 revolution, he at the most managed to become its principal beneficiary, and even then proved incapable of either retaining his functions as president or preserving the Republic that he had founded in 1912. His ardent nationalism accommodated some very dubious transactions with foreign powers and their representatives, both unofficial and authorized. Wilbur has shown clearly that in 1923–24, at the very point at which he entered into alliance with the Chinese communists, Sun had still not given up hope of cooperation with Great Britain or the United States. Behind the figure of the hero emerges that of a muddled and boastful politician, rushing headlong from one failure into another, an opportunist whose thought oscillated to suit the most short-term of circumstances, a hybrid product of unfortunate cross-breeding between two cultures; neither of which he ever fully mastered.

Monographs such as these have succeeded in sweeping the myth aside. However, the void left has not been filled. No general biography has come up with a redefinition of Sun's role in the revolutionary movement and revolutionary thought. And although most Western historians no longer recognize Sun Yat-sen as the sole guide or even the predominant leader of the Chinese revolution, neither does any of them venture explicitly to deny him any importance at all. Having settled on a positivism that lacks any wide perspective, which some scholars go so far as to consider "a debased form of history" (John Fitzgerald), Western studies on Sun Yat-sen seem to have got stuck in an impasse.

Once stripped of its legendary aura, the figure of Sun Yat-sen arouses little interest. The many colloquia devoted to him in recent years in China, Taiwan, and Japan have produced virtually no echoes in the West. This lack of interest, which may initially have reflected a reaction of lassitude and rejection in the face of the excesses of the myth, has now been reinforced by the conclusions reached in recent works by historians of eighteenth- and nineteenth-century Chinese society. Nowadays it is not just Sun Yat-sen, the individual, who is criticized, but everything that, rightly or wrongly, he symbolizes: the role of Western influences in the rise of the coastal provinces during the nineteenth and twentieth centuries; the elaboration of a new culture in those provinces, a culture at once cosmopolitan and nationalist, which animated the project of modernization and the revolutionary ideal; and, finally, the whole strategy of challenging the inland, rural, bureaucratic, despotic China by the peripheral China of the treaty ports and overseas communities that brought new values with them. The emphasis now tends, on the contrary, to be laid on the vitality of the Chinese tradition. It is claimed that it was within the traditional framework that, as early as the beginning or middle of the nineteenth century, plans began to take shape for the rationalization of the system of production and distribution, the diversification of social groups, and the diffusion of political responsibilities and initiatives. All these diverse developments are said to have led to the emergence of a "public sphere," in defense of which local elites became mobilized. The presence of this "public sphere" (to borrow the terminology of Jürgen Habermas) is said to have encouraged those elites to move from philanthropic to political action, and from the local to the national level at the very moment, at the end of the last century, when the Chinese crisis was deepening. It is within this process, it is claimed, that the *direct* origin of the 1911 revolution should be sought.[24]

Such a reading of history, which relegates the role of coastal China to the background, completely sweeps away the importance of Sun Yat-sen. It is perfectly normal that new generations should criticize the theories developed by their predecessors and should question the results of the cross-breeding between China and the West in the treaty ports. But it is more paradoxical to see these historians, so keen to help deep, old China to reappropriate the credit for the part it has played in its country's history, also opposing the theses being defended, through the symbolic figure of Sun Yat-sen, in the People's Republic of China and in Taiwan. Whether judged in terms of cooperation or in terms of imperialist exploitation, the foreign presence in China from 1842 to 1949 remains an essential historical fact. Equally, a response to the heroic cult that cannot limit itself simply to demolishing the heroic image should not be converted into radical rejection of everything that the cult stood for. What would be the point of opposing the mythical version of history created by the Chinese by an equally mythical counterversion of history featuring a contemporary China (of the nineteenth and twentieth centuries) in which foreign influence played no more than a secondary role? For dialogue to be possible between cultures, they must have a space in which to meet where they can compare their cognitive behavior. The study of Sun Yat-sen, at present a source of mutual incomprehension, might provide contemporary history with just such a special space.

Reference Matter

Biographical Sketches

This section gives basic information about important figures mentioned in the text. For more detail, see Lucien Bianco and Yves Chevrier, eds., Dictionnaire biographique du Mouvement ouvrier international, La Chine *(Paris: Éditions ouvrières et Presses de la Fondation nationale des sciences politiques, 1985); and Howard L. Boorman et al.,* Biographical Dictionary of Republican China, *4 vols. (New York: Columbia University Press, 1967–71).*

Mikhail Markovitch Borodin (alias Gruzenberg) (1884–1951)

Borodin was born in the province of Vitebsk and seems to have been set to work at an early age as a docker in Riga and to have acquired most of his education through his own efforts. He joined the Bund (the General Union of Jewish Workers) in 1900, and in 1903 joined Lenin's Bolshevik faction. He took part in the revolutionary events of 1905, following which he was obliged to go into exile in the United States.

The 1917 revolution drew him back to Russia. He became an agent of the Communist International and accomplished various missions in the United States, Mexico, and Europe before being appointed by the Central Committee in February 1923 to serve as adviser to Sun Yat-sen. Once in Canton, where he arrived in October 1923, he worked to strengthen the united front and use the influence he had acquired over Sun to impose his own views. The Guomindang's Reorganization Congress in January 1924 set the seal upon the success of his policies. Although the death of Sun Yat-sen the next year deprived him of a precious if difficult ally, he continued to play an essential role in the shaping of the Chinese revolution up until the summer of 1927. At this point he returned to Moscow, where the remainder of his career lacked any kind of glory. In 1949 Stalin had him sent to a camp, where he died two years later.

Sir James Cantlie (1851–1926)

James Cantlie was born into a Scottish family of modest means and studied first literature, then medicine at the University of Aberdeen and in London. He then pursued the career of a missionary and doctor, traveling in the Far East, southern Asia, the Near East, and elsewhere. He was of an open-hearted and liberal nature and took to Sun Yat-sen while the latter was a student of his at the College of Medicine for the Chinese in Hong Kong from 1887 to 1892. Dr. Cantlie welcomed Sun Yat-sen in London in 1896 and played a crucial role in securing the release of the young revolutionary when he was abducted and held prisoner in the Chinese Legation.

In later years Sun Yat-sen continued to correspond regularly with Dr. Cantlie and his wife. After the 1911 revolution, Dr. Cantlie produced (in collaboration) and published a work entitled *Sun Yat-sen and the Awakening of China*, in which he exalted the personality and role of the Chinese leader.

Chen Jiongming (1878–1933)

A Cantonese, born into a family of literati. He took part in the movement for local reforms, was elected deputy to the Provincial Assembly of Guangdong (1909), joined the Revolutionary Alliance in 1910, and took part in the 1911 revolution. At the beginning of the Republic, he was governor of Guangdong. In 1913, Yuan Shikai dismissed him from this post, and Chen Jiongming then campaigned against Yuan and joined the Constitution Protection Movement, led by Sun Yat-sen. In 1920, he conquered Canton and then worked alongside Sun Yat-sen to establish a provincial base there. In June 1922, Chen Jiongming ejected Sun Yat-sen from Canton, but six months later, in January 1923, he was himself ejected by Sun's mercenaries. After two years of resistance in eastern Guangdong, Chen Jiongming was finally defeated by Guomindang forces in the summer of 1925. Chen Jiongming, who was strongly influenced by the anarchists, was a partisan of regional autonomy, who wanted to make Guangdong a model province.

Chen Qimei (1876–1916)

This anti-Manchu revolutionary was a native of Zhejiang who undertook military studies in Japan where, in 1906, he joined the Revolutionary Alliance. In November 1911, he conquered Shanghai and became military governor of the city. After the failure of the Second Revolution, he fled to Japan where he helped Sun Yat-sen to organize the Chinese Revolutionary Party. Chen Qimei then returned to China, where he continued clandestine opposition and organized terrorist action. Yuan Shikai had him assassinated in Shanghai in May 1916.

Chen Qimei, who was an ardent partisan of Sun Yat-sen, was also the protector and friend of Chiang Kai-shek, whose career he directed and helped along. Chiang Kai-shek always remained faithful to the memory of his patron and made Chen's two nephews, Chen Guofu and Chen Lifu, his close collaborators and important leaders of the nationalist regime.

Chen Shaobai (1869–1934)

This anti-Manchu revolutionary was a Cantonese Christian and an excellent scholar who was closely associated with the earliest political activities of Sun Yat-sen, alongside whom he was a student at the Hong Kong College for Medicine for the Chinese. He was one of the "Four Great Bandits" who discussed revolution with Sun Yat-sen. As one of Sun's chief lieutenants at the time of the Revive China Society, he played an active part in organizing the Canton uprising of 1895 and the

Huizhou uprising of 1900 and in publishing in Hong Kong the revolutionary newspaper *Zhongguo ribao* (China Daily). After 1905, his political activity declined and it ceased altogether following the 1911 revolution.

Chen Tianhua (1875–1905)

Chen Tianhua was a native of Hunan, arrived in Japan in 1903, and took part in mobilizing patriotic anti-Russian opposition. Upon his return to Hunan, he helped Huang Xing and Song Jiaoren to set up the Society for China's Revival, in Changsa, in 1904, and produced two anti-Manchu pamphlets, *Wake Up!* and *Alarm to Arouse the Age*, which enjoyed great success.

He returned to Japan, where he helped to found the Revolutionary Alliance in 1905 and to define its program. But in December of the same year, he committed suicide in protest against the repressive Japanese policy adopted against the Chinese students and their militant activities.

Chiang Kai-shek (1887–1975)

He was a native of Zhejiang. While attending a course of military studies in Japan, he met Chen Qimei, who encouraged him to join the Revolutionary Alliance. In 1911, Chiang Kai-shek alongside Chen Qimei took part in the revolutionary struggles of Shanghai. He took refuge in Tokyo after the failure of the Second Revolution of 1913 and became a member of the Chinese Revolutionary Party. Then he returned to China to continue the struggle of resistance against Yuan Shikai. The assassination of Chen Qimei in May 1916 left Chiang Kai-shek deeply shocked. He entered upon a series of financial speculations and established closer ties with the secret society of the Green Gang.

In June 1922 he joined up with Sun Yat-sen, who had been ejected from Canton by Chen Jiongming and had taken refuge on a gunboat in the middle of the Pearl River. When Sun Yat-sen regained possession of Canton in the spring of 1923, he made Chiang Kai-shek the head of his General Staff, then sent him off to Moscow to negotiate military and financial aid (September–November 1923). He then made him responsible for the organization of the Huangpu Military Academy and appointed him as its director (in 1924).

Following Sun Yat-sen's death, Chiang Kai-shek, using his support from the army, triumphed over his rivals in the Guomindang, and then, in 1927, turned on his communist allies. At the head of the Nanking government (1927–37), he worked for the unification and modernization of China. Japanese aggression obliged him to form a new united front with the communists. In the civil war that broke out again after the Allied victory in 1945, Chiang Kai-shek's forces were defeated. Chiang Kai-shek took refuge in Taiwan, where, until his death in 1975, he continued to head the Republic of China, whose effective sovereignty was by then limited to the island.

Duan Qirui (1865–1930)

Duan Qirui was one of the principal military leaders of the Beiyang army and the head of one of the factions that contended for control of the Peking government after the death of Yuan Shikai.

He had formerly been an officer in the imperial armies but proved less loyal to the dynasty than to Yuan Shikai, his patron and protector, in whose political footsteps he followed. At Yuan Shikai's death, he became prime minister and, with the aid of Japan and the northern generals, tried to impose his authority and break the opposition of Parliament. He was ousted from power by the Zhili faction in 1920 but made a comeback to the political scene in 1924 as the provisional head of the Peking government. Lacking any military power, however, he played no more than a secondary role in the clashes between the Northern warlords, and he retired altogether from political life in 1926.

Feng Ziyou (1881–1958)

At the tender age of fourteen, Feng Ziyou joined the Revive China Society, following the example of his father, Feng Jingru, a Cantonese bookseller settled in Yokohama, who had founded the Japanese branch of the party. As a student at Waseda University, he took part in the patriotic activities of the Chinese students of Tokyo. He was one of the first members of the Revolutionary Alliance. Sun Yatsen appointed him its representative in Hong Kong and southern China. During Sun Yat-sen's brief administration as President of the Republic in 1912, Feng Ziyou was his private secretary. He later withdrew from political life, abandoning it completely after the formation of the united front with the communists, to whom he was hostile.

His interest then turned to history. Using the many materials (reports, correspondence, etc.) that he had acquired, as well as his own memories, between 1928 and 1944 he produced the three volumes of his *History of the Revolution Before the Founding of the Republic*, to which he added his *Anecdotes on the Revolution* (five volumes, published between 1939 and 1945).

Henry George (1839–1897)

A self-taught American reformer from a modest background, who practiced many professions, including those of a journalist on the *San Francisco Times* and a gas company employee. Moved by the social distress surrounding him, "with evangelical enthusiasm" he produced a project for reform, which he entitled *Progress and Poverty* (1879). He proposed that, to fight speculation, land rent should be appropriated by the state by means of a single tax levied on unearned increments. Although his ideas were criticized by professional economists, they met with great success in England and in Germany. Sun Yat-sen came under their influence while visiting London in 1896–97 and also through the suggestions of Miyazaki's brother, who had become one of George's principal Japanese disciples.

The success of his book encouraged Henry George to launch himself into politics and run for election as mayor of New York. He died in 1897, during his second electoral campaign.

Ho Kai (He Qi) (1859–1917)

Ho Kai was the son of a Cantonese pastor and businessman established in Hong Kong. He studied law and medicine in Great Britain. Upon his return to Hong

Kong, he became a lawyer and one of the colony's prominent Chinese figures. He was a member of the Legislative Council and also a great philanthropist. He founded the Alice Memorial Hospital and the College of Medicine for the Chinese, where Sun Yat-sen was to become a student. Ho Kai advocated China's adoption of Western institutions. The reformist views that he expressed both in essays written in Chinese and in the British press of the colony, in particular the *China Mail*, greatly influenced Sun Yat-sen at the time of the Revive China Society.

Hu Hanmin (1879–1936)

Hu Hanmin was born in Canton into a family from Jiangxi province. He studied the Classics, obtaining a degree before going to Japan to continue his education. He joined the Revolutionary Alliance as soon as it was founded and placed his brilliant talents as an essayist at the service of the *People's Journal*, the organ of the new party. In the years that followed, he was closely associated with the activities of Sun Yat-sen, whom he accompanied to Hanoi in 1907 and to Singapore in 1908 and whom he represented in Hong Kong in 1909, fund-raising, launching publications, and organizing insurrections. After the 1911 revolution, he became the first republican governor of Guangdong.

The failure of the Second Revolution forced him to flee to Japan with Sun Yat-sen, whom he continued to assist in his struggle against Yuan Shikai, and later in his efforts to establish his control over the Cantonese base. Hu Hanmin held a number of posts of responsibility in the successive governments that Sun Yat-sen established in Canton between 1917 and 1924. He was elected to the Central Executive Committee of the Guomindang by the Reorganization Congress and was hostile to the communists' growing influence in the party. After the death of Sun Yat-sen, he tried unsuccessfully to become his successor. In 1931 he entered into open conflict with Chiang Kai-shek. He died five years later without resuming any political role at a national level.

Huang Xing (1874–1916)

A native of Hunan. He obtained the top grade in the mandarin examinations before leaving in 1902 to continue his studies in Japan, where he took part in the patriotic and anti-Manchu demonstrations. Upon his return to Hunan in 1903, he founded the Society for China's Revival. After the failure of a planned insurrection in Changsha (1904), Huang Xing returned to Japan. Together with Sun Yat-sen, he was co-founder of the Revolutionary Alliance in 1905 and became its vice-president. Between 1905 and 1911, he organized and led the revolutionary insurrections in the southern provinces.

After the Wuchang uprising, in October 1911, he joined the insurrectional forces and took over their command. When Sun Yat-sen became President of the Republic in January 1912, he made Huang Xing Prime Minister of the provisional government. At the time of the crisis provoked by the assassination of Song Jiaoren on March 20, 1913, Huang Xing, in opposition to Sun Yat-sen, advocated recourse to legal, nonviolent solutions and it was with reluctance that he took part in the military clashes of the Second Revolution. When this revolution failed, he took refuge in Japan; a short time later he broke with Sun Yat-sen over the reorganization of the party and the swearing of a personal oath of allegiance.

Kang Youwei (1858–1927)

This Cantonese scholar was the inspiration for and leader of the reformist movement that culminated in the Hundred Day Reform of 1898. When forced into exile, Kang Youwei visited many overseas communities and, not without success, tried to mobilize them in the defense of the emperor Guangxu (then imprisoned by the dowager empress) and in favor of a constitutional monarchy. His Society to Protect the Emperor enjoyed great success, a fact that seriously affronted Sun Yat-sen. The rivalry between the reformists and the revolutionaries became very bitter once the Revolutionary Alliance was created, in 1905.

The 1911 revolution did not reconcile Kang Youwei with the Republic, but since he was now considered an old-fashioned monarchist and a reactionary Confucian, he had little political influence. On the other hand, his philosophical works, his radical reinterpretation of Confucianism to adapt it to the constraints of modernization, and his reflections on the world communism of Great Harmony continued to inspire many intellectuals.

Kong Xiangxi (H. H. Kung) (1881–1967)

Kong Xiangxi was born into a rich family of Shanxi bankers. His education began in a local missionary school, then, after converting to Christianity, he left for the United States where he studied at Yale University, among other places. He does not appear to have played any active part in the revolutionary movement and events. At the beginning of the Republic, he was in Tokyo, where, as secretary of the Chinese Young Men's Christian Association (YMCA), he became friendly with the Song family. In 1914, he married the eldest of the daughters, Song Ailing. It was a marriage that later on made him Sun Yat-sen's brother-in-law. At the same time as managing the family's banks and the modern school that he had founded in his native province, Kong Xiangxi collaborated with Sun Yat-sen, mediating between the Cantonese leader and the northern generals. In 1924, he joined Sun Yat-sen in Canton. He accompanied him on his journey to Peking and assisted him in his last moments. After Sun's death, Kong Xiangxi rallied to Chiang Kai-shek, who became another of his brothers-in-law by marrying the youngest of the Song sisters. Under the Nationalist regime, Kong Xiangxi became a minister (for Industry, Trade, and Finance). After the 1949 revolution, he emigrated with his family to the United States.

Homer Lea (1876–1912)

An American adventurer who, after studying Chinese at Stanford University, became involved with Kang Youwei and his San Francisco followers, who were members of the Society to Protect the Emperor.

Passionately interested in military strategy, Lea took the title of General and organized military training for the Chinese militias of New York and Philadelphia. He met Sun Yat-sen in 1904 and renewed contact with him in 1910, after breaking with Kang Youwei. The two men then hatched a great plot to overthrow the Manchu dynasty, which was supposed to be financed by New York bankers and effected with the aid of American mercenaries. In spite of the failure of this project, which never even got off the ground, Sun Yat-sen continued to trust Homer Lea, who was to be found at his side when the Republic was established in 1912. The death of Lea, who was carried off by a disease that same year, deeply affected Sun Yat-sen.

Li Liejun (1882–1946)

Li Liejun was born into a wealthy family of tea merchants from Jiangxi province. He was trained in a military academy in Japan, where he met revolutionary students and in 1906 became a member of the Revolutionary Alliance. He was actively involved in revolutionary fighting in Jiangxi and the Yangzi Valley in 1911–12. He became the military governor of Jiangxi and led the Second Revolution in 1913. In 1915–16, he joined the Yunnan generals and launched the antimonarchic campaign against Yuan Shikai. In 1917, he joined Sun Yat-sen in Canton when the latter set up his military government there. In the years that followed, he became one of the principal military leaders of the Guomindang, remaining constantly loyal to Sun Yat-sen. In January 1924, the Reorganization Congress elected him to the party's Central Executive Committee. After the death of Sun Yat-sen, he rallied to Chiang Kai-shek and held a number of important posts under the Nationalist regime.

Li Yuanhong (1864–1928)

This imperial officer was given the task of modernizing the military units of Hubei. When the uprising of October 10, 1911, broke out, the leaderless rebels forced their commanding officer to head the movement and become the military governor of Hubei. The success of the revolution confirmed Li Yuanhong's political commitment. He was elected vice-president under Sun Yat-sen, a post that he retained under Yuan Shikai. At Yuan's death, Li Yuanhong took over the presidency, in conformity with the constitution. However, in the face of opposition from the northern generals, he was unable to impose his authority and was forced to resign in 1917. Although he returned to the presidency in 1922–23, Li Yuanhong never again played a political role of any importance.

Liang Qichao (1873–1929)

This Cantonese scholar, a disciple of Kang Youwei, took part in the reformist attempt of the Hundred Days in 1898. When this failed, he took refuge in Japan, where he emerged as the leader of the anti-imperialist patriots and the radical young intelligentsia. After a brief period of closer relations with Sun Yat-sen, at the beginning of 1899, Liang Qichao then reverted to supporting Kang Youwei and his Society to Protect the Emperor. From 1905 to 1907, he defended the constitutionalists' cause in his *New People's Review* and led the polemic against the Revolutionary Alliance's *People's Journal* with talent and force.

Liang Qichao subsequently broke away from Kang Youwei and rallied to the new republican regime established in 1912. He was active in its parliament as the leader of the Progressive Party, accepted a number of posts of responsibility under Yuan Shikai, but supported the antimonarchist movement of 1916. Discouraged by the decline of republican institutions, in 1918 he retired from political life to devote himself to study, travel, writing, and teaching. He was the most incisive and influential Chinese thinker of the early twentieth century.

Liao Zhongkai (1878–1925)

Liao Zhongkai was born into a Cantonese family living in San Francisco. He began his studies in the United States, then continued them in Japan where, in 1903, he met Sun Yat-sen, became interested in socialist ideas, and wrote for the *People's Journal*. Following the 1911 revolution, the military governor of Guangdong, Hu Hanmin, made him responsible for the financial administration of the province. After the Second Revolution of 1913, he accompanied Sun Yat-sen into exile in Tokyo and returned to China with him in 1916. He was a member of the various governments that Sun set up in Canton from 1917 on. His particular responsibility was to raise funds for the military activities of the Guomindang. In the spring of 1923, he took part in the negotiations with the Soviet Ambassador Adolf Joffe, designed to form a united front between the Guomindang, Soviet Russia, and the Chinese Communist Party. In May 1923, Liao Zhongkai was appointed Minister of Finance in the Canton government and Governor of Guangdong. He then played an important political role as the principal leader of the Guomindang's left wing, favoring the united front policy.

After Sun Yat-sen's death, Liao Zhongkai was a contender for the succession, anxious to continue the policy of alliance with Russia and the communists. However, in August 1925 he was assassinated.

Lu Haodong (1872–1895)

Lu Haodong was the son of a Cantonese trader established in Shanghai and in his adolescence was Sun Yat-sen's friend, sharing his village life; he was his accomplice in the attack against the idols of the Cuiheng temple in 1883.

Following several years spent in Shanghai, in 1894 Lu Haodong again met up with Sun Yat-sen, never to leave him. He accompanied him to Tianjin in the hope of meeting Li Hongzhang, in early 1895, and designed the revolutionary emblem: a white sun on a blue background. In the field, in Canton, he helped Sun prepare the uprising of October 1895, then became its hero and martyr. He was arrested and tortured by the imperial police, and died proclaiming his faith in the revolution.

Hans Maring (alias Hendricus Sneevliet) (1883–1942)

The first activist experience of this militant of Dutch origin was in Indonesia, where he worked to establish an alliance between the nationalist bourgeoisie and the radical revolutionary movement, pursuing the strategy of a united front, which, together with Lenin, he defended ardently at the Second Congress of the Communist International in 1920.

Between 1921 and 1923 he was sent by the comintern to China on several missions, to explore the possibility of using the same strategy there and to identify possible partners. He took part in the congress that founded the Chinese Communist Party in July 1921, and in December of that same year went to Guilin to meet Sun Yat-sen. His conversations with Sun convinced him that he would be the most suitable ally. Over the next eighteen months, Maring tried to persuade the young Chinese Communist Party (which was more tempted by the proletarian option) of the advantages of a united front and to get Sun Yat-sen accepted by the still dubious Comintern. His efforts were rewarded by the Sun-Joffe declaration of January 1923, which sealed the Guomindang's alliance with the Soviets, and by the Second Congress of the CCP (in Canton in June 1923), which overcame all opposition to the united front. The go-between for this first Chinese united front then continued his revolutionary activities in the Netherlands, to which he returned in 1924. There, he broke away from communism and Stalin and in 1929 founded a Trotskyist party. He was one of the first members of the Dutch resistance and was shot by the Germans in 1942.

Miyazaki Torazō (Tōten) (1870–1922)

The Japanese adventurer and militant, Miyazaki Torazō came from a samurai family. He had received a liberal education, marked by a fervent but fleeting conversion to Christianity. His desire to save Asia and China from Western imperialism attracted him to Sun Yat-sen, whom he met for the first time in Yokohama in 1897 and whose adviser and very close friend he became, placing his relations with the higher Japanese bureaucracy at Sun's service.

Miyazaki helped to prepare the Huizhou uprising of 1900, and in 1905, in Tokyo, he helped Sun Yat-sen to found the Revolutionary Alliance. He was himself one of the earliest members of the Alliance and he played an active part in its organization and action.

In December 1911, he was with Sun Yat-sen on his triumphal return to China. But his influence appears to have been partly supplanted by that of other Japanese, chiefly businessmen and bureaucrats. When the revolution failed and Sun was again living in exile in Japan, Miyazaki was still at his side. Their old friendship endured, though it now carried little political weight. In the memoirs that he published in 1902, *The Thirty-three Years' Dream*, Miyazaki recalled the years of his youth and his early adventures alongside Sun Yat-sen, of whom he painted a picture full of affection and admiration.

Song Jiaoren (1882–1913)

Song Jiaoren was born in Hunan. In 1904 he enrolled in the Society for China's Revival, founded by Huang Xing. He was forced into exile in Japan, where he took part in the establishment of the Revolutionary Alliance. In 1910, after completing his studies in law, he returned to Shanghai where he published *The People's Stand* newspaper and set up the Central China Bureau of the Revolutionary Alliance.

During the 1911 revolution, he was the deputy for Hunan in the provisional

Parliament that elected Sun Yat-sen as President of the Republic. As an advocate of the system of ministerial responsibility, Song Jiaoren believed that the best way to limit the ambitions of Yuan Shikai was to create a powerful, united majority in Parliament. To this end, he created the Guomindang party, which took over from the Revolutionary Alliance and under Song Jiaoren's direction was victorious in the legislative elections of the winter of 1912–13. Song Jiaoren, who was universally expected to become prime minister, was assassinated at the Shanghai railway station on March 20, 1913, in all likelihood at the instigation of Yuan Shikai.

Song Qingling (1892–1981)

Song Qingling, the second daughter of Charlie Soong, was born in Shanghai. Her education began in a Methodist school in the International Settlement. At the age of sixteen she was sent to the United States where she attended Miss Clara Potwin's school in Summit, New Jersey, then Wesleyan College in Macon, Georgia, from which her elder sister Ailing had graduated.

When Song Qingling returned from the United States, the Second Revolution was in the process of failing, and she accompanied her family into exile in Japan. In Tokyo, she became Sun Yat-sen's assistant, taking care of his correspondence in English. She married him on October 25, 1914, in the face of her parents' opposition. From that time on, she was constantly at her husband's side, sharing his activities and his travels, and both his honors and his dangers, although never really exercising any political influence. After Sun Yat-sen's death, Song Qingling identified herself with the left wing of the Guomindang. But her role remained above all symbolic, as was the title of vice-president of the People's Republic of China with which the communist regime honored her in 1949.

Sun Fo (Sun Ke) (1891–1973)

Sun Fo, Sun Yat-sen's only son, was born in Guangdong and brought up in his uncle's home in Hawaii. Between 1911 and 1917, he studied in the United States. As mayor of Canton, a position that he held virtually without interruption from 1921 to 1925, he tried to implement a policy of modernization and urban renovation. Although somewhat less than enthusiastic about the united front policy, he did help to prepare for the Reorganization Congress of January 1924.

After Sun Yat-sen's death, Sun Fo held a number of responsible posts in the Nationalist government—presiding over the legislative Yuan from 1932 to 1948—but he was not always in agreement with Chiang Kai-shek. After the communist victory in 1949, he retired from public life.

Tao Chengzhang (1878–1912)

Tao Chengzhang, a native of Zhejiang, was trained at a military academy in Japan between 1902 and 1904. Upon returning to China, he organized the Restoration Society, the aim of which was to develop revolutionary action in the provinces of the lower Yangzi. This organization, which was closely involved with the secret societies, was active above all in Zhejiang. At the end of 1906 or the beginning of 1907, it merged with the Revolutionary Alliance. But from the autumn of 1907 on,

Tao Chengzhang undertook a grand tour of Southeast Asia, competing with Sun Yat-sen in his search for providers of funds. In November 1909, he attacked Sun's dictatorial style and financial operations in an *Open Letter* that was widely circulated. In 1910, the Restoration Society split off from the Revolutionary Alliance and concentrated further attacks on Sun Yat-sen. As soon as he heard of the Wuchang insurrection (October 10, 1911), Tao Chengzhang returned to China and played an active role in the revolutionary mobilization of Jiangsu and Zhejiang. On January 14, 1912, he was murdered on his sickbed in the Sainte-Marie hospital, in the French concession of Shanghai. The assassination had been ordered by Chen Qimei and is said to have been carried out by Chiang Kai-shek.

Wang Jingwei (1883–1944)

Wang Jingwei was born in Canton and began his classical education at home. In 1903, he received a provincial government scholarship to continue his studies in Japan, where, in 1906, he obtained a diploma in constitutional law and political science. He had meanwhile joined the Revolutionary Alliance and, a brilliant polemicist, he argued in the *People's Journal* against Liang Qichao and the reformists. He was influenced by anarchist ideas, and in Peking, in 1910, he organized an assassination attempt against the Prince Regent, which failed and for which he received a prison sentence.

The 1911 revolution brought him liberation, after which he traveled and lived in France during World War I, devoting himself chiefly to literature. He returned to China at the end of 1917, joined Sun Yat-sen's entourage, and played an important role within the Guomindang. The 1924 Reorganization Congress elected him to the party's Central Executive Committee. The following winter he accompanied Sun Yat-sen to the North. He was at his bedside as he died, and helped to compose (or actually himself composed) Sun's political testament.

Though he was considered the leader of the left wing of the Guomindang, and in 1925–26 appeared to be Sun's heir at the head of the party, he was supplanted by Chiang Kai-shek. He continued to clash with Chiang throughout the Nanking decade but meanwhile remained active in the Nationalist party and government. In 1940 he decided on collaboration with the Japanese and established in Nanking a rival government to that of Chiang Kai-shek, who had taken refuge in Chongqing (Sichuan).

Wu Peifu (1874–1939)

In the early 1920's, this officer of the Beiyang Army became one of the principal warlords. As leader of the Zhili faction, he controlled the Peking government from 1922 to 1924 and extended his territorial base toward central China as far as Hubei. His proclaimed liberal ideas and objective of pacific reunification won him popularity in intellectual circles and made him a daunting rival to Sun Yat-sen. However, in October 1924, he was betrayed by one of his subordinates. His fall totally upset the relations of the political forces in the North and determined Sun Yat-sen's decision to travel to Peking in an attempt to get himself recognized as the president of a reunified China. Up until 1926, Wu Peifu continued his efforts to regain power in the North, from his base in the central provinces. But in 1927 he was defeated definitively by the Guomindang troops of the Northern Expedition. He then retired from military and political life.

Yang Quyun (1861–1901)

Yang Quyun was born in Hong Kong, educated in an English school in the colony, and worked for various local trading companies. He acquired a good mastery of the English language and Western literature. His nationalism was expressed in his hostility to the Manchu dynasty. In 1895, he created the Literary Society for the Development of Benevolence, whose very Confucian name was a cover for its activities of political opposition. In 1895, this society merged with Sun Yat-sen's group to form the Hong Kong branch of the Revive China Society, of which Yang Quyun became president, despite Sun's rivalry. A few months later, the two men were mutually recriminating over responsibility for the failure of the Cantonese uprising launched by the Revive China Society.

After this failure, Yang Quyun at first sought refuge in Johannesburg, then, in 1898, he joined up with Sun Yat-sen in Japan, finally agreeing to abandon the presidency of the Revive China Society. He returned to Hong Kong and took an active part in preparing the Huizhou uprising (1900). In the repression that followed this latest revolutionary attempt, a price was put on Yang Quyun's head by the Cantonese authorities and he was assassinated in his classroom, in Hong Kong, on January 16, 1901.

Yuan Shikai (1859–1916)

Before the revolution, this officer and high-ranking mandarin held a wide variety of posts of responsibility: from 1882 to 1884 he was engaged on a lengthy diplomatic mission in Korea, defending Chinese rights and interests there in the face of Japanese ambitions; later he was involved in the modernization of the Chinese military forces and the creation of a New Army, out of which Yuan shaped the Beiyang Army, the principal instrument of his power. After the failure of the Hundred Day Reform, he became a favorite of the dowager empress Cixi and played an active part in the New Policy of reforms launched by the imperial government.

In 1908, the empress's death plunged Yuan Shikai into disgrace and he was dismissed from his post. But in the autumn of 1911, the Court, threatened by the revolution, turned to him for help. Yuan was more concerned to establish his own power than to serve the dynasty, however. After obtaining an imperial edict of abdication from the Court (on February 12, 1912), he had himself elected president of the Republic, thereby taking over from Sun Yat-sen, who voluntarily stepped down. After this, Yuan Shikai worked to eliminate all influence of the revolutionary party and to establish his own dictatorship. But his dream of a monarchical restoration alienated public opinion, which, out of a longing for order and peace, had initially resigned itself to accepting his power. Faced with revolt in the southern provinces and opposition from the foreign powers and many of the officers of the Beiyang Army, he died before he could be ejected from power.

Zhang Binglin (1868–1936)

Zhang Binglin, who was a native of Zhejiang, possessed philological and literary gifts that were as precocious as they were dazzling. In 1895, China's defeat at the hands of Japan brought him out of his ivory tower and he made contact with the reformists Kang Youwei and Liang Qichao. After the failure of the Hundred Day Reform, he found refuge in Japan. There, he met Sun Yat-sen, whose anti-Manchu sentiments he shared.

Back in Shanghai in 1902, he established a Patriotic School designed for revolutionary students. As the editor-in-chief of *Subao* (the Shanghai Newspaper), he included in its columns the incendiary tract by Zou Rong, *The Revolutionary Army*, which turned him into the hero of a *cause célèbre* and landed him in prison for three years.

Following his release in 1906 he joined Sun Yat-sen and the Revolutionary Alliance in Tokyo, where he took over the direction of the *People's Journal*. But in 1907, he accused Sun Yat-sen of incompetence and misuse of funds and supported the campaigns that Tao Chengzhang was then pursuing in Southeast Asia in a bid to strip the president of the Revolutionary Alliance of his functions.

After the 1911 revolution, Zhang Binglin left the Revolutionary Alliance to found his own, more moderate party. He did renew contact with Sun Yat-sen, however, and collaborated with him from time to time until he retired from politics in 1918. Despite the important role that he played as a popularizer of ideas and a revolutionary leader, Zhang Binglin remained famous mainly for his talents and erudition as a scholar and philosopher.

Zheng Shiliang (d. 1901)

This Cantonese Christian, a fellow student and friend of Sun Yat-sen, whom he met at the Medical School of the Canton Hospital in 1886, became one of Sun's chief lieutenants during the Revive China Society period. He had close links with the Triads of eastern Guangdong, and it was he who helped Sun recruit fighters to engage in the Canton uprising of 1895. He took refuge in Japan with Sun Yat-sen after the failure of the uprising, but soon returned to Hong Kong, where he continued to work with the secret societies.

In 1900, during the Huizhou uprising of which he was "the true hero" (Schiffrin), Zheng Shiliang again acted as liaison between Sun Yat-sen and the Triads and directed operations in the field, in eastern Guangdong, from which he originated. When the uprising failed, he fled to Hong Kong where he died suddenly in August 1901, probably poisoned by an agent of the Manchus.

Zhu Zhixin (1885–1920)

Zhu Zhixin was born in Guangdong and received an education in the Classics and mathematics. In 1904 he won a provincial government scholarship to continue his studies in Tokyo. In Japan, he mingled with the group of patriotic students from

Canton and joined the Revolutionary Alliance as soon as it was founded. He wrote numerous articles for the *People's Journal*, arguing with Liang Qichao and introducing his readers to Marx's philosophy.

Upon his return to Canton at the end of 1907, he became a professor, but this did not prevent him from continuing with clandestine resistance to the Manchus or from taking part in the insurrection of April 1911. After the revolution, he entered the provincial administration under Hu Hanmin. The failure of the Second Revolution of 1913 sent him back to Japan. There he worked closely with Sun Yat-sen, helping him to organize the Chinese Revolutionary Party. Between 1914 and 1916, he led a series of armed revolts against Yuan Shikai, in Guangdong. In 1917, he joined Sun Yat-sen's military government in Canton. The next year, he was in Shanghai, where he created and ran the Guomindang's theoretical periodical, *Reconstruction*, in which he expounded and defended Sun's program. When he died, in Guangdong, in the course of a local skirmish between militarists, Sun Yat-sen lamented this "brutal loss which is like the loss of [one's] two hands."

Notes

CHAPTER ONE

1. The term gentry designates the dominant class of traditional Chinese society, composed on the one hand of degree holders mostly from landowning families, some with public positions, others not, and, on the other, of large-scale merchants with purchased official titles of some kind. At the end of the nineteenth century, fusion between the literati wing of the gentry and its merchant wing was almost complete. The effect of this was to reinforce the solidarity and cohesion of the traditional elites.

2. Zhili is the ancient name of the province in which the nation's capital is situated. The province was renamed Hebei after the 1911 revolution.

3. John K. Fairbank, "The Early Treaty System in the Chinese World Order," in John K. Fairbank, ed., *The Chinese World Order*, 2d ed. (Cambridge, Mass., Harvard University Press, 1970), p. 261.

4. The viceroys generally exercised authority over two or several provinces.

5. To simplify, here and in the rest of the text the emperor will be given the name of the era during which he reigned.

6. The terms are from *Heshang* (The River Elegy), a television series by Su Xiaokang and Wang Luxiang shown in China in 1988, the script of which has been published.

7. The account of Sun's early life here is taken mainly from Schiffrin, *Sun Yat-sen*, chapter 2, "Early Influences."

8. Interview with Sun Yat-sen in the *New York Herald*, Sept. 10, 1922, cited by Lyon Sharman, *Sun Yat-sen, His Life and Its Meaning*, 2d ed. (Stanford, Calif.: Stanford University Press, 1968), p. 4.

9. *The Classics in Three Characters* (*Sanzijing*) was a reading textbook intended for beginners.

10. Cited in Ng Lun Ngai-ha et al., *Historical Traces of Sun Yat-sen's Activities in Hong Kong, Macao, and Overseas* (Hong Kong: United College, The Chinese University, Sun Yat-sen Research Institute, The Zhongshan University, 1986), p. 7.

11. In 1884, China abandoned the policy of conciliation and compromise that it

had practiced since the end of the Opium Wars. It now tried to use force to oppose French expansion in Tonking. In spite of successes at sea won by Admiral Amédée Courbet, France obtained no more than a semivictory. Nevertheless, in 1885 China, through the treaty of Tianjin, renounced all rights in Vietnam, which had become a French protectorate. This war provoked many antiforeigner incidents in southern China.

12. "Youzhi jingcheng" (Ambition fulfilled), in Sun Yat-sen, *Complete Works*, 1: 229. This work is, in effect, Sun Yat-sen's *Autobiography* (*Zizhuan*), which is included in Part I of his *Plan for National Reconstruction* (*Jianguo fanglüe*). This Part I is known by a number of different titles: "The Philosophy of Sun Wen," "The Plan for Psychological Reconstruction," and "The Memoirs of a Chinese Revolutionary." The *Autobiography* is sometimes called "Ambition Fulfilled" ("Youzhi jingcheng"). This is the title adopted by the editors of the *Complete Works* of Sun Yat-sen, published in 1981 by the Academy of Social Sciences of China and the Zhongshan University of Canton. It is also the title used in references in the present work.

13. The Welsh missionary Timothy Richard (1845–1919) arrived in China in 1870. He maintained close relations with a number of high dignitaries in Peking and also endeavored to spread reformist ideas through brochures and books published by the Society for the Diffusion of Christian and General Knowledge (Guangxuehui). From 1889 on, this society also published an influential review, *Globe Magazine* (*Wanguo gongbao*), of which Young Allen was the editor-in-chief.

14. The Triads provided the principal organization of secret societies in southern China. Unlike the sects in northern China, which were much given to religious superstition, the southern lodges were deeply involved with politics. They proclaimed their allegiance to the Ming dynasty, which had been toppled in the seventeenth century, and were opposed to the ruling dynasty of the Manchus. Most of the members were recruits from the lower peasant society or social dropouts and marginal individuals, altogether what amounted to a countersociety. Many literati and local elites collaborated with them discreetly, however, with the aim of controlling them and eventually exploiting to their own profit the force of the popular masses that they attracted.

15. Chen Xiqi and Luo Xianglin opted for the second interpretation, Harold Schiffrin, whom I am following here, for the first.

16. "Zai Xianggang daxuede yanshuo" (Speech given at the University of Hong Kong), Feb. 19, 1923, *C.W.* 7: 115–17.

17. "Youzhi jingcheng" (Ambition fulfilled), *Jianguo fanglüe* (Plan for national reconstruction), *C.W.* 6: 228.

18. This is Schiffrin's interpretation (see, e.g., *Sun Yat-sen*, pp. 35–40), in my view the most convincing one.

19. Letter signed "Sinensis," *China Mail*, Feb. 16, 1887.

20. The degree holders (*juren*), laureates in the provincial examinations, occupied a place in the hierarchy in between the bachelors (*xiucai*), who had passed the

prefecture examinations, and the doctors (*jinzhi*), who were admitted to the examinations organized by the imperial palace at Peking.

21. "Shang Li Hongzhang shu" (Petition to Li Hongzhang), *C.W.* 1: 8–18.

22. Ibid., p. 8.

CHAPTER TWO

1. This description of the founding of the Revive China Society relies mainly on Schiffrin, *Sun Yat-sen*, pp. 46–53.

2. Harold Z. Schiffrin, *Sun Yat-sen and the Origins of the Chinese Revolution* (Berkeley: University of California Press, 1968), p. 70.

3. Telegram from Consul O'Conor, dated Apr. 16, 1895, cited in ibid., pp. 80–81.

4. "Ni chuangli nongxuehui shu" (Manifesto on the creation of the Society of Agricultural Research), *C.W.* 1: 24–26, cited in ibid., p. 63.

5. Chinese text in Zou Lu, *Zhongguo Guomindang shigao* (Project for a history of the Chinese Nationalist Party), pp. 659–60, cited in ibid., p. 88.

6. Schiffrin supports the version according to which Sun Yat-sen voluntarily entered the Legation. He follows the interpretation of the episode given in 1930 by Luo Jialun. Other historians, such as Wu Xiangxiang, on the contrary, confirm that there certainly was a kidnapping, just as Sun Yat-sen claimed at the time of the drama. That is also the view of the most recent specialist to have investigated this episode, John Y. Wong, who denies any personal manipulation by Sun Yat-sen suggesting that there was a kidnapping, the better to enhance his own role in the affair (see John Y. Wong, *The Origins of an Heroic Image: Sun Yat-sen in London, 1896–1897* [Hong Kong: Oxford University Press, 1986], pp. 19, 172–73). I myself am not convinced by Wong's arguments and prefer Schiffrin's interpretation, which holds that the story of the kidnapping resulted from manipulation on the part of Sun, the most interested party.

7. Cited from Schiffrin, *Sun Yat-sen*, p. 119.

8. According to Dr. Cantlie, cited from ibid., pp. 134–35.

9. Letter from Minakata Kumagusu, cited from Wong, *The Origins of an Heroic Image*, pp. 280–81.

10. "Youzhi jingcheng" (Ambition fulfilled), in *Jianguo fanglüe* (Plan for national reconstruction), *C.W.* 6: 232–33, cited from Schiffrin, *Sun Yat-sen*, pp. 136–37.

11. This text, discovered by the historian Schiffrin in the 1960's, has not appeared in any collection of Sun Yat-sen's works. It was included (in its Chinese version) in the edition of Sun Yat-sen's *Complete Works* published in 1981 by the Academy of Chinese Social Sciences and the Zhongshan University of Canton; see *C.W.* 1: 87–108.

12. Cited from Schiffrin, *Sun Yat-sen*, p. 130.

13. The Japanese historian Nakamura Tadashi drew attention to this text in 1982; see Wong, *The Origins of an Heroic Image*, p. 224.

14. Cited from ibid., p. 233.

15. "Zhi Qu Fengzhi han" (Letter to Qu Fengzhi), *C.W.* 1: 46, cited from Schiffrin, *Sun Yat-sen*, p. 129.

CHAPTER THREE

1. Marius B. Jansen, *The Japanese and Sun Yat-sen* (Cambridge, Mass.: Harvard University Press, 1954), p. 59.

2. See, for example, the very critical judgment of Reginald d'Auxion de Ruffé in his work *Chine et Chinois d'aujourd'hui* (Paris: Berger-Levrault, 1926).

3. The Open Door doctrine was summarized in a note dated 1899, presented by the American Secretary of State John Hay. It insisted on equal commercial chances for all the foreigners present in China; powers that had obtained zones of influence were not to establish preferential conditions favorable to their own entrepreneurial nationals.

4. In the following paragraphs, the account of this policy of Sun's cooperation with Japanese early pan-Asianists are taken mainly from Marius Jansen, *The Japanese and Sun Yat-sen*, and "Japan and the Chinese Revolution of 1911," pp. 347 and following.

5. Etō Shinkichi and Marius B. Jansen, ed. and trans., *My Thirty-three Years' Dream: The Autobiography of Miyazaki Tōten* (Princeton, N.J.: Princeton University Press, 1982), p. 136.

6. Cited by Jansen, *The Japanese and Sun Yat-sen*, p. 67.

7. According to the testimony of a Japanese adviser, cited in ibid., p. 80.

8. The following account of the Triads' activities in eastern Guangdong is taken from Winston Hsieh, "Salt Smugglers and Local Uprising: Observations on the Social and Economic Background of the Waichow Revolution of 1911."

9. Cited from Edwards J. M. Rhoads, *China's Republican Revolution: The Case of Kwangtung, 1895–1913* (Cambridge, Mass.: Harvard University Press, 1975), p. 42.

10. Cited from Lilian Borokh, "Les débuts du mouvement républicain de Sun Yat-sen et les sociétés secrètes," in Jean Chesneaux, ed., *Mouvements populaires et sociétés secrètes en Chine aux XIXe et XXe siècles* (Paris: Maspéro, 1970), p. 356.

11. Letter from Sun Yat-sen to Cai Yuanpei and Zhang Xiangwen, cited in ibid., p. 358.

12. Rhoads, *China's Republican Revolution*, p. 289.

13. Ibid., p. 43.

CHAPTER FOUR

1. Michael Gasster, "The Republican Revolutionary Movement," in John K. Fairbank and Liu Kwang-ching, eds., *The Cambridge History of China*, vol. 11, *Late Ch'ing, 1800–1911* (Cambridge University Press, 1980), 2: 463.

2. The relations between the public sphere and the state bureaucracy are a controversial subject. Many historians of modern China believe that the development of the sphere of community interests in the second half of the nineteenth century coincided with the decline of the bureaucratic apparatus and that the institutions established by the local elites filled the gap created by the decline or retreat of state structures. The period of the New Policy is, on the contrary, marked by a simultaneous expansion in the initiatives of both local elites and the role of the state, a fact that would seem to bring us back to the analysis that Jürgen Habermas gives of European evolution in the eighteenth century, which is characterized by a simultaneous expansion of the public sphere and of the state apparatus. However, the reforming empire was unable to apply most of the reforms that it decreed. The New Policy revealed interventionist ambitions but mostly failed to realize them. In this respect, it is perhaps Philippe Ariès's analysis that proves to be the most pertinent for illuminating Chinese evolution. In Ariès's view, the "public sphere" began to expand in Europe at the dawn of modern times, at a point when the state was claiming ever greater jurisdiction but lacked the institutional means to exercise it. See Philippe Ariès, "Introduction," in Philippe Ariès and Georges Duby, eds., *Histoire de la vie privée*, vol. 3, *Passions de la Renaissance*. On the debates and problems raised by the application of Habermas's analyses of the public sphere to the Chinese case, see William T. Rowe, "The Public Sphere in Modern China," *Modern China* 16, no. 3 (July 1990): 309–29.

3. See Michael Gasster, "The Republican Revolutionary Movement," pp. 476–83.

4. Wuhan is the name given to the conurbation on the mid-Yangzi that includes Wuchang, the provincial capital of Hubei, Hanyang, the industrial city, and Hankou, the great river port catering to international trade.

5. *Jingshi zhong* (Alarm to arouse the age), cited here from Ernest Young, "Ch'en T'ien-hua (1875–1905): A Chinese Nationalist," *Papers on China*, Center for East Asian Studies, Harvard University, 13 (Dec. 1959): 120–21.

6. Tsou Jung (Zou Rong), *The Revolutionary Army: A Chinese Nationalist Tract of 1903*, introd., trans., and notes by John Lust (The Hague: Mouton, 1968), p. 59.

7. This biographical sketch is drawn from Wong Young-tsu, *Search for Modern Nationalism: Zhang Binglin and Revolutionary China 1889–1936*, pp. 4–45.

8. The term *minzu* is a Japanese neologism that entered Chinese political vocabulary after the beginning of the reformist movement of 1898. The term is ambiguous: it refers to the nation but has strong racial and ethnic connotations. In Zhang Binglin's work, it designates the nation in the sense of the human group whose collective identity is based on the combined links of blood, history, and customs.

9. Cited by Yves Chevrier, "Des réponses à la révolution," in Marie-Claire Bergère, Lucien Bianco, and Jürgen Domes, eds., *La Chine au XXe siècle*, vol. 1, *D'une révolution à l'autre, 1895–1949* (Paris: Fayard, 1989), p. 112.

10. Cited from Chün-tu Hsüeh, *Huang Hsing and the Chinese Revolution* (Stanford, Calif.: Stanford University Press, 1961), p. 35.

11. Cited by Harold Z. Schiffrin, *Sun Yat-sen*, p. 353.

12. For an overview of this cooperation, see Jeffrey G. Barlow, *Sun Yat-sen and the French, 1900–1908*, and J. Kim Munholland, "The French Connection that Failed: France and Sun Yat-sen, 1900–1908."

13. Report by Paul Doumer to the Minister for Colonies, dated Mar. 22, 1897, as cited in Paul Doumer, *L'Indo-Chine française (Souvenirs)* (Paris: Vuibert et Nony, 1905), p. 383.

14. Auguste François, *Le Mandarin blanc* (Paris: Calmann-Lévy, 1990), p. 279.

15. Ibid., p. 292. ·

16. Ibid., p. 293.

17. Archives du ministre des Affaires étrangères, Chine, Direction politique, Série A, carton 27, dossier 1, conversations with Sun Yat-sen between February 9 and May 18, 1905.

18. The history of the Boucabeille mission can be pieced together by studying the nine long monthly reports that the captain sent to the Ministry of War between December 1905 and October 1906. These reports are kept in the Archives du Service historique de l'armée, État-major de l'armée, Chine, Service des renseignements, carton 7N1676. These reports are summed up and analyzed by Bergère in "Ershi shijichi Faguo dui Sun Zhongshan zhengce: Bujiabei shijian (1905–1906)" ("French Policies toward Sun Yat-sen: The Boucabeille Affair").

19. Cited by Lyon Sharman, *Sun Yat-sen*, pp. 77–78.

20. Cited by Schiffrin, *Sun Yat-sen*, p. 321.

21. Liew Kit-siong, *Struggle for Democracy: Sung Chiao-jen and the 1911 Chinese Revolution* (Berkeley: University of California Press, 1971), p. 43.

22. "Zhina baoquan genge helun" (On the preservation or dismemberment of China), Sept. 21, 1923, *C.W.* 1: 218–24.

23. Schiffrin, *Sun Yat-sen*, p. 362.

24. See Hsüeh, *Huang Hsing*, p. 44.

25. See Liew, *Struggle for Democracy*, p. 47.

CHAPTER FIVE

1. About 1650, when they were still in college, Charles Perrault and his two brothers, Claude and Nicolas, wrote *The Travestite Aeneid*, a parody of Virgil's poem.

2. Michael Gasster, *Chinese Intellectuals and the Revolution of 1911: The Birth of Modern Chinese Radicalism* (Seattle: University of Washington Press, 1969), p. 229.

3. See Liew, *Struggle for Democracy*, pp. 68–70.

4. On the Cantonese friends and supporters of Sun within the Revolutionary Alliance, see Rhoads, *China's Republican Revolution*, pp. 101–3.

5. Cited from Noriko Tamada, "Sung Chiao-jen and the 1911 Revolution," *Papers on China*, Center for East Asian Studies, Harvard University, 21 (1968): 189.

6. Cited in Liew, *Struggle for Democracy*, p. 71.

7. Ibid., p. 80.

8. Ibid., p. 93.

9. Ibid., p. 98.

10. Chen Tianhua, "Lun Zhongguo yi gaichuang minzhu zhengti" (China must change and adopt a republican regime), *Minbao*, no. 1 (Nov. 26, 1905): 49; cited from Gasster, *Chinese Intellectuals and the Revolution of 1911*, p. 77. *Zuo Zhuan* (traditions of Zuo) is a chronicle of the Zhou period (eleventh to eighth centuries B.C.), probably put together in the fifth and fourth centuries B.C.

11. Han Min (Hu Hanmin), "*Minbao* zhi liu dazhuyi" (The six great principles of the *People's Journal*), *Minbao*, no. 3 (Apr. 18, 1906): 8.

12. Charlotte Furth, "The Sage as Rebel: The Inner World of Chang Ping-lin," in Charlotte Furth, ed., *The Limits of Change: Essays on Conservative Alternatives in Republican China* (Cambridge, Mass.: Harvard University Press, 1976), p. 117.

13. Zhu Zhixin, "Lun Manzhou sui yu lixian er bu neng" (Although the Manchu want to establish a Constitution, they are incapable of doing so), *Minbao*, no. 1 (Nov. 26, 1905): 36–38. Partial translation in Gasster, *Chinese Intellectuals and the Revolution of 1911*, p. 86.

14. Cited by Gasster, *Chinese Intellectuals and the Revolution of 1911*, pp. 89, 91.

15. Cited by Ernest Young, "Ch'en T'ien-hua (1875–1905): A Chinese Nationalist," *Papers on China*, Center for East Asian Studies, Harvard University, 13 (Dec. 1959): 124. This vision of modernity reduced to its most obvious material aspects uncannily evokes that of the reformists of the early 1980's, who dreamed of a Beijing bristling with skyscrapers.

16. Cited by Wong Young-tsu, *Search for Modern Nationalism: Zhang Binglin and Revolutionary China, 1869–1936* (Hong Kong: Oxford University Press, 1989), p. 59.

17. Young, "Ch'en T'ien-hua," pp. 144–45. The *Shujing* (Book of Documents) is one of the six Classics. It is a collection of texts dating from the ninth to the fifth centuries B.C., which reflect the tradition of the scribes, analysts, and diviners of Antiquity. Mencius, the philosopher of the fourth century B.C., considers that the prince's virtue is the basis of his power, since it wins him the support of the people, without which there can be no legitimate government. The writings of Mencius served as a reference to the neo-Confucian orthodoxy that dominated political thought at the time of the Manchu dynasty.

18. See Gasster, *Chinese Intellectuals and the Revolution of 1911*, pp. 115–16.

19. Jelléneck's thought is principally devoted to the role of the state as an instrument of liberation and national unification. He defended the idea that the state should submit voluntarily to the law and impose upon itself limits to its sovereignty.

20. "Zai Dongjing *Minbao* chuangkan zhounian qingzhudahui yanshuo" (Speech given at the meeting in Tokyo to celebrate the first anniversary of the foundation of the *People's Journal*), Dec. 2, 1906, *C.W.* 1: 330.

21. George died suddenly a few days before the elections.

22. Zi You (Feng Ziyou), "Lu *Zhongguo ribao* minshengzhuyi yu Zhongguo

zhengzhi geming zhi qiantu" (The principle of the people's livelihood and the future of the Chinese Revolution, an article originally published in the *Chinese Daily*), *Minbao*, no. 4 (May 1, 1906): 97–122. See comment by Harold Z. Schiffrin, "Sun Yat-sen's Early Land Policy: The Origin and Meaning of 'Equalization of Land Rights,' " *Journal of Asian Studies* 16, no. 4 (Aug. 1956): 551–52.

23. *Xinmin congbao* (New People's Miscellany), no. 14 (Sept. 3, 1906); the article is summarized and partially translated in Robert A. Scalapino and Harold Z. Schiffrin, "Early Socialist Currents in the Chinese Revolutionary Movement: Sun Yat-sen versus Liang Ch'i-Ch'ao," *Journal of Asian Studies* 18, no. 3 (May 1959): 335.

24. Xian Jie (pseud. for Zhu Zhixin), "Lun shehuigeming dang yu zhengzhigeming bing xing" (The social revolution must keep in step with the political revolution), *Minbao*, no. 5 (June 30, 1906): 43–66.

CHAPTER SIX

1. These Chinese bands of pirates and outlaws had established themselves in the mountainous zones surrounding the middle reaches of the Red River. In the early 1880's, they had resisted the penetration of the French. After the treaty of 1885 in which China recognized the French protectorate of Annam and the military occupation of Tonking, the Black Pavillions continued their resistance, which was crushed in 1896, after a series of campaigns led by Joseph Gallieni and Louis Lyautey.

2. But not all that close; 750 kilometers separated Haiphong and Kunming, and these were as yet incompletely served by the Tongking-Yunnan railway.

3. The Sunist strategy of Southern rebellions has been thoroughly studied by authors such as Barlow, *Sun Yat-sen and the French*; Hsueh, *Huang Hsing*; Munholland, "The French Connection That Failed"; and Rhoads, *China's Republican Revolution*.

4. Cited by Wong Young-tsu, *Search for Modern Nationalism*, p. 70, from Zhang Binglin's *Autobiography*.

5. Letter from Huang Xing, dated May 13, 1910, cited here from Chün-tu Hsüeh, *Huang Hsing and the Chinese Revolution*, p. 81.

6. Cited in ibid., p. 93.

7. Ibid.

8. In the following paragraphs, the account of the Singaporian-Malaysian revolutionary activities is taken chiefly from Yen Ching Hwang, *The Overseas Chinese and the 1911 Revolution*.

CHAPTER SEVEN

1. Cited by Chün-tu Hsüeh, *Huang Hsing*, p. 108.

2. The activities of these groups are described by Liew, *Struggle for Democracy*, pp. 105–16, and by Hsüeh, *Huang Hsing*, pp. 96–97.

3. The provincial assemblies had been instituted in July 1908 within the framework of constitutional reorganization undertaken by the reforming empire. An electorate limited to the elites had chosen as its representatives literati, members of the gentry, or students recently returned from studying abroad.

4. "Youzhi jingcheng" (Ambition fulfilled), *C. W.* 6: 244.

5. Lyon Sharman, *Sun Yat-sen*, p. 127.

6. The purpose of this consortium, formed in 1908, was to finance Chinese loans designed to ensure railway and economic development for the empire and also to finance its administration.

7. Albert Maybon, *La République chinoise* (Paris: Colin, 1914), pp. 166–67.

8. Cited by Hsüeh, *Huang Hsing*, p. 127.

9. Later known as Henry Puyi.

10. Edmond Rottach, *La Chine en révolution* (Paris: Perrin, 1914), pp. 145–46.

11. The name of the official buildings for the officials of the empire.

12. Rottach, *La Chine en révolution*, p. 151.

13. Fernand Farjenel, *A travers la révolution chinoise* (Paris: Plon-Nourrit, 1914), p. 275.

14. "Youzhi jingcheng" (Ambition fulfilled), *C. W.* 6: 246.

15. Lo Hui-min, ed., *The Correspondence of G. E. Morrison* (Cambridge: Cambridge University Press, 1976), 1: 667.

16. Cited by Earl Albert Selle, *Donald of China* (New York: Harper & Bros., 1948), p. 123.

17. Cited by Samuel Chu, *Reformer in Modern China: Chang Chien, 1853–1926* (New York: Columbia University Press, 1965), p. 78.

18. Cited by Hsüeh, *Huang Hsing*, p. 132.

19. Cited in Li Chien-Nung, *The Political History of China, 1840–1928* (Princeton, N.J.: Van Nostrand, 1956), p. 260.

20. Ernest P. Young, "Yuan Shik-k'ai's Rise to Presidency," in Mary C. Wright, ed., *China in Revolution: The First Phase, 1900–1913* (New Haven, Conn.: Yale University Press, 1968), pp. 422–23, n. 1.

21. Rottach, *La Chine en révolution*, p. 144.

22. Ibid., p. 147.

23. This was situated to the south of the imperial residence and the administrative quarters and was the district inhabited by merchants and the common people.

24. Cited by Farjenel, *A travers la révolution chinoise*, p. 194.

25. On the growing political and ideological influence of Song Jiaoren, see Liew, *Struggle for Democracy*, pp. 153–58 and 169–90, and Noriko Tamachi Yamada, "Sung Chiao-jen and the 1911 Revolution."

26. This analysis, favored by many contemporaries and historians of the period, began to be challenged in the 1960's.

27. Farjenel, *A travers la révolution chinoise*, pp. 274, 286.

28. "Zai Shanghai Guomindang huanyinghuide yanshuo" (Speech given at the

welcoming meeting organized by the Shanghai Guomindang), *C.W.* 2: 484–85. Partial translation in Hsüeh, *Huang Hsing*, pp. 141–42.

29. Interview cited in Sharman, *Sun Yat-sen*, p. 150.

30. Charles Albert, "La révolution chinoise et le socialisme," *L'Effort libre*, cahiers 5, 6, 7, February 1913, p. 165.

31. Cited in Edward Friedman, *Backward Toward Revolution: The Chinese Revolutionary Party* (Berkeley: University of California Press, 1974), p. 17.

32. Maybon, *La République chinoise*, p. 180.

33. Ibid., p. 164.

34. Ibid., pp. 163, 165.

35. "Zai Shanghai Zhongguo shehuidangde yanshuo" (Speech to the Chinese Socialist Party in Shanghai) October 14–16, 1912, *C.W.* 2: 506–24.

36. Ibid., p. 510.

37. Selle, *Donald of China*, pp. 135–37.

38. Morrison, *Correspondence*, 2: 101.

39. Cited in Marius Jansen, *The Japanese and Sun Yat-sen*, p. 160.

40. Ibid.

41. Cited in Tang Leang-Li, *The Inner History of the Chinese Revolution* (Westport, Conn.: Hyperion, 1977), p. 112.

42. "Zhi Huang Xing han" (Letter to Huang Xing), March 1915, *C.W.* 3: 165.

43. Cited in Jansen, *The Japanese and Sun Yat-sen*, p. 162.

44. Letter from Chen Qimei to Huang Xing, cited in Chen Xiqi, *Sun Zhongshan nianpu changpian* (Chronological biography of Sun Yat-sen) (Beijing: Zhonghua shuju, 1991), 1: 793.

45. Cited in Hsüeh, *Huang Hsing*, p. 159.

46. Marie-Claire Bergère, *La Bourgeoisie chinoise et la Révolution de 1911* (La Haye-Paris: Mouton, 1968), p. 114.

CHAPTER EIGHT

1. Cited by Edward Friedman, *Backward Toward Revolution*, p. 51.

2. "Zhi Nanyang gemingdangren han" (Letter to the revolutionaries of Southeast Asia), Apr. 18, 1914, *C.W.* 3: 81–82.

3. Letter from Kong Xiangxi (H. H. Kung), Apr. 3, 1915, in *The Correspondence of G. E. Morrison*, 2: 391.

4. Sterling Seagrave, *The Soong Dynasty* (New York: Harper & Row, 1985), p. 8.

5. Cited by Emily Hahn, *The Soong Sisters* (New York: Doubleday, Doran, 1941), p. 70.

6. Cited in Earl Albert Selle, *Donald of China*, pp. 139–40.

7. Typed letter, addressed to Mrs. Cantlie and dated Oct. 17, 1918, "Letters and Telegrams to Sir James and Lady Cantlie, 1913–1921" (a collection of photo-

copies of the original manuscripts or typescripts kept in the library of Hong Kong University).

8. Cited in Chang Jung and Jon Halliday, *Madame Sun Yat-sen (Soong Ching-ling)* (Harmondsworth-Penguin, 1986), p. 33.

9. T'ang Leang-li, *The Inner History of the Chinese Revolution*, p. 19.

10. For the text of the oath, see Zou Lu, *Zhongguo Guomindang shigao* (Project for a history of the Chinese Nationalist Party, Shanghai, 1929), 1: 163–64.

11. Testimony of Ju Zheng, cited by Friedman, *Backward Toward Revolution*, p. 57.

12. "Zhi Nanyang gemingdang han" (Letter to the revolutionaries of Southeast Asia), Apr. 18, 1914, *C. W.* 3: 81–82.

13. Cited by Friedman, *Backward Toward Revolution*, p. 58.

14. T'ang, *The Inner History*, p. 252.

15. Letter from Chen Qimei to Huang Xing, cited by Chün-tu Hsüeh, *Huang Hsing*, p. 160.

16. Cited by Friedman, *Backward Toward Revolution*, p. 52.

17. Pichon P. Y. Loh, *The Early Chiang Kai-shek: A Study of His Personality and Politics, 1887–1924* (New York: Columbia University Press, 1971), p. 132 n. 77, gives the text of the confidential letter from the United States consul general in Shanghai, dated Nov. 29, 1926, about "Chaing Kai-shek's criminal activities."

18. See the telegram from Dejean de La Bâtie, French consul general in Shanghai, dated Jan. 17, 1912, Archives of the Quai d'Orsay.

19. Friedman, *Backward Toward Revolution*, p. 208.

20. "Zhi Deng Zeru han" (Letter to Deng Zeru), Sept. 1, 1914, *C. W.* 3: 114.

21. At the time, the text of this letter only became known owing to leaks in the Shanghai foreign press. The original letter was found among Ōkuma Shigenobu's papers in 1943, after his death, but the text has yet to appear in any edition of Sun's *Complete Works*, including the most recent, published in Beijing in the 1980's.

22. Letter partially cited and translated in Marius Jansen, *The Japanese and Sun Yat-sen*, pp. 188–89. A copy of this letter is also to be found in the correspondence of G. E. Morrison, to whom it had been sent for diffusion in the foreign press. See Morrison, *Correspondence*, 2: 323 ff.

23. Letter from Kong Xiangxi (H. H. Kung), Apr. 3, 1915, in Morrison, *Correspondence*, 2: 389.

24. This letter remained hidden in the Japanese diplomatic archives until these archives were forcibly opened at the end of World War II. It is cited in Jansen, *The Japanese and Sun Yat-sen*, pp. 192–93.

25. Cited by Friedman, *Backward Toward Revolution*, p. 54.

26. On Cai E, the Yunnanese militarism, and the anti-Yuan rebellion, see Donald Sutton, *Provincial Militarism and the Chinese Republic: The Yunnan Army 1905–1925* (Ann Arbor: University of Michigan Press, 1980), pp. 143–61 and 186–92.

27. Cited by Albert A. Altman and Harold Z. Schiffrin, "Sun Yat-sen and the Japanese, 1914–1916," *Modern Asian Studies* 6, no. 4 (1972): 396.

28. Ibid., p. 398.

29. Cited in Li Shou-kung, "Dr. Sun Yat-sen's Constitution-Protection Campaign and the Establishment of the Military Government in Canton, 1917–1918," *China Forum* 4, no. 2 (July 1977): 261–62.

30. Telegram dated June 6, 1917, *C. W.* 4: 101.

31. "Zai Guangzhou Huangpu huanyinghuishangde yanshuo" (Speech delivered at the welcoming meeting in Huangpu [Canton], July 17, 1917), *C. W.* 4: 114–15.

32. Namely, the interim president, Feng Guochang, to whom Li Yuanhong legally passed on his functions when he retired.

33. Cited in Li Shou-kung, "Dr. Sun Yat-sen's Constitution-Protection Campaign," p. 290.

34. Zhang Binglin's *Autobiography*, cited in ibid., p. 292.

35. Testimony of Wu Tiecheng, an adviser to the military government, cited in ibid., pp. 300–301.

36. Cited in ibid., p. 296.

37. Cited in Chang and Halliday, *Madame Sun Yat-sen*, pp. 37–38.

38. Ibid.

39. This theme is taken up by Josef Fass, "Sun Yat-sen and the May 4th Movement," *Archiv Orientalny* 36, no. 4 (1968): 577–84.

40. The Versailles peace conference did in fact transfer to Japan the German territories and interests in Shandong whose restitution the Chinese were demanding. These were restored to China in 1922.

41. Speech made by Sun, Nov. 14, 1920, cited in George T. Yu, *Party Politics in Republican China: The Kuomintang, 1912–1924* (Berkeley: University of California Press, 1966), pp. 156–57.

42. Before being attached to the *Plan for National Reconstruction*, the articles that make up "Psychological Reconstruction" had been published, in December 1918, under the title *The Philosophy of Sun Yat-sen (Sun Wen Xueshuo)*.

43. *Sun Wen Xueshuo* (The philosophy of Sun Yat-sen), *C. W.* 6: 159.

44. Ibid.

45. Sun Yat-sen, *The International Development of China* (1921; 2d ed., London: Hutchinson, 1928). Subsequent quotations in the text are from the 1928 edition.

46. Cited by C. Martin Wilbur, *Sun Yat-sen: Frustrated Patriot* (New York: Columbia University Press, 1976), p. 324 n. 74.

CHAPTER NINE

1. For Sun's political activities during these years, the standard Western reference is C. Martin Wilbur's *Sun Yat-sen: Frustrated Patriot*, on which I relied for this chapter.

2. This is the view held by some Beijing students, as quoted by Winston Hsieh, "The Ideas and Ideals of a Warlord: Ch'en Chiung-ming 1878–1933," *Papers on China*, vol. 6 (Cambridge, Mass.: East Asian Research Center, 1962), pp. 198–252.

3. These cliques took their names from the provinces in which their principal military forces were based. Zhili is the ancient name for Hebei, the province of Peking, and Fengtian designates the provinces of Manchuria.

4. Cited in C. Martin Wilbur, *Frustrated Patriot*, p. 330 n. 2.

5. Ibid., p. 126.

6. "Jiuren dazongtong zhi dui wai xuanyan" (Address to the powers on the occasion of assuming the functions of president), May 5, 1921, *C. W.* 5: 532–33.

7. The administration of the Maritime Customs was placed under Chinese jurisdiction but was managed by the foreigners. It collected the taxes on imports, which were used primarily to repay debts contracted toward the foreign powers. Once those debts were paid off, the funds remaining, or "surplusses," were handed over to the Chinese government.

8. *New York Times*, Sept. 26, 1920, cited here from Sydney H. Chang and Leonard H. D. Gordon, *All Under Heaven: Sun Yat-sen and His Revolutionary Thought* (Stanford, Calif.: Hoover Institution Press, 1991), p. 67.

9. Telegram from Charles R. Crane, Peking, Feb. 28, 1921, cited in Wilbur, *Frustrated Patriot*, p. 324 n. 74.

10. Cited in ibid., p. 107.

11. Cited by Allen S. Whiting, *Soviet Policies in China, 1917–1924* (New York: Columbia University Press, 1954), p. 305 n. 21. The Comintern's favorable disposition toward Chen Jiongming is confirmed by those who have had access to the Comintern archives, such as Professor Roland Felber.

12. Telegram dated June 25, 1922, cited by F. Gilbert Chan, "Sun Yat-sen and the Origins of the Kuomintang Organization," in Gilbert F. Chan et al., eds., *China in the 1920's: Nationalism and Revolution* (New York: Franklin Walls, 1976), pp. 24–25.

13. Ibid.

14. Cited in Emily Hahn, *The Soong Sisters*, pp. 94–97.

15. Cited in Chan, "Sun Yat-sen and the Origins of the Kuomintang Organization," p. 25.

16. Ibid., pp. 25–26.

17. *New York Times*, Aug. 19, 1922, cited in Wilbur, *Frustrated Patriot*, p. 128.

18. The Chinese Eastern Railway was built by Russia across Manchuria at the end of the nineteenth century, but after their defeat in the war against Japan (1905), the Russians controlled only the northern and central stretches.

19. Cited here from Leng Shao-chuan and Norman D. Palmer, *Sun Yat-sen and Communism* (New York: Praeger, 1960), p. 53.

20. Cited in Lydia Holubnychy, *Michael Borodin and the Chinese Revolution, 1923–1925* (Ann Arbor, Mich.: University Microfilm International, 1979), pp. 139–40.

21. Ibid., p. 140.   22. Holubnychy, *Borodin*, pp. 141–47.

23. Wilbur, *Frustrated Patriot*, p. 112.   24. Cited in ibid., pp. 115–16.

25. Cited in Leng and Palmer, *Sun Yat-sen and Communism*, p. 56.

26. Dov Bing's interpretation is presented and argued in "Sneevliet and the Early

Years of CCP," *China Quarterly* 48 (Oct.–Dec. 1971): 677–97, and in "Was There a Sneevlitian Strategy" *China Quarterly* 54 (Apr.–June 1973): 345–53.

27. "Zhi Jiang Zhongzheng han" (Letter to Chiang Kai-shek), *C.W.* 6: 616–17; partially translated in Leng and Palmer, *Sun Yat-sen and Communism*, p. 60.

28. See Donald D. Sutton, *Provincial Militarism and the Chinese Republic: The Yunnan Army, 1905–1925* (Ann Arbor: University of Michigan Press, 1980), pp. 274–75.

29. "Zai Xianggang daxuede yanshuo" (Speech given to the University of Hong Kong), *C.W.* 7: 115–17. A number of newspaper reports of the visit to Hong Kong are cited in Wilbur, *Frustrated Patriot*, p. 336 n. 59, and in F. Gilbert Chan, "An Alternative to Kuomintang-Communist Collaboration: Sun Yat-sen and Hong Kong, January–June 1923," *Modern Asian Studies* 13, no. 1 (1979): 132–33.

30. *North China Herald*, Mar. 24, 1923, cited in Chan, "Sun Yat-sen and Hong Kong," p. 133.

31. Cited in A. I. Cherepanov, *Notes of a Military Adviser in China*, trans. by Alexandra O. Smith (Taipei: U.S. Army, Office of Military History, 1970), p. 111.

32. Ibid.

33. Ibid., p. 117.

34. Sutton, *Provincial Militarism*, p. 281.

35. Wilbur, *Frustrated Patriot*, pp. 168–69.

36. Vera V. Vishnyakova-Akimova, *Two Years in Revolutionary China*, trans. by Steven I. Levine (Cambridge, Mass.: Harvard University Press, 1971), p. 154.

37. Testimony cited by Holubynchy, *Michael Borodin*, p. 227.

38. According to unofficial but unconflicting (Chinese and Soviet) reports, cited in ibid., p. 270.

39. Ibid., p. 275.

40. Ibid., p. 310.

41. Ibid., p. 311.

42. See N. Mitarevsky, *Worldwide Soviet Plots* (Tianjin: Tientsin Press, 1927), cited here from ibid., p. 372.

43. Cited in Vishnyakova-Akimova, *Two Years*, p. 158.

44. Cited in Cherepanov, *Military Adviser*, p. 30.

45. Cited in Holubynchy, *Borodin*, pp. 283–84.

46. See N. Mitarevsky, *Worldwide Soviet Plots*, cited here from Wilbur, *Frustrated Patriot*, pp. 173–74.

47. Cited by Wilbur, *Frustrated Patriot*, p. 175.

48. Letter from Sun Yat-sen to Zou Lu, ibid., but not included in *C.W.*

49. Holubynchy, *Borodin*, pp. 304–5.

50. "Zai Guangzhou dabenying Guomindang yuande yanshuo" (Speech to members of the Guomindang party at the Canton headquarters), Nov. 25, 1923, *C.W.* 8: 437–38. Partial translation in Wilbur, *Frustrated Patriot*, p. 178.

51. "Zhongguo xianzhuang ji Guomindang gaizu wenti" (The present situation in

China and the problem of the Reorganization of the Guomindang), Jan. 24, 1924, *C.W.* 9: 100. Partial translation in Tsui Shu-chin, "The Influence of the Canton-Moscow Entente upon Sun Yat-sen's Revolutionary Tactics," *Chinese Social and Political Science Review* 20, no. 1 (1936): 106 n. 24.

52. "Guan yu Liening shishide yanshuo" (Speech on the death of Lenin), *C.W.* 9: 136–37. Partial translation in Dan N. Jacobs, *Borodin: Stalin's Man in China* (Cambridge, Mass.: Harvard University Press, 1981), p. 132.

53. Cited in Wilbur, *Frustrated Patriot*, p. 180.

54. *Tanhe Gongchandang liang da Yao'an* (Two important cases of Impeachment of the Chinese Communist Party), partial translation in Tsui, "Sun Yat-sen's Revolutionary Tactics," p. 127 n. 106.

55. "Pi Deng Zeru dengde shangshu" (Commentaries on the memorandum by Deng Zeru and others), *C.W.* 8: 458–59. Partial translation in Conrad Brandt, Benjamin Schwartz, and John K. Fairbank, *A Documentary History of Chinese Communism* (Cambridge, Mass.: Harvard University Press, 1952), pp. 72–73.

56. Cited in Cherepanov, *Military Adviser*, p. 48.

57. "Zhongguo Guomindang di yi ci quanguo daibiao dahui xuanyan" (Manifesto of the First National Congress of the Guomindang), Jan. 23, 1924, *C.W.* 9: 114–25.

58. "Guan yu minshengzhuyi zhi shuoming" (Explanations on the principle of the livelihood of the people), Jan. 21, 1924, *C.W.* 9: 110–13.

59. Cherepanov, *Military Adviser*, pp. 56–57.

60. Cited in Leng and Palmer, *Sun Yat-sen and Communism*, p. 71.

61. Cited in ibid., pp. 70–71.

62. Ibid., p. 76.

63. Letter to Liao Zhongkai, Mar. 14, 1924. Partial translation in ibid., pp. 72–73.

64. "Guan yu shixing dangjide mingling" (Circular on respect for party discipline), *C.W.* 9: 618.

65. Cited from Wilbur, *Frustrated Patriot*, p. 235.

66. Cited from Keiji Furuya, *Chiang Kai-shek: His Life and Times*, trans. by Chang Chun-ming (Annapolis, Md.: St. John's University Press, 1981), pp. 145–46.

67. Retz, *Mémoires* (Paris: Gallimard, collection "Pléiade," 1984), p. 677. The quotations that follow can be found on pages 729 and 630.

68. "Zai Huangpu junguan xuexiaode gaobie yanshuo" (Farewell speech to the cadets of the Huangpu Military Academy), Nov. 3, 1924, *C.W.* 11: 270.

69. Cited in Xenia Joukoff Eudin and Robert C. North, *Soviet Russia and the East, 1920–1927: A Documentary Survey* (Stanford, Calif.: Stanford University Press, 1957), pp. 344–46.

70. Peng Pai was the first Chinese communist leader to assign an essential role to the peasantry in the revolution. By 1921 he had already organized peasant associations in the Haifeng and Lufeng districts (eastern Guangdong).

71. "Zai Guangzhou nongming yundong jiangxisuo di yi jie biyeli yanshuo" (Speech on the occasion of the ceremony for the awarding of diplomas to the first

31. Élia, *Le Triple Démisme*, p. 180; *C. W.* 9: 267; Taipei ed., p. 63.

32. Élia, *Le Triple Démisme*, p. 197; *C. W.* 9: 274; Taipei ed., p. 70.

33. Élia, *Le Triple Démisme*, p. 208; *C. W.* 9: 281; Taipei ed., p. 75.

34. Élia, *Le Triple Démisme*, p. 209; *C. W.* 9: 281; Taipei ed., p. 75.

35. Élia, *Le Triple Démisme*, p. 201; *C. W.* 9: 277.

36. Élia, *Le Triple Démisme*, p. 207; *C. W.* 9: 280; Taipei ed., p. 74.

37. Élia, *Le Triple Démisme*, p. 253; *C. W.* 9: 304.

38. Élia, *Le Triple Démisme*, p. 219; *C. W.* 9: 286; Taipei ed., p. 97.

39. Élia, *Le Triple Démisme*, p. 219; *C. W.* 9: 286; Taipei ed., p. 81.

40. Élia, *Le Triple Démisme*, p. 219; *C. W.* 9: 286; Taipei ed., p. 82.

41. Clumsy though they sound, the English translations for the terms denoting the three categories of citizens do quite faithfully reflect the Chinese terms used by Sun Yat-sen.

42. Élia, *Le Triple Démisme*, p. 240; *C. W.* 9: 298; Taipei ed., p. 89.

43. Élia, *Le Triple Démisme*, p. 241; *C. W.* 9: 299; Taipei ed., pp. 90–91.

44. Élia, *Le Triple Démisme*, p. 309; *C. W.* 9: 333; Taipei ed., p. 129.

45. Élia, *Le Triple Démisme*, p. 293; *C. W.* 9: 324.

46. Élia, *Le Triple Démisme*, p. 305; *C. W.* 9: 330.

47. Élia, *Le Triple Démisme*, p. 305; *C. W.* 9: 331.

48. Élia, *Le Triple Démisme*, p. 288; *C. W.* 9: 321; Taipei ed., p. 113.

49. Élia, *Le Triple Démisme*, pp. 305–6; *C. W.* 9: 330–31; Taipei ed., p. 128.

50. An English translation (with a bilingual text) of this speech exists in *The Fundamentals of National Reconstruction* (Taipei: China Cultural Service, 1953), pp. 19–24.

51. "Zai Guangzhou dui Guomindangyuande yanshuo" (Speech to the Guomindang members of Canton), Dec. 30, 1924, *C. W.* 8: 573. See also, Chen Yuan-chyuan, "Elements of an East-West Synthesis in Dr. Sun Yat-sen's Concept of the 'Five-Power Constitution,'" in G. K. Kindermann, ed., *Sun Yat-sen: Founder and Symbol of China's Revolutionary Nation-Building* (Munich: Günter Olzog, 1982), pp. 143–72.

52. Élia, *Le Triple Démisme*, p. 343; *C. W.* 9: 351.

53. See Corinna Hana, "The Development of the *San-min chu-i* During the May Fourth Movement," in Kindermann, ed., *Sun Yat-sen: Founder and Symbol*, p. 137.

54. Élia, *Le Triple Démisme*, p. 341; *C. W.* 9: 350.

55. Élia, *Le Triple Démisme*, p. 343; *C. W.* 9: 352; Taipei ed., p. 129.

56. Élia, *Le Triple Démisme*, p. 290; *C. W.* 9: 322.

57. Élia, *Le Triple Démisme*, p. 312.

58. Élia, *Le Triple Démisme*, p. 343; *C. W.* 9: 352.

59. Élia, *Le Triple Démisme*, p. 271; *C. W.* 9: 314.

60. "Zhongguo gemingshi" (History of the Chinese Revolution), Jan. 29, 1923, *C. W.* 7: 66–67.

61. Ibid., p. 62.

62. "Guan yu zuzhi guominzhengfu an zhi shuoming" (Declaration on the plan for Organization of the National Government), *C. W.* 9: 103–4.

63. Cited by Tsui Shu-chin, "The Influence of the Canton-Moscow Entente upon Sun Yat-sen's Political Philosophy, II. The Principle of Democracy," *Chinese Social and Political Science Review* 18, no. 2 (July 1934): 190 n. 30.

64. "Zhonghua minguo jianshezhi jichu," cited in *Fundamentals of National Reconstruction*, pp. 121, 123.

65. Ibid., p. 118.

66. Ibid., p. 124.

67. *Fundamentals of National Reconstruction*, p. 7.

68. Ibid., p. 30.

69. See Allen S. Whiting, "A New Version of the *San-min-chu-i*," *Far East Quarterly* 14 (May 1955): 389–90.

70. Ramon Myers, "The Principle of People's Welfare: A Multidimensional Concept," in Cheng Chu-yuan, ed., *Sun Yat-sen's Doctrine in the Modern World* (Boulder, Colo.: Westview Press, 1989), p. 225.

71. The embarrassment of Pascal M. d'Élia is reflected in a note (p. 354 n. 1) in which he explains that the term "vital" should here be understood not in the biological or psychological, but in the economic sense.

72. Élia, *Le Triple Démisme*, pp. 354, 415; *C. W.* 9: 355, 386.

73. Élia, *Le Triple Démisme*, pp. 412, 415, 416; *C. W.* 9: 384, 386.

74. Élia, *Le Triple Démisme*, p. 406; *C. W.* 9: 381.

75. Élia, *Le Triple Démisme*, p. 375; *C. W.* 9: 365; Taipei ed., pp. 155–56.

76. Ibid.

77. Élia, *Le Triple Démisme*, p. 381; *C. W.* 9: 369.

78. Élia, *Le Triple Démisme*, pp. 381–82; *C. W.* 9: 369.

79. See Chap. 8, p. 246.

80. Élia, *Le Triple Démisme*, p. 381; *C. W.* 9: 369.

81. Élia, *Le Triple Démisme*, p. 391; *C. W.* 9: 374.

82. Cited in Maurice Zolotow, *Maurice William and Sun Yat-sen* (London: Robert Hall, 1948), p. 98.

83. See Maurice William, *Sun Yat-sen Versus Communism* (Baltimore, Md.: Williams & Wilkins, 1932).

84. Élia, *Le Triple Démisme*, p. 421; *C. W.* 9: 388; Taipei ed., p. 183.

85. Élia, *Le Triple Démisme*, p. 432; *C. W.* 9: 394; Taipei ed., p. 183.

86. Élia, *Le Triple Démisme*, p. 433; *C. W.* 9: 394; Taipei ed., p. 184.

87. Élia, *Le Triple Démisme*, p. 406; *C. W.* 9: 381; Taipei ed., p. 172.

88. Élia, *Le Triple Démisme*, pp. 406–7; *C. W.* 9: 381–82; Taipei ed., pp. 172–73.

89. Élia, *Le Triple Démisme*, p. 428; *C. W.* 9: 392; Taipei ed., p. 181.

90. Élia, *Le Triple Démisme*, p. 428; *C. W.* 9: 392; Taipei ed., p. 182.

91. Élia, *Le Triple Démisme*, p. 399; *C. W.* 9: 377. D'Élia's translation, "égaliser la propriété" (to equalize property) is not close to the Chinese text, which has *ping didequan*: "to equalize rights to land."

92. Élia, *Le Triple Démisme*, p. 446; *C. W.* 9: 399.

93. Élia, *Le Triple Démisme*, p. 411; *C. W.* 9: 384.

94. Élia, *Le Triple Démisme*, p. 417; *C. W.* 9: 387; Taipei ed., p. 183.

95. Élia, *Le Triple Démisme*, p. 421; *C. W.* 9: 390.

96. Élia, *Le Triple Démisme*, p. 425; *C. W.* 9: 391; Taipei ed., p. 180.

97. Élia, *Le Triple Démisme*, pp. 265–66; *C. W.* 9: 310.

98. Élia, *Le Triple Démisme*, pp. 425–26; *C. W.* 9: 391; Taipei ed., p. 181.

99. Élia, *Le Triple Démisme*, p. 431; *C. W.* 9: 393; Taipei ed., p. 182.

100. Élia, *Le Triple Démisme*, p. 431; *C. W.* 9: 393 (but the text of the *C. W.* differs from that translated by Élia).

101. Élia, *Le Triple Démisme*, p. 497; *C. W.* 9: 424; Taipei ed., p. 209.

102. *The Nation*, May 11, 1932, p. 548. Cited by Tsui, "The Influence of the Canton-Moscow Entente, III. The Principle of Livelihood," *Chinese Social and Political Science Review* 18, no. 3 (Oct. 1934): 345 n. 18.

103. *London Times Literary Supplement*, Dec. 17, 1931, p. 1016, cited by Tsui, ibid., p. 345.

104. Lyon Sharman, *Sun Yat-sen*, p. 328.

105. Élia, *Le Triple Démisme*, p. 191; *C. W.* 9: 271.

106. Élia, *Le Triple Démisme*, p. 433; *C. W.* 9: 394; Taipei ed., p. 183.

107. In the interests of simplicity, I have left aside the (in truth, essential) fact that the intellectuals of the transition were for the most part themselves introduced to Western ideas by Japanese translators and thinkers.

108. Cited by A. M. Woodruff, "Progress and Poverty: A Hundred Years' Perspective," in Richard W. Lindon and Sein Lin, eds., "Henry George and Sun Yat-sen: Application and Evolution of Their Land Use Doctrine" (Cambridge, Mass.: Lincoln Institute of Land Policy, 1977), 141 typed pages, ff. 27, 38.

CHAPTER ELEVEN

1. *Xiangdao zhoukan* (The weekly guide), no. 89, p. 786, English translation by Jerome Chen, "Dr Sun Yat-sen's Trip to Peking, 1924–1925," p. 85.

2. Words reported by the *Guangzhou guomin ribao* (Canton Nationalist Weekly), cited here from Chen Xiqi, *Sun Zhongshan nianpu changpian* (Chronological biography of Sun Yat-sen; Beijing: Zhonghua shuju, 1991), 2: 2050.

3. "Zai Huangpu junguan xuexiaode gaobie yanshuo" (Farewell speech to the Huangpu Military Academy), Nov. 3, 1924, *C. W.* 11: 264–65.

4. *North China Daily News*, Nov. 8, 1924, p. 224; cited from "Saggitarius" (H. G. W. Woodhead), *The Strange Apotheosis of Sun Yat-sen* (London: Heath, Cranton, 1939), p. 116.

5. "Zai Shanghai yu huanyingzhede tanhua" (Conversation in Shanghai with those who came to welcome [Sun]), Nov. 17, 1924, *C. W.* 11: 319.

6. Cited by Sidney Chang and Leonard H. D. Gordon, *All Under Heaven*, p. 85.

7. "Dui Shenhu shangye huiyisuo deng tuantide yanshuo" (Speech given to the members of the [Chinese] chamber of commerce of Kobe and other groups), Nov. 28, 1924, *C.W.* 11: 401–9.

8. Cited by Marius Jansen, *The Japanese and Sun Yat-sen*, p. 264 n. 15.

9. Interview with Duan Qirui on Dec. 7, 1924, at the Eastern News Agency, cited from "Saggitarius," *The Strange Apotheosis of Sun Yat-sen*, p. 119.

10. C. Martin Wilbur, *Frustrated Patriot*, pp. 272, 369 n. 29.

11. "Guoshi yizhu" (Political Testament), Mar. 11, 1924, *C.W.* 11: 639–40.

12. The text, written in English, is cited by Wilbur, *Frustrated Patriot*, pp. 279–80.

13. *Peking Press*, Mar. 20, 1925, cited from Léon Wieger, S. J., *La Chine moderne*, vol. 6, *Le Feu aux poudres 1925* (Hien-Hien [Hebei], 1926), p. 171.

14. Testimony of L. Carrington Goodrich, cited by Wilbur, *Frustrated Patriot*, p. 281.

15. Comment by Eugene Chen, cited from "Saggitarius," *The Strange Apotheosis of Sun Yat-sen*, pp. 125–26.

16. Cited from Pichon P. Y. Loh, "The Ideological Persuasion of Chiang Kai-shek," *Modern Asian Studies* 4, no. 3 (1970): 216.

17. Jansen, *The Japanese and Sun Yat-sen*, p. 1.

18. Élia, *Le Triple Démisme de Suen Wen*, Intro., p. xc.

19. Chiang Kai-shek, speech of Apr. 21, 1952, "Tudi guoyoude yaoyi" (Conditions and meaning of the nationalization of land).

20. See James Gregor, Maria Hsia Chang, and Andrew Zimmerman, *Ideology and Development: Sun Yat-sen and the Economic History of Taiwan* (Berkeley, Calif.: Center for Chinese Studies, 1981). The same "Sunist" interpretation of the Taiwanese economic success is to be found in Cheng Chu-yuan, "The Doctrine of the People's Welfare: The Taiwan Experiment and Its Implication for the Third World," in Cheng Chu-yuan, ed., *Sun Yat-sen's Doctrine in the Modern World*.

21. Arlen V. Meliksetov, "La modernisation de la Chine et le confucianisme," *Cahiers d'études chinoises* (Paris: INALCO, 1992), no. 10.

22. On the many publications and colloquia devoted to Sun Yat-sen during the 1980's, see Marie-Claire Bergère, "L'effet Sun Yat-sen: quand Orient et Occident se tournent le dos," *Études chinoises* 11, no. 1 (Spring 1992): 87–108.

23. See Schiffrin, *Sun Yat-sen and the Origins of the Chinese Revolution*; Wilbur, *Frustrated Patriot*.

24. See in particular, William Rowe, *Hankow*, vol. 1, *Commerce and Society in a Chinese City, 1796–1889* (Stanford, Calif.: Stanford University Press, 1984), p. 13: "The gradual change that those [traditional social and economic] structures underwent in the course of the 19th century led directly . . . into the political revolution of 1911."

Bibliography

WORKS IN WESTERN LANGUAGES

Albert, Charles. "La révolution chinoise et le socialisme." *L'Effort libre*, cahiers 5, 6, 7, February 1913.

Altman, Albert A., and Harold Z. Schiffrin. "Sun Yat-sen and the Japanese, 1914–1916." *Modern Asian Studies* 6, no. 4 (1972): 385–400.

Anschel, Eugène. *Homer Lea: Sun Yat-sen and the Chinese Revolution.* New York: Praeger, 1986.

Auxion de Ruffé, Reginald d'. *Chine et Chinois d'aujourd'hui.* Paris: Berger-Levrault, 1926.

Barlow, Jeffrey G. *Sun Yat-sen and the French, 1900–1908.* Berkeley, Calif.: Institute of East Asian Studies, Center for Chinese Studies, Research Monograph 14, 1979.

Bastid, Marianne. "La diplomatie française et la Révolution chinoise." *Revue d'histoire moderne et contemporaine,* 1969: 221–45.

——. "Faguode yinxiang ji geguo gonghezhuyizhe tuanjie yizhi: lun Sun Zhongshan yu Faguo zhengjiede guanxi" ("French Influences and the Alliance of Republicans from Every Country: On Sun Yat-sen and His Links with French Political Figures"). In Zhongguo Sun Zhongshan yanjiuhui, ed., *Sun Zhongshan he tade shidai* (*Sun Zhongshan yanjiuhui guoji xueshu taolunhui wen ji*), vol. 1 (Beijing: Zhonghua Shuju, 1989), pp. 454–70.

——. "L'ouverture aux idées d'Occident: quelle influence de la Révolution française sur la révolution républicaine de 1911?" *Extrême-Orient–Extrême-Occident.* Paris: Presses et Publications de l'université de Paris 8 (1983), 2: 21–40.

Bergère, Marie-Claire. *La Bourgeoisie chinoise et la Révolution de 1911.* La Haye-Paris: Mouton, 1968.

——. "L'effet Sun Yat-sen: quand Orient et Occident se tournent le dos." *Etudes chinoises* 11, no. 1 (Spring 1992): 87–108.

——. *The Golden Age of the Chinese Bourgeoisie, 1911–1937.* Cambridge: Cambridge University Press, 1989.

——. "Modernisation économique et société urbaine." In Marie-Claire Bergère, Lucien Bianco, and Jürgen Domes, eds., *La Chine au XXe siècle*. Vol. 1, *D'une révolution à l'autre, 1895–1949*, chap. 10. Paris: Fayard, 1990.

Bai Ji'er [Bergère]. "Ershi shijichu Faguo dui Sun Zhongshande zhengce" (A French policy toward Sun Yat-sen in the early twentieth century). "Bujiabei shijian 1905–1906" (The Boucabeille affair, 1905–1906). In Zhongguo Sun Zhongshan yanjiuhui, ed., *Sun Zhongshan he tade shidai* (*Sun Zhongshan yanjiuhui guoji xueshu taolunhui wenji*) (Sun Yat-sen and his time. A collection of the papers presented at the international academic conference on Sun Yat-sen), 1: 442, 453. 3 vols. Beijing: Zhonghua shuju, 1989.

Bianco, Lucien. *Origins of the Chinese Revolution, 1915–1949*. Translated from the French by Muriel Bell. Stanford, Calif.: Stanford University Press, 1971.

Bing, Dov. "Chang Chi and Ma-lin's First Visit to Dr. Sun Yat-sen." *Issues and Studies* 9, no. 6 (1973): 57–62.

———. "Sneevliet and the Early Years of the CCP." *China Quarterly* no. 48 (Oct.-Dec. 1971): 667–97.

———. "Was There a Sneevlitian Strategy?" *China Quarterly* no. 54 (Apr.-June 1973): 345–53.

Borokh, Lilian. "Les débuts du mouvement républicain de Sun Yat-sen et les sociétés secrètes." In Jean Chesneaux, ed., *Mouvements populaires et sociétés secrètes en Chine aux XIXe et XXe siècles*, pp. 344–59. Paris: Maspéro, 1970.

Brandt, Conrad, Benjamin Schwartz, and John K. Fairbank. *A Documentary History of Chinese Communism*. Cambridge, Mass.: Harvard University Press, 1952.

Broué, Pierre. *La question chinoise dans l'Internationale communiste*. Paris: Etudes et Documentation Internationales, 1976.

Bruguière, Michel. "Le chemin de fer du Yunnan. Paul Doumer et la politique d'intervention française en Chine, 1889–1902." *Revue d'histoire diplomatique*, 1963: 23–61, 129–62, 252–78.

Cantlie, James, and C. Sheridan Jones. *Sun Yat-sen and the Awakening of China*. New York: Fleming H. Revell, 1912.

Cantlie, Neil, and George Seaver. *Sir James Cantlie: A Romance in Medicine*. London: John Murray, 1939.

Chan, F. Gilbert. "An Alternative to Kuomintang-Communist Collaboration: Sun Yat-sen and Hong Kong, January-June 1923." *Modern Asian Studies* 13, no. 1 (1979): 127–39.

———. "Sun Yat-sen and the Origins of the Kuomintang Organization." In F. Gilbert Chan et al., eds., *China in the 1920's: Nationalism and Revolution*. New York: Franklin Walls, 1976.

Chan Lau Kit-ching. *China, Britain, and Hong Kong, 1895–1945*. Hong Kong: The Chinese University Press, 1990.

Chang, Sidney H., and Leonard H. D. Gordon. *All Under Heaven: Sun Yat-sen and His Revolutionary Thought*. Stanford, Calif.: Hoover Institution Press, 1991.

Chang Hao. *Chinese Intellectuals in Crisis: Search for Order and Meaning, 1890–1911*. Berkeley: University of California Press, 1987.

Chang Jung (with Jon Halliday). *Madame Sun Yat-sen (Soong Ching-ling)*. Harmondsworth: Penguin, 1986.

Chen, Jerome. "Dr. Sun Yat-sen's Trip to Peking, 1924–1925." *Readings on Asian Topics*, Scandinavian Institute of Asian Studies Monograph Series. Lund: Student Literature, 1970.

——. "The Left Wing Kuomintang: A Definition." *Bulletin of the School of Oriental and African Studies* 25, no. 3 (1962): 557–76.

——. *Yuan Shih-k'ai, 1859–1916*. Stanford, Calif.: Stanford University Press, 1961.

Chen Yuan-chyuan. "Elements of an East-West Synthesis in Dr. Sun Yat-sen's Concept of the 'Five-Power Constitution' and in the Chinese Constitution of 1946." In Gottfried-Karl Kindermann, ed., *East-West Syntheses*. Vol. 1. *Sun Yat-sen: Founder and Symbol of China's Revolutionary Nation-Building*, pp. 143–72. Munich: Günter Olzog, 1982.

Cheng, Shelley H. "The T'ung-meng-hui: Its Organization, Leadership, and Finances, 1905–1912." Ph.D. diss., University of Washington, 1962.

Cheng Chu-yuan, ed. *Sun Yat-sen's Doctrine in the Modern World*. Boulder, Colo.: Westview Press, 1989.

Cherepanov, A. I. *Zapiski voennogo sovetnika v Kitae* (Notes of a military adviser to China). Moscow: Academy of Sciences of the U.S.S.R., Nauka, 1964. Consulted here is the English translation by Alexandra O. Smith, *Notes of a Military Adviser in China*. Taipei: U.S. Army, Office of Military History, 1970.

Chesneaux, Jean. "Le mouvement fédéraliste en Chine, 1920–1923." *Revue historique*, no. 480 (Oct.-Dec. 1966): 347–84.

——. *Le mouvement ouvrier chinois de 1919 à 1927*. La Haye-Paris: Mouton, 1962. English translation by H. M. Wright, *The Chinese Labor Movement, 1919–1927*. Stanford, Calif.: Stanford University Press, 1968.

——et al., eds. *Mouvements populaires et sociétés secrètes en Chine aux XIXe et XXe siècles*. Paris: Maspéro, 1970. English translation, *Popular Movements and Secret Societies in China, 1840–1950*. Stanford, Calif.: Stanford University Press, 1972.

Ch'i Hsi-sheng. *Warlord Politics in China, 1916–1928*. Stanford, Calif.: Stanford University Press, 1976.

Choa, Gerald Hugh. *The Life and Times of Sir Kai Ho Kai: A Prominent Figure in Nineteenth-Century Hong Kong*. Hong Kong: The Chinese University Press, 1981.

Chong, Key Ray. "The Abortive American-Chinese Project for Chinese Revolution, 1908–1911." *Pacific Historical Review* 41 (1972): 54–70.

——. *Americans and Chinese Reform and Revolution, 1898–1922: The Role of Private Citizens in Diplomacy*. Lanham, Md.: University Press of America, 1984.

Chu, Samuel. *Reformer in Modern China: Chang Chien, 1853–1926*. New York: Columbia University Press, 1965.

Dikötter, Frank. *The Discourse of Race in Modern China*. Hong Kong: Hong Kong University Press, 1992.

Doumer, Paul. *L'Indo-Chine française (Souvenirs)*. Paris: Vuibert et Nony, 1905.

Élia, Pascal M. d', S.J. *Le Triple Démisme de Suen Wen*. Shanghai: Bureau sinologique de Zi-Ka-wei, 1930.

Esherick, Joseph W. *Reform and Revolution in China: The 1911 Revolution in Hunan and Hubei*. Berkeley: University of California Press, 1976.

Eto Shinkichi and Harold Z. Schiffrin, eds. *The 1911 Revolution in China: Interpretive Essays*. Tokyo: University of Tokyo Press, 1984.

Eudin, Xenia Joukoff, and Robert C. North. *Soviet Russia and the East, 1920–1927: A Documentary Survey*. Stanford, Calif.: Stanford University Press, 1957.

Fairbank, John K., ed. *The Cambridge History of China*. Vol. 12, *Republican China, 1912–1949*. Cambridge: Cambridge University Press, 1983.

Fairbank, John K., and Liu Kwang-ching, eds. *The Cambridge History of China*. Vol. 11, *Late Ch'ing, 1800–1911*. Cambridge: Cambridge University Press, 1980.

Farjenel, Fernand. *A travers la révolution chinoise*. Paris: Plon-Nourrit, 1914.

Fass, Josef. "Sun Yat-sen and Germany in 1921–1924." *Archiv Orientalni* 36 (1968): 134–48.

——. "Sun Yat-sen and the May-4th Movement." *Archiv Orientalni* 36, no. 4 (1968): 577–84.

——. "Sun Yat-sen and the [*sic*] World War I." *Archiv Orientalni* 35, no. 1 (1967): 111–20.

Felber, Roland. "Authoritarianism versus Premature Liberalism: Controversies Among Chinese Intellectuals at the Beginning of the Twentieth Century on China's Political Prospects." Paper presented at the 34th International Conference of Studies on Asia and North Africa, Hong Kong, Aug. 22–28, 1993.

Fincher, John. *Chinese Democracy, Statist Reform, the Self-Government Movement, and Republican Revolution*. Tokyo: Institute for the Study of Languages and Cultures of Asia and Africa, 1989.

Fogel, Joshua. "Race and Class in Chinese Historiography: Divergent Interpretations of Zhang Binglin and Antimanchuism in the 1911 Revolution." *Modern China* 3, no. 3 (July 1977).

François, Auguste. *Le Mandarin blanc. Souvenirs d'un consul en Extrême-Orient, 1886–1904*. Paris: Calmann-Lévy, 1990.

Friedman, Edward. *Backward Toward Revolution: The Chinese Revolutionary Party*. Berkeley: University of California Press, 1974.

Fung, Edmund S. K. "The T'ung-meng-hui Central China Bureau and the Wuchang Uprising." *Zhongguo wenhua yanjiusuo xuebao* (Bulletin of the Institute of Chinese Culture, The Chinese University of Hong Kong) 7, no. 2 (1974): 477–96.

Furth, Charlotte. "The Sage as Rebel: The Inner World of Chang Ping-lin." In Charlotte Furth, ed., *The Limits of Change: Essays on Conservative Alternatives in Republican China*, pp. 113–50. Cambridge, Mass.: Harvard University Press, 1976.

Furuya Keiji. *Chiang Kai-shek: His Life and Times*. Translated from the Japanese and abridged by Chang Chun-ming. Annapolis, Md.: St. John's University Press, 1981.

Gasster, Michel. *Chinese Intellectuals and the Revolution of 1911: The Birth of Modern Chinese Radicalism*. Seattle: University of Washington Press, 1969.

——. "The Republican Revolutionary Movement." In John K. Fairbank and Liu Kwang-ching, eds., *The Cambridge History of China.* Vol. 11, *Late Ch'ing, 1800–1911*, bk 2. Cambridge: Cambridge University Press, 1980.

Gregor, James A., and Maria Hsia Chang. "Chiang Kai-shek, China, and the Concept of Economic Development." *Proceedings of the Conference on Chiang Kai-shek and Modern China.* 5 vols. Vol. 3, *Chiang Kai-shek and China's Modernization*, pp. 616–35. Tapei, 1987.

Gregor, James A., Maria Hsia Chang, and Andrew Zimmerman. *Ideology and Development: Sun Yat-sen and the Economic History of Taiwan.* Berkeley, Calif.: Center for Chinese Studies, 1981.

Hahn, Emily. *The Soong Sisters.* New York: Doubleday, Doran, 1941.

Hana, Corinna. "The Development of the *San-min chu-i* During the May Fourth Movement." In G. K. Kindermann, ed., *East-West Syntheses.* Vol. 1, *Sun Yat-sen: Founder and Symbol of China's Revolutionary Nation-Building*, pp. 128–42. Munich: Günter Olzog, 1982.

Hao Yen-ping. "The Abortive Cooperation Between Reforms and Revolutionaries." *Papers on China*, Harvard University, East Asian Research Center, 15 (1961): 91–114.

Holubynchy, Lydia. *Michael Borodin and the Chinese Revolution, 1923–1925.* Ann Arbor, Mich.: University Microfilm International, 1979.

Hsieh, Winston. *Chinese Historiography on the Chinese Revolution of 1911: A Critical Survey and Selected Bibliography.* Stanford, Calif.: Stanford University Press, 1975.

——. "The Ideas and Ideals of a Warlord: Ch'en Chiung-ming, 1878–1933." *Papers on China.* Center for East Asian Studies, Harvard University, 16 (Dec. 1962): 198–252.

——. "Salt Smugglers and Local Uprisings: Observations on the Social and Economic Background of the Waichow Revolution of 1911." In Jean Chesneaux, ed., *Popular Movements and Secret Societies in China, 1840–1950*, pp. 154–64. Stanford, Calif.: Stanford University Press, 1972.

Hsüeh Chün-tu. "Un démocrate chinois: la vie de Song Jiaoren." In Hsüeh Chün-tu, ed., *Les Dirigeants de la Chine révolutionnaire, 1850–1972* (translated from the English), pp. 183–200. Paris: Calmann-Lévy, 1973.

——. *Huang Hsing and the Chinese Revolution.* Stanford, Calif.: Stanford University Press, 1961.

——. "Sun Yat-sen, Yang Ch'u-yun, and the Early Revolutionary Movement in China." *Journal of Asian Studies* 19, no. 3 (May 1960): 307–18.

Jacobs, Dan N. *Borodin: Stalin's Man in China.* Cambridge, Mass.: Harvard University Press, 1981.

Jansen, Marius B. "Japan and the Chinese Revolution of 1911." In John K. Fairbank and Liu Kwang-ching, eds., *The Cambridge History of China.* Vol. 11, *Late Ch'ing, 1800–1911*, bk. 2. Cambridge: Cambridge University Press, 1980.

——. *The Japanese and Sun Yat-sen.* Cambridge, Mass.: Harvard University Press, 1967.

——. "Yawata, Hanyehping, and the Twenty-one Demands." *Pacific Historical Review* 23, no. 1 (Feb. 1954): 31–48.

Jen Yu-wen. "The Youth of Sun Yat-sen." In Jen Yu-wen and Lindsay Ride, *Sun Yat-sen: Two Commemorative Essays*, pp. 1–22. Hong Kong: University of Hong Kong Center of Asian Studies, 1970.

Kindermann, Gottfried-Karl, ed. *East-West Syntheses*. Vol. 1, *Sun Yat-sen: Founder and Symbol of China's Revolutionary Nation-Building*. Munich: Günter Olzog, 1982.

Lam Man-sun. "Hong Kong and China's Reform and Revolutionary Movements: An Analytical Study of the Reports of Four Hong Kong English Newspapers (1895–1912)." Ph.D. diss., University of Hong Kong, 1984.

Leng Shao-chuan and Norman D. Palmer. *Sun Yat-sen and Communism*. New York: Praeger, 1960.

"Letters and Telegrams to Sir James and Lady Cantlie, 1913–1921." Collection of photocopies of original manuscripts or typescripts kept in the Library of Hong Kong University.

Levenson, Joseph R. *Liang Ch'i-Ch'ao and the Mind of Modern China*. London: Thames and Hudson, 1953.

———. "The Province, the Nation, and the World." In Albert Feurwerker et al., eds., *Approaches to Modern Chinese History*, pp. 268–88. Berkeley: University of California Press, 1967.

Li Shou-kung. "Dr. Sun Yat-sen's Constitution-Protection Campaign and the Establishment of the Military Government in Canton, 1917–1918." *China Forum* 4, no. 2 (July 1977): 255–311.

Liew Kit-siong. *Struggle for Democracy: Sung Chiao-jen and the 1911 Chinese Revolution*. Berkeley: University of California Press, 1971.

Linebarger, Paul. *The Political Doctrines of Sun Yat-sen*. Baltimore, Md.: Johns Hopkins University Press, 1937.

———. *Sun Yat-sen and the Chinese Republic*. New York: Century, 1925.

Lo Chia-lun [Luo Jialun]. *The Pictorial Biography of Dr. Sun Yat-sen*. Taipei: Historical Archives Commission of the Kuomintang, 1955.

Lo Hui-min, ed. *The Correspondence of G. E. Morrison*. 2 vols. Cambridge: Cambridge University Press, 1976.

Loh, Pichon P. Y. *The Early Chiang Kai-shek: A Study of His Personality and Politics, 1887–1924*. New York: Columbia University Press, 1971.

———. "The Ideological Persuasion of Chiang Kai-shek." *Modern Asian Studies* 4, no. 3 (1970): 211–30.

Lust, John. "Secret Societies, Popular Movements, and the 1911 Revolution." In Jean Chesneaux, *Popular Movements and Secret Societies in China, 1840–1950*, pp. 165–200. Stanford, Calif.: Stanford University Press, 1972.

Maybon, Albert. *La République chinoise*. Paris: Colin, 1914.

Meliksetov, Arlen V. "La modernisation de la Chine et le confucianisme." *Cahiers d'études chinoises*, no. 10: 71–80. Paris: INALCO, 1992.

Min Tu-ki. "An Inquiry into the Nature of the 1923 Renovation of the KMT."

Proceedings of the Conference on the Early History of the Republic of China, 1912–1927, Taipei, Academia Sinica, Institute of Modern History, Aug. 20–22, 1983, vol. 2: 787–95.

——. "Daitō Gappon Ron and the Chinese Response: An Inquiry into Chinese Attitudes Toward Early Japanese Pan-Asiansim." In Eto Shinkichi and Harold Z. Schiffrin, eds., *The 1911 Revolution in China: Interpretive Essays*, pp. 83–94. Tokyo: University of Tokyo Press, 1984.

Mitarevsky, N. *Worldwide Soviet Plots*. Tianjin: Tientsin Press, [1927]. This work, based on documents seized in a raid by the Chinese authorities on the Soviet Embassy in Peking on April 6, 1927, provides new information, but the author often fails to give precise sources. The work is nevertheless considered trustworthy by most specialists, including C. Martin Wilbur.

Miyazaki Tōten [Torazō]. *My Thirty-three Years' Dream: The Autobiography of Miyazaki Tōten*. Translated from the Japanese and with an Introduction by Eto Shinkichi and Marius B. Jansen. Princeton, N.J.: Princeton University Press, 1982.

Morrison, George E. *Correspondence*. See Lo Hui-min, ed.

Munholland, J. Kim. "The French Connection That Failed: France and Sun Yat-sen, 1900–1908." *Journal of Asian Studies* 32, no. 1 (Nov. 1972): 177–95.

Muntjewerf, A. C. "Was There a 'Sneevlietian Strategy'?" *China Quarterly* no. 53. (Jan.–Mar. 1973): 159–68.

Myers, Ramon. "The Principle of People's Welfare: A Multidimensional Concept." In Cheng Chu-yuan, ed., *Sun Yat-sen's Doctrine in the Modern World*. Boulder, Colo.: Westview Press, 1989.

Nathan, Andrew J. "A Constitutional Republic: The Peking Government, 1916–1928." In John K. Fairbank, ed., *The Cambridge History of China*. Vol. 12, *Republican China, 1912–1949*, bk. 1. Cambridge: Cambridge University Press, 1983.

——. "The Place of Values in Cross-Cultural Studies: The Example of Democracy and China." In Paul A. Cohen and Merle Goldman, *Ideas Across Cultures*, pp. 293–316. Cambridge, Mass.: Harvard University Press, 1990.

Ng Lun Ngai-ha et al. *Historical Traces of Sun Yat-sen's Activities in Hong Kong, Macao, and Overseas*. Hong Kong: United College, The Chinese University, Sun Yat-sen Research Institute, The Zhongshan University, 1986.

Pearl, Cyril. *Morrison of China*. Sydney: Angus and Robertson, 1967.

Price, Don. "Sung Chiao-jen's Political Strategy, 1912–1913." *Proceedings of the Conference on the Early History of the Republic of China, 1912–1927*. Taipei, Academia Sinica, Institute of Modern History, Aug. 20–22, 1983, vol. 2: 33–51.

Rankin, Mary Backus. *Early Chinese Revolutionaries: Radical Intellectuals in Shanghai and Chekiang, 1902–1911*. Cambridge, Mass.: Harvard University Press, 1971.

——. *Elite Activism and Political Transformation in China: Zhejiang Province, 1865–1911*. Stanford, Calif.: Stanford University Press, 1986.

Restarick, Henry Bond. *Sun Yat-sen: Liberator of China*. New Haven, Conn.: Yale University Press, 1931.

Rhoads, Edwards J. M. *China's Republican Revolution: The Case of Kwangtung, 1895–1913*. Cambridge, Mass.: Harvard University Press, 1975.

Rottach, Edmond. *La Chine en révolution*. Paris: Perrin, 1914.

Rowe, William T. *Hankow*. Vol. 1, *Commerce and Society in a Chinese City, 1796–1889*. Stanford, Calif.: Stanford University Press, 1984.

——. "The Public Sphere in Modern China." *Modern China* 16, no. 3 (July 1990): 309–29.

"Saggitarius" [H. G. W. Woodhead]. *The Strange Apotheosis of Sun Yat-sen*. London: Heath, Cranton, 1939.

Scalapino, Robert A., and Harold Z. Schiffrin. "Early Socialist Currents in the Chinese Revolutionary Movement: Sun Yat-sen versus Liang Ch'i Ch'ao." *Journal of Asian Studies* 18, no. 3 (May 1959): 321–42.

Schiffrin, Harold Z. "The Enigma of Sun Yat-sen." In Mary C. Wright, ed., *China in Revolution: The First Phase, 1900–1913*, pp. 462–74. New Haven, Conn.: Yale University Press, 1968.

——. *Sun Yat-sen and the Origins of the Chinese Revolution*. Berkeley: University of California Press, 1968.

——. *Sun Yat-sen: Reluctant Revolutionary*. Boston: Little, Brown, 1980.

——. "Sun Yat-sen's Early Land Policy: The Origin and Meaning of 'Equalizalism of Land Rights.'" *Journal of Asian Studies* 16, no. 4 (Aug. 1957): 549–64.

Schwartz, Benjamin. *In Search of Wealth and Power: Yen Fu and the West*. Cambridge, Mass.: Harvard University Press, 1964.

Seagrave, Sterling. *The Soong Dynasty*. New York: Harper & Row, 1985.

Selle, Earl Albert. *Donald of China*. New York: Harper & Bros., 1948.

Sharman, Lyon. *Sun Yat-sen: His Life and Its Meaning*. New York: John Day, 1934. Reissued Stanford, Calif.: Stanford University Press, 1968.

Sheridan, James E. *China in Disintegration: The Republican Era*. New York: Free Press, 1975.

——. "The Warlord Era: Politics and Militarism Under the Peking Government, 1916–1928." In John K. Fairbank, ed., *The Cambridge History of China*. Vol. 12, *Republican China, 1912–1949*, bk. 1. Cambridge: Cambridge University Press, 1983.

Shieh, Milton J. *The Kuomintang: Selected Historical Documents, 1894–1969*. New York: St. John's University Press, 1970.

Shimada Kenji. *Pioneer of the Chinese Revolution: Zhang Binglin and Confucianism*. Translated from the Japanese by Joshua A. Fogel. Stanford, Calif.: Stanford University Press, 1990.

Snow, Edgar. *Journey to the Beginning*. London: Gollancz, 1960.

Soulié de Morant, Georges. *Soun Iat-senn*. Paris: Gallimard, 1932.

Sun Yat-sen. *The Fundamentals of National Reconstruction*. Taipei: China Cultural Service, 1953.

——. *The International Development of China*. London: Hutchinson, 1921; reissued 1928.

——. *Kidnapped in London.* Bristol: Arrowsmith, 1897; reissued London, 1969.

——. *Le Triple Démisme.* Translated from the Chinese; see Pascal M. D'Élia.

Sutton, Donald D. *Provincial Militarism and the Chinese Republic: The Yunnan Army, 1905–1925.* Ann Arbor: University of Michigan Press, 1980.

Tamada Kamachi Noriko. "Sung Chiao-jen and the 1911 Revolution." *Papers on China,* Center for East Asian Studies, Harvard University, 21 (Feb. 1968): 184–229.

T'ang Leang-li. *The Inner History of the Chinese Revolution.* Westport, Conn.: Hyperion, 1977. (First issued 1930.)

Tchang Fou-jouei. "L'opinion publique française et la révolution de 1911." Doctoral thesis, Paris, faculté des lettres, n.d.

Teng Ssu-yü. "Dr. Sun Yat-sen and Chinese Secret Societies." *Studies on Asia* 4 (1963): 81–99.

Teng Ssu-yü and John K. Fairbank. *China's Response to the West: A Documentary Survey, 1839–1923.* Cambridge, Mass.: Harvard University Press, 1954.

Treadgold, Donald W. "Sun Yat-sen and Modern Christianity." In David C. Buxbaum and Frederick W. Mote, *Transition and Permanence: Chinese History and Culture,* pp. 123–54. Hong Kong: Cathay Press, 1972.

Tsai Jung-fang. "Comprador Ideologists in Modern China: Ho Kai and Hu Li-Yuan." Ph.D. diss., University of California, 1975.

Tse Tsan Tai [Xie Zuantai]. *The Chinese Republic: Secret History of the Revolution.* Hong Kong: South China Post, 1924.

Tsou Jung [Zou Rong]. *The Revolutionary Army: A Chinese Nationalist Tract of 1903.* Introduction, translation, and notes by John Lust. The Hague-Paris: Mouton, 1968.

Tsui Shu-chin. "The Influence of the Canton-Moscow Entente upon Sun Yat-sen's Political Philosophy." *Chinese Social and Political Science Review* 18 (1934), no. 1 (Apr.): 96–145; no. 2 (July): 177–209; no. 3 (Oct.): 341–88.

——. "The Influence of the Canton-Moscow Entente upon Sun Yat-sen's Revolutionary Tactics." *Chinese Social and Political Science Review* 20, no. 1 (Jan. 1936): 101–39.

Vishnyakova-Akimova, Vera V. *Two Years in Revolutionary China.* Translated from the Russian by Steven I. Levine. Cambridge, Mass.: Harvard University Press, 1971.

Wang, Y. C. [Wang Yiju]. *Chinese Intellectuals and the West, 1872–1949.* Chapel Hill: University of North Carolina Press, 1966.

Wang Ching-wei, ed. *China and Japan: Natural Friends–Unnatural Enemies.* Shanghai, 1941.

Wang Gungwu. "Sun Yat-sen and Singapore." *Journal of the South Seas Society (Nanyang Hsueh Pao)* 15, no. 1 (Dec. 1959): 55–68.

Weale, B. C. Putnam [Lenox Simpson]. *The Fight for the Republic of China.* New York: Dodd, Mead, 1917.

Whiting, Allen S. "A New Version of the *San-min-chu-i.*" *Far East Quarterly* 14 (May 1955): 389–91.

——. *Soviet Policies in China, 1917–1924*. New York: Columbia University Press, 1954.

Wieger, Léon, S.J. *La Chine moderne*. Vol. 6, *Le Feu aux poudres, 1925*. Hien-Hien (Hebei): Imprimiere de Sienhsien, 1926.

Wilbur, C. Martin. "Forging the Weapons: Sun Yat-sen and the Kuomintang in Canton, 1924." Mimeograph. New York: Columbia University, East Asia Institute, 1966.

——. "Problems of Starting a Revolutionary Base: Sun Yat-sen and Canton, 1923." *Bulletin of the Institute of Modern History*, Academia Sinica (Taipei) 2, no. 4 (1975): 1–63.

——. *Sun Yat-sen: Frustrated Patriot*. New York: Columbia University Press, 1976.

Wilbur, C. Martin, and Julie How Lien-ying. *Missionaries of Revolution: Soviet Advisers and Nationalist China*. Cambridge, Mass.: Harvard University Press, 1989.

Will, Pierre-Etienne. "L'ère des rébellions et de modernisation avortée." In Marie-Claire Bergère, Lucien Bianco, and Jürgen Domes, eds., *La Chine au XXe siècle*. Vol. 1, *D'une révolution à l'autre, 1895–1949*, chap. 2. Paris: Fayard, 1990.

Wong, John Y. *The Origins of an Heroic Image: Sun Yat-sen in London, 1896–1897*. Hong Kong: Oxford University Press, 1986.

——, ed. *Sun Yat-sen: His International Ideas and International Connections*. Broadway, N.S.W.: Wild Peony, 1987.

Wong Young-tsu. *Search for Modern Nationalism: Zhang Binglin and Revolutionary China, 1896–1936*. Hong Kong: Oxford University Press, 1989.

Woodruff, A. M. "Progress and Poverty: A Hundred Years' Perspective." In Richard W. Lindon and Sein Lin, eds., "Henry George and Sun Yat-sen: Application and Evolution of Their Land Use Doctrine." Cambridge, Mass.: Lincoln Institute of Land Policy, 1977. 141 typed pages.

Wright, Mary Clabaugh, ed. *China in Revolution: The First Phase, 1900–1913*. New Haven, Conn.: Yale University Press, 1968.

Yen Ching Hwang. *The Overseas Chinese and the 1911 Revolution*. London: Oxford University Press, 1976.

Young, Ernest P. "Ch'en T'ien-hua (1875–1905): A Chinese Nationalist." *Papers on China*, Center for East Asian Studies, Harvard University, 13 (Dec. 1959): 113–63.

——. "Politics in the Aftermath of Revolution: The Era of Yuan Shikai, 1912–1916." In John K. Fairbank, ed., *The Cambridge History of China*. Vol. 12, *Republican China, 1912–1949*, bk. 1. Cambridge: Cambridge University Press, 1983.

——. *The Presidency of Yuan Shik-k'ai: Liberalism and Dictatorship in Early Republican China*. Ann Arbor: University of Michigan Press, 1977.

——. "Yuan Shik-k'ai's Rise to Presidency." In Mary C. Wright, ed., *China in Revolution: The First Phase, 1900–1913*, pp. 420–42. New Haven, Conn.: Yale University Press, 1968.

Yu, George T. *Party Politics in Republican China: The Kuomintang, 1912–1924*. Berkeley: University of California Press, 1966.

Zolotow, Maurice. *Maurice William and Sun Yat-sen*. London: Robert Hall, 1948.

WORKS IN CHINESE

There are numerous studies of Sun Yat-sen in Chinese, and many repeat what others say. To limit the critical apparatus of a work not primarily aimed at specialists, I cite here only a few titles of fundamental importance. Similarly, I have omitted references to the rich Japanese bibliography as well as to the bibliography in Russian, also very extensive but frequently dominated by ideological preoccupations.

Cao Yabo. *Wuchang geming zhenshi* (True history of the uprising of Wuchang). 3 vols. Shanghai, 1930.

Chai Degeng et al., comp. *Xinhai geming* (The 1911 revolution). 8 vols. Shanghai, 1957.

Chen Shaobai. *Xingzhonghui geming shiyao* (Revolutionary history of the Revive China Society). Shanghai, 1929–30.

Chen Xiqi. *Sun Zhongshan nianpu changpian* (Chronological biography of Sun Yat-sen). 2 vols. Beijing: Zhonghua shuju, 1991.

——. *Tongmenghui chengliqiande Sun Zhongshan* (Sun Yat-sen before the founding of the Tongmenghui). Canton, 1957.

Chiang Kai-shek. "Tudi guoyoude yaoyi" (Conditions and meaning of the nationalization of land). *Jiang Zongtong sixiang yanlunji* (Collection of essays and speeches on the thought of President Chiang). Taipei: Zhongyang wenwu gongyingshe, 1966.

Feng Ziyou. *Geming yishi* (Anecdotes on the Revolution). 5 vols. Shanghai, 1939–45.

——. *Zhonghua minguo kaiguoqian gemingshi* (History of the Revolution before the founding of the Republic). Shanghai, 1928.

Guangdongsheng Sun Zhongshan yanjiuhui, ed. *Sun Zhongshan yanjiu* (Research on Sun Yat-sen), vol. 1. Canton, 1986.

Luo Jialun. *Guofuzhi daxue shidai* (The universities of Sun Yat-sen). Zhongqing, 1945.

——. *Zhongshan xiansheng Lundun beinan shiliao kaoding* (Critical analysis of the sources of the kidnapping of Sun Yat-sen in London). Shanghai, 1930.

Luo Xianglin. *Guofu yu Ou-Mei zhi youhao* (Sun Yat-sen and his European and American friends). Taipei, 1951.

Mao Sicheng, comp. *Minguo shiwu nian yiqian zhi Jiang Jieshi xiansheng* (Chiang Kai-shek, before 1926). 1936; reissued in 2 vols., n.p., n.d.

Song Jiaoren. *Wo zhi lishi* (My life). Taoyuan (Hunan), 1920; reissued Taipei, 1962.

Sun Yat-sen. *Guofu quanji* (Complete works of Sun Yat-sen). Edited by the Archives of Guomindang. 3 vols. Taipei, 1957. Rev. ed., 6 vols., 1965.

——. *Sun Zhongshan quanji* (Complete works of Sun Yat-sen). Comp. by Zhongshan daxue lishixi, Guangdongsheng shehuikexueyuan lishi yanjiusuo, Zhonguo shehuikexueyuan jindaishi yanjiusuo. 11 vols. Beijing: Zhonghua shuju, 1981–86.

——. "Youzhi jingcheng" (Ambition fulfilled). Written in 1918, published under various titles: "Geming yuanqi" (The origins of the revolution) and *Sun Zhongshan xiansheng zizhuan* (Autobiography of Sun-Yat Sen), in *Sun Zhongshan quanji* (Complete works of Sun Yat-sen), 6: 228–46. Beijing: Zhonghua shuju, 1981–86.

———. *Zhongguo gemingshi* (History of the Chinese Revolution). Canton, 1923.

Tanhe Gongchangdang liang da Yao'an (Two important cases of impeachment of the Communist Party). Central Control Commission of the Guomindang, September 1927. Republished in *Geming wenxian* (Documents on the Revolution), 9: 1278–86.

Wu Xiangxiang. *Song Jiaoren, Zhongguo minzhu xianzhengde xiangu* (Song Jiaoren, the precursor of China's constitutional democratic government). Taipei, 1964.

———. *Sun Yixian xiansheng zhuan* (The Life of Sun Yat-sen). 2 vols. Taipei, 1984.

Zhongguo Guomindang, Zhongyang dangshi shiliao bianzuan weiyuanhui, ed. and comp. *Geming wenxian* (Documents on the Revolution). Taipei: 61 vols. since 1953.

———, ed. *Guofu nianpu* (Chronological biography of Sun Yat-sen). 2 vols. Taipei, 1958. 2d ed. rev. 1969.

Zhongguo renmin zhengzhi xieshang huiyi, Quanguo weiyuanhui, Wenshi ziliao yanjiu weiyuanhui, ed. *Xinhai geming huiyilu* (Memories of the revolution of 1911). 5 vols. Beijing, 1961–63.

Zhongguo shehuikexueyuan jindai yanjiusuo, ed. *Huigu yu zhanwang. Guo nei wai Sun Zhongshan yanjiu shuping* (Retrospectives and perspectives. Evaluation of research work in China and abroad on the subject of Sun Yat-sen). Beijing: Zhonghua shuju, 1986.

Zhongguo Sun Zhongshan yanjiuhui, ed. *Sun Zhongshan he tade shidai (Sun Zhongshan yanjiuhui guoji xueshu taolunhui wen ji* (Sun Yat-sen and his age. Collection of contributions to the international conference on Sun Yat-sen). 3 vols. Beijing: Zhonghua shuju, 1989.

Zhonghua minguo kaiguo wushinian wenxian bianzuan weiyuanhui, comp. *Zhonghua minguo kaiguo wushinian wenxian* (Collection of documents in commemoration of the 50th anniversary of the founding of the Chinese Republic). Taipei, 1961–.

Zou Lu. *Zhongguo Guomindang shigao* (Project for a history of the Chinese Nationalist Party). Shanghai, 1929.

Index

In this index an "f" after a number indicates a separate reference on the next page, and an "ff" indicates separate references on the next two pages. A continuous discussion over two or more pages is indicated by a span of page numbers, e.g., "57–59."

Library of Congress Cataloging-in-Publication Data

Bergère, Marie-Claire.
Sun Yat-sen / by Marie-Claire Bergère ; translated from the French
by Janet Lloyd.
p.   cm.
Includes bibliographical references and index.
ISBN 0-8047-3170-5 (alk. paper)
1. Sun, Yat-sen, 1866–1925.   2. Presidents—China—Biography.
I. Lloyd, Janet.   II. Title.
DS777.B47   1998
951.04′1′092—dc21
[B]   97-35504

Original printing 1998

Last figure below indicates year of this printing:

06   05   04   03   02   01   00   99